THE OXFORD HANDBOOK OF

QUANTITATIVE ASSET MANAGEMENT

OXFORD HANDBOOKS IN FINANCE

SERIES EDITOR: MICHAEL DEMPSTER

THE OXFORD HANDBOOK OF BANKING
Edited by Allen N. Berger, Philip Molyneux, and John O.S. Wilson

THE OXFORD HANDBOOK OF CREDIT DERIVATIVES
Edited by Alexander Lipton and Andrew Rennie

THE OXFORD HANDBOOK OF QUANTITATIVE ASSET MANAGEMENT
Edited by Bernd Scherer and Kenneth Winston

THE OXFORD HANDBOOK OF

QUANTITATIVE ASSET MANAGEMENT

Edited by

BERND SCHERER

and

KENNETH WINSTON

OXFORD
UNIVERSITY PRESS

OXFORD
UNIVERSITY PRESS

Great Clarendon Street, Oxford OX2 6DP

Oxford University Press is a department of the University of Oxford.
It furthers the University's objective of excellence in research, scholarship,
and education by publishing worldwide in

Oxford New York

Auckland Cape Town Dar es Salaam Hong Kong Karachi
Kuala Lumpur Madrid Melbourne Mexico City Nairobi
New Delhi Shanghai Taipei Toronto

With offices in

Argentina Austria Brazil Chile Czech Republic France Greece
Guatemala Hungary Italy Japan Poland Portugal Singapore
South Korea Switzerland Thailand Turkey Ukraine Vietnam

Oxford is a registered trade mark of Oxford University Press
in the UK and in certain other countries

Published in the United States
by Oxford University Press Inc., New York

First published 2012

British Library Cataloguing in Publication Data
Data available

Library of Congress Cataloging in Publication Data
Data available

Typeset by SPI Publisher Services, Pondicherry, India
Printed in Great Britain
on acid-free paper by
MPG Books Group, Bodmin and King's Lynn

ISBN 978-0-19-955343-3

1 3 5 7 9 10 8 6 4 2

Series Editor's Preface

Recently two series of Oxford Handbooks covering financial topics have been merged into one under a single editorship – those in Finance found under Business and Economics and those in Quantitative Finance found under Mathematics. This is as it should be, for in spite of all the accusations regarding their role in the recent crisis and recession, financial services are both necessary and critical to the successful development of a global economy facing environmental and pension crises on top of the current one. It can also be argued that banking, insurance, and fund management are the last post war industries to go "high tech" and that the esoteric topics involved need exposition to a more general audience than simply that of their creators. The aim of this handbook series is therefore to cover recent developments in financial services, institutions, and markets in an up to date, accurate, and comprehensive manner which is clear and comprehensible to the interested reader. This will be achieved by careful choice of editors for, and exacting selection of contributors to, each handbook.

It is my hope that over time the volumes in this series will help to create a better understanding of financial topics by the educated public, including financial services managers, regulators, and legislators. Such an understanding appeared to be lacking in the run-up to the recent crisis, but it will be crucial to successful management of the global economy in the future.

Michael Dempster

Acknowledgments

This Handbook was commissioned by Sarah Caro at Oxford University Press in 2008. At Oxford University Press, Sarah guided the early construction of the Handbook; Emma Lambert the next phase; and Aimee Wright the final phase. We are grateful to Sarah, Emma, and Aimee for much hard work and for participation in many conference calls across many time zones. The editors would like to thank the book's contributors for their tolerance of the editors' suggestions, for their patience, and above all for the fine work that they have contributed in these chapters.

Contents

PART III INVESTMENT MANAGEMENT BEHAVIOR

PART IV PARAMETER ESTIMATION

PART V RISK MANAGEMENT

PART VI MARKET STRUCTURE AND TRADING

PART VII INVESTMENT SOLUTIONS

List of Figures

List of Tables

List of Contributors

Heiko M. Bailer is Head of Quantitative Solutions at Clariden Leu, the private bank of Credit Suisse. He is also a partner of Corepoint Capital AG and the developer of their Q2 products. Dr. Bailer began his financial career in 1999 at Deutsche Bank, Global Markets Fixed Income in New York. In 2005, he joined ABN AMRO's Delta One Trading Group in London. In 2007, he moved to Zurich as a Deputy CRO of Harcourt AG, a $5 billion fund of hedge funds. In 2005, Dr Bailer received his Ph.D. in Statistics from the University of Washington for his dissertation on financial robust factor models, and additionally earned a Certificate in Computational Finance. He also holds a master's degree in mathematics and physics from the University of Munich.

Dan diBartolomeo is President and Founder of Northfield Information Services, Inc., a provider of quantitative models of financial markets. He is a visiting professor at the CARISMA research center of Brunel University in London. In addition, he serves on the Board of Directors of the Chicago Quantitative Alliance and the advisory board of the International Association of Financial Engineers. Mr. diBartolomeo also continues his several years of service as a judge in the Moscowitz Prize competition, given for excellence in academic research on socially responsible investing by the University of California, Berkeley. He has written extensively for the CFA Research Foundation. This work includes "The risk of equity securities and portfolios" published in *Equity Specialization Program Readings*, 1997 and a wealth management textbook *Investment Management for Private, Taxable Wealth* (with Jarrod Wilcox and Jeffrey Horvitz). He has contributed chapters to eight other finance textbooks and published more than a dozen research papers in refereed journals. His most recent publications are "Equity portfolio volatility with market information and sentiment" (with G. Mitra and L. Mitra, *Quantitative Finance*, December 2009) and "Equity risk, default risk, default correlation and corporate sustainability," *Journal of Investing*, Winter 2010). Mr. diBartolomeo holds a B.Sc. degree from Cornell University in Applied Physics.

Jules H. van Binsbergen is Assistant Professor of Finance at the Kellogg School of Management at Northwestern University and the Stanford Graduate School of Business. Professor Binsbergen conducts theoretical and empirical research in finance. His current work focuses on asset pricing, in particular consumption-based asset pricing, return predictability, and quantitative portfolio management. Some of his recent research focuses on the implications of good-specific habit formation for asset prices, the interaction between cash flow growth predictability and stock return predictability, and the maturity structure of risk and return in financial markets. His research has appeared in leading academic journals such as the *Journal of Finance*. He is also a Faculty Research Fellow of the National Bureau of Economic Research (NBER).

Yossi Brandes is a managing director at Investment Technology Group, Inc., responsible for ITG's European Analytical Products & Research group as well as its business development. Prior to that, he ran the Trading Analytics Group within the Analytical Products and Research group. He has coauthored several articles on market microstructure, transaction costs, and portfolio construction. Mr. Brandes holds a master's in business administration from the Stern School of Business at NYU and a B.Sc. in computer science and economics from Haifa University.

Michael W. Brandt is Professor of Finance and the IBM Research Fellow at the Fuqua School of Business at Duke University. Professor Brandt conducts theoretical and empirical research in finance. His work on quantitative portfolio management, the response of financial markets to news, the role of order flow in price discovery, and the link between financial markets and the macro-economy has appeared in leading academic journals, including *The Journal of Business, Journal or Finance, Journal of Financial Economics, Journal of Monetary Economics,* and *Review of Financial Studies.* He serves as co-editor of the *Review of Finance*, the official journal of the European Finance Association, and as associate editor of the *Journal of Finance*, the official journal of the American Finance Association. He is also a faculty research associate of the National Bureau of Economic Research (NBER). Prior to joining the Fuqua School of Business in 2003, Professor Brandt was at the Wharton School of the University of Pennsylvania for six years.

Francis Breedon is Professor of Economics and Finance at Queen Mary College, University of London. His research focuses mainly on exchange rate economics and policy. Professor Breedon has extensive industry and policy experience including a period as Global Head of Currency Research at Lehman Brothers and before that as a senior economist at the Bank of England. He acts as a consultant to a number of financial institutions including hedge funds, central banks and ministries of finance on foreign exchange issues.

Sebastián Ceria is the Chief Executive Officer of Axioma. Before founding Axioma, he was an Associate Professor of Decision, Risk, and Operations at Columbia Business School from 1993 to 1998. Dr. Ceria has worked extensively in the area of optimization and its application to portfolio management. He is the author of many articles in publications including *Management Science, Mathematical Programming, Optima,* and *Operations Research.* Most recently, Ceria's work has focused on the area of robust optimization in portfolio management. He has co-authored numerous papers on the topic, including, "Incorporating estimation errors into portfolio Selection: robust portfolio construction," which was published in *The Journal of Asset Management.* He is a recipient of the Career Award for Operations Research from the National Science Foundation. Ceria completed his Ph.D. in operations research at Carnegie Mellon University's Graduate School of Industrial Administration.

Ian Domowitz is a managing director at Investment Technology Group, Inc., responsible for analytical and network products, and a member of the company's Management and Executive Committees. Prior to joining the company in 2001, he served as the Mary Jean and Frank P. Smeal Professor of Finance at Pennsylvania State University and previously was the Household International Research Professor of Economics at Northwestern University. A former member of the NASD's Bond Market Transparency Committee, he also served as chair of the Economic Advisory Board of the NASD. Mr. Domowitz has held positions with Northwestern's Kellogg Graduate School of Management, Columbia University, the Commodity Futures Trading Commission, the International Monetary Fund and the World Bank. He is currently a Fellow of the Program in the Law and Economics of Capital Markets at Columbia University.

Daniel Giamouridis is an assistant professor in the Department of Accounting and Finance of the Athens University of Economics and Business. He is also a senior visiting fellow at Sir John Cass Business School of City University and a research associate at the EDHEC-Risk Institute. His specialties are quantitative asset management and alternative investments on which he has published in journals, such as the *European Financial Management Journal, Journal of Alternative Investments, Journal of Asset Management, Journal of Banking and Finance, Journal of Financial Research, Journal of Derivatives, Journal of Futures Markets,* and *Journal of Portfolio Management*, among others, and has advised financial institutions covering areas such as quantitative equity research, hedge fund replication, asset management, and derivatives valuation.

Campbell R. Harvey is the J. Paul Sticht Professor of International Business at the Fuqua School of Business, Duke University, and a Research Associate of the National Bureau of Economic Research in Cambridge, Massachusetts. Professor Harvey obtained his doctorate at the University of Chicago in business finance. He has served on the faculties of the Stockholm School of Economics, the Helsinki School of Economics, and the Graduate School of Business at the University of Chicago. He has also been a visiting scholar at the Board of Governors of the Federal Reserve System. He has published over 100 scholarly articles. One focus of his research is on the implications of changing risk and higher moments for both asset allocation strategies and risk management. Harvey is the Editor of *The Journal of Finance* – the leading scientific journal in his field and one of the premier journals in the economic profession through 2012. He is the past-President of the Western Finance Association and serves on both the Board of Directors and the Executive Committee of the American Finance Association.

Thomas Hewett is the Chief Risk Officer of the Morgan Stanley Traditional Asset Management business and heads up the Global Risk and Analysis Team responsible for managing investment, credit, and operational risk. Prior to taking on this role Dr. Hewett managed the quantitative research group responsible for the development, testing, and enhancement of quantitative analytics relating to risk, portfolio construction, performance measurement, and attribution. Before joining Morgan Stanley, he was a senior manager in the Quantitative Services Group at Deloitte & Touche responsible for model validation and quantitative risk consulting. Previously, he was on the mathematics faculties at the Massachusetts Institute of Technology and Princeton University. He holds a B.Sc. with honors in mathematics and applied mathematics from the University of Cape Town and a Ph.D. in mathematics from Stanford University.

Roy P. M. M. Hoevenaars is Senior Portfolio Manager Global Tactical Asset Allocation at APG Asset Management in Amsterdam, the Netherlands. His responsibilities include the portfolio management, development, and research of cross-asset systematic absolute return strategies. He also focuses on volatility and correlation markets. Prior to joining GTAA in 2007, he was Coordinator ALM modeling. Dr. Hoevenaars joined APG Asset Management in 2001 and worked in various roles on asset liability management, asset allocation, hedge funds, and quantitative equity modeling. His expertise includes quantitative investment strategies, derivatives, asset allocation, asset liability management, hedge funds, and risk management. He holds a Ph.D. in financial econometrics and an M.Sc. degree in econometrics and operations research from the University of Maastricht. His Ph.D. dissertation is entitled "Strategic asset allocation and asset liability management." Dr. Hoevenaars is a lecturer on post-graduate courses. He has published numerous book chapters and articles in international refereed academic journals.

Bruce I. Jacobs is Co-founder and Principal of Jacobs Levy Equity Management, a provider of quantitative equity strategies. He is Co-chief Investment Officer, Portfolio Manager, and Co-director of Research. He is the author of *Capital Ideas and Market Realities: Option Replication, Investor Behavior, and Stock Market Crashes*; *Equity Management: Quantitative Analysis for Stock Selection* (with Ken Levy) and co-editor of *Market Neutral Strategies* (with Ken Levy) and *The Bernstein Fabozzi/Jacobs Levy Awards: Five Years of Award-Winning Articles* from the *Journal of Portfolio Management*. Dr. Jacobs' writing has received numerous awards including *Financial Analysts Journal* Graham and Dodd Awards. Dr. Jacobs is an Associate Editor of the *Journal of Trading* and serves on the *Journal of Portfolio Management* Advisory Board and the *Financial Analysts Journal* Advisory Council. He also served on the Committee to Establish the National Institute of Finance and is a member of its successor, the Office of Financial Research Discussion Forum. Dr. Jacobs has a B.A. from Columbia College, and an M.S. in operations research and computer science from Columbia. He also has an M.S.I.A. from Carnegie Mellon, and an M.A. in applied economics and a Ph.D. in finance from the Wharton School.

Ralph S. J. Koijen is Assistant Professor of Finance at the Booth School of Business at the University of Chicago. Professor Koijen conducts theoretical and empirical research in finance. His current work focuses on asset pricing, in particular quantitative portfolio management, return predictability, and performance measurement. Some of his recent research focuses on the interaction between cash flow growth predictability and stock return predictability, and the maturity structure of risk and return in financial markets, and performance measurement. His research has appeared in leading academic journals such as the *Journal of Finance, Review of Financial Studies*, and the *Journal of Financial*

Economics. He is also a faculty research fellow of the National Bureau of Economic Research (NBER).

Petter N. Kolm is the Director of the Mathematics in Finance Masters Program and Clinical Associate Professor at the Courant Institute of Mathematical Sciences, New York University. Previously, he worked in the Quantitative Strategies Group at Goldman Sachs Asset Management where his responsibilities included researching and developing new quantitative investment strategies for the group's hedge fund. Professor Kolm co-authored the books *Financial Modeling of the Equity Market: From CAPM to Cointegration* (Wiley, 2006), *Trends in Quantitative Finance* (CFA Research Institute, 2006), *Robust Portfolio Management and Optimization* (Wiley, 2007), and *Quantitative Equity Investing: Techniques and Strategies* (Wiley, 2010). He holds a Ph.D. in mathematics from Yale, an M.Phil. in applied mathematics from The Royal Institute of Technology, and an M.S. in mathematics from ETH Zurich. He is a member of the editorial board of the *Journal of Portfolio Management*. As a consultant and expert witness, he has provided his services in areas such as algorithmic and quantitative trading strategies, econometrics, forecasting models, portfolio construction methodologies incorporating transaction costs, and risk management procedures.

Robert Kosowski is Director of the Risk Management Lab and Centre for Hedge Fund Research and Assistant Professor in the Finance Group of Imperial College Business School, Imperial College London. His research focuses on asset pricing and hedge fund strategies. Dr. Kosowski's research has been published in top peer-reviewed finance journals such as *The Journal of Finance* and *The Journal of Financial Economics* and has been awarded best paper awards from the European Finance Association (2007) and INQUIRE UK (2008). Prior to joining Imperial College London he was an Assistant Professor of Finance at INSEAD. He holds a B.A. and M.A. in economics from Cambridge University and an M.Sc. and Ph.D. from the London School of Economics. Dr. Kosowski consults for private and public sector organizations and he was Specialist Advisor to the UK House of Lords and Expert Technical Consultant to the IMF. He has worked for Goldman Sachs, the Boston Consulting Group, and Deutsche Bank.

Mark Kritzman is President and CEO of Windham Capital Management, LLC, and the Chairman of Windham's investment committee. He is responsible for managing research activities and investment advisory services. He is also a founding partner of State Street Associates, and he teaches a graduate course in financial engineering at the Massachusetts Institute of Technology. He serves on several corporate and non-profit boards, including the Institute for Quantitative Research in Finance, The Investment Fund for Foundations, and State Street Associates. He is a member of several advisory and editorial boards, including the Center for Asset Management at Boston College, the Advisory Board of the MIT Sloan Finance Group, the Emerging Markets Review, the International Association of Financial Engineers, the *Journal of Alternative Investments*, the *Journal of Derivatives*, and the *Journal of Investment Management*, where he is Book Review Editor. He has written numerous articles for academic and professional journals and is the author of six books including *Puzzles of Finance* and *The Portable Financial Analyst*. Mr. Kritzman won Graham and Dodd awards in 1993 and 2002, the Research Prize from the Institute for Quantitative Investment Research in 1997, and the Bernstein Fabozzi/Jacobs Levy Award in 2003 and 2006. In 2004, he was elected a Batten Fellow at the Darden Graduate School of Business Administration, University of Virginia. He received a master's in business administration from New York University.

Kenneth N. Levy is Co-founder and Principal of Jacobs Levy Equity Management, a provider of quantitative equity strategies. He is Co-chief Investment Officer, Portfolio Manager, and Co-director of Research. He is the co-author with Bruce Jacobs of *Equity Management: Quantitative Analysis for Stock Selection*; co-editor with Bruce Jacobs of *Market Neutral Strategies*; and co-editor of *The Bernstein Fabozzi/Jacobs Levy Awards: Five Years of Award-Winning Articles* from *the Journal of Portfolio Management*. Levy's writing has received numerous awards including *Financial Analysts Journal* Graham and Dodd Awards. Mr. Levy is a CFA charterholder and has served on the CFA Candidate Curriculum Committee, the POSIT Advisory Board, and the investment board of a community foundation. Mr. Levy has a B.A. in economics from Cornell University; an M.B.A. and an M.A. in business economics from the University of Pennsylvania's Wharton School; and has completed all requirements short of a dissertation for a Ph.D. at Wharton.

John C. Liechty is a professor at the Smeal College of Business at Penn State University and has extensive experience developing solutions for top investment banks and marketing research firms. He is an expert in derivative pricing and asset allocation, computational statistics and high-performance computing, and marketing research. He has extensive experience in organizing and leading research efforts and has experience in creating production level pricing and analysis systems. He has consulted extensively for top investment banks, including Morgan Stanley and Goldman Sachs, helping develop models and parallel computing software solutions for calibrating basket, credit derivatives, and statistical based trading strategies. He has also helped lead software development efforts at In4mation Insights, a quantitatively focused marketing research firm, where software for leading edge marketing research models was integrated into a high-performance/parallel computing platform. In addition, he is a founding member and a leading organizer of an effort that resulted in a provision in the Dodd–Frank Act of 2010 that creates a new Office in the U.S. Treasury, the Office of Financial Research, which has the mandate to provide better data and analytic tools to the regulatory community in order to safeguard the U.S. financial system (see www.ce-nif.org). Dr. Liechty has a Ph.D. from the Statistical Laboratory at Cambridge University.

Merrill W. Liechty is an associate professor of clinical practice at the LeBow College of Business, Drexel University. Dr. Liechty has done research in Bayesian statistics applied to higher moment estimation, computationally intensive problems, and finance related topics. He has a Ph.D. from the Department of Statistical Science at Duke University.

Lee Maclin is Adjunct Professor at the Courant Institute of Mathematical Sciences, New York University and Founding Partner of Pragma Financial Systems. He has over 20 years of experience on Wall Street and has worked and consulted for some of its largest and best known firms. Since 1999, he has taught in The Courant Institute's Master of Science Program in Mathematics in Finance including classes on algorithmic trading and quantitative strategies, computing in finance, econometrics and statistical inference, and computational methods. In 2002, he was one of the founding partners of Pragma Financial Systems and, for the next six years, served as its Director of Research. At Pragma, his work focused on the development of optimal execution and dynamic portfolio management tools. He is a frequent speaker on the topic of algorithmic trading and computational finance.

Tatiana A. Maravina is a Ph.D. student in the Department of Statistics at the University of Washington. She is working on her dissertation with Professor R. Douglas Martin. Her research interests are in the area of post-modern statistics in finance, including robust and Bayesian methods for portfolio optimization. She has a master's degree with honors in mathematical statistics from Moscow State University, Russia.

R. Douglas Martin is Professor of Statistics, Adjunct Professor of Finance, and Director of Computational Finance at the University of Washington, and former Chairman of the Department of Statistics. He was a consultant in the Mathematics and Statistics Research Center at Bell Laboratories from 1973 to 1983. He founded Statistical Sciences to commercialize the S language for data analysis and statistical modelling in the form of S-PLUS. Subsequently he was a co-founder and Chairman of FinAnalytica, Inc., developer of the Cognity portfolio construction and risk management system, and served as CEO from 2006 to 2008. Professor Martin has authored numerous publications on time series and robust statistical methods, and is co-author of two books: *Modern Portfolio Optimization* (2005), and *Robust Statistics: Theory and Methods* (2006). His research is on applications of modern statistical methods in finance and investment. He holds a Ph.D. in electrical engineering from Princeton University.

Simon Myrgren is a vice president at State Street Associates in Cambridge. He is primarily involved with research concerning portfolio allocation and portfolio risk models. Before joining State Street Associates he devised mathematical and computational models for theoretical physics applications at the University of California, Berkeley. He received his Ph.D. in theoretical chemistry in August 2004. Dr. Myrgren has published several papers in several leading physics and finance journals.

Colm O'Cinneide is a partner and head of portfolio construction at QS Investors, an independent asset management firm with approximately $13 billion under management formed in 2010 from the Quantitative Strategies group of Deutsche Bank's institutional asset management arm, DB Advisors. Dr. O'Cinneide had joined Deutsche in 2000 after a 17-year career in academia featuring tenured faculty positions in Mathematical Sciences at the University of Arkansas and Industrial Engineering (Operations Research area) at Purdue University. He has 40 refereed academic publications and was sole

Principal Investigator on several National Science Foundation grants supporting his research in applied probability. He holds a Ph.D. in statistics from the University of Kentucky and B.Sc. and M.Sc. degrees in mathematical sciences from the National University of Ireland. He is a former president of the Society of Quantitative Analysts in New York.

Sébastien Page is an executive vice president and head of the client analytics group in PIMCO's Newport Beach office. Prior to joining PIMCO in 2010, he was a senior managing director and head of the portfolio and risk management group at State Street Associates, where he managed the firm's asset allocation advisory and currency management activities. He joined State Street in 2000 as a research associate and subsequently held a number of roles with increasing responsibility. Mr. Page has written and spoken extensively on issues pertaining to portfolio analytics throughout his career. He has more than 10 years of experience and holds a master's degree in finance and a bachelor's degree in business administration from Sherbrooke University in Quebec, Canada.

Michael Peskin is the CEO and founding partner of Hudson Pilot LLC, an advisory firm focused on delivering enterprise management solutions to corporations, insurance companies, and endowments and foundations. Prior to establishing Hudson Pilot, Mr. Peskin served in a senior capacity at Morgan Stanley in Investment Banking, Global Capital Markets, Asset Management, and the Fixed Income and Equity divisions. He has spoken and written extensively on a wide variety of pension finance and investment issues. He is an associate of the Society of Actuaries, and the Institute of Actuaries, a member of the American Academy of Actuaries and is a Chartered Enterprise Risk Analyst. He served as chair of the Joint Academy of Actuaries/Society of Actuaries Pension Finance Task Force, as a member of the Pension Practice Council of the Academy of Actuaries, as a member of the Public Plan Subcommittee and Social Security Committee, and is the Academy of Actuaries representative to the International Actuarial Task Force on Financial Economics.

Bernd Scherer Ph.D. is full time Professor of Finance at EDHEC Business School in London and a member of EDHEC Risk. Prior to joining EDHEC Risk, Professor Scherer was Managing Director and Global Head of Quantitative Structured Products at Morgan Stanley in London and Honorary Visiting Professor at the University of London, Birkbeck College. Previously, he was with Deutsche Asset Management where he successively headed the Investment Solutions and Overlay Management Group in Frankfurt, and Global Quantitative Research and Portfolio Engineering from New York. Bernd has 16 years of investment experience within top financial institutions. He has published eight books on quantitative finance and over 50 articles in leading academic and practitioner journals.

Vitaly Serbin is a director at Investment Technology Group, Inc. He manages the Portfolio Analytics subgroup which is a part of the Financial Engineering department in Boston, MA. Mr. Serbin joined the company in 2001 after receiving a Ph.D. in finance from the University of Illinois at Urbana-Champaign. He has co-authored articles that have appeared in the *Journal of Finance, the Journal of Portfolio Management, the Journal of Investment Management* and others.

George Skiadopoulos is Associate Professor in the Department of Banking and Financial Management of the University of Piraeus. He is also an associate research fellow at the Financial Options Research Centre of the University of Warwick and an honarary senior visiting fellow in the Faculty of Finance in Cass Business School. He has published in academic journals such as the *Journal of Business Finance, International Journal of Forecasting, Journal of Futures Markets*, and *Review of Derivatives Research*, among others, and is a speaker in international conferences and executive training courses. He is a member of the editorial board of the *Journal of Business Finance and Accounting* and serves on the Academic Advisory Council of the Professional Risk Managers International Association (PRMIA).

David Starer is a senior quantitative analyst at Jacobs Levy Equity Management. Previous to Jacobs Levy, he was Research Analyst, Investment Technology, at the Investment Management Division of Lend Lease Corporation in Sydney, Australia. There he developed stochastic models of stock returns, portfolio optimizers, and real-time portfolio management systems. Dr. Starer has received the *Journal of Portfolio Management* Outstanding Article Award. Previously he was a patent engineer and on the Faculty of Informatics, Department of Electrical Engineering, University of Wollongong, Australia. Dr. Starer has a B.S. in electrical engineering from the University of Cape Town, and a master's in electronic engineering from the University of Pretoria. He earned M.S., M.Phil., and Ph.D. degrees in electrical engineering from Yale University, where he was a research fellow at the Center for Systems Science.

Nils Tuchschmid is currently Professor of Banking and Finance at Haute École de Gestion, University of Applied Sciences in Geneva, Switzerland. He is also Invited Professor of Finance at HEC Lausanne University and lecturer at the University of Zurich and ULB in Bruxelles. He is the author of books and articles on traditional and alternative investments, on portfolio management, and on optimal decision making processes. Up to 1999, he was a Professor of Finance at HEC Lausanne. Prior to joining HEG in 2008, he worked for various financial institutions, among others, BCV, Credit Suisse, and UBS.

Reha H. Tütüncü is a managing director at Goldman Sachs Asset Management where he manages a team responsible for the optimization platform used for quantitative portfolio construction. Prior to joining GSAM, he was an associate professor in the Department of Mathematical Sciences at Carnegie Mellon University. He received his Ph.D. in operations research from Cornell University. He is the co-author of the book *Optimization Methods in Finance* and the author of many articles on the subjects of optimization and quantitative finance in academic and practitioner journals.

Erik Wallerstein is a quantitative analyst at Credit Suisse in Zurich, Switzerland. Previously he was a research fellow at Haute École de Gestion, University of Applied Sciences in Geneva, Switzerland. He holds an M.Sc. in applied mathematics from Lund University, Sweden, and a master's in advanced Studies in Finance from ETH-Zurich and University of Zurich. At HEG he was working together with Professor Nils Tuchschmid where they published in the area of hedge fund research.

Kenneth Winston is the Chief Risk Officer of Western Asset Management, a global fixed income investment manager headquartered in Pasadena, California. Dr. Winston's group assesses and manages investment risk, does quantitative research, and oversees enterprise and operational risk at Western Asset. Prior to Western Asset, Dr. Winston worked in firm risk management at Morgan Stanley and was Chief Risk Officer at Morgan Stanley Investment Management in New York. While he was at Morgan Stanley, he was an Adjunct Professor of Financial Mathematics at the Courant Institute of Mathematical Sciences at New York University. He began his financial career as a quantitative portfolio manager after having taught mathematics at Rutgers University. Dr. Winston is the author of a number of articles and papers, including "Buy side risk management" which won the 2006 Roger Murray Award for best paper at the Institute for Quantitative Research in Finance. Dr. Winston obtained his Ph.D. in pure mathematics from the Massachusetts Institute of Technology and a B.S. and M.S. in mathematics from the California Institute of Technology.

Michael Wolf is Professor of Econometrics and Applied Statistics at the University of Zurich. After obtaining a Ph.D. in statistics from Stanford University, he held previous academic positions at UCLA, Universidad Carlos III, and Universitat Pompeu Fabra. His research can be classified into three categories. First, inference methods which do not require overly strict parametric assumptions, such as bootstrap and subsampling methods; for example, such methods can be used for testing whether the Sharpe ratios of two investment strategies are different. Second, methods for multiple testing (which occurs whenever more than one test is carried out at the same time); for example, such methods can be used to find out which hedge fund managers deliver outstanding performance. Third, methods to estimate large-dimensional covariance matrices when the number of assets is of the same magnitude, or even larger, than the number of data points; for example, such methods can be used to construct Markowitz portfolios with superior out-of-sample performance. The methodological work of Dr. Wolf has been published in leading theory journals, such as *Econometrica, The Annals of Statistics*, and *Journal of the American Statistical Associaton*. On the other hand, his applied work has been published in practitioner journals, such as *Journal of Empirical Finance, Journal of Portfolio Management*, and *Willmott Magazine*. Dr. Wolf consults for private and public sector companies.

Dan Wunderli is a Ph.D. student in economics at the University of Zurich, where he also obtained his master's degree in Quantitative Finance. He has carried out research for Credit Suisse as part of a consulting project of the University of Zurich. He has given talks at the European Meeting of the Financial Management Association in Prague and at the Institute on Computational Economics at the University of Chicago. During his master's degree studies, he attended a summer school on advanced econometrics at the London School of Economics. Before starting his master's degree, he completed an internship at the Statistics Department of the Swiss National Bank.

Xiaodong Xu is a senior manager at the Alternative Asset Management division of Union Bank Privée (UBP). He is responsible for global quantitative asset allocation research. Prior to joining UBP in 2010, he spent five years as a quantitative analyst with the Quantitative Strategy group of Deutsche Bank. He received his Ph.D. from Northwestern University in 2005.

Sassan Zaker is a manager of Alternative Investments at Julius Bär. He joined Bank Julius Bär & Co. Ltd. in 2004 as Head Alternative Products and Advisory. Before joining Julius he worked for Swissca Portfolio Management, Finfunds Management AG, and UBS. Sassan Zaker has 17 years of business experience in quantitative analysis, portfolio management, and private and institutional client experience. He holds a master's and Ph.D. engineering degree from the Swiss Federal Institute of Technology (ETH) and is also a CFA charterholder.

CHAPTER 1

INTRODUCTION

BERND SCHERER AND KENNETH WINSTON

QUANTITATIVE portfolio management has advanced to a highly specialized discipline. Computing power and software improvements have driven this development: we can now solve large scale quadratic programs with mixed integer constraints in reasonable times that would not have been thinkable when Harry Markowitz began the modern era of quantitative portfolio management in 1952. But computing power and software would not have been sufficient without the major advances in financial economics and econometrics that have shaped academia and the financial industry over the last 60 years. While the idea of a general theory of finance is still only a distant hope, asset managers now have tools in the financial engineering kit that address specific problems in their industry. The present Handbook consists of seven sections that explore major themes in current theoretical and practical use. These themes span all aspects of a modern quantitative investment organization.

Both qualitative and quantitative investment organizations spend enormous resources on human capital and data intensive research so as to build superior portfolios. Quantitative managers often deploy this costly information using *Portfolio Optimization* methods. Thus Part I of the Handbook consists of three chapters on this subject. Reha Tütüncü (Goldman Sachs) provides in "Recent Advances in Portfolio Optimization" a comprehensive review of the field to help readers navigate this deep area. Bruce I. Jacobs, Kenneth N. Levy, and David Starer (all of Jacobs Levy Equity Management) extend Markowitz's 1956 critical line algorithm to the construction of enhanced active equity (that is, long/short) portfolios. Debates over quantitative versus qualitative methods for portfolio construction, and the efficacy of various quantitative measures, have raged for decades and no doubt will go on for decades more. Sebastian Ceria (Axioma) refers to "religious" camps in these debates in his chapter "To Optimize or Not to Optimize: Is that the Question?". His provocative piece argues that there is no alternative to the use of "MVO" (mean-variance optimization) methods.

Further aspects of the *Portfolio Construction Processes* used by quantitative asset management organizations are investigated in the next section of the Handbook. Mark Kritzman (Windham Capital Management), Simon Myrgren (State Street), and

Sébastien Page (PIMCO) use dynamic programming in "Adding the Time Dimension: Optimal Rebalancing" to assess when in the management process it is best to rebalance portfolios. Colm O'Cinneide (QS Investors) provides in "Bayesian Methods in Investing" an overview and a tutorial of the extensive field of Bayesian methods, in which prior views about parameters of future outcome distributions are carefully updated to take into account new information. A different approach to the decision-theoretic problem faced by portfolio engineers is put forward by Michael Wolf and Dan Wunderli (both of the University of Zurich). In "Fund-of-Funds Construction by Statistical Multiple Testing Methods" they offer a framework to avoid data mining and to incorporate only significant risk premia. Nils Tuchschmid, Eric Wallerstein (both of the University of Applied Sciences, Geneva), and Sassan Zuker (Bank Julius Baer & Co. Ltd) survey in their "Hedge Fund Clones" chapter the current processes used by institutions seeking to construct portfolios with properties similar to hedge funds, using purely quantitative and deterministic methods.

The behavioral and organizational aspects of asset management organization are explored in Part III of the Handbook. The chapter by Jules H. van Binsbergen (Stanford University and NBER), Michael Brandt (Duke University and NBER), and Ralph S. J. Koijen (University of Chicago and NBER), "Decentralized Decision Making in Investment Management" argues that the inherent decentralization in asset management decision processes is welfare distracting and needs to be modified. This has direct implications for popular methods such as core/satellite and portable alpha approaches. Bernhard Scherer (EDHEC) and Xiaodong Xu (Deutsche Asset Management) argue in "Performance Based Fees, Incentives and Dynamic Tracking Error Choice" that fee structures that incent managers to diverge from the best interests of their clients are an issue only for badly written single period contracts. With the right contract specification, Scherer and Xu argue, excessive risk taking can largely be mitigated.

The Handbook then considers the issue of *Parameter Estimation* – crucial for quantitative methods – in the next three chapters. Heiko Bailer (Clariden Leu- Credit Suisse Group), Tatiana Mariavina, and R. Douglas Martin (both of the University of Washington) describe in "Robust Betas in Asset Management" how instabilities in exposure measures can be tackled. Daniel Giamouridis (Athens University of Economics and Business) and George Skiadopolous (University of Piraeus) offer in "The Informational Content of Financial Options for Quantitative Asset Management: A Review" tools for the financial engineer to estimate and accommodate non-normal distributions. Campbell R. Harvey (Duke University), John Liechty (Pennsylvania State University), and Merrill Liechty (Drexel University) conduct a parameter estimation experiment in "Parameter Uncertainty in Asset Allocation." This chapter revisits a test pitting a Monte-Carlo-based resampling approach advocated by Richard Michaud versus a Bayesian approach. While the resampled approach was found to be superior by Markowitz and Usmen in 2003, Harvey, Liechty, and Liechty obtain different results when a more realistic Bayesian procedure is used.

The next section addresses risk and *Risk Management*. Dan diBartolomeo (Northfield Information Services) surveys the major approaches to estimating equity risk in "Equity

Factor Models: Estimation and Extensions." diBartolomeo also shows how equity factor models can be extended to cover some fixed income credit risk. Kenneth Winston (Western Asset Management) takes up the fixed income risk theme, surveying the size and scope of the global fixed income market and describing two key risks in this market: interest rate risk and credit risk. In the next chapter, Winston and Thomas Hewett (Morgan Stanley Investment Management) consider "Risk Management for Long-Short Portfolios." Winston and Hewett point out that long-short portfolios have outcome distributions very different from long-only portfolios, and (after characterizing these distributions) argue that stop losses are not the optimal risk management technique for such portfolios.

Purely theoretical approaches to markets often fail in practice if they do not take into account *Market Structure and Trading*, the subject of the next section of the Handbook. A whole sub-industry (high frequency trading) is based on the knowledge of market microstructure and transaction costs. Equally, investment capacity problems can be seen as applications of transaction cost economics. Petter Kolm and Lee Maclin (both of New York University) describe in "Algorithmic Trading, Optimal Execution, and Dynamic Portfolios" the current status of algorithmic trading and in managing and benchmarking trading processes. Yossi Brandes, Ian Domowitz, and Vitaly Serbin (all of Investment Technology Group) expand on this in "Transaction Costs and Equity Portfolio Capacity Analysis" by including the capacity dimension. This dimension is not only important for computing the decay of advantageous information, but also for the distribution function of an asset management firm, addressing the question of pricing limited capacity.

In the final section of the Handbook, three chapters attack the unique problems of the field of *Investment Solutions*. Investment solutions address the construction of the entire portfolio held by an owner of capital. Many other methods address only the construction of portfolios representing a specific part on the entire owner's capital. Michael Peskin (Hudson Pilot) applies corporate finance principles to corporate pension plans in "Pension Funds and Corporate Enterprise Risk Management." Peskin identifies dynamic asset allocation policies for these plans as a function of funding level and sponsor health, creating an intersection between corporate finance and investment theory. Roy Hoevenaars (APG Asset Management) derives asset allocation methods for sector-wide pension funds in "Pricing Embedded Options in Value-Based Asset Liability Management." Such sector-wide funds are typical in Canada and in some European jurisdictions. While pension funds (also known as retirement funds and superannuation schemes) represent one of the largest concentrated pools of capital in the world, sovereign wealth funds are growing fast as another pool of highly concentrated capital. Such funds convert some of the wealth of a nation, which is often in the form of a non-renewable natural resource such as oil, into financial holdings that will provide for future generations as the stock of the natural resource dwindles. Francis Breedon (Queen Mary College, University of London) and Robert Kosowski (Imperial College London) provide a normative framework for sovereign wealth funds in "Asset Liability Management for Sovereign Wealth Funds."

We hope that readers of the *Handbook of Quantitative Asset Management* will use this Introduction both as a tour guide and as selected reading advice. As the variety of subjects, authors, and authors' backgrounds suggests, quantitative asset management is a field undergoing vigorous investigation and development. While no one book could cover all parts of this robust field, the Handbook explores some of the most important aspects of the theory and practice of quantitative asset management.

PART I

PORTFOLIO OPTIMIZATION

CHAPTER 2

RECENT ADVANCES IN PORTFOLIO OPTIMIZATION

REHA H. TÜTÜNCÜ

2.1 Introduction

When awarding the Nobel Prize in Economic Sciences to Harry Markowitz in 1990 (along with Merton Miller and William Sharpe), the prize committee praised Markowitz for having developed "a theory for households' and firms' allocation of financial assets under uncertainty, the so-called theory of portfolio choice. This theory analyzes how wealth can be optimally invested in assets which differ in regard to their expected return and risk, and thereby also how risks can be reduced" (Royal Swedish Academy of Sciences 1990). Markowitz' work, introduced in a 1952 article titled *Portfolio Selection* (Markowitz 1952) and further developed in the seminal book *Portfolio Selection: Efficient Diversification of Investments* (Markowitz 1959), formalized the diversification principle in portfolio selection and provided a "rigorously formulated, operational theory for portfolio selection under uncertainty – a theory which evolved into a foundation for further research in financial economics" (Royal Swedish Academy of Sciences 1990).

This influential theory remains at the center of the debates on quantitative portfolio selection more than five decades later. Markowitz' theory suggests that portfolios providing the optimal utility to the investor can be computed by focusing on two dimensions: the expected return of the portfolio and its variance. This reduces the portfolio selection problem into the so-called *mean-variance optimization* (MVO) problem, which belongs to a special case of a class of optimization problems known as *quadratic programming* problems. Through time, the explosive growth of computational resources as well as advances in optimization algorithms, turned MVO into a ubiquitous tool easily available to any interested investor. This pervasive use (and misuse) of MVO also led to criticisms, tests of efficacy, and countless proposals to improve the original methodology. This debate continues to this day and in this chapter, we will review some of the main threads in this debate.

In Section 2.2, we focus on the formulation of the portfolio selection problem, and in particular, on the measure of risk used in the trade-off function. Following the recent literature, we frame this discussion in the context of utility maximization versus mean-variance optimization. We interpret MVO and its variants as approximations to expected utility maximization problems with general utility functions. This interpretation allows us to consider the generalizations of the MVO problem that involve higher moments of the returns that have received attention recently.

In Section 2.3, we turn to the issue of estimation errors and their impact on mean-variance optimization. We focus on two strategies. First, we discuss robust optimization as an example of approaches that modify the optimization methodology used to generate the optimal portfolios. Second, we discuss the Black–Litterman model as an example of approaches that modify the inputs to the MVO problem with the aim of producing more intuitive and better behaved portfolios. Both the application of robust optimization methodology to portfolio selection and the Black–Litterman model were introduced in the 1990s. During the past decade both approaches have received increasing interest and their variations as well as extensions continue to appear in the literature on a regular basis.

When using the MVO methodology for portfolio construction, most managers impose various constraint on the portfolio weights or trade variables. These constraints can lead to portfolios with dramatically different composition and performance in comparison to unconstrained optimal portfolios. Several recent studies focused on the measurement of the impact of these constraints and we review these efforts in Section 2.4. After briefly discussing the *transfer coefficient* concept introduced by Clarke *et al.* (2002), we focus on what we call the *shadow cost decomposition* approach. This approach is based on the first-order optimality conditions for the MVO problem and the related concept of constraint shadow costs.

In Section 2.5, we discuss some of the recent developments related to the modeling of the portfolio construction problem as a multi-period decision problem. These models not only capture the effects of trading costs on portfolios more accurately, but also consider concepts such as information decay and investment horizon that cannot be easily modeled in the traditional single-period MVO setting. While the multi-period models often suffer from the curse of dimensionality, recent algorithmic and computational advances have enabled the solution of problems of growing size.

2.2 The Portfolio Optimization Problem

In order to develop a mathematical model of the portfolio selection problem, let us first introduce our notation. We consider an investment universe of n securities $S_1, S_2, \ldots, S_n$

with uncertain future returns $r_1, r_2, \ldots, r_n$. Let $r = [r_1, \ldots, r_n]^\top$ be the vector of these returns. A portfolio is represented with the n-dimensional vector $\omega = [\omega_1, \ldots, \omega_n]^\top$ where ω_i denotes the proportion of the total funds invested in security i. Let Ω, a subset of $\boldsymbol{R}^n$, denote the set of permissible portfolios. The set Ω is often defined through explicit constraints on the allocation of weights as we discuss later in the chapter; we use this generic representation to simplify the exposition. The (uncertain) return of the portfolio, r_P, depends linearly on the weights:

$$r_P(\omega) = \omega_1 r_1 + \ldots + \omega_n r_n = \omega^\top r. \tag{2.1}$$

Let α_i and σ_i denote the expected value and the standard deviation of r_i, the return of security S_i. For $i \neq j$, ρ_{ij} denotes the correlation coefficient of the returns of assets S_i and S_j. Let

$$\alpha = \begin{bmatrix} \alpha_1 \\ \vdots \\ \alpha_n \end{bmatrix}, \text{ and } \Sigma = \begin{bmatrix} \sigma_{11} & \sigma_{12} & \ldots & \sigma_{1n} \\ \sigma_{21} & \sigma_{22} & \ldots & \sigma_{2n} \\ \vdots & \vdots & \ddots & \vdots \\ \sigma_{n1} & \sigma_{n2} & \ldots & \sigma_{nn} \end{bmatrix}.$$

Here, Σ is the symmetric $n \times n$ covariance matrix of the returns with $\sigma_{ii} = \sigma_i^2$ and $\sigma_{ij} = \sigma_{ji} = \rho_{ij}\sigma_i\sigma_j$ for $i \neq j$.

2.2.1 Utility Functions

Most economic studies of investor behavior start with a model of investor's preferences, typically represented as a utility function of the investor's wealth. After choosing a utility function, one may derive optimal decisions for a rational investor who would try to maximize the expected utility of her decisions. The portfolio selection problem can be expressed in this manner also: The rational investor chooses a portfolio ω that maximizes the expected utility of the total return $r_P(\omega)$ of her investments at the end of the investment period.

Let us consider a utility function $u\,(r_P(\omega))$ that measures the utility of the outcome $r_P(\omega)$ for the investor. For simplicity, we will often write $u(\omega)$ instead of $u\,(r_P(\omega))$. It is customary to assume that the utility functions reflect some axioms of rational behavior, such as the von Neumann–Vorgenstern axioms, or at least the assumptions that the function is increasing and concave. Since $r_P(\omega)$ is an uncertain quantity that depends on the uncertain returns r_i, the utility function $u(\omega)$ is an uncertain quantity as well. We can create an index of utility for the portfolio ω by computing the expected value $u(\omega)$ and express the portfolio selection problem as the problem of maximizing expected utility:

$$\max_{\omega \in \Omega} E\,[u(\omega)]. \tag{2.2}$$

Here, the expectation is computed with respect to a multivariate distribution of the return vector r. This distribution is typically estimated using statistical techniques and may be based on a factor-model of returns.

2.2.2 Mean-Variance Optimization

The tractability of problem (2.2) depends on two important factors: the mathematical form of the utility function $u(\omega)$ and the properties of the set Ω of permissible portfolios. Targeting a simple and intuitive objective function, Markowitz' theory of mean-variance optimization reduces the problem of portfolio selection into a trade-off between the mean return α_P of the portfolio and its variance σ_P^2. This simplification is achieved by assuming that investors choose among risky securities on the basis of these two quantities only. In our notation these quantities can be computed as follows:

$$\alpha_P(\omega) = E\left[r_P(\omega)\right] = \omega_1\alpha_1 + \ldots + \omega_n\alpha_n = \alpha^\top \omega,$$

and

$$\sigma_P^2(\omega) = E\left[(r_P(\omega) - \alpha_P(\omega))^2\right] = \sum_{i,j} \rho_{ij}\sigma_i\sigma_j\omega_i\omega_j = \omega^\top \Sigma\omega,$$

where $\rho_{ii} \equiv 1$.

Markowitz' assumption that investors choose portfolios only based on the trade-off between α_P and σ_P^2 holds if the investors exhibit concave quadratic utility of the form

$$u(r_P(\omega)) = r_P(\omega) - \lambda\left(r_P(\omega) - E\left[r_P(\omega)\right]\right)^2.$$

In this expression, λ is a *risk-aversion* coefficient and is used to penalize the deviation of portfolio returns from their mean. When u is given in this manner, we observe that the expected utility function has the familiar mean-variance form:

$$\begin{aligned} E\left[u(r_P(\omega))\right] &= E\left[r_P(\omega)\right] - \lambda E\left[(r_P(\omega) - E[r_P(\omega)])^2\right] \\ &= \alpha_P(\omega) - \lambda\sigma_P^2(\omega). \end{aligned} \tag{2.3}$$

Substituting this expression as the objective function in (2.2), we obtain the generic form of the mean-variance optimization problem:

$$\max_{\omega\in\Omega} \phi(\omega) := \alpha_P(\omega) - \lambda\sigma_P^2(\omega) = \alpha^\top\omega - \lambda\omega^\top\Sigma\omega. \tag{2.4}$$

The function ϕ in (2.4) is sometimes called the *risk-adjusted expected return* function.

The simplest variant of the MVO problem is obtained in the case when $\Omega = \boldsymbol{R}^n$, meaning that there are no portfolio constraints and all portfolio allocations are permissible. In this case, the optimal solution to (2.4) is available in a simple analytical form:

$$\omega_u^* = \frac{1}{2\lambda}\Sigma^{-1}\alpha. \tag{2.5}$$

The subscript u in (2.5) is used to indicate that ω_u^* is the *unconstrained* optimal solution to (2.4). One feature of the unconstrained case is that the optimal weights satisfy an important equilibrium condition; namely that ratio of the marginal contribution to return to marginal contribution to risk is equal for all securities at optimality. In the constrained case that we will address in Section 2.4, this condition no longer holds.

One of the most debated aspects of the MVO formulation is its dependence on the quadratic utility assumption. Critics point out, in particular, the unintuitive implication of this assumption that beyond a critical level of return, investors will prefer less return to more return. The MVO formulation is consistent with non-quadratic utility maximization only when the returns can be assumed to follow a multi-dimensional elliptical distribution.[1] When this assumption holds, the form of the utility function becomes irrelevant and mean-variance optimality leads to maximum expected utility. Nevertheless, this also is a restrictive assumption and is often refuted by empirical analyses of security return distributions.

2.2.3 Alternative Formulations

Given the debate about the assumptions of the MVO formulation, it was natural that alternative formulations emerged. In these alternative formulations one usually replaces the variance of the portfolio return with a different measure of risk in the statement of the trade-off function used in optimization. An early example of these different measures was the measure of lower semivariance discussed by Markowitz (1959):

$$SV_P(\omega) = E\left[\min(r_P(\omega) - \alpha_P(\omega), 0)^2\right]. \tag{2.6}$$

Using this *downside risk measure*, one can replace the MVO problem (2.4) with the following *mean-semivariance optimization* problem:

$$\max_{\omega\in\Omega} \hat{\phi}(\omega) := \alpha_P(\omega) - \lambda SV_P(\omega). \tag{2.7}$$

Downside risk-measures such as semivariance are intuitively appealing because of their focus on losses which is more in line with a colloquial notion of risk. However, their use in practice has been limited because of the computational burden of optimizing with such measures. There are no simple formulas for aggregating such measures from securities to portfolios and their computation requires working with the entire joint distribution of the returns rather than a few moments as in standard MVO.

[1] Elliptical distributions are generalizations of normal distributions and have the property that their characteristic functions can be expressed using only the first two moments of the distribution.

Another measure of portfolio risk that is found often in the literature is the *mean absolute deviation* measure proposed by Konno (1990):

$$MAD_P(\omega) = E\left[|r_P(\omega) - \alpha_P(\omega)|\right]. \tag{2.8}$$

Optimizing portfolios using an objective function that combines expected return with mean absolute deviation is relatively simple as this problem can be expressed as a linear optimization problem.

Recent years have also seen an increase in interest for tail measures of risk such as value-at-risk (VaR) and conditional value-at-risk (Rockafellar and Uryasev 2000). VaR is a measure based on the percentiles of loss distributions and represents the predicted maximum loss with a specified probability level over a certain period of time. Given a probability level α, α-VaR of a random variable X is defined as follows:

$$\mathrm{VaR}_\alpha(X) := \min\{\gamma : P(X \geq \gamma) \leq 1 - \alpha\}. \tag{2.9}$$

In the portfolio selection setting, where ω denotes the portfolio weight vector and r denotes the random future returns of the securities, we can let $f(\omega, r)$ denote the loss function, e.g., $f(\omega, r) = -r^\top \omega$. If $p(r)$ represents the probability density function of r, then $\Psi(\omega, \gamma) := \int_{f(\omega,r)<\gamma} p(r)dr$ is the cumulative distribution function of f and we can rewrite (2.9) as follows:

$$\mathrm{VaR}_\alpha(\omega) := \min\{\gamma : \Psi(x, \gamma) \geq \alpha\}. \tag{2.10}$$

Then, one can combine expected returns with VaR in the objective function and obtain the *mean-VaR optimization* problem for portfolio selection. Despite its popularity among practitioners, as a risk measure VaR has several well-known problems. In particular, it is easy to construct examples where it is possible to increase the riskiness of a portfolio as measured by VaR while diversifying it, a counterintuitive result. Furthermore, VaR pays no attention to the magnitude of the losses beyond the VaR value and this can cause VaR optimized portfolios to have concentrated catastrophic risks.

These concerns led to the development of a variant of VaR called the conditional VaR that measures the expected value of the loss given that the loss exceeds VaR. The α-CVaR associated with portfolio ω is defined as:

$$\mathrm{CVaR}_\alpha(\omega) := \frac{1}{1-\alpha} \int_{f(\omega,r) \geq \mathrm{VaR}_\alpha(\omega)} f(\omega, r)p(r)dr. \tag{2.11}$$

In general, it is difficult to optimize either the VaR or CVaR of portfolios directly in a portfolio optimization setting because of the implicit description of the VaR value. Instead, one considers the following auxiliary function:

$$F_\alpha(\omega, \gamma) := \gamma + \frac{1}{1-\alpha} \int_{f(\omega,r) \geq \gamma} \left(f(\omega, r) - \gamma\right) p(r)dr. \tag{2.12}$$

This function is convex in the argument γ and has additional desirable properties that imply the following important observation (Rockafellar and Uryasev 2000):

$$\min_{\omega \in \Omega} \mathrm{CVaR}_\alpha(\omega) = \min_{\omega \in \Omega, \gamma} F_\alpha(\omega, \gamma). \tag{2.13}$$

Consequently, one can minimize CVaR directly, without needing to compute VaR first. These observations have been the basis of the *mean-CVaR optimization* models discussed by Rockafellar and Uryasev (2000) who also provide sampling based solution techniques for these formulations.

2.2.4 Utility Maximization vs. MVO

As we stated earlier, mean-variance optimization is consistent with utility maximization only with quadratic utility functions and such functions are problematic because of the negative marginal utility they imply at high levels of returns. Does this matter? Does the MVO formulation need to be consistent with expected utility maximization? One can argue that mean-variance optimization is nothing more than the quantification of a trade-off between two characteristics of portfolios and has no inevitable connection to utility maximization. Indeed, in his 1959 book, Markowitz (1959, ch. X) claims that "it is logically possible to accept the use of mean and variance and either accept or reject the expected utility maxim." As a result, in a considerable portion of the studies on portfolio optimization, and in the development of most of the alternative formulations we discussed in Section 2.2.3, MVO became the point of departure and utility maximization (with its "inconvenient" axioms) was either completely ignored or relegated to a secondary role.

It is possible to take a different approach and treat utility maximization as the natural anchor for portfolio selection. From this perspective, MVO and its multitude of variations can be viewed as mathematical approximations of the true expected utility maximization problem rather than simplistic trade-offs on two portfolio characteristics that is disconnected from rational investor behavior. Take, for example, the mean-semivariance optimization model (2.7) we discussed above. The semivariance measure (2.7) reflects the view that investors distinguish between good (upside) and bad (downside) variance and are mainly concerned with downside variance. Since the quadratic utility function that is used in the standard MVO formulation does not allow for this asymmetry, the mean-semivariance optimization problem in (2.7) can be seen as an imperfect approximation to an expected utility optimization problem with a utility function that is steeper for losses than it is for gains.

Along these lines, it is instructive to interpret the MVO approach as a mathematical approximation to the general expected utility maximization formulation, as was done in several recent books on portfolio optimization (Meucci 2005; Scherer 2002; Fabozzi *et al.* 2007). Indeed, for any analytical utility function, the expected utility can be expressed as an infinite sum of the raw moments of the return distribution:

$$E\left[u(r_P(\omega))\right] = \gamma_0 + \gamma_1 E\left[r_p(\omega)\right] + \gamma_2 E\left[r_p(\omega)^2\right] + \ldots = \sum_{i=0}^{\infty} \gamma_i M_i(\omega), \quad (2.14)$$

where

$$M_i(\omega) = E\left[r_P(\omega)^i\right]$$

represent the raw moments of the portfolio return $r_P(\omega) = \omega^\top r$.

Alternatively, the expected utility function can be expressed in terms of the central moments

$$CM_i(\omega) = E\left[\left(r_P(\omega) - E\left[r_P(\omega)\right]\right)^i\right].$$

A natural way to develop this representation is to consider a Taylor series approximation to $u(r_P(\omega))$ around the point $\alpha_P(\omega) = E\left[r_P(\omega)\right]$ and then take expectations on both sides:

$$\begin{aligned} u(r_P(\omega)) &= u(\alpha_P(\omega)) + u'(\alpha_P(\omega))\left(r_P(\omega) - \alpha_P(\omega)\right) \\ &\quad + \frac{1}{2}u''(\alpha_P(\omega))\left(r_P(\omega) - \alpha_P(\omega)\right)^2 + \sum_{i=3}^{\infty} \delta_i u^{(i)}\left(r_P(\omega) - \alpha_P(\omega)\right)^i, \quad (2.15) \end{aligned}$$

and

$$\begin{aligned} E\left[u(r_P(\omega))\right] &= u(\alpha_P(\omega)) + u'(\alpha_P(\omega))E\left[r_P(\omega) - \alpha_P(\omega)\right] \\ &\quad + \frac{1}{2}u''(\alpha_P(\omega))E\left[\left(r_P(\omega) - \alpha_P(\omega)\right)^2\right] + \sum_{i=3}^{\infty} \delta_i u^{(i)} E\left[\left(r_P(\omega) - \alpha_P(\omega)\right)^i\right], \\ &= u(\alpha_P(\omega)) + \delta_2 CM_2(\omega) + \sum_{i=3}^{\infty} \delta_i CM_i(\omega). \quad (2.16) \end{aligned}$$

In the expressions above, γ_i and δ_i are the coefficients of the corresponding moments in these expansions. In this setting, the MVO approach can be interpreted as maximizing an approximation of the expected utility function where the approximation is obtained simply by dropping the third and higher order terms from the infinite series expansion in (2.16).

This interpretation also allows us to judge the suitability of mean-variance optimization for approximating general expected utility maximization. Omitting the higher order terms in (2.16) cannot be justified if the coefficients δ_i are not small for some $i \geq 3$ (meaning that the actual utility function is not close to a quadratic utility function), and if the central moments of order $i \geq 3$ are not approximately spanned by the first and second moments (meaning that the return distribution is far from normal). Given that the empirical security return distributions often exhibit negative skewness (more downside extremes than upside extremes) as well as excess kurtosis, it can be argued that the two term approximation of a generic expected utility maximization as in MVO is not adequate and portfolio selection models can be improved by considering additional terms from the expansion in (2.14) or (2.16).

In the MVO setting, the objective function of the problem (2.4) implies that, of two portfolios with identical expected returns, one would prefer the one with smaller variance. Pursuing this idea further, it is reasonable to assume that of two portfolios with identical expected returns and variances, a rational investor would prefer the one with higher skew; and when the first three central moments match, she prefers the portfolio with lower kurtosis. These preferences can be expressed in a portfolio selection model by using more than the first two terms in the expansion (2.16) when forming an objective function. This is precisely the approach taken by Harvey *et al.* (2004) as well as by Jondeau and Rockinger (2006). Harvey *et al.* formulate an objective function that considers the skewness and co-skewness of the returns when comparing alternative portfolios, while Jondeau and Rockinger use formulations that incorporate the first four central moments. Similarly, Fabozzi *et al.* (2007) devote a section of their book on robust portfolio selection to portfolio selection with higher moments and demonstrate, for example, how a logarithmic utility function can be approximated using a four-term objective function that rewards higher expected returns and skew while penalizing higher variance and kurtosis. In a related study, Adler and Kritzman (2007) consider what they call the *full-scale optimization* approach for constructing portfolios. They consider the expected utility maximization problem, without any approximations, using sampling ideas and sophisticated search algorithms. They report that in tests where return distributions demonstrate persistent higher moments, a full-scale optimization approach produces better portfolio performance both in- and out-of-sample.

It is important to note that the additional model flexibility afforded by using higher order moments in a portfolio selection optimization does not come for free. Not only are there many additional parameters that need to be estimated, but also the estimation error with these parameters tends to be larger, increasing the estimation risk in the resulting optimizations. Furthermore, solving portfolio optimization problems involving higher order moments is often quite difficult. Inclusion of the skewness and co-skewness terms destroys the concavity property of the objective function and this impacts the computational cost and stability of optimization methods in a negative way.

2.3 Handling Estimation Errors in the Optimization Inputs

One of the persistent debates about mean-variance optimization focuses on the well established sensitivity of the methodology to perturbation of the inputs (Chopra and Ziemba 1993) and its tendency to amplify the effects of input mis-estimation, a property referred to as *estimation error maximization* (Michaud 1989). Critics of MVO argue that small changes in the inputs of the problem tend to generate portfolios with vastly different compositions – a counterintuitive behavior at best, and a potentially devastating deficiency at worst. Given that the inputs to the MVO are statistical estimates of the moments of non-stationary return distributions, the magnitude of the estimation error can be significant. Combined with the input sensitivity of MVO, these errors may lead to portfolios far from truly optimal ones, potentially with poor performance and excessive turnover.

A number of approaches have been proposed to address these issues in MVO. Some of these approaches try to model the estimation error in the MVO inputs and tweak the optimization algorithms to incorporate this additional element. Stochastic programming methods that develop a probabilistic model of the input uncertainty and attack the portfolio construction problem through scenario generation are examples of this approach; see the survey by Yu *et al.* (2003). The steady stream of research on the application of robust optimization methodology to portfolio selection during the last decade also belongs to this category and is the subject of the recent book by Fabozzi *et al.* (2007).

Other approaches focus on improving the inputs of the portfolio selection problem before any optimization is conducted. The best known of these approaches is the Black–Litterman (1990) methodology that aims to generate a *consistent* set of return and risk forecasts by blending the investor's subjective views with the implied views of the market. We briefly review robust optimization and Black–Litterman methods in the remainder of this section.

2.3.1 Robust Optimization

The observation that the results of an optimization problem may change greatly in response to small changes in the inputs is not specific to MVO and in fact this behavior is encountered often in various classes of optimization problems. The problem is the potentially discontinuous and ill-behaved mapping between the inputs and the outputs of optimization problems (Bonnans and Shapiro 2000). Furthermore, both theoretical and computational evidence suggests that the input sensitivity issue of optimization algorithms can be more pronounced in the presence of constraints.

In addition, in many optimization models including the MVO model, the inputs to the problem are either not known at the time the problem must be solved, are computed inaccurately, or are otherwise uncertain. The combination of this fact with the input sensitivity of optimization algorithms leads to the serious concern that one is solving the wrong problem, and finding a solution that is far from optimal for the correct problem.

Robust optimization is a methodology that is developed to address these concerns and refers to the modeling of optimization problems with data uncertainty to obtain a solution that is guaranteed to be "good" for all or most possible realizations of the uncertain parameters. Uncertainty in the parameters is described through *uncertainty sets* that contain many possible values that may be realized for the uncertain parameters. The size of the uncertainty set is determined by the level of desired robustness.

For *robust portfolio optimization* one typically considers a model where return and covariance matrix information is uncertain and is defined through an uncertainty set, say $\mathcal{U}$. For example, this information may take the form "the expected return on security j is between 3% and 5%" rather than claiming that it is, say, 4%. More generically, an interval type uncertainty set for the inputs α and Σ take the following form:

$$\mathcal{U} = \{(\alpha, \Sigma) : \alpha^L \leq \alpha \leq \alpha^U, \ \ \Sigma^L \leq \Sigma \leq \Sigma^U, \ \ \Sigma \text{ is positive semidefine}\}, \qquad (2.17)$$

where $\mu^L, \mu^U, \Sigma^L, \Sigma^U$ are the extreme values of the intervals. The positive semidefiniteness restriction is necessary for Σ to be a valid covariance matrix. Other popular choices for uncertainty sets in portfolio optimization include ellipsoidal uncertainty sets (Ceria and Stubbs 2006; Goldfarb and Iyengar 2003) polyhedral uncertainty sets, and histogram-based uncertainty sets (Bienstock 2007).

Given an uncertainty set $\mathcal{U}$, the robust portfolio optimization problem is formulated in an adversarial setting. One takes the view that, once the investor makes a portfolio selection, say ω, an adversary ("nature") will choose a set of *true* values for the mean-variance objective function parameters α and Σ from the set $\mathcal{U}$ to minimize the investor's utility value. The choice of the adversary can be seen as the worst case realization of the input parameters α and Σ from their uncertainty set $\mathcal{U}$. Then, the objective of the investor is to choose a portfolio ω that maximizes this worst case objective value:

$$\max_{\omega \in \Omega}\{ \min_{(\alpha,\Sigma)\in\mathcal{U}} \alpha^\top \omega - \lambda \omega^\top \Sigma \omega\}. \qquad (2.18)$$

Note that, unlike stochastic programming models where the parameter uncertainty is modeled through probabilistic descriptions, robust optimization does not associate a probability with elements of the uncertainty set. While this approach avoids the often difficult task of finding an appropriate probability distribution to model the parameter uncertainty, it also treats every element of the uncertainty set in a uniform manner, potentially attaching too much importance to extreme but very unlikely scenarios in the set. This represents a more conservative perspective on uncertainty that does not always match investor behavior and is one of the most debated aspects of robust optimization.

Given that the values of the parameters α and Σ will depend on the selection of ω, the two-level optimization formulation in (2.18) results in a significantly more difficult problem to solve than the standard problem (2.4). Fortunately, modern optimization techniques such as conic optimization and software tools utilizing these techniques make robust portfolio optimization problems tractable. We refer the reader to Cornuejols and Tütüncü (2007) and Fabozzi *et al.* (2007) and the references listed in these books for additional details.

One important property of most robust optimization models is that the input-output mapping becomes smoother and more stable compared to the standard optimization methods, meaning that as inputs are perturbed, outputs (optimal allocations) change in predictable and continuous fashion. Schöttle and Werner (2006a,b) provide empirical and theoretical evidence on these properties of robust optimization.

2.3.2 Black–Litterman Model

One important determinant of the solution quality in MVO is the consistency of the return and risk forecasts used in optimization. For example, two securities with nearly identical risk profiles but very different expected return estimates can lead to portfolios with extreme weights as the optimizer would interpret such inputs as an indication of a near-arbitrage opportunity. Even if the issues of input uncertainty and the sensitivity of the optimization algorithms to such uncertainty can be addressed using the approaches we already mentioned in Section 2.3.1, one still has to be concerned about the misalignment of return and risk estimates and the effect of such misalignment on optimal portfolios generated.

In two influential articles in the early 1990s, Black and Litterman (1990, 1992) diagnosed the inconsistency of the return and risk estimates used as optimization inputs as the main reason for the unintuitive portfolios often generated by the MVO approach and provided an innovative methodology to address this problem. Their solution was to combine the market's implied view with the investor's subjective views to generate a blended return forecast that is better aligned with the risk forecasts.

The Black–Litterman (BL) model provides an effective mechanism to improve the *inputs* used in the MVO approach rather than changing the optimization methodology itself, as in stochastic programming or robust optimization techniques. The BL methodology is often very effective in practice. It produces intuitive and balanced portfolios that are tilted toward the investor's views. The improved consistency of the return and risk estimates provided by the BL model also makes the MVO approach less prone to error maximization. The success of the model continues to attract attention in the academic and practitioner literature; see, for example, Idzorek's (2004) detailed description of the implementation of the BL model.

The focus of the BL approach on Markowitz' MVO model has been seen as its limitation and some of the recent developments regarding the BL model has focused on extending its application to other portfolio construction strategies than the MVO approach and to cases where the investors' views can be on various market risk and return factors, instead of the returns of the securities in the investment universe. For example, Martellini and Ziemann (2007) consider the application of the BL approach to construction of portfolios using skewness and higher moments in addition to mean and variance in the optimization process. They argue that the use of the higher moments is particularly useful in hedge fund style portfolio allocation since the hedge fund returns show significant deviations from normality.

Jones, Lim, and Zangari (2007) discuss the use of the BL model in constructing structured equity portfolios based on a factor return model. In their methodology, the investor views are expressed on the factors of the return model. They show how these views can be used to generate so-called *view portfolios*, which are then combined to create an *optimal tilt portfolio* that captures all views of the investor. In a separate study, Meucci (2009) offers a generalization of the BL approach to address cases where the investor expresses views on risk factors effecting the returns rather than directly on the returns themselves or on return factors. His extension covers cases where the views may be expressed in terms of stress-test scenarios and he provides an interesting case study where the BL approach is applied to option trading by expressing views on implied volatilities of underlying securities.

2.4 Understanding the Impacts of Constraints in Portfolio Optimization

Portfolio managers using a quantitative portfolio optimization approach often impose constraints on portfolio weights and exposures while constructing portfolios. In some cases, these constraints reflect the requirements of the investor (e.g., the investment universe to be used or the ability to take short positions) or regulatory restrictions and, as such, they are non-discretionary pieces of the portfolio optimization problem. In other cases, the constraints are discretionary and may originate from the portfolio manager's desire to limit exposure to certain securities, industries, countries, etc., or her aversion to excessive trading. Whatever their origin, constraints affect the portfolio construction process and the optimal portfolios generated in a material way. This, in turn, impacts the performance of the portfolios constructed.

Understanding and quantifying this impact is an important need for portfolio managers. Recognizing this need, there has been a focused effort in the quantitative portfolio construction literature during the last decade to develop useful diagnostic measures and tools to evaluate the impact of various types of constraints on portfolio performance. In this section, we review some of this literature and provide guidance on its future directions.

2.4.1 Transfer Coefficient

While the impact of constraints on portfolio composition was discussed in earlier studies (e.g., Grinold and Easton 1998), it was the 2002 article by Clarke *et al.* (2002) and their introduction of the concept of the *transfer coefficient* that refocused attention on constraints in quantitative portfolio optimization. Clarke *et al.* define the transfer coefficient, *TC*, to be the cross-sectional correlation coefficient between the risk-adjusted active weights in an optimized portfolio and the risk-adjusted forecasted active returns ("alphas") for the corresponding securities.

This definition is motivated by an observation in a simplified setting where the active returns are assumed to be uncorrelated. In this setting, unconstrained optimal risk-adjusted active weight allocations are proportional to the alphas. Indeed, if we assume that the matrix Σ in the unconstrained MVO problem (2.4) is diagonal with diagonal elements σ_i^2, then optimal weights ω_i^* satisfy

$$\omega_i^* = \frac{\alpha_i}{\sigma_i^2} \frac{1}{2\lambda}. \tag{2.19}$$

The identity in (2.19) follows directly from (2.5) and the assumption that Σ is a diagonal matrix. As a result, in this unconstrained case, the risk-adjusted active weights $\left(\omega_i^* \cdot \sigma_i\right)$ and the risk-adjusted alphas (α_i/σ_i) are perfectly correlated, and the transfer coefficient of this base case is 1. When the portfolio optimization problem includes trading costs or constraints, the identity (2.19) no longer holds and the transfer coefficient depends on how well the resulting active weights line up with their risk-adjusted alphas.

In practice, most portfolio optimization problems have multiple constraints: long-only constraint, exposure limits, trading limits, etc. Each of these constraints distorts the optimal weights away from their values in the unconstrained case; some higher, others lower. Furthermore, the impact of one constraint may change depending on the presence of other constraints. To address these complexities, Clarke *et al.* (2002) compute this coefficient in a number of hypothetical scenarios involving the long-only constraint, market-cap neutrality constraint, and turnover constraint. They find that the long-only constraint has, by far, the most noticeable impact.

2.4.2 Shadow Cost Decomposition

While the analysis described by Clarke *et al.* provides important insights into the impact of different constraints on portfolio characteristics, their approach is enumerative and does not offer a scalable strategy to decompose the effects of multiple constraints when there are may be tens or hundreds of them. Such a decomposition is obtained by considering the first-order optimality conditions of constrained optimization problems. Since the first-order conditions involve the shadow costs (Lagrange multipliers) of the portfolio construction constraints, we will refer to this approach as *shadow cost decomposition.*

Let us start by considering a more general form of the MVO problem (2.4) that incorporates trading costs into the objective function and has an explicit description of the set Ω of permissible portfolios through linear constraints:

$$\begin{aligned} &\max_\omega \ \phi(\omega) := \alpha^\top \omega - \lambda \omega^\top \Sigma \omega - \gamma TC(\Delta\omega) \\ &\text{s.t.} \ A\omega \leq b. \end{aligned} \tag{2.20}$$

In the problem above $\Delta\omega = \omega - \omega^0$ represents the changes in weights (i.e., trades), $TC(\cdot)$ is the trading cost function, and γ is a parameter of aversion to trading costs. The matrix A is an $m \times n$ dimensional matrix of linear constraint coefficients. To simplify the presentation, we stick to this generic notation for constraints and do not discuss various constraint categories such as exposure, holding, trading, etc., separately.

The solution ω^* of (2.20) satisfies the following set of first-order optimality conditions:

$$\alpha - 2\lambda\Sigma\omega^* - \gamma\nabla TC(\Delta\omega^*) - A^\top\pi = 0, \tag{2.21}$$

with additional conditions on π:

$$\pi^\top(b - A\omega) = 0,\ \pi \geq 0. \tag{2.22}$$

In the optimality conditions listed above, π is the m-dimensional vector of *shadow costs* (Lagrange multipliers) associated with the linear constraints $A\omega \leq b$. Using (2.21) one can write

$$2\lambda\Sigma\omega^* = \alpha - \gamma\nabla TC(\Delta\omega^*) - A^\top\pi. \tag{2.23}$$

Solving for ω^*, and recalling from equation (2.5) that $\omega_u^* = \frac{1}{2\lambda}\Sigma^{-1}\alpha$ represents the unconstrained optimal solution, we get

$$\begin{aligned}\omega^* &= \frac{1}{2\lambda}\Sigma^{-1}\alpha - \frac{\gamma}{2\lambda}\Sigma^{-1}\nabla TC(\Delta\omega^*) - \frac{1}{2\lambda}\Sigma^{-1}A^\top\pi \\ &= \omega_u^* - \frac{\gamma}{2\lambda}\Sigma^{-1}\nabla TC(\Delta\omega^*) - \frac{1}{2\lambda}\Sigma^{-1}A^\top\pi.\end{aligned} \tag{2.24}$$

One can further decompose (2.24) into contributions from individual constraints. Letting A_i represent the transpose of the ith row of the constraint matrix A, and letting π_i denote the corresponding element of the shadow cost vector π, one can write:

$$\omega^* = \frac{1}{2\lambda}\Sigma^{-1}\alpha - \frac{\gamma}{2\lambda}\Sigma^{-1}\nabla TC(\Delta\omega^*) - \sum_{i=1}^{m}\frac{\pi_i}{2\lambda}\Sigma^{-1}A_i. \tag{2.25}$$

Comparing with the solution (2.5) in the unconstrained case, we immediately observe that equations (2.24) and (2.25) can be seen as a decomposition of the optimal portfolio weights into contributions from alpha, transaction costs, and constraint terms. In this setting, the first term on the right-hand side of (2.25) is seen as the set of ideal weights, and the additional terms as the distortion of these ideal weights because of the presence of constraints and transaction costs. Equivalently, it is possible to view each one of the terms on the right-hand side of equation (2.25) as different portfolios. With this view, the managed portfolio is the aggregation of a pure unconstrained mean-variance optimal portfolio, a *transaction-cost portfolio*, and *constraint portfolios* corresponding to each binding constraint.

The decomposition (2.23)–(2.25) was studied recently by various researchers including Grinold (2005), Scherer and Xu (2007), and Stubbs and Vandenbussche (2008). In a related study, Bender *et al.* (2009) represent the constrained optimal portfolio using its beta with respect to the unconstrained portfolio:

$$\omega^* = \beta\omega_u^* + \omega_r, \text{ where } \beta = \frac{(\omega^*)^\top \Sigma\omega_u^*}{\left(\omega_u^*\right)^\top \Sigma\omega_u^*}. \tag{2.26}$$

Note that ω_r, the residual of this beta decomposition, is orthogonal to the unconstrained optimal portfolio ω_u^* by construction. Next, Bender *et al.* use the shadow-cost decomposition (2.25) to write the residual portfolio as follows:

$$\omega_r = \gamma\left[\beta_{TC}\omega_u^* - \frac{1}{2\lambda}\Sigma^{-1}\nabla TC(\Delta\omega^*)\right] + \sum_{i=1}^m \pi_i\left[\beta_i\omega_u^* - \frac{1}{2\lambda}\Sigma^{-1}A_i\right].$$

Above, β_{TC} and β_i represent the beta of the shadow cost portfolio of the transaction-cost term and constraint i with respect to the unconstrained optimal portfolio. This approach decomposes the optimal portfolio into one aligned with alphas $\left(\beta\omega_u^*\right)$ and distortionary effects from costs and constraints that add risk to the portfolio without changing its alpha. Note that the β in (2.26) is closely related to the notion of transfer coefficient.

Next, we review various uses of the shadow-cost decomposition discussed in the studies listed above.

2.4.2.1 *Utility Decomposition*

Scherer and Xu (2007), pose the following question: "What harm can constraints do to value added, i.e., investor utility?" They observe that constraints can sometimes affect individual security weights significantly without having much impact on utility and that their impact is best measured in the utility dimension. They proceed to answer this question using shadow cost decomposition.

To compute the impact of constraints on utility, we can compute the utility of the unconstrained optimal portfolio ω_u using the quadratic utility function $\phi(\omega)$ from (2.4):

$$\phi\left(\omega_u^*\right) = \alpha^\top\omega_u^* - \lambda\left(\omega_u^*\right)^\top \Sigma\omega_u^*,$$

and compare that to the utility of the constrained optimal solution ω^* of problem (2.20). Note that $\omega_u^* = \frac{1}{2\lambda}\Sigma^{-1}\alpha$ implies $\alpha = 2\lambda\Sigma\omega_u^*$. Therefore,

$$\alpha^\top\omega_u^* - \alpha^\top\omega^* = 2\lambda\left(\omega_u^*\right)^\top \Sigma\omega_u^* - 2\lambda\left(\omega_u^*\right)^\top \Sigma\omega^*.$$

Using this identity, Scherer and Xu perform the following computation:

$$\begin{aligned}
\phi\left(\omega_u^*\right) - \phi(\omega^*) &= \left(\alpha^\top \omega_u^* - \lambda\left(\omega_u^*\right)^\top \Sigma\omega_u^*\right) - \left(\alpha^\top\omega^* - \lambda(\omega^*)^\top\Sigma\omega^*\right) \\
&= \lambda\left(\omega_u^* - \omega^*\right)^\top \Sigma\left(\omega_u^* - \omega^*\right) \\
&= \lambda\left(\frac{\gamma}{2\lambda}\Sigma^{-1}\nabla TC(\Delta\omega^*) + \frac{1}{2\lambda}\Sigma^{-1}A^\top\pi\right)^\top \\
&\quad \Sigma\left(\frac{\gamma}{2\lambda}\Sigma^{-1}\nabla TC(\Delta\omega^*) + \frac{1}{2\lambda}\Sigma^{-1}A^\top\pi\right) \\
&= \frac{1}{4\lambda}\left(\gamma\nabla TC(\Delta\omega^*) + A^\top\pi\right)^\top \Sigma^{-1}\left(\gamma\nabla TC(\Delta\omega^*) + A^\top\pi\right).
\end{aligned}$$

Above, we used the identity (2.24) to express $\omega_u^* - \omega^*$ in terms of the transaction cost and constraint contributions. Separating the final equation above into two parts, we obtain

$$\begin{aligned}
\phi\left(\omega_u^*\right) - \phi(\omega^*) = \frac{1}{4\lambda}&\left[\gamma\nabla TC(\Delta\omega^*)^\top\Sigma^{-1}\left(\gamma\nabla TC(\Delta\omega^*) + A^\top\pi\right)\right. \\
&\left. +\pi^\top A\Sigma^{-1}\left(\gamma\nabla TC(\Delta\omega^*) + A^\top\pi\right)\right].
\end{aligned} \tag{2.27}$$

In this last expression, the first term on the right-hand side represents the utility loss due to the presence of transaction costs in the MVO formulation and the second term represents the utility loss due to constraints. As we have seen in (2.25), the constraint contribution term can be further decomposed into contribution terms from each individual constraint.

Using this methodology, Scherer and Xu (2007) analyze the impact of the long-only constraint as well as beta-neutrality and size-neutrality constraints in a mean-variance optimization setting and find that, as long as the alphas of the securities are not correlated with their market-cap categorizations, the majority of the utility loss can be attributed to the long-only constraint.

2.4.2.2 *Active Weight Decomposition*

When analyzing a mean-variance optimized portfolio, investment managers are often puzzled by the appearance of over-weights in low or negative alpha securities, or conversely, of under-weights in high alpha securities. Clearly, the risk and covariance structure of an asset may lead to an optimal weight not perfectly aligned with its alpha. In other cases, this type of unintuitive weight can be explained through the presence of trading costs or constraints. For example, one may have a neutral weight or an under-weight in a high alpha security because of the high cost of trading into that security. Or, the portfolio may be prevented from under-weighting a negative alpha security because of the need to satisfy a beta-neutrality constraint. The decomposition in equation (2.25) is an effective tool in providing such explanations in a systematic way in the analysis and interpretation of individual security weights.

It should, however, be noted that the conclusions derived through shadow-cost decomposition are not always intuitive in a security level analysis. For example, we may see that the weight of a technology stock is being distorted because of an industry exposure constraint on the airline industry. The main reason for such occurrences and the difficulty of interpreting decomposition results is the presence of the inverse of the covariance matrix in equation (2.25). This inverse matrix carries the correlation information about cross-sectional returns and *spreads* the impact of a constraint on one security (or security group) to the remaining, correlated securities.

For this reason, it is often useful to consider the *implied alpha decomposition* given in (2.23). The expression on the right-hand side of this equation is the *implied alpha* of the security. For a given set of weights, a risk-aversion parameter, and a covariance matrix of returns, the implied alpha of the given weights is the set of alphas that would make these weights optimal in an unconstrained MVO problem. The implied alphas of the unconstrained optimal weights in (2.5) are clearly the alphas themselves. For weights determined through a constrained optimization, the decomposition (2.23) provides the impact of each constraint on the implied alpha. The absence of the Σ^{-1} on the right-hand side of this equation makes the decomposition easier to interpret and the magnitude of the constraint impacts easier to measure and compare.

2.4.2.3 *Return Factor Analysis*

One of the common methods for developing estimates of alphas is through the use of a multiple-factor model. For example, one may develop a return model involving multiple factors or *signals* such as valuation, growth, etc., and then compute the expected return of each security as a weighted sum of the expected signal returns where the weights are the *loadings* or *exposures* of that security to the signal. This model can be represented as follows:

$$\alpha = B^{\top} f = \sum_{i=1}^{k} f_i B_i, \tag{2.28}$$

where f is a k-dimensional vector of expected factor returns, and B is the $k \times n$ matrix of the exposures. The B_i are the transposes of the rows of the matrix B corresponding to the exposures to signal i. Given this factor model for the returns, one can compute the aggregate exposure to the return factors in an optimal portfolio by multiplying the exposure matrix with the optimal weights:

$$e^* = B\omega^* = \begin{bmatrix} B_1^{\top}\omega^* \\ \vdots \\ B_k^{\top}\omega^* \end{bmatrix}, \text{ and } \alpha^* = \alpha^{\top}\omega^* = f^{\top}e^* = \sum_{i=1}^{k} f_i e_i^*.$$

In other words, the exposure of a portfolio ω^* to factor i is $e_i^* = B_i^{\top}\omega^*$, the expected return contribution of factor i for this portfolio is $f_i e_i^*$, and the expected return of the portfolio is the sum of all expected factor contributions, that is $\sum_{i=1}^{k} f_i e_i^*$.

Given that the constraints and transaction costs can decrease the expected return of the optimal portfolio, it becomes important to determine whether the impact is uniform across different return factors or not. The decomposition (2.25) can be very useful in this analysis. We can write:

$$e_i^* = g_i^* + h_i^*,$$

where

$$g_i^* = B_i^\top \omega_u^* = \frac{1}{2\lambda} B_i^\top \Sigma^{-1} \alpha$$

is the exposure of the unconstrained optimal portfolio ω_u^* to factor i and

$$h_i^* = -\frac{\gamma}{2\lambda} B_i^\top \Sigma^{-1} \nabla TC(\Delta\omega^*) - \sum_{i=1}^{m} \frac{\pi_i}{2\lambda} B_i^\top \Sigma^{-1} A_i$$

is the distortion of the unconstrained optimal exposure introduced by the presence of the trading costs and constraints. By comparing, for example, the ratios e_i^*/g_i^*, or some other relative exposure measure, one can determine the factors most affected by the presence of constraints. This type of analysis has strategic implications for the portfolio manager. For example, a signal that is mostly neutralized by a long-only constraint might not be useful for managing long-only portfolios.

2.4.2.4 *Performance Attribution*

In addition to understanding the impact of constraints and trading costs on optimal portfolios constructed in an *ex ante* fashion as we have seen above, the shadow cost decomposition can be used for evaluating the impact of constraints/costs on realized, *ex post* performance. As we discussed above, the managed portfolio can be seen as an aggregation of the optimal unconstrained portfolio, a transaction cost portfolio and constraint portfolios corresponding to each active constraint. Then, the performance of the managed portfolio is also an aggregate quantity, namely the sum of the performance of each of the portfolios in the decomposition. Using standard portfolio performance measurement techniques, we can measure how much each constraint portfolio contributes to the performance of the final portfolio. A return based analysis conducted in this manner complements the *ex ante* analysis we discussed in the previous paragraphs.

Recall that some constraints serve a *model insurance* function. If the portfolio manager is concerned about the accuracy of the model inputs of the MVO problem (expected returns and the covariance matrix) and the extreme bets these inaccuracies may lead to in an optimized portfolio, she may prefer to limit the size of the bets explicitly using constraints. On an *ex ante* basis, such constraints can only decrease the utility of the optimized portfolio. However, on an *ex post* basis, a decomposition analysis may reveal that an insurance constraint actually improves performance by preventing the portfolio from taking bets that turn out to be harmful to the portfolio performance.

As with any insurance strategy, such an evaluation must be made on an on-going basis and using observations from a relatively long history.

2.5 Dynamic Portfolio Optimization

The portfolio management problem is not a single-period problem. Portfolio weights move through market movements and portfolio characteristics such as alpha and risk drift away from their previously optimized levels. A portfolio manager must periodically reevaluate her portfolio and make adjustments to it to bring it back in line with its stated objectives. As such, the proper formulation of the portfolio optimization problem requires a dynamic, multi-period approach.

More often than not, a manager treats each portfolio rebalance as a single-period problem independent of the earlier or future rebalances. This approach does not look further than one-period ahead and the only memory of the previous rebalances is contained in the starting portfolio. Nevertheless, many of the decisions made in one rebalance have repercussions on the future rebalances, especially if one considers the effects of trading costs and taxes on performance. For example, a position opened at one rebalance must eventually be closed, potentially at a higher cost of trading. Given these concerns, the "one period at a time" approach leads to sub-optimal portfolio rebalancing strategies.

The problem, of course, is the difficulty of adding the time dimension to the portfolio optimization problem. This not only introduces the difficult task of estimating the future evolution of expected returns and risks but also the burden of solving a dynamic optimization problem.

2.5.1 Dynamic Programming

Dynamic programming is a term used to describe both a modeling methodology and the associated solution approaches in the context of sequential decision problems. Dynamic programming models consist of decision *stages*, typically representing different time periods, and a set of possible *states* for the variables of interest in each stage. The output of a dynamic programming model is a *policy* or a *strategy* that represents the collection of actions a decision-maker would take at each state, should she ever reach that state. Actions or events lead to *transitions* from one state in one stage to a state in the following stage. A *value function* measures the best possible objective one can achieve starting from a particular state.

Dynamic programming models and methods are based on Bellman's *Principle of Optimality*. This principle states that for overall optimality in a sequential decision process, all the decisions made in the future stages after reaching a particular state must be optimal with respect to that state. Using this principle, the value function can be expressed in a recursive manner and much of the mathematical study of dynamic programming models focus on this recursion.

Dynamic programming models are pervasive in the study of portfolio problems. In the continuous time setting, closed form solutions were derived under restrictive assumptions in classical studies; see, e.g., Merton (1971). Similarly, in a discrete-time multi-period optimal portfolio selection model, closed form solutions can be derived by making simplifying assumptions (Li and Ng 2001). These simplified models often ignore the significant effects of transaction costs or the portfolio constraints to make the dynamic problem tractable. In a more recent study, Grinold (2006) considers a dynamic programming model for optimal portfolio construction with transaction costs and information decay. To make the model tractable, Grinold must make an assumption that relates the transaction cost model to the risk model. Under this assumption, he demonstrates that the optimal portfolios are a mixture of a scaled-back "ideal" portfolio and the current position. The scaling parameter represents the ability of the manager to add value in the long run in the presence of transaction costs.

One aspect of portfolio construction that is neither well understood nor sufficiently studied is the problem of optimal mixing of different return generating signals. Consider, for example, an investor who constructs a return model that contains both valuation or quality based slow-moving long horizon signals, and price reversal or event based fast-moving short horizon signals. Dynamic programming models, such as that of Grinold (2006), are providing new tools for improving the risk budgeting decisions in these scenarios.

2.5.2 Stochastic Programming

We have already discussed the use of stochastic programming techniques in decision problems with uncertain inputs in Section 2.3. Stochastic programming approaches are especially powerful when they are applied in a multi-stage setting and allow for adaptive solutions. The flexibility of the stochastic programming approach coupled with the availability of computational implementations that can solve stochastic programs of ever-increasing dimensions, make it a good choice for modeling dynamic decisions in portfolio management. For example, stochastic programming has become the method of choice for most asset-liability management models (Zenios and Ziemba 2006). We briefly review this powerful methodology in this subsection.

Stochastic programming refers to an optimization problem where some of the input parameters are not known with certainty and can be described using a stochastic model. Stochastic programming models can include both *anticipative* and *adaptive* decision variables. Anticipative variables correspond to those decisions that must be made before any future observations. In contrast, adaptive variables correspond to decisions that can be made after realizations of some or all of the uncertain parameters are observed.

Stochastic programming models that include both anticipative and adaptive variables are called *recourse* models. One can model a dynamic decision environment where information is revealed progressively and the decisions are adapted to the new information using a multi-stage stochastic programming formulation. In the context of portfolio management, each portfolio rebalancing opportunity represents a decision stage and such problems can be conveniently formulated as multi-stage stochastic programs with recourse.

To illustrate the concept of multi-stage stochastic programs we consider a two-period portfolio selection problem, with decision variables ω^1 corresponding to the period 1 portfolio allocations, r^1 representing the vector of realized security returns at the end of period 1, and decision variables $\omega^2(r^1)$ corresponding to the period 2 portfolio allocations. Note that the notation $\omega^2(r^1)$ indicates that period 2 decisions are adaptive, i.e., they can depend on period 1 returns. In this setting, a two-stage stochastic programming formulation of the problem can be written as follows:

$$\begin{aligned} \max\nolimits_{\omega^1} \ & \phi^1(\omega^1) + E[\max\nolimits_{\omega^2(r^1)} \phi^2(\omega^2(r^1))] \\ & \omega^1 \in \Omega^1 \\ & \omega^2(r^1) \in \Omega^2(\omega^1, r^1). \end{aligned} \tag{2.29}$$

Above, ϕ^1 and ϕ^2 represent the utility functions corresponding to the first and second periods, respectively. In this representation, the objective function is a combination of the utility of the first period allocations and the expected utility of the second period allocations, where the expectation is taken over all realizations of the first period returns, r^1. The constraints that must be satisfied by the first period decisions are represented through membership of the set Ω^1. Note that the second-period decisions must be linked to both the first period allocations and first period returns; for example, the starting value of the second period portfolio must match the ending value of the first period portfolio. Therefore, both the first period portfolio positions and the realized returns from the first period affect the constraints that must be satisfied by the recourse variables ω^2. That is precisely why we represent the second period feasible portfolio set Ω^2 as a function of both ω^1 and r^1.

It is straightforward, but notationally cumbersome, to generalize the two-period model to an arbitrary number of stages/periods. To solve these problems, one typically generates scenario trees, corresponding to possible different paths the unknown parameters may have followed between stages. When using multiple stages and multiple scenarios for each stage, the total number of different scenarios to be considered can easily grow up to tens of thousands or even millions. The solution techniques for solving problems of that dimension exploit the rich structure in multi-stage stochastic programs. In particular, decomposition techniques that take advantage of the block-diagonal constraint matrix structure and parallelization of the computations on different branches of the scenario tree allow the solution of stochastic programming problems with millions of variables and constraints (Gondzio and Kouwenberg 2001).

2.5.3 Approximate Dynamic Programming

Finally, one should mention the emerging field of *approximate dynamic programming* and its application to optimal multi-period portfolio construction. This field has grown out of the recognition that in traditional dynamic programming, the computational burden of the value function calculation can grow exponentially with the size of the problem, making it unsuitable for large-scale decision making problems. However, the value function can sometimes be approximated reasonably well using a computationally inexpensive approximation scheme. Approximate dynamic programming generally refers to strategies that use such approximate value functions in a dynamic programming framework (Powell 2007). Portfolio construction methodologies utilizing the approximate dynamic programming strategy have also started to appear in the literature (Haugh and Kogan 2008) and provide an exciting avenue for future research.

References

Adler, T. and Kritzman, M. (2007). Mean-variance versus full-scale optimisation: In and out of sample. *Journal of Asset Management*, 7(5), 302–311.

Bender, J., Lee, J., and Stefek, D. (2009). Decomposing the impact of portfolio constraints. *MSCI Barra Research Insights*, August.

Bienstock, D. (2007). Histogram models for robust portfolio optimization. *Journal of Computational Finance*, **11**, 1–64.

Black, F. and Litterman, R. (1990). Asset allocation: Combining investor views with market equilibrium. *Goldman Sachs Fixed Income Research.*

Black, F. and Litterman, R. (1992). Global portfolio optimization. *Financial Analysts Journal*, **48**, 28–43.

Bonnans, J.F. and Shapiro, A. (2000). *Perturbation Analysis of Optimization Problems.* Springer-Verlag, New York.

Ceria, S. and Stubbs, R. (2006). Incorporating estimation errors into portfolio selection: Robust portfolio construction. *Journal of Asset Management*, 7(2), 109–127.

Chopra, V.K. and Ziemba, W.T. (1993). The effects of errors in mean, variances, and covariances in optimal portfolio choice. *Journal of Portfolio Management*, **19**(2), 6–11.

Clarke, R, de Silva, H., and Thorley S. (2002). Portfolio constraints and the fundamental law of active management. *Financial Analyst Journal*, **58**, 48–66.

Cornuejols, G. and Tütüncü, R. (2007). *Optimization Methods in Finance.* Cambridge University Press, Cambridge.

Fabozzi, F.J., Kolm, P.N. Pachamanova, D.A., and Focardi, S.M. (2007). *Robust Portfolio Optimization and Management.* John Wiley & Sons, Hoboken, New Jersey.

Goldfarb, D. and Iyengar, G. (2003). Robust portfolio selection problems. *Mathematics of Operations Research*, **28**, 1–38.

Gondzio, J. and Kouwenberg, R. (2001). High performance computing for asset liability management. *Operations Research*, **49**, 879–891.

Grinold, R.C. and Easton, K.A. (1998). Attribution of performance and holdings. In *Worldwide Asset Liability Modeling* (ed. W. T. Ziemba and J. M. Mulvey). Cambridge University Press, Cambridge.

Grinold, R.C. (2005). Implementation efficiency. *Financial Analysts Journal*, **61**, 52–64.

Grinold, R.C. A dynamic model of portfolio management. *Journal of Investment Management*, **4**(2), 1–18.

Harvey, C.R., Liechty, J.C., Liechty, M.W., and Müller, P. (2004). Portfolio selection with higher moments. *Quantitative Finance*, **10**(5), 469–85.

Haugh, M.B. and Kogan, L. (2008). Duality and approximate dynamic programming for pricing American options and portfolio optimization. In *Handbooks in OR and MS*, Vol. 15. (eds J.R. Birge and V. Linetsky), pp. 925–948. Elsevier, Amsterdam.

Idzorek, T. (2004). A step-by-step guide to the Black–Litterman model. Working Paper, Zephyr Associates.

Jondeau, E. and Rockinger, M. (2006). Optimal portfolio allocation under higher moments. *European Financial Management*, **12**(1), 29–55.

Jones, R., Lim, T., and Zangari, P.J. (2007). The Black–Litterman model for structured equity portfolios. *Journal of Portfolio Management*, **33**(2), 24–33.

Konno, H. (1990). Piecewise linear risk functions and portfolio optimization. *Journal of the Operations Research Society of Japan*, **33**(2), 139–156.

Li, D. and Ng, W. (2001). Optimal dynamic portfolio selection: Multiperiod mean-variance formulation. *Mathematical Finance*, **10**(3), 387–406.

Markowitz, H.M. (1952). Portfolio selection. *Journal of Finance*, **7**, 77–91.

Markowitz, H.M. (1959). *Portfolio Selection: Efficient Diversification of Investments*. John Wiley & Sons, New York.

Martellini, L., and Ziemann, V. (2007). Extending Black–Littermnan analysis beyond the mean-variance framework. *Journal of Portfolio Management*, **33**(4), 33–44.

Merton, R. (1971). Optimum consumption and portfolio rules in a continuous time model. *Journal of Economic Theory*, **3**, 373–413.

Meucci, A. (2005). *Risk and Asset Allocation*. Springer-Verlag, Berlin.

Meucci, A. (2009). Enhancing the Black–Litterman and related approaches: Views and stress-test on risk factors. *Journal of Asset Management*, **10**(2), 89–96.

Michaud, R. (1989). The Markowitz optimization enigma: Is optimized optimal? *Financial Analysts Journal*, **45**, 31–42.

Powell, W. (2007). *Approximate Dynamic Programming: Solving the Curses of Dimensionality*. John Wiley & Sons, Hoboken.

Rockafellar R.T. and Uryasev, S. (2000). Optimization of conditional value-at-risk. *The Journal of Risk*, **2**, 21–41.

The Royal Swedish Academy of Sciences (1990). Press release announcing the recipients of 1990 Nobel Prize in Economic Sciences, October 16, 1990 (available from http://nobelprize.org).

Scherer, B. (2002). *Portfolio Construction and Risk Budgeting*. Risk Books, Pamplona, Navarra.

Scherer, B. and Xu, X. (2007). The impact of constraints on value-added. *Journal of Portfolio Management*, **33**(4), 45–54.

Schöttle, K. and Werner, R. (2006a). Towards reliable efficient frontiers. *Journal of Asset Management*, **7**(2), 128–141.

Schöttle, K. and Werner, R. (2006b). Consistency of robust portfolio estimators. Technical Report, Munich University of Technology.

Stubbs, R. and Vandenbussche, D. (2008). Constraint attribution. *Axioma Research Report*, No. 4.

Yu, L., Ji, X. and Wang, S. (2003). Stochastic programming models in financial optimization: A survey. *Advanced Modeling and Optimization*, 5(1), 1–26.

Zenios, S.A. and Ziemba, W.T. (eds) (2006). *Handbook of Asset and Liability Management, Volume 1: Theory and Methodology*. North-Holland, Amsterdam.

CHAPTER 3

PRACTICAL OPTIMIZATION OF ENHANCED ACTIVE EQUITY PORTFOLIOS

BRUCE I. JACOBS, KENNETH N. LEVY, AND DAVID STARER

3.1 Introduction

We have long advocated the use of integrated optimization for long-short portfolios (see, for example, Jacobs, Levy, and Starer, 1998, 1999). For an unconstrained problem, closed-form expressions exist for the optimum portfolio, and the most demanding computational burden imposed by integrated optimization is the inversion of a covariance matrix. Even when linear equality constraints (such as budget constraints) are added to the problem, closed-form solutions still exist, and it is still a simple matter to find the optimum integrated portfolio. These simple closed-form solutions are often used as the basis for further theoretical study.

In practice, however, long-short portfolio management cannot operate without constraints, or even with only equality constraints. Practical long-short portfolio management requires that the portfolio be subject to inequality constraints, nonlinear constraints, or both. Inequality constraints arise, for example, when upper or lower bounds are placed on security holdings. These could include short-sales restrictions or restrictions on large holdings. Such constraints make the optimization problem more difficult, and generally call for optimization by quadratic programming. Nonlinear constraints arise, for example, in the optimization of enhanced active equity (EAE) portfolios, in which the total weight of securities held long should equal some predetermined amount, and the total weight of the securities sold short should equal another predetermined amount.[1] Although methods exist for solving problems with nonlinear constraints, they are not specifically tailored to the portfolio optimization problem. Thus, an analyst who uses these optimization methods loses insight and tends to regard the optimizer simply as a "black box."

In this chapter, we address the problem of performing integrated optimization subject to the most common inequality and nonlinear constraints; specifically the EAE portfolio optimization problem. We keep the approach as simple as possible so as to retain insight. First we formulate the EAE portfolio optimization problem by starting with the most basic mean-variance portfolio optimization problem and successively adding simple constraints until we arrive at a minimally constrained EAE problem. We then show how this problem can be solved using existing fast portfolio optimizers, or using an approximate approach that makes use of standard quadratic programming. Finally, we provide a numerical example using the method derived.

3.2 Developing the Enhanced Active Equity Model

In this section, we formulate the EAE portfolio optimization problem by starting with the most basic mean-variance portfolio optimization problem and successively adding simple constraints until we arrive at a minimally constrained EAE problem.

The simplest mean-variance portfolio optimization problem is to minimize[2] an objective function

$$\mathcal{O} = \tfrac{1}{2}\sigma_P^2 - \tau\mu_P, \tag{3.1}$$

which is a linear combination of the portfolio's return variance σ_P^2 and its expected return μ_P. The parameter $\tau \geq 0$ is the investor's risk tolerance. When the risk tolerance is zero, the objective is to minimize portfolio return variance, and when it tends to infinity, the objective is to maximize portfolio expected return. As τ varies over the range from zero to infinity, the pair (μ_p, σ_P) trace out the efficient frontier.

The investor optimizes the objective function for given τ by choosing proportions of wealth allocated to available securities. Let μ_i be the expected return of security i, σ_{ij} be the covariance between the returns of securities i and j, and x_i be the proportion of wealth that the investor allocates to security i. Suppose there are n securities available. The portfolio's expected return is then

[1] Enhanced active equity portfolios are also known by various other names such as active extension portfolios, or 120–20, 130–30, etc., portfolios.

[2] The portfolio optimization problem can be framed interchangeably as a minimization problem as in Equation (3.1), or as a maximization, as in Jacobs, Levy, and Starer (1998). Although the intuition of portfolio managers usually favors the maximization of risk-adjusted return, we work extensively here with the critical line algorithm (CLA) of Markowitz (1956) and therefore, in this chapter, prefer to adhere to the CLA's convention of minimization.

$$\mu_p = \boldsymbol{\mu}^\top \boldsymbol{x}, \tag{3.2}$$

and the variance of its return is

$$\sigma_p^2 = \boldsymbol{x}^\top \boldsymbol{\Omega} \boldsymbol{x}, \tag{3.3}$$

where $\boldsymbol{\mu}$ is the expected return vector with ith entry μ_i, $\boldsymbol{\Omega}$ is the covariance matrix with ijth entry σ_{ij}, and $\boldsymbol{x}$ is the portfolio vector with ith entry x_i.

Substituting Equations (3.2) and (3.3) into Equation (3.1), and minimizing, leads to the solution

$$\boldsymbol{x} = \tau\, \boldsymbol{\Omega}^{-1} \boldsymbol{\mu} \tag{3.4}$$

if, as is usually the case for a universe of risky assets, the covariance matrix is positive definite. This unconstrained solution shows that for zero risk tolerance, the investor puts no wealth into any of the risky securities, but that the magnitude of the amount invested grows linearly with risk tolerance. In the simple case where covariances between different securities are all zero (i.e., where the covariance matrix is diagonal), the amount invested in each security is proportional to the security's expected return, and inversely proportional to the variance of its return. The unconstrained solution in Equation (3.4) often forms the basis for further theoretical analysis, such as that performed by Jacobs, Levy, and Starer (1998, 1999), where we examined the conditions under which an optimal long-short portfolio would naturally be neutral and derived formulas for optimally equitizing a long-short portfolio to a benchmark.

3.2.1 Linear Constraints

Even though the solution given in Equation (3.4) provides a good intuitive feel for the way in which risk, return, and investor preferences should be combined to form an optimal portfolio, there are a number of issues that limit its use in practice. For example, it does not include a budget constraint; i.e., a constraint that requires the invested proportions to sum to 100%. In fact, some would argue that $\boldsymbol{x}$ given in Equation (3.4) is not a portfolio by definition because it does not satisfy the budget constraint.

The budget constraint can be written as

$$\sum_{i=1}^{n} x_i = \boldsymbol{\iota}^\top \boldsymbol{x} = 1, \tag{3.5}$$

where the symbol $\boldsymbol{\iota}$ denotes a vector of ones. This, and many other constraints, are all special cases of the general linear constraint

$$\boldsymbol{A}\boldsymbol{x} = \boldsymbol{b} \tag{3.6}$$

where $\boldsymbol{A}$ is a given constant matrix and $\boldsymbol{b}$ is a given constant vector.

The problem now becomes one of minimizing the objective function $\mathcal{O}$ subject to the constraint in Equation (3.6). A simple way to do this is to form the Lagrangian,

$$\mathcal{L}(x) = \tfrac{1}{2}x^\top \boldsymbol{\Omega} x - \tau \boldsymbol{\mu}^\top x + \boldsymbol{\lambda}^\top (Ax - b), \tag{3.7}$$

to differentiate the Lagrangian with respect to x and the Lagrange multiplier vector $\boldsymbol{\lambda}$, and to set the result equal to zero, giving the Karush–Kuhn–Tucker conditions

$$\begin{bmatrix} \boldsymbol{\Omega} & A^\top \\ A & O \end{bmatrix} \begin{bmatrix} x \\ \boldsymbol{\lambda} \end{bmatrix} = \begin{bmatrix} 0 \\ b \end{bmatrix} + \begin{bmatrix} \boldsymbol{\mu} \\ 0 \end{bmatrix} \tau. \tag{3.8}$$

If, as is usual, the covariance matrix is positive definite, the solution is

$$x(\tau) = x_0 + x_1 \tau \tag{3.9}$$

where

$$x_0 = \boldsymbol{\Omega}^{-1} A^\top \left[A \boldsymbol{\Omega}^{-1} A^\top \right]^{-1} b, \tag{3.10}$$

$$x_1 = \boldsymbol{\Omega}^{-1} \left[\boldsymbol{\Omega} - A^\top \left[A \boldsymbol{\Omega}^{-1} A^\top \right]^{-1} A \right] \boldsymbol{\Omega}^{-1} \boldsymbol{\mu}. \tag{3.11}$$

Again, the portfolio weights are linearly related to risk tolerance; but now they vary with τ in such a way that the constraints are always satisfied.

In the special case where the only constraint is the budget constraint (i.e., $A = \boldsymbol{\iota}^\top$ and $b = 1$), Equations (3.10) and (3.11) reduce to

$$x_0 = \frac{1}{\boldsymbol{\iota}^\top \boldsymbol{\Omega}^{-1} \boldsymbol{\iota}} \boldsymbol{\Omega}^{-1} \boldsymbol{\iota} \tag{3.12}$$

$$x_1 = \boldsymbol{\Omega}^{-1} \left[\boldsymbol{\mu} - \frac{\boldsymbol{\iota}^\top \boldsymbol{\Omega}^{-1} \boldsymbol{\mu}}{\boldsymbol{\iota}^\top \boldsymbol{\Omega}^{-1} \boldsymbol{\iota}} \boldsymbol{\iota} \right]. \tag{3.13}$$

Unfortunately, although the portfolio given in Equation (3.9) satisfies the budget constraint and any other linear constraints expressed by Equation (3.6), it is still not practical because it allows for positions with unlimited size. For example, consider a budget constraint that restricts the sum of all holdings to be \$1 million. A portfolio consisting of \$101 million held long in one security and \$100 million sold short in another security would satisfy this constraint, even though the portfolio is clearly not realistic.

3.2.2 Inequality Constraints: Bounds on Holdings

In order to prevent the creation of unrealistic portfolios as described above, it is necessary to place bounds on the portfolio holdings. Such bounds could be written as elementwise vector inequalities of the form

$$0 \leq \boldsymbol{d} \leq \boldsymbol{x} \leq \boldsymbol{u}$$

where $\boldsymbol{d}$ is the vector of smallest allowable holdings, and $\boldsymbol{u}$ is the vector of largest allowable holdings. The inclusion of such bounds increases the complexity of the problem considerably. No longer can a single matrix inversion suffice to find the optimal portfolio.

A particularly important specific form of the bounded portfolio optimization problem is the following:

$$\begin{aligned} &\text{Find } \boldsymbol{x} \text{ to minimize} \quad && \mathcal{O} = \tfrac{1}{2}\boldsymbol{x}^\top \boldsymbol{\Omega} \boldsymbol{x} - \tau\, \boldsymbol{\mu}^\top \boldsymbol{x} \\ &\text{subject to} && \boldsymbol{A}\boldsymbol{x} = \boldsymbol{b}, \\ & && \boldsymbol{x} \geq \boldsymbol{0}. \end{aligned} \tag{3.14}$$

This problem is solved by the well-known technique of quadratic programming.[3] The critical line algorithm (CLA) of Markowitz (1956) is a form of quadratic programming that is particularly relevant to portfolio optimization. As described, for example, in Jacobs, Levy, and Markowitz (2005), the constraint set in (3.14) can represent weak linear inequalities (i.e., inequalities such as $\boldsymbol{A}\boldsymbol{x} \geq \boldsymbol{b}$ or $\boldsymbol{A}\boldsymbol{x} \leq \boldsymbol{b}$) by use of slack variables.

3.2.3 Nonlinear Constraints: Enhanced Active Equity Portfolios

For a long-short portfolio, the sign of the holding x_i is not constrained. A positive value of x_i is interpreted as a long position, and a negative value is interpreted as a short position. Generally, though, while the sign is not constrained, there are limits on the magnitudes of these holdings. Therefore, potentially, the objective function and constraint set described in Section 3.2.2 could be used to obtain the efficient frontier for long-short portfolios.

A recently introduced class of portfolios that both holds securities long and sells them short, but which cannot be optimized directly as described above, is the class of enhanced active equity (EAE) portfolios. Jacobs and Levy (2006, 2007a, b) provide detailed descriptions of these portfolios and their properties. The main problem that arises in the optimization of EAE portfolios is that, for a portfolio with enhancement ϵ, the sum of the long weights should be $1 + \epsilon$, and the sum of the (absolute values of the) short weights should be ϵ. This is an inherently nonlinear constraint on the weights, and it cannot be written in the standard form of Equation (3.6). To date, perhaps because of this nonlinear constraint, no simple and practical methods have been presented for mapping out the efficient frontier of EAE portfolios. In this section, we provide mechanisms for doing so.

[3] See, for example, Wolfe (1959) or Nocedal and Wright (1999). Best and Kale (2000) provide a clear and succinct description. For an up-to-date and relatively comprehensive survey of quadratic programming as applied to portfolio optimization, see Mitra, Ellison, and Scowcroft (2007a, b).

To our knowledge, all relevant constraints on long-short portfolios, including the nonlinear one pertaining to EAE portfolios, can be accommodated in a linear framework if one adopts the convention of representing an n-security long-short portfolio in terms of $2n$ nonnegative variables, $x_1, \ldots, x_{2n}$, in which the first n variables, $x_1, \ldots, x_n$, represent the securities in a given set held long, and the second n variables, $x_{n+1}, \ldots, x_{2n}$, represent short sales in the *same* set of securities (see Jacobs, Levy, and Markowitz, 2005, 2006). Let $\boldsymbol{x}$ now represent the extended portfolio vector containing all $2n$ variables. Also, let $\boldsymbol{l}$ represent the first n variables (i.e., the long part of the portfolio), and let $\boldsymbol{s}$ represent the second n variables (i.e., the short part of the portfolio). Thus

$$\boldsymbol{x} = \begin{bmatrix} \boldsymbol{l} \\ \boldsymbol{s} \end{bmatrix}. \tag{3.15}$$

With this convention, the portfolio's expected return is[4]

$$\mu_P = \begin{bmatrix} \boldsymbol{\mu}^\top & -\boldsymbol{\mu}^\top \end{bmatrix} \boldsymbol{x} = \boldsymbol{\theta}^\top \boldsymbol{x}, \tag{3.16}$$

the variance of the portfolio's return is

$$\sigma_P^2 = \boldsymbol{x}^\top \begin{bmatrix} +\boldsymbol{\Omega} & -\boldsymbol{\Omega} \\ -\boldsymbol{\Omega} & +\boldsymbol{\Omega} \end{bmatrix} \boldsymbol{x} = \boldsymbol{x}^\top \boldsymbol{Q} \boldsymbol{x}, \tag{3.17}$$

and the standard linear constraint set becomes

$$\begin{bmatrix} A & -A \end{bmatrix} \begin{bmatrix} \boldsymbol{l} \\ \boldsymbol{s} \end{bmatrix} = \mathcal{A}\boldsymbol{x} = \boldsymbol{b}, \tag{3.18}$$

$$\boldsymbol{x} \geq \boldsymbol{0}. \tag{3.19}$$

Among the many constraints that this set can accommodate are the budget constraint and a constraint that the beta of the portfolio should be equal to some desired value, β_D. In addition, $\mathcal{A}$ can be extended further to accommodate the important constraints that apply to EAE portfolios with enhancement ϵ; that is, that the sum of the long weights should be $1+\epsilon$, and the sum of the (absolute values of the) short weights should be ϵ. The beta and enhancement constraints are accommodated with

$$\mathcal{A} = \begin{bmatrix} \beta_1 & \cdots & \beta_n & -\beta_1 & \cdots & -\beta_n \\ 1 & \cdots & 1 & 0 & \cdots & 0 \\ 0 & \cdots & 0 & 1 & \cdots & 1 \end{bmatrix}, \quad \boldsymbol{b} = \begin{bmatrix} \beta_D \\ 1+\epsilon \\ \epsilon \end{bmatrix} \tag{3.20}$$

where β_i is the beta of the ith security.

In summary, the EAE portfolio optimization problem consists of finding $\boldsymbol{x}$ that maximizes $\mathcal{O} = \frac{1}{2}\sigma_P^2 - \tau\mu_P$ (with μ_P and σ_P^2 given in Equations (3.16) and (3.17), respectively), subject to the constraints given in Equations (3.18), (3.19), and (3.20). In the following section, we describe methods for solving this problem.

[4] This assumes no financing charge for purchasing an ϵ of longs with the cash proceeds from an ϵ of shorts.

3.3 Optimizing Enhanced Active Equity Portfolios

We want to optimize the Lagrangian

$$\mathcal{L}(x) = \tfrac{1}{2}x^\top Qx - \tau\boldsymbol{\theta}^\top x + \boldsymbol{\lambda}^\top(\mathcal{A}x - b) \tag{3.21}$$

with $x, \boldsymbol{\theta}, Q$, and $\mathcal{A}$ defined in Equations (3.15) through (3.18). Unfortunately, the structure of the matrix Q introduces a complication; the matrix is singular because its second block column is the negative of its first block column. Therefore, the set of equations (3.16) through (3.20) cannot be used directly (for example, using a standard quadratic program) to find the optimal EAE portfolio. Below, we demonstrate techniques that can be used to solve the problem. In Section 3.3.1, we show how the objective function can be modified such that standard quadratic programming can be used to find the optimal EAE portfolio for a particular choice of risk tolerance τ. This solution, however, provides only one point on the efficient frontier, and cannot be used efficiently to tell where securities change between the IN, UP, and DN states (i.e., it cannot efficiently find the corner portfolios). In Sections 3.3.2 and 3.3.3 we show how to trace out the entire efficient frontier by stepping efficiently from corner portfolio to corner portfolio. In Section 3.3.2, we show how existing fast algorithms (which make use of structured covariance matrices) can be used for the problem, and then in Section 3.3.3, we show how the critical line algorithm can be used for general covariance matrices (including singular ones).

3.3.1 Imposing Nonsingularity

One simple trick to solving the problem of a singular $2n$ covariance matrix in Equation (3.17) is to modify it by adding off-diagonal terms as follows,

$$Q_k = \begin{bmatrix} +\boldsymbol{\Omega} & kI - \boldsymbol{\Omega} \\ kI - \boldsymbol{\Omega} & +\boldsymbol{\Omega} \end{bmatrix}. \tag{3.22}$$

For scalar $k > 0$, this modified covariance matrix is no longer singular, so when Q_k is substituted for Q in Equation (3.21), a standard quadratic program will find a unique solution. Furthermore, as demonstrated below, this unique solution is the correct solution.

The modified Lagrangian is

$$\mathcal{L}_k(x) = \tfrac{1}{2}x^\top Q_k x + \tau\boldsymbol{\theta}^\top x + \boldsymbol{\lambda}^\top(\mathcal{A}x - b), \tag{3.23}$$

$$= \mathcal{L}(x) + k \sum_{i=1}^{n} l_i s_i. \tag{3.24}$$

Since l and s are both constrained to have all nonnegative entries, the term involving the summation in Equation (3.24) serves to penalize any attempt to produce both a long and a short position in the same security. That is, it penalizes any attempt to produce overlapping long and short positions. If k is large enough, the penalty will be such that the quadratic program will produce a portfolio with no overlapping long and short positions (i.e., a trim portfolio). Note that for trim portfolios, the term $\sum_{i=1}^{n} l_i s_i$ is zero, and the term has no effect on the Lagrangian. In that case, $\mathcal{L}_k(x) \equiv \mathcal{L}(x)$. Thus, an algorithm that optimizes $\mathcal{L}_k(x)$ to produce a trim portfolio will also optimize the original Lagrangian $\mathcal{L}(x)$.

This trick is useful, for example, if one wishes to find one particular efficient portfolio corresponding to a specified risk tolerance without mapping out the entire efficient frontier.

Empirically, we have found that a value of $k \approx 0.5$ is usually sufficient to produce trim portfolios. Much smaller values of k may result in untrim portfolios, and very much larger values of k can result in numerically unstable results.

3.3.2 Using the Trimability Property

Jacobs, Levy, and Markowitz (2005, 2006) showed that if fairly mild trimability conditions are satisfied, fast algorithms can be used to optimize long-short portfolios using the $2n$ representation, even though the covariance matrix in this representation is singular. In this section, we briefly summarize the operation of fast algorithms for factor models of covariance. Such models are commonly used in quantitative management, and incorporate the common single factor model as a special case.

Markowitz and Perold (1981) provide a description of factor and scenario models, and indicate how such models are diagonalized to provide fast algorithms. The essential idea is to introduce new artificial or fictitious securities, one for each common factor (see Sharpe, 1963; Cohen and Pogue, 1967). The amount invested in each fictitious security is constrained to be a linear combination of the investments in the real securities. With the model thus augmented, the covariance matrix becomes diagonal, or nearly so, and the equations for the pieces of the efficient set become much easier to solve.

Consider first a simple single-factor model as used by Sharpe (1963) and Cohen and Pogue (1967). The securities' returns are assumed to obey the model

$$r = \boldsymbol{\alpha} + \boldsymbol{\beta} r_m + \boldsymbol{\varepsilon} \tag{3.25}$$

$$\mathbb{E}[r] = \boldsymbol{\alpha} + \boldsymbol{\beta} \mu_m \tag{3.26}$$

where r is the vector of security returns, $\boldsymbol{\alpha}$ and $\boldsymbol{\beta}$ are parameter vectors, r_m is the market return, μ_m is the expected value of the market return, and $\boldsymbol{\varepsilon}$ is a vector of idiosyncratic returns. Each idiosyncratic return is assumed to have mean $\mathbb{E}[\varepsilon_i] = 0$, variance $\mathbb{V}[\varepsilon_i] = \sigma_i^2$, and to be uncorrelated with all other idiosyncratic returns, $\mathbb{E}[\varepsilon_i \varepsilon_j] = 0$ for all $i \neq j$. With this model, the covariance matrix $\boldsymbol{\Omega}$ of $\boldsymbol{r}$ is

$$\boldsymbol{\Omega} = \boldsymbol{\beta}\sigma_m^2\boldsymbol{\beta}^\top + V \tag{3.27}$$

where σ_m^2 is the variance of r_m, $\boldsymbol{v}$ is a vector with σ_i^2 in its ith position, and $V = \text{diag}(\boldsymbol{v})$ is a diagonal matrix with the elements of $\boldsymbol{v}$ along its main diagonal.

Substituting Equations (3.26) and (3.27) into Equations (3.2) and (3.3) gives the following expressions for the portfolio's expected value and variance of return:

$$\mu_P = \boldsymbol{x}^\top\boldsymbol{\alpha} + \boldsymbol{x}^\top\boldsymbol{\beta}\mu_m \tag{3.28}$$

$$\sigma_P^2 = \boldsymbol{x}^\top\boldsymbol{\beta}\sigma_m^2\boldsymbol{\beta}^\top\boldsymbol{x} + \boldsymbol{x}^\top V\boldsymbol{x}. \tag{3.29}$$

Now define a new, fictitious, $(n+1)$st security with expected return $\mu_{n+1} = \mu_m$, variance $\sigma_{n+1}^2 = \sigma_m^2$, and whose weight is constrained to be $x_{n+1} = \boldsymbol{\beta}^\top\boldsymbol{x}$. With these definitions, μ_P and σ_P^2 can be written as

$$\mu_P = \begin{bmatrix} \boldsymbol{x} \\ x_{n+1} \end{bmatrix}^\top \begin{bmatrix} \boldsymbol{\mu} \\ \mu_{n+1} \end{bmatrix}, \quad \sigma_P^2 = \begin{bmatrix} \boldsymbol{x} \\ x_{n+1} \end{bmatrix}^\top \begin{bmatrix} V & \boldsymbol{0} \\ \boldsymbol{0}^\top & \sigma_{n+1}^2 \end{bmatrix} \begin{bmatrix} \boldsymbol{x} \\ x_{n+1} \end{bmatrix}.$$

The important property imparted by this definition is that the variance of the portfolio's return now involves a diagonal matrix. This greatly simplifies the computation of the optimal weights. To use this property for long-only portfolios, one employs an algorithm specifically tailored for the purpose such as that presented by Sharpe (1963). Such an algorithm has as its inputs only the vector of expected returns of the securities and the market $[\boldsymbol{\mu}^\top, \mu_{n+1}]^\top$, the idiosyncratic variances of the securities and the market $\left[\boldsymbol{v}^\top, \sigma_{n+1}^2\right]^\top$, the securities' betas $\boldsymbol{\beta}$, and any constraints (including the constraint $x_{n+1} = \boldsymbol{\beta}^\top\boldsymbol{x}$ that couples the fictitious security to the real ones). Importantly, the dense covariance matrix, $\boldsymbol{\Omega}$, is not presented directly to the algorithm. The algorithm uses the sparse nature of the diagonalized covariance matrix to compute the efficient frontier in a computationally efficient manner.

In the multi-factor case with

$$\boldsymbol{r} = \boldsymbol{\alpha} + B\boldsymbol{f} + \boldsymbol{\varepsilon},$$

where $\boldsymbol{f}$ is a vector of factor returns and B is a matrix of factor loadings, the analysis above extends naturally to

$$\mu_P = \begin{bmatrix} \boldsymbol{x} \\ \boldsymbol{y} \end{bmatrix}^\top \begin{bmatrix} \boldsymbol{\mu} \\ \boldsymbol{\phi} \end{bmatrix}, \quad \sigma_P^2 = \begin{bmatrix} \boldsymbol{x} \\ \boldsymbol{y} \end{bmatrix}^\top \begin{bmatrix} V & O \\ O^\top & W \end{bmatrix} \begin{bmatrix} \boldsymbol{x} \\ \boldsymbol{y} \end{bmatrix}$$

where $\boldsymbol{\phi} = \mathbb{E}[\boldsymbol{f}]$ is the expected factor return, $W = \mathbb{V}[\boldsymbol{f}]$ is the covariance matrix of the factor returns, and

$$\boldsymbol{y} = B^\top\boldsymbol{x}$$

is a vector of fictitious securities; one for each factor. The variance of the portfolio's return again involves only a diagonal matrix (or an almost diagonal matrix if W is not diagonal).

As shown in Jacobs, Levy, and Markowitz (2005, 2006), this diagonalization procedure applied to portfolios with both long and short positions gives

$$\mu_P = \begin{bmatrix} l \\ s \\ y \end{bmatrix}^\top \begin{bmatrix} +\boldsymbol{\mu} \\ -\boldsymbol{\mu} \\ \boldsymbol{\phi} \end{bmatrix}, \tag{3.30}$$

$$\sigma_P^2 = \begin{bmatrix} l \\ s \\ y \end{bmatrix}^\top \begin{bmatrix} V & O & O \\ O & V & O \\ O & O & W \end{bmatrix} \begin{bmatrix} l \\ s \\ y \end{bmatrix} + \begin{bmatrix} l \\ s \\ y \end{bmatrix}^\top \begin{bmatrix} O & -V & O \\ -V & O & O \\ O & O & O \end{bmatrix} \begin{bmatrix} l \\ s \\ y \end{bmatrix}, \tag{3.31}$$

with the artificial security vector defined as

$$y = B^\top (l - s).$$

Although the second term on the right-hand side of Equation (3.31) distorts the diagonal form of the variance, for trimable models, as shown in Jacobs, Levy, and Markowitz (2005, 2006), one can effectively ignore it. One simply presents the appropriate fast algorithm with the $2n$ vector of expected security returns $[+\boldsymbol{\mu}^\top, -\boldsymbol{\mu}^\top]^\top$, the vector of expected factor returns $\boldsymbol{\phi}$, the $2n$ vector of idiosyncratic variances $[+\boldsymbol{\nu}^\top, +\boldsymbol{\nu}^\top]^\top$, the covariance matrix of the factor returns W, the $2n$ vector of betas $[+\boldsymbol{\beta}^\top, -\boldsymbol{\beta}^\top]$, and any constraints (including the constraint that couples the fictitious security vector to the real ones). Again, importantly, the dense covariance matrix of the real securities' returns is not presented directly to the algorithm. The fast algorithm will then find the correct efficient frontier.

3.3.3 Using the Critical Line Algorithm

Another method for optimizing EAE portfolios is to use the critical line algorithm (CLA) of Markowitz (1987) and Markowitz and Todd (2000). Unlike the fast algorithms described above, the CLA does not depend on the particular structure of the covariance matrix. In fact, a major advantage of the CLA is that it still maps out the entire, and correct, efficient frontier even when the covariance matrix is singular. It is, therefore, ideally suited to optimizing EAE portfolios.

In this section, we summarize the CLA with a presentation based on the use of 0-1 matrices (see, e.g., Magnus and Neudecker, 1986). This helps to clarify the structure of the algorithm, and to assist in its translation to matrix-oriented programming languages. In Section 3.3.3.1 we demonstrate how the standard CLA can be modified to apply to benchmark-sensitive portfolios such as EAE portfolios.

There is a perception among some researchers that the CLA cannot accommodate upper bounds on security holdings (see, e.g., Stein, Branke, and Schmeck, 2008, page 3949) without the addition of slack variables. Exercise 7.3 on page 179 of Markowitz and Todd (2000), however, shows how the algorithm can be modified so as to incorporate such bounds directly without the use of slack variables. In this section, we demonstrate the use of the CLA with upper bound modifications.

Our objective is to:

$$\begin{aligned} \text{Find } \boldsymbol{x} \text{ to minimize } \mathcal{O} &= \tfrac{1}{2}\boldsymbol{x}^\top \boldsymbol{\Omega} \boldsymbol{x} - \tau\, \boldsymbol{\mu}^\top \boldsymbol{x} \\ \text{subject to} \qquad A\boldsymbol{x} &= \boldsymbol{b}, \\ \boldsymbol{x} &\geq \boldsymbol{d}, \\ \boldsymbol{x} &\leq \boldsymbol{u}. \end{aligned} \tag{3.32}$$

Notice that, with an obvious change in notation, the EAE problem in Equation (3.23) can be formulated in this way.

Define the following three sets: IN to represent the securities that are currently between their lower and upper limits (i.e., that are in the portfolio, or IN), UP to represent those securities that are currently at their upper limit (i.e., that are UP), and DN to represent those securities that are currently at their lower limit (i.e., that are DN). That is,

$$\text{IN} = \{i \mid d_i < x_i < u_i\}, \quad \text{UP} = \{i \mid x_i = u_i\}, \quad \text{DN} = \{i \mid x_i = d_i\}. \tag{3.33}$$

We will use an IN, DN, or UP subscript on a vector to indicate that the vector contains only elements from the corresponding set.

Also define three operators $\mathbb{N}$, $\mathbb{D}$, and $\mathbb{U}$ corresponding to IN, DN, and UP. $\mathbb{N}$'s domain is the set of all portfolio vectors $\boldsymbol{x}$, and its range is the set of vectors whose dimension is the cardinality of IN, with $|\text{IN}| \leq n$. $\mathbb{N}\boldsymbol{x}$ is a vector that contains only the elements of $\boldsymbol{x}$ that are IN. $\mathbb{D}$ and $\mathbb{U}$ are defined analogously with respect to DN and UP, respectively. Thus, $\mathbb{N}\boldsymbol{x} = \boldsymbol{x}_{\text{IN}}$, $\mathbb{D}\boldsymbol{x} = \boldsymbol{x}_{\text{DN}}$, and $\mathbb{U}\boldsymbol{x} = \boldsymbol{x}_{\text{UP}}$. It can be useful to interpret the $\mathbb{N}$, $\mathbb{D}$, and $\mathbb{U}$ operators as multiplications by identity matrices that contain only the rows from their corresponding sets.[5] The matrix $\mathbb{N}$, for example, is generated using an identity matrix from which all rows have been removed except those that are in the set IN. By definition, $\mathbb{D}\boldsymbol{x} = \mathbb{D}\boldsymbol{d} = \boldsymbol{d}_{\text{DN}}$, and $\mathbb{U}\boldsymbol{x} = \mathbb{U}\boldsymbol{u} = \boldsymbol{u}_{\text{UP}}$.

While multiplication by $\mathbb{N}$, $\mathbb{D}$, or $\mathbb{U}$ removes elements not belonging to the corresponding sets, and therefore generally results in shortened vectors, multiplication by these matrices' transposes causes vector re-lengthening, with zeros inserted for all

[5] For computational purposes, the multiplication interpretation should not be used literally. In matrix-oriented programming languages, the operations can be accomplished with simple subscripting. For example, if the vector `k` contains the numbers in the set IN, then the operation $\boldsymbol{x}_{\text{IN}} = \mathbb{N}\boldsymbol{x}$ is implemented in Matlab using the statement `xin = x(k,:)`.

elements not belonging to the corresponding set. Using these properties, it is easy to show that x can be decomposed as follows:

$$\begin{aligned} x &= \mathbb{N}^\top x_{\text{IN}} + \mathbb{D}^\top d_{\text{DN}} + \mathbb{U}^\top u_{\text{UP}}, \\ &= \mathbb{N}^\top x_{\text{IN}} + \mathbb{D}^\top \mathbb{D} d + \mathbb{U}^\top \mathbb{U} u, \\ &= \mathbb{N}^\top x_{\text{IN}} + k, \end{aligned} \tag{3.34}$$

where we have defined

$$k = \mathbb{D}^\top \mathbb{D} d + \mathbb{U}^\top \mathbb{U} u \tag{3.35}$$

to be the vector whose elements are zero for IN securities, equal to the lower bound for DN securities, and equal to the upper bound for UP securities.

We now use the definitions of $\mathbb{N}$, $\mathbb{D}$, and $\mathbb{U}$ in the analysis of the Lagrangian in Equation (3.7), which applies to the problem in equation set (3.32). Let η be the gradient of the Lagrangian:

$$\eta = \frac{\partial \mathcal{L}}{\partial x} = \boldsymbol{\Omega} x - \mu\tau + A^\top \lambda. \tag{3.36}$$

For securities that are between their upper and lower limits, i.e., for $i \in \text{IN}$, the gradient must be zero. Thus, premultiplying Equation (3.36) by $\mathbb{N}$ to select only the IN securities,

$$\mathbb{N}\boldsymbol{\Omega} x - \mathbb{N}\mu\tau + \mathbb{N}A^\top \lambda = 0$$

which, with the use of Equation (3.34), gives

$$\mathbb{N}\boldsymbol{\Omega}\mathbb{N}^\top x_{\text{IN}} + \mathbb{N}A^\top \lambda = \mathbb{N}\mu\tau - \mathbb{N}\boldsymbol{\Omega} k. \tag{3.37}$$

Using Equation (3.34), the general linear constraint, Equation (3.6), becomes

$$A\mathbb{N}^\top x_{\text{IN}} = b - Ak. \tag{3.38}$$

Finally, combining Equations (3.37) and (3.38) gives

$$\begin{bmatrix} \mathbb{N}\boldsymbol{\Omega}\mathbb{N}^\top & \mathbb{N}A^\top \\ A\mathbb{N}^\top & \mathbf{O} \end{bmatrix} \begin{bmatrix} x_{\text{IN}} \\ \lambda \end{bmatrix} = \begin{bmatrix} 0 \\ b \end{bmatrix} - \begin{bmatrix} \mathbb{N}\boldsymbol{\Omega} \\ A \end{bmatrix} k + \begin{bmatrix} \mathbb{N}\mu \\ 0 \end{bmatrix} \tau. \tag{3.39}$$

This is the equation that defines the straight-line segment along the efficient frontier for the given IN, UP, and DN sets. As τ changes, the solution reaches discrete critical points (i.e., corner portfolios) at which the compositions of these sets change. The critical line algorithm provides a computationally efficient way to step from corner portfolio to corner portfolio, thereby tracing out the entire efficient frontier.

3.3.3.1 *CLA with a Benchmark*

In the discussion thus far, we have not been specific about the precise nature of the portfolio weights. The CLA as originally formulated is very general and can be applied to virtually any weight representation. However, for institutional portfolio management, it is useful to distinguish between total, benchmark, and active weights. More specifically, a portfolio's total weight vector $\boldsymbol{h}$ comprises the sum of two components: a benchmark or market component $\boldsymbol{m}$ and an active component $\boldsymbol{x}$. The skill of the active portfolio manager is focused on choosing the best active component. The Lagrangian in this case is

$$\mathcal{L}(\boldsymbol{h}) = \tfrac{1}{2}\left(\boldsymbol{h}-\boldsymbol{m}\right)^{\top} \boldsymbol{Q}\left(\boldsymbol{h}-\boldsymbol{m}\right) - \tau\boldsymbol{\theta}^{\top}\left(\boldsymbol{h}-\boldsymbol{m}\right) + \boldsymbol{\lambda}^{\top}\left(\boldsymbol{A}\boldsymbol{h}-\boldsymbol{b}\right). \tag{3.40}$$

Repeating the process of optimizing this Lagrangian, but now choosing the variable of interest to be the total weight vector $\boldsymbol{h}$ rather than $\boldsymbol{x}$, shows that all expressions remain identical except for the constant on the right-hand side of Equation (3.39). In particular, Equation (3.39) becomes

$$\begin{bmatrix} \mathbb{N}\boldsymbol{\Omega}\mathbb{N}^{\top} & \mathbb{N}\boldsymbol{A}^{\top} \\ \boldsymbol{A}\mathbb{N}^{\top} & \mathrm{O} \end{bmatrix} \begin{bmatrix} \boldsymbol{h}_{\mathrm{IN}} \\ \boldsymbol{\lambda} \end{bmatrix} = \begin{bmatrix} \boldsymbol{0} \\ \boldsymbol{b} \end{bmatrix} - \begin{bmatrix} \mathbb{N}\boldsymbol{\Omega} \\ \boldsymbol{A} \end{bmatrix}\boldsymbol{k} + \begin{bmatrix} \mathbb{N}\boldsymbol{\Omega} \\ \mathrm{O} \end{bmatrix}\boldsymbol{m} + \begin{bmatrix} \mathbb{N}\boldsymbol{\mu} \\ \boldsymbol{0} \end{bmatrix}\tau. \tag{3.41}$$

3.3.3.2 *Algorithm Implementation*

Markowitz (1987) showed that the matrix (which we will call $\boldsymbol{M}_{\mathrm{IN}}$) on the left-hand side of Equations (3.39) and (3.41) is nonsingular, so these equations can be solved for $\boldsymbol{x}_{\mathrm{IN}}$ and $\boldsymbol{\lambda}$ to give[6]

$$\begin{bmatrix} \boldsymbol{h}_{\mathrm{IN}} \\ \boldsymbol{\lambda} \end{bmatrix} = \boldsymbol{\alpha} + \boldsymbol{\beta}\tau, \tag{3.42}$$

where, in our case,

$$\boldsymbol{\alpha} = \boldsymbol{M}_{\mathrm{IN}}^{-1}\left[\begin{bmatrix} \boldsymbol{0} \\ \boldsymbol{b} \end{bmatrix} - \begin{bmatrix} \mathbb{N}\boldsymbol{\Omega} \\ \boldsymbol{A} \end{bmatrix}\boldsymbol{k} + \begin{bmatrix} \mathbb{N}\boldsymbol{\Omega} \\ \mathrm{O} \end{bmatrix}\boldsymbol{m}\right], \tag{3.43}$$

$$\boldsymbol{\beta} = \boldsymbol{M}_{\mathrm{IN}}^{-1}\begin{bmatrix} \mathbb{N}\boldsymbol{\mu} \\ \boldsymbol{0} \end{bmatrix}. \tag{3.44}$$

Equations (3.43) and (3.44) can be substituted into Equation (3.36) to give

$$\boldsymbol{\eta} = \boldsymbol{\gamma} + \boldsymbol{\delta}\tau, \tag{3.45}$$

where, in our case,

$$\boldsymbol{\gamma} = \boldsymbol{G}\boldsymbol{\alpha} + \boldsymbol{\Omega}\left(\boldsymbol{k}-\boldsymbol{m}\right), \tag{3.46}$$

and

$$\boldsymbol{\delta} = \boldsymbol{G}\boldsymbol{\beta} - \boldsymbol{\mu}, \tag{3.47}$$

[6] In this section and the next, we use the symbol $\boldsymbol{\beta}$ to refer to the slope of the portfolio holding vector with respect to investor risk tolerance, as used in Markowitz (1987).

with

$$G = \left[\, \boldsymbol{\Omega} \mathbb{N}^{\top} \quad A^{\top} \,\right]. \tag{3.48}$$

The CLA traces out the efficient set as risk tolerance τ is reduced in discrete steps from infinity down to zero.[7] That is, the algorithm steps from corner portfolio to corner portfolio. At a typical step, the algorithm has available the sets IN, UP, and DN. With these sets, it can solve for $\boldsymbol{\alpha}$, $\boldsymbol{\beta}$, $\boldsymbol{\gamma}$, and $\boldsymbol{\delta}$. With this information it can compute which of the following events takes place at the next corner:

1. An IN security can reach its upper bound, and move from IN to UP. In this case, since the security is initially in IN, it must satisfy Equation (3.42), and as it attains the upper bound, it must satisfy $u_i = \alpha_i + \beta_i \tau$, from which we obtain that the corner portfolio occurs when τ reaches

$$\tau_1 = \frac{u_i - \alpha_i}{\beta_i}, \quad \beta_i < 0. \tag{3.49}$$

2. An IN security can reach its lower bound, and move from IN to DN. In this case, since the security is initially in IN, it must satisfy Equation (3.42), and as it attains the lower bound, it must satisfy $d_i = \alpha_i + \beta_i \tau$, from which we obtain that the corner portfolio occurs when τ reaches

$$\tau_2 = \frac{d_i - \alpha_i}{\beta_i}, \quad \beta_i > 0. \tag{3.50}$$

3. A security at its upper bound could move from UP to IN. In this case, for the security to enter IN, its gradient must increase to zero as τ decreases. From Equation (3.45), this occurs when τ reaches

$$\tau_3 = -\frac{\gamma_i}{\delta_i}, \quad \delta_i < 0. \tag{3.51}$$

4. A security at its lower bound could move from DN to IN. In this case, for the security to enter IN, its gradient must decrease to zero as τ decreases. From Equation (3.45), this occurs when τ reaches

$$\tau_4 = -\frac{\gamma_i}{\delta_i}, \quad \delta_i > 0. \tag{3.52}$$

The largest of $\{\tau_1, \tau_2, \tau_3, \tau_4\}$ determines the value of τ at the next corner, or if the algorithm terminates.

We now have all information necessary to implement the CLA for EAE portfolios with a constraint set that includes both lower and upper bounds.

[7] We use the symbol τ instead of the symbol λ_E used in Markowitz (1987); Markowitz and Todd (2000); and Jacobs, Levy, and Markowitz (2005).

3.4 Example

To illustrate the use of the method described in Section 3.3.3, we found the efficient frontier for a portfolio of $n = 100$ securities whose excess returns were generated by the model

$$r = \boldsymbol{\alpha} + \boldsymbol{\beta} r_m + \boldsymbol{\varepsilon},$$

where, for each realization, $\boldsymbol{\alpha}$ and $\boldsymbol{\beta}$ were normally distributed with means of zero and one, respectively, and standard deviations of 5% and 20%, respectively. The idiosyncratic return vector, $\boldsymbol{\varepsilon}$, was normally distributed with a mean of zero and a standard deviation of $\sigma_\varepsilon = 30\%$. The market excess return, r_m, had a mean of $\mu_m = 5\%$ and a standard deviation of $\sigma_m = 15\%$. We formed the expected return vector using $\boldsymbol{\mu} = \boldsymbol{\alpha} + \boldsymbol{\beta}\mu_m$, and the covariance matrix using $\boldsymbol{\Omega} = \boldsymbol{\beta}\sigma_m^2\boldsymbol{\beta}^\top + \sigma_\varepsilon^2 \boldsymbol{I}$.

To produce the efficient frontier for a long-only portfolio with a beta of one, we used a CLA program with $\boldsymbol{\mu}$ and $\boldsymbol{\Omega}$, together with the following constraint matrix and vector:

$$A = \begin{bmatrix} \beta_1 & \cdots & \beta_n \\ 1 & \cdots & 1 \end{bmatrix}, \quad b = \begin{bmatrix} 1 \\ 1 \end{bmatrix}.$$

We imposed lower and upper position constraints of zero and one, respectively.

To produce the efficient frontier for an EAE portfolio with a beta of one and enhancement of ϵ, we used the quantities defined above, together with the constraint set defined in Equation (3.20) in a CLA program using the $2n$ representation.

The resulting efficient frontiers for $\epsilon \in \{10\%, 20\%, 30\%, 40\%, 50\%\}$ are shown in Figure 3.1. As expected, the figure shows that, from high to moderate portfolio risks, a larger enhancement provides a larger expected return. As the portfolio risk reduces, the efficient frontiers converge to one another.

The optimal level of enhancement is a function of risk tolerance. Ignoring upper and lower bounds on portfolio holdings for simplicity, the Lagrangian for an EAE portfolio can be written in the form

$$\mathcal{L} = \tfrac{1}{2}\boldsymbol{x}^\top \boldsymbol{\Omega}_k \boldsymbol{x} - \tau \boldsymbol{\mu}^\top \boldsymbol{x} + \boldsymbol{\lambda}^\top (A\boldsymbol{x} - b - c\varepsilon)\,.$$

Regarding $\boldsymbol{x}$, $\boldsymbol{\lambda}$, and ϵ as variables to be controlled, and rearranging the first-order conditions for optimality of the Lagrangian gives

$$\begin{bmatrix} x \\ \boldsymbol{\lambda} \\ \epsilon \end{bmatrix} = M^{-1} \begin{bmatrix} \boldsymbol{\mu} \\ 0 \\ 0 \end{bmatrix} \tau + M^{-1} \begin{bmatrix} 0 \\ b \\ 0 \end{bmatrix},$$

where

$$M = \begin{bmatrix} \boldsymbol{\Omega}_k & A^\top & \mathrm{O} \\ A & \mathrm{O} & -c \\ 0 & -c^\top & 0 \end{bmatrix}.$$

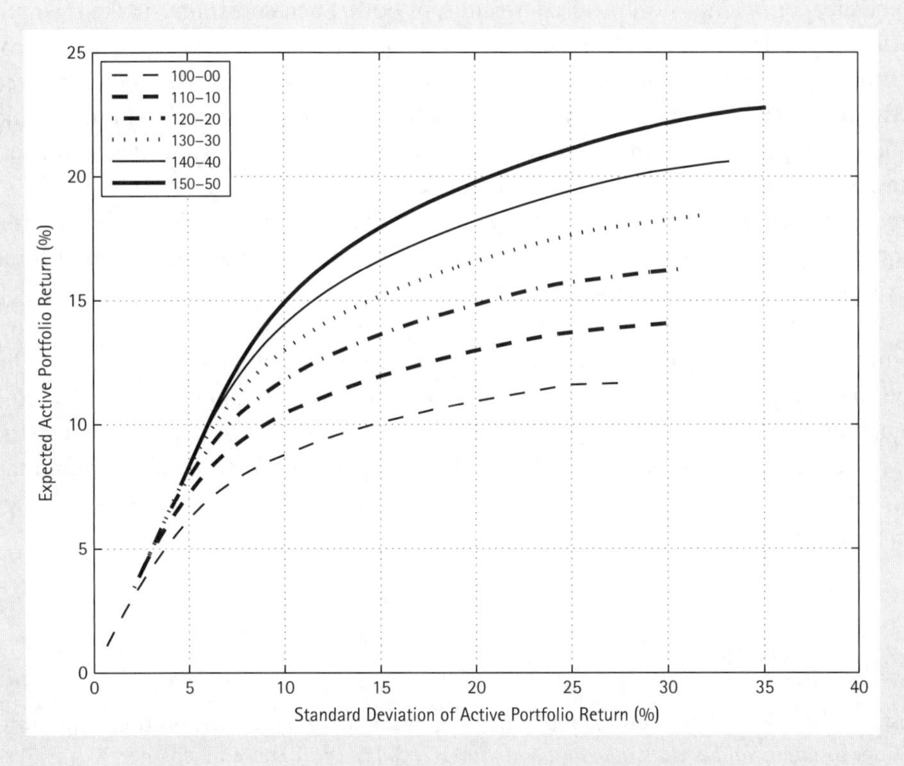

FIGURE 3.1 Efficient frontiers for EAE portfolios with 100 securities.

Therefore, in the simple case where bounds are ignored, enhancement ϵ is a linear function of risk tolerance τ. In the more realistic case where bounds are incorporated, ϵ will be a piecewise linear function of τ. As one's risk tolerance increases, so one's chosen enhancement should increase. Conversely, as one's risk tolerance decreases, so one's chosen enhancement should decrease.

At very low levels of risk tolerance ($\tau \approx 0$), the optimization approaches a variance minimization problem. For the long-only portfolio, the solution to this problem is to set the portfolio equal to the benchmark, at which point the active variance is zero. As higher levels of enhancement are imposed, the portfolio is forced away from the benchmark, and this introduces positive active variance.

3.5 Conclusion

Although for an unconstrained or linearly constrained portfolio optimization problem, closed-form expressions exist for the optimum portfolio, similar expressions are not available for practical long-short portfolios because these portfolios require the use of inequality constraints, nonlinear constraints, or both. Such constraints make the optimization problem more difficult, and generally call for optimization by quadratic programming. Nonlinear constraints arise, for example, in the optimization of enhanced active equity (EAE) portfolios, in which the total weight of securities held long should equal some predetermined amount, and the total weight of the securities sold short should equal another predetermined amount. We have shown how EAE portfolios evolve mathematically out of the simplest mean-variance portfolio as one imposes sequentially more realistic constraints, while, at the same time granting oneself some flexibility to sell securities short.

We addressed the problem of performing integrated optimization subject to the most common inequality and nonlinear constraints, and specifically for the EAE portfolio optimization problem. We presented a slightly generalized version of the critical line algorithm for solving the EAE problem, in which we allowed for upper as well as the more traditional lower bounds on the portfolio weights, and we used these to find the efficient frontiers for a range of enhanced active equity portfolios, from 100–00 (long-only) through 150–50.

References

Best, M. J. and Kale, J. K. (2000). Quadratic programming for large-scale portfolio optimization. In *Financial Services Information Systems* (ed. J. Keyes) 2nd edn. chapter 30, pp. 513–529. Auerbach.

Cohen, K. J. and Pogue, J. A. (1967). An empirical evaluation of alternative portfolio-selection models. *Journal of Business*, **40** (2), 166–193.

Jacobs, B. I. and Levy, K. N. (2006). Enhanced active equity strategies: Relaxing the long-only constraint in the pursuit of active return. *Journal of Portfolio Management*, **32** (3), 45–55.

Jacobs, B. I. and Levy, K. N. (2007a). 20 myths about enhanced active 120-20 strategies. *Financial Analysts Journal*, **63** (4), 19–26.

Jacobs, B. I. and Levy, K. N. (2007b). Enhanced active equity portfolios are trim equitized long-short portfolios. *Journal of Portfolio Management*, **33** (4), 19–25.

Jacobs, B. I., Levy, K. N., and Starer, D. (1998). On the optimality of long-short strategies. *Financial Analysts Journal*, **54** (2), 40–51.

Jacobs, B. I., Levy, K. N., and Starer, D. (1999). Long-short portfolio management: An integrated approach. *Journal of Portfolio Management*, **25** (2), 23–32.

Jacobs, B. I., Levy, K. N., and Markowitz, H. M. (2005). Portfolio optimization with factors, scenarios, and realistic short positions. *Operations Research*, **53** (4), 586–599.

Jacobs, B. I., Levy, K. N., and Markowitz, H. M. (2006). Trimability and fast optimization of long-short portfolios. *Financial Analysts Journal*, **62** (2), 36–46.

Magnus, J. R. and Neudecker, H. (1986). Symmetry, 0-1 matrices and jacobians: A review. *Econometric Theory*, **2** (2), 157–190.

Markowitz, H. M. (1956). The optimization of a quadratic function subject to linear constraints. *Naval Research Logistics Quarterly*, **III**, 111–133.

Markowitz, H. M. (1987). *Mean-Variance Analysis in Portfolio Choice and Capital Markets*. Basil Blackwell, Cambridge, MA.

Markowitz, H. M. and Perold, A. F. (1981). Portfolio analysis with factors and scenarios. *Journal of Finance*, **36** (14), 871–877.

Markowitz, H. M. and Todd, G. P. (2000). *Mean-Variance Analysis in Portfolio Choice and Capital Markets*. Frank J. Fabozzi, New Hope, PA.

Mitra, G., Ellison, F., and Scowcroft, A. (2007a). Quadratic programming for portfolio planning: Insights into algorithmic and computational issues Part I—Solving a family of QP models. *Journal of Asset Management*, **8** (3), 200–214.

Mitra, G., Ellison, F., and Scowcroft, A. (2007b). Quadratic programming for portfolio planning: Insights into algorithmic and computational issues Part II—Processing of portfolio planning models with discrete constraints. *Journal of Asset Management*, **8** (4), 249–258.

Nocedal, J. and Wright, S. J. (1990) *Numerical Optimization*. Springer, New York.

Sharpe, W. F. (1963). A simplified model for portfolio analysis. *Management Science*, **9** (2), 277–293.

Stein, M., Branke, J., and Schmeck, H. (2008). Efficient implementation of an active set algorithm for large-scale portfolio selection. *Computers and Operations Research*, **35** (12), 3945–3961.

Wolfe, P. (1959). The simplex method for quadratic programming. *Econometrica*, **27** (3), 382–398.

CHAPTER 4

TO OPTIMIZE OR NOT TO OPTIMIZE: IS THAT THE QUESTION?*

SEBASTIÁN CERIA

4.1 Introduction

The debate of whether to optimize or not to optimize when building equity portfolios has flared up again during the last few years, especially as quantitative strategies that rely heavily on optimization for portfolio construction have been faltering. In this chapter we address the basic question of whether optimization helps or hurts in the construction of equity portfolios, i.e. "should we optimize or not optimize?"

As with most black and white questions, the answer undoubtedly lies in between. Indeed, the real question may be not whether to optimize or not optimize, but how and when we should optimize. Most researchers and practitioners favoring optimization do not necessarily recognize the perils of using optimization based techniques for portfolio construction in certain situations; similarly, the anti-optimization crowd is completely against using optimization, even in cases where there is no obvious alternative. Researchers and practitioners seem to fall into two religious camps: either they believe in optimization or they don't.

The literature is full of arguments against the use of optimization for portfolio construction, see, for example Jobson (1991) and Michaud (1999). They cover a wide spectrum, from the very soft "the optimized portfolios lack intuition" to the very technical "optimized portfolios have an extreme over-reliance on parameters which are estimated

* The author would like to thank Anthony Renshaw for his valuable comments on an early version of this chapter; and Anureet Saxena for his various suggestions and contributions to Section 4.4, and for performing the computational experiments included in this chapter.

with significant estimation error." Detractors of optimization also argue that the best proof that optimization is not useful is the fact that most equity portfolio managers do not rely on optimization when building their portfolios. Part of the challenge of defending optimization in this debate is that, faced with criticisms such as these, it is not really clear what the alternative is that non-optimization proponents recommend in place of optimization. What does *non-optimization* really mean? Is it *rules of thumb* that are applied during the portfolio construction process? If so, what are those rules of thumb? And on the other side of the debate, what do we really mean by optimization? Is it the original mean-variance optimization (MVO) model as first introduced by Markowitz, or is optimization as commonly used by today's portfolio managers, sometimes termed *enhanced MVO*, which recognizes and incorporates a wide range of real world portfolio construction requirements as well as the mathematical and computational improvements of the last 50 years?

Early research suggested that it is not possible to distinguish the performance of naïve portfolio construction techniques and those built by using MVO. But those arguments were tested on very simplistic cases involving small asset universes with little, if any, limits on asset and factor exposures. These simplistic cases are not representative of modern day portfolio management challenges, and certainly not of the optimization techniques that modern portfolio managers use. More recently, there has been renewed interest in studying the performance of equally weighted portfolios. De Miguel, Garlappi, and Uppal (2009) argue that $1/N$ portfolios (equally weighted portfolios for a universe of N assets) outperform MVO generated portfolios in a set of practical experiments. Unfortunately, this research, like other comparisons between equally weighted portfolios and MVO, is not of much value to today's portfolio managers because of its lack of applicability to the current environment. As far as we know, no portfolio manager that favors optimization would use the unadulterated, original MVO framework, and no naïve portfolio construction technique applied in practice will be as simple as equal weighting. At the very least, equally weighted portfolios may not satisfy compliance restrictions imposed by asset owners.

Any comparison of optimization vs. an alternative depends crucially on how the input parameters – namely, the expected returns and, to a lesser extent, risk – are estimated. This is illustrated by the recent debate over whether the $1/N$ portfolio construction strategy outperforms MVO. While De Miguel, Garlappi and Uppal (2009) argue that $1/N$ outperforms optimized portfolios: "Of the fourteen (optimization-based) models we evaluate over seven empirical datasets, we find that none is consistently better than the $1/N$ rule in terms of Sharpe ratio, certainty-equivalent return, or turnover, indicating that, out of sample, the gain from optimal diversification is more than offset by estimation error." Kritzman, Page, and Turkington (2010), in "In defense of optimization: The fallacy of $1/N$" demonstrate exactly the opposite: "The ostensible superiority of the $1/N$ approach arises not from limitations in optimization, but rather, from reliance on rolling short-term samples for estimating expected returns . . . By relying on longer-term samples for estimated expected returns or even naively contrived but yet plausible assumptions, optimized portfolios outperform equally weighted ($1/N$) portfolios out of sample".

This chapter makes the argument that even though the use of optimization may have disadvantages, it still adds value to the portfolio management process. Our examples compare "good" optimization and "better" optimization: that is, the performance of optimized portfolios with varying degree of optimization quality and accuracy. We believe that showing that better optimization outperforms good optimization demonstrates the value of optimization. We would contend that, in the majority of cases, good optimization is robust as a proxy for rules of thumb, and that better optimization is superior to rules of thumb. For example, a commonly used rule of thumb for matching portfolio exposures to desired targets can be easily mimicked by using an optimization proxy. The methodology of comparing good to better optimization is repeatable and realistic for the complexities of modern portfolio management. Indeed, while our "less optimized" portfolios may not be "optimal," they will satisfy all the constraints that are normally imposed as part of the portfolio construction process, yielding results which are – at a minimum – realistic and implementable.

4.2 MVO and its Extensions – The Optimization Model

In 1952 Harry Markowitz introduced mean-variance optimization (MVO) in an article titled "Portfolio selection" published in the *Journal of Finance*, see (Markowitz 1952). Since then, those ideas have been extended to form the basis of what is now called modern portfolio theory, or MPT. MPT and MVO provide a solid foundation for the basic problem that portfolio managers have to tackle on a daily basis, namely, what is the optimal tradeoff between risk and return. In 1990, Markowitz received the ultimate recognition for his contributions when the Swedish Academy awarded the Sveriges Riksbank Prize in Economic Sciences in Memory of Alfred Nobel jointly to Markowitz, Miller, and Sharpe *"for their pioneering work in the theory of financial economics,"* see (The Royal Swedish Academy of Sciences 1990).

Markowitz's MVO is essentially the formulation of an optimization problem that resolves the issue of optimal tradeoff of risk and return by modeling expected returns as a linear function in the weights of the portfolio, and risk, or variance, as a quadratic function of those weights. Risk and expected return are then traded off by solving a quadratic optimization problem, with a *utility function* of the form:

$$\text{Max}_w \alpha^T w - \mu w^T Q w$$

where α is the vector of expected returns, w the weights of the assets in the optimal portfolio, μ is a parameter that represents the investor's "risk aversion," and Q is the covariance matrix of returns. In practice, Q is never estimated as a full covariance matrix of asset returns, but rather a factor decomposition of this matrix is used (Grinold and Kahn 1990). The factor-based version of the Q matrix is also commonly referred to as the *risk model*. The term w^TQw represents the variance of the portfolio, and it is also referred to as the *risk* of the portfolio. The original MVO model also included non-negativity (i.e., no-shorting) constraints on the weights of the portfolio.

The MVO model contains two critical parameters that need to be estimated: (1), expected returns or α, which are used to represent the forecasted return of the portfolio; and (2), the covariance of returns or Q, that is used to compute the risk of the portfolio. As is well known, the stochastic relationship between return and risk makes estimating expected returns much more challenging than estimating risk. For this reason, a significant portion of the optimization research literature has addressed the impact of estimation error in the expected returns.

Another improvement to the MVO model comes from advances in the techniques used for estimating the parameters used for expected returns and covariances of returns. Indeed, it is possible to create more stable mean-variance optimal portfolios by utilizing more stable expected return estimators. In some cases (but not always!), optimized portfolios utilizing these alternative estimation techniques lead to improve realized performance. One of the more common techniques is Bayesian shrinkage of the estimates towards a more stable mean. James–Stein estimators (Jobson and Korkie 1981) shrink the expected returns towards the average expected return based on the volatility of the asset and the distance of its expected return from the average. Jorion (1985) shrinks the expected return estimate towards the minimum variance portfolio, and Black and Litterman (1990) developed a Bayesian approach for producing stable expected return estimates that combine equilibrium expected returns and investor's views on specific assets or weighted groups of assets. Black and Litterman's solution blended return forecast is better aligned with the risk forecasts and the investor's view. For a detailed overview of the Black and Litterman model and a guide to its implementation, see Litterman *et al.* (2003), Idzorek (2004), or Meucci (2007). Several extensions of the Black and Litterman approach have been introduced over the last few years; see for example Jones, Lim, and Zangari (2007), Martellini and Ziemann (2007), and Meucci (2009).

The basic MVO model has been extended over time to incorporate realistic assumptions that appear in practice. A large number of practical restrictions can be added to the basic MVO model without altering the quadratic programming structure of the model or changing its complexity. Any linear constraint on the weights of the portfolio can be added to the model. Additional quadratic or linear terms in the weights of the portfolio can also be added to the utility function with corresponding aversion parameters. While adding additional terms to the objective function does not complicate the solution of the quadratic programming problem, in practice, it adds the challenge of calibrating an aversion parameter corresponding to each added term to quantitatively indicate the relative importance of each of the terms. The quadratic programming structure of Markowitz's original MVO model is not preserved when quadratic constraints are allowed. These constraints are typically used to represent a risk target such as a tracking error target with respect to one or multiple benchmarks. Such problems are not as easily solvable but can still be efficiently tackled with modern optimizers.

Over the last 10 years, as optimizers have become more powerful and more widely accessible, practitioners have further extended MVO to include objectives and constraints that are neither linear nor quadratic, or even convex. For example, the predicted market impact of a trade measured as transaction costs is often modeled as a nonlinear function of the trade size. Almgren (2005) used empirical data from hundreds of thousands of trades to conclude that market impact cost was best approximated by a function that is a fractional power in the size of the trade (1.6, in fact, which is widely cited as 5/3). Another class of constraints that has become popular is limiting the number of names held in the final portfolio. Unfortunately, modeling such constraints is non-trivial and involves the addition of indicator variables to decide whether a certain stock is or is not in the portfolio. The addition of such constraint results in a non-convex problem commonly referred to as a mixed-integer (nonlinear) programming problem. For a comprehensive study of MVO's extensions, see Tütüncü (2011).

Defenders of optimization would argue that the new constraints and objective terms are natural enhancement to the model, and that they increase its value. Further, when making comparisons, researchers should also use the best parameter estimation techniques available. Detractors, on the other hand, would argue that the use of additional constraints or non-standard estimation techniques is living proof that MVO is flawed, and that the constraints essentially "correct" its deficiencies by directing the solution to align it with the portfolio managers desires. Detractors would further argue that if you add enough constraints, the optimal portfolio will be driven by the constraints and not by the basic foundation of MVO and MPT. Note that this line of reasoning is not a criticism of optimization at all but rather a criticism of a very narrow interpretation of MVO. While such a semantic debate may be theoretically amusing, it defies belief to suggest that investment practitioners would be interested in anything less than the best available techniques in practice. In other words, who cares if the solution is driven by constraints? Surely the arguments for and against optimization must be based on real world results, not constitutional originalism.

4.3 The Value of Optimization

In this section we present a series of experiments illustrating how realized performance improves when the underlying optimization approach is improved.

4.3.1 Passive Portfolio Construction

The objective of a passive portfolio manager is to track a benchmark as closely as possible, so as to provide investors with returns which are equivalent, if not equal, to the return of the benchmark. While the easiest way to track a benchmark is to hold all of the securities in the benchmark with their corresponding weights, it may be impractical or too costly to do so in practice.

Let b represent the weights in the benchmark to be tracked, Q the covariance matrix, and w the vector of weights for the securities in the tracking portfolio; the mathematical formulation of the passive problem is then as follows:

$$Min(w-b)^T Q(w-b),\ subject\ to\ w \geq 0,\ additional\ constraints.$$

The most common *additional constraints* of this model used by passive portfolio managers include:

- limits on the number of names held (do not hold more than Y securities in the portfolio);
- threshold holdings on positions (if the security is held, hold at least X bps);
- liquidity constraints (limit the holding in any security to Z% of the ADV);
- limits on transaction costs and/or market impact (penalize securities that would incur significant trading costs or market impact).

The optimization-based model of the problem is straightforward and does not involve the proprietary estimation of any parameters (the covariance matrix and market impact model can be licensed from third-party vendors). However, the addition of some of the constraints, especially those related to limiting the number of names or threshold holdings, significantly adds to the complexity of the problem, since they are non-convex.

Since the objective in a passive strategy is to minimize predicted tracking error to the benchmark, an optimized portfolio will tend to have lower predicted tracking error than a portfolio that is produced heuristically. But does a lower predicted tracking error imply a lower realized tracking error? In other words, would an optimized passive portfolio have better realized performance (i.e. better realized tracking error) than a non-optimized, or "less-optimized" portfolio?

To answer this question we performed a series of experiments for a passive strategy where we varied the quality of the solution obtained by Axioma's optimizer, thus providing solutions that are gradually "less optimal," yielding a higher predicted tracking error. The experiment was set up as follows:

- Selection universe: Names in the Russell 3000 Index.
- Objective: Minimize tracking error to the Russell 3000 Index.
- Maximum names held = 50.
- Long only.

Additional constraints included liquidity constraints, in order to limit the holdings in illiquid names. In order to produce solutions that are less optimized we parameterized the optimization algorithm in Axioma's optimizer so as to produce heuristic solutions of varying quality.

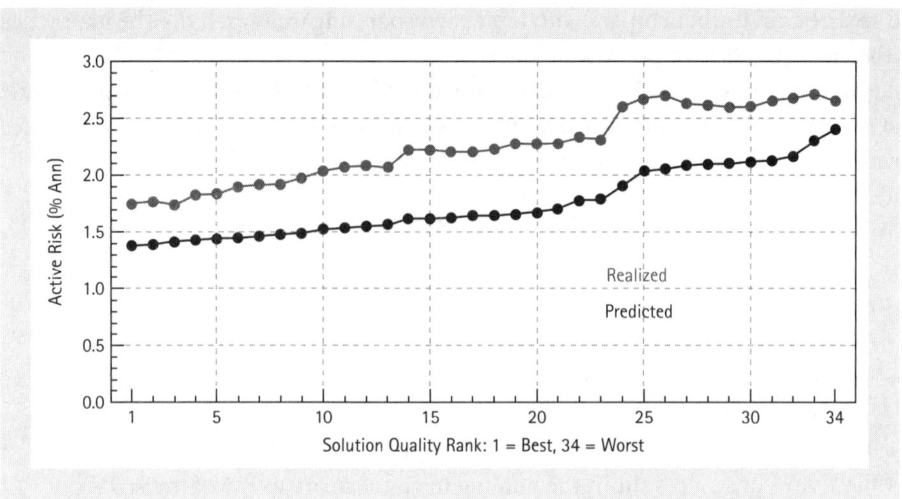

FIGURE 4.1 Predicted and realized active risk for optimized solutions of varying quality.

Figure 4.1 shows predicted vs. realized risk for 2006 for the various solutions we obtained. The quality of the solution produced by the parameterized algorithm varies along the x-axis from 1 (best solution) to 35 (worst solution).

As the quality of the solution deteriorates on an *ex ante* basis, the quality of the realized tracking error also deteriorates. Figure 4.2 quantifies this by plotting the *ex ante* vs. *ex post* ranking of the solutions obtained.

For this passive example, the better the quality of the optimizer, the better the *ex post* performance.

Figure 4.1 illustrates a well-known bias of optimized portfolios: optimized portfolios consistently underestimate the realized tracking error (i.e. the difference between

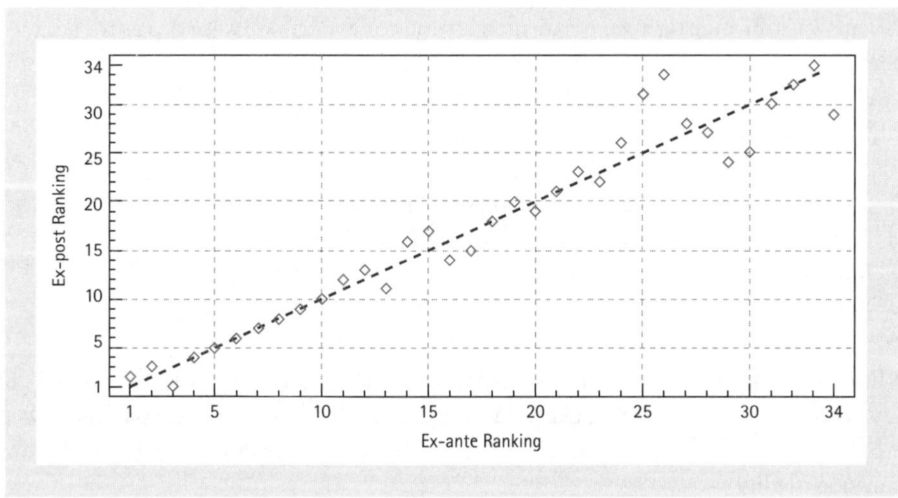

FIGURE 4.2 *Ex post* vs. *ex ante* solution quality rankings.

the realized and predicted tracking error is always positive, and always large). This phenomenon is easily explained in terms of selection bias: since the optimizer searches for low tracking error solutions, it prefers assets whose risk and tracking error is low, and hence have the largest probability of being underestimated. In other words, optimized portfolios that reduce or limit risk bias any risk estimation errors towards underestimation.

In the literature, optimization is sometimes criticized as an "error-maximization" procedure, since errors in both the expected returns and covariance are usually biased in the optimized portfolios even if they are unbiased throughout the selection universe of the optimization problem. In fact, some of the most impassioned (and publicized) critiques of optimization have focused on the tendency of optimized portfolios to have estimation error biases.

The pragmatic response to such critiques is to ask whether error biases affect realized performance. For this example, the answer is no. The better the optimization, the lower the predicted tracking error, and the lower realized tracking error, even though the optimization has maximized risk underestimation.

4.3.2 Active Portfolio Management

The goal of an active portfolio manager is to "beat" the return of a benchmark while managing to a target tracking error, typically between 4% and 6%. One of the key inputs to the portfolio construction process for active management is the expectation of the return of each of the stocks in the eligible universe. Such expectations can be represented as a vector of expected returns, as relative rankings, price targets, or as simple buy, sell and hold recommendations.

The strongest debate over whether to optimize or not occurs in the area of active portfolio management. To a large extent, that debate has been fueled by the fact that expected returns are difficult to estimate and the MVO framework will tend to be very sensitive to any estimation error.

While sensitivity to inputs may produce quite diverse portfolios, an interesting question is whether these sensitivities have implications in portfolio performance. Michaud, who has coined the phrase that "optimizers are error maximizers," when he introduced his re-sampling approach to portfolio construction, see also Scherer (2002), argues that MVO overweights those assets with a large estimated return to estimated variance ratio (underweights those with a low ratio) and that these are precisely the assets likely to have large estimation errors. More recently, in an article called "Are optimizers error maximizers?," Kritzman (2006) shows that while "errors in the estimates of these values may substantially misstate optimal allocations, the return distributions of the correct and incorrect portfolios will nevertheless likely be quite similar." Kritzman concludes, without any doubt that "The hype that mean-variance optimizers are error maximizers seems to be just that – hype. Conventional wisdom may be conventional, but not always correct." Essentially, Kritzman argues that even if we accept that optimizers are very sensitive to estimation errors and that estimation errors severely affect the composition of the optimal portfolios, the realized performance of optimized portfolios, however flawed, is better than the alternatives.

To illustrate the value of optimization when compared with heuristic portfolio construction techniques, we performed a number of experiments on actual portfolio manager's data.

The data we used for the experiment includes expected returns, as provided by the portfolio managers, and a set of constraints. In the experiments illustrated in Figures 4.3 and 4.4, we compared the realized performance (realized tracking error vs. realized returns) of Axioma's optimizer vs. the performance of a heuristic process that builds optimal portfolios as follows: In the first step, we rank assets by their expected returns. Then, from largest expected return to smallest expected return, we replace the assets in the portfolio with the lowest expected return with an asset with higher expected return (with a fixed set of weights) while making sure that the exposures in the portfolio to the risk model factors are closely matched to the exposures of the benchmark.

4.3.3 The Portfolio Factory

Another broadly accepted use of optimization is in the context of separately managed accounts (or SMA) both for institutional and private wealth management. Institutional asset managers usually provide their clients with the flexibility to impose additional constraints on the portfolios that they manage for them. For example, a "health conscious" endowment may impose that their portfolio holds no tobacco stocks, and a "green" pension fund that investments are only made in companies with a small carbon

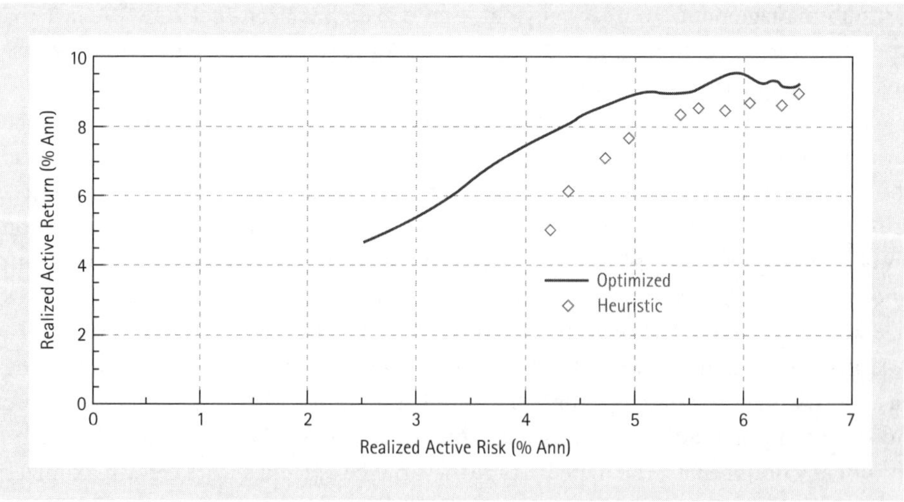

FIGURE 4.3 Optimized and heuristic realized efficient frontiers – Example 1.

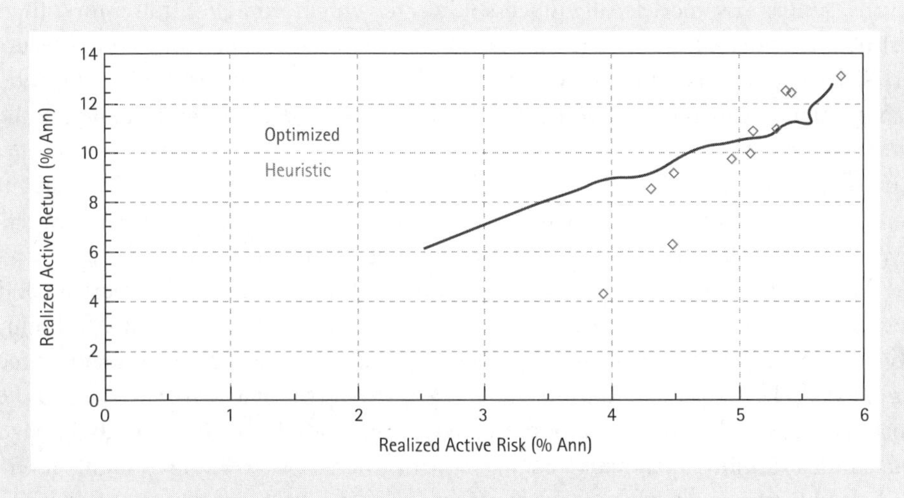

FIGURE 4.4 Optimized and heuristic realized efficient frontiers – Example 2.

footprint. However, it's not possible for a portfolio manager to incorporate all of these constraints on their model portfolios simultaneously, since those restrictions may be subtracting real alpha. An optimization based portfolio construction process provides an elegant answer to this problem, by allowing the portfolio manager to maximize the transfer of information from their model portfolios to the client portfolio, while still satisfying all of the client constraints.

It is important to note that the proposed approach is independent of how the model portfolio is actually built. In fact, this optimization-based approach to managing a large number of portfolios is widely used in a broad range of financial institutions, regardless of whether the firm builds the model portfolio following a fundamental or quantitative process.

4.4 The Perils of Optimization

Although we have argued that portfolios that are generated through optimization tend to outperform portfolios generated with heuristic methodologies, there are some cases where optimization must be used with care.

4.4.1 Trade Crowding

In recent years, concerns have been raised over *trade crowding* of quantitative strategies. Because most quantitative managers use similar models for estimating expected returns, similar risk models, all embedded into the enhanced MVO framework, their portfolios tend to look similar. As a result, quantitive managers often attempt to execute very similar trade lists, thus "crowding" the trade. In fact, many quantitative portfolio managers have blamed the crowding of the quant space for the poor performance of the last few years.

In August 2007, quantitative managers experienced what we characterized as a "quant scare." In a note to our clients in late August of 2007, we wrote: "quantitative managers have experienced a trifecta of unprecedented changes in the magnitude, direction and correlations of factor returns, driving (negative) returns in the equity markets and increased risk for quant managers... There is general agreement in the quant community that the recent scare was caused by a liquidity crunch stemming from the sub-prime lending debacle. Matthew S. Rothman (2007) was among those who first articulated the most plausible explanation linking these two events, as follows: Many multi-strategy hedge funds running quantitative equity strategies were also investing in highly leveraged credit instruments. When the value of these credit instruments began to fall due to the sub-prime crisis, the funds were forced to raise cash to cover margin calls. Since the market values of these illiquid instruments were hard to gauge, the multi-strategy funds moved to generate cash by selling equities instead. This liquidation triggered a steep decline in the equity assets held by quant managers as a whole. The decline increased the overall volatility in the market, thus forcing even those managers not invested in the credit instruments to begin reducing leverage in an attempt to manage risk. Due to similarities in the positions that quant managers held, the effects of the reduction in leverage spilled well beyond the world of market-neutral hedge fund strategies."

What really happened during the quant scare of August 2007? One potential explanation is that what caused the unprecedented drop in factor returns is a combination of quant managers using similar risk models and optimization-based rebalancing of their portfolios. A plausible sequence of events is as follows: In the last days of the month of July, some quantitative funds, as hypothesized by Rothman, started liquidating their equity positions, probably to gain cash to cover losses in their sub-prime portfolios. (Little did they know of the sub-prime debacle that would occur a year later.) As a consequence, volatility rapidly increased. Quantitative managers then waited until the beginning of August, to perform the usual rebalancing of their portfolios. Given the unusual increase in volatility, and the extreme movements in those factor returns (which are part of every risk model), the optimizer consumed most of the available turnover to bring those measures into line, thus reducing the predicted tracking error and re-aligning the factor exposures.

Effectively, the optimization was driven by constraints: the optimizer had no choice but to ignore estimates of expected returns, since it needed to significantly reduce the predicted risk of the portfolios and the factor exposures. That means that the trades of most quantitative managers were completely dominated by the structure of their risk models. And since most quantitative managers use similar risk models, their risk reduction trades ended up being similar to each other. Our thesis is that the combination of the optimizer and the risk model ended up being lethal for many managers.

Their trades exacerbated the drop, and the returns of quant managers during the months of July and August were disastrous, except, of course, for those managers who decided not to optimize during those days.

If volatility increases rapidly and factor returns have extraordinary changes, the user of an optimizer should understand that the trade may be dominated by the need to reduce the predicted risk of the portfolio, essentially ignoring the expected returns. Moreover, since the risk model will dominate the trade, the likelihood of trade crowding is large. When this happens, optimizers should either be avoided or used with extreme caution. In fact, the best advice for such situations may be to do nothing until the calm settles.

4.4.2 Factor Alignment Problems

Construction of optimized portfolios entails the complex interaction between three key entities, namely, the risk factors, the alpha factors, and the constraints within an optimization framework. The problems that arise due to mutual misalignment between these three entities are collectively referred to as factor alignment problems (FAPs). The FAP manifests itself through risk underestimation, undesirable exposures to factors with hidden and unaccounted systematic risk, consistent failure in achieving *ex ante* performance targets, inability to harvest high quality alphas into above-average IR, etc. FAPs have received a lot of attention in the recent literature (see Lee and Stefek 2008, Saxena and Stubbs 2010a, b, c). The following discussion is based on the work of Saxena and Stubbs.

For the sake of illustration, consider a portfolio manager (PM) whose risk model is defined by the Fama–French risk factors while his alpha model is derived from Pastor and Stambaugh's extension to the Fama–French model. Recall that the Pastor–Stambaugh model has a liquidity factor in addition to the market sensitivity, size, and value factors which are also present in the Fama–French model. Suppose the PM's expected returns are obtained by equally weighting all the factors in Pastor–Stambaugh model. When the mentioned alpha and risk model are used within an optimization framework, the relative weighing of various alpha factors gets reassigned during the portfolio construction phase. Specifically, since the optimizer perceives no systematic risk in the liquidity factor, it is likely to overload on the liquidity factor relative to other factors. As an unintended consequence, it follows that the optimal portfolio will have excessive exposure to the liquidity factor. Since the systematic risk arising from the liquidity factor is not correctly accounted for during the portfolio construction process, the *ex ante* risk estimates are likely to underestimate the realized risk values, leading to estimation errors in risk prediction and depressed risk adjusted performance.

The above example captures the essence of FAP in its purest form. In a more practical setting, however, the misalignment between the alpha and risk factors is usually more complicated. For instance, the alpha model can use an S/P factor which is only partially spanned by the regular risk factors such as E/P or B/P. The presence of constraints adds another layer of complication and introduces additional sources of misalignment. For example, even when both the risk model and the alpha model may have a liquidity factor, a constraint on average daily volume may affect the manner in which the optimizer gives the optimal portfolio exposure to the liquidity factor.

To summarize, factor alignment problems are the result of an optimizer's propensity to neutralize the exposure of the portfolio to any known systematic risk factors. In doing so, the optimizer takes excessive exposure to factors that have systematic risk but which are missing from the factor risk model that is used to construct the optimal portfolios, thus resulting in a downward bias in risk prediction. This phenomenon was recently verified empirically by Saxena and Stubbs (2010a, b, c), who showed that the problem of risk-underestimation is not present if the risk of the optimal portfolio is measured by a different risk model which is not used in portfolio construction.

Recent research into FAP has revealed some novel techniques to correctly account for the systematic risk of such "hidden" factors. For instance, Axioma's patented Alpha Alignment Factor as described by Renshaw *et al.* (2006) corrects for this misalignment by penalizing the portion of the portfolio which is not spanned by the user risk factors. Interestingly, augmenting the traditional MVO approach with enhancements such as the Alpha Alignment Factor (AAF) not only improves the accuracy of the risk prediction but also the *ex post* performance of the optimal portfolios. Saxena and Stubbs (2010b) investigate these issues analytically and show that the AAF approach, in fact, pushes the *ex post* efficient frontier upwards thereby empowering a PM to access portfolios that lie above the traditional risk-return frontier.

4.5 Conclusions

In this chapter we have described the thesis that portfolio managers should not be concerned with the question of whether to optimize or not to optimize, but rather whether optimization-based approaches to portfolio construction provide value when compared to the alternatives. We have shown that, in spite of its flaws, optimization techniques can provide demonstrable value in realistic portfolio construction cases, not only when measuring *ex ante* performance, but also when comparing *ex post* performance.

Finally, we would like to mention that use of optimization in equity portfolio construction is making a slow but steady transition from being an "approach favored by choice" to an "approach dictated by necessity." For example, in the area of risk management, any contemporary portfolio manager that needs to monitor the risk of a truly global portfolio needs to hedge away exposures to systematic risk factors – a task which is best accomplished by means of an optimizer.

REFERENCES

Almgren, R., Thum, C., Hauptmann, E., and Li, H. (2005). Equity market impact. *Risk*, **18**, 21–28.

Black, F. and Litterman, R. (1990). Asset allocation: Combining investors views with market equilibrium. Technical report, Goldman, Sachs, & Company. Fixed Income Research.

De Miguel, V., Garlappi, L., and Uppal, R. (2009). Optimal versus naïve diversification: How inefficienct is the $1/N$ porfolio stratetgy? *Review of Financial Studies*, **22**(5), 1915–1953.

Grinold, R. and Kahn, R. (2000). *Active Portfolio Management: A Quantitative Approach for Providing Superior Returns and Controlling Risks*. Mc Graw Hill, New York.

Idzorek, T (2002). A step-by-step guide to the Black–Litterman model. Technical report, Duke University.

Jobson, J.D., and Korkie, B. (1981). Putting markowitz theory to work. *Journal of Portfolio Management*, **36**, 70–74.

Jones, R., Lim, T., and Zangari, P. (2007). The Black–Litterman model for structured equity portfolios. *Journal of Portfolio Management*, **33**(2), 24–33.

Jorion, P. (1985). International portfolio diversification with estimation risk. *The Journal of Business*, **58**(3), 259–278.

Kritzman, M. (2006). Are optimizers error maximizers? *Journal of Portfolio Management* **32**(4), 66–69.

Kritzman, M., Page, S., and Turkington, D. (2010). In defense of optimization: The fallacy of $1/N$, *Financial Analysts Journal*, **26**(2), 31–39.

Lee, J. and Stefek, D. (2008). Do risk factors eat alpha? *Journal of Portfolio Management*, **34**(4), 12–25.

Litterman, R. and the Quantitative Resources Group Goldman Sachs Asset Management (2003). *Modern Investment Management. An Equilibrium Approach*. John Wiley and Sons, New York.

Markowitz, H. (1952). Portfolio selection. *The Journal of Finance*, **VII**(1), 77–91.

Meucci, A. (2007). *Risk and Asset Allocation*. Springer Finance, New York.

Meucci, A. (2009). Enhancing the Black–Litterman and related approaches: Views and stress-test on risk factors. *Journal of Asset Management*, **10**(2), 89–96.

Michaud, R. (1999). *Efficient Asset Management: A Practical Guide to Stock Portfolio Optimization and Asset Allocation*. Harvard Business School Press, Cambridge, MA.

Renshaw, A., Stubbs, R., Schmieta, S., and Ceria, S. (2006). Axioma Alpha factor method: Improving risk estimation by reducing risk model portfolio selection bias. Technical report, Axioma, Inc. Research Report.

Rothman, M. (2007). Turbulent times in quant land, Lehman Brothers Memo.

Saxena, A., and Stubbs, R. (2010a). Alpha alignment factor: A solution to the underestimation of risk for optimized active portfolios, Axioma Technical Report No. 15.

Saxena, A., and Stubbs, R. (2010b). Pushing the frontier (literally) with the alpha alignment factor, Axioma Technical Report No. 22.

Saxena, A., and Stubbs, R. (2010c). Finance, statistics, accounting, optimization and some alignment Problems, Axioma Technical Report.

Scherer, B. (2002). Portfolio resampling: Review and critique. *Financial Analysts Journal*, **45**, 98–109.

The Royal Swedish Academy of Sciences (1990). Press release announcing the recipients of 1990 Nobel Prize in Economic Sciences (http://www.nobelprize.org).

Tütüncü, R. (2011). Recent advances in portfolio optimization, Chapter 2 of this volume.

PART II

PORTFOLIO CONSTRUCTION PROCESSES

CHAPTER 5

ADDING THE TIME DIMENSION: OPTIMAL REBALANCING[1]

MARK KRITZMAN, SIMON MYRGREN, AND SÉBASTIEN PAGE

SOPHISTICATED investors employ some variation of mean-variance analysis to determine the optimal allocation of their portfolios. Yet when price changes cause the actual mix to drift away from the optimal target even the most sophisticated investors resort to naïve heuristics, such as calendar or range based rules to determine when to rebalance. A calendar heuristic calls for rebalancing at the end of an arbitrary period such as a month, a quarter, or a year. Implicitly, this approach assumes that prices change about the same amount each period, but this is far from true. A range based heuristic calls for investors to restore the optimal weights whenever the actual weights drift outside of ranges set around the optimal weights. By establishing uniform ranges investors implicitly assume that a 5% misallocation to stocks introduces the same degree of distortion to the portfolio as a 5% misallocation to cash. Although these heuristics are preferable to the extremes of no rebalancing and continual rebalancing, they are almost certainly suboptimal. To determine the optimal rebalancing schedule we must employ a technique called dynamic programming.

5.1 DYNAMIC PROGRAMMING

Dynamic programming was introduced by Richard Bellman (1952), the same year that Markowitz published his landmark article on portfolio selection.[2] Dynamic

[1] This chapter synthesizes two articles: Kritzman, Mary, Myrgren, and Page (2007, 2009).

[2] Coincidently, both Richard Bellman and Harry Markowitz worked at the Rand Corporation at the same time.

programming provides solutions to multi-stage decision processes in which the decisions made in prior periods affect the choices available in later periods. This approach is particularly suitable to portfolio rebalancing because whether or not we rebalance today influences what happens to our portfolio in the future. Perhaps the best way to understand dynamic programming is to consider how we can use it to find a partner, of all things (see, for example, Smith 1997).

5.2 Partner Search

Imagine you have 10 years to find a partner and you meet one potential partner each year. You rank each companion on a scale from 0 to 100 and assume that scores are uniformly distributed, which means you are as likely to meet someone you rank as a 10 as you are someone you rank as a 60. At the end of each year, you must decide to marry your current companion or leave that person and continue searching. You are not allowed to revert to previous companions, and if you have not found your partner by year 10, your parents force you to marry the person you are with at that time.

Dynamic programming provides the optimal year-by-year decision policy by working backwards from year 10. The expected score of your companion in year 10 is 50; hence you should marry in year 9 only if your companion at the time scores above 50. There is thus a 50% chance you will marry your companion in year 9. If you marry in year 9, your companion's expected score is 75 given that it must be above 50 in order for your companion to be marriageable. There is also a 50% likelihood that you will not marry in year 9 and settle in year 10 for a companion with an expected score of 50. The expected score and therefore hurdle at year 9 equals 62.5 (50% × 75 + 50% × 50).

In year 8, you should marry your current companion only if he or she scores above 62.5. The likelihood that your companion in year 8 will score above 62.5 is 37.5%, and the expected score of marriageable candidates in year 8 is 81.3, given that his or her score must surpass 62.5. There is a 62.5% chance that you will continue your search into year 9 which has an expected score of 62.5. The expected score for year 8 therefore equals 69.5 (37.5% × 81.25 + 62.5% × 62.5), and this score is the hurdle for your companion in year 7.

By proceeding in this fashion we determine the scores for each year, as shown in Table 5.1.[3] Your strategy for finding a partner is to marry if your current companion scores higher than the expected score for the subsequent year.

[3] Recursively the score for year k can be expressed as $score(k) = 50 \times \left(1 + \left(\frac{score(k+1)}{100}\right)^2\right)$.

Table 5.1 Partner search.

Year	1	2	3	4	5	6	7	8	9	10
Expected score	86.1	84.9	83.6	82.0	80.0	77.5	74.2	69.5	62.5	50.0

5.3 Simplified Solution to Portfolio Rebalancing

Now let us turn to a still simple but more relevant illustration of dynamic programming. Suppose we own a portfolio that has a 60% allocation to stocks and a 40% allocation to bonds and that the possible returns for each asset along with their probabilities are given by Table 5.2.

If in the subsequent period stocks and bonds both return 8%, our asset mix will remain at 60/40. If either of the other scenarios prevails, our asset mix will drift away from our 60/40 target mix. Table 5.3 shows how the asset mix might change after one and two periods given the probabilistic returns in Table 5.2.

If stocks increase by 26% and bonds rise by 1%, for example, our asset mix will shift from 60/40 to 65/35. In order to decide whether to remain at 65/35 or to rebalance to 60/40, we must compare the cost of being misallocated with the trading costs we would incur to restore the optimal weights. It is straightforward to estimate the trading costs. It is anything but straightforward to estimate the cost of being misallocated. We start by estimating the utility of our initial 60/40 portfolio. To do so, we must define a utility function, which converts wealth into a measure of happiness or satisfaction. In this example, we assume that our expected utility is equal to the natural logarithm of wealth. This particular utility function means that we are risk averse and prefer to preserve the same asset mix irrespective of our wealth. Table 5.4 shows how we apply the return assumptions displayed in Table 5.2 to determine the utility of a 60/40 stock/bond portfolio. We compute the natural logarithm of a 60/40 mix under each of the three return scenarios and take the weighted sum of these values.

Table 5.2 Return distribution.

	Probability	Stock Return	Bond Return
Scenario 1	25%	26%	1%
Scenario 2	50%	8%	8%
Scenario 3	25%	−11%	10%

Table 5.3 Probable asset mixes over two periods.

Start	End of period 1		End of period 2	
	Asset mix	Probability*	Asset mix	Probability*
			70/30	1/4
	65/35	1/4	65/35	1/2
			60/40	1/4
			65/35	1/4
60/40	60/40	1/2	60/40	1/2
			55/45	1/4
			60/40	1/4
	55/45	1/4	55/45	1/2
			50/50	1/4

*given prior state

Table 5.4 Expected utility for 60/40 portfolio.

$$25\% \times \ln((1 + .26) \times .60 + (1 + .01) \times .40) = 0.0371$$
$$50\% \times \ln((1 + .08) \times .60 + (1 + .08) \times .40) = 0.0385$$
$$25\% \times \ln((1 - .11) \times .60 + (1 + .10) \times .40) = -0.066$$

Expected Utility: 0.069

As it turns out, a portfolio of 60% stocks and 40% bonds yields the highest expected utility (0.0690) of any possible mix of stocks and bonds for a log-wealth investor and given our return assumptions. Stated differently, a 60/40 mix exactly balances our aversion to loss with our desire to grow wealth. Any deviation from this mix reduces expected utility. We can therefore think of the cost of being misallocated, which we call the sub-optimality cost, as the difference between the maximum utility we derive from a 60/40 mix and the lower utility we derive from a 65/35 mix. If we switch the weights in Table 5.3 to 65% stocks and 35% bonds, we find that expected utility falls to .068969. Therefore the sub-optimality cost expressed in units of utility equals .0031 (.069000 − .068969). The problem with this definition of cost is that we cannot directly compare it to trading costs, which are expressed in monetary units. We therefore need to convert units of utility into monetary units so that we can compare them directly to trading costs. We accomplish this conversion by taking the certainty equivalent of utility.

A certainty equivalent is the value of a certain prospect that yields the same utility as the expected utility of an uncertain prospect.[4] Consider an investor who has log wealth

[4] This notion was introduced by the famous mathematician, Daniel Bernoulli in 1738. For an English translation, see: Bernoulli, Daniel, "Exposition of a new theory on the measurement of risk,"

utility and is faced with a risky investment that has an equal probability of increasing by 1/3 or falling by 1/4. The utility of this investment equals the sum of the probability weighted utilities of the two outcomes. If the initial investment is \$100.00 the expected utility of this investment equals 4.60517 as shown:

$$4.60517 = \ln(133.33) \times .50 + \ln(75.00) \times .50.$$

This investment has an expected value of \$104.17, but this expectation is uncertain. How much less should the investor be willing to accept for sure, such that she would be indifferent between this amount and an uncertain value of \$104.17? It turns out that \$100.00 also yields a utility of 4.6052 ($\ln(100) = 4.60517$). Therefore, if her utility function equals the logarithm of wealth, she would be indifferent between receiving \$100.00 for sure and an equal probability of receiving \$133.33 or \$75.00.

For a log wealth utility function, we find the certainty equivalent by raising e, the base of the natural logarithm, to the power of expected utility.

$$100.00 = e^{\ln(133.33) \times .50 + \ln(75) \times .50}.$$

The sub-optimality cost of the 65/35 mix, therefore, is the difference in the certainty equivalents of the two portfolios, which equals 0.00328% ($e^{.069000} - e^{.068969}$). How does this sub-optimality cost compare to the cost of rebalancing to the optimal weights? Let us assume it costs 5 basis points to trade stocks and 7 basis points to trade bonds; hence the cost of restoring the optimal weights equals 0.00700% ($0.05 \times 0.0005 + 0.05 \times 0.0007$). It is thus cheaper to remain sub-optimal than to trade.

But this analysis is incomplete because it ignores what might happen in the future. If we remain sub-optimal given a 65/35 mix after one period we face a different set of outcomes in period 2 than if we restore the optimal weights. We must therefore take into account the cost of future choices between rebalancing and remaining sub-optimal in order to decide what to do in prior periods. Just as in the partner problem, we start by working backwards from the end of period 2.

We calculate the sub-optimality costs and the rebalancing costs for all of the possible portfolios at the end of period 2. Then in order to calculate the total cost of a particular choice at the end of period 1, we add the cost of future choices, assuming we always act optimally. This is the essence of dynamic programming.

Table 5.5 extends Table 5.3 to include the cost of rebalancing and the cost of sub-optimality for each possible portfolio at each state throughout the investment horizon,

Econometrica, January 1954. Also, for more about Daniel Bernoulli's contributions to finance and mathematics, see Bernstein, Peter L., *Against the Gods: The Remarkable Story of Risk*, John Wiley & Sons, Inc., 1996. While a risk-neutral probability measure might be an alternative to using certainty equivalents, it only works if the probability distribution is known and the asset to be priced can be perfectly replicated. Also, this approach might be difficult to scale. On the other hand, to calculate the certainty equivalent requires a utility function. Because optimal rebalancing assumes the optimal portfolio is known, the utility function is also known, making it a convenient way to link sub-optimality cost to the optimal asset allocation.

Table 5.5 Rebalancing versus sub-optimality costs (basis points) and optimal rebalancing roadmap.

	End of period 1				End of period 2			
Start	Asset mix	Probability*	Rebalacing cost**	Sub-Optimality cost**	Asset mix	Probability*	Rebalancing cost**	Sub-Optimality cost**
					70/30	25%	1.20	1.27
	65/35	25%	0.75	0.76	65/35	50%	0.60	0.32
					60/40	25%	0.00	0.00
					65/35	25%	0.60	0.32
60/40	60/40	50%	0.00	0.15**	60/40	50%	0.00	0.00
					55/45	25%	0.60	0.30
					60/40	25%	0.00	0.00
	55/45	25%	0.75	0.73	55/45	50%	0.60	0.30
					50/50	25%	1.20	1.22

*Given prior state
**Discount rate = 5%

Table 5.6 The curse of dimensionality.

Number of assets	Number of portfolios	Number of calculations to perform
2	101	5,620,751
3	5,151	14,619,573,351
4	176,851	17,233,228,186,751
5	4,598,126	11,649,662,254,243,700
6	96,560,646	5,137,501,054,121,460,000
7	1,705,904,746	1,603,471,162,336,350,000,000
8	26,075,972,546	374,655,945,665,079,000,000,000
9	352,025,629,371	68,281,046,097,460,800,000,000,000
10	4,263,421,511,271	10,015,396,403,505,300,000,000,000,000

and it presents the optimal choices for all of these portfolios, which represent the dynamic programming solution.

This example is unrealistically simple because it assumes we allocate between only two assets over only two periods with only three possible return scenarios. Moreover, it assumes that we either rebalance fully or not at all. With realistic assumptions, the computational challenge rises sharply and becomes intractable with just a few assets. Table 5.6 shows how many portfolios we must consider and how many calculations we must perform as we increase the number of assets and the granularity with which we rebalance. This computational challenge is called the curse of dimensionality.[5]

5.4 Formal Solution to Portfolio Rebalancing

Let us assume an investor with log-wealth utility wishes to select a set of portfolio weights that maximize expected utility over a forthcoming period. The expected utility $E(U)$ of the portfolio is written as the weighted sum of the n security expected returns under m scenarios, each with associated p probability

$$E(U) = \sum_{i=1}^{m} p_i \ln\left(1 + \sum_{j=1}^{n} X_j \mu_{ij}\right) = p \ln\left(1 + \mu X'\right) \tag{5.1}$$

[5] The term "curse of dimensionality" is due to Richard Bellman.

where

$$\mu = \begin{bmatrix} \mu_{11} & \mu_{12} & \cdots & \mu_{1n} \\ \mu_{21} & \mu_{22} & \cdots & \mu_{2n} \\ & & \vdots & \\ \mu_{m1} & \mu_{m2} & \cdots & \mu_{mn} \end{bmatrix}$$

is the matrix of expected returns, $X = [X_1, \ldots, X_n]$ are the current portfolio weights in percentage, and $p = [p_1, \ldots, p_m]$ are the probabilities associated with the m scenarios. Let $X^{opt} = \left[X_1^{opt}, \ldots, X_n^{opt}\right]$ denote the optimal portfolio weights. $E(U)$ is then maximized when $X = X^{opt}$ and denoted $E(U^*)$. With the passage of time asset prices change, and X deviates from X^{opt} resulting in a loss of expected utility. As we have shown in the context of our simple three-scenario example, for a given sub-optimal $E(U)$, the certainty equivalent cost (CEC) is given by:

$$CEC = e^{E(U^*)} - e^{E(U)}. \tag{5.2}$$

The transaction costs (TC) at period t are written as

$$TC_t = \sum_{i=1}^{n} C_j \left|X_{jt} - X_{jt-1}\right| \tag{5.3}$$

where C_j is the cost per unit of trading security j from the previous weights X_{jt-1} to the new weights X_{jt}.

The general portfolio rebalancing problem is therefore to minimize the combined costs associated with deviations from X^{opt} as defined in (5.2) while also minimizing transaction costs as defined in (5.3).

We define the dynamic programming solution to portfolio rebalancing as the recursive minimization of the cost function

$$J_t(X_t, X_{t-1}) = Min\{CEC_t + TC_t + J_{t+1}(X_{t+1}, X_t)\} \tag{5.4}$$

where the total cost for the current period, $J_t(X_t, X_{t-1})$, is a function of the current CEC and TC, but also of future costs $J_{t+1}(X_{t+1}, X_t)$.

In our experiments we use a 28-processor grid computing platform. Grid computing relies on parallel processing to facilitate large-scale computation. Even with grid computing, it is computationally intractable to derive the optimal rebalancing schedule for a 10-asset portfolio if we rebalance in increments as small as 1%. On a regular workstation, for example, the computing time required to solve this problem would be nearly 12,000 times the age of the universe.[6] Fortunately, Harry Markowitz pointed us to an algorithm he developed with Erik van Dijk (see Markowitz and van Dijk, 2004) which reduces

[6] If, instead, you are one of the 80% of Americans who believe the universe was created only 6,000 years ago, the computing time would be 2.65×10^{10} times the age of the universe. In either case, grid computing would be of no use.

the dimensionality of the problem and enables us to derive rebalancing solutions for portfolios of up to 100 assets.

5.5 The Markowitz–van Dijk Algorithm

The Markowitz–van Dijk algorithm replaces $J_t(X_{t+1}, X_t)$ in (5.4) by a quadratic function of the current and optimal portfolio weights. In general, a quadratic approximation Q to $J_t(X_{t+1}, X_t)$ has the following form:

$$Q = \sum a_i X_i + \sum b_i^2 X_i^2 + \sum_i \sum_{j>i} c_{ij} X_i X_j. \tag{5.5}$$

To simplify our experiments, however, we conjecture that Q is proportional to the squared deviations (the "drifts") multiplied by a coefficient d:[7]

$$Q_t = d \sum_{i=1}^{n} \left(X_{it} - X^{opt'} \right)^2. \tag{5.6}$$

The cost function (5.4) then becomes

$$J_t(X_t, X_{t-1}) = CEC_t + TC_t + Q_t. \tag{5.7}$$

To determine the value of the coefficient d in (5.6) we use Monte Carlo simulations. We generate 200 return paths. We minimize cost as defined in (5.7)[8] at each decision point during the simulation and we continue to run simulations and change d until we find its best performing value. Computational intensity, which is low to begin with, remains manageable as we add more assets.[9]

5.6 Results

We test the relative efficacy of dynamic programming and the MvD heuristic with data on domestic equities, domestic fixed income, non-U.S. equities, non-U.S. fixed

[7] The quadratic approximation in Equation (5.6) helps overcome computational challenges. While it is possible that calibration of the approximation using a more general form of the quadratic approximation to the future costs could yield even better results, this approximation performs remarkably well. We thank Harry Markowitz for this insight.

[8] There are a variety of optimization algorithms to minimize this cost function. We use the fmincon function which is available in the optimization toolbox of MatLab.

[9] For example, finding the best coefficient d for a 100 asset case would take slightly more than 10 days without grid computing.

income, and emerging market equities. For these portfolios the expected portfolio return is

$$E_p = \sum_{i=1}^{n} X_i \mu_i = X\mu' \tag{5.8}$$

and the expected portfolio variance is

$$V_p = \sum_{i=1}^{n} \sum_{j=1}^{n} X_i X_j \sigma_{ij} = XCX' \tag{5.9}$$

where $X = [X_1, \ldots, X_n]$ is the set of asset weights, $\mu = [\mu_1, \ldots, \mu_n]$ is the set of expected returns on the n assets, σ_{ij} is the covariance between assets i and j, and C is the covariance matrix (σ_{ij}). We use monthly returns from October, 2001 through September, 2006 to measure standard deviations and correlations. Table 5.7 shows our standard deviations and transaction cost assumptions.

Table 5.8 shows our correlation assumptions.

To estimate expected returns we solve for the implied returns under the assumption that the allocations in Table 5.9 are optimal under mean-variance utility and a fully invested budget constraint:

$$\begin{aligned} E(U) &= X\mu' - \tfrac{\lambda}{2} XCX' \\ \text{s.t.} X1_n' &= 1. \end{aligned} \tag{5.10}$$

Table 5.7 Standard deviation and transaction cost assumptions.

Rebalancing asset class	Index	Standard deviation	Transaction cost
Domestic equities	S&P 500	12.74%	0.40%
Domestic fixed income	lehman US Agg	3.96%	0.45%
Foreign developed equity	MSCI EAFE + Canada	13.41%	0.50%
Foreign bonds	CGBI World ex U.S.	8.20%	0.75%
Foreign emerging equity	MSCI EM	18.51%	0.75%

Table 5.8 Correlations.

	Domestic equities	Domestic fixed income	Foreign dev. equities	Foreign fixed income
Domestic fixed income	-0.31			
Foreign developed equity	0.84	-0.19		
Foreign bonds	-0.14	0.53	0.16	
Foreign emerging equity	0.77	-0.17	0.83	−0.05

Table 5.9 Optimal portfolios.

	Two assets	Three assets	Four assets	Five assets
Domestic equities	60.00%	40.00%	40.00%	40.00%
Domestic fixed income	40.00%	40.00%	25.00%	25.00%
Foreign developed equity		20.00%	20.00%	15.00%
Foreign bonds			15.00%	15.00%
Foreign emerging equity				5.00%

Here λ is the risk aversion parameter, which here has been set to 7.5, and 1_n is a vector of ones.[10] We thus calculate the implied returns as follows (see Sharpe, 1974):

$$\mu_{impl} = \lambda CX' + \frac{-\lambda + 1_n C^{-1} \mu'}{1_n C^{-1} 1_n{}'} 1_n'. \tag{5.11}$$

We use domestic stocks and domestic fixed income for the two-asset case. We add non-U.S. equities for the three-asset case, non-U.S. fixed income for the four-asset case, and emerging market equities for the five-asset case. Table 5.9 shows the assumed optimal portfolio weights, which as stated before are optimal under the standard mean-variance utility function. The choice of the initial portfolio weights is arbitrary. In our example, we use optimal portfolios based on a set of reasonable expectations and a mean-variance utility function.[11] We could just as well substitute optimal weights based on other descriptions of expected utility. Long-only investment managers, for example, would rely on a mean-tracking error utility function, while behavioral investors might use an S-shaped value function. Investors mostly concerned with large losses would use a kinked utility function (see Cremers, Kritzman, and Page, 2005). Also, the assumption that returns are normally distributed is convenient but not necessary for optimal rebalancing – as long as the distributions can be generated via Monte Carlo simulations.

We assume that we have a two-year investment horizon over which we wish to minimize the aggregate total cost; that is, the cumulative sum of trading costs and sub-optimality costs. For the calendar heuristics, we fully rebalance the portfolio at pre-determined time intervals. For the tolerance band heuristics, we fully rebalance the portfolio when asset weights breach predetermined thresholds of 0.25, 0.5, 0.75, 1, 2, 3, 4, and 5%. Although we cannot extend the dynamic programming algorithm beyond five assets, we test the MvD heuristic and the other heuristics for portfolios of 10, 25, 50, and 100 assets using individual stocks, which are listed in the appendix.

[10] Although here the risk aversion was set to 7.5, our methodology works equally well for any other choice of risk aversion.

[11] Others have shown that results of comparisons between optimal rebalancing and industry heuristics are not sensitive to changes in utility function or changes in risk and return assumptions (see Sun *et al.* 2006).

Table 5.10 Performance comparison – Total costs (bps).

Rebalancing strategy	Two assets	Three assets	Four assets	Five assets	Ten assets	Twenty Five assets	Fifty assets	Hundred assets
Dynamic Programming	6.31	6.66	7.33	8.76	NA	NA	NA	NA
MvD Heuristic	6.90	7.03	7.58	8.61	25.57	20.38	17.92	12.46
0.25% bands	15.19	17.01	19.81	21.37	41.93	42.96	41.53	26.88
0.50% bands	14.11	15.75	17.81	18.92	41.73	38.42	31.15	21.82
0.75% bands	12.80	14.09	15.32	16.27	40.05	32.95	31.46	25.02
1% bands	11.54	12.52	13.15	14.13	37.71	31.95	36.74	29.47
2% bands	8.73	9.20	9.79	10.73	41.94	48.59	66.96	39.33
3% bands	8.51	8.66	10.14	11.43	61.29	73.78	89.03	41.54
4% bands	9.46	9.52	12.08	13.78	88.49	93.23	98.55	41.96
5% bands	11.20	11.21	14.80	16.77	120.19	106.38	102.38	42.03
Monthly	15.65	17.25	20.07	21.85	41.92	42.92	43.34	39.75
Quarterly	11.05	11.86	13.51	14.76	45.17	34.32	33.12	26.54
Semi-annually	11.13	11.53	12.67	13.95	69.97	40.75	37.33	24.41

As indicated in Section 5.3, for each portfolio we sample several hundred values for d until we find the d which yields the lowest average figure of merit (AFOM),[12] which we define as the average total cost over the 200 Monte Carlo runs:

$$AFOM = \frac{1}{200} \sum_{i=1}^{200} \sum_{p=1}^{24} CEC_{i,p}^{MV} + TC_{i,p} \tag{5.12}$$

where $CEC_{i,p}^{MV}$ is the certainty equivalent cost for the ith portfolio path in the pth period under mean-variance utility and $TC_{i,p}$ are the transaction costs (5.3) for the ith portfolio path in the pth period.

Table 5.10 summarizes the results. It shows that the MvD heuristic performs quite well compared to the dynamic programming solution for the two-asset case and substantially better than other heuristics.[13] As we increase the number of assets we find that the advantage of dynamic programming over the MvD heuristic shrinks and is reversed at five assets. We are not able to apply dynamic programming beyond five assets, but we are able to extend the MvD heuristic up to 100 assets. We find that the MvD heuristic reduces total costs relative to all of the other heuristics by substantial amounts. In the

[12] The term "figure of merit" is from in Markowitz and van Dijk (2003).

[13] Some investors might use more sophisticated heuristics. For example they might use different bands for each asset, or rebalance partially, for example to the edge of the band, rather than back to the optimal weights. Our approach will be useful to these investors, as it will help them optimize these decision rules.

Table 5.11 Dynamic programming discretization scheme.

Number of assets	Number of discreetization points	Number of portfolios
2	5,000	5,001
3	60	3,323
4	14	2,174
5	7	1,508

appendix we present a more detailed cost analysis that partitions costs into trading and sub-optimality components.

Although the performance of the MvD heuristic improves relative to the dynamic programming solution as more assets are added, this improvement reflects a growing reliance on approximation for the dynamic programming approach. For the two-asset case the dynamic programming solution searches within an interval of ±5% around the optimal portfolio, and divides this range into 5,000 units. For greater than two assets, the search is confined to ±3% around the optimal portfolio, and this space is divided into increasingly coarser units, as shown in Table 5.11.

We have no way of knowing how well the MvD heuristic would track the ideal but unobtainable dynamic programming solution, but we are encouraged that its advantage over the next best heuristic increases as we add more assets. Moreover, we would not know *ex ante* which heuristic is the next best; hence a fairer assessment of the relative efficacy of the MvD heuristic might be to compare it to the average result of the other heuristics.

5.7 Conclusion

Portfolio allocations drift from their optimal weights as prices shift. Most investors employ naïve heuristics to rebalance their portfolios. We describe how dynamic programming can be used to identify an optimal rebalancing schedule, which significantly reduces rebalancing and sub-optimality costs compared to naïve heuristics.

Unfortunately the curse of dimensionality prevents us from applying dynamic programming to more than a few assets. As an alternative we examine the efficacy of a more sophisticated heuristic called the MvD heuristic, which scales up to several hundred assets. Our tests show that the MvD heuristic performs almost as well as dynamic programming for up to four assets and better than dynamic programming for five assets. In theory, of course, dynamic programming always yields the best result, but we cannot observe these results beyond a few assets. Therefore, we have no way of determining how the MvD heuristic would compare to the unobservable "correct" dynamic programming solution. To the extent of our knowledge, however, the MvD heuristic is the best alternative by far for rebalancing portfolios with more than just a few assets.

The scalability of the MvD heuristic opens the door to several new applications of portfolio rebalancing. Passive managers could use the MvD heuristic to optimize the tradeoff between tracking error and transaction costs. Quantitative asset managers could use it to minimize alpha decay between rebalancing dates.

Asset owners in particular could benefit from the MvD heuristic, as they are continually confronted with asset mix rebalancing decisions. Moreover, asset owners could customize the optimal rebalancing process to existing tolerance bands, tracking error targets, cash inflows, and benefit payments.

APPENDIX

Table 5.A.1 shows the securities used to create the stock portfolios for the 10, 25, 50, and 100 asset cases.

For example, the first 10 securities in column 1 constitute the 10-asset portfolio, and the securities in the first column constitute the 25-asset portfolio.

We determine the risks and correlations of the securities in Table 5.A.1 based on daily historical returns from January 2005 through January 2006 and estimate the expected returns as the implied returns under the assumption that the equally weighted portfolio is optimal under mean-variance optimization.

Table 5.A.2–5.A.9 show the trading cost and sub-optimality cost components for the various rebalancing algorithms.

Table 5.A.1 Securities used for stock portfolios.

MICROSOFT	SLM	SIGMA ALDRICH	MORGAN STANLEY
IBM	GOLDEN WEST FINANCIAL	GENERAL DYNAMICS	GOLDMAN SACHS
CISCO SYSTEMS	PFIZER	DANAHER	FANNIE MAE
DELL	JOHNSON & JOHNSON	CENDANT	US BANCORP
ORACLE	AMGEN	GENERAL ELECTRIC	WASHINGTON MUTUAL
EBAY	UNITEDHEALTH GROUP	UNITED TECHNOLOGIES	PRUDENTIAL FINL.
YAHOO	MEDTRONIC	BOEING	LEHMAN BROTHERS
FIRST DATA	ELI LILLY	3M	METLIFE
ADOBE SYSTEMS	WYETH	TYCO INTL.	ALLSTATE
HOME DEPOT	CARDINAL HEALTH	UNITED PARCEL SER.	SAINT PAUL TRAVELERS
LOWE'S COMPANIES	GILEAD SCIENCES	CATERPILLAR	SUNTRUST BANKS
TARGET	SCHERING-PLOUGH	HONEYWELL INTERNATIONAL	BANK OF NEW YORK
STARBUCKS	GUIDANT	EMERSON ELECTRIC	FRANK.RES.
BEST BUY	CAREMARK RX	LOCKHEED MARTIN	HARTFORD FINANCIAL SERVICES
SEARS HOLDINGS	STRYKER	FEDEX	INTEL
NIKE	VALERO ENERGY	BURLINGTON NORTHERN SANTA FE CORPORATION	HEWLETT-PACKARD
AMAZON.COM	BURLINGTON RES	ILLINOIS TOOL WORKS	QUALCOMM
KOHLS	DEVON ENERGY	UNION PACIFIC	APPLE COMPUTERS
CLEAR CHANNEL COMMUNICATIONS	ANADARKO PETROLEUM	CITIGROUP	MOTOROLA
OMNICOM GROUP	PROCTER & GAMBLE	BANK OF AMERICA	TEXAS INSTRUMENTS
HARLEY-DAVIDSON	WAL MART STORES	AMERICAN INTERNATIONAL GROUP	CORNING
YUM! BRANDS	PEPSICO	JP MORGAN CHASE & COMPANY	EMC
AMERICAN EXPRESS	WALGREEN	WELLS FARGO & COMPANY	APPLIED MATERIALS
FREDDIE MAC	ANHEUSER-BUSCH	WACHOVIA	AUTOMATIC DATA PROCESSING
CAPITAL ONE FINANCIAL	ECOLAB	MERRILL LYNCH & COMPANY	ADVANCED MICRO DEVICES

Table 5.A.2 Performance comparison – Two assets (5,000 Monte Carlo simulations).

	Costs (bps)		
Rebalancing strategy	Trading	Sub-optimality	Total
Dynamic Programming	4.87	1.44	6.31
MvD heuristic	4.86	2.04	6.90
0.25% bands	15.18	0.01	15.19
0.50% bands	14.06	0.05	14.11
0.75% bands	12.63	0.17	12.80
1% bands	11.19	0.34	11.54
2% bands	7.18	1.55	8.73
3% bands	5.17	3.34	8.51
4% bands	3.88	5.58	9.46
5% bands	3.00	8.20	11.20
Monthly	15.65	0.00	15.65
Quarterly	9.31	1.74	11.05
Semi-annually	6.70	4.43	11.13

Table 5.A.3 Performance comparison – Three assets (5,000 Monte Carlo simulations).

	Costs (bps)		
Rebalancing strategy	Trading	Sub-optimality	Total
Dynamic programming	4.68	1.98	6.66
MvD heuristic	4.73	2.30	7.03
0.25% bands	17.00	0.00	17.01
0.50% bands	15.71	0.04	15.75
0.75% bands	13.94	0.15	14.09
1% bands	12.20	0.32	12.52
2% bands	7.69	1.50	9.20
3% bands	5.40	3.26	8.66
4% bands	4.03	5.49	9.52
5% bands	3.16	8.05	11.21
Monthly	17.25	0.00	17.25
Quarterly	10.24	1.61	11.86
Semi-annually	7.38	4.15	11.53

Table 5.A.4 Performance comparison – Four assets (5,000 Monte Carlo simulations).

	Costs (bps)		
Rebalancing strategy	Trading	Sub-optimality	Total
Dynamic programming	5.10	2.23	7.33
MvD heuristic	4.94	2.64	7.58
0.25% bands	19.80	0.00	19.81
0.50% bands	17.73	0.08	17.81
0.75% bands	15.05	0.27	15.32
1% bands	12.57	0.58	13.15
2% bands	7.29	2.50	9.79
3% bands	4.82	5.32	10.14
4% bands	3.33	8.75	12.08
5% bands	2.29	12.51	14.80
Monthly	20.07	0.00	20.07
Quarterly	11.87	1.64	13.51
Semi-annually	8.50	4.17	12.67

Table 5.A.5 Performance comparison – Five assets (5,000 Monte Carlo simulations).

	Costs (bps)		
Rebalancing strategy	Trading	Sub-optimality	Total
Dynamic programming	6.21	2.55	8.76
MvD heuristic	5.30	3.31	8.61
0.25% bands	21.36	0.01	21.37
0.50% bands	18.81	0.11	18.92
0.75% bands	15.92	0.35	16.27
1% bands	13.41	0.72	14.13
2% bands	7.70	3.02	10.73
3% bands	5.09	6.33	11.43
4% bands	3.55	10.23	13.78
5% bands	2.46	14.31	16.77
Monthly	21.85	0.00	21.85
Quarterly	12.95	1.82	14.76
Semi-annually	9.29	4.66	13.95

Table 5.A.6 Performance comparison – Ten assets (5,000 Monte Carlo simulations).

	Costs (bps)		
Rebalancing strategy	Trading	Sub-optimality	Total
MvD heuristic	19.59	5.98	25.57
0.25% bands	41.93	0.00	41.93
0.50% bands	41.68	0.05	41.73
0.75% bands	39.21	0.83	40.05
1% bands	34.47	3.24	37.71
2% bands	20.76	21.18	41.94
3% bands	14.11	47.19	61.29
4% bands	10.14	78.35	88.49
5% bands	7.42	112.76	120.19
Monthly	41.92	0.00	41.92
Quarterly	24.83	20.34	45.17
Semi-annually	17.69	52.28	69.97

Table 5.A.7 Performance comparison – Twenty-five assets (5,000 Monte Carlo simulations).

	Costs (bps)		
Rebalancing strategy	Trading	Sub-optimality	Total
MvD heuristic	14.16	6.22	20.38
0.25% bands	42.96	0.00	42.96
0.50% bands	37.07	1.34	38.42
0.75% bands	27.60	5.35	32.95
1% bands	21.63	10.32	31.95
2% bands	10.56	38.02	48.59
3% bands	5.91	67.87	73.78
4% bands	3.35	89.88	93.23
5% bands	1.78	104.59	106.38
Monthly	42.92	0.00	42.92
Quarterly	25.32	9.01	34.32
Semi-annually	17.97	22.78	40.75

Table 5.A.8 Performance comparison – Fifty assets (5,000 Monte Carlo simulations).

	Costs (bps)		
Rebalancing strategy	Trading	Sub-optimality	Total
MvD heuristic	12.05	5.86	17.91
0.25% bands	41.22	0.31	41.53
0.50% bands	25.23	5.92	31.15
0.75% bands	17.46	14.00	31.46
1% bands	12.93	23.73	36.66
2% bands	5.15	61.82	66.96
3% bands	1.80	87.23	89.03
4% bands	0.59	97.95	98.55
5% bands	0.23	102.16	102.38
Monthly	43.34	0.00	43.34
Quarterly	25.57	7.55	33.12
Semi-annually	18.14	19.19	37.33

Table 5.A.9 Performance comparison – Hundred assets (5,000 Monte Carlo simulations).

	Costs (bps)		
Rebalancing strategy	Trading	Sub-optimality	Total
MvD heuristic	7.55	4.91	12.46
0.25% bands	24.75	2.13	26.88
0.50% bands	12.95	8.88	21.82
0.75% bands	8.13	16.89	25.02
1% bands	5.39	24.08	29.47
2% bands	0.71	38.61	39.33
3% bands	0.10	41.44	41.54
4% bands	0.02	41.94	41.96
5% bands	0.01	42.02	42.03
Monthly	39.75	0.00	39.75
Quarterly	23.46	3.08	26.54
Semi-annually	16.63	7.78	24.41

References

Bellman, R. E. (1952). On the theory of dynamic programming. *Proceedings of the National Academy of Sciences*, **38**, 716–719.

Cremers, J.-H., Kritzman, M. and Page, S. (2003). Portfolio formation with higher moments and plausible utility. *Revere Street Working Paper Series. Financial Economics* 272–12 (2003).

Cremers, J.-H., Kritzman, M. and Page, S. (2005). Optimal hedge fund allocations. *Journal of Portfolio Management*, **31**, 70–81.

Kroll, Y., Levy, H. and Markowitz, H. M. (1984). Mean variance versus direct utility maximization. *Journal of Finance*, **39** 47–61.

Kritzman, M., Myrgren, S., and Page, S. (2007). Portfolio rebalancing: A test of the Markowitz-Van Dijk Heuristic. MIT Sloan Research Paper No. 4641–07.

Kritzman, M., Myrgren, S., and Page, S. (2009). Optimal rebalancing: A scalable solution. *Journal of Investment Management*, 7, 9–19.

Levy, H. and Markowitz, H. M. (1979). Approximating expected utility by a function of mean and variance. *American Economic Review*, **69**, 308–317.

Markowitz, H. M. (1952). Portfolio selection. *Journal of Finance*, **7**, 77–91.

Markowitz, H. M. and van Dijk, E. L. (2003). Single-period mean–variance analysis in a changing world (corrected). *Financial Analysts Journal*, **59**, 30–44.

Sharpe, W. F. (1974). Imputing expected returns from portfolio composition. *Journal of Financial and Quantitative Analysis*, **9**, 463–472.

Smith, D. K. (1997). Dynamic programming: an introduction. PASS Maths, http://plus.maths.org/issue3/dynamic/.

Sun, W., Fan, A. Chen, L. W. Schouwenaars, T. and Albota, M. (2006). Optimal rebalancing for institutional portfolios. *Journal of Portfolio Management*, Winter, 33–43.

CHAPTER 6

BAYESIAN METHODS IN INVESTING

COLM O'CINNEIDE

6.1 Introduction

This chapter is in part an overview and in part a tutorial on the Bayesian approach to investment decisions, emphasizing its foundations, its most practical uses, and the computational techniques that are essential to its effective implementation. A disciplined investment process requires that all decision be well founded, and this necessitates a rigorous methodology. The Bayesian approach is founded on utility theory and the concept of subjective probability. The likelihood principle provides further justification. These three ideas form a solid basis for adopting the Bayesian paradigm. The popularity of Bayesian methods owes as much to computational tools as it does to conceptual elegance, and the Markov Chain Monte Carlo framework for Bayesian computations is another cornerstone of the approach. In broad outline, this chapter explains the basics of the Bayesian approach, reviews its foundations, presents the Markov Chain Monte Carlo method, and then presents some examples. The first example deals with techniques for dealing with the mundane messy data challenges that Wall Street quantitative analysts face daily. The second is a regime-shifting analysis of U.S. equity markets, illustrating the subtlety in modeling that the Bayesian approach makes possible.

Here is a brief overview of the approach. The starting point is a statistical model relating observed data and future outcomes to unknown parameters. Next, the investor expresses her views about the parameters in the form of a prior distribution describing how likely she considers various possible parameter values to be. Once the prior distribution is specified, the next step is to take account of the information contained in the observed data, leading to what is called the posterior distribution. Bayes' theorem is used here, and this gives the approach its name. The posterior distribution combines the information content of the data with that of the prior distribution. The penultimate step is to identify the distribution of future outcomes that are relevant to investment performance. This distribution is called the predictive distribution. Finally, the portfolio that maximizes the investor's expected utility with respect to the predictive distribution is identified. This completes a brief description of the Bayesian approach to investment decisions. Section 6.2 provides more details. This approach was articulated in the finance literature in the 1950s by Markowitz (see Chapter 12 of Markowitz 1991). Since that time it has become broadly accepted by academics. It has also been used fairly widely by practitioners, in asset allocation and manager selection decisions, and in alpha strategies.

The Bayesian approach appeals to the large cohort of scientifically trained analysts who have entered the financial-services industry over the past 25 years. This appeal is tempered by the fact that, while good investment decisions often depend on rigorous mathematical modeling, they cannot be made solely on the basis of mathematical models. Emanuel Derman's lament that "Trained economists have never seen a really first-class model..." (Derman 2004: 266) is emblematic of the mixing of the scientific and financial cultures. The limits of analysis as applied to financial markets has been a theme of many authors. George Soros's (1988) concept of reflexivity, the feedback loop between market prices and market participants, is an expression of the inscrutability of markets. Paul Krugman (1997) bluntly conveyed his skepticism about market rationality with the lines: "I like the theory of efficient markets as much as anyone. I don't begrudge Robert Merton and Myron Scholes the Nobel Prize..." The message of all this is that to participate in financial markets is to face ambiguity, or Knightian uncertainty, rather than measurable odds. To use Bayesian methods effectively in investing, the limits of mathematical modeling must be borne in mind.

Despite the shortcomings of science-as-applied-to-markets, there is a vast amount of data of relevance to investment decisions, and decision-makers are charged with making best use of it. A coherent methodology is needed, and the Bayesian approach provides one. The Bayesian approach also provides a convenient framework for incorporating subjective information and views into an investment decision, through the prior distribution. Another powerful reason to adopt a Bayesian approach is the undeniable presence of parameter uncertainty. In an investment decision based on a quantitative analysis, we make the leap of faith that our summaries of past experience are relevant to the future. But we know that the summaries are at best approximations, subject to randomness and error that manifests as a component of investment risk known as estimation risk. Decisions that ignore estimation risk are clearly flawed, and any analysis that simply substitutes parameter estimates for true parameter values is subject to this flaw.

This chapter is organized as follows. Section 6.2 sets out the Bayesian approach to investment decisions and explains the main concepts. Section 6.3 focuses on estimation risk and presents a basic example. Sections 6.4 and 6.5 concern the foundations of the approach, namely, utility theory, subjective probability, and the likelihood principle. Sections 6.6 and 6.7 present the Markov Chain Monte Carlo methodology and illustrate it with simple but important examples showing how to handle common data challenges that plague Wall Street analysts, such as combining quarterly data with monthly. Section 6.8 presents a regime-shifting model. This section is more demanding mathematically than the others. Section 6.9 contains some concluding notes. The appendix presents the standard Bayesian analysis for the multivariate normal statistical model.

6.2 The Bayesian Approach to Investment Decisions

The Bayesian approach to investment decisions begins with a statistical model that relates historical data, such as past returns, to important parameters, such as expected future returns. We denote our historical data by x. We view this as an observation of a random variable X. We use θ to represent the unknown parameters of our model. We do not distinguish notationally between the unknown θ and one of its possible values. X and θ may be quite complex in structure. The statistical model of X is presented in the form of a probability density function[1] $f(x;\theta)$. The archetypal example, however imperfect, is the multivariate normal model of returns X, independent over time, in which case the parameter $\theta = (\mu, \Sigma)$ is comprised of the mean vector and covariance matrix. The parameter θ is of interest because it is assumed to have a bearing on the future, although we have yet to specify that relationship. Before we do so, we describe how we analyze the data x to extract information about θ.

The Bayesian paradigm requires us to specify a prior distribution $\pi(\theta)$ expressing how likely we believe each possible value of θ to be, before we have looked at the data x. This is sometimes challenging, as for example when x includes the history of the U.S. stock market index, a history that is ingrained in our psyches due to its relationship with economic and financial outcomes. Another challenge is to identify a prior distribution that reflects a lack of information about θ – that is, a noninformative prior. Identifying a satisfactory prior distribution requires some effort but the benefits are significant because once it is specified we can identify the joint distribution of X and θ as

$$\pi(\theta)f(x;\theta) \tag{6.1}$$

and, more importantly, the conditional distribution of θ given the observed history $X = x$ as

$$f(\theta|x) = \frac{\pi(\theta)f(x;\theta)}{\int \pi(\theta)f(x;\theta)d\theta}. \tag{6.2}$$

(Here and throughout, all integrals are over the full range of the variable being integrated on.) This is called the posterior distribution of θ and it contains all the information we have about θ, combining the information content of the prior distribution $\pi(\theta)$ with that of the data x. The posterior distribution is effectively a revision of

[1] Here and throughout, the mathematics is kept as simple and informal as possible, and we refrain from commenting on assumptions and generalizations.

the prior distribution in light of what we learn about θ from the data x. This calculation is where Bayes' theorem is used – in fact the formula (6.2) is a version of Bayes' theorem. Bayes' theorem is a simple relationship between the probability of an event A conditional on another event B and the probability of B conditional on A. It states that $P(A|B) = P(B|A)P(A)/P(B)$, and this follows directly from the definition $P(A|B) \equiv P(A \cap B)/P(B)$ of conditional probability ($\equiv$ means "equals by definition"). Analogously, (6.2) above shows us how to move from the distribution of X conditional on θ to the distribution of θ conditional on X.

The posterior distribution encapsulates the information content of both the data and the prior and is often the central focus of a Bayesian statistical analysis. However, for investment decisions we must assess what this information about the unknown parameters means for the future, and this leads us to the predictive distribution (6.3) below. Y will represent future returns or any other future outcomes relevant to our decision-making. The model $f(x;\theta)$ of X must be extended to a model $f(x,y;\theta)$ of (X,Y). Then the joint distribution of X, Y and θ is

$$\pi(\theta)f(x,y;\theta)$$

and the conditional distribution of Y given $X = x$ is

$$f(y|x) = \frac{\displaystyle\int \pi(\theta)f(x,y;\theta)d\theta}{\displaystyle\iint \pi(\theta)f(x,y;\theta)d\theta\, dy} = \int f(y|x,\theta)f(\theta|x)d\theta. \tag{6.3}$$

This is what is called the predictive distribution of Y, and, parallel to the posterior distribution, it is all the investor needs to know about the future in order to make a decision. The second expression also shows explicitly how estimation risk is taken into account. Rather than computing some estimate $\hat{\theta}$ of θ and taking $f(y|x,\hat{\theta})$ as the distribution of future outcomes Y on the basis of which to select a portfolio, Equation (6.3) shows how the various possible values of θ, weighted by their probabilities $f(\theta|x)$ under the posterior distribution, contribute to forming our beliefs about future outcomes Y.

Now we introduce the investor's utility $U(Y,w)$, a function of future outcomes Y and her portfolio w. In our examples this will be a function of her return over her investment horizon, but it is not necessary to specialize to that case at this point. Her goal is to choose w to maximize expected utility, making use of all available information. Her investment decision comes down to choosing the portfolio weights w that maximize

$$\mathbb{E}\Big(U(Y,w) \,\Big|\, X = x\Big) = \int U(y,w)f(y|x)dy. \tag{6.4}$$

This is her expected utility under the predictive distribution.

To summarize, the Bayesian approach requires the following ingredients: a prior distribution $\pi(\theta)$ containing any *a priori* information; a model $f(x,y;\theta)$ relating θ to observed data x and future outcomes y; and finally a utility function U describing the investor's preferences. The analysis consists of identifying the predictive distribution

$f(y|x)$ of Y, and then choosing the portfolio that maximizes the expected utility with respect to that distribution. The predictive distribution contains all information about the future that is of interest to the investor, combining the information content of the prior distribution with that of the historical data x.

6.3 Estimation Risk

Estimation risk is a term meaning the investment risk associated with not knowing the true values of parameters and is a focus of a Bayesian investment analysis. Perhaps Klein and Bawa (1976) were the first authors to address estimation risk systematically in the context of investments. Barberis (2000) lists many subsequent studies. The concept of estimation risk can be given a precise meaning based on Equation (6.3) if we take variance as the definition of risk. Let W denote any random quantity defined in terms of our model for X, Y, and θ. We write $\mathbb{E}_x$ and Var_x for expected values and variances conditional on the observed data $X = x$. Then the predictive variance of W may be decomposed as

$$\mathrm{Var}_x(W) = \mathrm{Var}_x(\mathbb{E}_x(W|\theta)) + \mathbb{E}_x(\mathrm{Var}_x(W|\theta)). \tag{6.5}$$

This formula is a generalization of the standard one-way analysis of variance in statistics. What is of interest here is that the first term on the right arises from the randomness of θ and so may be attributed to estimation risk. The second term is an average of the variances of W evaluated as if θ were known, and this we view as the risk arising from the statistical model itself.

Here is a standard example of a Bayesian analysis of an investment decision, presented with a focus on the role of estimation risk. Suppose that annual excess returns on the equity market are normally distributed with unknown mean θ, which is the equity risk premium, and known volatility σ_0. Suppose also that our prior beliefs about θ are described by a normal distribution with mean m and standard deviation s. Taking as our data the past T years of equity returns $x = (x_1, x_2, \ldots, x_T)$, the joint probability density function of θ and x is identified through Equation (6.1) as

$$\varphi(\theta; m, s^2) \prod_{t=1}^{T} \varphi\left(x_t; \theta, \sigma_0^2\right) = \frac{1}{(2\pi)^{(T+1)/2} s \sigma_0^T} \exp\left(-\frac{1}{2}\left\{\frac{(\theta - m)^2}{s^2} + \sum_{t=1}^{T} \frac{(x_t - \theta)^2}{\sigma_0^2}\right\}\right),$$

where $\varphi(x; \mu, \sigma^2) \equiv \left(1/\sqrt{2\pi}\sigma\right) \exp\{-(x - \mu)^2/2\sigma^2\}$ is the normal probability density function. After some reorganization of terms to express the exponent as a quadratic in θ in a standard form, we find using (6.2) that the posterior distribution of θ is again normal, with mean and variance given by

$$\tilde{m} = \frac{\dfrac{m}{s^2} + \dfrac{T\bar{x}}{\sigma_0^2}}{\dfrac{1}{s^2} + \dfrac{T}{\sigma_0^2}} \quad \text{and} \quad \tilde{s}^2 = \left(\frac{1}{s^2} + \frac{T}{\sigma_0^2}\right)^{-1}. \tag{6.6}$$

(Here and below, we use a tilde to indicate a parameter of the posterior distribution.) This means that the posterior mean $\tilde{m}$ of θ is a weighted average of the prior mean m and "sample mean" $\bar{x}$, with weights proportional to precisions (i.e., inverse variances) and the "sample size" T in a natural way. It also shows that the posterior variance $\tilde{s}^2$ of θ is smaller than either the prior variance s^2 or the variance of the sample mean σ_0^2/T, reflecting the combining of information from prior and data. As this historical window T increases to infinity, $\tilde{s}$ approaches zero and the posterior distribution becomes ever more concentrated around a single point, namely $\bar{x}$.

We denote by Y the future return over a horizon of H years, taking returns to be additive over time rather than multiplicative for simplicity. Conditional on θ, the distribution of Y is normal with mean $H\theta$ and variance $H\sigma_0^2$. Taking account of parameter uncertainty represented by the posterior distribution given in (6.6), the predictive distribution of Y has mean and variance given by

$$m_{\text{pred}} = H\tilde{m} \quad \text{and} \quad s_{\text{pred}}^2 = H^2\tilde{s}^2 + H\sigma_0^2. \tag{6.7}$$

The two terms in the formula for the predictive variance here correspond in turn to the two terms on the right side of Equation (6.5). The first term is the posterior variance of the H-period mean $H\theta$. The second is the variance of the H-period return conditional on θ. The presence of the factor H^2 in the first term highlights an important phenomenon: unlike equity risk, estimation risk does not diversify over time here. A low value of θ will affect equity returns negatively throughout the investment horizon H, just as a high value will affect returns positively throughout the horizon. In contrast, the "intrinsic" component of the predictive variance, that is, the component that remains when all parameters are known (namely $H\sigma_0^2$) grows only linearly because returns are independent over time conditional on θ.

The case of a noninformative prior, in which we have no opinion about θ prior to looking at the data, may be analyzed by letting the prior variance of θ, namely s^2, tend to infinity. The limiting results are simple and intuitive. The posterior mean and variance of θ become $\tilde{m} = \bar{x}$ and $\tilde{s} = \sigma_0^2/T$, which are simply the "classical" sample mean and its variance. The predictive mean and variance of Y are

$$m_{\text{pred}} = H\bar{x} \quad \text{and} \quad s_{\text{pred}}^2 = H^2\frac{\sigma_0^2}{T} + H\sigma_0^2 = \left(\frac{H}{T} + 1\right)H\sigma_0^2,$$

by (6.6) and (6.7). The predictive variance is the variance of the return over H periods conditional on θ, $H\sigma_0^2$, scaled up by the factor $H/T + 1$ to account for estimation risk; the larger the historical window T, the smaller the effect of estimation risk.

With Markowitz preferences and risk aversion λ, our optimal holdings of equity are given by

$$w = \frac{m_{\text{pred}}}{\lambda s^2_{\text{pred}}} = \frac{T}{T+H}\frac{\bar{x}}{\lambda s_0^2} = \frac{T}{T+H} w_0 \text{ where } w_0 \equiv \frac{\bar{x}}{\lambda s_0^2},$$

the balance of our wealth being invested in riskless bonds. At the second equality we have assumed the noninformative prior. The quantity w_0 is what we would hold in equities if we took θ to be known and equal to $\bar{x}$ – that is, if we ignored estimation risk. This is the naïve equity allocation. The factor $T/(T+H)$ is where the investment horizon H and the historical window T fight it out. If they are equal, then the estimation risk causes us to reduce our holdings of equity to exactly one half of the naïve weight. As the horizon increases, estimation risk dominates any possible benefit from the predictive expected return and the optimal equity holdings tend to zero.

Figures 6.1–6.3 present a simple example of a Bayesian analysis of equity excess returns based on a five-year window ($T = 5$) of historical annual returns and assuming normality. The sample mean excess return over the five years is taken to be $\bar{x} = 8\%$ and the annual volatility of returns σ_0 is taken to be known and equal to 15%. We consider two prior distributions, the first noninformative and the second optimistic with mean excess return $m = 10\%$ and "margin of error" $s = 3\%$ around this mean. Under the noninformative prior, the posterior and predictive means are again 8%, the same as the sample mean. The posterior standard deviation of the expected excess return is 6.71% and this estimation risk boosts the predictive volatility from 15% to 16.43%.

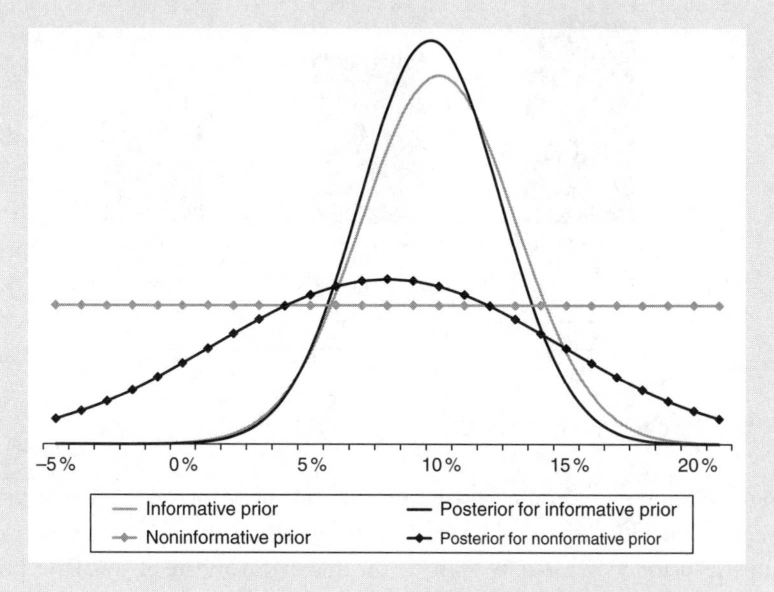

FIGURE 6.1 Prior distributions and posterior distributions.

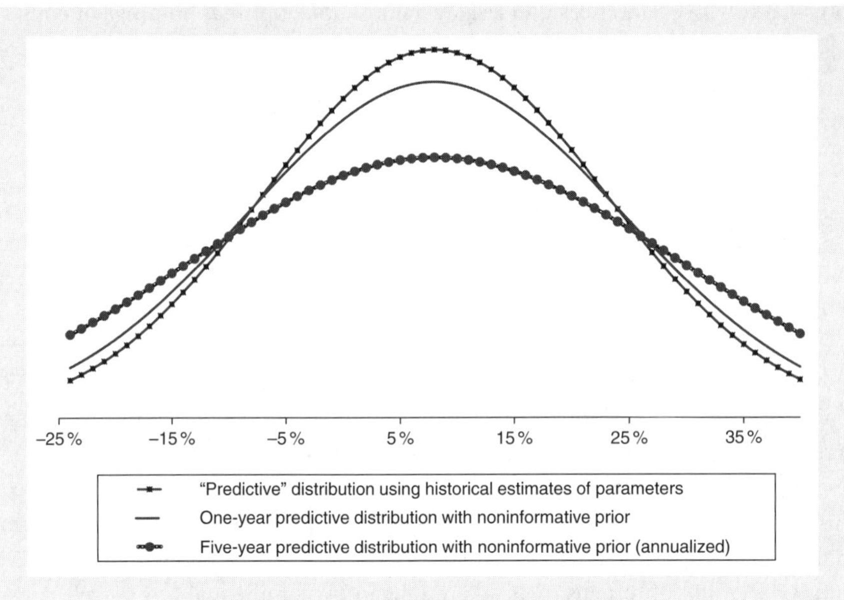

FIGURE 6.2 Predictive distributions in three scenarios.

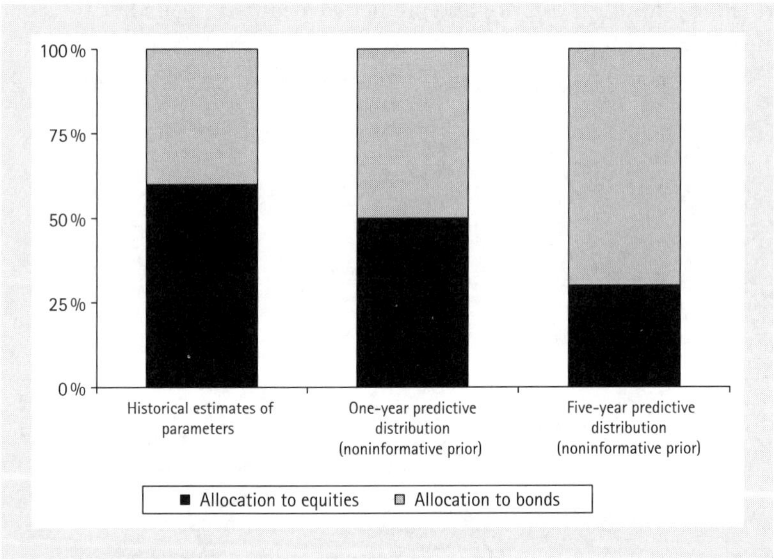

FIGURE 6.3 Allocation to equities and bonds in three scenarios.

The high conviction embodied in the informative prior overwhelms the historical data, as is evidenced by the fact that the posterior mean of 9.67% is much closer to the optimistic prior view of 10% than to the historical mean of 8%. The posterior standard deviation of the expected excess return is 2.74%, slightly smaller than the margin of error of 3% associated with the informative view and this small estimation risk results in a predictive volatility of 15.25%, only marginally higher than the 15% specified in the statistical model. The prior and posterior distributions are shown in Figure 6.1.

Turning now to portfolio choice, we first calibrate risk aversion so that the naïve allocation to equities is $w_0 = 60\%$, leaving 40% of wealth in riskless bonds. With this calibration, the optimal allocation to equities with a one-year horizon ($H = 1$) assuming the noninformaive prior – and taking estimation risk into account – is $w = 50\%$. If we increase the horizon to $H = 5$ years, the allocation to equities drops to $w = 30\%$, one-half of the naïve allocation. The predictive distributions on which these allocations are based are shown in Figure 6.2. The "annualized five-year predictive distribution" in this figure is the normal distribution such that the distribution of the sum of five years of independent returns with that distribution is the same as the five-year predictive distribution. See Figure 6.3 for the allocation to equities and bonds in the three scenarios discussed.

Barberis's (2000) study of estimation risk encompassed periodic rebalancing and predictability of returns. He identifies several phenomena that are not apparent in the simple example discussed here. He shows that predictability of the stock index based on dividend yield can lead to mean reversion that makes stocks more attractive to a buy-and-hold investor, but that estimation risk weakens this effect considerably. He also points out that an investor who rebalances periodically will learn about the parameters between rebalancings, and to hedge against bad news about future opportunities – such as arises from poor performance between rebalancings – she will tend to reduce her exposure to equities. Estimation risk also reduces the sensitivity of equity holdings to the initial level of the dividend yield. For more on the effects of estimation risk on investment decisions, see Xia (2001).

6.4 Foundations: Utility Theory and Subjective Probability

Utility theory and subjective probability are two of the central concepts in the Bayesian approach to investment decisions, and we present a brief review of these topics. A third key concept is the likelihood principle, and this will be discussed in the next section. The von Neumann–Morgenstern (1944) theory of utility centers on the discovery that, under reasonable consistency assumptions about preferences, agents always behave as if they have a utility function whose expectation they wish to maximize. This result gives the concept of utility a foundation that it lacked when it was first introduced in the eighteenth century.

To convey a sense of the von Neumann–Morgenstern ("VNM") theory, suppose an experimenter proposes various gambles to an agent who then reports her preferences among them. The gambles have three possible outcomes, x, y, and z, which correspond to rewards for the agent. The experimenter controls the probabilities $p = (p_x, p_y, p_z)$ of the outcomes and reveals them to the agent. For example, the experimenter may set $p = (1, 0, 0)$ to make outcome x a certainty. Suppose the agent prefers x to y and y to z. Then it would seem inconsistent if she were to prefer z to x, and this exemplifies the kind of consistency condition that von Neumann and Morgenstern took as axiomatic. Similarly, but more subtly, suppose she prefers $p = (.5, .5, 0)$ to $p = (1, 0, 0)$. That is to say, she prefers an equal chance of x and y to a guarantee of x. If so, there is an apparent inconsistency because if she prefers x to y, then surely she should prefer a guarantee of x to a gamble that sometimes produces the less favorable y instead. What von Neumann and Morgenstern proved was that if the agent's preferences do not exhibit inconsistencies such as these then there exists a function U such that her preferences may be completely summarized as a desire for the highest possible value of $U(x)p_x + U(y)p_y + U(z)p_z$ – that is, her decisions are identical to those of an agent whose goal is to maximize this expected utility. In other words, von Neumann and Morgenstern proved that consistent decision-making, as they defined it, could always be characterized as maximizing expected utility.

This surprisingly strong result has not led the world of finance and economics to reject all other models of decision-making. The Markowitz preferences, summarized as a desire for higher expected return and lower volatility, have proved useful due to their simplicity and mathematical tractability despite their being inconsistent with the VNM axioms – this inconsistency is due to the fact that variance is quadratic rather than linear as a function of the probabilities. Recursive utility functions, such as the Epstein–Zinn utility, also lie outside the scope of the VNM framework, but are useful in breaking the link between an agent's elasticity of intertemporal substitution and her risk aversion, a feature that is important in asset allocation (Campbell and Viceira 2002).

Cognizant of skepticism that preferences could be reduced to a numerical measure, von Neumann and Morgenstern (1944: 17) drew an analogy between their theory of utility and how the sensation of warmth became quantifiable in terms of the concepts of heat and temperature in physics:

> Even if utilities look very unnumerical today, the history of the experience in the theory of heat may repeat itself, and nobody can foretell with what ramifications and variations.

Modern fMRI technology is opening up the tantalizing possibility of measuring utility directly by observing blood flow in the brain. See Harbaugh *et al.* (2007) for an indication of the current state of this branch of neuroscience. In light of this, the above remark appears prophetic.

While von Neumann and Morgenstern's theory showed how consistent preferences imply utility-maximizing behavior, it took the probabilities as given. This left open the question of how agents arrive at the probabilities of various outcomes of interest, such as the chance that the stock market will rise. Leonard J. Savage (1962), building on the foundation laid by F.P. Ramsey and others, stepped into this breach with his theory of subjective probabilities. Savage proposed that agents are imbued with a subjective sense of the chances of various outcomes, such as whether the stock market will go up today, and that these subjective views may be elicited by offering gambles with payoffs based on the outcomes. If an agent expresses a willingness to pay 50 cents for a payoff of $1 if a coin toss results in heads, it is generally reasonable to conclude that she thinks there is at least a 50-50 chance of heads. Savage imposed consistency axioms on preferences that were sufficiently strong to allow him to deduce the existence not only of a utility function but also of probabilities, such that consistent behavior meant maximizing expected utility with respect to those probabilities. This extended VNM utility theory by providing a rationale for assigning probabilities to outcomes. The result was a model of behavior that was much in evidence in the theory of portfolio selection developed by Markowitz, who had studied under Savage at the University of Chicago.

In a recent interview, Markowitz (2004) described his view of the subjective probability framework thus:

> As of 1959 I was convinced that the proper way a rational decision-maker should act was to maximize expected utility using personal probabilities. In other words, I had been thoroughly brainwashed by Leonard J. Savage's Foundations of Statistics.

In the same interview, he went on to acknowledge that the intellectual edifice of utility maximization and subjective probability is imperfect. Its failings become apparent when we introduce ambiguity, or Knightian uncertainty. This form of uncertainty leads most people to make choices that are inconsistent with expected utility maximization no matter what probabilities are assigned. Consider the four games described in Table 6.1, all based on an experiment in which a ball is drawn at random from an urn containing 100 balls, 50 of which are either red or blue and 50 of which are either yellow or green. We have introduced Knightian uncertainty by making the number balls of each color unknown. With the information provided, there is little to choose between games A and B. Now games C and D differ from the first two only in providing a payoff of $1 rather than $0 if a green ball is drawn. Under Savage's axioms, this additional payoff should not tip the balance either way. However, most people prefer D to C because D now provides a true 50% chance at $1, whereas the odds of a win in game C are still ambiguous. The preference for D over C is called ambiguity aversion. This feature of human behavior

Table 6.1 The Ellsberg paradox.

	50 balls		50 balls	
	Red	Blue	Yellow	Green
Payoff of game A	0	1	0	0
Payoff of game B	0	0	1	0
Payoff of game C	0	1	0	1
Payoff of game D	0	0	1	1

in the presence of Knightian uncertainty is known as Ellsberg's[2] (1961) paradox, and is a feature that is inconsistent with Savage's axioms. See Machina (2009) for a recent discussion and pointers to the literature.

Just as the additional payoff for a green ball in game D resolves the ambiguity in game B, so also does moving down the efficient frontier towards cash or treasuries because Knightian uncertainty about the equity risk premium and the performance of speculative investments is removed. There are theories of decision-making that account for ambiguity aversion at the expense of sacrificing the simplicity of expected-utility maximization. See, for example Bassett (2004).

6.5 Foundations: The Likelihood Principle and Bayesian Statistical Analysis

The likelihood principle is a simple but radical idea in statistics, supported by a compelling argument and yet not widely accepted by statisticians. It is also the third foundation stone of the Bayesian approach to investments, along with utility theory and subjective probability. To explain this principle in proper context, a few words about statistical practice are in order.

Undergraduate statistics courses typically deal with the "frequentist" approach, centering on hypothesis testing and confidence intervals. This approach is based on statements about the frequency of certain events under hypothetical repetitions of an experiment. A 95% confidence interval for a parameter is an interval determined according to a procedure applied to the results of an experiment which ensures that, under independent repetitions of the experiment, the interval will contain the parameter with probability at least 95%, whatever the values of the unknown parameters may be. The phrase "whatever the values of the unknown parameters . . . " is the calling card of the frequentist approach. It means that the 95% confidence level is not just the probability that the interval contains the unknown parameter in repetitions of the experiment, but the minimum of such probabilitilities across all possible values of the unknown parameters. This defining requirement of any 95% confidence interval is so difficult to satisfy that no such interval exists for some common estimation problems. For example, there is no confidence interval for the difference in the means of two normal populations, based on independent random samples from each; the textbook method is valid only under the assumption that the population variances are equal. This gap in the frequentist toolkit is known as the Behrens–Fisher problem. Challenges such as this have led some statisticians to seek more flexible frameworks. The Bayesian approach has been a beneficiary of this trend.

[2] Daniel Ellsberg is perhaps best known for releasing the *Pentagon Papers* in 1971.

Statistics has many uses, ranging from analyzing the results of clinical trials, where objectivity is a primary concern, to investment decision-making, where the subjective views of an experienced market participant often play a key role. The Bayesian approach offers a framework for incorporating subjective information into decisions, and this is a pragmatic reason for investors to use that approach. The heart of the frequentist approach to statistics is that parameters are viewed as unknown constants – think of seventeenth century astronomers making observations of the positions of the fixed stars. In this approach, rather than the parameters being random, we are in a state of Knightian uncertainty with respect to them. However, an investor faces a gamble on the values of parameters such as the equity risk premium, and to characterize these as "fixed but unknown" does not bring her closer to a decision. Savage's theory of subjective probability, and indeed common sense, lead the investor to make decisions based on the probabilities she assigns to the various possible values of parameters.

Complementing these pragmatic reasons for taking a Bayesian rather than a frequentist approach, the likelihood principle offers a theoretical reason. The likelihood function associated with the data x is defined as

$$L(\theta; x) \equiv f(x; \theta). \tag{6.8}$$

This is simply the probability density function viewed as a function of θ for fixed x, rather than the other way around. The likelihood principle states that the information content of data depends only on the likelihood function. The three central facts about this principle are that (a) it is inconsistent with standard statistical procedures such as tests of hypotheses and confidence intervals, (b) it is consistent with the Bayesian approach, and (c) there are compelling reasons for believing that it is true. To explain (a), for example confidence intervals and tests of hypothesis are inconsistent with the likelihood principle simply because they are defined in terms of probabilities of various outcomes in hypothetical repetitions of the experiment, and not just in terms of the observed outcome. That (b) is true may be seen at once from the analysis of Section 6.2. The posterior and predictive distributions given in Equations (6.2) and (6.3) clearly depend only on the likelihood. See Berger and Wolpert (1988) for extensions to the case where unknown future outcomes Y are present. Indeed, the Bayesian approach provides a good answer to the question: If we accept the likelihood principle and agree that conclusions from experiments should only depend on the likelihood, how should we proceed to draw those conclusions?

Turning to (c) above, here is a brief exposition of the basis for the likelihood principle following a surprising paper by Allan Birnbaum (1962). The central theme of the argument is that "randomizations," such as tossing coins and rolling dice, whose outcomes have known probabilities not depending on the unknown parameters θ, have no bearing on the information content of data.

We will argue first that if two outcomes x_1 and x_2 of an experiment have the same likelihoods, so that $L(\theta, x_1) = L(\theta, x_2)$ for all θ, then they should always lead to the same conclusions about the unknown θ. This preliminary step is the "sufficiency principle." (It is enough to assume that the likelihoods are proportional, rather than strictly equal, but we assume equality in the interests of brevity.) Suppose that an assistant carries out the experiment and reports that either x_1 or x_2 has occurred but doesn't tell us which. Then because the likelihoods are the same for all θ, the probability that the outcome was actually x_1 rather than x_2 is simply 1/2 irrespective of θ. Since this probability doesn't depend on θ, knowing which of x_1 and x_2 was the true outcome is equivalent to observing a coin toss and so surely cannot be relevant to our conclusions about θ. This argument convinces many of the truth of the sufficiency principle, and there is broad agreement on it among statisticians.

The sufficiency principle says in essence that in a given experiment only the likelihood matters. The likelihood principle extends this idea across different experiments on the same unknown parameters θ. The justification due to Birnbaum (1962) is simple and ingenious, and hinges on combining two experiments into one with a coin toss. Suppose we can perform two experiments to study θ. This situation arises for example in deciding how to carry out a survey or in choosing an apparatus with which to make a measurement. Suppose that the likelihood function of the outcome x_1 of experiment 1 is equivalent (i.e., proportional) to that of the outcome x_2 of experiment 2. We create a compound experiment by first tossing a coin to choose one of the two experiments, and then carrying out the chosen experiment. Now x_1 and x_2, as two possible outcomes of the compound experiment, should lead to the same conclusions by the sufficiency principle. To deduce the likelihood principle we invoke the intuition that the initial coin toss should have no bearing on our conclusions. This is to say, the process of tossing the coin, choosing experiment 1, and then observing x_1 should produce the same information as doing experiment 1 directly and observing x_1, without ever considering experiment 2. Again, many people find this statement intuitive and natural. If we agree with this, then doing the first experiment and observing x_1 must produce exactly the same information as doing the second experiment and observing x_2. This establishes the likelihood principle.

In summary, there are convincing arguments to support the likelihood principle, and the likelihood principle in turn provides a compelling reason to adopt the Bayesian paradigm. The trinity of utility theory, subjective probability, and the likelihood principle gives the Bayesian approach a consistency that is not enjoyed by some other approaches. This consistency is key in investment management, where decisions are subject to careful scrutiny. Practitioners are familiar with the challenges of explaining quantitative investments, for example the common but puzzling phenomenon of a short position in an asset that has a high alpha or expected return. Often the explanation is that the risk benefit of the short position exceeds the return benefit of a long position. What the Bayesian approach assures us of is that there is a sound answer to any such conundrum, ultimately founded on the axioms of consistent preferences and beliefs, and the likelihood principle. Approaches that are not meticulously thought out from first principles can lead to situations in which a "short-high-alpha problem" exposes a flaw in the methodology rather than a subtle implication of it.

6.6 Markov Chain Monte Carlo and the Gibbs Sampler

The success of the Bayesian approach owes a great deal to computational feats made possible by Monte Carlo methods. Monte Carlo methods are random experiments run on a computer. The technique was first proposed in 1946 by Stanislaw Ulam, a mathematician working at the Los Alamos National Laboratories. According to an account by Roger Eckhardt (in Cooper 1989), he struck upon the idea as he was pondering the problem of estimating the probability of winning the solitaire game Canfield. He realized that the ENIAC, the first digital computer which had been unveiled just the year before, could be programmed to simulate a large number of Canfield games, allowing a good estimate of the probability to be made. He quickly saw more important applications, such as simulating neutron diffusion in a fission reaction. John von Neumann, on hearing Ulam's idea, initiated serious investigation of the method in a hand-written 1947 letter, reproduced in Cooper (1989), to Robert Richtmyer, the Theoretical Division Leader at Los Alamos National Laboratories, complete with an ENIAC program for implementing what he had in mind. The Monte Carlo method soon contributed to assessments of the feasibility of fusion bombs.

The simplest form of Monte Carlo involves independent repetitions of a computer experiment. Ulam's proposed Canfield experiments would have been of this type. The Markov Chain Monte Carlo (MCMC) method instead allows each experiment to depend on the outcome of the preceding one. In the early Los Alamos applications, the experiments represented stages in the progress of a fission reaction and each stage indeed depended on the preceding one. The benefit of relaxing the independence requirement is the ease with which we can devise easily-simulated Markov Chains with desired long-run behavior. We will take the Gibbs sampler (Geman and Geman 1984) as our central example of MCMC.

The key to the long-run behavior of a Markov Chain is that, quite generally, it is characterized by a unique stationary distribution. A stationary distribution is a distribution such that, if the initial state of the chain X_1 follows that distribution, then so will the next state X_2, and the next, and so forth. Moreover the long-run statistics of the states $X_1, X_2, X_3, \ldots$ typically also follow that distribution. This last statement means for example that the mean $\bar{X}_n$ of the first n of the X's converges to the expected value of the stationary distribution as $n \to \infty$, and the same applies to means of any function of the X's. Moreover, these long-run averages typically converge to expectations over the stationary distribution no matter how we initialize the Markov Chain.[3]

The Gibbs sampler will be our main example of the MCMC approach because it is especially suited to statistical applications. To illustrate Gibbs sampling, suppose we have a probability density function $f_{X,Y}(x, y)$ of two random variables X and Y, and

[3] We omit various qualifications and conditions here, as has been the style of this chapter. See Meyn and Tweedie (1993) for a thorough and general discussion.

we wish to simulate them. Suppose moreover that while we have no direct method for simulating (X, Y) jointly, it is easy to simulate X given $Y = y$ and to simulate Y given $X = x$. To the uninitiated, this may seem an unnatural requirement, but we will find no end of natural and important examples of such pairs (X, Y) in the next two sections. We define a Markov Chain as follows. Beginning by setting X_1 to an arbitrary value x_1, we choose Y_1 according to $f_{Y|X}(y_1|x_1)$, the conditional distribution of Y given $X = x_1$. Then we choose X_2 according to $f_{X|Y}(x_2|y_1)$, the conditional density of X given $Y = y_1$. These conditional probability density functions are defined by

$$f_{X|Y}(x|y) = \frac{f_{X,Y}(x,y)}{f_Y(y)} \text{ and } f_{Y|X}(y|x) = \frac{f_{X,Y}(x,y)}{f_X(x)} \tag{6.9}$$

where the denominators are the marginal distributions given by

$$f_X(x) = \int f_{X,Y}(x,y)dy \text{ and } f_Y(y) = \int f_{X,Y}(x,y)dx. \tag{6.10}$$

This proceeds, each time choosing the next X value according to the conditional distribution of X given the previous Y, and similarly choosing the next Y according to the conditional distribution of Y given the previous X. The Markov Chain here is not the sequence $X_1, Y_1, X_2, Y_2, \ldots$ but rather the sequence of pairs $(X_1, Y_1), (X_2, Y_2), \ldots$. This is a typical Gibbs sampler and what makes it interesting is that its long-run distribution is indeed the desired joint distribution $f_{X,Y}(x, y)$. The key to seeing why is to show that $f_{X,Y}(x, y)$ is a stationary distribution, and we prove this by evaluating the joint distribution of (X_2, Y_2) assuming that X_1 and Y_1 have been initialized according to $f_{X,Y}$, as follows:

$$\begin{aligned}
\iint f_{X_1,Y_1,X_2,Y_2}(x_1, y_1, x_2, y_2)dx_1dy_1 &= \iint f_{X,Y}(x_1, y_1)f_{X|Y}(x_2|y_1)f_{Y|X}(y_2|x_2)dx_1dy_1 \\
&= \int f_Y(y_1)f_{X|Y}(x_2|y_1)f_{Y|X}(y_2|x_2)dy_1 \\
&= \int f_{X,Y}(x_2, y_1)f_{Y|X}(y_2|x_2)dy_1 \\
&= f_X(x_2)f_{Y|X}(y_2|x_2) = f_{X,Y}(x_2, y_2).
\end{aligned}$$

(Justification: The first equality follows from the description of the steps of the chain and its initial distribution. The second integrates out over x_1 using (6.10). The third uses the definition (6.9) of the conditional probability density functions. The fourth integrates out over y_1 using (6.10) again. The fifth uses (6.9) again.) Having shown that $f_{X,Y}(x, y)$ is a stationary distribution, we conclude that the long-run statistics of the Markov Chain may be used to estimate expectations and probabilities associated with that joint distribution. This is how the Gibbs sampler works.

We illustrate the Gibbs sampler in the next section by applying it to some messy-data challenges that arise frequently in quantitative analysis for investments. Later we present a regime-shifting model, which demonstrates the flexibility of the Bayesian approach as well as the computational capabilities of the Gibbs sampler.

6.7 Handling Messy Data with the Gibbs Sampler

One of the most important applications of MCMC is in dealing with messy data, such as missing or incomplete observations. We begin with three common examples, encountered routinely in quantitative analysis. Then we present a magic bullet that resolves them all, and illustrate it in one particular case.

Example 1: Missing returns Computing means and covariance matrices for historical return data is a daily chore in quantitative analysis. In the ideal case, we have returns on all assets in every period in the historical window. However, sometimes the most recent returns are missing for some fund managers. This is common because the returns of different managers typically won't become available at the same time. The expedient of dropping the most recent periods for all the assets is one way to make the data more amenable to analysis, but this discards the freshest and most relevant data, and if markets have been especially turbulent we may be reluctant to do this. Another cause of missing return data is that we may have a longer history on some assets or managers than on others, because of different inception dates. Truncating the data to the shortest common history may mean discarding useful data. A typical example is an asset allocation study, in which long histories on stock and bond indices are combined with shorter histories on hedge funds, real estate, private equity, and infrastructure. Another example, perhaps the first to receive attention in the finance literature, is that of asset allocation to different emerging markets based on return histories with different start dates (Stambaugh 1997).

Example 2: Data with different frequencies Some data is easily available monthly, weekly, or daily – prices of liquid assets, for example. Other data, such as GDP estimates and returns on illiquid assets such as infrastructure and private equity, may be available only quarterly. Combining data with different frequencies leads to a problem of incomplete observations. Quarterly data may often be viewed as partially observed monthly data.

Example 3: Asynchronous data Markets around the world close at different times. At day's end in New York, the latest available Asian stock exchange prices are roughly 12 hours old. Correlations between daily returns of the TOPIX and the S&P 500 indices are anomalously small due to the asynchronicity of the closing times. The problem may be treated by postulating a world of 24-hour pricing that is only partially observed.

We denote the observed data by X_O and the unobserved data by Z so that $X = (X_O, Z)$ is the full data. In Example 1, Z represents the latest returns of managers who have not yet reported results. In Example 2, Z represents the GDP in the first two months of each quarter – GDP in the third month is then inferred from the quarterly number. In Example 3, Z represents the prices that would be observed on Asian markets if they were open at 4:00 pm New York time.

The Gibbs sampler provides a meta-algorithm for dealing with these situations and it works as follows. We propose a model $f(x|\theta)$ for the complete data $X = (X_O, Z)$ and a prior $\pi(\theta)$ on the parameter θ. We can set θ to some arbitrary value θ_1 initially, and then simulate the unobserved Z given x_O and θ_1. Call the resulting imputed data z_1. This step is typically easy because it is based on the full model distribution $f(x|\theta_1)$ which is often chosen with tractability in mind. Now we have complete data $x_1 = (x_O, z_1)$ and simulating a new parameter value θ_2 from the posterior distribution of θ given $X = x_1$ is a standard Bayesian analysis without missing data. We continue as in the previous section to produce $\theta_1, z_1, \theta_2, z_2, \theta_3, z_3$, and so forth. The distribution of the resulting θ_i's is the posterior distribution for the original missing data problem. The predictive distribution may be computed also by including relevant future outcomes Y as part of the unobserved Z. The power of this approach is that it allows us to take any Bayesian analysis for a complete-data problem and extend it to an incomplete-data problem. For a fuller discussion see Tanner (1998).

Let us illustrate this with an analysis of four investments, the Fama–French (1992) porfolios MKT, SMB, and HML, along with an international stock index labeled INTL. Returns on MKT, SMB, and HML are available from Kenneth French's website at (mba.tuck.dartmouth.edu/pages/faculty/ken.french). For INTL we used returns on the MSCI ex-U.S. index from the MSCI website (www.mscibarra.com). We base the analysis on monthly returns on the Fama–French portfolios, but quarterly returns on INTL. Note how cumbersome an *ad hoc* analysis of this data can be. The obvious approach is to reduce all data to quarterly, but this immediately reduces the information content of the data with respect to the Fama–French portfolios by a factor of three. To compute covariances for the Fama–French portfolios using monthly returns but to compute covariances with INTL using quarterly returns can lead to covariance matrix estimates that are not positive definite, which in turn can lead to negative variance estimates. The Gibbs sampler avoids all these problems and makes full use of the available data, exploiting monthly detail where possible and still producing positive definite covariance matrices. Here is one way to implement this analysis.

We adopt the standard model that returns are normal with parameter $\theta = (\mu, \Sigma)$. We choose the inverse Wishart distribution $\mathrm{IW}'(V, \nu)$ as our prior on the covariance matrix Σ (see the appendix for notation). Roughly speaking, this means that our prior information about Σ is equivalent to what we would learn if we took a sample of size ν from a normal population with mean 0 covariance Σ and found the sample covariance to be V. (The standard noninformative prior results if we take $\nu = 0$.) We choose the normal distribution with mean m and covariance matrix $\tau^{-1}\Sigma$ as the conditional prior distribution of μ given Σ. Again, this prior information is roughly equivalent to what we would learn by taking a sample of size τ from a normal population with parameter (μ, Σ) and observed only the mean of the sample. The full prior distribution so defined is called the inverse Wishart-Normal distribution and we denote it by $\text{IWN}'(V, \nu, m, \tau)$. (The prime in IWN′ indicates that this parametrization is slightly non-standard. See the appendix for an explanation.)

Suppose now that we observe all monthly returns over an interval of T time periods, and we write $\bar{x}$ and s^2 for the sample mean and sample covariance matrix (with divisor T), respectively. Then the posterior distribution is known explicitly. It is $\text{IWN}'(\tilde{V}, \nu + T, \tilde{m}, \tau + T)$ where

$$\tilde{m} = \frac{\tau m + T\bar{X}}{\tau + T} \quad \text{and} \quad \tilde{V} = \frac{\nu V + Ts^2 + \left(\frac{1}{T} + \frac{1}{\tau}\right)^{-1} (\bar{x} - m)'(\bar{x} - m)}{\nu + T}. \tag{6.11}$$

The posterior mean is a natural combination of the prior and historical means. The posterior covariance matrix is a natural combination of the prior covariance V and the sample covariance s^2, plus a term that captures the implications for Σ of the disagreement between the sample mean $\bar{x}$ and the prior mean m – a large disagreement suggests large variances, for example. The essence of the Bayesian analysis with full data is the simple transformation from the prior $\text{IWN}'(V, \nu, m, \tau)$ to the posterior $\text{IWN}'(\tilde{V}, \nu + T, \tilde{m}, \tau + T)$. The appendix fills in the details of this analysis.

The Gibbs sampler enables us to extend this complete-data analysis to the case of quarterly data combined with monthly, by applying the meta-algorithm described above. The key step is to compute the conditional distribution of the monthly returns on our quarterly series, given the parameter $\theta = (\mu, \Sigma)$ and the observed data. Let I denote the indices of the monthly return series and J those of the quarterly series (of which there is only one in the present example). Then this conditional distribution of the unobserved monthly returns in period t is normal with mean vector and covariance matrix given by

$$\mu_{tJ|I} = \mu_J + \Sigma_{J|I}\Sigma_{II}^{-1}(x_{tI} - \mu_I) \quad \text{and} \quad \Sigma_{J|I} = \Sigma_{JJ} - \Sigma_{JI}\Sigma_{II}^{-1}\Sigma_{IJ}$$

where x_{tI} denotes the observed returns in month t and the subscripts I and J indicate the indices over which submatrices of μ and Σ are defined. Note that the conditional means vary across time due to the presence of the term x_{tI}, but the conditional covariances do not because of the assumed multivariate normality. We have identified the conditional distribution of the monthly returns of the quarterly series given the monthly series, but now we have to condition further on the observed quarterly returns of the quarterly series. Since the monthly returns of the quarterly series have the same covariance matrix $\Sigma_{J|I}$ given the monthly series, we can simulate the monthly returns of the quarterly series conditional on all observed data as follows. Simulate normal vectors U_t with time-varying mean vectors $\mu_{tJ|I}$ and constant covariance matrix $\Sigma_{J|I}$ for each monthly return. Now de-mean these series within each quarter, and add one-third of the observed quarterly return to each monthly observation in the quarter. This clearly ensures that the quarterly returns of the imputed data match the observed quarterly returns, but it also ensures that the generated data follows the correct conditional distribution of monthly returns of the quarterly series. This shows how to impute the full monthly data for the quarterly series. The Gibbs sampler then proceeds by doing a complete-data Bayesian analysis based on the imputed monthly data for the quarterly series, drawing a new θ from the posterior, imputing again, and so forth.

In our example, the data consists of the 24 monthly returns on MKT, SMB, and HML for the years 2008–2009 and quarterly returns on INTL for the same period. The Gibbs sampler described above was run for 20,000 iterations with the noninformative prior (best thought of as the IWN' prior with $\tau = \nu = 0$). The upper left chart of Figure 6.4 shows the posterior distribution of the correlation between MKT and INTL based on this simulation. The lower left chart shows the posterior distribution of the same correlation but using the monthly returns on INTL. Note that the loss of information about the correlations due to using quarterly returns on INTL has quite a dramatic effect on the posterior distribution. While the posterior distribution of the correlation based on quarterly INTL returns is diffuse and centered approximately on .5, the posterior distribution using monthly INTL returns is tightly centered around .9. On the one hand

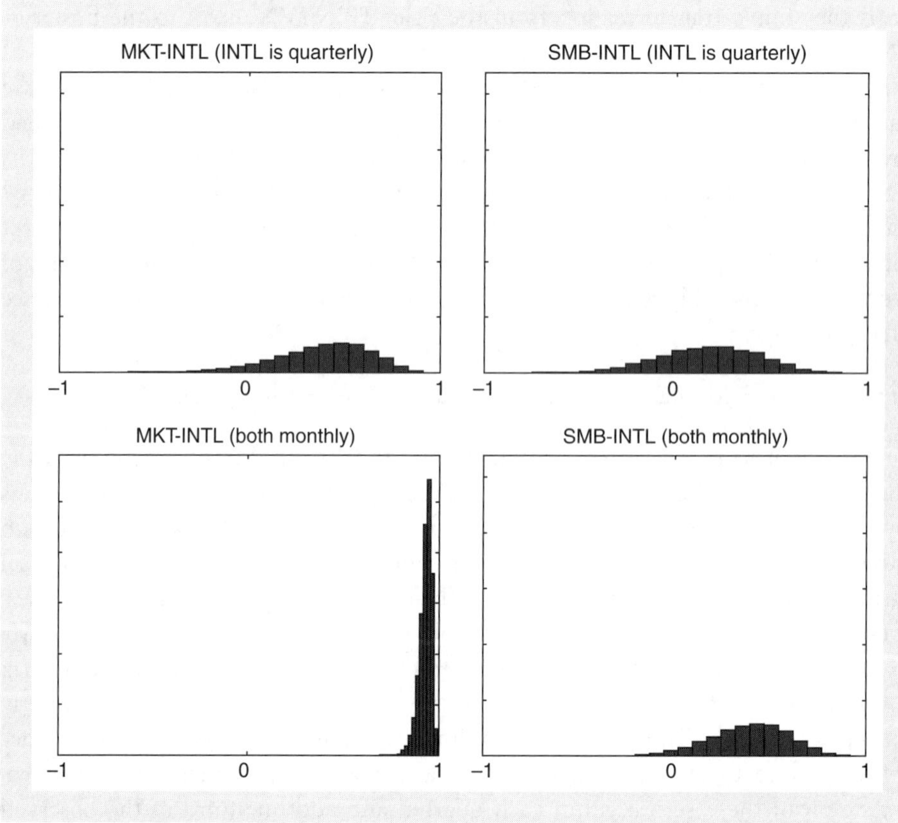

FIGURE 6.4 The posterior distribution of the correlation between an international portfolio INTL and the Fama–French MKT and SMB portfolios based on return data for 2008–2009. In the upper two charts, monthly returns are used for MKT and SMB while quarterly returns are used for INTL. In the lower two charts, all returns are monthly.

this is intuitive: we lose 75% of our information about correlations between INTL and MKT when we have monthly data rather than quarterly. On the other hand, this analysis calls into question our choice of a noninformative prior. Realized correlations between MKT and INTL have been high for several decades, and unless we believe this situation has changed it would be erroneous to base an investment decision on an analysis that promises excellent international diversification opportunities. The two charts on the right in Figure 6.4 display the posterior distribution of the correlations between SMB and INTL, again using first quarterly and then monthly INTL returns, and here the impact of the loss of information due to observing only quarterly returns on INTL is much less severe due mainly to the fact that the realized correlation is lower in this case. While this example shows the power of the Gibbs sampler in handling messy data, it also highlights the challenges of choosing an appropriate prior.

6.8 A Regime-Switching Model

In this section we present a more sophisticated example of a Bayesian MCMC analysis. This will illustrate the range and flexibility of the MCMC approach as well as some of the more subtle modeling ideas that Bayesian methods can bring to investment decisions.

Financial markets go through regimes characterized by expansion and contraction, high and low risk tolerance, and so forth. The regime-switching model conjures up an unobserved Markov process representing the state of the economy. A simple model takes the economy to be in one of two states, say expansion and contraction. Fitting such a model to market data allows investors to make decisions that take account of the probability of a future regime change. See Ang and Bekaert (2002) for a full example of such a model.

We present a simple Gibbs sampler for a regime-shifting model. For more on these algorithms see Scott (2002) and references therein. The historical window consists of T time periods $1, 2, \ldots, T$. We denote the Markov Chain that determines the state of the economy by Z, and so $(Z_1, Z_2, \ldots, Z_T)$ is the sequence of states of the economy over the historical window. We emphasize that Z is not directly observed, but rather is inferred from the behavior of asset prices. K denotes the number of states of Z.

We write $P = \left(p_{ij}\right)$ for the transition matrix of the Markov Chain Z. This means that p_{ij} is the probability that Z moves to state j next period given that this period it is in state i, irrespective of any previous history. The matrix P is stochastic, which is to say its rows add to 1. To specify the behavior of Z it remains only to specify how it is initialized at time 1. We denote the initial distribution by $\rho = (\rho_1, \rho_2, \ldots, \rho_K)$. Then the probability that Z visits the sequence of states $z = (z_1, z_2, \ldots, z_T)$ is given by

$$\mathbb{P}(Z = z) = \rho_{z_1} p_{z_1,z_2} p_{z_2,z_3} \cdots p_{z_{T-1},z_T} = \rho_{z_1} \prod_{t=2}^{T} p_{z_{t-1},z_t}. \tag{6.12}$$

This is the probability of the economy starting in state z_1 multiplied by the probability of next entering state z_2 given that it started in state z_1, and so forth.

We write $\theta_i = (\mu_i, \Sigma_i)$ for the mean vector and covariance matrix of returns in a period when the economy is in state i; returns are assumed multivariate normal and independent conditional on the sequence of states of Z. The number of assets whose returns are observed will be denoted by d. Let $x_1, x_2, \ldots, x_T$ denote the observed returns over time, each one a row vector of length d, and x a $T \times d$ matrix that stacks all these row vectors. The factor that appears in the likelihood corresponding to the return vector at time t assuming that the economic state is i is

$$\varphi_i^t \equiv \varphi\left(x_t; \mu_i, \Sigma_i\right),$$

where φ is the multivariate normal probability density function defined in Equation (6.15) in the appendix. With this notation the likelihood of both the returns and the unobserved sequence of regimes (x, z) is

$$L(r, z; \Theta) = \rho_{z_1}\varphi_{z_1}^1 \prod_{t=2}^{T} p_{z_{t-1}z_t}\varphi_{z_t}^t. \tag{6.13}$$

Here, Θ represents the full set of parameters of the model, consisting of all the θ_i's, the transition matrix P, and the initial distribution ρ.

We next assign a prior distribution to these parameters. First we assign the standard prior to θ_j, namely $\text{IWN}'(V_j, \nu_j, m_j, \tau_j)$. We want this to be somewhat informative to avoid divergence of the Gibbs sampler, as will be explained below. For our prior on ρ, the initial distribution of the chain, we could adopt a uniform distribution as a natural noninformative choice. For example, if there are only two states, then ρ_1 is taken to be uniformly distributed on [0,1], so that $\rho_2 = 1 - \rho_1$ is also uniform. A more general alternative is the Dirichlet distribution, and because this choice does not lead to a more complex analysis we adopt it here. A stochastic vector $\rho = (\rho_1, \rho_2, \ldots, \rho_K)$ follows the Dirichlet distribution with parameter $b = (b_1, b_2, \ldots, b_K)$ if the probability density function is

$$f(\rho_1, \rho_2, \ldots, \rho_{K-1}) = C\rho_1^{b_1-1}\rho_2^{b_2-1}\cdots\rho_K^{b_K-1}$$

for a constant C that makes this integrate to 1. Note that ρ_K is determined by the condition that all the ρ_k's add to 1. If $b = e$, a vector of 1's, then this becomes the uniform prior distribution, the natural noninformative prior. Otherwise, the distribution of ρ_k is concentrated around b_k/B, where B is the sum of the b_k's. The larger the value of B, the more concentrated the distribution. By choosing B large, we can express strong confidence in our prior guesses b_k/B at the ρ_k's.

To complete the specification, we must consider the prior distribution of the transition matrix P of the Markov Chain. Again the Dirichlet distribution is a convenient choice. Like ρ, each row of P adds to 1. We assume that the rows of P are independent, and that each one follows its own Dirichlet distribution, row k having parameter vector

A_k. The matrix A formed by stacking the A_k's serves as the parameter for this prior distribution on P. The main reasons for choosing Dirichlet priors here are that they include the noninfomative uniform distribution and that they lead to an analytically tractable Bayesian model.

We can now write down the full prior distribution, up to a scaling constant to make it integrate to 1:

$$\prod_{k=1}^{K} \rho_k^{b_k-1} \prod_{j=1,k=1}^{K} p_{jk}^{a_{jk}-1} \prod_{k=1}^{K} \Big[|\Sigma|^{-(\nu_k+d+2)/2} \dots$$

$$\times \exp\left(-\frac{1}{2}\left\{\mathrm{tr}\left(\nu_k \Sigma_k^{-1} V_k\right) + \tau_k(\mu_k - m_k)\Sigma_k^{-1}(\mu_k - m_k)'\right\}\right)\Big]. \quad (6.14)$$

The first product here is the Dirichlet prior on the initial distribution ρ of the regime. The second combines the Dirichlet priors on the rows of the transition matrix P. The third is the prior on the means and covariance matrices in the K regimes. The product of the likelihood (6.13) and the prior (6.14) is the full joint law of the parameters and data, which corresponds to Equation (6.1) above. A Gibbs sampler may be developed readily based on it. The Gibbs sampler is based on three variables, the Dirichlet parameters (ρ, P) describing the Markov Chain, the θ_j's, and finally the sequence of states $Z = (Z_1, Z_2, \dots, Z_T)$ of the unobserved Markov Chain. The steps of the chain are based on the distribution of each one of the three, conditional on knowing the other two. These steps are described in the next three paragraphs.

Conditional distribution of (ρ, P) In this step of the Gibbs sampler, we are treating z and the θ_i's as known. We view the product of (6.13) and (6.14) as a function of ρ and P only, keeping everything else fixed. Now (6.14) is a product of powers of ρ_j's and p_{ij}'s, and multiplying by (6.13) simply contributes T more factors to this product, namely ρ_{z_1} and p_{z_{t-1},z_t} for $t = 2, 3, \dots, T$, one factor for each state visited. We count the number of transitions n_{jk} that z makes from state j to state k over the time period $1, 2, \dots, T$. These form a matrix $N = (n_{jk})$, and the conditional posterior distribution of P given z and the θ_j's is simply that its rows are independent and follow Dirichlet distributions with parameters given by the rows of $A + N$. It couldn't be simpler. Similarly, the posterior distribution of ρ given "everything else" is Dirichlet with parameter $b + n$, where n is a vector with a 1 in the z_1 position and zeros elsewhere.

Conditional distribution of the θ_j**'s** In this step, we are treating z and (ρ, P) as known. Since z is known, we can group the time periods according to regime, for example separating returns in the expansion state into one sample and returns in the contraction state into another. The result is K random samples from K normal populations, each with an IWN$'$ prior, and the posterior distribution for each is again IWN$'$ with parameters easily calculated according to (6.11). We can simulate the θ_j's for the next iteration of the Gibbs sampler by generating them as independent IWN$'$ variates. The analysis is no more difficult than that of the appendix. It is here that we need somewhat informative priors on $(\theta_j, j = 1, 2, \dots, K)$. Otherwise, from time to time in the MCMC iterations we will produce a realization z of the Markov Chain Z in which a particular regime is not observed at all. In this case, one of our K samples is empty and the corresponding θ_j is drawn from the prior, and if the prior is noninformative the Gibbs sampler will diverge, though perhaps only very slowly.

Conditional distribution of Z Given (ρ, P) and the θ_j's, the conditional distribution of Z is given by (6.13). While this looks complicated, it is of a similar form to (6.12). In fact it is again a Markov Chain. We can see this as follows. We define a sequence of matrices Q_t by $Q_t = \left(q_{ij}^t\right)$ where $q_{ij}^t = p_{ij}\varphi_j^t$. Now (6.13) relates to the Q_t's as (6.12) relates to P. In other words, the conditional law of Z is again a Markov Chain, one whose transition rules change with time. Those transition rules are represented by transition matrices $\dot{P}_1, \dot{P}_2, \ldots, \dot{P}_T$. The $\dot{P}_t$'s will be determined by making the Q_t's stochastic – that is, by making their rows sum to 1 – by pre- and post-multiplying them by suitable diagonal matrices. We define δ_T to be the vector of row sums of Q_T, given by $\delta_T \equiv Q_T e$. Here again e denotes a vector of ones. Then we divide each row of Q_T by its row sum to produce the stochastic matrix

$$\dot{P}_T \equiv \Delta_T^{-1} Q_T \quad \text{where} \quad \Delta_T \equiv \text{diag}(\delta_T).$$

We proceed to define the stochastic matrices $\dot{P}_t$ recursively by $\delta_t \equiv Q_t \delta_{t+1}$, $\Delta_t \equiv \text{diag}(\delta_t)$, and $\dot{P}_t \equiv \Delta_t^{-1} Q_t \Delta_{t+1}$ for $t = T-1, T-2, \ldots, 1$. The $\dot{P}_t$'s are the stochastic matrices that govern the transitions of Z conditional on θ_i's and (ρ, P). It remains only to specify the initial distribution and that is given by

$$\dot{\rho} \equiv \frac{\rho \Delta_1}{\rho \Delta_1 e}.$$

The denominator on the right scales the entries to add to 1. To validate the claim that the conditional distribution of Z is given by the initial distribution $\dot{\rho}$ and transition matrices $\dot{P}_t$, one only has to confirm that the probability of any sequence of states under this specification is proportional to the quantities (6.13), and this follows simply because all the δ_t's cancel out. So we have identified the conditional distribution of the unobserved sequence of regimes Z as a time-inhomogeneous Markov Chain, which is easily simulated. This completes the description of the Gibbs sampler.

We next apply this Gibbs sampler to a specific situation. For our data we take weekly returns on the Fama–French portfolios MKT, SMB, and HML, for the 10-year period from January 2000 to December 2009. We choose a three-state model with noninformative priors and run 1000 iterations of the Gibbs sampler described above. In Figure 6.5 we present the predictive probability of each state over the decade. The states are identified as low, moderate, and high volatility, according to the posterior mean volatility of MKT. A technical problem in regime models is that the regime labels are actually arbitrary and with a sufficiently long run of the sampler we may observe random relabelings. Fortunately, for many problems these relabelings are so rare that their probability is negligible. By monitoring our iterations we verified to a high degree of confidence that no relabeling occurred in this example.

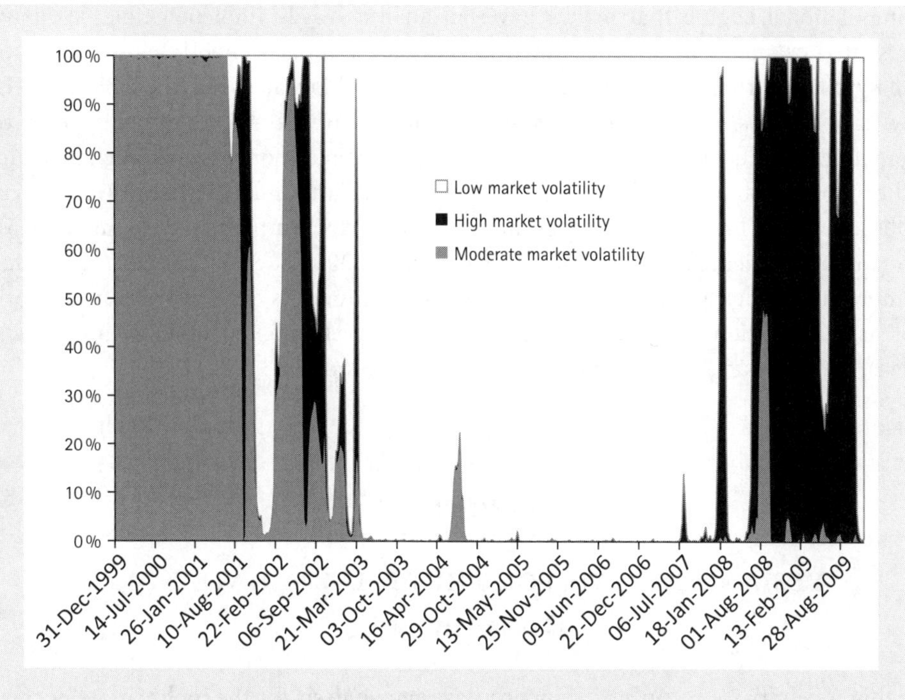

FIGURE 6.5 A three-regime model for U.S. stocks based on weekly returns on the Fama–French portfolio MKT, SMB, and HML, from January 2000 to December 2009.

As may be seen from Figure 6.5, the Gibbs sampler identified the early years of the decade as a moderate volatility regime interrupted by brief high-volatility periods associated with the 9/11 attacks of 2001 and the accounting scandals of 2001–2002. It also identifies the "quant crisis" of August 2007 and the global financial crisis following the Lehman collapse in September 2008 as high-volatility regimes. The economic expansion from 2003 to 2006 appears as a low volatility regime. By extracting the predictive distribution of future returns from the Gibbs sampler, investment decisions can be based on the likelihood of the current regime continuing and of a change of regime during the investment holding period. A weakness of such an analysis is that we observe only a few regime changes in the data and so our information on the transition probabilities between the regimes is quite weak. Despite the many shortcomings, the analysis provides insights and food for thought.

6.9 Concluding Remarks

In this chapter we have surveyed the foundations of the Bayesian approach to investing. We have also described the Markov Chain Monte Carlo methodology, which is the computational engine that makes Bayesian analysis easily implementable. We have presented examples illustrating how the Bayesian approach enables us to deal with messy data and enhances our ability to devise sophisticated but tractable models. We have emphasized foundations and computation in this chapter at the expense of modeling techniques. A fuller discussion tailored for practitioners would include many other topics such as the Black–Litterman method (Black and Litterman 1991; Meucci 2006), dynamic linear models (West and Harrison 1989; Putnam and Quintana 1985), and priors on pricing models (Pastor and Stambaugh 2002). See Rachev *et al.* (2008) for a more comprehensive introduction. Whether one's focus is on a rigorous framework for asset allocation or on creative modeling in developing quantitative investment ideas, the Bayesian approach provides an invaluable toolkit.

APPENDIX

Bayesian Analysis for the Multivariate Normal Distribution

In this appendix we record the standard Bayesian analysis for the multivariate normal distribution. The multivariate normal probability density function with mean μ and covariance matrix Σ is given by

$$\varphi(x;\mu,\Sigma) = (2\pi)^{-d/2}|\Sigma|^{-1/2}\exp\left(-\frac{1}{2}(x-\mu)\Sigma^{-1}(x-\mu)'\right), \tag{6.15}$$

where x and μ are d-dimensional row vectors. If, instead, x is a $T \times d$ matrix whose rows form a random sample of size T from this multivariate normal distribution then the probability density function of x may be written as

$$f(x;\mu,\Sigma) = (2\pi)^{-dT/2}|\Sigma|^{-T/2}\exp\left(-\frac{1}{2}\mathrm{tr}\left\{\Sigma^{-1}(x-e\mu)'(x-e\mu)\right\}\right) \tag{6.16}$$

where e denotes a column vector of ones of dimension T and tr denotes the trace of a square matrix, that is, the sum of the diagonal entries.

The inverse Wishart prior on Σ is given by

$$f_{\mathrm{IW}}(\Sigma;V,\nu) = C|\Sigma|^{-(\nu+d+1)/2}\exp\left(-\frac{1}{2}\left\{\mathrm{tr}\left(\Sigma^{-1}(\nu V)\right)\right\}\right).$$

Here, C is a scaling constant ensuring that the density integrates to 1. We denote this distribution by $\mathrm{IW}'(V,\nu)$. This parametrization of the inverse Wishart has the benefit of making the distribution centered roughly on V, and more concentrated around V the greater ν is. The expected value of Σ under the $\mathrm{IW}'(V,\nu)$ distribution is

$$\mathbb{E}(\Sigma) = \frac{\nu V}{\nu - d - 1},$$

and so is roughly equal to V when the degrees of freedom ν are large.

The standard Bayesian analysis of a multivariate normal random sample assumes an inverse Wishart prior on Σ, and, conditional on Σ, takes the prior on μ to be normal with a particular mean m and covariance matrix $\tau^{-1}\Sigma$. This distribution of μ is centered on m, and is more concentrated around m the greater τ is. The combined prior on $\theta \equiv (\mu, \Sigma)$ is known as the "inverse Wishart-Normal distribution." It may be characterized by the four parameters (V, ν, m, τ); it is denoted here by $\text{IWN}'(V, \nu, m, \tau)$

The posterior distribution is proportional to the product of the prior on Σ, the conditional prior on μ given Σ (the product of these two is the full prior distribution), and the probability density function of x, so the posterior distribution of (μ, Σ) is given up to a scaling constant by

$$|\Sigma|^{-(\nu+d+T+2)/2} \exp\left(-\frac{1}{2}\text{tr}\left\{\Sigma^{-1}\left(\nu V + (\mu - m)'(\mu - m) + (x - e\mu)'(x - e\mu)\right)\right\}\right) \ldots$$

Write $\bar{x}$ for the row vector of means and s^2 for the sample covariance matrix (defined with divisor T rather than $T - 1$). Then the final term in the exponent above may be written $(x - e\mu)'(x - e\mu) = Ts^2 + T(\mu - \bar{x})'(\mu - \bar{x})$ and after substituting this and reorganizing terms to separate those involving μ we reduce the last expression above to

$$\cdots = |\Sigma|^{-(\nu+d+T+1)/2} \exp\left(-\frac{1}{2}\text{tr}\left\{\Sigma^{-1}\left(\nu V + Ts^2 + \frac{(\bar{x} - m)'(\bar{x} - m)}{1/T + 1/\tau}\right)\right\}\right)$$
$$|\Sigma|^{-1/2} \exp\left(-\frac{1}{2}\text{tr}\left\{\Sigma^{-1}(\mu - \tilde{m})'(\mu - \tilde{m})\right\}\right)$$

where $\tilde{m}$ is given in (6.11). This final result may be recognized as being of the same IWN′ form as the prior, but with parameters $\tilde{V}$ and $\tilde{m}$ given by (6.11) and with $\tilde{\tau} = \tau + T$ and $\tilde{\nu} = \nu + T$. So the "effective sample sizes" τ and ν of the prior have each been increased by T and the prior mean and covariance matrix have been blended in a natural way with the mean and covariance matrix of the data. For further discussion see the paragraph containing (6.11).

References

Ang, A. and Bekaert, G. (2002). Regime switches in interest rates. *Journal of Business and Economic Statistics*, **20**(2), 163–182.

Barberis, N. (2000). Investing for the long run when returns are predictable. *Journal of Finance*, **55**(1), 45–48.

Bassett, G. W. Jr., Koenker R. and Kordas, G. (2004). Pessimistic portfolio allocation and Choquet expected utility. *Journal of Financial Econometrics*, **2**(4), 477–492.

Berger, J.O. and Wolpert, R.L. (1988). *The Likelihood Principle* (second edition). The Institute of Mathematical Statistics, Hayward, California (available for download at http://projecteuclid.org/euclid.lnms/1215466210).

Birnbaum, A. (1962). On the foundations of statistical inference. *Journal of the American Statistical Association*, 57(298), 269–326.

Black, F. and Litterman, R. (1991). Asset allocation: Combining investor views with market equilibrium. *Journal of Fixed Income*, **1**(2), 7–18.

Campbell, J.Y. and Viceira, L.M. (2002). *Strategic Asset Allocation: Portfolio Choice for Long-term Investors.* Oxford University Press, Oxford.

Chen, M.-H., Shao Q.-M. and Ibrahim, J.G. (2000). *Monte Carlo Methods in Bayesian Computation.* Springer-Verlag. New York.

Cooper, N.G. (ed.) (1989). *From Cardinals to Chaos: Reflection on the Life and Legacy of Stanislaw Ulam.* Cambridge University Press, Cambridge

Derman, E. (2004). *My Life as a Quant.* John Wiley, Hoboken, NJ.

Ellsberg, D. (1961). Risk, ambiguity and the Savage axioms. *Quarterly Journal of Economics*, 75(4), 643–669.

Fama, E.F. and French, K.R. (1992). The cross-section of expected stock returns. *Journal of Finance*, **47**(2), 427–465.

Feynman, R.P. (1972). *Statistical Mechanics.* Perseus Books, New York.

Geman, S. and Geman, D. (1984). Stochastic relaxation, Gibbs distributions, and the Bayesian restoration of images. *IEEE Transactions on Pattern Analysis and Machine Intelligence*, **6**, 721–741.

Gilks, W.R., Richardson, S., and Spiegelhalter, D. (1995). *Markov Chain Monte Carlo in Practice.* Chapman & Hall/CRC, Boca Raton.

Harbaugh, W., Mayr, U., and Burghart, D. (2007). Neural responses to taxation and voluntary giving reveal motives for charitable donations. *Science*, **316**, 1622–25.

Hastings, W.K. (1970). Monte Carlo sampling methods using Markov chains and their applications. *Biometrika*, **57**(1), 97–109.

Klein, R.W. and Bawa, V.S. (1976). The effect of estimation risk on optimal portfolio choice. *Journal of Financial Economics*, **3**(3), 215–231.

Krugman, P. (1997). Seven habits of highly defective investors. *Fortune*, December 29.

Machina, M.J. (2009). Risk, ambiguity, and the rank-dependence axioms. *American Economic Review*, **99**(1), 385–392.

Markowitz, H. (1991). *Portfolio Selection* (second edition). Blackwell. Malden, Massachusetts.

Markowitz, H. (2004). Transcript of interview available from the American Finance Association (at http://www.afajof.org/association/historyfinance.asp). Interviewed by Stephen Buser.

Meucci, A. (2006). Beyond Black–Litterman: views on non-normal markets. *Risk*, **19**(2), 96–102.

Meyn, S.P. and Tweedie, R.L. (1993). *Markov Chains and Stochastic Stability.* Springer-Verlag, London (available for download at: http://probability.ca/MT).

Neumann, J. von and Morgenstern, O. (1944). *Theory of Games and Economic Behavior.* Princeton University Press, Princeton

Pastor, L. and Stambaugh, R. (2002). Investing in equity mutual funds. *Journal of Financial Economics*, **63**(3), 351–80.

Putnam, B.H. and Quintana, J.M. (1995). Debating currency markets efficiency using dynamic multiple-factor models. *American Statistical Association: Proceedings of the Section on Bayesian Statistical Science*, pp. 199–205.

Rachev, S.T., Hsu, J.S.J., Bagasheva, B.S. and Fabozzi, F.J. (2007). *Bayesian Methods in Finance.* John Wiley: Frank J. Fabozzi Series, Hoboken.

Savage, L.J. (1962). *The Foundations of Statistical Inference.* Methuen, London.

Scott, S.L. (2002). Bayesian methods for hidden Markov models: Recursive computing in the 21st century. *Journal of the American Statistical Association*, **97**(457), 337–351.

Soros, G. (1988). *The Alchemy of Finance.* Simon & Schuster, New York. (Paperback by John Wiley, New York, 2003.)

Stambaugh, R.F. (1997). Analyzing investments whose histories differ in length. *Journal of Financial Economics*, **45**(3), 285–331.

Tanner, M.A. (1998). *Tools for Statistical Inference: Methods for the Exploration of Posterior Distributions and Likelihood Functions.* Springer Series in Statistics, New York.

West, M. and Harrison, P.J. (1989). *Bayesian Forecasting and Dynamic Models.* Springer-Verlag, New York.

Xia, Y. (2001). Learning about predictability: The effects of parameter uncertainty on dynamic asset allocation. *Journal of Finance*, **56**(1), 205–246.

CHAPTER 7

FUND-OF-FUNDS CONSTRUCTION BY STATISTICAL MULTIPLE TESTING METHODS*

MICHAEL WOLF AND DAN WUNDERLI

7.1 The Challenge

A fund-of-funds (FoF) manager or an institutional investor faces the challenge of selecting a (relatively) small number of "good" hedge funds from a large universe of candidate funds. We shall address the problem of fund selection from a statistical point of view. The analysis will be based solely on the track records of the individual managers. Arguably, the track record constitutes the single most important piece of information to judge the quality of a fund manager.[1] But making sense of the track records is a non-trivial task.

If we want to answer the question whether a particular fund manager is skilled based on his track record, we can use a statistical test. Such a test declares a fund manager skilled if his alpha with respect to a suitable benchmark is statistically proven to be positive "beyond a reasonable doubt," say a doubt threshold of 5%. This doubt threshold, say 5%, is denoted by the *significance level* of the test. By design, there is only a small

* M.W.: Research supported by the Swiss National Science Foundation (NCCR FINRISK, Module A3).
D.W.: Many thanks to Ashok Kaul, Andrea Heuson, Iwan Meier, and Chayawat Ornthalanai for helpful comments. I would also like to thank Eurekahedge Inc. for the kind support and the FMA for organizing the FMA European Conference 2008 in Prague and the LSE for organizing the LSE Alternative Investments Conference 2011. I gratefully acknowledge financial support from the Swiss Banking Institute.

[1] To be sure, there may be other pieces of information as well, such as the general background of the manager, his investment philosophy, the size and location of his office, etc. However, such factors are not easily quantifiable and/or available and so they will be left out of the statistical analysis.

chance then, say 5%, that a lucky manager passes the test, that is, gets wrongly identified as skilled.[2] Importantly, this logic assumes that *only one* manager is tested. If *many* managers are tested at the same time, the small individual doubts accumulate to a large global doubt. In other words, it now becomes very likely that some lucky managers will pass the test. This is undesirable for investment purposes. In general, only skilled managers will continue to outperform, while lucky managers will not.

The following analogy might help illustrate this dilemma. Imagine a person claims to have – some, though not necessarily perfect – extrasensory perception (ESP). A possible test consists of secretly tossing a coin 10 times and having the person predict the outcome of each toss. It would then be reasonable to identify the person as possessing ESP if she scores at least nine correct predictions. The logic is that somebody guessing completely at random has a chance of about 1.1% of scoring at least nine correct predictions. As a result, there is only a small chance that an "ignorant" person passes the test by chance.[3] But now consider 1,000 persons taking the test at the same time (perhaps because we put out a related job ad) and assume they are all ignorant. One would expect $0.011 \times 1,000 =$ 11 persons to pass the test by chance alone, that is, to get lucky. And the probability that at least one person will pass the test by chance alone, if they all guess independently of each other, is $1 - (1 - 0.011)^{1000} = 99.998\%$.

If our goal is to select the skilled managers from a large universe of candidates, we face a similar challenge to Cinderella: we want to identify the skilled managers ("*The good ones into the pot*") but exclude at the same time the lucky managers ("*The bad ones into the crop*"). But, unlike her, we must face the imperfect nature of statistical tests.[4] As a result, naïve testing, without taking the multiple evaluations into account, will allow lucky managers to creep in. This pitfall is rephrased by Grinold and Kahn (2000):

> The fundamental goal of performance analysis is to separate skill from luck. But, how do you tell them apart? In a population of 1,000 investment managers, about 5 percent, or 50, should have exceptional performance by chance alone. None of the successful managers will admit to being lucky; all of the unsuccessful managers will cite bad luck.

7.2 The Solution

We now discuss the solution to the challenge. In doing so, we first need to introduce some notation. There are N funds in the universe and the (common) return history comprises T observations. The alpha of a given fund manager with respect to his corre-

[2] Imposing a significance level of 0% is not possible, as it would imply that no manager, based on a finite track record, could ever be found skilled, no matter how impressive his track record may be.

[3] Again, if we did not allow for a small chance of an ignorant person passing the test, based on a finite number of tosses, no one could be declared as having ESP even if she predicts all outcomes correctly.

[4] Cinderella enjoyed the help of pigeons who could perfectly tell whether a particular lentil was "good" or "bad."

sponding benchmark is denoted by α_n, for $n = 1, \ldots, N$. The choice of the appropriate benchmark is up to the FoF manager, not the statistician. For example, the benchmark could simply be the riskfree rate. Or it could be a hedge fund index, comprised of funds that have a similar investment style. More generally, multi-factor benchmarks as in Kosowski *et al.* (2007) are also possible.

We look at individual hypotheses of the form:

$$H_n : \alpha_n \leq 0 \quad \text{vs.} \quad H'_n : \alpha_n > 0 \,. \tag{7.1}$$

So for each fund, the null hypothesis corresponds to a non-skilled manager (that is, his alpha is negative or zero), while the alternative corresponds to a skilled manager (that is, his alpha is positive). The two sets of non-skilled (or potentially lucky) managers and skilled managers are denoted by $\mathcal{I}$ and $\mathcal{I}'$, respectively:

$$\mathcal{I} = \{n : \alpha_n \leq 0\} \quad \text{and} \quad \mathcal{I}' = \{n : \alpha_n > 0\} \,.$$

The goal is to make individual decisions about each testing problem (7.1) while controlling the probability of lucky managers to pass the test by chance. A particular manager n is declared skilled by our statistical method if H_n is rejected in favor of H'_n. Depending on the (unknown) state of nature, there are two possibilities if this happens. On the one hand, if H_n is actually true, we made a mistake in the sense of declaring a non-skilled manager as skilled. Or, in the lingo of the statistician, we made a *false discovery*. On the other hand, if H_n is actually false, we correctly identified a skilled manager as skilled. Or, in the lingo of the statistician, we made a *true discovery*.

7.2.1 Formal Description of the Solution

For the purpose of this chapter, accounting for multiple testing means that we are concerned about the possibility of even one lucky manager passing the test or, in other words, of making even a single false discovery.[5]

Let F denote the number of false discoveries that our statistical method is going to make. Then the *familywise error rate* (FWE) is defined as the probability of making even one false discovery:

$$\text{FWE} \equiv P\{F > 0\} = P\{\text{Reject at least one } H_n \text{ with } n \in \mathcal{I}\} \,.$$

An appropriate statistical multiple testing method then ensures that this probability lies below some small, prespecified level, say 5% or 10%. Usually this level is denoted by α in the statistical literature but here we shall denote it by δ instead in order to avoid any confusion with the α's of the fund managers. Therefore, the goal is to ensure that:

$$\text{FWE} \leq \delta.$$

[5] Put in the context of Cinderella, we do not want even one bad one ending up in the pot.

By limiting the probability that even one lucky manager passes the test, we can in turn be confident that all managers identified by the statistical method are truly skilled. More specifically, assume $\delta = 10\%$. Then, after applying the method, we can be $1 - \delta$, or 90%, confident that all identified managers are truly skilled. As a result, with a high probability, our statistical FoF portfolio will only consist of skilled managers.

7.2.2 Implementation of the Solution

Implementing the solution in practice is anything but trivial. A host of statistical problems arise, among others:

- The non-normality of hedge fund returns.
- The time series nature of hedge fund returns.
- The choice of the individual performance measures: raw alpha estimate $\hat{\alpha}$ vs. t-statistic. The t-statistic is obtained by dividing the raw alpha estimate by its estimation uncertainty, which is quantified via a standard error.
- Accounting for the dependency across managers in order to improve the power of the statistical method, that is, its ability to detect skilled managers.

For each fund we compute an estimate of α_n, denoted by $\hat{\alpha}_n$, and a corresponding standard error $\hat{\sigma}_n$.[6] The "studentized" test statistic for testing H_n vs. H'_n is then given by

$$t_n = \frac{\hat{\alpha}_n}{\hat{\sigma}_n}.$$

The funds are ranked according to their test statistics, that is, the fund with the largest t_n statistic is the top fund according to this ranking and so on.

Alternatively, it would be possible to rank the fund managers simply according to their non-studentized test statistics $\hat{\alpha}_n$, that is, according to the "raw" alpha estimates. While this is actually the more common approach in the mainstream finance media, we consider it misguided. Ranking by the $\hat{\alpha}_n$ does not account for the (wildly) varying risks taken on by the various fund managers. On the other hand, ranking by the t_n does, since a larger risk will be reflected by a larger standard error $\hat{\sigma}_n$. This is in the very same spirit as using the Sharpe ratio (that is, a risk-adjusted performance measure) to judge the performance of a fund manager rather than the raw excess return (that is, a not-risk-adjusted performance measure).

How to compute $\hat{\alpha}_n$ and the corresponding standard error, $\hat{\sigma}_n$, respectively, depends on the given benchmark. A very general setup covering most practical applications is multi-factor benchmarks as in Kosowski *et al.* (2007). In such cases, $\hat{\alpha}_n$ can be computed from a standard OLS time series regression, based on the observed fund return and factor data. But care must be taken in computing the standard error $\hat{\sigma}_n$. It would be

[6] The standard error $\hat{\sigma}_n$ is an estimate of the unknown standard deviation of $\hat{\alpha}_n$.

generally wrong to simply use the standard error provided by the OLS output, since it does not properly account for the time series nature of hedge fund returns (and potentially also some of the factors). Instead one should use a HAC standard error[7] employing kernel estimation techniques; for example, see Andrews (1991) and Andrews and Monahan (1992).

Once the test statistics t_n have been obtained, it is the task of the multiple testing method to compute a cutoff value, denoted by d, from the joint track records of all managers in the investment universe and then declare those managers as skilled for which $t_n > d$. Crucially, this has to be done in a way such that the FWE is controlled. Of course, controlling a multiple testing criterion is only one side of the coin. It could be trivially achieved by never declaring any fund manager as skilled (that is, by choosing $d = \infty$). Naturally, there is also the other side of the coin. At the same time, we wish to identify as many skilled managers as possible. So in the lingo of the statistician, we want to employ a multiple testing method with as much *power* as possible. The current state of the art is developed (Romano and Wolf 2005) and can be summarized as follows.

It turns out that the ideal critical value d would be given by the $1 - \delta$ quantile of the following random variable:

$$\max_{1 \leq n \leq N} \frac{(\hat{\alpha}_n - \alpha_n)}{\hat{\sigma}_n} \,. \tag{7.2}$$

Importantly, the value of d is not only determined by the N marginal distributions of the individual statistics $(\hat{\alpha}_n - \alpha_n)/\hat{\sigma}_n$ but also by their cross-dependence structure. Such a procedure is not realistic, nevertheless, since the distribution of the random variable (7.2) is not known in practice. However, a consistent estimator of d, denoted by $\hat{d}$, can be obtained by a bootstrap method. Namely, $\hat{d}$ is obtained as the $1 - \delta$ quantile of the following random variable:

$$\max_{1 \leq n \leq N} \frac{(\hat{\alpha}_n^* - \hat{\alpha}_n)}{\hat{\sigma}_n^*} \,. \tag{7.3}$$

To this end, artificial return data are generated by an appropriate time series bootstrap mechanism. The estimator of α_n and its corresponding standard error computed from this artificial data set are denoted by $\hat{\alpha}_n^*$ and $\hat{\sigma}_n^*$, respectively. The algorithm to compute $\hat{\sigma}_n^*$ generally depends on the particular bootstrap mechanism chosen. We refer the interested reader to Romano and Wolf (2005) for the details. The *bona fide* decision rule is then to declare all funds managers as skilled for which $t_n > \hat{d}$.

The price one has to pay for replacing d by $\hat{d}$ is that control of the FWE is replaced by *asymptotic* control of the FWE:

$$\limsup_{T \to \infty} \text{FWE} \leq \delta \,.$$

[7] HAC stands for "heteroskedasticity and autocorrelation consistent."

However, simulation studies show that for practically relevant sample sizes T, the finite-sample control of the FWE is very satisfactory; see Romano and Wolf (2005) and Romano *et al.* (2008).

Remark 7.1. A key innovation of Romano and Wolf (2005) is to develop a *stepwise* method to detect as many skilled managers as possible. Instead of using a formal algorithm, it can be quite easily described in English. Assume there are $N = 100$ managers under test simultaneously and that 10 of them are detected as skilled using the procedure described above. We are left then with a smaller universe of 90 managers. The "trick" now is to use the same formal procedure on the remaining smaller universe, which might lead to the detection of some further skilled managers.

The reason is as follows. The individual test statistics t_n will stay the same, of course. However, the critical value $\hat{d}$ in this second step will generally be smaller, since now we are looking at the maximum over 90 statistics, rather than over 100 statistics, and so the resulting $1 - \delta$ quantile will be at most as large but typically strictly smaller. So some further rejections may result. In which case we continue to play the same game in the third step and so on, until no further rejections result.

This more powerful stepwise method still provides asymptotic control of the FWE.

For the empirical analysis of this chapter, we use the riskfree rate as the common benchmark for all hedge funds. In this case, the corresponding alpha is simply the expected excess return of the fund (over the riskfree rate). For a given fund, $\hat{\alpha}_n$ is computed as the sample average excess return over the observed investment period. The corresponding standard error $\hat{\sigma}_n$ is a standard HAC standard error employing a kernel estimation technique. In particular, we use the method of Andrews and Monahan (1992), based on the QS (quadratic spectral) kernel.

7.2.3 Comparison to Related Approaches

Needless to say, we are not the first ones to suggest carrying out hedge fund selection based on the managers' track records. We lack the time and the space to discuss all previously suggested approaches in detail and so limit ourselves to two selected comparisons.

Our method will, with a high probability, only identify skilled managers. As described above, the method works in the following way. Rank the fund managers by a certain performance criterion computed from their respective track records. Then based on the chosen input parameter δ, the method selects an *a priori* random number of the top funds, which are then declared as skilled. In other words, the threshold a manager must pass is actually computed from the joint track records themselves and is therefore stochastic. Knowing the number of funds in the investment universe will not tell us how many funds will end up in the FoF portfolio until we actually jointly examine all the track records.

This is in contrast to some previous approaches that suggest picking either an *a priori* fixed percentage or an *a priori* fixed number of the top funds for the FoF portfolio;

see Joehri and Leippold (2006) and Gregoriou *et al.* (2006), respectively. In discussing such approaches, we will focus on the fixed-percentage strategies; the critique would be similar for the fixed-number strategies.

The obvious question is how to pick the percentage *ex ante*? When backtesting the strategy, for a given investment universe and a given investment period, there usually will be a certain percentage leading *ex post* to a very good performance. But there is no universally "optimal" percentage. The results will vary with the investment universe and/or the investment period. To put it in the context of non-skilled vs. skilled managers to select two (overly) extreme scenarios just to make the point: if all managers are non-skilled, the optimal percentage is zero; if all the managers are skilled, the optimal percentage is 100. Knowing from previous published studies that a certain percentage worked well for a certain investment universe during a certain investment period, is not overly helpful to a FoF manager faced with a different universe and a different period. In fact, such information might actually be quite misleading.

On the other hand, the use of our multiple testing methods gives the FoF manager the confidence that for his specific investment universe and investment period, the selected fund managers are all skilled. And such a selection should result in continued attractive future performance for the corresponding FoF portfolio. Whether this indeed is the case will be examined in the next section by means of some backtesting exercises. Importantly, these exercises do not require any hindsight knowledge but instead yield true "out-of-sample" performances.

7.3 Investment Universes and Portfolio Construction

We use the CISDM database from http://wrds.wharton.upenn.edu and a customized Eurekahedge datafeed from http://www.eurekahedge.com to get monthly series of net-of-fees hedge fund returns.

We apply an "observe ten years–invest one year" strategy with a three-month sell lag, moving at an annual frequency. More specifically, on October 1, of every year y, we feed 117 months of past return data into the multiple testing method. It then detects the statistically significantly skilled fund managers. We then invest in the equal-weighted portfolio of the detected hedge funds from January to December in year $y + 1$. Then the procedure repeats, that is, on October 1 of year $y + 1$, we already need to decide which hedge funds we want to invest in over the next year $y + 2$. Given the annually moving "observe ten years–invest one year" strategy, six investment periods from year 2000 to 2005 (for CISDM) and from year 2002 to 2007 (for Eurekahedge), respectively, are obtained.

At any given investment point in time, we are only selecting from a certain sub-universe of all funds contained in the respective database (CISDM or Eurekahedge).

First, we restrict attention to funds which both have a complete 117-month return history *and* are open to investment at this point. Second, we exclude funds that (overall) lost money over this 117-month period.[8] Third, we exclude all funds that have at least one recorded monthly return exceeding 50% in absolute value.[9] Fourth, to avoid the inclusion of funds which are "too similar" to each other, we impose that all the pairwise sample correlations over the 117-month period lie below 0.95, so some further funds might have to be excluded.[10]

In addition to the equal-weighted portfolio of the outperforming funds, we build a global minimum variance portfolio (GMV) with the outperforming funds. Specifically, given K outperforming funds over 117 months detected by our multiple testing method, we solve the following optimization problem within each 117-month window

$$\begin{aligned} \min_{\mathbf{w}} \quad & \mathbf{w}'\hat{\Sigma}\mathbf{w} \\ \text{s.t.}\ & \mathbf{w} \geq \mathbf{0} \\ & \mathbf{w}'\mathbf{1} = 1, \end{aligned} \tag{7.4}$$

using quadratic programming methods. Since the true covariance matrix Σ is unknown, we estimate it using a suitable shrinkage estimator from the joint track records of the K funds over the last 117 months; see the appendix for details. Optimization problem (7.4) returns an optimal weight $\mathbf{w}^*$ for each 117-month window. In the following year, one then invests in the $\mathbf{w}^*$-weighted portfolio of the outperforming funds. The equal-weighted portfolio is simply the $\mathbf{w}^* = [1/K \ldots 1/K]$ weighted portfolio of the outperforming funds. The rebalancing and the three months sell-lag are as before.

As pointed out before, selecting an appropriate benchmark for a given hedge fund is the task of the FoF manager, not of the statistician. Since we are "ignorant" in this respect, we simply chose the riskfree rate as the universal benchmark. Such a choice certainly appears reasonable and may even be the natural one from certain viewpoints. In practice, the particular riskfree rate we use is from the CRSP Risk Free Rates file.[11]

The multiple testing criterion we employ is the control of the FWE with parameter $\delta = 10\%$. So at any given point in time, we can be 90% confident that all identified managers are truly skilled.

It is then natural to ask whether there is any "value" in our statistical technique of constructing a FoF. An obvious competitor is the $1/N$ portfolio, that is, the equal-weighted portfolio of all available hedge funds. Recent work by DeMiguel *et al.* (2009), in the context of building equity portfolios, shows that this simple-minded portfolio

[8] Since we are benchmarking against the risk-free rate always, no fund manager that lost money overall could possibly be considered outperforming.

[9] The motivation here is two-fold. On the one hand, such recorded returns might simply correspond to data-entry mistakes. On the other hand, even if such returns are true, they may have a large impact on the data analysis because of their undue effect on sample means, sample standard deviations, and sample Sharpe ratios.

[10] The motivation here is that sometimes "basically the same fund" can appear under slightly different names. We implicitly take the stance that the FoF manager would only want to invest in one such fund.

[11] We employ the average rate of *ask* and *bid*.

is actually surprisingly difficult to outperform for statistical methods that construct portfolios based on the past return data. However, in contrast to equity investing, the $1/N$ portfolio is often not feasible for a FoF manager, given the various minimum investments of the individual funds. Hence, it is of interest to see whether statistical FoF portfolios, based on a much smaller investment universe, can do (at least) as well as the $1/N$ portfolio. So for each investment universe, we also include the $1/N$ portfolio in our study.

Remark 7.2. Having a smaller investment universe by applying a multiple testing method rather than investing in all available funds is particularly important when portfolio optimization, such as choosing the global minimum variance portfolio, is used. In this case, the smallest weight (or investment portion) will often be much smaller than the inverse of the number of funds to invest in. So the larger the number of funds, given the various minimum investments, the less feasible such an "optimized" strategy becomes.

Furthermore, we consider two investable hedge fund indices for comparison. The HFRX Global Investable Hedge Fund Index is from www.hedgefundresearch.com and the CS/Tremont Investable Hedge Fund Index from www.hedgeindex.com. Note that the inclusion of these indices somewhat amounts to comparing apples to oranges, since they correspond to investment universes different from both the CISDM and the Eurekahedge databases. Nevertheless it is interesting to see how our statistical FoF portfolios fare against some "real life" competitors.

7.3.1 Idealistic Setup

In a first analysis, all hedge funds that have a complete return history of 192 months are part of our chosen investment universes. This is idealistic, since we will never know in January 2000, say, which funds will survive until December 2005 in order to restrict our attention to them. Nevertheless, it is also of interest to compare our statistical FoF portfolio to the $1/N$ portfolio in this context.

Remark 7.3. Constructing investment portfolios based on statistical multiple testing methods, investing in assets which are established as outperforming, is certainly not restricted to the hedge fund industry. More generally, this approach could also be applied to equities, bonds, foreign exchange, etc. The frequency of individual assets "dying" in such alternative markets will often be much reduced compared to the hedge fund industry, or even (close to) zero. So including the results for a world without dying individual funds/assets is not only of academic interest.

In a second step, we will make the investment setup more realistic with respect to the characteristics of the hedge fund industry and not using any future knowledge about fund survivorship.

Either way, we always impose a realistic sell lag of three months. That is, we have to decide at October 1 in year $y-1$ which funds to sell at January 1 of year y. For simplicity, we synchronize the buy decisions with the sell decisions. So on October 1 of year $y-1$, the portfolio to be held throughout year y is chosen.

Our CISDM investment universe comprises 97 hedge funds, ranging from January 1990 to December 2005. The Eurekahedge investment universe contains 61 hedge funds over the period January 1992 to December 2007. Restricting attention to the hedge funds actually open to investment throughout the 16-year period further reduces the sizes of the two universes to 91 and 54, respectively.

7.3.2 Realistic Setup

In the second part of our analysis, we evaluate a realistic strategy, both for the FoF and the $1/N$ portfolios as follows. In October of a given year, we take as the investment universe all funds that have a complete 117-month history. As before, we impose a reasonable sell lag of three months and synchronize the sell decisions with the buy decisions.

We then construct both our statistical FoF portfolios and the $1/N$ portfolio and hold them for a year. During that year, some funds might "die" of course. Not all funds will generally return all money to the investors. We, therefore, assume a uniform recovery rate of 90% of the investments at the time a fund closes down.[12] The recovered money is then invested in the riskfree rate for the remainder of year. Then we play the same game again next October. So in this way, the size of the investment universe–actually varies over time. Finally, we impose a disinvest-reinvest restriction, as many fund managers are not willing to tolerate a come-and-go-as-you-please behavior of investors. If we disinvest from fund n in October of any year, we are no longer allowed to reinvest in fund n in any of the following years.[13]

The sizes of the CISDM investment universes only containing open funds are 86, 116, 160, 211, 268, 371 for the years 2000, 2001, … , 2005, respectively. The sizes of the Eurekahedge investment universes with only open funds are 92, 118, 137, 138, 136, 119 for the years 2002, 2003, … , 2007, respectively.

7.3.3 Statistical Significance of Portfolio Outperformance

Of course, we must keep in mind that any performance measures computed from a finite investment period are only sample-based estimates rather than true "population

[12] Of course, recovery rates vary in practice. But this additional knowledge is not available to us. So to impose a fixed "average rate" appears the best feasible solution.

[13] The results do not change much if this disinvest-reinvest restriction is not imposed. For the sake of brevity, the results without this restriction are not reported.

numbers" (or *parameters* in the lingo of the statistician). So when comparing two portfolios based on a given performance measure, we cannot necessarily conclude that the portfolio with the higher sample-based estimate is indeed better. In other words, we cannot claim any statistical significance based on the sample-based estimates only. To this end, rather, we need to employ a proper statistical test.

Let us focus on the Sharpe ratio which, arguably, is the single most important performance measure. We want to establish whether the true "underlying" Sharpe ratio of the statistical FoF portfolio is indeed larger than that of the $1/N$ portfolio in the realistic setup. Denote these two parameters by SR_{FoF} and $\text{SR}_{1/N}$, respectively. Further, denote their difference by Δ, that is,

$$\Delta = \text{SR}_{\text{FoF}} - \text{SR}_{1/N} .$$

Since we have an *a priori* belief that $\Delta > 0$ and would like to "verify" this belief by a statistical test, we consider a one-sided test of the kind:

$$H : \Delta \leq 0 \quad \text{vs.} \quad H : \Delta > 0 .$$

For both investment universes, the sample-based estimates $\hat{\Delta}$ are indeed positive: for the CISDM universe, we obtain $\hat{\Delta} = 0.37 - 0.32 = 0.05$; for the Eurekahedge universe, we obtain $\hat{\Delta} = 0.37 - 0.27 = 0.10$, as reported in Table 7.3 below. But again, this does not "prove" that the two population Δ's are also positive.

Testing for the difference between two population Sharpe ratios is a non-trival matter. The most commonly used method in the finance literature is the test of Memmel (2003), which is a corrected version of the earlier test of Jobson and Korkie (1981). Unfortunately, this test was derived using the overly strict assumptions of return data that follow a normal distribution and are additionally independent over time. At least one of these two assumptions is generally violated in practice. For hedge fund return data, typically both assumptions are violated. As a result, the test of Memmel (2003) tends to overstate the statistical evidence that is really contained in the observed data. Therefore, since we want to demonstrate that our FoF portfolios outperform the $1/N$ portfolios with respect to the Sharpe ratio, using the test of Memmel (2003) would actually be tempting. However, it would not be correct.

Ledoit and Wolf (2008) propose a bootstrap test that instead yields reliable inference in the presence of non-normal return distributions and time series effects. In other words, it gives a fair appraisal of the statistical significance actually contained in the observed data. Note that their bootstrap test is designed for two-sided hypotheses of the kind

$$H : \Delta = 0 \quad \text{vs.} \quad H' : \Delta \neq 0,$$

but it can be easily modified to apply to the one-sided case as well.

As stated, we believe that the Sharpe ratio is the single most important performance measure. Looking at measures that are not adjusted for the risk taken out by the fund manager, such as the average (excess) return, can be quite misleading. Nevertheless, we can apply a statistical test to the difference between average (excess) returns as well. Again, we propose to use a bootstrap test that yields reliable inference in the presence of non-normal return distributions and time series effects. Testing for means is easier than testing for Sharpe ratios. Therefore, the test of Ledoit and Wolf (2008) can be "simplified" in a straightforward manner to deal with means.

7.4 RESULTS

The results are summarized in Tables 7.1 and 7.2 for the idealistic setup and in Tables 7.3 and 7.4 for the realistic setup, respectively. Importantly, all summary statistics are on a monthly basis, that is, they are not annualized.[14] In addition, Figures 7.1 and 7.2 provide some graphical representation of the various return distributions.

7.4.1 Idealistic Setup

First, we report the number of hedge funds making up the statistical FoF portfolio in each of the six annual investment periods. For the CISDM portfolio this number

Table 7.1 Performance of portfolios: Idealistic setup.

	# of hedge funds in each of the 6 years	average exc. return	average return	Sharpe ratio	maximum drawdown
	CISDM data, investment period: Jan 2000 – Dec 2005.				
EW-FoF	9, 9, 3, 7, 5, 8	0.38%	0.60%	0.28	−4.22%
GMV-FoF	9, 9, 3, 7, 5, 8	0.42%	0.61%	0.59	−1.47%
$1/N$	91	0.51%	0.73%	0.20	−10.02%
HFRX Global	> 60	0.39%	0.64%	0.28	−3.92%
CS/Tremont	60	0.38%	0.60%	0.48	−2.06%
	Eurekahedge data, investment period: Jan 2002 – Dec 2007.				
EW-FoF	1, 1, 1, 3, 5, 5	0.40%	0.63%	0.57	−1.89%
GMV-FoF	1, 1, 1, 3, 5, 5	0.38%	0.60%	0.64	−0.56%
$1/N$	54	0.64%	0.86%	0.31	−7.52%
HFRX Global	> 60	0.27%	0.49%	0.23	−3.57%
CS/Tremont	60	0.35%	0.57%	0.40	−2.68%

[14] While annualizing (excess) returns is straightforward, annualizing Sharpe ratios is not. The usual method of multiplying the monthly Sharpe rations by $\sqrt{12}$ is misleading for hedge funds due to the autocorrelation of the returns over time; see Lo (2002).

Table 7.2 Statistical significance of outperformance: Idealistic setup.

	Alternative hypothesis	i = CISDM	i = Eureka
j=mean excess return	$\mu^{exc}_{\text{EW-FoF}} < \mu^{exc}_{1/N}$	$p = 0.35$	$p = 0.18$
j=Sharpe ratio	$SR_{1/N} < SR_{\text{EW-FoF}}$	$p = 0.36$	$p = 0.09$
j=mean excess return	$\mu^{exc}_{\text{GMV-FoF}} < \mu^{exc}_{1/N}$	$p = 0.38$	$p = 0.17$
j=Sharpe ratio	$SR_{1/N} < SR_{\text{GMV-FoF}}$	$p = 0.20$	$p = 0.11$

Note: If a p-value is smaller than α, then the data supports the alternative hypothesis at significance level α.

Table 7.3 Performance of portfolios: Realistic setup.

	# of hedge funds in each of the 6 years	average exc. return	average return	Sharpe ratio	maximum drawdown
	CISDM data, investment period: Jan 2000 – Dec 2005.				
EW-FoF	10, 14, 13, 14, 10, 11	0.36%	0.58%	0.37	−1.83%
GMV-FoF	10, 14, 13, 14, 10, 11	0.20%	0.41%	0.33	−3.66%
$1/N$	86,116,160,211,268,371	0.54%	0.76%	0.32	−5.62%
HFRX Global	> 60	0.39%	0.61%	0.28	−3.92%
CS/Tremont	60	0.38%	0.60%	0.48	−2.06%
	Eurekahedge data, investment period: Jan 2002 – Dec 2007.				
EW-FoF	18, 21, 21, 21, 10, 9	0.26%	0.48%	0.37	−3.55%
GMV-FoF	18, 21, 21, 21, 10, 9	0.30%	0.53%	0.67	−0.60%
$1/N$	92,118,137,138,136,119	0.46%	0.68%	0.27	−5.73%
HFRX Global	> 60	0.27%	0.49%	0.23	−3.57%
CS/Tremont	60	0.35%	0.57%	0.40	−2.68%

Table 7.4 Statistical significance of outperformance: Realistic setup.

	Alternative hypothesis	i = CISDM	i = Eureka
j=mean excess return	$\mu^{exc}_{\text{EW-FoF}} < \mu^{exc}_{1/N}$	$p = 0.27$	$p = 0.17$
j=Sharpe ratio	$SR_{1/N} < SR_{\text{EW-FoF}}$	$p = 0.34$	$p = 0.33$
j=mean excess return	$\mu^{exc}_{\text{GMV-FoF}} < \mu^{exc}_{1/N}$	$p = 0.11$	$p = 0.26$
j=Sharpe ratio	$SR_{1/N} < SR_{\text{GMV-FoF}}$	$p = 0.54$	$p = 0.11$

Note: If a p-value is smaller than α, then the data supports the alternative hypothesis at significance level α.

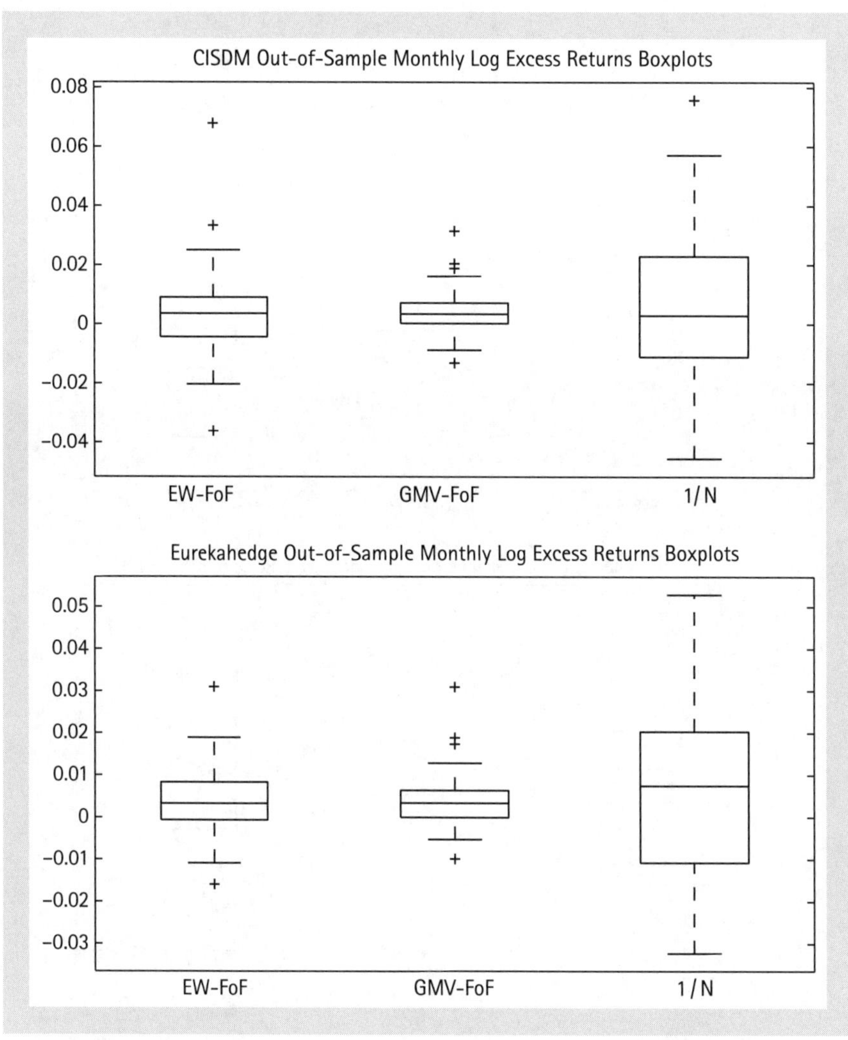

FIGURE 7.1 Box plots of out-of-sample log excess returns: Idealistic setup.

varies between 3 and 9, compared to a universe size of 91. For the Eureka portfolio, this number varies between 1 and 5, compared to a universe size of 54. The size of the HFRX index varies over time, always being larger than 60. The size of the CS/Tremont index is 60.

Second, we report the mean of the monthly excess log returns over the six annual investment periods. We find that for both investment universes (and their slightly different respective investment periods), the statistical FoF portfolios yield a lower excess return than the $1/N$ portfolio. However, these differences are not statistically significant, as reported in Table 7.2.

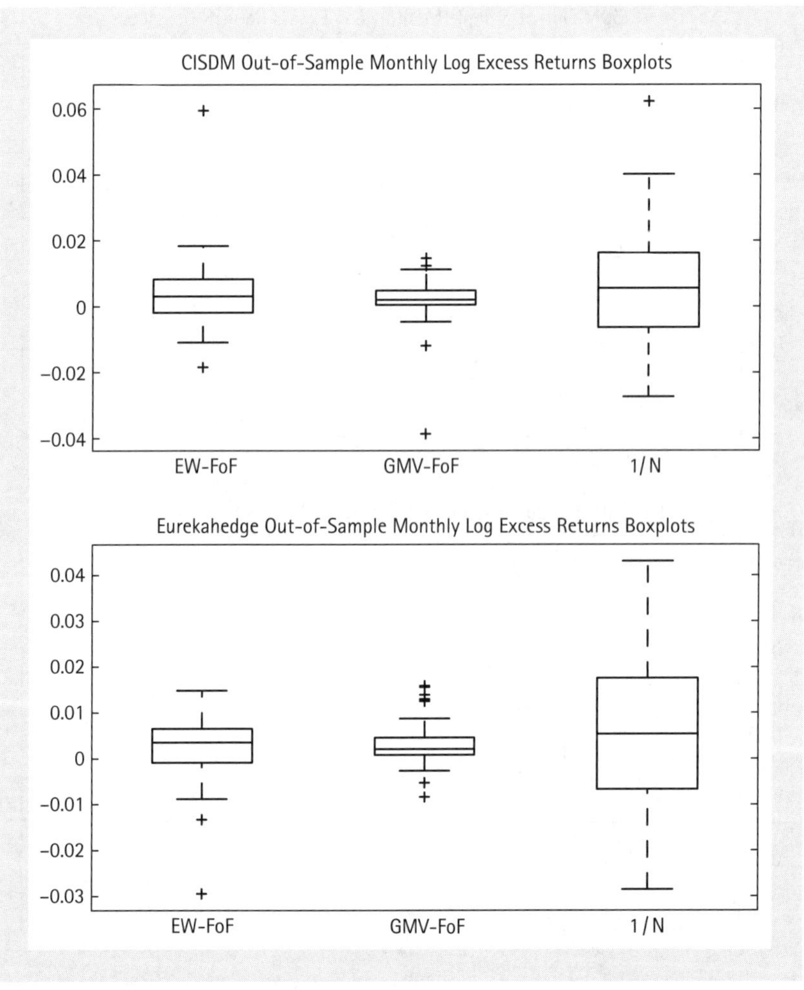

FIGURE 7.2 Box plots of out-of-sample log excess returns: Realistic setup.

Third, we report the mean of the "raw" log annual returns (that is, not in excess of the riskfree rate). Not surprisingly, the comparisons are qualitatively very similar to those for the excess returns.

Fourth, we report the Sharpe ratios of the monthly log excess returns. As already stated, for both investment universes, our statistical FoF portfolios have a (somewhat) smaller excess return and a (much) smaller portfolio size than the $1/N$ portfolio. Typically, one would expect smaller portfolios to have less favorable Sharpe ratios than larger ones due to diversification effects. However, the opposite is the case for both investment universes, with the differences being rather large at times. This is especially remarkable in case of the Eurekahedge universe where the size of the statistical FoF portfolios ranges from 1 to 5. Statistical significance at the 10% level is only achieved in one case, though: namely for the EW-FoF portfolio with the Eureka data.

Fifth, we report the maximum drawdown over the out-of-sample investment period of $6 \cdot 12 = 72$ months. Again, for both investment universes, the statistical FoF portfolios outperform the $1/N$ portfolio, adding further evidence to the claim that a multiple testing technique successfully identifies a small number of skilled managers from the large investment pool.

The boxplots in Figure 7.1 clearly show that the $1/N$ portfolio, despite its larger universe size, yields returns that are much more variable compared to the two statistical portfolios. In addition, portfolio optimization appears successful in the sense that the returns of GMV-FoF are somewhat less variable compared to EW-FoF.

We finally note that the statistical portfolios generally compare favorably to the investable indices as well.

7.4.2 Realistic Setup

First in Table 7.3, we report the number of hedge funds making up the statistical FoF portfolio in each of the six annual investment periods. We observe that the sizes of the CISDM FoF portfolios vary between 10 and 14. The Eureka FoF portfolios contain between 9 and 21 funds. The size of the HFRX index varies over time, always being larger than 60. The size of the CS/Tremont index is 60.

Second, we report the mean of the monthly excess log returns over the six annual investment periods. We see again that the mean excess monthly returns are lower than their $1/N$ counterparts. However, these differences are not statistically significant; see Table 7.4.

Third, we report the mean of the "raw" log monthly returns (that is, not in excess of the riskfree rate). Not surprisingly, the comparisons are qualitatively very similar to those for the excess returns.

Fourth, we report the Sharpe ratios of the monthly log excess returns. As before, the statistical portfolios yield consistently higher Sharpe rations compared to the $1/N$ portfolio, though not at a level of statistical significance.

Fifth, we report the maximum drawdown over the out-of-sample investment period of $6 \cdot 12 = 72$ months. Again, for both investment universes, the statistical FoF portfolios outperform the $1/N$ portfolio, with the differences being rather large. In fact, for both universes, the $1/N$ portfolio has the worst drawdown of all five portfolios.

The boxplots in Figure 7.2 clearly show that the $1/N$ portfolio, despite its larger universe size, yields returns that are much more variable compared to the two statistical portfolios. In addition, portfolio optimization appears successful in the sense that the returns of GMV-FoF are somewhat less variable compared to EW-FoF.

We finally note that the statistical portfolios generally compare favorably to the investable indices as well.

Remark 7.4. We generally fail to find statistical significance when testing for outperformance. This may not be surprising, given that it is notoriously difficult to find statistical significance in small samples of noisy financial returns (our out-of-sample period only comprises 72 months). There is, nevertheless, a clear and strong pattern. For each performance criterion (average excess return, Sharpe ratio, or maximum drawdown), there is a total of eight comparison cases (two setups, two data sets, and two statistical portfolios). In all eight cases, the story is always the same: the statistical portfolio yields a lower average excess return but outperforms the $1/N$ portfolio both in terms of the Sharpe ratio and the maximum drawdown. The latter two criteria are probably more relevant, as most FoF managers promote their ability to manage the risk in their portfolios.

We can also ask the question whether portfolio optimization via the GMV portfolio yields further benefits. Here the results are a bit mixed, but they suggest that the general answer may be yes. In terms of the Sharpe ratio and maximum drawdown, the GMV statistical portfolio does better than the equal-weighted statistical portfolio in three cases (both data sets in the idealistic setup and the Eurekahedge data set in the realistic setup) and worse in one case (the CISDM data set in the realistic setup). In addition, the gains in the cases of outperformance are larger than the losses in the case of underperformance.

7.5 Conclusions

We have studied whether it is possible to construct hedge fund portfolios with attractive return properties based on the past track records of all managers in the investment universe alone. Importantly, such a strategy must not rely on any hindsight knowledge, say about which fixed percentage of top managers for a given investment universe and investment period would have worked well.

Our approach consists of comparing each manager to a given benchmark (which could be common or be allowed to vary with managers) and then to determine which managers statistically outperform their benchmark. Such managers are deemed "skilled" and we simply go on to hold an equal-weighted or a global-minimum-variance portfolio of all skilled managers as our FoF portfolio. This process is repeated, and the portfolios thus updated, every year.

Crucially, in determining which managers statistically outperform their benchmark, one must take into account that a large number of managers are examined at the same time. In other words, one must account for the problem of multiple comparisons (of managers against benchmark). We do this by employing some state-of-the-art statistical multiple testing methods. These methods take the non-normal return distributions and time series nature of hedge fund returns into account to properly control the chance of non-skilled managers creeping into our FoF portfolio. On the other hand, these methods are also optimized with respect to detecting as many skilled managers as possible in order to build a well-diversified portfolio.

We backtested this strategy (without using any hindsight knowledge) on two hedge fund universes. When comparing the performance of the statistical FoF portfolios to their most natural competitor, namely the $1/N$ portfolio, we found that they deliver consistent improvements both in terms of the Sharpe ratio and the maximum monthly drawdown. The return properties are also attractive when compared to two investable hedge fund indices (based on different investment universes).

While traditional approaches to construct FoFs, such as due diligence, will remain vital, we believe that statistical selection techniques based on the past track records alone can be an attractive (and cost efficient) alternative method. Of course, there is no reason not to combine these two approaches. Indeed, while clearly beyond the scope of this chapter, the combination of more complex traditional approaches with statistical selection techniques might well result in the best of both worlds.

Research supported by the Swiss National Science Foundation (NCCR FINRISK, Module A3).

Many thanks to Ashok Kaul, Andrea Heuson, Iwan Meier, and Chayawat Ornthalanai for helpful comments. I would also like to thank Eurekahedge Inc. for the kind support and the FMA for organizing the FMA European Conference 2008 in Prague. I gratefully acknowledge financial support from the Swiss Banking Institute.

APPENDIX

New Shrinkage Estimator for Σ

When estimating a covariance matrix based on (limited) past track records, one should not use the sample covariance matrix. This is especially true when the estimated covariance matrix is used for purposes of portfolio optimization. The intuitive reason is that the optimizer will latch on to the large estimation error contained in the sample covariance matrix and produce very unstable portfolios that often yield poor out-of-sample performance. This important point is discussed by Ledoit and Wolf (2003, 2004) who also offer a remedy. Namely, shrink the sample covariance matrix to a highly structured estimator, called the *shrinkage target*. Such an estimator will be biased, unlike the sample covariance matrix, but in return will contain very little estimation error. Combining the two estimators via shrinkage will result in an optimal bias-variance trade-off.

Ledoit and Wolf (2003, 2004) suggest shrinkage targets for a universe of stocks: the single-factor model and the single-correlation model. But the targets have a common feature: the diagonal of the matrix is the same as the diagonal of the sample covariance matrix. As a result, only the sample covariances get shrunken/modified but not the sample variances.

We feel that such an approach is sub-optimal when dealing with hedge funds instead of stocks. Due to the wildly varying amounts of risk taken on by the various funds, already the differences between the sample variances will be overstated. It, therefore, appears useful to shrink the sample variances in addition to the sample covariances.

Therefore, we propose the *two-parameter* model as a shrinkage target. It has one common variance and one common covariance. The estimation of these two parameters is straightforward. One simply takes the average of all sample variances and the average of all sample covariances, respectively. One is then left to find a formula for the optimal shrinkage intensity. The general methodology is outlined by Ledoit and Wolf (2003) and the details are left to the reader. Computer code in the Matlab language can be downloaded for free from the following website: http://www.ledoit.net/ole2_abstract.htm.

References

Andrews, D.W.K. (1991). Heteroskedasticity and autocorrelation consistent covariance matrix estimation. *Econometrica*, **59**, 817–858.

Andrews, D.W.K. and Monahan, J. C. (1992). An improved heteroskedasticity and autocorrelation consistent covariance matrix estimator. *Econometrica*, **60**, 953–966.

DeMiguel, V., Garlappi, L., and Uppal, R. (2009). Optimal versus naive diversification: How inefficient is the $1/N$ portfolio strategy? *Review of Financial Studies*, **22**, 1915–1953.

Gregoriou, G.N., Hübner, G., Papageorgiou, N., and Rouah, F. (2006). Simple hedge fund strategies as an alternative to funds of funds: evidence from large-cap funds. In *Funds of Hedge Funds* (ed. Gregoriou, G.N.) Quantitative Finance Series, pp. 117–131. Elsevier, Amsterdam.

Grinold, R.C. and Kahn, R.N. (2000). *Active Portfolio Management* (second edition). McGraw-Hill, New York.

Jobson, J.D. and Korkie, B.M. (1981). Performance hypothesis testing with the Sharpe and Treynor measures. *Journal of Finance*, **36**, 889–908.

Joehri, S. and Leippold, M. (2006). Quantitative hedge fund selection for funds of funds. In *Funds of Hedge Funds* (ed. Gregoriou, G.N.) Quantitative Finance Series, pp. 433–454. Elsevier, Amsterdam.

Kosowski, R., Naik, N., and Teo, M. (2007). Do hedge funds deliver alpha? A Bayesian and bootstrap analysis. *Journal of Financial Economics*, **84**, 229–264.

Ledoit, O. and Wolf, M. (2003). Improved estimation of the covariance matrix of stock returns with an application to portfolio selection. *Journal of Empirical Finance*, **10**(5), 603–621.

Ledoit, O. and Wolf, M. (2004). Honey, I shrunk the sample covariance matrix. *Journal of Portfolio Management*, **30**(4), 110–119.

Ledoit, O. and Wolf, M. (2008). Robust performance hypothesis testing with the Sharpe ratio. *Journal of Empirical Finance*, **15**, 850–859.

Lo, A. (2002). The statistics of Sharpe ratios. *Financial Analyst Journal*, **58**, 36–42.

Memmel, C. (2003). Performance hypothesis testing with the Sharpe ratio. *Finance Letters*, **1**, 21–23.

Romano, J.P. and Wolf, M. (2005). Stepwise multiple testing as formalized data snooping. *Econometrica*, 73(4), 1237–1282.

Romano, J.P., Shaikh, A.M., and Wolf, M. (2008). Formalized data snooping based on generalized error rates. *Econometric Theory*, **24**(2), 404–447.

CHAPTER 8

HEDGE FUND CLONES

NILS TUCHSCHMID, ERIK WALLERSTEIN, AND SASSAN ZAKER

In simple terms hedge fund replication refers to the process of replicating, or cloning, the returns of hedge funds through a statistical model or algorithmic trading strategy. A first step to better understand why and how it is possible to replicate hedge funds – famed for their complexity and sophistication – is to better understand the sources of hedge fund returns. Research on explaining hedge fund returns has in broad terms taken two approaches. The most common approach is to carefully select a set of asset factors and estimate how well these explain hedge fund returns with means of factor analysis (e.g. Fung and Hiseh, 1997; Ennis and Sebastian, 2003). The other approach tries to explain hedge fund returns by designing and testing generic trading strategies that certain groups of hedge funds employ (e.g. Mitchell and Pulvino, 2001).

Both of these approaches are also used to replicate hedge funds. They are not conflicting in any sense; Fung and Hiseh (2007) combine them for example. They do, however, serve two distinct goals in understanding hedge fund returns. Factor analysis helps understand when and where hedge funds invest, but without understanding why. A generic trading strategy, on the other hand, tries to explain the dynamics of hedge fund strategies and their associated sources of risk.

A third approach to look at hedge fund returns, but not directly caring about their source, is to understand why they are attractive to investors' portfolios. More precisely, the approach focuses on replicating distributional properties of hedge funds relative to the overall portfolio of an investor and is due to Kat and Palaro (2005). This implies that the approach does not aim to track hedge fund returns on a month-to-month basis.

Why should investors be interested in products replicating hedge funds? The answer is not as simple as saying that replication products are likely to track hedge funds in terms of return and risk level. Even if this may very well be the case, replication products have some attractive features which hedge funds usually do not have. Replication products are claimed to be liquid, transparent, and to low charge fees compared to hedge funds. However, none of these claims should be taken at their face value.

Liquidity proved indeed to be very valuable during the credit crises. However, bearing liquidity risk can also yield attractive returns and this is important to factor in. Replication products are in general transparent in that they publish their holdings or give detailed descriptions of their trading strategies. However, many approaches to hedge fund replication are very sophisticated and complex and it is not obvious how all of them will give investors transparency or better understanding of what they are investing into. Replication products do charge lower fees then hedge funds. Yet, and almost obvious, lower fees are not to the benefit of investors if performance (after fees) is not comparable with that of actual hedge funds.

This chapter will begin with a section of a detailed and critical assessment of the three approaches of hedge fund replication. This is followed by a survey of 19 replication products and their performance. The last section concludes.

8.1 Hedge Fund Replication Methods

There are in broad terms three approaches to hedge fund replication. The first method, factor replication, is a top-down approach which tries to estimate asset exposures of hedge funds with various statistical methods (e.g. Jaeger and Wagner, 2005; Hasanhodzic and Lo, 2007). The second is a bottom-up approach, which we will refer to as rule-based replication. It aims to isolate broad and fundamental characteristics of hedge fund strategies and implement these with automated trading algorithms (e.g. Mitchell and Pulvino, 2001). The third approach aims to replicate desirable distributional properties of hedge fund returns with dynamic trading techniques (e.g. Kat and Palaro, 2005).

8.1.1 Factor Replication

The underlying assumption of this method is that major parts of hedge fund returns can be captured by a set of common risk factors. That is, the hedge fund return generating process can be expressed as:

$$r_t = \text{alpha} + \sum_{i=1}^{K} \text{beta}_i f_{i,t} + \epsilon_t. \tag{8.1}$$

where r_t are the hedge fund returns, alpha is a constant, and beta_i is the exposure towards risk factor $f_{i,t}$. If the risk factors are chosen with consideration of being investable and liquid, then parts of the returns can be replicated by constructing a portfolio of the risk factors, weighted by beta_i. The claim by hedge funds is that most parts of the returns pertain to alpha and thus few, if any, parts of the returns can be replicated by such a model. There are, however, several academic articles (e.g. Jaeger and Wagner, 2005;

Hasanhodzic and Lo, 2007; Fung *et al.* 2008) showing that it is indeed possible to capture significant parts of hedge fund returns with a simple linear model as in (8.1).

A popular replication technique, which was first developed to analyze mutual fund performance, is called style analysis and is due to Sharpe (1992). A relaxed form of this model is used in analyzing hedge funds and is defined as:[1]

$$r_t = \sum_{i=1}^{K} w_i f_{i,t} + \lambda_t, \tag{8.2}$$

$$\text{s.t.} \sum_{i=1}^{K} w_i = 1 \tag{8.3}$$

where r_t are the monthly returns of the fund, K is the number of factors, w_i is the factor exposure towards the monthly return of factor $f_{i,t}$, and λ_t is the part of the monthly returns, unexplained by the factors. The constraint in (8.3) is the budget constraint. It yields an interpretation of w_i as portfolio weights.

However, as highlighted by ter Horst, Nijman, and de Roon (2004), the constraint in (8.3) will give biased estimates of the weights.[2] As a reminder, the objective function in the estimation process is to minimize the variance of λ_t with respect to w_i. Assume the linear regression estimation as a reference point to the estimation of fund of funds factor exposures. In order to get an appropriate portfolio interpretation of this estimation the exposures have to be scaled linearly to sum to 1. However, the benefit of instead imposing a constraint will cause the portfolio weights to only increase (decrease) the weight(s) to the factor(s) with the lowest (highest) variance (and covariance), thus creating a portfolio with lower risk than if the estimates from linear regression were to be used (and scaled to sum to 1). These biases are important to consider if the style analysis approach is used to replicate hedge fund returns.

It is far from straightforward to select which assets best capture the risk and return structure of hedge fund returns, that is specifying the $f_{i,t}$ in (8.1). While anyone would agree that most hedge funds trade in equity, commodities, and bonds, just including an index derived from these asset classes may be too simplistic. Many strategies are implemented through derivatives which will give nonlinear returns relative to the underlying asset. Thus the factor model should include derivative based factors to overcome nonlinearities. This, however, adds an enormous number of new factors to choose from and the selection process becomes more complex.

In the case of hedge funds, estimating the factor exposures contains several difficulties as well. The frequency of hedge fund data is in most cases monthly, thus requiring long-spanning sample periods. Hedge funds are often highly dynamical and have time

[1] The original model of Sharpe (1992) imposed the constraint $0 \leq w_i \leq 1, \forall i$. This is obvious in the case of mutual funds since they are restricted to hold short positions and use leverage but not in the case of hedge funds which do not have these restrictions.

[2] It is often incorrectly assumed that the exclusion of the intercept in style analysis has an impact on the estimation process as compared to linear regression. Omitting the intercept does not in fact change the solution at all, see Becker (2003).

varying exposure towards asset classes which is not captured by a linear factor model. The simplest extension to overcome this is to use a rolling-window over the time-series to estimate weights using data over, for example, the past 24 month. Again the low frequency of data requires unsatisfactory long estimations periods.[3]

There are several techniques to increase the degree of flexibility of a linear model to better capture time-varying exposures. Most notable are Bayesian techniques which have been developed in optimal control theory, like the Kalman or particle filter.[4] In brief Kalman filter methods are used to extend the model in (8.1) by allowing the beta_i, or portfolio weights, to change randomly over time. More precisely, let B_t be the vector of all portfolio weights beta_i, $i = 1, \ldots, K$, at time t. Then, in the Kalman filter model, it is assumed that B_t evolves according to

$$B_t = B_{t-1} + \gamma_t \tag{8.4}$$

where γ_t is a K-vector normal random variable with zero mean and covariance matrix Σ. Estimating Σ is fairly easy in the standard Kalman model, however, in the case of replication it is desirable to impose further assumptions on the model. For example, it is likely to assume that portfolio weights of hedge fund assets exhibit shifts, rather than normally distributed changes, during times of market dislocations. Extending the Kalman filter model as well as using the particle filter model is complex and demands a considerable amount of time to be implemented and calibrated in a satisfactory manner. For instance, the filters can easily be over-specified and consequently come up with nice, yet heavily data-mined results.

A general problem of factor analysis is spurious correlation, which means that a statically significant factor exposure does not imply a causal link between the estimated factor exposures and hedge fund returns. This becomes a particular issue for hedge fund replication due to their exposure to liquidity risk. The downside risk of liquidity often goes in tandem with the downside risk of other more liquid asset classes. The crisis of 2008 is a case in point. Many hedge funds posted terrible returns during October and November of that year due to holdings in illiquid assets. At the same time most market indices like equities and bonds had terrible performance as well. A factor replication model using hedge funds data would have likely over-estimated exposure towards equities or bonds if the illiquidity exposure was not properly accounted for.

The often highlighted problems of hedge fund data as backfill bias, selection bias, and survivorship bias (Fung and Hsieh, 2004) are of less concern for hedge fund replication since these biases all relate to the omission of hedge fund return samples and not to adding noise to the return data itself.

As a final remark, factor replication is certainly best suited to capture aggregate returns (i.e. hedge fund indices and fund of hedge funds) since the idiosyncratic risk

[3] Considering that some hedge funds employ high-frequency trading strategies where trades are executed in milliseconds, using a 24 month rolling-window of return data does not seem convincing to capture time-varying asset exposures.

[4] For further references to Kalman and particle filters, see Doucet, Freitas, and Gordon (2001) and Chui and Chen (2008).

exposures will diminish significantly and simplify the process of choosing an appropriate set of factors and estimating factor exposures.

8.1.2 Rule-Based Replication

This second method of hedge fund replication is a bottom-up approach which aims to implement well-known and well-understood hedge fund strategies with low-cost and relatively simple trading algorithms. An important difference between rule-based and factor replication is that it does not try to extract statistical patterns of hedge fund return time series but actually implements hedge fund strategies.

What has enabled this model of replication – as argued by, e.g. Berger, Kabiller, and Crowell (2008) – is that with time many hedge fund strategies become conventional wisdom. Growing academic research contributes to this evolution as well as the simple fact that over time knowledge about hedge fund strategies is spread across the financial industry. In other words, with time, parts of the alpha component of hedge fund returns becomes beta, also called by some alternative beta.

One example of academic research shedding light on hedge fund strategies is Mitchell and Pulvino (2001) who investigate merger arbitrage strategies. The strategy tries to capitalize on the outcome of corporate mergers. After the announcement of merger talks between two companies, the share price of the target firm will rapidly jump close to the bidder's price. However, a spread will persist until the deal is successfully consummated. To bet that the deal will go through and the spread will contract, the merger arbitrage strategy holds a long position in the target firm's share and hedges some market risk with a short position in the acquiring firm. The historical evidence shows that most merger deals indeed go through. This suggests that there may be little added value to spend (costly) time to estimate the probabilities of the result of merger talks, rather than using a rule based approach which employs the strategy on all announced merger negotiations. Mitchell and Pulvino (2001) employ this rule based approach on a data set of merger deals over the period 1963–1998 and found this strategy to explain a significant part of merger arbitrage hedge fund returns.

Durate, Longstaff, and Yu (2007) use a similar approach to unveil the risk and return of fixed-income arbitrage strategies. They specify trading rules for five common fixed-income arbitrage strategies and investigate to what extent these can be explained by market risk factors. As an example, they implement a fixed-income volatility arbitrage strategy. The intuition of the strategy is to try to exploit the well documented fact that implied (or perceived) volatility of options often exceeds that of realized volatility. In more technical terms the strategy consists of a short position in an at-the-money interest rate cap and a delta-hedge of the underlying interest rate securities. Durate, Longstaff, and Yu find that of the five strategies implemented, three of these generate positive excess returns after adjusting for market risks, transaction costs, and hedge fund fees.

It is possible to combine factor replication and rule-based trading strategies, and this is to some extent discussed by Fung and Hsieh (2007). In this context these trading strategies are referred to as alternative betas, as opposed to traditional betas like equity, bond, and commodity factors. As argued above, the alternative beta factors serve to better explain the "alpha" part of the hedge fund return generating process in (8.1).

However, constructing an investable alternative beta factor, as in the trading strategies outlined above, differs significantly from that of a traditional beta. The latter refers to exposures towards equities, bonds, or commodities. These factors represent parsimonious, long-only, buy and hold assets. Consequently investing into these assets is straightforward. Rule-based trading strategies, on the other hand, contain dimensions which do not follow straightforward rules. Most prevalent of these dimensions are the sizing of positions, leveraging, and increased risk management. Taking the example of the merger arbitrage strategy, what decides the size and leveraging of stock positions? Furthermore, managing short positions and trading in derivatives demands skilled portfolio and risk management.

8.1.3 Dynamic Trading

The third method of hedge fund replication differs from the above in that it tries to capture the distributional properties of hedge fund returns, as opposed to capturing time-series properties. That is, over a longer period of time the dynamic trading approach aims to match the distributional properties such as mean, volatility, and correlation of hedge fund return time-series relative to a portfolio of common assets. But on a monthly basis, return time-series of hedge funds are not expected to be replicated.

This method of hedge fund replication was first put forth by Kat and Palaro (2005; 2006ab).[5] It is based on the seminal work of Black and Scholes (1973) and Merton (1973) on pricing financial derivatives. More specifically, a payoff function, like a call option, of a security can be replicated with the dynamic trading of the security and a risk free asset. Kat and Palaro make use of this insight by constructing exotic pay-off functions which aim to concur, in distribution, with hedge fund returns.

At the center in implementing this method are the investor's portfolio and the reserve asset. The implementation consists in broad terms of three steps. First, the investor's portfolio is used to functionally define desirable dependence structures relative to hedge fund returns. One approach to the problem has been to fit returns of a hedge fund and the investor's portfolio to an appropriate bivariate copula. The second step is to derive the payoff function – where the reserve asset is the dependent variable – which will give the dependence structure relative to the investor's portfolio. The final and third step is to derive the dynamic trading strategy which replicates the payoff function.

[5] For extensions, see Papageorgiou, Remillard and Hocquard (2008) and Takahashi and Yamamoto (2009).

An important note on the first step is that it is by no means necessary to use hedge fund returns to define the dependence structure. It has been used in the literature mostly for pedagogical reasons. From a practical point of view it is rather preferable to stipulate (and define mathematically) which distributional properties the clone should have as well as dependence towards the investor's portfolio. This avoids many problems associated with the use of hedge fund data.

Papageorgiou *et al.* (2008) find that this replication method captures pre-specified higher moments and correlation with high precision regardless of the reserve asset. They do note, however, that the reserve asset "only" affects the mean return. The investment returns of replicating the payoff function are necessarily dependent on the reserve asset, as is the case for any derivative. The simplest illustration of this is a European call option where the link between the option's investment return at the exercise date and the underlying asset is indeed easy to understand. Hence there is consequently a need for security selection skills to construct a reserve asset. A successful dynamic trading fund must have a reserve asset which will yield attractive returns under the required distribution structure.

The model is very complex and it is indeed difficult to give economic meaning and interpretation to the asset allocations which the model produces. Furthermore, the theory of dynamic trading presupposes highly liquid markets in order to change the portfolio weights at small time-intervals. The difficulty of selecting a reserve asset as well as these two final remarks demands a substantial due diligence process for investors seeking investments in this approach.

8.2 Replication Products

With the growing academic support that hedge fund replication may be achievable theoretically, several large and small financial companies have launched replication products. These products are often launched as a replication index which is investable through tracker-funds or structured products. This chapter investigates 19 products from 17 companies, listed in Table 8.1, and based on any of the replication models in the previous chapter.[6] Note in Table 8.1 that the frequency of the data is mostly daily as compared to monthly which is standard in the hedge fund industry.

Table 8.1 shows that 12 companies use a factor replication model to capture hedge fund returns, four use rule-based replication, one uses distribution replication and two use a combination of factor and rule-based replication. Interviews with replication providers suggest that the current trend for new launches is towards highly sophisticated mathematical models, often where rule-based approaches complement factor analysis. The conclusions about performance presented in Table 8.1 of different products should

[6] There are at least 30 companies active in this market segment but we will limit our analysis to those in Table 8.1, since (1) other products have too short a sample period or (2) companies do not disclose return time-series.

Table 8.1 List of replication products, their methods, and inception date.

Company	Index/Fund name	Replication method	Frequency	Inception	Annulazied since incp.	
					Mean	S.D
Barclays Capital	BC-Long Barclays Alternatives Replicator Index	Factor replication	Daily	1-Oct-07	−0.039	0.087
Credit Suisse	CS-Long/Short Equity Replication Index (Net)	Factor replication	Daily	3-Mar-08	−0.008	0.199
Credit Suisse	CS-Inverse Long/Short Equity Replication Index (Net)	Factor replication	Daily	3-Mar-08	−0.031	0.196
Concept Fund Solutions	CON-DB Alternative Return Fund	Factor replication	Daily	18-Jun-08	−0.250	0.220
Desjardins Global Asset Management	DGAM-Enhanced Alternative Investments	Factor replication	Monthly	29-Jun-07	0.022	0.056
Goldman Sachs	GS-Aboslute Return Tracker Index	Factor replication	Daily	1-Mar-07	0.013	0.107
IceCapital Fund Management	ICE-Alternative Beta Fund	Factor replication	Daily	19-Mar-07	−0.027	0.116
Innocap Investment Management	IC-Salto Index	Factor replication	Daily	3-Jul-07	−0.043	0.090
Innocap Investment Management	IC-Verso Index	Factor replication	Daily	2-Mar-07	0.031	0.084
JP Morgan	JP-Alternative Beta Index	Factor replication	Daily	12-Feb-07	0.014	0.074
Merrill Lynch	ML-Factor index	Factor replication	Daily	3-Apr-06	0.033	0.081
Societe Generale	SGI-Alternative Beta Index	Factor replication	Daily	1-Mar-07	−0.016	0.120
Deutsche Bank	DB-Absolute Return beta Index	Rule based	Daily	1-May-07	−0.146	0.189
Fulcrum Asset Management	FLC-Alternative Beta Fund	Rule based	Bi-weekly	17-Oct-07	0.035	0.069
Index IQ	IQ-Hedge Composite Beta Index	Rule based	Daily	31-Oct-07	0.002	0.131
Rydex SGI	RYD-Multi-Hedge Strategies Fund	Rule based	Daily	19-Sep-05	−0.046	0.110
Morgan Stanley	MS-altera Index	Factor replication / Rule based	Daily	1-Aug-07	0.027	0.086
Partners Group	PG-Alternative beta strategies Index	Factor replication / Rule based	Daily	6-Oct-04	0.028	0.112
Aquila Capital	AC-Statistical Value Market Neutral 7 Vol Fund	Distribution approach	Daily	5-Feb-08	0.017	0.048

Note: The mean and standard deviation (S.D.) is calculated over the sample period from respective inception date to 30 September 2009.

be made with some considerations of the tough months they had to weather during the credit crisis.

Fee-levels of replication investment vehicles vary and are dependent on the targeted clientele. Most products charge a flat fee of 1–2% on asset under management and no performance fee. Some companies, like Fulcrum Asset Management, differ on this point by charging fund of funds like fees of 1% on asset under management (AUM) and 10% on performance, abbreviated 1/10. Furthermore, some companies also charge a so-called penalty fee of 1–3% on investments if disinvestments are made within 1–3 years after initial investments. The overall trend is still to charge significantly lower than the 2/20 charged by hedge funds combined with the 1/10 charged by fund of funds. Liquidity terms are in general much better than for traditional hedge funds where replication products offer daily, weekly, or bi-weekly liquidity.

The size of the replication industry is difficult to estimate, primarily because many companies do not want to disclose their size for marketing reasons. Furthermore, during the credit crisis AUM of many replication products became very volatile, not due to their own performance, but because they were the most liquid instruments among hedge fund assets. One product, for example, faced redemptions of 80% of AUM. During the same period, however, shortable replication products had large inflows which subsequently were disinvested when markets stabilized in 2009. A conservative lower bound on the aggregate AUM of the replication space is around 3 billion USD in 2009, to be compared with the overal hedge fund industry that managed an estimated $1.4 trillion at the same time according to Hedge Fund Research.

The general opinion of hedge fund replication providers is that replication products will offer better liquidity and lower fees for portfolio managers seeking hedge fund like returns. However, there are two different opinions of which role replication products should have in a portfolio; either as a complement or a replacement of hedge fund investments. Some, such as Societe Generale, Barclays, Innocap, and Credit Suisse, aim their product to complement hedge fund portfolios. They also offer shortable replication products. Shorting hedge fund exposure may sound counterintuitive, but with the limited liquidity of hedge funds it offers asset managers the possibility to hedge, for example, duration mismatches, from the point they desire to redeem fund shares up until this is realized. Other companies, such as Blue White Alternative Investments and Fulcrum Asset Management, have benchmarked their products to outperform hedge fund composite indices on a risk-adjusted basis and consequently aim to replace actual hedge fund investments.

Many companies have close collaboration with academics. For example, Professors Fung, Hsieh, and Naik cooperated with two companies (Credit Suisse and JP Morgan) in this survey as well as two other companies (State Street Global Advisors and Blue White Alternative Investments). Professor Kat is cooperating with Aquila Capital.

The distribution approach, as mentioned in the previous section, does not necessarily have to be directly targeted to replicate hedge fund performance. This is also the case for the Aquila Capital fund which targets zero correlation towards equities, 7% volatility, and 10% annual returns.

8.2.1 Performance

This section will evaluate and compare the performance of the replication products over the sample period from March 2008 to September 2009, over which period all products where operating live. Due to the unusually volatile markets of 2008 and 2007 a fixed sample period is necessary in order to facilitate more comparable performance measures. Most data have been accessed through Bloomberg, except for Barclays and Societe Generale, which have been accessed through the companies' homepages. Data of all products which are listed as indices are gross of fees, except Credit Suisse, and all products listed as funds are net of fees.

Table 8.2 presents some performance statistics of the replication products and some market indices. The cross-sectional performance, regardless of measure, is in general heterogeneous. The annualized continuously compounded mean returns vary between −20.9% and 5.9%, excluding short versions. The risk, or annualized standard deviation (S.D.), also varies significantly between 7.8% and 20.6%. Tail risk, proxied by kurtosis, seems to be present in many products, with many having kurtosis of around 10.

The lower panel of Table 8.2 presents performance statistics of some market indices. Compared to hedge fund indices, more than 50% of the products (excluding the short versions) performerd better than the aggregate composite indices from HFR and CS/Tremont. Furthermore, more than 80% of the products outperformed HFRI's fund of funds index. This hedge fund index is to some extent more representative than the other two since fund of funds is easier to invest in than hedge funds and thus better represents actual hedge fund investment experiences net of all fees. Hedge fund indices have significantly lower S.D. than replication products in general. The indices, however, have also significantly higher positive autocorrelation (ρ_1 and ρ_2) than replication products. Hedge fund indices have around 60% autocorrelation while all replication products have far less and many even negative autocorrelation. As noted by Lo (2002), positive (negative) autocorrelation will bias S.D. downward (upward) and hence the interpretation of this measure and the Sharpe ratio for the hedge fund indices in particular should be made with this in mind. When evaluating the mean return and S.D. it is again worth emphasizing that not all products are benchmarked to outperform but to track an index.

This data set only includes two shortable products, from Innocap and Credit Suisse.[7] Evaluating a short index towards its long index is, however, somewhat complicated. The short index has to be defined to mirror the return of the long index over a specific time period. In the case of hedge fund replication this often seems to be on a monthly basis. Furthermore this implies that over longer intervals the compounded returns of the short

[7] Barclays Capital and Societe Generale both have short versions of their replication index. However, their short index data is posted as a long index and the performance of the shortable index is close to that of the long. Hence we have refrained from including the performance of this index.

Table 8.2 Performance statistics of replication products and some market indices over the period March 2008 to September 2009.

		Annualized						
	Tot. Return	Mean	S.D.	Sharpe	Kurt.	Skew.	ρ_1	ρ_2
BC-Long Barclays Alternatives Replicator Index	-12.2	-0.082	0.110	-0.75	7.0	-0.4	-4.6	-3.2
CS-Long/Short Equity Replication Index (Net)	-2.6	-0.017	0.199	-0.08	11.2	0.9	-19.8*	-16.9*
CS-Inverse Long/Short Equity Replication Index (Net)	-3.6	-0.023	0.197	-0.12	10.0	-0.9	-19.6*	-15.9*
CON-DB Alternative Return Fund	-28.2	-0.209	0.206	-1.01	9.5	-0.6	-14.4*	-10.1
DGAM-Enhanced Alternative Investments	7.9	0.048	0.053	0.91	2.4	0.5	12.0	32.2
GS-Aboslute Return Tracker Index	-6.2	-0.040	0.108	-0.37	9.5	-0.2	-5.2	-14.8*
ICE-Alternative Beta Fund	2.2	0.014	0.132	0.10	9.9	0.2	-1.0	-12.6*
IC-Salto Index	-11.3	-0.076	0.102	-0.74	7.9	-0.6	8.3	-11.0*
IC-Verso Index	11.5	0.068	0.100	0.68	6.7	0.4	14.3	-11.3*
JP-Alternative Beta Index	1.2	0.007	0.083	0.09	5.7	-0.3	-0.4	6.7
ML-Factor index	0.6	0.004	0.101	0.03	6.1	-0.1	4.5	1.3
SGI-Alternative Beta Index	-9.6	-0.063	0.139	-0.46	12.4	0.2	-39.9*	13.2*
DB-Absolute Return beta Index	-23.3	-0.167	0.206	-0.81	10.6	-0.4	-22.7*	-9.8
FLC-Alternative Beta Fund	9.8	0.059	0.070	0.84	2.6	0.5	10.8	21.7
IQ-Hedge Composite Beta Index	2.1	0.013	0.139	0.09	10.0	0.2	-2.6	-15.4*
RYD-Multi-Hedge Strategies Fund	-17.4	-0.120	0.152	-0.79	10.6	0.1	-11.9*	-11.3*
MS-altera Index	-3.4	-0.022	0.095	-0.23	40.5	0.9	2.0	-22.6*
PG-Alternative beta strategies Index	-9.3	-0.062	0.126	-0.49	9.0	-0.1	-11.5*	-3.5
AC-Statistical Value Market Neutral 7 Vol Fund	8.3	0.051	0.082	0.61	6.6	0.2	-6.0	-9.7
S & P 500	-20.6	-0.145	0.379	-0.38	6.5	-0.1	-14.2*	-13.5*
MSCI EAFE	-25.0	-0.182	0.330	-0.55	6.6	-0.2	9.9*	-11.3*
C.S/T Comp	-7.1	-0.004	0.030	-0.13	2.9	-0.8	62.2*	36.8
HFRI Fund Weighted Composite	-4.0	-0.002	0.031	-0.07	3.0	-0.6	60.3*	31.5
HFRI Fund of Funds Composite	-12.3	-0.007	0.027	-0.26	3.3	-1.0	60.7*	33.4
HFRX Equal Weighted Strategies	-14.8	-0.008	0.013	-0.66	14.9	-1.4	29.1	18.1

Note: ρ_1 and ρ_2 are the first- and second-order autocorrelation, where an asterisk indicates significance at the 95% level.

index are not necessarily the opposite of the long index.[8] Hence, correlation is a more appropriate metric to evaluate the short indices where these should have the opposite sign to their long counterpart. In this respect, judging from Table 8.3, both short indices seem to meet their goals.

Correlations of the products towards various asset classes, proxied by market and hedge fund indices, are presented in Table 8.3. Most products exhibit high correlation towards both the more traditional market indices as well as hedge fund indices. The clear exceptions are from Ice Capital, Fulcrum, and Aquila Capital, which all show low or negative correlation across all indices. High correlation towards hedge fund indices is, however, not necessarily desirable. Some replication products have absolute return targets, as most hedge funds, and these products should not be expected to have low or negative correlation towards hedge fund indices which have negative returns.

Figure 8.1 presents the cumulative returns of a selection of replication products as well as the S&P 500 and HFRI Fund Weighted Composite over the period March 2008–September 2009. The plot illustrates well the cross-sectional heterogeneity of replication products. The worst performing product is very close to the S&P 500. On the other hand, the best performing product in this figure has a distinctly different path from either the HFRI or S&P 500 index.

Given the small sample of products as well as the short sample period it is not possible to come to any conclusive judgment of whether any replication technique is preferable. It is equally difficult to see any performance pattern with respect to any of the replication techniques. Of the five best performing products, two use factor replication, two rule-based replication, and one distribution replication.

All replication products are to a large extent susceptible to model risk. That is, the risk that a trading model will not perform as expected live, under real market conditions, as compared to backtested data. Wallerstein, Tuchschmid and Zaker (2009) tested statistical differences in return time-series of six replication products before and after inception and found no statistical patterns which indicate model risk.

Having a large well-known firm (and all their resources) behind a replication product does not seem to push the performance in any certain direction. For instance, Deutsche Bank's product has the second worst annualized return while JP Morgan's has the sixth best performance. All the top five products, ranked by return and disregarding shortable products, were developed by niched asset management firms. Again, the limited sample needs to be taken into consideration and more thorough analysis of firm characteristics and performance will require more observations.

[8] Consider an index which has the following monthly returns $r = \{-20\%, 25\%\}$. The total return of the index is 0%, while a short index mirroring these returns on a monthly basis will have a total return of −10%.

Table 8.3 Linear correlation of replication products and some market indices over the period March 2008 to September 2009.

	SP500	RSL2000	EAFE	CMDTY	BOND	C.S/T.	HFRI	HFRI FoF	HFRX
BC-Long Barclays Alternatives Replicator Index	73	66	76	72	72	87	94	87	51
CS-Long/Short Equity Replication Index (Net)	75	64	43	38	38	81	85	80	40
CS-Inverse Long/Short Equity Replication Index (Net)	−75	−64	−43	−39	−39	−81	−85	−80	−39
CON-DB Alternative Return Fund	72	59	58	45	45	81	85	83	44
DGAM-Enhanced Alternative Investments	67	58	74	72	72	65	75	66	56
GS-Aboslute Return Tracker Index	51	41	85	65	65	73	83	73	44
ICE-Alternative Beta Fund	7	9	8	15	15	29	28	24	5
IC-Salto Index	79	72	80	68	68	83	88	83	54
IC-Verso Index	−78	−71	−81	−67	−67	−84	−89	−83	−55
JP-Alternative Beta Index	1	−3	60	38	38	85	89	81	42
ML-Factor index	35	30	88	48	48	80	91	77	49
SGI-Alternative Beta Index	59	53	43	36	36	80	88	80	28
DB-Absolute Return beta Index	75	63	56	42	42	79	83	80	45
FLC-Alternative Beta Fund	11	10	20	42	42	27	22	31	26
IQ-Hedge Composite Beta Index	79	67	70	58	58	75	85	73	55
RYD-Multi-Hedge Strategies Fund	92	84	52	44	44	71	77	69	48
MS-altera Index	54	50	59	39	39	80	86	82	48
PG-Alternative beta strategies Index	82	75	49	35	35	75	81	72	51
AC-Statistical Value Market Neutral 7 Vol Fund	−1	−3	−5	−10	−10	−14	−8	−11	−3
S & P 500	100	94	48	37	37	71	82	68	33
MSCI EAFE	48	39	100	56	56	79	89	76	52
C.S/Tremont Composite	71	65	79	84	84	100	96	97	92
HFRI Fund Weighted Composite	82	74	89	84	84	96	100	96	90
HFRI Fund of Funds Composite	68	59	76	83	83	97	96	100	94
HFRX Equal Weighted Strategies	33	25	52	40	40	92	90	94	100

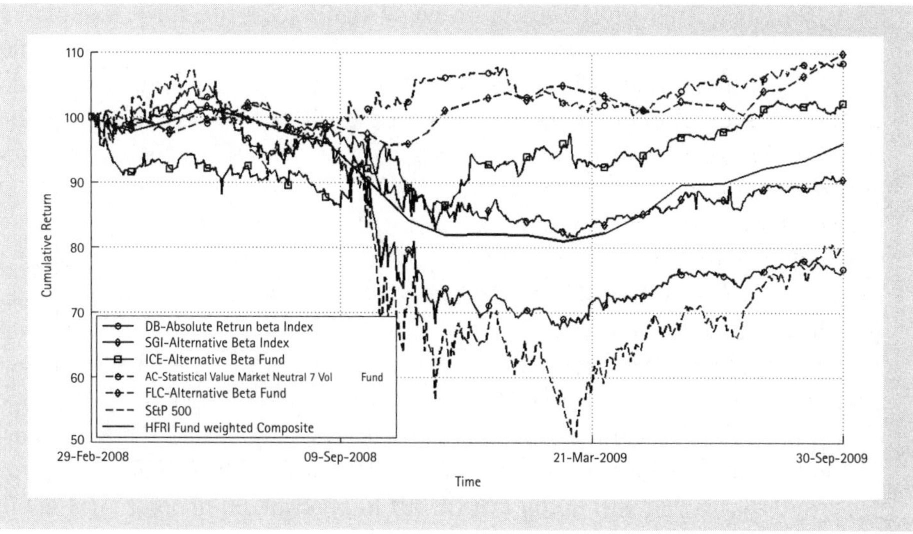

FIGURE 8.1 Cumulative returns of five replication products, S&P 500, and HFRI Composite Index.

8.2.2 Selection Risk

The cross-sectional heterogeneity in the performance of replication products is problematic for investors since it raises concerns for selection risk. That is, difficulties in selecting which products to invest in among an asset class. The risk-return scatter plot of the products in Figure 8.2 highlights selection risk. The figure plots each product in Table 8.1 according to its S.D., along the x-axis, and the mean along the y-axis. This picture illustrates well the large dispersion of both mean and S.D. Furthermore, the data points reveal a downward sloping risk-return slope which can be explained by the general negative performance of financial assets over the sample period. Again, caution should be observed on the interpretation given the small number of data points and the sample period.

Table 8.4 presents the performance of the replication products (short versions excluded) over two disjoint sample periods: March 2008 to March 2009 and April 2009 to September 2009. This gives some insight into the time-varying performance of replication products and the selection risk. The sample periods are divided to represent bear and bull market environments. Again, the performance over both sample periods is heterogeneous. In the first period continuously compounded annualized mean returns vary between −38.7% and 3.1% and the S.D. between 4.0% and 24.0%. In the second periods the mean varies between 5.2% and 31.1% and S.D. varies between 4.3% and 10.4%.

The Ranking column in each Period panel presents the relative ranking with respect to mean returns of the replication products. This league table is significantly altered over

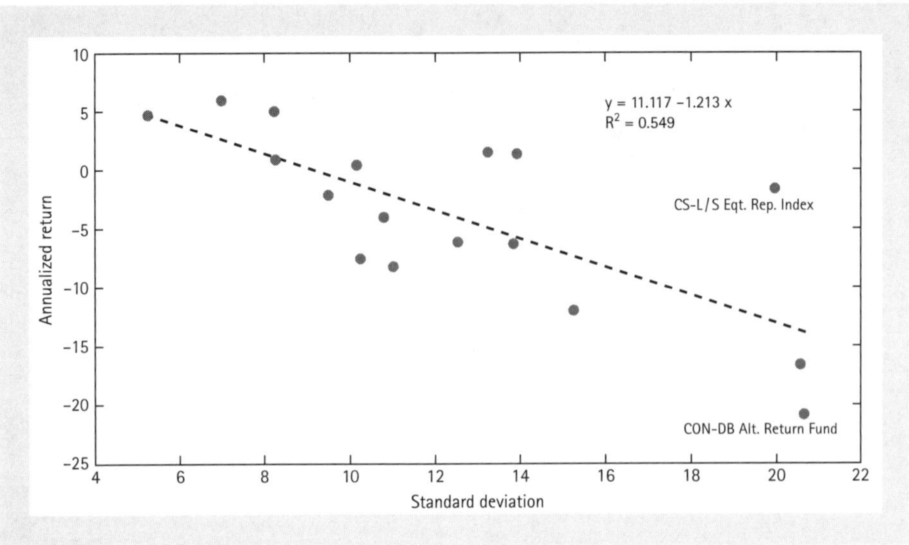

FIGURE 8.2 Scatter plot of the risk (S.D.) and annualized return (Mean) of replication products from Table 8.1.

the two periods. For instance, Fulcrum and Aquila Capital's products have the best and second best mean performance over Period 1 but the second worst and worst performance over Period 2, respectively. Index IQ's product has the best mean performance in Period 2 while only ranking 9 in Period 1. Given the different market environments in the two periods and the underlying strategies of the products these rankings are not too surprising. Aquila Capital's product aims for low correlation towards market indices which paid off well during the bear market of Period 1 but less so during the bull market of Period 2. Barclays's is a factor based product and is likely to be exposed to general asset classes. This is reflected in negative returns (−20.1%) in the bear market period and postive (17.7%) in the bull market period. Yet, too much should not be read into the ranking in Table 8.4 for two reasons. Firstly, the short sample period. Secondly, some products, like Credit Suisse's, target a specific index, rather than to have the overall best performance. It does, however, raise warning signs if past success is to forecast good future performance.

Can the underlying methods of replication perhaps guide investors on the selection of replication products? The replication methodologies differ significantly on a theoretical level. However, the implications of methodologies on performance are more subtle. Factor analysis is not likely to be able to capture strategies with idiosyncratic return patterns or based on illiquid assets. Rule-based replication adds some dimensions to the management of the replication portfolio, which are the sizing of positions, level of leverage, and complex risk management. This consequently demands seasoned professionals to manage a rule-base replication product. Finally, distribution replication is likely to be the most demanding technique. While it may be an excellent method to capture

Table 8.4 Performance statistics of replication products over the two following sample periods: March 2008 to March 2009 and April 2009 to September 2009.

	Period 1				Period 2			
	Mean	S.D.	Sharpe	Ranking	Mean	S.D.	Sharpe	Ranking
BC-Long Barclays Alternatives Replicator Index	−0.201	0.121	−1.67	15	0.177	0.081	2.18	7
CS-Long/Short Equity Replication Index	−0.084	0.236	−0.36	5	0.131	0.073	1.81	14
CON-DB Alternative Return Fund	−0.387	0.239	−1.62	17	0.180	0.098	1.84	6
DGAM-Enhanced Alternative Investments	−0.014	0.040	−0.35	3	0.181	0.060	3.00	5
GS-Aboslute Return Tracker Index	−0.136	0.124	−1.10	10	0.168	0.060	2.80	8
ICE-Alternative Beta Fund	−0.071	0.153	−0.46	4	0.198	0.065	3.07	4
IC-Salto Index	−0.176	0.116	−1.51	13	0.144	0.060	2.39	12
JP-Alternative Beta Index	−0.094	0.092	−1.02	6	0.230	0.053	4.30	3
ML-Factor index	−0.114	0.111	−1.02	8	0.259	0.074	3.50	2
SGI-Alternative Beta Index	−0.163	0.152	−1.08	12	0.155	0.104	1.49	10
DB-Absolute Return beta Index	−0.314	0.240	−1.31	16	0.152	0.095	1.60	11
FLC-Alternative Beta Fund	0.031	0.068	0.45	1	0.121	0.075	1.61	15
IQ-Hedge Composite Beta Index	−0.124	0.158	−0.78	9	0.311	0.080	3.87	1
RYD-Multi-Hedge Strategies Fund	−0.199	0.182	−1.10	14	0.052	0.043	1.21	17
MS-altera Index	−0.104	0.110	−0.95	7	0.158	0.045	3.52	9
PG-Alternative beta strategies Index	−0.151	0.149	−1.01	11	0.133	0.036	3.71	13
AC-Statistical Value Market Neutral 7 Vol Fund	0.024	0.092	0.26	2	0.109	0.056	1.94	16

Notes: All performance measures are annualized. The Ranking column gives the relative ranking of the Mean performance over the sample period.

correlation, variance, skewness, or other higher moment distributional properties, it is more troublesome to replicate the returns.

8.3 Conclusion

Academic research supports a sound foundation for the rationale of hedge fund replication. How large a role it will play in the industry is yet to be seen and is of course closely linked to the performance of hedge fund replication products themselves. The performance of the replication products analyzed in this chapter is mixed with large cross-sectional differences in returns and volatility. However, some products do deliver competitive hedge fund like returns. This is a strong indicator that some risk premiums earned by hedge funds are realizable at a lower cost.

The benefit of replication products is, however, not only related to their risk-return performance. They can provide valuable liquidity in contrast to the illiquidity inherent with hedge fund vehicles. Going forward, however, the lack of liquidity risk may prove to be costly on returns. Another valuable feature is the ability to hedge hedge fund exposure through shortable replication products, when redemption is not possible.

Yet, there seems to be a significant level of selection risk in choosing a good replication product. This implies high due diligence costs for investors, and it is also reminiscent of actual hedge fund investments.

Investors should also question the promise of better transparency in replication products. The trend seems to be that replication models are becoming increasingly complex and there is necessarily a need to also understand why models allocate to certain assets. The distribution approach is a case in point. While Aquila performed well over the sample period it is not in our view straightforward to understand under which market conditions this method will deliver its best returns, especially given the low target correlation with equity markets.

As a final remark, the short sample period and number of available replication products have been taken into consideration for these conclusions. The hedge fund replication industry is at the time of writing still an industry in its infancy.

References

Becker, T. (2003). Exploring the mathematical basis of return-based style analysis. In *Handbook of Equity Style Management* (ed. T.D. Coggin and F.J. Fabozzi). John Wiley & Sons, New York.

Berger, A.L., Kabiller, D., and Crowell, B. (2008). Is alpha just beta waiting to be discovered? *White paper, AQR Capital Management, LLC.*

Black, F. and Scholes, M. (1973). The pricing of options and corporate liabilities. *The Journal of Political Economy*, **81**(3), 637–654.

Chui, C.K. and Chen, G. (2008). *Kalman Filtering: with Real-Time Applications* (4 edn). Springer Verlag, Berlin.

Doucet, A., de Freitas, N., and Gordon, N. (2001). *Sequential Monte Carlo Methods in Practice*. Springer Verlag, Berlin.

Durate, J., Longstaff, F.A., and Yu, F. (2007). Risk and return in fixed-income arbitrage: Nickels in front of a steamroller. *The Review of Financial Studies*, **20**(3), 769–811.

Ennis, R.M. and Sebastian, M.D. (2003). A critical look at the case for hedge funds. *The Journal of Portfolio Management*, **29**(4), 103–112.

Fung, W. and Hsieh, D.A. (1997). Empirical characteristics of dynamic trading strategies: The case of hedge funds. *Review of Financial Studies*, **10**(2), 275–302.

Fung, W. and Hsieh, D.A. (2004). Hedge fund benchmarks: A risk-based approach. *Financial Analysts Journal*, **60**, 65–80.

Fung, W. and Hsieh, D.A. (2007). Will hedge funds regress towards index-like products? *Journal of Investment Management*, **5**(2), 46–65.

Fung, W., Hsieh, D.A., Naik, N.Y., and Ramadorai, T. (2008). Hedge funds: Performance, risk and capital formation. *Journal of Finance*, **63**(4), 1777–1803.

Hasanhodzic, J. and Lo, A.W. (2007). Can hedge-fund returns be replicated? The linear case. *Journal of Investment Management*, **5**(2), 5–45.

Jaeger, L. and Wagner, C. (2005). Factor modeling and benchmarking of hedge funds: Can passive investments in hedge fund strategies deliver? *The Journal of Alternative Investments*, **8**(3), 9–36.

Kat, H.M. and Palaro, H.P. (2005). Who needs hedge funds? A copula-based approach to hedge fund return replication. *Alternative Investment Research Centre Working Paper # 0024*.

Kat, H.M. and Palaro, H.P. (2006a). Replication and evaluation of fund of hedge funds returns. *Alternative Investment Research Centre Working Paper # 0028*.

Kat, H.M. and Palaro, H.P. (2006b). Superstars or avarage joes? A replication-based performance evaluation of 1917 individual hedge funds. *Alternative Investment Research Centre Working Paper # 0030*.

Lo, A.W. (2002). The statistics of sharpe ratios. *Financial Analysts Journal*, **58**(4), 36–52.

Merton, R.C. (1973). Theory of rational option pricing. *The Bell Journal of Economics and Management Science*, **4**(1), 141–183.

Mitchell, M.L. and Pulvino, T.C. (2001). Characteristics of risk and return in risk arbitrage. *Journal of Finance*, **56**(6), 2135–2175.

Papageorgiou, N., Remillard, B., and Hocquard, A. (2008). Replicating the properties of hedge fund returns. *The Journal of Alternative Investments*, **11**(2), 11–38.

Sharpe, W.F. (1992). Asset allocation: Management style and performance measurement. *Journal of Portfolio Management*, **18**(2), 7–19.

Takahashi, A. and Yamamoto, K. (2009). Generating a target payoff distribution with the cheapest dynamic portfolio: An application to hedge fund replication. *Working Paper*.

ter Horst, J.R., Nijman, T.E., and de Roon, F.A. (2004). Evaluating style analysis. *Journal of Empirical Finance*, **11**(1), 29–53.

Wallerstein, E., Tuchschmid, N., and Zaker, S. (2009). How do hedge fund clones manage the real world? *Journal of Alternative Investments*, **12**(3), 37–50.

PART III

INVESTMENT MANAGEMENT BEHAVIOR

CHAPTER 9

DECENTRALIZED DECISION MAKING IN INVESTMENT MANAGEMENT*

JULES H. VAN BINSBERGEN, MICHAEL W. BRANDT, AND RALPH S.J. KOIJEN

9.1 Introduction

The investment management division of pension funds is typically structured around traditional asset classes such as equities, fixed income, and alternative investments. For each of these asset classes, the fund employs asset managers who use their skills to outperform passive benchmarks. The Chief Investment Officer (CIO) subsequently allocates the fund's capital to the various asset classes, taking into account the liabilities that the fund has to meet. As a consequence, asset allocation decisions are made in at least two stages. In the first stage, the CIO allocates capital to the different asset classes, each managed by a different asset manager. In the second stage, each manager decides how to allocate the funds made available to him, that is, to the assets within his class. This two-stage process can generate several misalignments of incentives between the CIO and his managers, which can have a substantial effect on the fund's performance. Alternatively, the CIO could restrict attention to passive benchmarks and ignore active management altogether. The CIO of the fund therefore faces a tradeoff between the benefits of decentralization, driven by the market timing and stock selection skills of the managers, and the costs of delegation and decentralization. In this chapter, we first

* We thank Keith Ambachtsheer, Rob Bauer, Lans Bovenberg, Ned Elton, Marty Gruber, Niels Kortleve, and Theo Nijman for useful discussions and suggestions. This project has been sponsored by the International Center for Pension Fund Management (ICPM) at the Rotman School.

quantify this tradeoff by computing the level of managerial skill, as measured by the information ratio, that each manager needs to have to offset the costs of decentralized asset management. We assume in this case that managers are compensated on the basis of their performance relative to a cash benchmark. Next, we show how optimally designed benchmarks for the managers can help to reduce the costs of decentralization, while still allowing the managers to capitalize on their informational advantage. These benchmarks reflect the risk in the fund's liabilities, leading to an integrated framework to develop liabilities-driven investment (LDI) strategies.

Decentralization of investment decisions leads to the following important, if not exhaustive, list of misalignments. First, in the case of a defined-benefits plan, the fund has to meet certain liabilities. The risks in these liabilities affect the optimal portfolio choice of the CIO. By compensating managers using cash benchmarks, they have no incentive to hedge the risks in the liabilities. This increases the mismatch risk between the fund's assets and liabilities. Second, the two-stage process can lead to severe diversification losses. The unconstrained (single-step) solution to the mean-variance optimization problem is likely different from the optimal linear combination of mean-variance efficient portfolios in each asset class.[1] Third, there may be considerable, but unobservable, differences in appetites for risk between the CIO and each of the asset managers. When the CIO only knows the cross-sectional distribution of risk appetites of investment managers but not where in this distribution a given manager falls, delegating portfolio decisions to multiple managers can be very costly. We use a stylized representation of a pension plan to quantify the tradeoff between these costs and the benefits of decentralization. We assume that the CIO acts in the best interest of the pension holders, whereas the investment managers only wish to maximize their personal compensation.

This chapter is central to the debate on LDI strategies. So far, the main focus has been to determine the strategic allocation to the various asset classes, taking into account the risks in the liabilities.[2] In particular, most pension funds face specific risk factors that cannot be hedged perfectly using the strategic allocation. One can think of inflation risk in countries in which inflation-linked bonds are not traded, illiquidly traded, or tied to a different price index than that used to index the liabilities: for instance in most European countries in which the liabilities adjust to wage inflation, whereas inflation-linked bonds are tied to price inflation. We show however that benchmarks can be very effective in minimizing mismatch risk. The benchmarks that we design reflect the risks in the liabilities. This introduces implicitly an incentive for each asset manager to search for a hedge portfolio using the assets in his class. With this portfolio, the CIO can use the strategic allocation to the different asset classes to efficiently manage mismatch risk.

The optimal benchmarks that we derive look dramatically different from cash benchmarks. Cash benchmarks have been popularized recently in response to the observed risk attitudes of asset managers. As it turns out, asset managers tend to hold portfolios that are close to their benchmark. This "benchmark-hugging" behavior is potentially

[1] See Sharpe (1981) and Elton and Gruber (2004).

[2] See e.g. Binsbergen and Brandt (2006); Hoevenaars, Molenaar, Schotman; Steenkamp (2008).

costly to the CIO because the manager does not fully exploit the informational advantage he may have. Indeed, the average risk aversion coefficient that we estimate is much higher than one would expect from standard economic theory. We show however that cash benchmarks are a sub-optimal response to such behavior of asset managers. Our benchmarks explicitly take a position in the active portfolio that the manager holds. This in turn motivates the manager to deviate from the passive benchmarks and to allocate more of its capital to the active strategy, which forms the motivation to hire the manager to begin with. Clearly, by introducing such benchmarks, it could be the case that some managers take on too much active risk. We therefore introduce tracking error constraints to rule out investment strategies that are too aggressive from the fund's perspective. We therefore show how to solve for the strategic allocation, performance benchmarks, and risk constraints for pension funds.

This chapter is extends Binsbergen, Brandt and Koijen (2008), where we argue that decentralization has a first-order effect on the performance of investment management firms. Using two asset classes (bonds and stocks) and three assets per class (government bonds, Baa-rated corporate bonds, and Aaa-rated corporate bonds in the fixed income class, and growth stocks, intermediate, and value stocks in the equities class) the utility costs can range from 50 to 300 basis points per year. We further demonstrate that when the investment opportunity set is constant and risk attitudes are observable, the CIO can fully align incentives through an unconditional benchmark consisting only of assets in each manager's asset class. In other words, cross-benchmarking is not required. When relaxing the assumption that the CIO knows the asset managers' risk appetite, by assuming that the CIO only knows the cross-sectional distribution of investment managers' risk aversion levels but does not know where in this distribution a given manager falls, we find that the qualitative results on the benefits of optimal benchmarking derived for a known risk aversion level apply to this more general case. In fact, we find that uncertainty about the managers' risk appetites increases both the costs of decentralized investment management and the value of an optimally designed benchmark.

The main difference between our chapter and Binsbergen, Brandt and Koijen (2008) is that we focus on pension plans by including liabilities as an additional potential misalignment between the CIO and the asset managers. Furthermore, in Binsbergen, Brandt and Koijen (2008) the only way that managers can add value is by their market timing skills. In this chapter we consider the case where the managers have stock selection skills. As such we can derive the minimum information ratio the managers need to have to overcome the costs of decentralization. Quantifying this tradeoff can help pension plans in designing the organizational structure of their plan as well as in the hiring decisions of their investment managers. Finally, in this chapter, we estimate the empirical cross-sectional distribution of risk preferences using a manager-level database following Koijen (2008). In Binsbergen, Brandt and Koijen (2008) we have not estimated the distribution, but instead have assumed that this distribution is a truncated normal distribution.

Using this model, we find that managers need to be very skilled to justify decentralized investment management. The information ratio that each manager needs to have is between 0.40 and 1.30, depending on the risk attitude of the pension fund. Such information ratios exceed the Sharpe ratio on the aggregate stock market and are rarely observed for fund managers over longer periods after accounting for management fees. We therefore show that one needs to have rather strong prior beliefs on the benefits of active management to decentralize asset management.

In practice, the performance of each asset manager is measured against a benchmark comprised of a large number of assets within his class. In the literature, the main purpose of these benchmarks has been to disentangle the effort and achievements of the asset manager from the investment opportunity set available to him. In this chapter we show that an optimally designed unconditional benchmark can also serve to improve the alignment of incentives within the firm and to substantially mitigate the utility costs of decentralized investment management. By lowering the costs of decentralization, the information ratio required to justify a decentralized organizational structure will decrease.

Our results provide a different perspective on the use of performance benchmarks. Admati and Pfleiderer (1997) take a realistic benchmark as given and show that when an investment manager uses the conditional return distribution in his investment decisions, restricting him by an unconditional benchmark distorts incentives.[3] In their framework, this distortion can only be prevented by setting the benchmark equal to the minimum-variance portfolio. That is, if managers can hold cash positions, cash benchmarks would be optimal. We show that the negative aspect of unconditional benchmarks can be offset, at least in part, by the role of unconditional benchmarks in aligning other incentives, such as liabilities, diversification, and risk preferences.

The negative impact of decentralized investment management on diversification was first noted by Sharpe (1981), who shows that if the CIO has rational expectations about the portfolio choices of the investment managers, he can choose his investment weights such that diversification is at least partially restored. However, this optimal linear combination of mean-variance efficient portfolios within each asset class usually still differs from the optimally diversified portfolio over all assets. To restore diversification further, Sharpe (1981) suggests that the CIO impose investment rules on one or both of the investment managers to solve an optimization problem that includes the covariances between assets in different asset classes. Elton and Gruber (2004) show that it is possible to overcome the loss of diversification by providing the asset managers with investment rules that they are required to implement. The asset managers can then implement the CIO's optimal strategy without giving up their private information.

Both investment rules described above interfere with the asset manager's desire to maximize his individual performance, on which his compensation depends. Furthermore, when the investment choices of the managers are not always fully observable, these *ad hoc* rules are not enforceable. In contrast, we propose to change managers' incentives by introducing a return benchmark against which the managers are evaluated for the purpose of their compensation. When this benchmark is implemented in the

[3] See also Basak, Shapiro, and Teplá (2006).

right way, it is in the managers' own interest to follow investment strategies that are (more) in line with the objectives of the CIO.

9.2 THEORETICAL FRAMEWORK

9.2.1 The Model

Before presenting our model, we first need to specify (i) the financial market the managers can invest in, (ii) the evolution of the liabilities of the plan, and (iii) the preferences of both the CIO and his managers.

Financial market The financial market is as in Black–Scholes–Merton in which we have $2 \times k$ assets with dynamics:

$$\frac{\mathrm{d}S_{it}}{S_{it}} = \left(r + \sigma_i'\Lambda\right) \mathrm{d}t + \sigma_i'\mathrm{d}Z_t,$$

and a cash account earning a constant interest rate r:

$$\frac{\mathrm{d}S_{0t}}{S_{0t}} = r\mathrm{d}t.$$

Z_t is a $(2k+3)$-dimensional standard Brownian motion. Define $\Sigma_C \equiv (\sigma_1, \ldots, \sigma_{2k})'$ and, without loss of generality, we assume it is lower triangular.

We consider a model with two asset classes each consisting of k (different) assets. The CIO employs two managers to manage each of the k assets. The managers may have stock picking ability, which may be a motivation for hiring them to begin with. To capture this, we endow each manager with a different idiosyncratic technology:

$$\frac{\mathrm{d}S_{it}^A}{S_{it}^A} = \left(r + \sigma_i^{A\prime}\Lambda\right) \mathrm{d}t + \sigma_i^{A\prime}\mathrm{d}Z_t,$$

in which only $\sigma_{1(2k+1)}^A$ and $\sigma_{2(2k+2)}^A$ are non-zero. The corresponding prices of risk in Λ, denoted by λ_{A1} and λ_{A2}, are referred to as prices of active risk. It is a measure of stock picking ability in dynamic models (Nielsen and Vassalou 2005; and Koijen 2008). Also, define Λ_C as the vector of prices of risk in which λ_{A1} and λ_{A2} are zero. This would be the vector of prices of risk that the CIO would use if he were to form the portfolio himself. Finally, define the full volatility matrix as $\Sigma \equiv \left(\Sigma_C', \sigma_1^A, \sigma_2^A\right)'$.

Liabilities We consider a rather flexible model for the fund's liabilities, L_t:

$$\frac{\mathrm{d}L_t}{L_t} = \mu_L \mathrm{d}t + \sigma_L'\mathrm{d}Z_t,$$

in which the last Brownian motion, $Z_{2k+3,t}$, is assumed to capture idiosyncratic risk that is present in the liabilities, like mortality risk or unspanned inflation risk.

Preferences of the CIO Denote the fund's assets at time t by A_t and define the funding ratio as the ratio of assets and liabilities:

$$F_t = \frac{A_t}{L_t}.$$

The funding ratio is the central state variable for most pension funds. For that reason, the CIO's preferences depend on the future funding ratio. We assume that the CIO has power utility over the funding ratio of the fund:

$$E_t\left(\frac{1}{1-\gamma_C}F_T^{1-\gamma_C}\right),$$

in which γ_C denotes the CIO's risk aversion. Because we abstract from the potential agency problems between the beneficiaries of the fund and the CIO of the fund, one could think of γ_C as the risk preferences of the fund's beneficiaries.

Preferences of the asset managers The asset managers of the various asset classes have no incentive to account for the fund's liabilities. Typically, asset managers are compensated relative to a cash benchmark or some conventional benchmark like the S&P500 for large-cap stocks. We assume that the manager's preferences reflect their benchmark in a similar way as the CIO's preferences reflect the fund's liabilities:

$$E_t\left(\frac{1}{1-\gamma_i}\left(\frac{A_{iT}}{B_{iT}}\right)^{1-\gamma_i}\right),$$

in which A_{it} denotes the assets available to manager i, B_{it} the value of the benchmark of manager i, and γ_i his coefficient of relative risk aversion. We assume that the benchmark satisfies the dynamics:

$$\frac{\mathrm{d}B_{it}}{B_{it}} = (r + \beta_i\Sigma_i\Lambda)\,\mathrm{d}t + \beta_i\Sigma_i\mathrm{d}Z_t,$$

where we have the standard restrictions on the benchmark (no cross-benchmarking and no cash). In addition, the managers are assumed to be myopic.

9.2.2 Centralized Problem

If the CIO invests in all the assets himself, henceforth called the centralized investment problem, the optimal strategy of the CIO reads:

$$x_C = \frac{1}{\gamma_C}\left(\Sigma_C\Sigma_C'\right)^{-1}\Sigma_C\Lambda_C + \left(1-\frac{1}{\gamma_C}\right)\left(\Sigma_C\Sigma_C'\right)^{-1}\Sigma_C\sigma_L,$$

which implies that for $\gamma_C = 1$, the CIO ignores the risk in the liabilities. If, by contrast, $\gamma_C \longrightarrow \infty$, the CIO simply implements the liabilities-hedging strategy. The value function corresponding to the optimal strategy is given in the appendix. Note that the CIO has no access to the idiosyncratic technologies and uses Λ_C in his portfolio choice as a result.

9.2.3 Decentralized Problem with Cash Benchmarks

In this section, we study the impact of cash benchmarks, which in effect means that managers care about absolute returns rather than relative returns. Despite the fact that these benchmarks do not satisfy the restrictions we impose on the optimal benchmarks we derive in the next section, it provides an important point of reference. After all, there has been a recent trend towards cash benchmarks in several pension funds. We study the implications of choosing cash benchmarks, accounting for the organizational structure of pension funds. If the managers are compared to the cash account, they act as asset-only managers.

The first asset manager has the mandate to decide on the first k assets and the second asset manager manages the remaining k assets. Neither of the asset managers has access to a cash account. If they did, they could hold highly leveraged positions or large cash balances, which is undesirable from the CIO's perspective.[4] The CIO allocates capital to the two asset managers and invests the remainder, if any, in the cash account.

The optimal strategy of manager i is given by:

$$x_i^{Cash} = \frac{1}{\gamma_i} x_i + \left(1 - \frac{x_i' \iota}{\gamma_i}\right) x_i^{MV},$$

in which:

$$x_i = \left(\Sigma_i \Sigma_i'\right)^{-1} \Sigma_i \Lambda,$$

$$x_i^{MV} = \frac{\left(\Sigma_i \Sigma_i'\right)^{-1} \iota}{\iota' \left(\Sigma_i \Sigma_i'\right)^{-1} \iota}.$$

The optimal portfolio of the asset managers can be decomposed into two components. The first component, x_i, is the standard myopic demand that optimally exploits the risk-return trade-off. The second component, x_i^{MV}, minimizes the instantaneous return variance and is therefore labeled the minimum-variance portfolio. The minimum variance portfolio substitutes for the riskless asset in the optimal portfolio of the asset manager. The two components are then weighted by the risk attitude of the asset manager to arrive at the optimal portfolio.

[4] A similar cash constraint has been imposed in investment problems with a CIO and a single investment manager (e.g., Brennan 1993; Gómez and Zapatero 2003).

Provided with these optimal strategies, the CIO needs to decide upon the optimal allocation to the two asset classes. This problem is as before, but now with a reduced asset space. Define:

$$\bar{\Sigma} \equiv \begin{bmatrix} x_1^{Cash\prime} \Sigma_1 \\ x_2^{Cash\prime} \Sigma_2 \end{bmatrix}.$$

The optimal strategic allocation now reads:

$$x_C^{Cash} = \frac{1}{\gamma_C} \left(\bar{\Sigma}\bar{\Sigma}'\right)^{-1} \bar{\Sigma}\Lambda + \left(1 - \frac{1}{\gamma_C}\right) \left(\bar{\Sigma}\bar{\Sigma}'\right)^{-1} \bar{\Sigma}\sigma_L.$$

It is important to note that decentralization is harmful along at least two dimensions. First, the risk-return trade-off available to the CIO deteriorates, which is captured by the term $\frac{1}{\gamma_C} \left(\bar{\Sigma}\bar{\Sigma}'\right)^{-1} \bar{\Sigma}\Lambda$. However, the second effect, which is not present in Binsbergen *et al.* (2008), is purely due to risk in the liabilities. Decentralization reduces the possibilities to hedge the risk in the liabilities, which is captured by the term $\left(1 - \frac{1}{\gamma_C}\right) \left(\bar{\Sigma}\bar{\Sigma}'\right)^{-1} \bar{\Sigma}\sigma_L$. This suggests that we want to give the managers an incentive to account for the risks in the liabilities. Also note that we now use the price of risk Λ that exploits the skills managers potentially have. We solve this problem in the next section.

Finally, we note that the same optimal strategy arises when the CIO give the minimum variance portfolio in the respective asset classes as the benchmark.

9.2.4 Decentralized Problem with Optimal Benchmarks

We now consider the decentralized investment problem in which the CIO designs a performance benchmark for each of the investment managers in an attempt to align incentives. We restrict attention to benchmarks in the form of portfolios that can be replicated by the asset managers. This restriction implies that only the assets of the particular asset class are used and that the benchmark contains no cash position. There is no possibility and, as we show later, no need for cross-benchmarking. We derive optimal benchmarks (β_1 and β_2) as well as the CIO's optimal allocation to the two managers. As before, we first derive the optimal strategy of the managers. The optimal policy for manager i is given by:

$$x_i^B = \frac{1}{\gamma_i} x_i + \left(1 - \frac{1}{\gamma_i}\right) \beta_i + \frac{1}{\gamma_i} \left(1 - x_i'\iota\right) x_i^{MV}.$$

The optimal benchmarks subsequently read:

$$\beta_i = x_i^{MV} + \frac{\gamma_i}{\gamma_i - 1} \left(\frac{\tilde{x}_i^C}{\tilde{x}_i^{C\prime}\iota} - x_i^{Cash} \right)$$

and the optimal strategic allocation to the different asset classes is given by $\tilde{x}_i^{C\prime}\iota$. It is important to note that this solution implements the **first-best solution** as if asset management is centralized and the CIO has access to the idiosyncratic technology as well:

$$\tilde{x}_C = \frac{1}{\gamma_C}\left(\Sigma\Sigma'\right)^{-1}\Sigma\Lambda + \left(1 - \frac{1}{\gamma_C}\right)\left(\Sigma\Sigma'\right)^{-1}\Sigma\sigma_L.$$

Because x^C reflects the risk in the liabilities, the benchmarks will inherit this adjustment. To gain some further intuition, consider the case in which the CIO and the manager are very conservative, that is, $\gamma_i \longrightarrow \infty$ and $\gamma_C \longrightarrow \infty$. In this case, we have:

$$\tilde{x}_C = \left(\Sigma\Sigma'\right)^{-1}\Sigma\sigma_L,$$

which is the liabilities-hedging portfolio. The optimal benchmark now reads:

$$\beta_i = \frac{\tilde{x}_i^C}{\tilde{x}_i^{C\prime}\iota},$$

which is the normalized liabilities hedging portfolio, which is exactly what the manager will implement. This result shows that managers now have the incentive to explore within their respective asset classes which portfolio is the best hedge against liabilities risk.

9.3 Practical Implementation

In this section we discuss how to implement our methodology in practice. To bring the model to the data we need to estimate (i) the return dynamics of the different asset classes and (ii) the risk preferences of asset managers. It seems realistic that the CIO is not able to elicit the coefficient of relative risk aversion from the managers directly. We consider the more realistic case in which the CIO has a view on the distribution of risk preferences, but does not know where in this distribution a particular manager falls. We present here how to estimate this distribution from data on actively-managed, U.S. equity mutual funds.

9.3.1 Estimation Return Dynamics

We follow Binsbergen *et al.* (2008) and consider the case with two asset classes, equities and fixed income, and three assets per class. The estimates for the return dynamics are displayed in Table 9.1.

Panel A shows estimates of the parameters Λ and Σ. Panel B shows the implied instantaneous expected return and correlations between the assets. In the fixed income

Table 9.1 Constant investment opportunities.

Panel A: Model parameters

Source of risk	Z_1	Z_2	Z_3	Z_4	Z_5	Z_6
Λ	0.331	0.419	-0.0291	0.126	0.477	0.305
Σ						
Gov. bonds	13.5%	0	0	0	0	0
Corp. bonds, Baa	8.2%	5.6%	0	0	0	0
Corp. bonds, Aaa	9.1%	2.7%	2.4%	0	0	0
Growth stocks	3.7%	6.3%	0.3%	16.5%	0	0
Int. stocks	3.6%	6.8%	0.3%	11.7%	7.3%	0
Value stocks	3.6%	7.7%	0.1%	10.4%	6.8%	5.9%

Panel B: Implied parameters

	Expected return	Correlation					
Gov. bonds	9.5%	100%	82%	93%	20%	23%	22%
Corp. bonds, Baa	10.1%	82%	100%	92%	37%	43%	45%
Corp. bonds, Aaa	9.1%	93%	92%	100%	29%	34%	34%
Growth stocks	10.9%	20%	37%	29%	100%	88%	80%
Int. stocks	14.0%	23%	43%	34%	88%	100%	93%
Value stocks	15.7%	22%	45%	34%	80%	93%	100%

Notes: This table gives the estimation results of the financial market in Section 9.1 over the period January 1973 through November 2004 using monthly data. The model is estimated by maximum likelihood. The asset set contains government bonds ("Gov. bonds"), corporate bonds with credit ratings Baa ("Corp. bonds, Baa") and Aaa ("Corp. bonds, Aaa"), and three equity portfolios ranked on their book-to-market ratio (growth/intermediate ("Int.")/value). Panel A provides the model parameters and Panel B portrays the implied instantaneous expected returns ($r + \Sigma\Lambda$) and correlations. In determining Λ, we assume that the instantaneous nominal short rate equals $r = 5\%$.

asset class, we find an expected return spread of 1% between corporate bonds with a Baa versus Aaa rating. In the equities asset class, we estimate a high value premium of 4.8%. The correlations within asset classes are high, between 80% and 90%. Furthermore, there is clear dependence between asset classes, which, as we show more formally later, implies that the two-stage investment process leads to inefficiencies.

9.3.2 Estimating Distribution of Risk Aversion

To bring the model to the data, we need to take a stance on the risk preferences of the managers. We not only consider the case in which the CIO knows the risk appetites of the managers but also the case where the CIO only knows the cross-sectional distribution of risk preferences, but does not know where in this distribution a particular manager falls. In this section, we estimate this cross-sectional distribution of risk preferences using mutual fund data.

We follow Koijen (2008) who shows within the preference structure we have how to estimate the cross-sectional distribution of risk preferences and managerial ability. We use data on actively-managed, U.S. equity mutual funds. Monthly mutual-fund returns come from the Center for Research in Securities Prices (CRSP) Survivor Bias Free Mutual Fund Database. The CRSP database is organized by fund rather than by manager, but contains manager's names starting in 1992. The identity of the manager is used to construct a manager-level database. The sample consists of monthly data over the period from January 1992 to December 2006.[5] For the active fund managers, we consider a set of nine style benchmarks that are distinguished by their size and value orientation. For large-cap stocks, we use the S&P 500, Russell 1000 Value, and Russell 1000 Growth; for mid-cap stocks, we take the Russell Midcap, Russell Midcap Value, and Russell Midcap Growth; for small-cap stocks, we select the Russell 2000, Russell Value, and Russell 2000 Growth. The style indexes are taken from Russell, in line with Chan, Chen, and Lakonishok (2002) and Chan, Dimmock, and Lakonishok (2006). The sample consists of 3,694 unique manager-fund combinations of 3,163 different managers who manage 1,932 different mutual funds. For 1,273 manager-fund combinations we have more than three years of data available. We impose a minimum data requirement of three years to estimate all models so that performance regressions deliver reasonably accurate estimates. For mutual funds, we consider a model in which the manager can trade the style benchmark, an active portfolio, and a cash account. This resembles the model we have, without the cash restriction and we consider the case where the managers can trade multiple passive portfolios. In such a model and with the preferences we have, the manager *i*'s alpha, beta and active risk are given by:

$$\alpha_i = \frac{\lambda_{Ai}^2}{\gamma_i},$$

$$\beta_i = \frac{\lambda_B}{\gamma_i \sigma_B} + \left(1 - \frac{1}{\gamma_i}\right),$$

$$\sigma_{\varepsilon i} = \frac{\lambda_{Ai}}{\gamma_i};$$

see Koijen (2008) for further details. One can think of the active risk as the residual risk in a standard performance regression. λ_B denotes the Sharpe ratio on the benchmark and σ_B denotes the benchmark volatility. These two moments suffice to estimate the manager's risk aversion (γ_i) and ability (λ_{Ai}). We use these moments to estimate the two attributes of the manager and focus on the implied cross-sectional distribution of risk aversion across all mutual fund managers. Figure 9.1 displays a non-parametric estimate of the cross-sectional distribution of the coefficient of relative risk aversion. The average risk aversion across all managers equals 25.92 and its standard deviation 51.19. The

[5] We refer to Koijen (2008) for further details on sample construction.

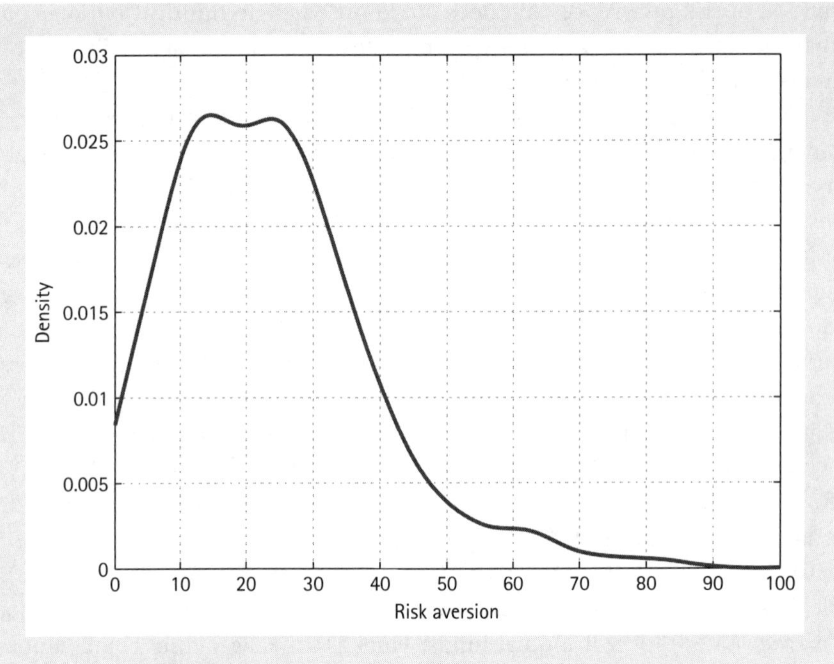

FIGURE 9.1 Cross-sectional distribution of risk preferences.

distribution is clearly right-skewed. The high estimates for risk aversion resonate with the findings of Becker, Ferson, Myers, and Schill (1999). The findings are also consistent with the ideas in the investment management industry that managers are often rather conservative and act closely around their benchmarks.

9.4 Main Empirical Results

To calibrate the model, we will assume that the return on the liabilities is like the return on government bonds, that is, $\sigma_L = \sigma_1$. Also, in computing the optimal portfolios with cash benchmarks and the optimal benchmarks, we assume the managers are unskilled: $\lambda_{A1} = \lambda_{A2} = 0$. We subsequently compute which levels of managerial ability would be required to justify decentralized asset management.

9.4.1 Known Preferences

Optimal portfolios We first consider the case where asset management in centralized. Figure 9.2 displays the optimal allocation to the six assets for different risk aversion levels of the CIO ranging from $\gamma_C = 2, \ldots, 10$. It is important to note that all allocations

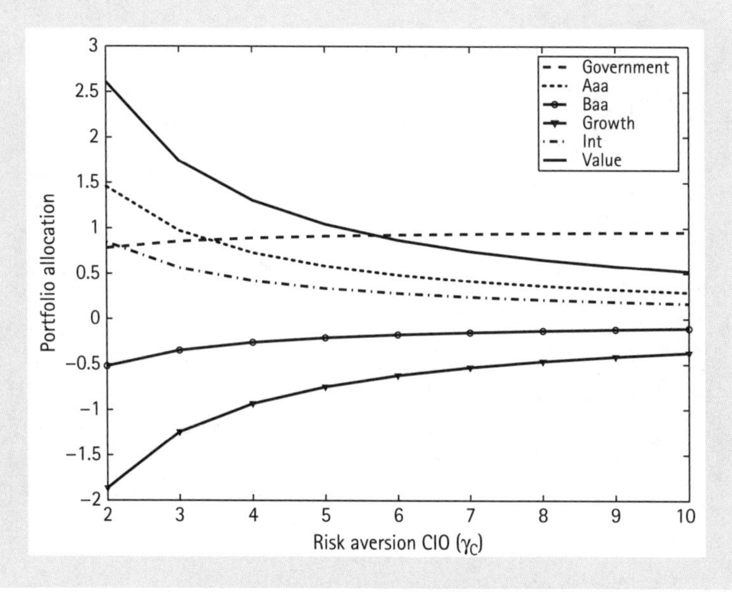

FIGURE 9.2 Optimal centralized allocation.

converge to zero if γ_C tends to infinity, apart from the allocation to government bonds. In our model, returns on the liabilities are tied to the return on long-term government bonds, and a more conservative CIO therefore tilts the optimal allocation to government bonds to reduce the mismatch risk with the liabilities.

Next, we consider the case in which asset management is decentralized and managers are compared to cash benchmarks. We display in Figure 9.3 the optimal overall allocation of the CIO to the assets in both asset classes. The coefficients of relative risk aversion of both managers are set to $\gamma_i = 10$ and the asset managers have $\gamma_1 = \gamma_2 = 5$. The key observation is that we find it to be optimal to *short* government bonds for the bond manager. This leaves the CIO with the trade-off to short the bond manager, which will be very costly from a risk-return perspective, or to hedge the liabilities. However, the managed portfolio of the bond manager also invests in Aaa- and Baa-rated corporate bonds, and a perfect hedge, as we had before, cannot be achieved. It turns out to be optimal to exploit the risk-return trade-off in the fixed income class, introducing a substantial amount of mismatch risk due to imperfectly hedging the liabilities.

Motivation to decentralize asset management The previous section suggests that decentralization severely complicates managing the risks in the liabilities properly. However, it could in fact be the case that the costs for the CIO are rather small compared to the value-added managers have due to their stock-picking skills. We now compute the skill (λ_{A1} and λ_{A2}) that managers need to have to justify decentralization. To this end, we assume symmetry in skills ($\lambda_{A1} = \lambda_{A2}$) and compute which levels of ability are required to make the CIO indifferent between (i) centralized asset management, but no

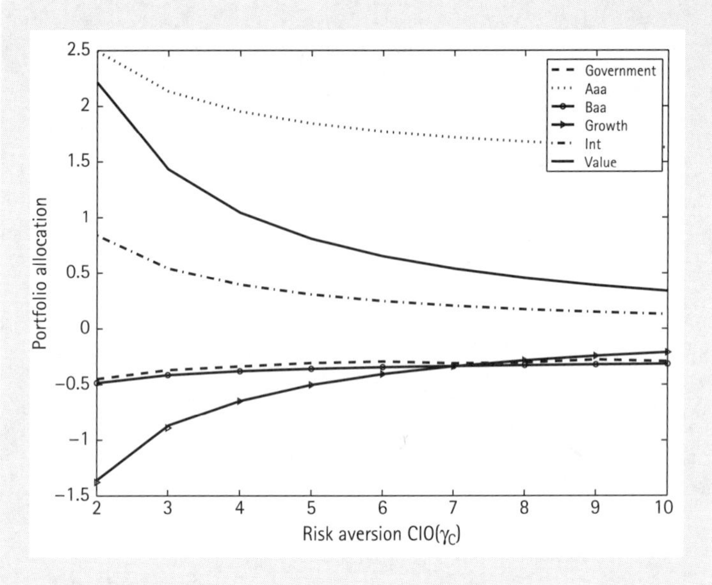

FIGURE 9.3 Optimal decentralized allocation without benchmarks.

access to the active portfolios of the managers and (ii) decentralized asset management. The required prices of risk are displayed in Figure 9.4, in which we assume that either $\gamma_1 = \gamma_2 = 5$ or $\gamma_1 = \gamma_2 = 25$. To compute these skill levels, we use the value functions that we derive in the appendix.

First, we find that the costs induced by decentralization are high. The required level of managerial ability ranges from $\lambda_A = 0.4$ to $\lambda_A = 1.3$. Recall that these numbers are information ratios, and there is little evidence that managers are able to produce such levels of outperformance, if at all. Second, the costs are higher if the CIO is more conservative. In this case, the CIO is more concerned about hedging liabilities and cares less about the risk-return trade-off. To make the CIO indifferent between centralization and decentralization, managers should be even more skilled. Third, if the asset managers are more conservative, we find that the required level of managerial ability is lower. One possible explanation for this is that the minimum variance portfolio is less sub-optimal than the mean-variance portfolio from the CIO's perspective. As such, the CIO prefers to hire more skilled managers in this case.

Optimal benchmarks In Figures 9.5 and 9.6 we compute the optimal performance benchmark for different risk aversion levels of the CIO ranging over $\gamma_C = 2, \ldots, 10$. Two aspects are worth noting. First, the benchmark in the fixed income class reflects the risk preferences of the CIO, while this is not the case for the equity asset class. The reason is that $\left(\Sigma\Sigma'\right)^{-1}\Sigma\sigma_L = 0_{4\times 1}$ for the equity asset class and, as a result, $\tilde{x}_C / \left(\tilde{x}_C'\iota\right)$ does not depend on γ_C. Second, the benchmarks induce the bond manager to tilt its

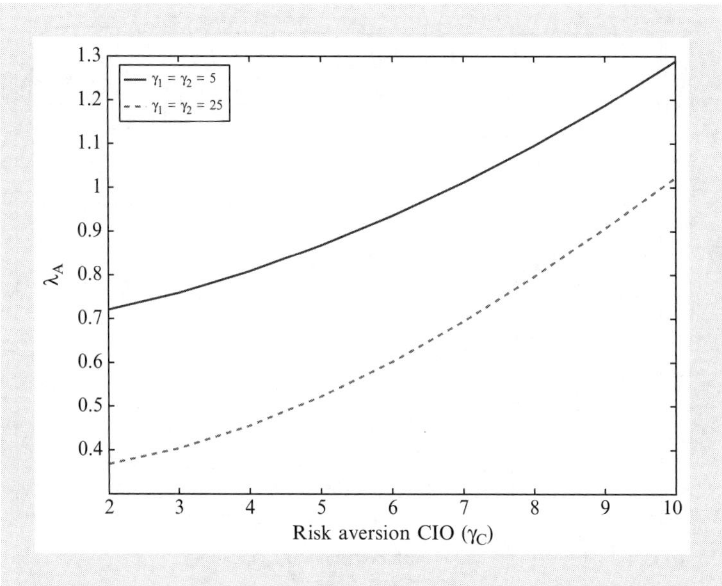

FIGURE 9.4 Required levels of managerial ability to justify decentralization.

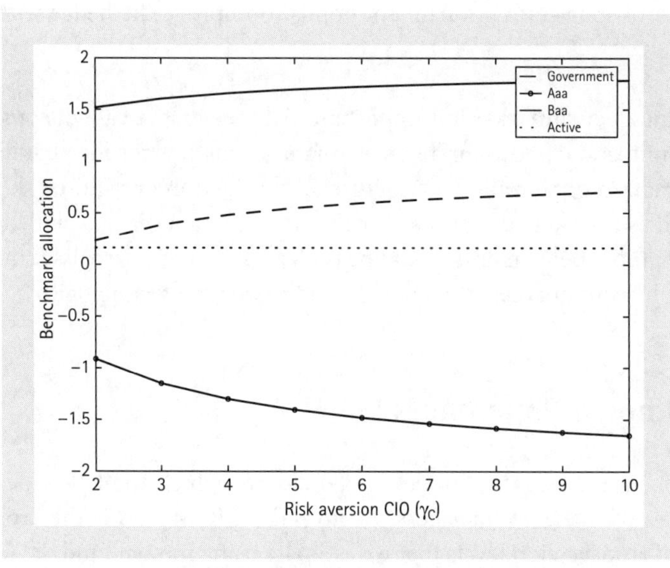

FIGURE 9.5 Optimal benchmarks fixed income manager.

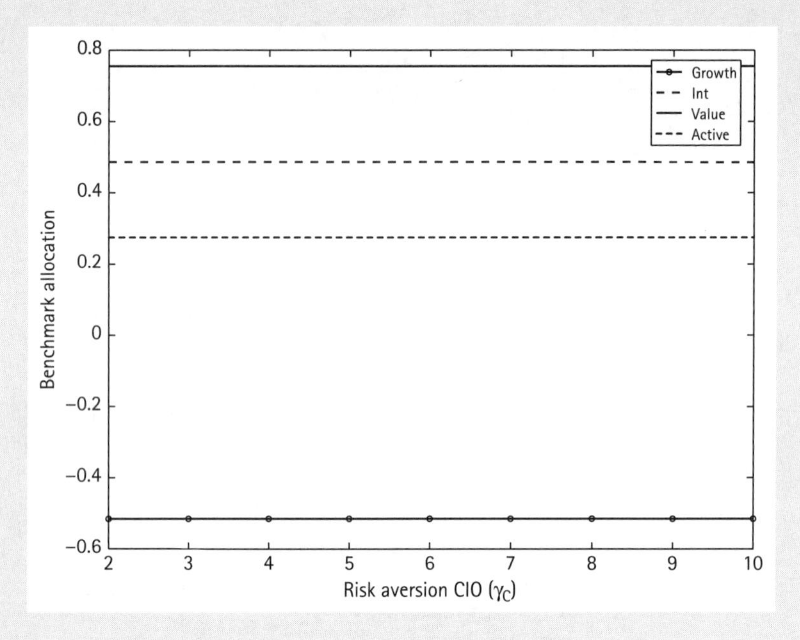

FIGURE 9.6 Optimal benchmarks equity manager.

portfolio towards long-term government bonds to improve the hedge with the fund's liabilities.

Value of optimal benchmarks It is important to notice that in case of constant investment opportunities and known preferences, managers do not need to be skilled to motivate a decentralized organizational structure. The reduction in required skill levels can be interpreted as the value of optimal benchmarks. If managers are skilled, decentralization with optimal benchmarks would be preferred to centralized asset management, because the CIO cannot access the managers' idiosyncratic technologies.

9.4.2 Unknown Preferences

In this section, we extend the model to the case in which the CIO does not know the preferences of the asset managers. All that the CIO knows is the cross-sectional distribution of risk aversion levels that we estimate using mutual fund data. This cross-sectional distribution is displayed in Figure 9.1. For simplicity, we assume that the risk aversion levels of both managers are perfectly correlated.

Motivation to decentralize asset management In this case, we solve numerically for the CIO's allocation to both asset classes:

$$\max_{x_C} E_0 \left(\frac{1}{1-\gamma_C} W_T^{1-\gamma_C} \right). \tag{9.1}$$

It is important to note that the expectation integrates out both uncertainty about future asset returns and uncertainty about the risk appetites of asset managers.

We can simplify the problem by using the analytical value function derived earlier and reported in the appendix:

$$\max_{x_C} E_0 \left(E \left(\frac{1}{1-\gamma_C} W_T^{1-\gamma_C} \middle| \gamma_1, \gamma_2 \right) \right) = \max_{x_C} \frac{1}{1-\gamma_C} W_0^{1-\gamma_C} E_0 \left(\exp \left(a(x_C, \gamma) T_C \right) \right). \tag{9.2}$$

Along these lines, we are able to solve for the optimal strategic allocation to both asset classes. With the optimal strategy of the CIO in hand, we compute the skill levels ($\lambda_A = \lambda_{A1} = \lambda_{A2}$) that ensure that the CIO is indifferent between centralized and decentralized asset management.

9.5 Extensions

We briefly discuss two extensions of our model.

9.5.1 Portfolio Constraints

Although institutional investors may be less restricted by short sales constraints, see for instance Nagel (2005), it is plausible that shorting assets is costly for certain asset classes. In this section, we briefly summarize how such constraints can be incorporated.

In case of constant investment opportunities, Tepla (2000) shows that the dynamic problem can be solved using standard static techniques, i.e., solving for the optimal portfolio of the asset managers entails solving a sequence of problems as before, but with a reduced asset space. Once the portfolio constraints have been satisfied, we obtain a candidate solution and finally optimize over all candidate solutions. If investment opportunities are time-varying, we have to resort to numerical techniques, but these are particularly simple once we impose the assumption of managerial myopia. After all, investors only incorporate current investment opportunities, implying that we can determine the managers' optimal portfolio without solving a dynamic program.

The empirical application used throughout is not particularly suited for imposing portfolio constraints, as the fixed income manager optimally shorts Aaa-rated bonds to finance investments in Baa-rated bonds and similarly for the equity manager for growth and value stocks. Consequently, we only obtain corner solutions.

9.5.2 Time-Varying Investment Opportunities

In the model we have considered to far, risk premia are assumed to be constant. However, it is well known that risk premia tend to move over time, see Cochrane (2007) and Binsbergen and Koijen (2008) for stocks and Cochrane and Piazzesi (2005) for government bonds. Binsbergen *et al.* (2008) incorporate return predictability in a model that does not feature liabilities and managerial ability as we have. From a technical perspective, however, the same derivations suffice to extend our model to account for time-varying investment opportunities. Binsbergen *et al.* (2008) show that in this case the costs of decentralized asset management, and the value of optimally designed benchmarks, both increase. We refer to their paper for a detailed analysis of a model with time-varying risk premia.

9.6 Conclusions

In this chapter, we have studied the investment problem of a pension fund in which a centralized decision maker, the Chief Investment Officer (CIO), for example, employs multiple asset managers to implement investment strategies in separate asset classes. The CIO allocates capital to the managers who, in turn, allocate these funds to the assets in their asset class. We assume that managers have specific stock selection and market timing skills which allow them to outperform passive benchmarks. However, the decentralized organizational structure also induces several inefficiencies and misalignments of incentives including loss of diversification and unobservable managerial appetite for risk. We show that if the CIO leaves the behavior of the asset managers unaffected, which happens for instance if managers are remunerated relative to a cash benchmark, the information ratio required to justify this organizational structure ranges from 0.4 to 1.3. However, by using optimally designed benchmarks, we can mitigate the inefficiencies induced by decentralization and can still realize the potential benefits of managerial ability. Our framework suggests that the ability and performance of the managers can influence the choice of organizational design of the fund, which in turn influences the performance of the fund as a whole.

Appendix

I. Value functions

Centralized problem The value function takes the form:

$$J(F, \tau_C) = \frac{1}{1-\gamma_C} F^{1-\gamma_C} \exp\left(a(x)\tau_C\right),$$

with $\tau_C = T_C - t$ and x the (implied) portfolio choice of the CIO, which equals:

$$x = \frac{1}{\gamma_C}\left(\Sigma_C\Sigma_C'\right)^{-1}\Sigma_C\Lambda_C + \left(1 - \frac{1}{\gamma_C}\right)\left(\Sigma_C\Sigma_C'\right)^{-1}\Sigma_C\sigma_L,$$

in this case. The function $a(x)$ reads:

$$a(x) = (1-\gamma_C)\left(r + x'\Sigma_C\Lambda_C - \mu_L + \sigma_L'\sigma_L - x'\Sigma_C\sigma_L\right)$$
$$-\frac{1}{2}\gamma_C(1-\gamma_C)\left(x'\Sigma_C - \sigma_L'\right)\left(\Sigma_C'x - \sigma_L\right),$$

which can be derived using standard dynamic programming techniques.

Decentralized with cash benchmarks The value function in this case takes the same form, but the function $a(x)$ changes because the CIO can now access the idiosyncratic technologies via the managers:

$$a(x) = (1-\gamma_C)\left(r + x'\Sigma\Lambda - \mu_L + \sigma_L'\sigma_L - x'\Sigma\sigma_L\right)$$
$$-\frac{1}{2}\gamma_C(1-\gamma_C)\left(x'\Sigma - \sigma_L'\right)\left(\Sigma'x - \sigma_L\right),$$

and the optimal (implied) portfolio reads:

$$x = \begin{bmatrix} x_{C(1)}^{Cash}x_1^{Cash} \\ x_{C(2)}^{Cash}x_2^{Cash} \end{bmatrix}.$$

Decentralized with optimal benchmarks In case of optimal benchmarks, the CIO can achieve first-best, but with access to the idiosyncratic technologies. As such, $a(x)$ is of the form:

$$a(x) = (1-\gamma_C)\left(r + x'\Sigma\Lambda - \mu_L + \sigma_L'\sigma_L - x'\Sigma\sigma_L\right)$$
$$-\frac{1}{2}\gamma_C(1-\gamma_C)\left(x'\Sigma - \sigma_L'\right)\left(\Sigma'x - \sigma_L\right),$$

with a portfolio:

$$x = \frac{1}{\gamma_C}\left(\Sigma\Sigma'\right)^{-1}\Sigma\Lambda + \left(1 - \frac{1}{\gamma_C}\right)\left(\Sigma\Sigma'\right)^{-1}\Sigma\sigma_L.$$

References

Admati, A.R. and Pfleiderer, P. (1997). Does it all add up? Benchmarks and the compensation of active portfolio managers. *Journal of Business*, **70**, 323–350.

Barberis, N.C. (2000). Investing for the long run when returns are predictable. *Journal of Finance*, **55**, 225–264.

Basak, S., Shapiro, A., and Teplá, L. (2006). Risk management with benchmarking. *Management Science*, **52**, 542–557.

van Binsbergen, J.H. and Brandt, M.W. (2007). Optimal asset allocation in asset liability management. Working paper, Duke University.

van Binsbergen, Jules H., Brandt, M.W. and Koijen, R.S.J. (2008). Optimal decentralized investment management. *Journal of Finance*, **63**, 1849–1895.

Brennan, M.J. and Xia, Y. (2001). Stock price volatility and equity premium. *Journal of Monetary Economics*, **47**, 249–283.

Cochrane, J.H. and Piazzesi, M. (2005). Bond risk premia. *American Economic Review*, **95**, 138–160.

Elton, E.J. and Gruber, M.J. (2004). Optimum centralized portfolio construction with decentralized portfolio management. *Journal of Financial and Quantitative Analysis*, **39**, 481–494.

Hoevenaars, R.P.M.M., Molenaar, R.D.J., Schotman, P.C., and Steenkamp, T.B.M. Strategic asset allocation with liabilities: Beyond stocks and bonds, *Journal of Economic Dynamics and Control*, **32**, 2939–297.

Koijen, R.S.J. (2008). The cross-section of managerial ability and risk preferences. Working paper, University of Chicago.

Ou-Yang, H. (2003). Optimal contracts in a continuous-time delegated portfolio management problem, *Review of Financial Studies*, **16**, 173–208.

Sharpe, W.F. (1981). Decentralized investment management. *Journal of Finance*, **36**, 217–234.

Stracca, L. (2006). Delegated portfolio management: A survey of the theoretical literature. *Journal of Economic Surveys*, **20**, 823–848.

Teplá, L. (2000). Optimal portfolio policies with borrowing and shortsale constraints. *Journal of Economic Dynamics & Control*, **24**, 1623–1639.

Vayanos, D. (2003). The decentralization of information processing in the presence of interactions. *Review of Economic Studies*, **70**, 667–695.

CHAPTER 10

PERFORMANCE BASED FEES, INCENTIVES, AND DYNAMIC TRACKING ERROR CHOICE

BERND SCHERER AND XIAODONG XU

INTRODUCTION

Mutual funds and corporate pension funds are increasingly using incentive fees, or performance-based fees (PBFs) to reward their fund managers. Janus Capital Group Inc established performance incentives for the managers of 13 of its 59 funds in September 2005. Vanguard and Fidelity are just another two examples of investment companies which use incentive fees. Even in the absence of explicit performance-based fees, Brown, Harlow, and Starks (1996) and Chevalier and Ellison (1997) have shown that an implicit performance-based compensation structure arises from proportional fees as a result of the fact that net investment flows into funds respond strongly to recent performance.

The effects of performance-based fees on investment decisions have been documented in a number of papers. Grinblatt and Titman (1989) apply option pricing theory to analyze the manager's risk incentives in a single-stage framework. They find that improperly designed performance-based fee contracts create incentives for gaming by varying the risk of the fund. Carpenter (2000) examines the optimal dynamic investment policy for a risk-averse fund manager and finds that the convexity of the option-like compensation structure can lead the manager to dramatically increase volatility in some circumstances. Goetzman, Ingersoll, and Ross (2003) focus primarily on valuing claims on a hedge fund's assets and show that convexity gives rise to a risk-shifting incentive on the part of the money manager. Ferguson and Leistikow (2003) also use a multi-period framework, but they treat it as a sequence of myopic single-period problems.

Basak, Pavlova, and Shapiro (2005) examine mutual fund managers' risk-taking behavior when compensation is a function of fund value, which in turn depends on flows.

Although these papers contain many useful insights, they focus either on a single-period model or assume a restrictive continuous-time framework. In either case, the model is motivated more by analytic tractability than by realistic investment considerations. For example, many investors expect their active risk relative to the benchmark to be maintained within a range. Investors also have limited tolerance for underperformance, and are likely to redeem their investments from funds that trail their benchmarks significantly. Ippolito (1992) finds that poor fund performance results in large money outflow while good performance leads to significant inflow of new money. Khorana (1996) shows that up to two years of below average performance significantly increases the probability that the mutual fund manager will be fired. We shall address these considerations in a multi-stage framework using stochastic programming techniques.

Recently, Hodder and Jackwerth (2006) analyzed a fund manager's risk taking behavior with liquidation barrier in consideration. However, their work mainly focuses on asymmetric compensation structure. The focus of this chapter is the behavior of active portfolio managers under different performance-based compensation structures, the most common examples of which are proportional fees and incentive fees, or a combination of these.[1] In practice, the incentive fee can be either of the asymmetric type (no loss participation) or fulcrum type (loss participation). Recognizing that the incentive fee is an option contingent on the performance of the fund, the problem of determining a fund manager's optimal active risk bears some relation to the problem of valuing a derivative.[2] However the investment manager cannot be allowed to hold a short position in this performance option, synthetic or otherwise, as this would subvert the investor's intended purpose in paying a performance fee. The portfolio manager cannot be allowed to delta hedge the option in his private portfolio.

Many papers have considered the optimal contract design problem in a multi-stage game-theoretic framework. Das and Sundaram (1999) and Stremme (2001) have attacked the problem from a signaling perspective. Their work centers around what they call "fee speech," i.e., what does a given fee structure tell us about the manager? Is there a pooling equilibrium in which every manager (good as well as bad) offers the same contract or is the market outcome separating, i.e., can we tell whether a manager has skill by looking at his fee structure?

Traditional analysis of performance-based fees does not consider the dynamic nature of active portfolio management. In reality, fund managers are more concerned about the renewal of their lucrative long-term contracts than about the marginal benefits

[1] We ignore the case of flat fees, independent of both asset and performance, as this does not appear to generate any interesting risk-shifting behavior.

[2] It is beneficial to elaborate on this point a bit further. Practitioners seem to prefer asset-based fees over fixed fees despite the fact that asset-based fees make them share a client's benchmark risk. They do this because their intuition tells them that asset-based fees benefit from the underlying trend in (equity) markets. However this intuition is wrong. Asset-based fees are among the most primitive of derivatives and as such the price of a derivative is independent of its (real-world) drift rate.

they may gain by varying risk in the short term. Our chapter addresses the effect of investor intolerance of negative fund performance on the valuation of incentive fees and the manager's optimal risk policy response in this setting. In our model, if the fund severely underperforms the benchmark then the manager is fired. Specifically, we assume that the investor has a minimum performance tolerance barrier, which he enforces based on periodic performance reports. At the end of any reporting period, the management contract will be terminated if performance is below the investor tolerance barrier. We refer to this as a knockout, or down-and-out, performance barrier. The core of our chapter is to address the multi-stage portfolio management problem for a utility-maximizing investment manager in the presence of a discrete knockout barrier, or down-and-out performance barrier. Even though determined exogenously, our underperformance tolerance assumptions are consistent with industry reality, especially in the case of mutual funds for which market forces play an important role. Since the performance history of mutual funds is public information, investors are well informed, and willing to act on news of poor returns.

10.1 Review of the Single-Stage Incentive Fee Model

We start with a review of the single-period model in which the money manager is subject to some form of performance-based compensation structure. While investors and portfolio managers use different performance-based fee contracts, which vary widely in terms of complexity and sophistication, we focus on two popular contract types. Hedge funds typically charge investors a fixed percentage of assets under management plus an asymmetric incentive fee, while mutual funds typically charge a fixed percentage plus a symmetric "fulcrum fee" (at least in the U.S.) as incentive.

Figure 10.1 gives the most commonly used compensation structure for hedge funds. It contains a proportional fee and an incentive fee. The proportional fee takes the form $B = k_1 W$, where k_1 is typically 1–2% and W denotes assets under management (AUM) at the end of the period. The incentive fee is typically a proportion of the outperformance of the portfolio over a pre-specified target (high watermark returns in the case of hedge funds). However, other targets are common, such as a hurdle point r_h above a benchmark.

Denote by r_M and r_B the returns of the managed portfolio and the benchmark portfolio, respectively. Then the managed fund's relative return[3] with respect to the benchmark at the end of the investment period can be expressed as $r_1 = \frac{1+r_M}{1+r_B} - 1$. If the manager outperforms the target return by an amount $r_1 - r_h$, the bonus compensation equals $k_2(r_1 - r_h)W_0$, where $0 < k_2 < 1$ is the fraction of the excess return over the hurdle rate that goes to the manager, and W_0 is the initial wealth of the fund. In all other

[3] For a single-period model it is often convenient to calculate arithmetic outperformance. However, to be consistent with our multi-period model in the rest of this chapter, we use geometric outperformance instead.

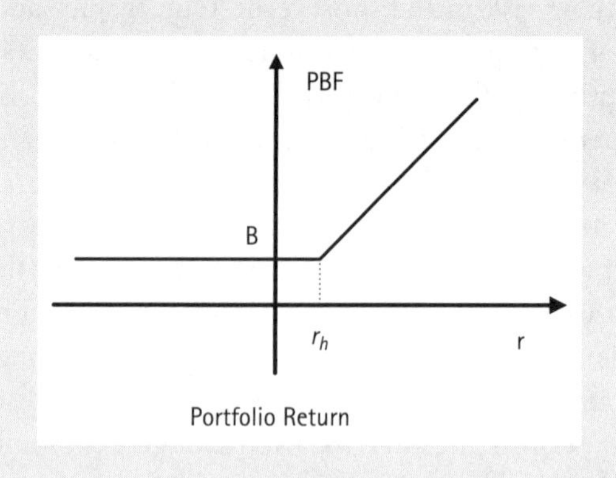

FIGURE 10.1 Portfolio manager's payoff under asymmetric fee compensation structure as a function of realized return. B is the flat fee, and r_h is the hurdle point for asymmetric fee.

cases, the manager only collects a proportional fee, i.e., a fee that is a certain percentage of the fund's assets W at the end of the investment period. The hedge-fund manager's compensation at the end of the period has the form

$$F(r_1) = k_1 W + \max[0, k_2(r_1 - r_h)W_0].$$

From Figure 10.1 we see that the fund manager's performance-based compensation incorporates a call option. Since this fee schedule effectively limits downside risk for the portfolio manager, we would expect the manager to prefer riskier portfolios to maximize his personal utility. Grinblatt and Titman (1989) have shown that performance-based compensation contracts as in Figure 10.1 provide an incentive for fund managers to deviate from the risk level which is optimal for the investor. Carpenter (2000) also points out that the convexity of the option makes the manager seek payoffs and can lead to dramatic increases in the portfolio's volatility.

To protect public investors' interest, the incentive fee structures in the U.S. mutual fund industry are regulated according to the Investment Company Amendments Act of 1970, an amendment to the Investment Company Act of 1940. This amendment requires all mutual fund managers wishing to charge performance-based fees to adopt a fulcrum fee structure. Figure 10.2 illustrates a typical fulcrum fee contract, which takes the form of a base proportional fee, B, plus an adjustment for outperforming or underperforming the benchmark. With a fulcrum fee, the compensation is symmetric around a chosen index, so that any increases in fees for performance in excess of the benchmark, r_B, must be matched by decreases in fees for performance that falls short of the benchmark by a like amount.

In case the return of the managed fund equals the benchmark return, i.e., $r_1 = 0$, the manager's payoff will only contain the proportional fee $k_1 W$. The incentive portion of the fulcrum fee has a cap hurdle rate, r_C, and a floor hurdle rate, r_F. To satisfy the legal requirement of symmetry of fulcrum fees, we must have $r_C = -r_F$. If the managed

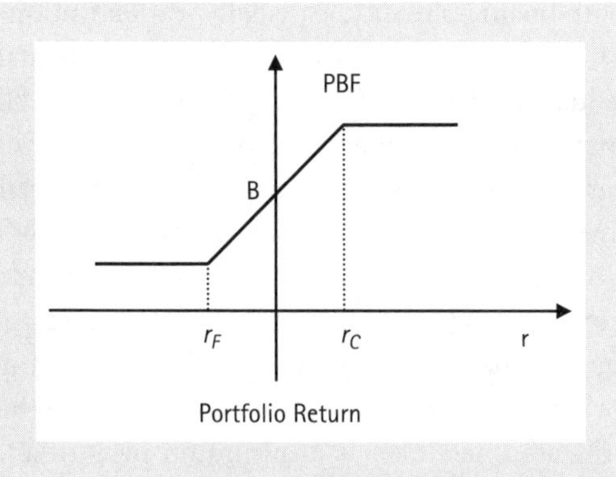

FIGURE 10.2 Portfolio manager's payoff as a function of realized return under a fulcrum fee compensation structure. B is the proportional fee, and r_F and r_C are the floor and cap rates for the fulcrum-fee contract.

portfolio's realized return is greater than r_C, the "cap" fee will be $k_1W + k_2r_CW_0$. Symmetrically, if the managed portfolio underperforms the benchmark by an amount greater than r_F, the manager's "floor" fee level is $k_1W + k_2r_FW_0$. When relative return is in the intermediate range $[r_F, r_C]$ the performance fee increases linearly from the floor to the cap. The manager's payoff can be expressed as follow

$$F(r_1) = k_1W + k_2W_0 \min[r_C, \max[r_F, r_1]].$$

Although the symmetric structure of the fulcrum fee mitigates the manager's risk-shifting incentive when the fund's return is near the benchmark, there is still a significant incentive to deviate from the client's preferred level of risks when his relative return is near r_F or r_C. In the case that the managed portfolio's performance is far behind the benchmark, the manager has a strong incentive to increase the fund's risk level because his downside risk is limited; he will also play it safe and act more like an index fund if he is considerably ahead of the benchmark. This applies in a single-period framework, because there is no opportunity for the investor to punish the manager for deviating from the optimal contract. We will relax this assumption in the next section.

10.2 Multi-Period Setting and Portfolio Manager's Optimization Problem

In the remainder of this chapter we formulate a multi-stage portfolio management problem with incentive fees and a knockout barrier for poor performance. The knockout feature is consistent with business reality, especially for institutional investors. Heinkel and Stoughton (1994) observe that almost all major institutional investors pay professional portfolio evaluation firms, such as Frank Russell or Wilshire Associates, to monitor and report managers' performance on a regular basis. Since the performance of the money managers (usually measured annually) can be easily observed and the cost of transferring money from one manager to another is not high, significantly underperforming the benchmark will result in redemptions from the fund. In the case of mutual funds where performance is public information, investors are well informed and will exit a fund if performance is poor compared with its competitors.

To consider investor's performance tolerance in a dynamic investment environment, our multi-period model assumes there is a minimum performance knockout barrier for the investor, and he can observe the performance of the fund dynamically. At the end of each period, the manager will be fired if the fund's relative performance is below the knockout barrier. A more formal specification of the model is as follows. Initially, the investor turns over a sum of money, W_0, to the fund manager and delegates fund investment decisions to him over a certain length of time. Assume the portfolio will be rebalanced T times over the investment horizon and the investor can observe the fund's performance at the end of each period (labeled as $1, 2, \ldots, T$.) At the beginning of each period, the manager will make a decision to maximize his expected utility at the end of the investment horizon, subject to any constraint imposed by the investor. His final payoff depends on the fund's performance over the investment horizon in a manner specified in the agreed compensation contract.

There is a pre-specified benchmark against which the performance of the managed portfolio will be evaluated. Let $r_t = \frac{1+r_{t,M}}{1+r_{t,B}} - 1$ be the relative return on the investment during period t, where $r_{t,M}$ and $r_{t,B}$ denote the returns of the managed and the benchmark portfolios, respectively. We assume that the manager will maximize his personal utility by adjusting the portfolio's active risk level, i.e., the volatility of the active returns. In our model, the level of active risk, σ, he chooses will determine the entire distribution of return; in particular, the active[4] expected return α will be a function of active risk.

We must explain the relationship between active risk, σ, and expected active return, α, before we formalize the manager's utility maximization problem. A key statistic for measuring the manager's investment skills is the information ratio, defined as $IR \equiv \alpha/\sigma$. This is a concept similar to the Sharp ratio. A larger information ratio indicates a higher active return per unit of active risk. The relationship between active risk and active return is specified by active efficient frontier, $\alpha(\sigma)$. For a given level of active risk, $\alpha(\sigma)$ is the largest alpha the manager can achieve. In another words, the active efficient frontier defines the quality of the opportunities available to a manager. Each active manager will have his own active efficient frontier. The active efficient frontier of a good manager will dominate that of a poor one. Through out this chapter, we assume that the manager's

[4] We assume throughout that the manager does no market timing, so that residual risk and active risk are equal.

frontier is static, i.e., that the manager's investment skill will not change during the investment horizon.

The active efficient frontier for an unconstrained investor is a straight line through the origin. In this case, the information ratio of the optimal portfolio is independent of active risk. This situation is fairly typical for a hedge-fund investor. However, for a constrained investor, for example a typical mutual-fund investor with a long-only constraint (more precisely, one who cannot borrow), the frontier becomes concave and the information ratio decreases as the portfolio's active risk increases. Since a long-only requirement incurs inequality constraints, there is no explicit formula for the loss in efficiency. Grinold and Kahn (2000) carried out a numerical experiment to explore the impact of such constraints. They summarized their conclusions in the form of an approximate formula showing how much IR is typically lost because of long-only constraints, as a function of the number of assets and the active risk. The sample efficient frontier we used to illustrate the effects of long-only constraints is based on Grinold and Kahn's simple model, which estimates the active efficient frontier with long-only constraints by

$$\alpha(\sigma) = 100 \cdot IR \cdot \left\{ \frac{[1+\sigma/100]^{1-\gamma(N)} - 1}{1-\gamma(N)} \right\},$$

where IR is the information ratio without long-only constraints (assumed to be 1.0), σ is the security's residual risk, N is number of securities, and $\gamma(N) = (53+N)^{0.57}$. This specification is used for asset based fee and fulcrum fee cases (typically with long-only constraint). For hedge funds we use $\alpha = IR \cdot \sigma$ instead.

In the examples to follow, we take our active efficient frontiers to be as in Figure 10.3. The long-only frontier is based on the Grinold–Kahn model with 500 assets and an unconstrained IR of 1. The long-short frontier is based on an IR of 1 – we imagine this to reflect an unconstrained strategy based on the same information set as the long-only frontier. The loss of efficiency as risk increases is clearly visible in the long-only case. The long-only frontier represents the mutual fund case, and will always be coupled with a fulcrum fee structure. The long-short frontier represents the hedge-fund case, and will always be coupled with the asymmetric fee structure.

Our analysis to follow assumes that r_t is normally distributed, specifically, that $r_t \sim N\left(\alpha_t(\sigma_t), \sigma_t^2\right)$. The normality assumption is largely one of convenience because the stochastic programming method we use applies equally well to any return distribution. We also assume that r_t is conditionally independent of the past given σ_t.

If the fund's cumulative relative performance from time 0 to time t, $R_t \equiv \prod_{t=1}^{t}(1+r_t)$, is below a pre-determined knockout barrier level,[5] $R_{t,Barrier}$, the portfolio manager will be fired. Let I_t denote the investor's knockout indicator:

[5] We assume that the knockout barrier is exogenously determined by the investors. It is natural to allow the barrier to be time-dependent since the variance of the fund's cumulative relative performance will increase as time progresses.

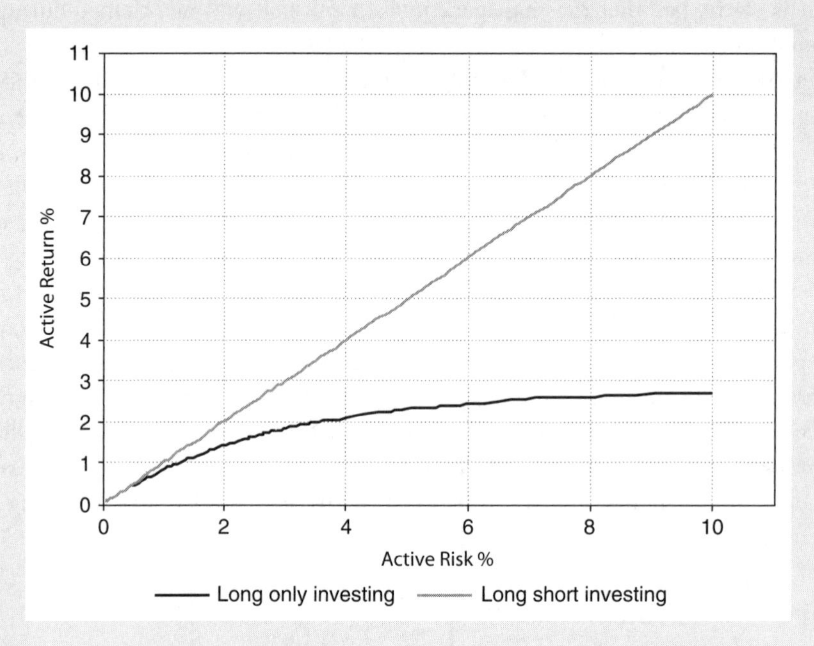

FIGURE 10.3 Active efficient frontiers for portfolios with and without long-only investment constraints.

$$I_t = \begin{cases} 1 & \textit{if } R_t \geq R_{t,Barrier} \\ 0 & \text{otherwise.} \end{cases}.$$

$I_t = 1$ indicates that the manager is not fired and may continue to run the fund through the next period, period $t+1$. If the manager has not been fired at the end of period T, he will be paid according to a pre-specified compensation structures and the realized relative return. Otherwise, the manager receives only the fixed proportional fee of the initial fund wealth, pro-rated according to how many periods he managed the fund before he was fired. We assume that the fee is received upon termination of the management contract and is invested at the risk-free rate until time T.

We assume that the manager's only decision in each period $t \in \{1, \ldots, T\}$ is the choice of the risk level $\sigma_t \in [\sigma_{t,L}, \sigma_{t,H}]$, where $[\sigma_{t,L}, \sigma_{t,H}]$ is the risk range specified for period t. In our model, σ also implicitly determines the portfolio's expected excess return α. Further, assume the portfolio manager's utility is based on the total fees accrued by time T (including fees received before time T, which are invested at the risk-free rate), and exhibits constant relative risk aversion (CRRA):

$$U(W_T) = \frac{W_T^{1-\gamma}}{1-\gamma}, \ \gamma > 0.$$

Given the above setting, the portfolio manager's utility maximization optimization problem[6] can be expressed as

$$\max_{\sigma} E[U(F(R))] \text{ where } \sigma_t = \sigma_t(R_t) \text{ for } t = 1, 2, \ldots, T$$

where F is the total accrued fee at the end of the horizon, which depends on the history of the fund's performance, R, and in particular on the investor's knockout indicator process, I. The maximal expected utility is a function of the contract parameters Φ, such as the initial assets under management, W_0, the time-dependent knockout barrier $R_{Barrier}$, and the different hurdle rates and fees.

The complexity of many real-world problems often means that we have to abandon hope of an elegant closed-form solution as our mathematical models are refined. Because the model presented here incorporates many of the practical nuances of investor demands, manager motivation, and investment skill, it has no closed-form solution. This is the price we pay for the realism of the model. We therefore developed a stochastic programming algorithm to solve the portfolio manager's active risk optimization problem.

10.3 Scenario Tree Generation and the Optimization Algorithm

We use dynamic programming to solve the portfolio manager's dynamic tracking error optimization problem. This section illustrates the scenario tree generation process and a solution algorithm we proposed. Similar to binomial or trinomial option pricing, we first generate a multinomial scenario tree to represent the possible realization of the managed portfolio's relative performance at the end of each stage, and then use the backward induction method to find the optimal solution.

The contract horizon is divided into T stages, each corresponding to a managerial evaluation period. For simplicity, we assume the managed portfolio has static active efficient frontier and constant risk range $[\sigma_L, \sigma_U]$ specified by the investor over the contract horizon. The starting point's cumulative relative performance is set to 1. Let P be the probability measure with respect to the distribution of the gross relative return, R, over a single investment stage associated with a node in the scenario tree. Denote by R_L and R_U the lower and upper ε percentile level (e.g., 1%) of the gross relative return assuming the maximum tracking error decision is taking and the alpha is equal to 0, i.e.,

[6] In order to capture alpha we need to deviate from a pure contingent claims approach. Remember that option pricing does not know the concept of alpha as it does not need fair valuation. In fact option pricing is relative pricing, i.e., all claims are priced correctly relative to each other, but every single claim could be far from its equilibrium value.

$$P[R \leq R_L | \alpha = 0, \sigma = \sigma_U] = \varepsilon$$

$$P[R \geq R_U | \alpha = 0, \sigma = \sigma_U] = \varepsilon.$$

To represent the investment uncertainty over a single stage, K discrete samples are taken from $[R_L, R_U]$. This is accomplished by multiplying the initial position by a factor u_k

$$u_k = R_L e^{(k-1)\Delta} \quad \forall\, k \in [1, \ldots, K],$$

where $\Delta \equiv \frac{1}{K-1} \log\left(\frac{R_U}{R_L}\right)$ is the discrete relative return interval. We first apply this process to the root node and then repeat the procedure for all other discrete realizations over the contract horizon. The total number of scenarios at stage t is give by $t(K-1)+1$. Notice that the adjacent nodes have $K-1$ common realizations, which significantly decreases the size of the scenario tree. Figure 10.4 illustrates a simple three-stage scenario tree with five possible realizations for each node.

A scenario, $\{s, t\}$, represents a path between time 0 and time t in the scenario tree. Denote by N_t^s a decision node associated with scenario $\{s, t\}$. Each node N_t^s has an immediate ancestor node N_{t-1}^{s-} and a set of immediate descendant nodes $N_{t+1}^{s+} \in D\left(N_t^s\right)$. Let $p_t^s > 0$ be the probability associated with a possible realization, r_t^s, in the scenario tree at time $t \in [0, T]$. The probability p_t^s can be calculated from the relative return probability distribution function as

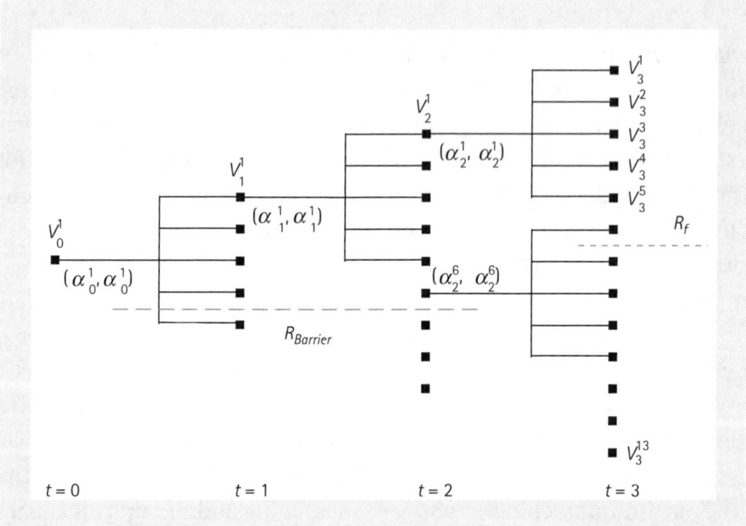

FIGURE 10.4 A simple three-stage-five-child scenario tree. The fund's investment horizon is separated into three stages. For each "parent" node (where decisions are taken) there are five children (where decisions are evaluated and new decisions are formed). $R_{Barrier}$ is the knock-out cumulative relative return level, and R_f is the floor level of the asymmetric compensation parameter.

$$p_t^s = \begin{cases} 1 - P\left(r_t \le a_t^{K-1} | R_{t-1}^{s-}, \sigma_{t-1}^{s-}\right) & \textit{if } s = K \\ P\left(a_t^{s-1} < r_t \le a_t^s | R_{t-1}^{s-}, \sigma_{t-1}^{s-}\right) & \textit{if } 1 < s < K \\ P\left(r_t \le a_t^1 | R_{t-1}^{s-}, \sigma_{t-1}^{s-}\right) & \textit{if } s = 1, \end{cases}$$

for a given parent node cumulative return position R_{t-1}^{s-} and tracking error decision σ_{t-1}^{s-}, where $a_t^s = \frac{r_t^s + r_t^{s+1}}{2} \forall s \in [1, \ldots, K-1]$.

The scenario-tree generated by the above procedure is a lattice approximation of the state space of relative returns. There are two sources of inaccuracy in using a lattice: quantization error and specification error. Quantization error is incurred by approximating a continuous distribution with discrete outcomes while mismatching between the barrier level and the available lattice points causes specification error. There is a tradeoff between these two types of errors. As the lattice space decreases, the errors get smaller and the solution converges to the true value. However, higher accuracy requirement makes the numerical calculation more cumbersome.

Our tree generation process provides an effective approach to mitigate both the quantization error and the specification error. Increasing the number of discrete samples does not incur too much calculation burden since the computational complexity is not high: the total number of node is $(T+1)\left[\frac{T}{2}(K-1)+1\right]$ and the performance of the managed portfolio is usually observed quarterly or annually. We can further align a lattice level with the barrier level by adjusting the truncation error specification ε or the number of scenarios K.

We further designed a backward induction algorithm to identify the manager's optimal tracking error policy under different scenarios. The detailed algorithm is described as follows:

Step 1: At the end of the last stage T, calculate the portfolio manager's payoff $F\left(R_T^s\right)$ for each realization r_T^s; identify the investor's knockout decision set $\left\{I_t^s | \forall\, t,\, s\right\}$ based on the exogenous tolerance barrier set $\{R_{t,Barrier}, t \in [1, T-1]\}$; if $I_t^s = 0$ for a certain node, calculate the manager's knockout utility based on a pre-specified contract.[7]

Step 2: Let $t = T-1$, and find the manager's optimal tracking error decision, σ_{T-1}^{s-}, at the beginning of the last period by solving the manager's utility maximization problem

$$V_{T-1}^s\left(R_{T-1}^s\right) = \underset{\sigma_{T-1}^s \in \left[\sigma_{T-1,L}^{\cdot}\sigma_{T-1,H}^{\cdot}\right]}{\text{Max}} \sum_{N_T^{s+} \in D\left(N_{T-1}^s\right)}^{p_T^{s+}} U_T^{s+}\left(F\left(R_T^{s+}\right)\right)$$

for all scenarios with $I_{T-1}^s = 1$.

[7] We assume the investor will pay a pro-rated portion of the fixed management fee which will be invested into a risk free account by the manager. The utility of a knockout realization is then calculated based on the future value of the prorated portion of the fixed fee at time T.

Step 3: Let $t = t - 1$, and find the manager's optimal tracking error decision, σ_t^s, by solving the following optimization problem

$$V_t^s\left(R_t^s\right) = \underset{\sigma_t^s \in [\sigma_{t,L}, \sigma_{t,H}]}{\text{Max}} \sum_{N_{t+1}^{s+} \in D(N_t^s)}^{p_{t+1}^{s+}} V_{t+1}^{s+}\left(R_{t+1}^{s+}\right)$$

for all scenarios with $I_t^s = 1$ at time t. If $t = 0$, go to step 4, otherwise, repeat step 3.

Step 4: Stop and identify the optimal tracking error decision rules for the manager's utility maximization problem.

The algorithm first calculates managers' utility at the end of contract period T based on the compensation contract and the ratio between the cumulative returns of the managed and benchmark portfolios. It then identifies the status of all the nodes at the beginning of the last stage, more specifically, if the managed portfolio has not hit the knockout barrier, an optimization problem is solved to find the optimal tracking error which maximizes the expected utility of the current node; otherwise, the manager is out. A similar procedure is then applied to the second last stage, and so on. The manager's optimal contingent tracking error strategy is obtained by working back through all the nodes in the scenario tree. Correspondingly, the object value of the root node optimization problem is the maximum expected utility at time T.

10.4 Dynamic Decision Making under Various Fee Schedules

This section illustrates a manager's risk-taking behavior in a multi-stage investment environment with a focus on the effects of time and performance. Our analyses include the three most popular compensation structures: proportional fees, asymmetric incentive fees, and symmetric incentive fees. We find that managers show a much richer range of risk behaviors than in the single-stage model as time progresses. The manager displays a remarkable prudence as he strives to preserve his long-term franchise (the present value of future fees) in the earlier stage; however, he prefer to increase the fund's risk exposure in the later stages. Our observations show that the shortsighted single-stage model exaggerates the effects of the incentive and that a well-defined knockout barrier further tempers the fund manager's risk appetite. While the presence of a knockout barrier aligns the manager's behavior with the investor's interests, our analyses also indicate that too little tolerance of underperformance will force the manager towards a passive position while the clients still pay active fees, and capping fees too earlier will cause a lock-in effect.

10.4.1 Proportional Asset -Based Fee

Although performance-based compensation structures have been adopted by many investment companies, the traditional and still dominant form of compensation in the mutual fund and institutional asset management industry is an asset-based fee, where the management firm receives a fraction of the total assets under management. Our analysis shows that even under such a traditional fee structure, with no explicit performance fee, the manager still shows a certain level of risk-shifting behavior.

Since most investors evaluate the performance of their money manager on an annual basis,[8] the investment horizon in our analyses is set to one year with quarterly rebalance, i.e., $T = 4$. We measure returns as of the start of the horizon, so that initially the manager's relative return is set equal to 1, i.e., $R_0 = 1$. To enable the manager to exhibit aggressive risk-shifting behavior, quarterly active risk is allowed to range from $\sigma_L = 0$ to $\sigma_U = 10\%$ per quarter (20% annually). The knockout barrier is set to 0.85, i.e., the management contract will be immediately terminated if the cumulative realized return at the end of a quarter is 15% below the benchmark portfolio at the end of any quarter before the last one. If the manager's contract is allowed to run through the last quarter, his final payoff will be 1% of the fund's wealth at the end of the year.[9] The risk-free rate is assumed to be 5% per annum. We also set the portfolio manager's relative risk aversion parameter equal to 4 and the initial wealth to 1. This will be referred to as the "base case" throughout this chapter.

Figure 10.5 examines the manager's optimal active risk choice at different times. The manager's active risk exposure depends both on time and the fund's cumulative relative return. The flat risk decision rule displayed for Q1 requires some explanation. The fund's starting cumulative relative performance is fixed at 1. Hence, the optimal active risk decision is made only at the point where relative return equals 1. However, we find it helpful to represent this decision as a horizontal line, so that the decisions made at the beginnings of each of the four quarters are displayed on an equal footing. We remind the reader, in this chart and in similar charts to follow, that this decision assumes a relative return of 1 by placing a triangle on the horizontal line representing the decision rule for Q1 where the relative return is 1.

Figure 10.5 shows that the fund manager chooses a conservative active risk policy in the earlier stages. At the beginning of Q1, the manager adopts a lower active risk than in later stages at the point where the fund's relative return is 1. At Q2, we observe the same trend across all the states. Contrary to popular belief, the manager prefers conservative investment decisions (low active risk), even when the performance is significantly behind the benchmark as the risk of being fired due to crossing the knockout barrier

[8] One-year evaluation period is considered as the most commonly used evaluation period for a money manager in industry.

[9] In practice, the asset-based fee is charged as a percentage of average assets under management over an investment period. For simplicity, we assume the fee is calculated based on the end of year asset only.

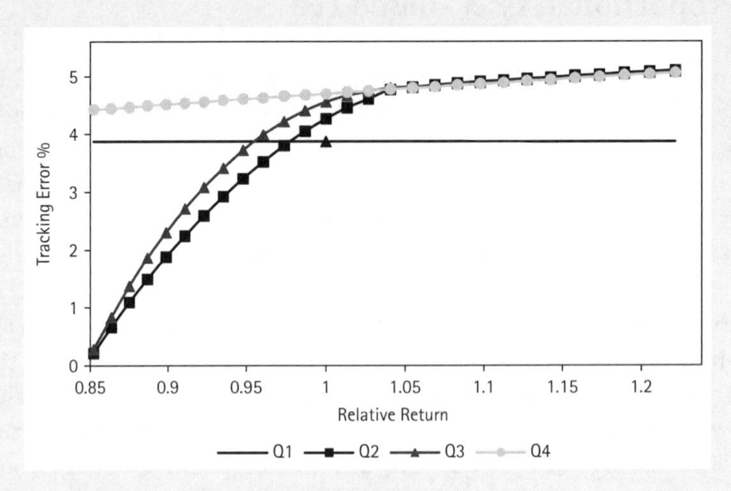

FIGURE 10.5 Active risk decisions at different investment stages under an asset-based fee structure. This figure shows the portfolio manager's state dependent active risk decision at the beginning of each quarter. The parameters for the fraction of fund fee contract are: $R_{Barrier} = 0.85$, $k = 1\%, \gamma = 4, \sigma_L = 0,\ \sigma_H = 10\%$.

hangs like the Sword of Damocles over him. As performance gets better, the manager gradually increases the fund's active risk to capture future upside returns. Dynamically this works like portfolio insurance on active returns. The manager switches dynamically between the risk-free asset (the index fund) and the risky asset (the active fund), taking higher active risk when returns are good.

As we enter later stages (Q3 and Q4), investment decisions become more aggressive. This reveals an important tradeoff between the knockout penalty and the asset-based fee compensation. The manager receives a percentage of the market value of the fund's assets as compensation and is therefore inclined to take higher risks in order to increase the probability of a larger management fee. However, a higher active risk also increases the probability of being fired and thus losing all future management fee flows. On top of this, risk aversion on the manager's part and information ratio decay also decrease the marginal contribution to revenues for larger active risks. When the fund's performance trails the benchmark significantly, the probability of being fired increases quickly. Soon the knockout penalty dominates the potential upside of positive performance on asset-based fees. Eventually the manager prefers a conservative investment strategy. As the fund's performance improves, the marginal knockout penalty decreases while the expected management fee increases and the manager tends to increase the level of active risk. While hitting the barrier early means losing future earnings ability and hence incurs a larger knockout cost, this is of less concern in later stages. The conservative strategy dominates in the earlier stages, especially when the fund's performance is close to the barrier.

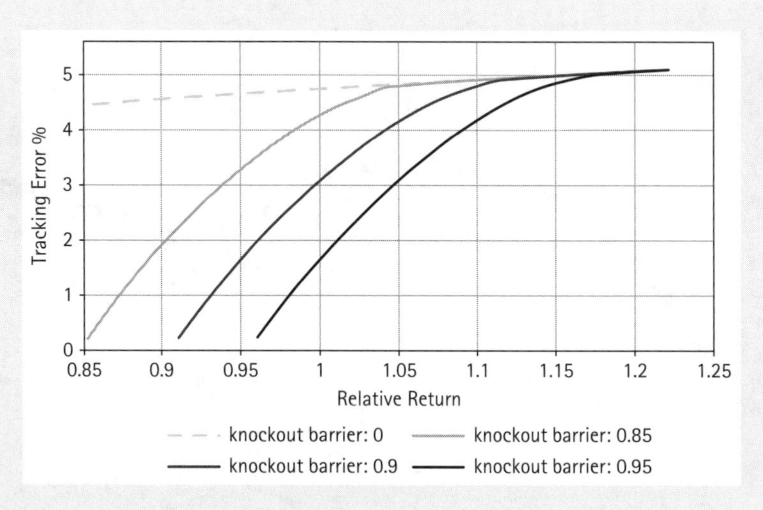

FIGURE 10.6 The effects of a knockout barrier on active risk decisions with a proportional asset-based fee structure. This figure shows the portfolio manager's active risk decision at the beginning of second investment stage with three different knockout barriers: 0, 0.85, 0.9, 0.95. All other parameters are as in Figure 10.3.

Figure 10.6 compares the manager's active risk decisions under different knockout barrier specifications. The line with a knockout barrier of zero corresponds to the case with no barrier at all, since in our model the value of the fund is always above zero. For a given relative return, the managed fund's active risk level increases as the knockout barrier decreases. A lower knockout barrier decreases the chance of termination, which in turn results in a smaller knockout penalty cost. Note that the gaps among all lines increase, when the fund's performance deteriorates. A fund with a higher knockout barrier adopts a more conservative investment strategy because of the increased danger of the manager being fired.

Our analysis has shown that even a proportional asset-based fee may provide incentives for a fund manager to eventually take higher risks. Imposing a knockout barrier mitigates the manager's risk-shifting incentive as higher active risk leads to a larger expected knockout penalty. The multi-stage setting further illustrates that it is not in the manager's best interests to adopt a myopic single-stage decision rule since it ignores the benefit of future fee flows.

10.4.2 Asymmetric Incentive Fee

Asymmetric incentive fee structures are very popular among hedge funds and commodity trading advisors (CTAs). The incentive fee is similar to a call option with the hurdle return corresponding to the strike price. Traditional single-period analysis indicates

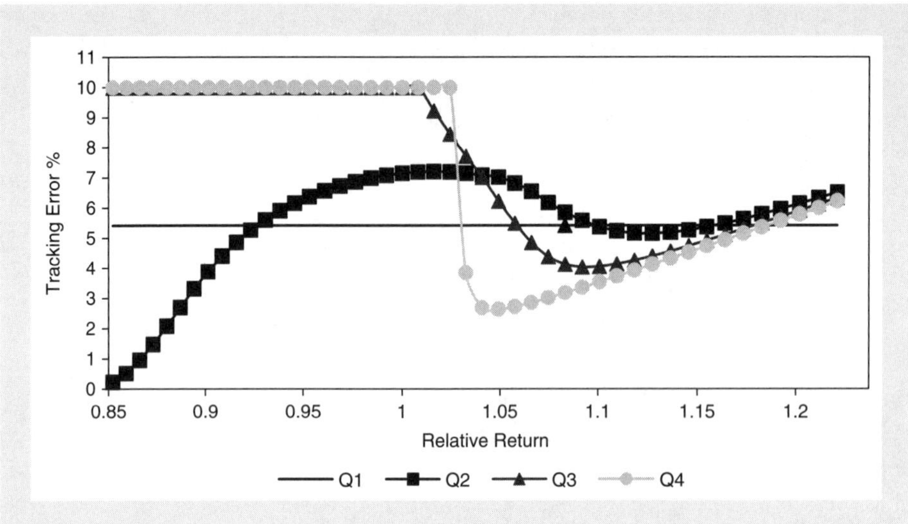

FIGURE 10.7 Active risk decisions at different investment stages under an asymmetric incentive fee structure. This figure shows the portfolio manager's state-dependent active risk decision at the beginning of each quarter. The parameters for the asymmetric incentive compensation contract are: $R_h = 1.0$, $R_{Barrier} = 0.85$, $k_1 = 1\%$, $k_2 = 20\%$, $\gamma = 4$, $T = 4$, $\sigma_L = 0$, $\sigma_H = 10\%$.

that within this structure a fund manager is tempted to invest more aggressively as this will increase the expected value of his performance option. Our analyses below will show that risk decisions are much more complicated in a multi-stage setting. As in the base case of a proportional asset-based fee, we still assume the manager faces a constant knockout barrier during the whole investment horizon. All other settings and parameters are the same, except the compensation structure. We assume the manager earns a fixed management fee of 1% of the initial assets, plus an incentive fee equal to 20% of the fund's excess return above the high watermark, which is set to 1.

Figure 10.7 shows the manager's risk rules as a function of his fund's performance status. While a manager with an asset-based compensation structure prefers to monotonically increase active risk as the fund's performance improves or as the investment horizon approaches, Figure 10.7 indicates that a hedge fund manager has a much more complex risk behavior (as in Figure 10.5, the flat active risk observation at stage 1 is for consistency of presentation). We start with the last stage's active risk decisions as depicted by the Q4 decision rule, which in fact is a single-stage utility maximization problem. The manager exhibits three areas of economic behavior.

Case 1: Poor performance When the fund's relative performance is less than 1, the manager takes the maximum allowed risk of 10%. As his performance option is out of the money, it is optimal for him to play aggressively to increase the option value.

Case 2: Intermediate performance As the performance option moves into the money, the manager tries to protect its terminal value by reducing investment risks. Figure 10.7 show that the portfolio's active risk drops sharply from 10% to 2.64% as relative performance increases from 1.02 to 1.05. Over this region, the manager abruptly reverses his strategy from aggressive to conservative. The major motive for this change is the incentive to lock in the realized option gain. For a lower risk aversion ($\gamma < 4$) this effect would be less pronounced.[10]

Case 3: Good performance If the option moves further into the money, the manager prefers to increase active risk again. With a positive information ratio and a performance sharing arrangement in place, there is a strong incentive to produce alpha.

Compared with the Q4 decision rule, the decisions at Q3 is qualitatively similar but less dramatic. The investment behaviors in the two investment stages are very similar when the option is either deeply in or deeply out of the money. At this stage, the manager is not as pressed for time, and this allows him to take more active risk. If risk taking pays off, he can lock in the gain in the last stage. If, on the other hand, the active investment suffers poor returns, he still has one more chance to bet in the last stage. Hence, the level of risk chosen in the decision rule for the next-to-last stage is generally above that of the last stage. This effect is more significant when the relative performance falls in the region between aggressive and conservative.

A surprising observation from Figure 10.7 is the manager's prudent investment behavior when his incentive option is deep out of the money, as it is at the beginning of the second investment stage. This finding stands in strong contrast with the existing literature on the single-stage asymmetric incentive fee contract. Grinblatt and Titman (1989) highlight the fact that, with limited liability, the manager has an incentive to take on a riskier portfolio than otherwise; see also Gollier, Koehl, and Rochet (1997). Of course, this behavior is not prudence *per se*. In fact, the reason the manager chooses such a low active risk is to avoid hitting the knockout barrier at an early stage, which would mean sacrificing not only the potential incentive compensation but also the present value of the future percentage fee. The option-like nature of the incentive compensation will dominate the knockout penalty as the fund's performance is far above the barrier. This leads to larger active risk as shown on the right side of the Q2 line.

Figure 10.8 illustrates the manager's active risk choices under different knockout barrier levels at the beginning of the second stage. Comparing cases with a knockout barrier to the case without, the manager shows prudent investment preferences, especially when the fund is significantly trailing the benchmark. When the fund's relative performance is far ahead of the benchmark, the effects of the knockout barrier will play a minor role in determining the optimal level of investment risk. Essentially, the knockout barrier serves as a control mechanism for unobserved volatility, i.e., even

[10] The authors can provide analysis to support this on request.

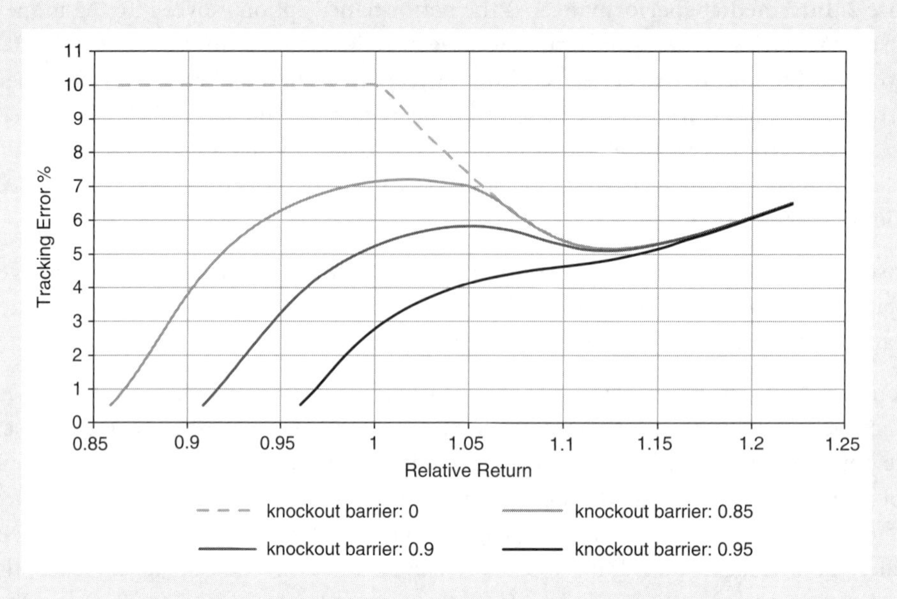

FIGURE 10.8 The effects of a knockout barrier on active risk decisions with an asymmetric incentive fee structure. This figure shows the portfolio manager's active risk decision at the beginning of the second investment stage with three different knockout barriers: 0, 0.85. 0.9, 0.95. All other parameters are as in Figure 10.5.

though the investor cannot observe volatility directly in our setting,[11] he can observe one of its consequences: unpleasantly large returns.

In summary, our analyses suggest that hedge-fund managers will follow a much more complex risk strategy in a multi-stage setting with a knockout barrier in force. More frequent observations will impose prudent behavior, i.e., to avoid risk shifting makes business sense.

10.4.3 Symmetric Compensation Structure

For practical purposes all fee arrangements that use a symmetric participation structure have a fixed component, as well as a variable component which is symmetric about the benchmark return. This compensation structure has recently gained popularity in the institutional and mutual fund industries. A typical fund with a fulcrum fee structure caps the maximum negative impact of the variable fee, and this also limits the maximum

[11] Of course, there would be no need for all this, if investors could perfectly monitor manager outcome, i.e., if there were neither hidden action nor hidden information.

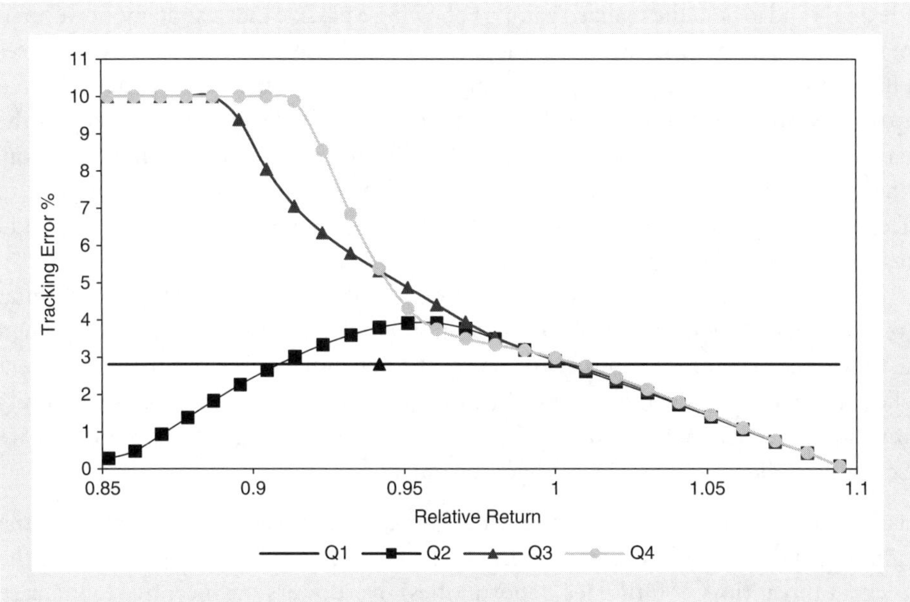

FIGURE 10.9 Active risk decisions at different investment stages under a fulcrum fee structure. This figure shows the portfolio manager's optimal active risk decision as a function of relative return at the beginning of each quarter. The parameters for the fulcrum fee are: $R_C = 1.1$, $R_F = 0.9$, $k_1 = 1\%$, $k_2 = 1\%$, $R_{Barrier} = 0.85$, $\gamma = 4$, $T = 4, \sigma_L = 0$, $\sigma_H = 10\%$.

attainable fee. Crucially, the floor will ensure that the manager's total compensation remains positive.

In our symmetric institutional fund example, the amount of the fixed fee is equivalent to 1% of the fund's initial wealth, and the proportional incentive part is 1% of the excess return over the benchmark. The floor and cap hurdle rates are set to 0.9 and 1.1, respectively, and the knockout barrier is set at 0.85. Note that a knockout barrier above the lower hurdle rate would make little sense as it would make the latter irrelevant until the last period.

The manager's optimal risk strategies at different decision times through the year are shown in Figure 10.9. (Again, at stage 1 we only make a decision at the point where relative return equals 1.) Based on the manager's active or passive risk-taking style, the fund's relative return space can be divided into two regions the passive, benchmark-tracking region, and the active risk management region.

The passive benchmark tracking region is located on the right side of the cap relative return point, which is $R_C = 1.1$ in these examples. The manager's optimal policy is to hold the benchmark portfolio and lock in the gains. The explanation of the passive benchmark tracking region is very intuitive. When the manager performs very well over the earlier investment stages, he is near or above the concave portion of the payoff schedule. Therefore, the best strategy is to closely track the benchmark ("closet indexing") and lock in the realized gain.[12] Following a passive index strategy, however, is not necessarily in the best interests of the investor who is paying active management fees in the expectation of receiving a positive alpha. Even though the manager has achieved superior performance in an earlier stage, it would be beneficial to the investor if the manager were to maintain the level of active risk for the rest of the investment horizon. Otherwise the breadth of an investment strategy clearly suffers. To avoid a gain-lock-in effect, the ceiling of the performance based fee should in generally not be too low. Good pragmatic advice is for the investor to set it where he thinks luck begins.

The active risk management region is located on the left side of the cap rate point. Over this region, the manager's decision is similar to the asymmetric case except when the fund's performance is significantly above the benchmark. The optimal investment policy depends both on the number of investment stages remaining and the fund's cumulative performance relative to the benchmark. To highlight the time effect, we discuss the earlier stages and later stages separately.

Case 1: Earlier stages The Q2 line shows the manager's optimal active risk policy at the beginning of the second investment period. The decision curve is humped because the knockout threat (loss of future fee opportunities) overpowers the incentive to increase the value of the implicit long call on out-performance in the region when the fund significantly underperforms its benchmark. As performance improves and compensation becomes more symmetric the manager gradually increases active risk in order to maximize utility. As performance approaches the determined performance cap, risk-taking only offers downside possibilities for the manager (but not for the client) and we see the familiar reigning in of active risk. Compared with the manager's active risk decision at stage 2 at the point where the portfolio's relative return is 1, the manager's decision at stage 1 is more conservative because the knockout penalty in stage 1 is larger that that in stage 2.

Case 2: Later stages The logic changes slightly in later stages, Q3 and Q4, when underperformance leads the manager to expect only the minimum (floor) fee. Now the threat of termination largely loses its disciplining influence, while the all-or-nothing feature of owning a call on out-performance makes the policy of maximizing active risk optimal. It is all the same to the manager whether he is terminated as a result of hitting the knockout barrier or loses his incentive fee because of bad performance. The level of active risk decreases almost monotonically as the fund's performance improves, because of the concave utility (large fee payments carry less utility) and the capped upside compensation (fee payments do not become very large anyway).

Compared with the optimal policy of the asymmetric compensation structure shown in Figure 10.7, the manager follows similar active strategies at the beginning of the third and the fourth investment stages in the middle region (between cap and floor), However,

[12] This result is consistent with a recent investigation by Elton et al. (2003). They find that outperforming funds show a much lower variance than other funds, although we acknowledge that there might be other reasons behind this.

the gap between the decision curves of these two stages become smaller. This can be explained by the concave nature of the collar option in the neighborhood of the cap, since limited cap compensation dampens the manager's anticipated compensation at an even earlier stage.

Overall, our observations confirm the manager's tendency to balance the knockout penalty and the option benefit. The manager optimally trades off termination risk against the anticipated fees. As relative performance moves away from the barrier, the marginal loss (adding one unit of risk) from termination risk decreases. Risk-taking, however, has an upper limit as both concave utility and concave compensation eventually make risk-taking less attractive.

As in the previous sections, we present a comparative analysis for different knockout barriers in Figure 10.10. Intuitively, for a given performance state, a higher barrier level increases the chance of knockout and the marginal penalty cost for an additional unit of risk. Therefore, the existence of the knockout barrier mitigates the manager's risk, taking incentives.

Just as too low a cap fee can push the manager to follow a passive index strategy, too low a tolerance of downside risk also provides an undesirable incentive: a passive index tracking strategy in earlier stages and an aggressive gamble at the last stage. If the earlier stage's poor performance brings the fund close to the knockout barrier, the manager

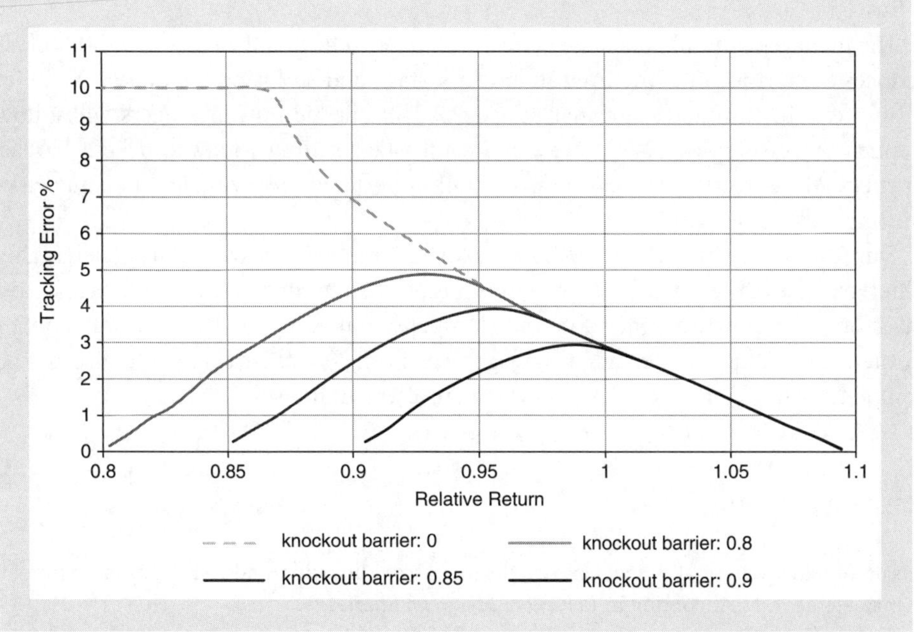

FIGURE 10.10 The effects of a knockout barrier on active risk decisions with a fulcrum fee structure. This figure shows the portfolio manager's active risk decision at the beginning of the second investment stage with three different knockout barriers: 0, 0.8, 0.85. 0.9. All other parameters are as in Figure 10.7.

has no room to take active risk. Instead, he will follow a strict indexing strategy because even a moderate active risk exposure may lead to a high chance of being fired (up to 50% in the case of the normal distribution).

10.5 Conclusions

This chapter investigated the determination of the optimal active risk policy as a function of time and relative performance (state variables) using stochastic programming techniques.

In contrast to previous research, we explicitly modeled the possibility that a management contract will be terminated if performance drops below a minimum acceptable target level. We find that this knockout barrier will encourage the manager to invest more conservatively. This result is explained by the tradeoff between the knockout penalty and the compensation incentive. Managers take little risk when the fund's performance is close to a knockout barrier, because of the large penalty cost of being fired. Essentially the knockout barrier serves as a control mechanism for unobserved volatility, i.e., even though volatility – in our setting – cannot be observed directly by the investor, we can observe one of its consequences: unpleasantly large returns.

The manager carefully maneuvers the fund to avoid hitting the barrier and therefore reduces the chance of being fired in an early stage and so losing the present value of future fees. In summary, our analyses suggest that hedge fund managers will follow a much more complex risk strategy in a multi-stage setting with a knockout barrier in effect. More frequent observations will impose prudent behavior, i.e., avoiding risk-shifting makes business sense.

Our results have important implications for active management, and are considerably different for each fee structure. At a minimum, this research will help managers and investors alike to write a more optimal compensation contract. This not only applies to the relationship between asset management firms and their clients but also to the compensation of portfolio managers within investment houses.

References

Basak, S., Pavlova, A., and Shapiro, A. Optimal asset allocation and risk shifting in money management. Forthcoming in *Review of Financial Studies*.

Bertsekas, D. (2001) *Dynamic Programming and Optimal Control*. Vol. I and II Athena Scientific, Belmont, Massachusetts.

Birge, J. and Louveaux, F. (1997). *Introduction to Stochastic Programming*. Springer, New York.

Black, C., Elton, E., and Gruber, M. (2003). Incentive fees and mutual funds. *Journal of Finance*, **58**, 779–804.

Brown, K., Harlow, W., and Starks, L. (1996). Of tournaments and temptations: An analysis of managerial incentives in the mutual fund industry. *Journal of Finance*, **51**, 85–110.

Carpenter, J. (2000). Does option compensation increase managerial risk appetite? *Journal of Finance*, **55**, 2311–2331.

Chevalier, J. and Ellison, G. (1997). Risk taking by mutual funds as a response to incentives. *Journal of Political Economy*, **105**, 1167–1200.

Das, S. and Sundaram, R. (1999). Fee speech: Adverse selection and the regulation of mutual funds. Working paper, *Center for Law and Business, New York University*.

Ferguson R. and Leistikow, D. (2003). Long-run investment management fee incentives and discriminating between talented and untalented managers. *Journal of Investment Management*, **1**, 47–72,

Goetzmann, W., Ingersoll, J., and Ross, S. (2003). High-water marks and hedge fund management contracts. *Journal of Finance*, **58**, 1685–1717.

Gollier, C., Koehl, P., and Rochet, J. (1997). Risk-taking behavior with limited liability and risk aversion. *Journal of Risk and Insurance*, **64**, 347–370.

Grinblatt, M. and Titman, S. (1989). Adverse risk incentives and the design of performance-based contracts. *Management Science*, **35**, 807–822.

Grinold, R. and Kahn, R. (2000). The efficiency gains of long-short investing. *Financial Analysts Journal*, **56**, 40–53.

Heinkel, R. and Stoughton, N. (1994). The dynamic of portfolio management contracts. *The Review of Financial Studies*, 7, 351–387.

Hodder, J. and Jackwerth, J.C. Incentive contracts and hedge fund management. Forthcoming in *Journal of Financial and Quantitative Analysis*.

Ippolito, R. (1992). Consumer reaction to measures of poor quality: Evidence from the mutual fund industry. *Journal of Law and Economics*, **35**, 45–70.

Khorana, A. (1996). Top management turnover: An emperical investigation of mutual fund managers. *Journal of Financial Economics*, **40**, 403–427.

Stremme A. (2001). Optimal compensation for fund managers of uncertain type: The information advantages of bonus schemes. Working paper, *Department of Finance, New York University*.

PART IV

PARAMETER ESTIMATION

CHAPTER 11

ROBUST BETAS IN ASSET MANAGEMENT*

HEIKO M. BAILER, TATIANA A. MARAVINA, AND R. DOUGLAS MARTIN

11.1 Introduction

In spite of its known shortcomings the capital asset pricing model (CAPM) and the corresponding single factor market model remain ubiquitous in asset management. This is reflected for example by the prominent place of CAPM and the market model for risk modeling in the first chapter of Connor *et al.* (2010). The standard practice of asset managers and financial data service providers is to compute beta estimates as the slope coefficient in a classical least squares (LS) fit of the market model to historical asset returns and market returns. Unfortunately one or more outliers in the asset returns or the market returns can have a very substantial influence on the values of a LS beta, leading to a very misleading assessment of the market risk premium. This flaw in classic beta estimates and the existence of alternative robust beta estimates need to be better known by asset managers and financial data service providers.

This chapter addresses the above need by introducing a theoretically justified robust beta estimate that is not much influenced by outliers, and illustrate by in-depth comparisons of LS and robust betas how often and when significant differences tend to occur between the two estimates. Our over-arching goal is to promote routine use of robust betas by asset managers and financial data service providers as a complement to LS betas for the following purposes: (a) identification of firms and time periods for

* Part of the research leading to this chapter appears in Bailer (2005). We wish to acknowledge with gratitude help from Professor Timothy Simin at Pennsylvania State University in the early stages of this research project.

which there are substantial differences between the two beta estimates, and (b) evaluating the market risk premia based on robust betas that reject one or a very small number of outliers, in comparison with that of LS betas that may be adversely influenced by outliers. In order to develop an in-depth understanding of the absolute and relative behaviors of robust and LS betas we compute, visualize, and analyze the time series of cross-section distributions of paired differences between LS and robust beta estimates of risk. These cross-sections are computed on contiguous two-year intervals of weekly returns over the period 1964 to March 2009, and we compute analogous cross-sections for differences in standard errors, t-statistics for null hypothesis of unity betas, and percentage contribution of market risk to total risk. Our results show that a very tiny fraction of outliers, often only one or two, will often have a huge impact on the value of an LS beta, resulting in a very different value from that of the robust beta. Furthermore the robust beta often involves rejecting only one or two outliers.

Computing the time series of cross-section distributions of the betas and their associated statistics allows us to achieve another goal: the identification and analysis of time-variation in these distributions. Not surprisingly our results show that the cross-section distributions exhibit significant temporal patterns, the most significant of which are associated with: (a) major market events such as the recession in the early to mid-1970s, the crash of 1987, the dot-com bubble collapse in 2000, and the financial markets collapse in 2008–9, and (b) time-varying market volatility. In some cases the resulting influence on the cross-sections of betas and related quantities seems reasonable, while in other cases the reason for the behavior is not clear and further research is required.

Since previous studies have indicated that outliers in equity returns are a small firm effect (see for example Martin and Simin 2003), we study this question here in more detail by computing the above cross-sections across four equal sized market capitalization groups. The results provide further confirmation that the prevalence of outliers is a small firm effect, and that correspondingly the largest differences between LS and robust betas tend to occur for the smaller sized firms.

The remainder of this chapter is organized as follows. Section 11.2 briefly recalls the inadequate optimality properties of least square estimates for non-normal distributions and introduces the proposed robust estimator of beta, including its key theoretical properties. Section 11.3 describes our method of selecting "liquid" stocks from the entire CRSP database of listed stocks, and reports on the temporal behavior of market volatility and of market capitalization (including its astonishing growth from 2003 through 2007 and subsequent dramatic drop). Section 11.4 presents detailed results on the cross-section distributions of the OLS and robust estimates and related quantities. Section 11.5 analyzes the behavior of the cross-section distributions of the systematic contribution to risk over time. Concluding comments appear in Section 11.6. Appendix A contains a review of existing research literature on robust betas. Appendices B and C provide computational details for the robust beta estimate introduced in Section 11.2, Appendix D contains some additional details on the stock returns data used for the study, and

Appendix E documents extensive non-normality in the cross-section of these returns as measured by the Jarque–Bera statistics.

11.2 Non-Robust Least Squares and a Robust Beta Alternative

Financial data service providers and practitioners invariably deliver beta estimates that are based directly or indirectly on OLS estimates, which may be quite misleading due to the influence of one or more returns outliers.[1] These providers and practitioners should not be blamed too much for uniformly relying on OLS beta estimates. After all OLS estimates are simple, widely available in software packages, and are best *linear* unbiased estimates under mild assumptions, where "best" means "minimum variance." In addition they are best estimates among both linear and nonlinear estimates when the errors are normally distributed. In this highly idealized case that J. W. Tukey called "utopian," OLS estimates also have a convenient distribution theory for inference, i.e., for t-statistics and p-values. This is something that is drilled into every graduate student in statistics, economics, and finance.

However, equity returns and market returns often have skewed and fat-tailed non-normal distributions that give rise to outliers, in which case OLS is no longer best among all linear and nonlinear estimates.[2] It is known that least squares parameter estimates for linear regression models are quite non-robust in the data-oriented sense – they can be very adversely influenced by outliers – and in the statistical sense – they can suffer from bias and inflated variance (alternatively, loss of efficiency) due to outlier-generating fat-tailed and skewed distributions. Fortunately good robust regression estimates exist that suffer relatively little from these problems. See for example the books by Huber (1981), Hampel *et al.* (1986), and Rousseeuw and Leroy (1987) and the more recent Maronna *et al.* (2006), and references therein. By now there is a substantial research literature on robust estimation of betas which we review in Appendix A.

A challenge to the user of robust regression is that there exist a number of proposed robust alternatives to OLS, and the asset manager is left in the uncomfortable state of not knowing which one to choose. While there are several theoretical arguments in support of alternative types of robust estimates, we believe that a particular type of regression

[1] Many financial service providers report an unadjusted OLS estimate while others report a shrinkage version designed to correct for the tendency of the OLS estimate to revert towards the market beta over time (Blume 1975). See also the Vasicek (1973) Bayesian argument for a shrinkage estimator. Martin and Simin (2003) provide a brief tabular survey of the type of betas delivered by financial data service providers.

[2] There is a considerable body of finance literature describing the skewness and fat-tails (kurtosis) of the distributions of the returns of various asset classes. See for example Bradley and Taqqu (2003), and Rachev *et al.* (2005), and the references therein.

M-estimate described below has a most attractive theoretical justification and therefore use it throughout this study.[3] The single-factor model for computing beta is

$$r_t = \alpha + \beta \cdot r_{M,t} + u_t, \quad t = 1, \ldots, T \tag{11.1}$$

where r_t are the equity returns and $r_{M,t}$ are market returns, both in excess of a risk-free rate, and with the conventional assumption that the errors u_t are serially uncorrelated and uncorrelated with the market returns. Regression M-estimates $\hat{\alpha}$ and $\hat{\beta}$ for the parameters α and β are obtained by minimizing

$$\sum_{t=1}^{T} \rho\left(\frac{r_t - \alpha - \beta \cdot r_{M,t}}{\hat{s}_u}\right) \tag{11.2}$$

with respect to α and β, where ρ is a symmetric robustifying loss function and $\hat{s}_u$ is a robust scale estimate for the residuals $\hat{u}_t = r_t - \hat{\alpha} - \hat{\beta} \cdot r_{M,t}$. With $\psi = \rho'$ the resulting $\hat{\alpha}$ and $\hat{\beta}$ satisfy the local minimum conditions

$$\sum_{t=1}^{T} r_{M,t} \cdot \psi\left(\frac{r_t - \hat{\alpha} - \hat{\beta} \cdot r_{M,t}}{\hat{s}_u}\right) \tag{11.3}$$

and

$$\sum_{t=1}^{T} \psi\left(\frac{r_t - \hat{\alpha} - \hat{\beta} \cdot r_{M,t}}{\hat{s}_u}\right) = 0. \tag{11.4}$$

Special cases of regression M-estimates include the least-absolute-deviations (LAD) estimate for which $\rho(u) = |u|$ and a robust residuals scale estimate is not needed, and the Huber (1964) min-max variance optimal loss function that is quadratic in a central region $(-c,\ c)$ and linear outside that region.

We note that the LAD and Huber functions are both convex and therefore lead to a relatively easy optimization problem. Unfortunately these functions are unbounded and it turns out that for unbounded loss functions the bias of a regression M-estimator is unbounded under reasonable outlier generating models. See for example Martin, Yohai and Zamar (1989) who showed that in order to obtain bias robustness toward outliers when the predictor variables are random one needs to use a bounded loss function. Three members of a particular family of bounded loss functions $\rho_c(u)$ that we advocate and use throughout this chapter are shown in the left-hand panel of Figure 11.1 and the corresponding "psi" functions $\psi_c = \rho_c'$ are shown in the right-hand panel.

The formulas for the functions $\rho_c(u)$ and $\psi_c(u)$ given in Appendix B confirm the shape of the functions in Figure 11.1: $\rho_c(u)$ is quadratic and $\psi_c(u)$ is linear in the central

[3] M-estimates are *maximum-likelihood type* estimates introduced by Huber (1964) for estimating location and by Huber (1973) for regression. They are obtained by replacing the logarithm of the density of the residuals $\ln f(u)$ with a "robustifying" loss function $\rho(u)$ that grows at most linearly for large u. Note that in the case of a normal density $\rho(u)$ is a quadratic, leading to the least squares estimate, and it is this rapid growth rate that results in a lack of robustness toward outliers of the least squares estimates.

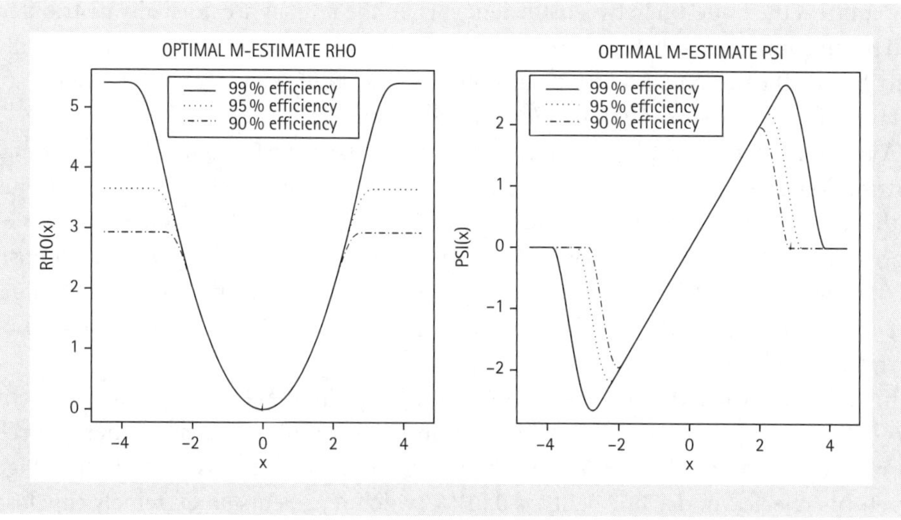

FIGURE 11.1 Optimal robust ρ and ψ for three normal distribution efficiencies.

region $|u| \leq 2c$, and these two functions are constant and zero, respectively, in the region $|u| \geq 3c$. The latter property results in residuals greater than $3c$ in magnitude being *rejected*, i.e., they are treated as outliers that have no influence on the estimate, in the solution (11.3)–(11.4). Robust estimators with this behavior are said to be *outlier-rejection* estimators. We note that the function $\psi_c(u)$ is an intuitively appealing improvement over a so-called *hard-rejection* function that is linear in a central region $(-c, c)$ and zero outside that region thereby treating all residuals in the central region as good while treating those outside the region as bad. By way of contrast the function $\psi_c(u)$ makes a smooth transition from treating sufficiently small residuals as good and sufficiently large residuals as bad. The above ρ_c is a good piecewise polynomial approximation to an optimal bias robust M-estimate loss function discovered by Svarc, Yohai and Zamar (2002). The optimality criteria they used was that in large sample sizes the resulting M-estimate should minimize the maximum bias due to outliers while at the same time paying only a small user-defined penalty in terms of reduced statistical *efficiency* when the data is normally distributed.[4] For normally distributed returns the OLS estimate has 100% efficiency while the efficiency of our robust estimate is simply the ratio of the variance of the OLS estimate to the variance of the robust estimate and therefore has efficiency less than 100%.

Note that as $c \to \infty$ then $\rho_c(u)$ becomes a pure quadratic function and the M-estimate becomes the fully-efficient OLS estimate when the returns are normally distributed. For finite c the robust estimate has a larger variance than the OLS estimate, hence efficiency less than 100%, when the returns are normally distributed. The choice

[4] Statistical *efficiency* of an estimator is defined as the ratio of the minimum attainable variance under a given distribution model to the variance of the estimator.

of c controls the trade-off between efficiency when the returns are normally distributed and the maximum bias that can be caused by outliers when the returns are not normally distributed. The normal distribution efficiencies of 90%, 95% and 99% in Figure 11.1 are obtained for the values $c = 0.944$, 1.06 and 1.29, respectively.

A natural way to view the increased variability of the robust estimate for the normal distribution is in terms of the reciprocal of the square root of the efficiency, i.e., in terms of the ratio of standard errors RSE(Robust, OLS) = S.E.(Robust)/S.E.(OLS) where S.E. represents standard error. The efficiencies 85%, 90%, 95%, and 99% give RSE(Robust, OLS) values of 1.085, 1.054, 1.026, 1.005, respectively. This gives standard error inflations of 8.5%, 5.4%, 2.6%, and 0.5% for the robust estimator relative to OLS in the case of normally distributed returns.

In our study we used an efficiency of 99%, obtained with the choice of tuning constant $c = 1.29$, in which case we pay virtually nothing in terms of inefficiency when returns are normally distributed. For example with this choice of tuning constant the percentage of returns rejected under normality is 0.011%, which represents an extremely tiny loss in information. At the same time our robust beta estimates turn out to deal well with non-normal returns containing outliers that can adversely influence the OLS betas.[5]

Figure 11.2 provides four examples of OLS estimates and robust beta estimates computed as described above with different outlier configurations. The four companies are Merrill Lynch and Co. (ME) during 2002–2003, Electronic Data Systems Corp. (EDS) during 2002–2003, Valhi, Inc. (VHI) during 1990–1991, and E.I. du Pont de Nemours and Co. (DD) during 1986–1987. These companies had average market capitalizations during those two-year intervals of \$40.0B, \$14.7B, \$1.1B, and \$22.3B, respectively. The dashed and solid lines show the OLS and robust fits. The two parallel dotted lines indicate the region outside of which data points are rejected by the robust regression described above and in more detail in Appendix C.

The MER example in the upper left contains two influential market return outliers that are not MER return outliers. The OLS beta estimate of 1.5 is smaller than the robust beta estimate of 1.8 because the latter estimate rejects these two outliers (plus two others). In this case the OLS estimate is an under-estimate of the typical systematic risk of MER. For the EDS example there are three outliers that are EDS return outliers that influence the OLS beta estimate in a positive direction resulting in the value 2.03. It may be noted that none of these three outliers are market return outliers, but the one in the lower left of the figure has considerable influence. By way of contrast the robust beta estimate is 1.41, indicating that EDS has a typically smaller risk than is indicated by the OLS beta estimate. In this case one might reasonably argue that the robust beta under-estimates the systematic risk of EDS.[6] In the case of VHI there are two outliers, one a

[5] In Section 11.4 we show that the median number of outliers rejected is about 1%. This is consistent with the findings of Knez and Ready (1997) who showed that the Fama and French (1992) risk premium on size completely disappears when 1% of the most extreme observations are deleted each month. By way of contrast Martin and Simin (2003) used 85% efficiency which results in a larger fraction of outlier deletions that we no longer believe is advisable.

[6] For further discussion of the influence of this type of outlier, see Section 11.6.

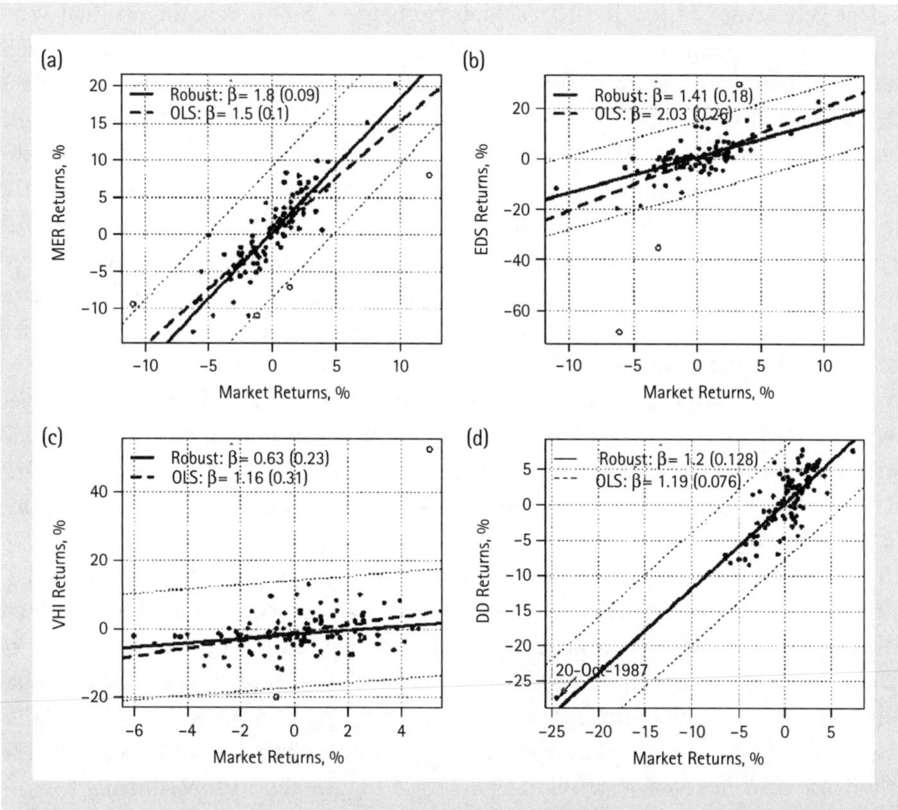

FIGURE 11.2 OLS and robust beta estimates for four different outlier configurations.

negative VHI return outlier whose market return value is in the middle of the market returns, and one a positive VHI return gross outlier that is the largest market return. The latter is highly influential on the OLS beta estimate whereas the former is not. In this case the OLS estimate of 1.16 indicates that VHI has a systematic risk slightly larger than that of the market, while the robust estimate rejects the two outliers, giving an estimate of .63. In this case the OLS estimate substantially over-estimates the risk of VHI and the robust estimate gives a more believable indication that VHI has considerably less risk than the market (in this case the most influential outlier is a huge positive return that an investor is happy to have).

In the case of DD there is a single data point that is a gross isolated outlier in both the market returns and the DD returns. It happens that this outlier is quite close to the robust straight-line fit and is not rejected as an outlier by the robust fitting method. As a result the OLS and robust beta estimates are very close to one another, and this is as it should be, for such an outlier can be considered to be a "good" outlier in that it is consistent with both linear single-factor model fits. It should be noted that except for DD the standard errors of the robust beta estimates are smaller than those of the OLS fits. This is because outliers in the residuals from an OLS fit inflate the residual sum-of-squares component of the coefficient standard error estimate in the case of OLS, while the robust beta estimate rejects such outliers. Furthermore, except for DD the OLS beta differs from the robust beta by more than two robust standard errors, and hence differences between the two estimates can be judged to be significant. On the other hand, for DD the opposite is true: the robust beta standard error is larger than the OLS beta standard error. This is because the robust estimate rejects the single outlier for purposes of computing the standard error, thereby reducing the sum-of-squared market returns relative to that of the OLS estimate (for details, see Appendix C). One might argue that this is quite reasonable: when the single gross outlier for DD is included in the sum-of-squared market returns in computing an OLS beta standard error, it may result in an unduly optimistic standard error estimate. Put differently, one may be wise not to trust a single outlier as in the case of DD as having exceptionally high information content. We also note that in the case of DD the difference between the OLS and robust beta is less than two standard errors whichever standard error estimate one chooses.

In concluding this section we point out that minimizing the objective function (11.2) is a non-convex optimization problem that requires a sophisticated method to insure finding a good solution. By a "good" solution we mean either a global minimum of (11.2) or else obtain a local minimum whose performance is nearly as good as a global minimum solution. The optimization method we use was proposed by Yohai, Stahel and Zamar (1991), as described in Appendix C and implemented in S-PLUS and R. The method also provides robust standard errors for $\hat{\beta}$ that we report subsequently.

11.3 Equity Selection and Temporal Behavior

The data for our study is from the Center of Research in Securities Prices (CRSP) U.S. Stock and U.S. Treasury Databases. We focus on all common stocks listed on the NYSE, AMEX, and NASDAQ exchanges and use the CRSP value-weighted NYSE/AMEX/NASDAQ composite as the market proxy. All computations are carried out using contiguous two-year intervals of weekly returns from the beginning of 1964 through March 2009.[7] Weekly returns were computed using end-of-Tuesday weekly returns obtained by aggregating all available daily total returns, so long as there is at least one daily return in a given week.[8] The risk-free rates were obtained from the CRSP

[7] The period from January 2008 through March 2009 contains 66 weeks.

[8] Missing daily returns are discarded in aggregating to weekly returns, and thus a weekly return will be missing if and only if all five daily returns in a given week are missing.

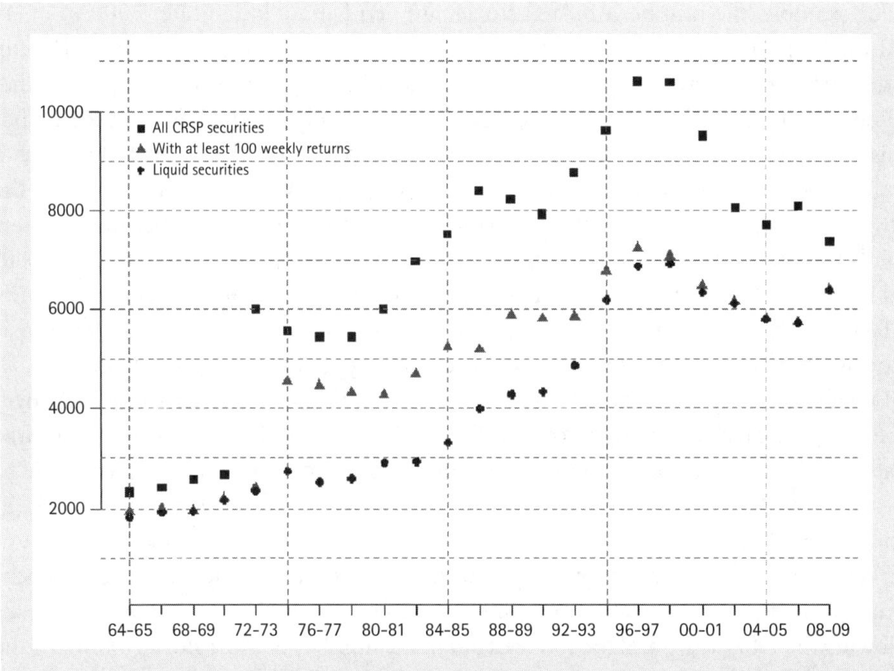

FIGURE 11.3 Number of securities in the study. Squares represent the total number of firms in the CRSP U.S. Stock Database that have at least one weekly return in each contiguous two-year period. Triangles represent the number of firms listed for at least 100 weeks in each such period. Round dots show the number of firms with at least 100 non-zero returns in each period.

Risk Free Rates File and are based on one-month T-bill rates converted to one-week risk-free returns.[9]

Our analysis is carried out on a "liquid" subset of the above securities, where liquidity is defined as having at least 100 non-zero weekly returns in a given two-year interval.[10] The number of such liquid firms over time is represented by the round dots in Figure 11.3. By way of comparison the squares represent the number of stocks in the CRSP database that had at least one weekly return for each two-year interval, which we refer to as "listed" stocks. The triangles represent the number of stocks that have returns for at least 100 weeks during each two-year interval but not necessarily at least 100 non-zero returns, which we refer to as "long-listed" stocks. Jumps, peaks, and valleys in the number of listed stocks, long-listed stocks, and liquid stocks are associated with market events and changes in regulations.

[9] For each month CRSP Risk-Free Rates File reports continuously compounded 365 day rates (we use the one based on the average of the bid and ask prices of a one-month T-Bill). Denote it as R. We assume that for all weeks in that month the one-week continuously compounded risk-free return is $R\frac{7}{365}$ percent.

[10] For the January 2008–March 2009 interval the requirement is at least 64 non-zero returns.

For example, the number of listed stocks jumped from a little under 3000 in 1970–1971 to about 6000 in 1972–1973 after the NASDAQ stock exchange opened. The dip in the number of these stocks in the mid-to-late 1970s reflects the deep recession that followed the oil crisis in 1973. This was followed by a steady rapid growth in the number of listed stocks until the stock market crash in October 1987, which was followed by a dip in the number of listed stocks until 1991. During the advent of the Internet and the increasing popularity of dot-com companies, the number of listed stocks again grew rapidly for most of the 1990s. Then the drop in the number of listed stocks in 2000–2001 and further in 2002–2003 is associated with the burst of the technology bubble and the 9/11/01 terrorist attacks. Finally, the dip in the number of listed stocks in 2008–2009 is associated with the financial market collapse that began in the summer of 2008.

The most striking features of the total number of liquid stocks versus listed stocks over time are: (1) the lack of a jump in the number of liquid stocks in 1972–1973; (2) the large relative difference between the number of liquid stocks and the number of listed stocks starting in 1972–1973 when NASDAQ opened as compared with prior to 1972–1973; (3) similar overall patterns before and after 1972–1973 except for an attenuated impact of market events on the liquid stocks, e.g., the smaller dip in the number of liquid stocks during the recession of the mid-1970s, the non-existent dip in the number of these stocks following the 1987 crash, and the reduced dip in the number of these stocks following the dot-com bubble burst and 9/11/01; and (4) the tendency for the number of liquid stocks to lag the number of listed stocks by roughly two years. The reason for the first behavior is that in 1972–1973 the new NASDAQ firms did not have enough history to satisfy our liquidity selection criteria, e.g., 90% of the excluded stocks were traded for 54 weeks or less. The second behavior reflects the fact that in any two-year interval subsequent to NASDAQ opening there are a very large number of listed stocks that do not satisfy our definition of being liquid, no doubt due to the large number of micro-cap and small-cap listings enabled by NASDAQ (though the proportion of such listed stocks appears to have decreased in recent years). The third behavior is due to the fact that the liquid stocks are nonetheless a significant subset of the listed stocks. The fourth behavior is hardly surprising in view of our definitions of listed stocks versus liquid stocks, and we note that the seemingly different pattern of listed stocks versus liquid stocks in the 2006–2007 and 2008–2009 periods may be due to this lag effect.

We note that the relative difference between long-listed stocks and liquid stocks is strikingly different from the relative differences between listed stocks and liquid stocks. Prior to 1974–1975 there is only a very small relative difference between long-listed stocks and liquid stocks. Then in 1974–1975 there is a substantial jump due to NASDAQ opening in 1972–1973, with the lag effect mentioned above. However, unlike the relative difference between the listed and liquid stocks, the relative difference between long-listed and liquid stock decreases over time until there is almost no difference subsequent to the dot-com collapse in 2000.

One might argue that our focus on liquid stocks induces a selection bias in our results and that the choice of 100 weeks of non-zero returns is arbitrary. However if we included stocks with shorter histories, possibly very short, we could have returns series with many zeros resulting in biased estimates; if we delete the zeros we end up with smaller sample sizes, with correspondingly larger estimator standard errors than when using 100 or more returns. Using sample sizes of 100–105 results in almost identical and nearly minimal standard errors. On balance we felt this was the best approach.

It is natural to expect that the behaviors of beta estimates differ for different market capitalization ranges. Therefore, we present our results in four equal sized groups based on firm size, where size is defined as the log of the market capitalization in millions of dollars. For each two-year period the stocks are split into four equal sized market capitalization groups called SIZE25, SIZE50, SIZE75, and SIZE100, based on their average market capitalization during each two-year interval. The resulting market capitalization lower quartile, median, and upper quartile break points for each two-year period are plotted in Figure 11.4 and displayed in Table 11.1. We note that using the Russell market cap segmentation methodology as reported on May 31, 2009, the largest micro-cap firm capitalization is $375M. This indicates that there are likely to be a fair number of micro-cap firms in our SIZE50 group (the lower quartile to median capitalization group) and at least some in the low end of the SIZE75 group (the median to upper-quartile capitalization group). A more detailed time profile of market capitalization quantiles is provided in Appendix D.

For purposes of reference in subsequent discussions it will be useful to refer to Figure 11.5, which displays the time series of market return volatility computed from the weekly market returns on each two-year interval.

Figure 11.5 reveals that the range of two-year average market volatilities is large, with local peaks in excess of 20% in the vicinity of well-known market events (an all-time

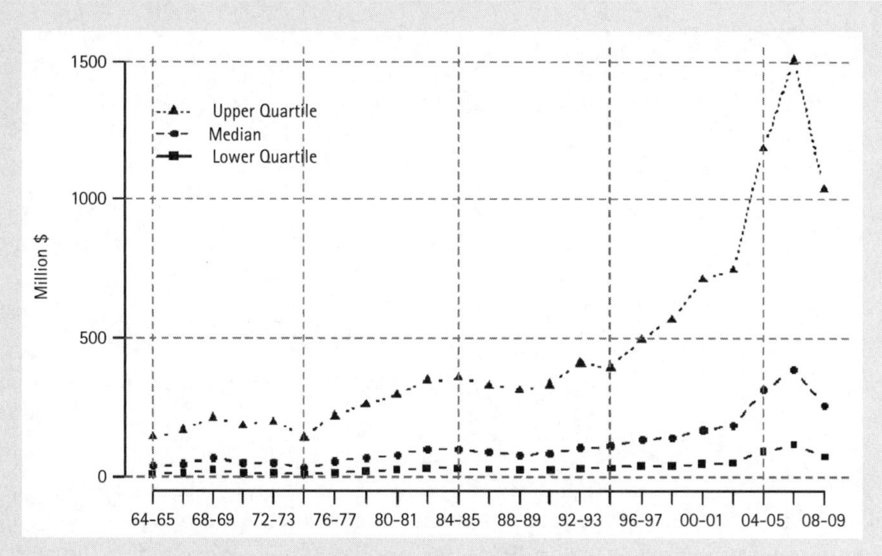

FIGURE 11.4 Market capitalization lower quartile, median, and upper quartile break points for the liquid stocks included in the study, in millions of dollars. These break points are based on average market capitalization over a given two-year interval. Triangles represent the upper quartile, circles the median, and squares the lower quartile.

Table 11.1 Market capitalization percentiles in millions of dollars.

	64–65	66–67	68–69	70–71	72–73	74–75	76–77	78–79
25%	12.2	15.7	25.7	16.2	16.5	12.2	17.9	24.2
50%	40.1	47.4	69.8	51.0	52.4	37.1	56.1	70.1
75%	146.5	172.9	216.9	186.3	200.0	144.9	223.3	263.5

	80–81	82–83	84–85	86–87	88–89	90–91	92–93	94–95
25%	27.7	35.1	34.3	30.6	27.9	27.9	35.0	36.3
50%	81.1	103.2	102.1	90.6	79.7	87.9	107.2	113.9
75%	298.3	350.0	358.8	332.3	315.3	335.6	413.6	397.6

	96–97	98–99	00–01	02–03	04–05	06–07	08–09
25%	43.5	44.9	48.6	52.8	94.3	120.7	75.0
50%	137.8	142.6	171.5	186.4	318.8	387.5	263.3
75%	498.5	568.6	712.6	746.6	1184.8	1504.4	1039.6

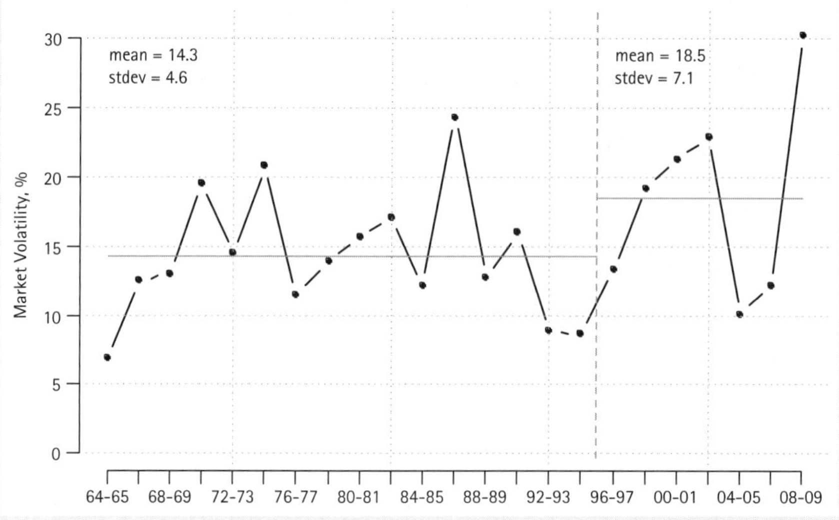

FIGURE 11.5 Annualized excess market returns volatility.

peak of 30% occurs during the recent financial market meltdown of 2008–2009), and with minimum values below 10% in 1964–1965 and 1992–1995. We note that the market volatilities are both higher on average and more volatile during 1996–2009 than during 1964–1995. As we discuss in the next two sections, it turns out that the market volatility levels influence the standard errors of the OLS and robust beta estimates as well as the market risk as a percentage of total risk. By way of contrast, the mean market returns have no such impact, and we provide a graph of their values over time in Appendix D for the interested reader.

11.4 OLS AND ROBUST BETAS CROSS-SECTIONS

This section studies the time series of cross-sections of OLS and robust estimates of beta, as well as the cross-section of standard errors of the estimates, on contiguous two-year intervals from 1964 to March of 2009. All estimates are based on weekly returns in excess of the risk-free rate. We first analyze the raw OLS and robust betas.

Figure 11.6 displays the cross-section distributions of OLS betas as represented by box-plots of all liquid stocks in each two-year interval from 1964 to March of 2009.[11] Figure 11.7 displays the time series of cross-sections of robust betas based on the same returns data used in Figure 11.6, and with the same vertical axis range. The pattern of

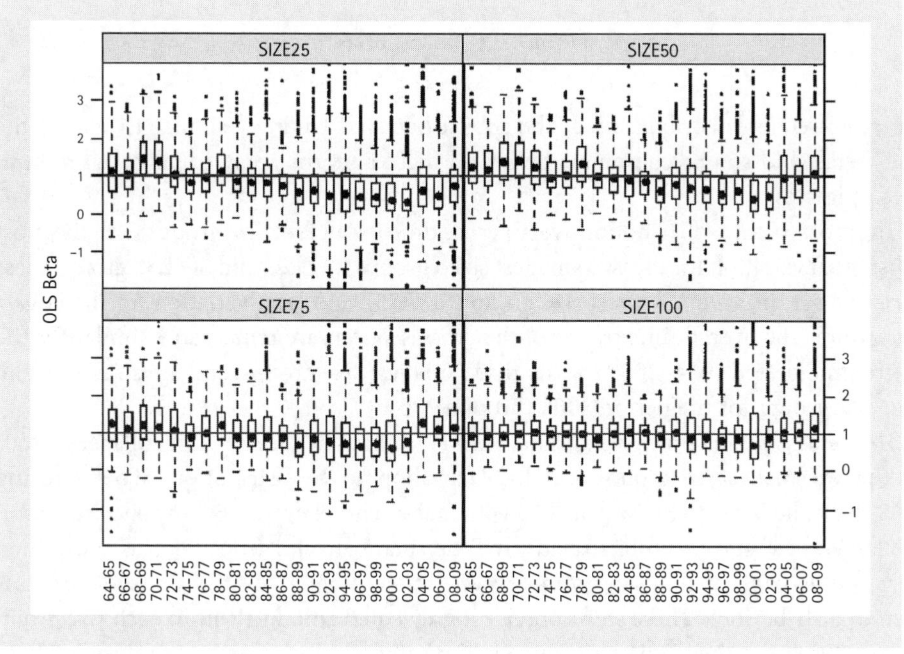

FIGURE 11.6 OLS betas.

[11] The dots in the middle of each box represent the median beta; the ends of the boxes represent the upper and lower quartiles of the betas. The "whiskers" are placed at the farthest value not beyond one-and-a-half times the inter-quartile range (i.e., the box height) from the nearest quartile (box end), and dots outside the fences are regarded as outliers in the tails of the distributions.

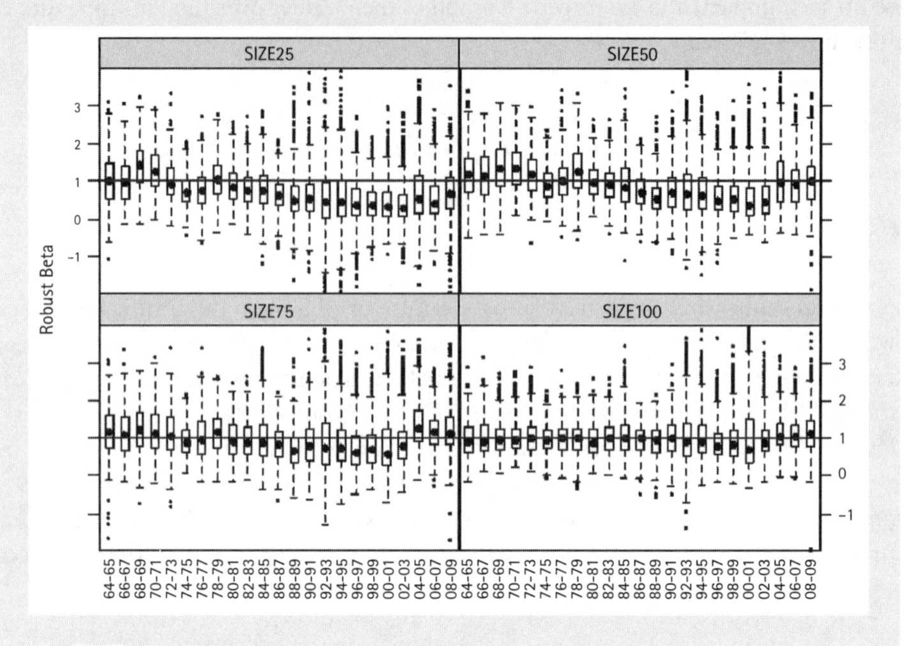

FIGURE 11.7 Robust betas.

the cross-section distributions of the robust betas is strikingly similar to that of the OLS betas, and so our comments below on these patterns apply equally well to both beta estimates.

The cross-section distributions vary across time for all four size groups with the most substantial variation for the two smallest sized groups (SIZE25 and SIZE50 groups), less variation for the second largest size group (SIZE75), and least variation for the largest size group. The overall time trends of the cross-sections are remarkably similar for the entire time period 1964–2009 for the three smallest size groups, and are similar for all four size groups for the period 2000 through 2009.

The betas exhibit a downward trend from 1968 through the dot-com collapse in 2001 for the two smallest size groups, with local variations in the distributions of betas during 1968–1979 and in 1986–1987 associated with major market events. By way of comparison the largest size group exhibits relatively little such behavior from 1964 to 2001. Then during 2004–2009 all four size groups experience substantial positive shifts in the cross-section distributions. These shifts are of roughly equal amounts within each size group during 2004, and there exists a transitional positive shift in distribution during 2002–2003 for the two largest size groups that is absent for the two smallest size groups. We note that for all size groups there is a tendency for some degree of positive skewness in the central part of the cross-sections, but the more striking effect is the increasingly fat right tail in the distribution in the latter portion of the period covered.

One might hope to draw firm conclusions about the relationship between the cross-sections of OLS and robust betas and the occurrence of market recessions and crashes.

However, Figures 11.6 and 11.7 send quite mixed messages. The three smallest size groups exhibit the following behaviors in response to recessions and crashes through 2001:

(a) During the four-year interval 1968–1971 (which includes the recession of 1969–70) the distributions of the betas abruptly increase: for the two smallest size groups, three-quarters of the betas are larger than one, and the median betas for each two-year period are about 1.5. The second largest group has similar such changes but smaller in magnitude, and the largest size group has essentially no such.
(b) In 1972–1973 and 1974–1975, which encompass the deep recession of 1973–1975, the distributions of the betas shift in an increasingly negative direction.
(c) During the 1976–1979 period of recovery from the previous recession, the distributions of the betas shift in an increasingly positive direction.
(d) In 1986–1987 which includes the crash of 1987 the distributions of the betas shift in a negative direction.
(e) During 1996–1999, which contained the Asia crisis and the Russian default, more than three-quarters of the betas for the two smallest size groups were negative, with median betas in the vicinity of .5 and only slightly larger betas for the second largest size group.
(f) During the dot-com buildup in 1998–1999 and collapse in 2000–2001, the distributions of betas shifted only slightly in a positive direction and then slightly in a negative direction, respectively. The latter behavior is also evident in the largest size group where the dispersion of the betas is also the largest among all four groups.

During the 2004–2007 period the distributions of betas shift in a positive direction in all size groups with roughly equal shifts within each group. For the largest two size groups the distributions are shifting toward their 2004 locations already in 2002–2003. It is quite puzzling that during the financial market collapse of 2008–2009 the distributions of betas remain roughly the same as in 2006–2007 for the three largest size groups and the distribution is shifted positively relative to 2006–2007 for the smallest size group. But we have seen similar behavior during the 1968–1971 period containing the recession of 1969–1970 when the distributions of betas shifted in a positive direction relative to 1966–1967 for the two smallest size groups. It remains an open question why betas move in a negative direction during some market recessions or crashes and move in a positive direction during other such events.

Although Figures 11.6 and 11.7 show that the cross-section distributions of the OLS and robust betas are similar, differences between the estimates may be obscured by the overall variability in each of the estimates. The statistical remedy to deal with this is to compute the cross-sections of paired differences between the two estimates and the results are presented in Figure 11.8. The distributions of the paired differences are concentrated rather close to zero for the two largest size groups, but less so for the two smallest size groups for which substantial positive differences occur. Furthermore all size groups have paired difference distributions with fat right and left tails that reflect

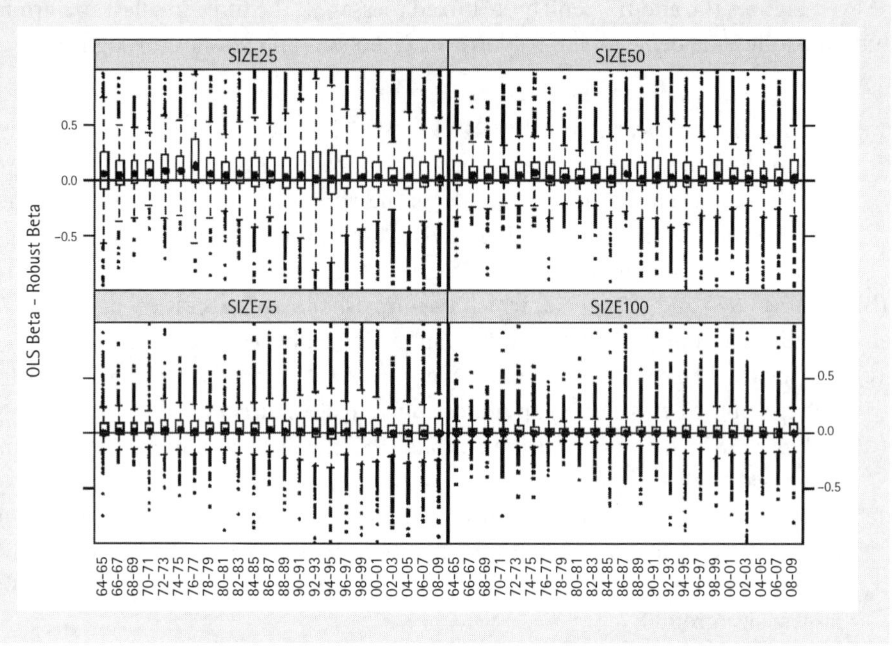

FIGURE 11.8 Paired differences between OLS and robust betas.

some very large differences between OLS and robust betas for the same firm, including some differences larger than one that are outside the plotting region.

Figure 11.9 displays the fraction of stocks having paired differences between OLS and robust betas that exceed financially meaningful values of .25, .5, .75, and 1. The results show that the fractions of exceedances increase with decreasing firm size and are quite variable across time.

The distribution of the paired differences between OLS and robust betas for each size group is provided in Figure 11.10 which displays the exceedance probabilities (one minus the usual cumulative distribution function) of these differences. The positive skewness of the distributions is evident, particularly so for the smaller size groups, and the distributions are increasingly concentrated around zero as the group size increases.

Table 11.2 provides the fraction of firms in each size group during the higher and more volatile market period 1986–2009, for which the absolute difference between OLS and robust beta, |DIFF|, is greater than $\Delta = .1,\ .2,\ \cdots,\ 1.0$. It is evident that |DIFF| decreases with increasing Δ and with increasing firm size. Differences greater than $\Delta = .3$ are likely to be significant to most investors and for the smallest size group 25% of the firms have |DIFF| larger than .3, while for the largest size group a non-ignorable 6% of the firms have such differences.

Table 11.3 presents similar results across all size groups for the time period 1992–1997 in order to facilitate comparison with Martin and Simin (2003). Our results are shown in the second column and those of Martin and Simin (2003) are shown in the third column.

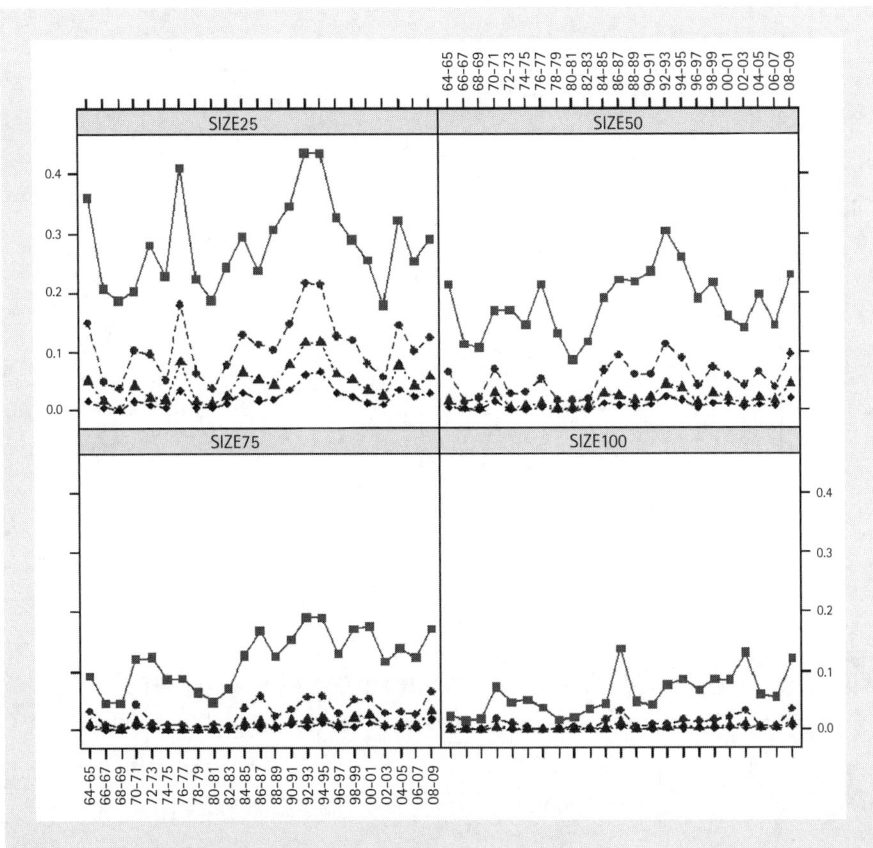

FIGURE 11.9 Fractions of pairwise OLS and robust beta differences exceeding 0.25 (squares), 0.5 (circles), 0.75 (triangles), and 1 (diamonds) in absolute value.

Compared to Martin and Simin (2003), our current study results in a smaller fraction of firms with absolute differences between OLS and robust betas greater than the various values of Δ. This is very likely due to the fact that although Martin and Simin (2003) used the same general type of robust regression method as we do, they used one with a normal distribution efficiency of 85%, which results in rejecting more returns as outliers than does our choice of 99% normal distribution efficiency.

We now examine how the standard errors of the OLS betas behave and how they compare with the robust betas' robust standard errors described in Appendix C. Figure 11.11 shows that the cross-section distributions of the OLS standard errors (S.E.s) vary considerably over time, with fat tails and very large standard errors for some stocks, particularly for the smaller size groups. The three largest median OLS S.E.s occur in the 1964–1965, 1992–1993 and 1994–1995 intervals for all four size groups, which is consistent with the fact revealed by Figure 11.5 that these three two-year intervals had the three smallest market volatilities.[12] The smallest median OLS S.E. occurs in

[12] The standard error for an OLS beta is inversely related to the volatility of market returns. Expression (11.C3) shows that this is also the case for robust betas.

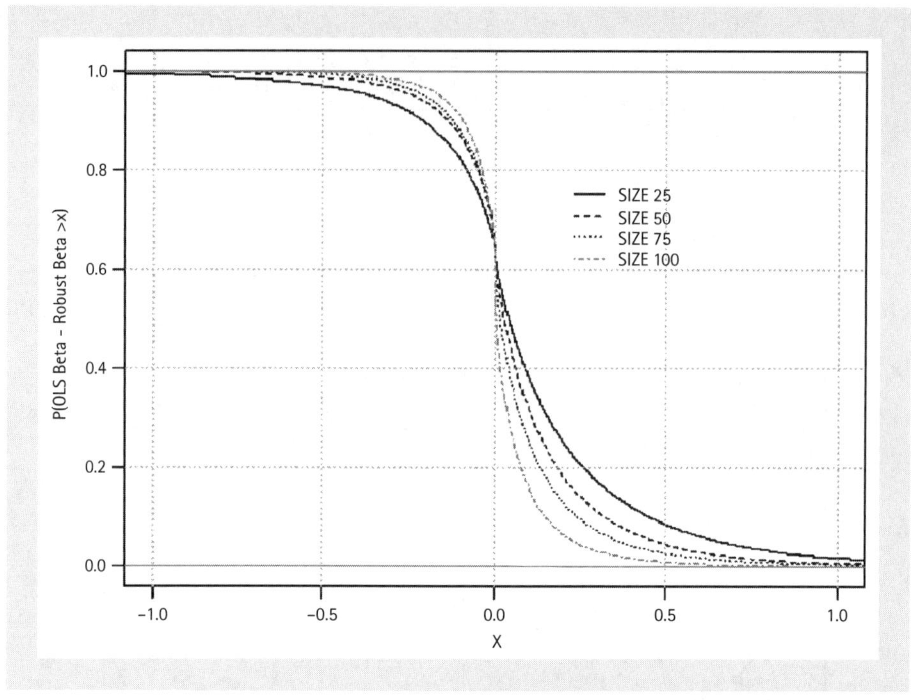

FIGURE 11.10 Distribution of paired differences between OLS and robust betas.

Table 11.2 Fraction of firms during 1986–2009 with |DIFF| greater than Δ.

Δ	SIZE25	SIZE50	SIZE75	SIZE100
0.1	0.56	0.46	0.4	0.28
0.2	0.37	0.26	0.21	0.12
0.3	0.25	0.16	0.11	0.06
0.4	0.18	0.1	0.07	0.03
0.5	0.13	0.07	0.04	0.02
0.6	0.09	0.04	0.03	0.01
0.7	0.07	0.03	0.02	0.01
0.8	0.05	0.02	0.01	0
0.9	0.04	0.01	0.01	0
1	0.03	0.01	0.01	0

Table 11.3 Comparison with |DIFF| values in Martin and Simin (2003) for 1992–1997.

Δ	|DIFF > Δ|	M&S 2003
0.1	0.47	0.62
0.2	0.28	0.39
0.3	0.18	0.26
0.4	0.12	0.18
0.5	0.08	0.13
0.6	0.06	0.10
0.7	0.04	0.07
0.8	0.03	0.05
0.9	0.02	0.04
1	0.02	0.03

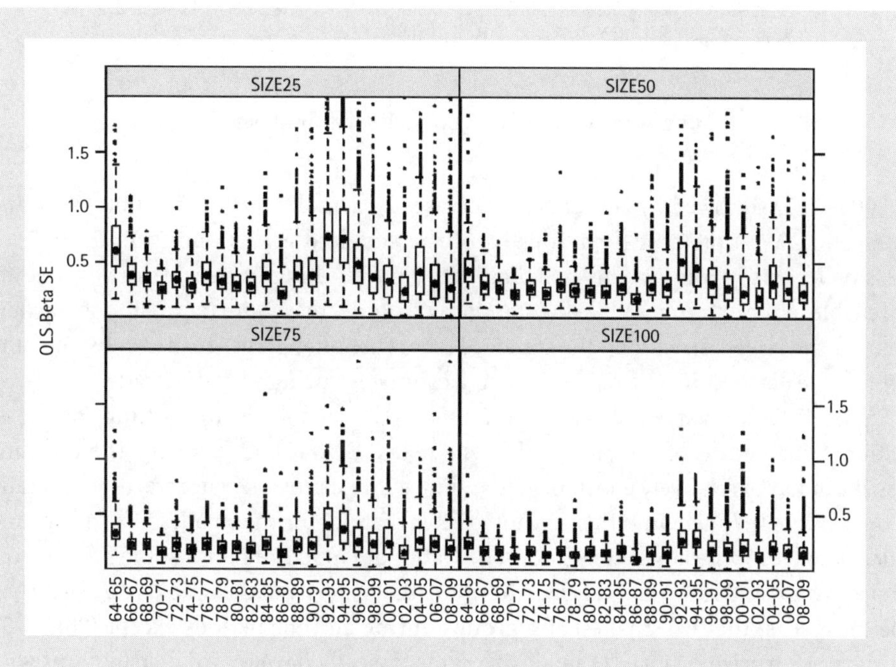

FIGURE 11.11 OLS beta standard errors.

1986–1987 for all four size groups, which is consistent with that period having a large market volatility that is second only to that in 2008–2009. The decreasing pattern of OLS S.E.s from 1994 through 2003 is consistent with the increasing market volatilities during that time interval. Similarly the increase in S.E.s in 2004–2005, followed by the subsequent decrease in S.E.s through 2009, is consistent with the drop in market volatility

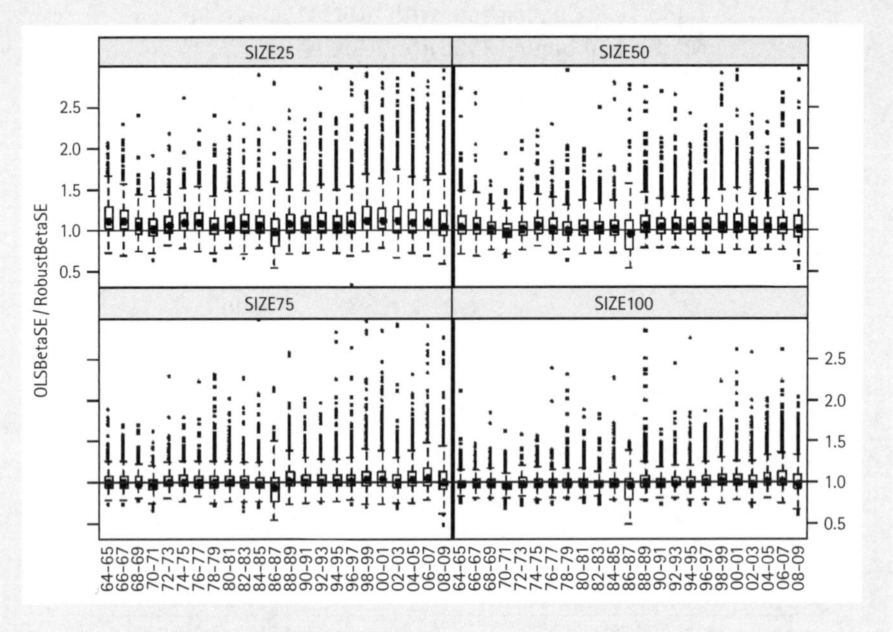

FIGURE 11.12 Ratios of OLS beta S.E.s to robust beta S.E.s.

in 2004–2005 followed by subsequent increases in market volatility in 2006–2007 and 2008–2009. We note that three-fourths of the standard errors during 1992–1995 for the smallest size group are greater than one-half, resulting in beta estimates that are unreliable in the extreme. While the standard errors decrease with increasing size group, even for the largest size group the standard errors are often larger than .2 subsequent to 1991; this leads to quite imprecise OLS beta estimates during the last decade.[13]

Figure 11.12 compares the S.E.s of the OLS and robust betas by plotting the cross-section distributions of the ratio of the OLS beta S.E. to robust beta S.E. The resulting distributions are relatively constant across time with positive skewness relative to a ratio of one. While the median ratios are not greater than 1.2 for the smallest size group and much smaller for the larger size groups, the ratios are much larger for some firms across all size groups and time intervals. Furthermore the majority of the ratios are greater than one for at least the two smallest size groups during all time periods except 1986–1987. This is not surprising since (1) small size firms typically have return distributions with fatter tails and more skewness than large size firms; and (2) robust regression coefficient standard errors are smaller than OLS standard errors under fat-tailed non-normality, the more so the fatter the tails. By way of contrast note that for the largest size group prior to 1986–1987 it appears that the ratios are not only very concentrated around one, but sometimes have a majority of values less than one, such as in 1970–1971.

[13] This lack of precision motivated Fama and French (1992) and other researchers to use grouping methods to average out the beta estimation errors in factor model asset pricing studies.

The interval 1986–1987 that contains the Black Monday market crash has cross-section distributions for all size groups that are significantly shifted toward ratios less than one, i.e., half of the OLS standard errors are smaller than the robust standard errors and sometimes substantially so. Twenty-five percent of the firms have ratios of S.E.s less than about .75 for all size groups during 1986–1987. Standard error ratios that small are not explained by normal distribution inefficiency of the robust betas (see the discussion in Section 11.2). It is more likely due to large "good" outliers that are consistent with the single factor model but are down-weighted by our robust regression method as in the case of the firm with ticker DD in Section 11.2 (cf. Figure 11.2). This situation can happen whenever a market crash yields one or more negative market return outliers along with one or more negative firm return outliers that are consistent with the fitted single-factor model. This is likely what happens during the market crash in 1987.

Finally we analyze the beta "t-statistic" formed by subtracting the market beta value of one from each beta estimate and dividing the result by the S.E. of the beta estimate. The cross-sections of the resulting OLS beta t-statistics are displayed in Figure 11.13 and the cross-sections of the robust beta t-statistics are shown in Figure 11.14. Beta t-statistics that fall outside the region defined by the horizontal lines at ± 1.96 in Figure 11.13 and Figure 11.14 are significantly different from the market beta value of one at an approximate 5% level. We say "approximate" in the case of the OLS betas because the distributions of the returns are not normal, and in the case of the robust betas because the t-distribution assumption is approximate under normality as well as non-normality.

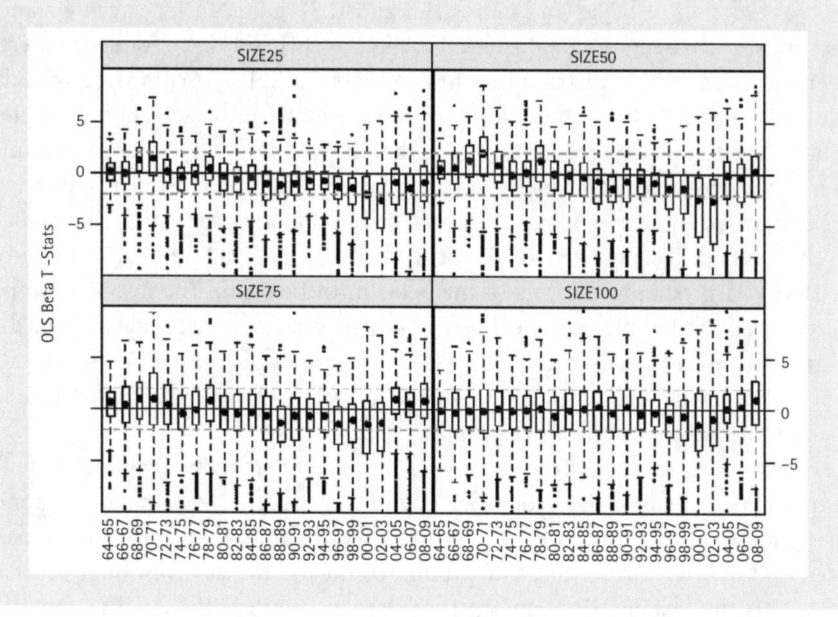

FIGURE 11.13 OLS beta t-statistics.

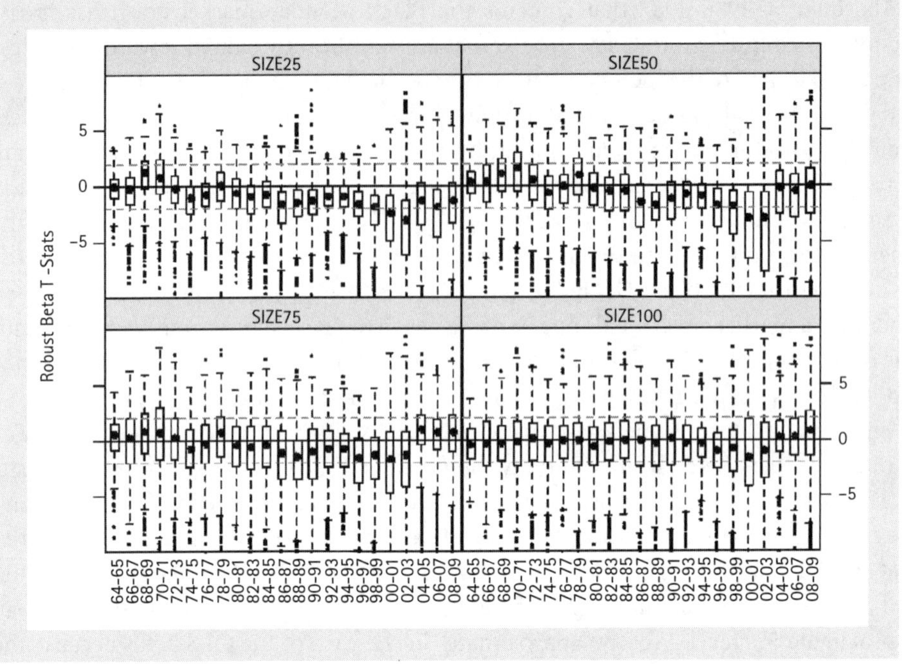

FIGURE 11.14 Robust beta t-statistics.

The time series patterns of the cross-sections of the beta t-statistics in Figures 11.13 and 11.14 are strikingly similar. These patterns are also similar to the time series patterns of the cross-section of betas (in Figures 11.6 and 11.7), adjusted for varying standard errors (whose cross-sections are displayed in Figures 11.11 and 11.12). A major difference between the cross-section distributions in Figures 11.6 and 11.7 as compared with those in Figures 11.13 and 11.14 is that the former have predominantly fat right tails while the latter have fat left tails. The reason for this is that the smallest and largest beta estimates are associated with relatively small and relatively large standard errors, respectively, as can be confirmed by scatter plots of estimated betas versus their standard errors. The relatively compact distributions of the beta t-statistics in 1992–1995 arise because of the relatively large standard errors of the betas in those years. The negative shift and increased dispersion in the cross-section of the distributions of the t-statistics in 2000–2003 arise because a large fraction of beta estimates have values less than one and at the same time have small standard errors. This latter behavior is particularly dramatic in 2002–2003 for the two smallest size groups.

The over-arching messages from Figures 11.13 and 11.14 are that: (a) almost half of the stocks in the two smallest size groups had significantly higher systematic components of risk than the market during 1970–1971, with the fraction of such stocks decreasing to about one-quarter for the SIZE100 group; (b) during the dot-com bubble collapse in 2000–2003 the systematic components of risk are significantly less than that of the market for about half the stocks in the two smallest size groups and somewhat less

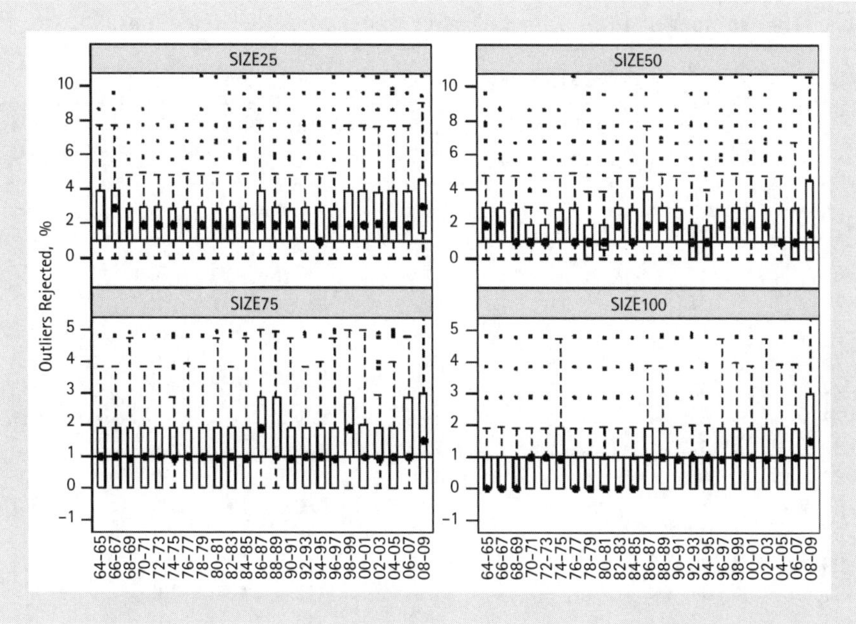

FIGURE 11.15 Percentage of observations rejected with 99% efficiency.

than half of the stocks in the two largest size groups; (c) rather remarkably the financial market collapse in 2008 had little impact on the distribution of standardized betas, the only noticeable effect being an increase in the number of betas significantly greater than one during 2008–2009 relative to the previous four years for the largest size group; (d) the distribution of the standardized betas is relatively constant from 1964 to 1999 for the largest size group.

In Section 11.2 we pointed out that under normality only 0.011% of the returns would be rejected as outliers, and it is of interest to understand how many returns are rejected as outliers by the robust beta due to the non-normality[14] of the returns in the above analysis. To this end Figure 11.15 shows the percentage of outliers rejected by our robust fitting method for each of the two-year intervals of our study. Since we always have between 100 and 105 returns in each two-year interval, the percentages shown are close to the number of outliers rejected. The overall median number of outliers rejected across all time periods and all size groups is .96%, and these percentages are on average larger for smaller size groups whose returns have more outliers than larger size groups. It is also not surprising to see a larger percentage of outliers rejected during 2008–2009 which contains the recent financial services meltdown and market crash.

Since the plots in Figure 11.15 do not reveal information about the tails of the cross-sections of the number of outliers, we provide such information in Table 11.4.

[14] The extent of non-normality of the liquid stocks used in this study is shown in Appendix E which displays the box-plots of Jarque–Bera and related statistics for the stocks included in this study.

Table 11.4 Number of firms with tail percentages of outlier rejections.

TIME INTERVAL	SIZE25+SIZE50			SIZE75+SIZE100		
	#of firms > 5% rejects	#of firms > 10% rejects	max % rejected	#of firms > 5% rejects	#of firms > 10% rejects	max % rejected
64-65	46	1	11.5	9	0	8.7
66-67	64	0	9.6	13	0	8.7
68-69	32	0	7.6	3	0	5.7
70-71	32	0	8.7	5	0	7.7
72-73	42	0	8.7	9	0	7.7
74-75	52	0	8.6	14	0	6.7
76-77	53	2	10.6	7	0	8.7
78-79	45	1	10.6	19	1	11.5
80-81	55	2	10.5	13	0	8.7
82-83	65	1	12.5	18	0	9.6
84-85	78	4	13.3	26	0	8.6
86-87	151	4	11.5	45	1	11.5
88-89	94	4	11.5	48	1	12.5
90-91	94	2	12.4	28	0	9.5
92-93	74	3	29.8	14	0	9.6
94-95	77	1	11.5	24	1	11.5
96-97	106	5	20	53	0	9.5
98-99	239	8	11.5	92	2	12.7
00-01	219	7	15.4	66	2	17.3
02-03	246	17	16.2	64	0	9.5
04-05	141	3	15.4	29	1	11.5
06-07	168	7	15.8	84	5	12.5
08-09	547	53	22.7	265	28	18.2

This table shows the number of firms in the two smallest size quartile groups combined (labeled SIZE25+SIZE50) with more than 5% and 10% of observations rejected (columns labeled "# rejects > 5%" and "# rejects > 10%") and the maximum percent rejected (labeled "max % rejected"), and similarly for the two largest size quartile groups combined.

The results reveal an increasing trend in the number of firms with greater than 5% outliers rejected for all size groups, with a larger number of such firms in the two smallest groups than the two largest groups for all time intervals. It is evident that the distribution of percentage outliers rejected beyond 5% is very highly concentrated between 5% and 10% prior to 2008–2009. For all size groups the number of firms with greater than 5% outliers nearly doubles in 1986–1987 relative to 1984–1985, but surprisingly decreases in 2000–2001, and very dramatically increases by more than 300% in 2008–2009 relative to 2006–2007. Thus there is not a uniform behavior in the number of firms rejecting more than 5% outliers across different market crashes, which implicitly suggests that the tail behavior of the joint distribution of market returns and stock returns is not consistent across different market crashes. We note that since there are about 4000 firms in our study in 1986–1987, the percentage of firms in the two smallest size groups with more than 5% outliers rejected is about 3.8%. In 2008–2009 we have about 6500 firms in our study, so the percent of firms in the two smallest size groups in 2008–2009 with more than 5% rejections is about 8.4%; this indicates that the 2008–2009 financial services meltdown and market crash exhibited an exceptionally wild character, as reflected in a large number of outliers.

11.5 Variation in Systematic Risk Over Time

It is natural to ask how the cross-sections of systematic risk as a fraction of overall risk behave across time for OLS and robust estimates of beta. Figures 11.16 and 11.17 provide the answer to this question by displaying the cross-sections of the ratio $|\beta| \cdot \sigma_M \div \sigma_{stock}$ of absolute beta times standard deviation of the market returns, divided by the standard deviation of the stock returns. The time series patterns of the cross-section distributions of these ratios are rather similar across the size groups and choice of OLS versus robust beta estimate. One sees that (1) the systematic contribution to total risk ratios increases with firm size; and (2) for all firm sizes the ratios increase monotonically from 1964 until 1971, followed by erratically lower levels until reaching record lows in 1992–1993, and then increase monotonically until 2008–2009 across all size groups, except for the peculiar positive jump in 2002–2003 for the largest size group.

Overall the single-factor model does not capture large percentages of market risk relative to total risk. For example, in the smallest size group the median percentage of market risk never exceeds 50% and is less than 20% for 1964–1965 and 1992 through 2007. Higher percentages of market risk are captured by the model for the largest size group, with cross-section median percentages of market risk in the 60–70% range occurring during 1986–1987 and 2008–2009. Nonetheless, during 1992–1995 three-fourths of the firms in the largest size group have market risk percentages less than about 40% of total risk. And the median percentage of market risk for the largest size group across the entire time interval studied is only about 50%.

We note that the percentage of market risk to total risk depends on the product $|\beta| \cdot \sigma_M$. Thus it is not surprising to see some clear relationships between the temporal patterns of systematic contributions to total risk in Figures 11.16 and 11.17 and the temporal patterns of market volatility in Figure 11.5 and betas in Figures 11.6 and 11.7. For example, the distributions in Figures 11.16 and 11.17 for 1970–1971 are shifted in a positive direction because that interval has betas that are among the largest across the entire time interval and the market volatility is fairly large. The

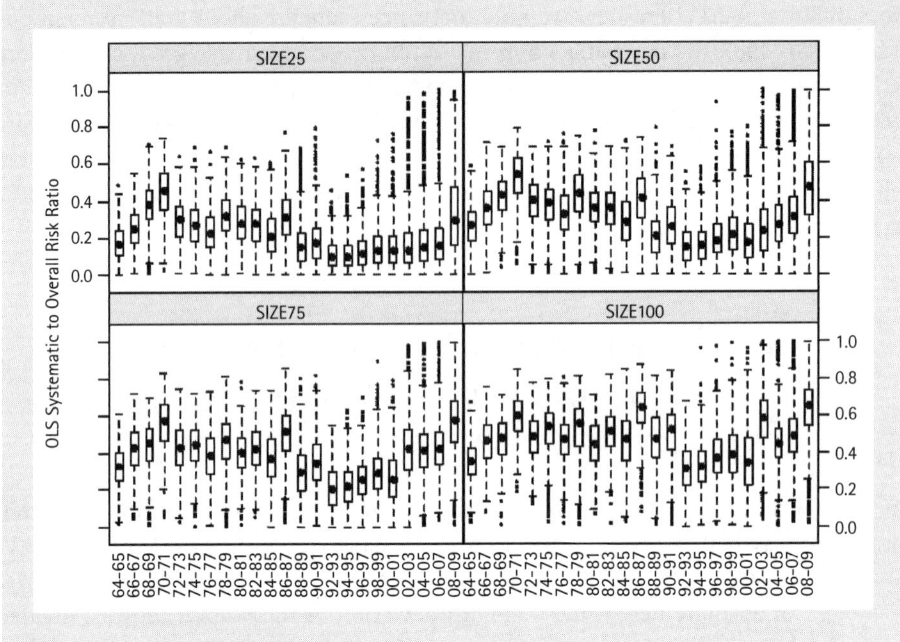

FIGURE 11.16 Ratio of systematic risk to total risk for OLS betas.

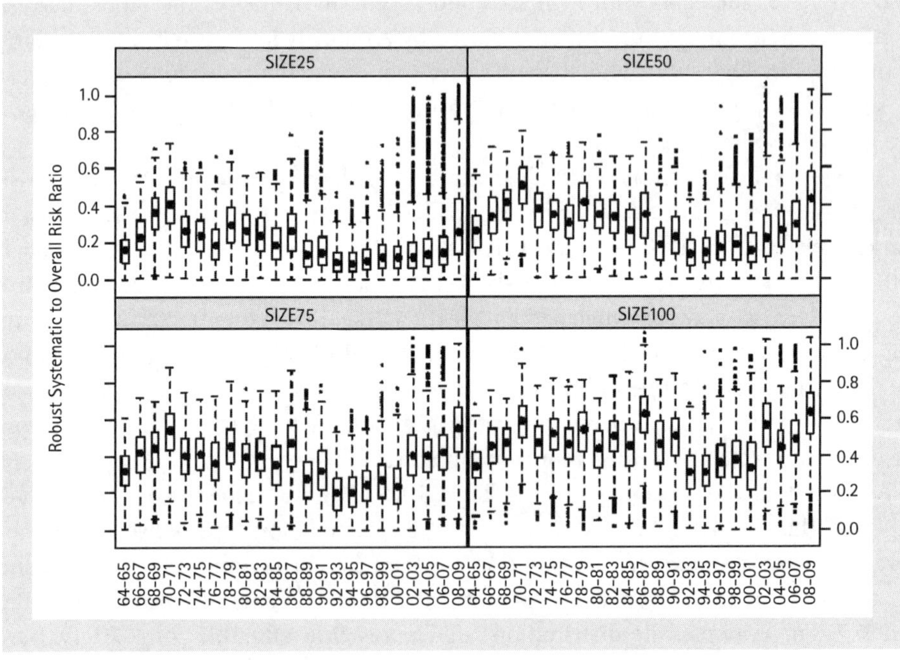

FIGURE 11.17 Ratios of systematic risk to total risk for robust betas.

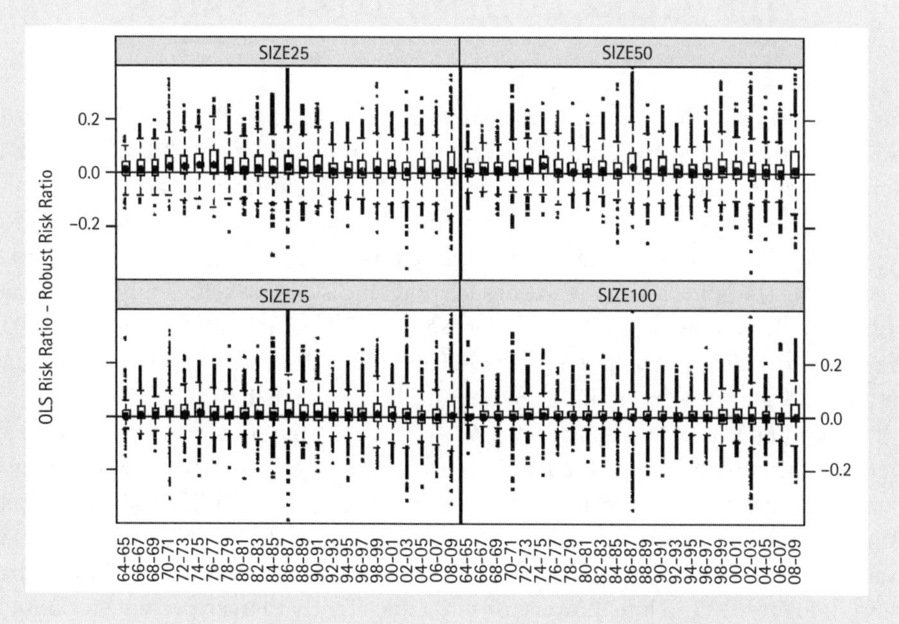

FIGURE 11.18 Paired differences between systematic and total risk ratios.

distributions during 1986–1987 and 2008–2009 are locally shifted in positive directions primarily because these time intervals locally have greatly increased market volatilities (cf. Figure 11.5).[15] The lowest systematic components of risk that occur in 1992–1995 are not surprising since these time intervals have the two lowest market volatilities other than 1964–1965.

While the time series of cross-section distributions of systematic to total risk ratios in Figures 11.16 and 11.17 for OLS and robust betas look quite similar, we examine the differences between the use of OLS and robust betas by plotting the cross-sections of paired differences between these ratios in Figure 11.18. The resulting cross-section distributions are relatively constant across time and group size, with medians quite close to zero. However there tends to be a shift and skewness in the positive direction, with three-quarters or so of the values being positive in many time intervals, particularly for the three smallest size groups. For such time intervals the OLS betas result in somewhat larger systematic contributions to total risk than do robust betas. However, except for the time periods 1970–1971, 1986–1987, 2002–2003 and 2008–2009, about half of the differences are less than about .05 and very rarely greater than .2 across all size groups. The latter time periods stand out by virtue of their largest dispersions and tail fatness, with a substantial number of differences greater than .2.

[15] It remains to determine why the systematic components of risk ratios are so much larger during 2002–2003 than during the adjacent intervals 2000–2001 and 2004–2005 for the largest size group.

11.6 Concluding Discussion

Our study reveals that during any two-year interval and over the entire period 1964–2009, the difference between the OLS and robust beta can be "large" for a small to moderate fraction of the firms, where by "large" we mean differences in excess of 0.3. Such distances can give investors and portfolio managers a misleading indication of beta risk. The use of a standard shrinkage estimator based on OLS and robust betas (see footnote 1) would reduce the size of such differences but not sufficiently to eliminate misleading indications of beta risk. See, for example, Table 2 of Martin and Simin (2003). The fraction of large distances between OLS and robust betas decreases with firm size, and this indicates that outlier influence on OLS betas is a small firm effect.

It is important to note that large differences between the robust and OLS estimates due to outlier influences on the latter are obtained using a robust estimator that is almost fully efficient for the normal distribution. Correspondingly the robust beta estimator typically rejects very few returns as outliers, and in particular the median number of returns rejected as outliers is typically one or two across time and all firm sizes (cf. Figure 11.15). Note, however, from Table 11.4 that larger percentages of outliers are rejected for some firms but that the number of firms with greater than 10% outliers rejected is quite negligible. Furthermore the number of firms with greater than 5% rejections is essentially negligible for the two largest size groups except for 2008–2009. The latter time period is quite exceptional for the large number of firms rejecting more than 5% for all firm sizes; further study is needed to understand this phenomenon.

The standard errors of OLS and robust estimates exhibit considerable variability over time and on average decrease with increasing firm size. The majority of the firms in the smallest size group have standard errors that render the betas unreliable in the extreme, and this is the case even for the largest size group of firms during some time periods. Market volatility has the most influence on cross-section distribution of beta estimates as may be seen by comparing Figures 11.5 and 11.11, which reveal that standard errors tend to be large when market volatility is low and vice versa. Figure 11.12 shows that OLS betas tend to have larger standard errors than robust betas, the more so for smaller size firms than larger size firms. The time period 1986–1987 is an anomaly in that for half the firms in all size groups the OLS beta standard errors are smaller than those of the robust betas (often substantially so). This is evidently because most of the outliers caused by the crash of 1987 are "good" outliers such as in Figure 11.2(d).

In spite of the frequent occurrence of large differences between paired OLS and robust betas, the cross-section distributions and the time series patterns of these distributions are strikingly similar within each size group. Thus one will draw almost identical conclusions about the behavior of the cross-section distributions of betas in relationship to market recessions, crashes, and volatilities when using OLS betas as when using robust betas. For example, conclusions about what fraction of betas are significantly larger or smaller than one in any given two-year interval are almost the same whether using OLS or robust betas (cf. Figures 11.13 and 11.14), and conclusions about the time variation in the systematic contribution to total risk are almost the same whichever of the two beta estimates you use (cf. Figures 11.16 and 11.17).

Our analysis of the systematic contribution to total risk in Section 11.5 shows that the single-factor market model captures a larger percentage of the total risk as firm size increases and during some but not all periods of time containing recessions or crashes. Perhaps interestingly, 1970–1971, 1986–1987, and 2008–2009 yield some of the highest such values. However on an overall basis the single-factor market model does not tend to capture market risk as a large percentage of total risk, with the largest such percentages being 60–70% for the largest size groups in the exceptional periods 1986–1987 and 2008–2009. Overall the market percentage of total risk captured by a single-factor model is probably considerably smaller than what many asset managers may imagine.

It is important to note that different outlier configurations have quite different influences on OLS beta risk. For example an OLS beta can under-estimate beta as in Figure 11.2(a) as well as over-estimate beta as in Figure 11.2(c), and in these two examples the robust beta provides a better estimate of beta risk. On the other hand, in Figure 11.2(b) the configuration of outliers is such that the robust beta value of 1.41 may be regarded as an under-estimate of beta risk relative to the OLS beta value of 2.03. Finally, one can have a gross outlier such as in Figure 11.2(d) that gives rise to virtually identical OLS and robust betas, hence identical estimates of beta risk.

In summary, the differences in OLS and robust beta estimates are sufficiently large frequently enough that both should be computed and compared on a routine basis. Upon identifying firms with large differences, e.g., greater than a user defined threshold, the time series of market and stock returns should be examined for the time of occurrence of influential outliers and their possible cause. Two-dimensional scatter plots (such as in Figure 11.2) should also be made in order to help decide whether the robust beta is a better or worse indicator of systematic risk.

It would be possible to automate the detection of configurations such as in Figure 11.2(b) where robust betas give optimistic indications of systematic risk. It may be that detection of large differences between OLS and robust betas will lead to identification of firms with specific characteristics of interest to investors.

APPENDIX A

Prior Research Literature on Robust Betas

The least absolute deviation (LAD) version of the M-estimate is the oldest and perhaps most widely known candidate alternative to least squares for dealing with non-normal returns. In the context of estimating beta, the LAD estimate was studied early on by Sharpe (1971), who considered 30 common stocks used to compute the Dow Jones Industrial Average and 30 mutual funds, both in the mid-to-late 1960s. Cornell and Dietrich (1978) also studied the LAD estimate using 100 companies randomly drawn from the S&P 500 from 1962 to 1975. Both studies were motivated by the knowledge that returns sometimes have fat-tailed and skewed non-normal distributions, and that an alternative to OLS might therefore perform better. Sharpe (1971) and Cornell and Dietrich (1978) concluded that the LAD alternative did little to improve the OLS estimate of beta.[16] These results are evidently due to the lack of influential outliers in the returns of large size equities and mutual funds for these early time periods.

Subsequently a number of studies focused on newer proposed robust alternatives to OLS for estimating beta in the single-factor model. Connolly (1989) studied the weekend effect using OLS, M-estimates, and regression-quantile estimates (Koenker and Bassett, 1978). Chan and Lakonishok (1992) showed that the regression-quantiles method could provide higher efficiency than OLS when estimating beta. Mills and Coutts (1996) studied a variety of robust beta estimates including regression-quantile estimates, a resistant line estimate, and LAD, with a focus on event studies applications. Bowie and Bradfield (1998) studied the performance of each of the major types of robust estimates on several different data sets and concluded that it was important to deal with market return outliers as well as asset return outliers. See also Bradfield (2003). Barnes and Hughes (2002) use regression quantile estimates to show that the market price of beta risk is significant in both tails. Cloete *et al.* (2002) examined the use of the Vasicek (1973) Bayes estimate in which the OLS estimate is replaced with three types of robust regression estimates. Genton and Ronchetti (2008) focused on prediction of beta and developed a shrinkage robust estimator with shrinkage of any available robust estimator for regression toward OLS.

In a precursor to the current study, Martin and Simin (2003) focused on estimating beta based on weekly returns with the same type of robust regression estimate used in the current chapter. Their study included all AMEX, NYSE, and NASDAQ stocks in the CRSP database having data for at least two years in the interval 1992–1996 and reported the following results: (1) the OLS and robust betas differ by more than 0.5 for about 13% of the firms; (2) robust betas predict future robust betas better than OLS betas; (3) the existence of influential outliers is mainly a small firm effect; and (4) the majority of financial data service providers deliver beta estimates without regard to dealing with the adverse influence of outliers.

APPENDIX B

Formulas for the Rho and Psi Functions

The analytic expressions for the ρ and ψ functions displayed in Figure 11.1 are

$$\rho(r;c) = \begin{cases} 3.25 \cdot c^2 & |r/c| > 3 \\ c^2 \cdot \left[1.792 - 0.972 \cdot \left(\frac{r}{c}\right)^2 + 0.432 \cdot \left(\frac{r}{c}\right)^4 - 0.052 \cdot \left(\frac{r}{c}\right)^6 - 0.002 \cdot \left(\frac{r}{c}\right)^8\right], & 2 < |r/c| \le 3 \\ 0.5 \cdot r^2 & |r/c| \le 2 \end{cases} \tag{11.B1}$$

[16] However, Sharpe (1971) mentioned that on the stock level the differences were significant.

and

$$\psi(r;c) = \begin{cases} 0 & |r/c| > 3 \\ c \cdot \left[-1.944 \cdot \left(\frac{r}{c}\right) + 1.728 \cdot \left(\frac{r}{c}\right)^3 - 0.312 \cdot \left(\frac{r}{c}\right)^5 + 0.016 \cdot \left(\frac{r}{c}\right)^7\right], & 2 < |r/c| \le 3 \\ r & |r/c| \le 2. \end{cases} \tag{11.B2}$$

We note that the above ρ_c is a good piecewise polynomial approximation to an optimal bias robust M-estimate loss function discovered by Svarc, Yohai and Zamar (2002) for the case of 95% normal distribution efficiency. We use this form for higher normal distribution efficiency even though the constants should be adjusted somewhat for efficiencies different from 95%.

APPENDIX C

THE COMPUTATIONAL METHOD

The first step in computing the robust estimate is to compute an initial estimate $\hat{\theta}^0 = \left(\hat{\alpha}^0, \hat{\beta}^0\right)$ of the true parameter values $\theta = (\alpha, \beta)$ using the highly robust regression S-estimate approach of Rousseeuw and Yohai (1984) as follows. Form the residuals $\tilde{u}_t(\theta) = \tilde{u}_t(\alpha, \beta) = r_t - \alpha - \beta \cdot r_{M,t}$ where for the moment we let $\theta = (\alpha, \beta)$ be *arbitrary* fixed parameter values. Compute a robust residuals scale estimate $\tilde{s}(\theta)$ by finding the value of $s(\theta)$ that solves the equation

$$\frac{1}{T-p}\sum_{t=1}^{T} \rho_c\left(\frac{\tilde{u}_1(\theta)}{s(\theta)}\right) = .5. \tag{11.C1}$$

The resulting estimate $\tilde{s}(\theta)$ is known as an M-estimate of scale and it can be shown to be unique for the ρ_c given in Appendix B. A regression S-estimate of the true parameter values $\theta = (\alpha, \beta)'$ is a value $\hat{\theta}^0$ that minimizes $s(\theta)$:

$$\hat{\theta}^0 = ar\, gmin_\theta s(\theta) \tag{11.C2}$$

The computation (11.C2) is a two-dimensional non-convex optimization problem for which a "good" solution is obtained using a random re-sampling method that computes a preliminary estimate $\hat{\theta}^0$ that minimizes $s(\theta)$ among a very large set of candidate perfect fit estimates of θ.[17] One then solves (11.C2) with $\theta = \hat{\theta}^0$ to obtain the initial scale estimate $\hat{s}^0 = s(\hat{\theta}^0)$. Finally, an M-estimate $\hat{\theta}$ is obtained as the local minimum of (11.2) nearest to $\hat{\theta}^0$.

We use the Yohai, Stahel and Zamar (1991) proposal for computing the standard errors of $\hat{\theta}$. The standard errors are computed as the square root of the diagonal elements of the two-by-

[17] Random samples of pairs (r_{t_1}, r_{t_1}) and (r_{t_2}, r_{t_2}) with $t_1 \neq t_2$ are taken for this purpose.

two robust covariance matrix given by

$$C_{\hat{\theta}} = \left((1, \tilde{r}_M)'(1, \tilde{r}_M)\right)^{-1}.$$
$$= \frac{1}{T \cdot (avg(\tilde{r}_M^2) - avg^2(\tilde{r}_M))} \begin{pmatrix} avg(\tilde{r}_M^2) & -avg\left(\tilde{r}_M\right) \\ -avg\left(\tilde{r}_M\right) & 1 \end{pmatrix} \qquad (11.C3)$$

where for a vector $\mathbf{x}$, $avg(\mathbf{x})$ is the average of the elements of $\mathbf{x}$, and the $T \times 2$ matrix $(\mathbf{1}, \tilde{\mathbf{r}}_M)$ and the scalar estimate $\hat{\nu}$ are computed as follows. First, we use the preliminary estimates $\hat{\theta}^0 = (\hat{\alpha}^0, \hat{\beta}^0)$ and $\hat{s}^0$ to compute

$$\tilde{\nu} = T \cdot \frac{(\hat{s}^0)^2 \sum_{t=1}^{T} \psi^2(z_t^0)}{\left(\sum_{t=1}^{T} \psi'(z_t^0)\right)^2}. \qquad (11.C4)$$

where

$$z_t^0 = \frac{\hat{u}_t^0}{\hat{s}^0} = \frac{r_t - \hat{\alpha}_0 - \hat{\beta}_0 r_{M,t}}{\hat{s}^0}. \qquad (11.C5)$$

Then we compute the weights

$$W_t = \frac{\psi(z_t^0)}{z_t^0}, i = 1, \ldots, T \qquad (11.C6)$$

and shrunken market returns

$$\tilde{r}_{M,t} = \frac{W_t \cdot r_{M,t}}{\bar{W}} \qquad (11.C7)$$

with

$$\bar{W} = \frac{1}{T} \sum_{t=1}^{T} w_t. \qquad (11.C8)$$

Referring to (11.B2) one sees that the effect of the weights in (11.C7) is to leave unaltered market returns for which scaled residuals at the preliminary robust estimates $\hat{\theta}^0 = (\hat{\alpha}^0, \hat{\beta}^0)$ are less than $2c$, and set equal to zero those for which these scaled residuals are greater than $3c$. The matrix $(\mathbf{1}, \tilde{\mathbf{r}}_M)$ consists of a column of 1s and a column of the shrunken values in (11.C7). Referring to (11.C3) one can see that the purpose of shrinking the market returns is to prevent market return outliers that give rise to residual outliers from biasing the $\hat{\beta}$ variance estimate (hence standard deviation estimate) toward an optimistically small value.

Figure 11.c1 illustrates the difference between the initial and final robust beta estimate for the DD ticker example in Figure 11.2 of Section 11.2. The dotted outlier rejection boundary lines for the initial estimate are based on $c = .4047$, which is the value required to have a highly robust initial estimate with breakdown point of one-half.

This leads to an initial estimator with the very low normal distribution efficiency of 24.3% and results in 35 data points rejected. However, rejection lines for the final estimates are based on $c = 1.29$ which corresponds to a normal distribution efficiency of 99%.[18]

[18] For details see Maronna, Martin, and Yohai (2006).

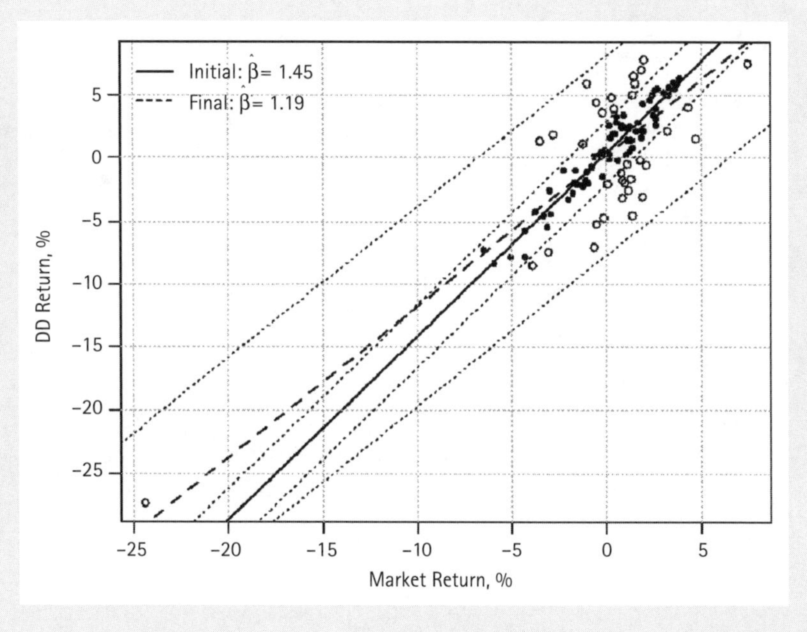

FIGURE 11.C1 Initial and final robust beta estimates for firm with ticker DD.

APPENDIX D

Time Series Behavior of Market Capitalization

While the growth in market capitalization of the liquid stocks from 2003 to 2007 is dramatic, it is useful to view it in the context of historical percent growth rates from one two-year period to the next as in Figure 11.D1. It is apparent that the quartiles and median all behave rather similarly over time and that there are two previous time periods of exceptional growth, one in 1968–1969 relative to 1966–1967 ranging from 20% for the upper quartile and a little over 60% for the lower quartile, and one in 1976–1967 relative to 1974–1975, all fairly close to 45%. The growth spurts in 2004–2005 relative to 2002–2003 of 60% for upper quartile and 80% for the lower quartile are not only larger than the earlier growth spurts in capitalization, they also occur relative to a much larger capitalization base than the earlier growth spurts (compare the 02–03 column of Table 11.1 with the 66–67 and 74–75 columns, particularly for the median and upper quartile capitalizations).

The similarities in the time series of quartiles and median market capitalizations in Figure 11.D1 suggest that the entire cross-sectional distribution of market capitalization growth behaves rather similarly. The suggestion is confirmed by Figure 11.D2 which displays the time series of sizes, i.e., logarithm of market capitalization in millions of dollars, for the 1%, 10%, 25%, 50%, 75%, 90%, and 99% market capitalization quantiles. The profiles of these quantile time series are remarkably similar, with the exception of the lowest 1% sized firms that had their

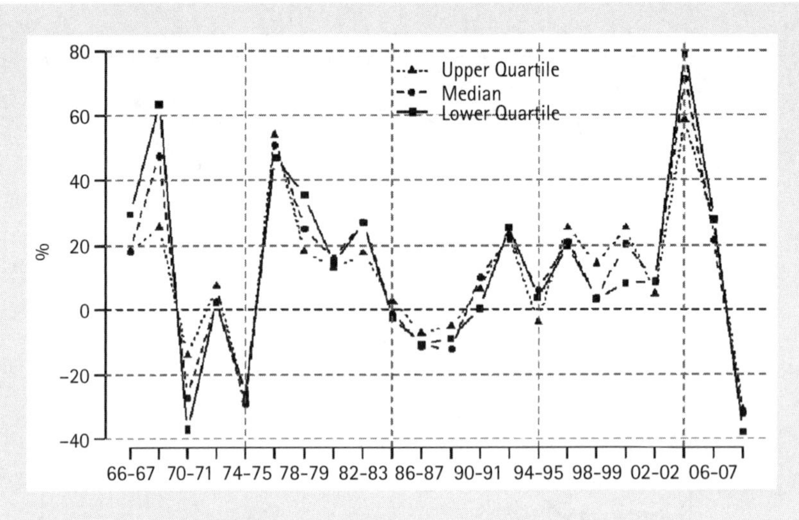

FIGURE 11.D1 Relative changes in market capitalization median and quartiles.

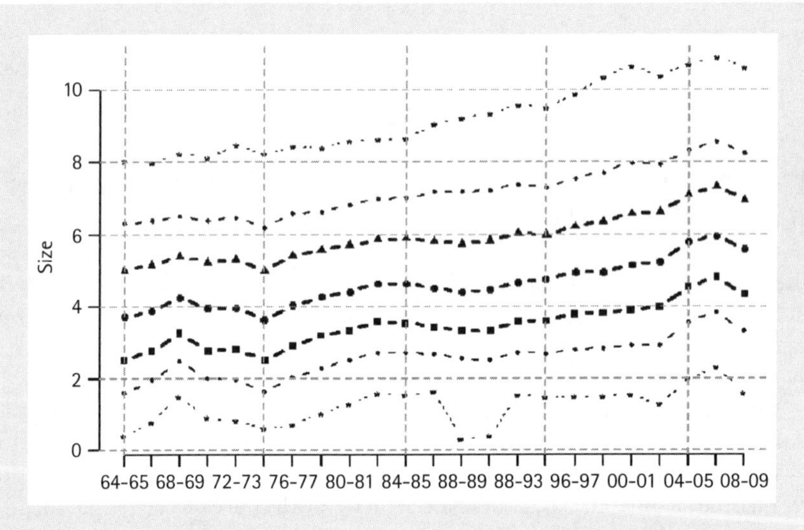

FIGURE 11.D2 Size (log of market capitalization in $M) percentiles for the liquid stocks. Solid lines are for the upper quartile (triangles), median (circles), and lower quartile (squares). Dotted light lines represent the 1st and 99th percentiles and dashed grey lines represent the 10th and 90th percentiles.

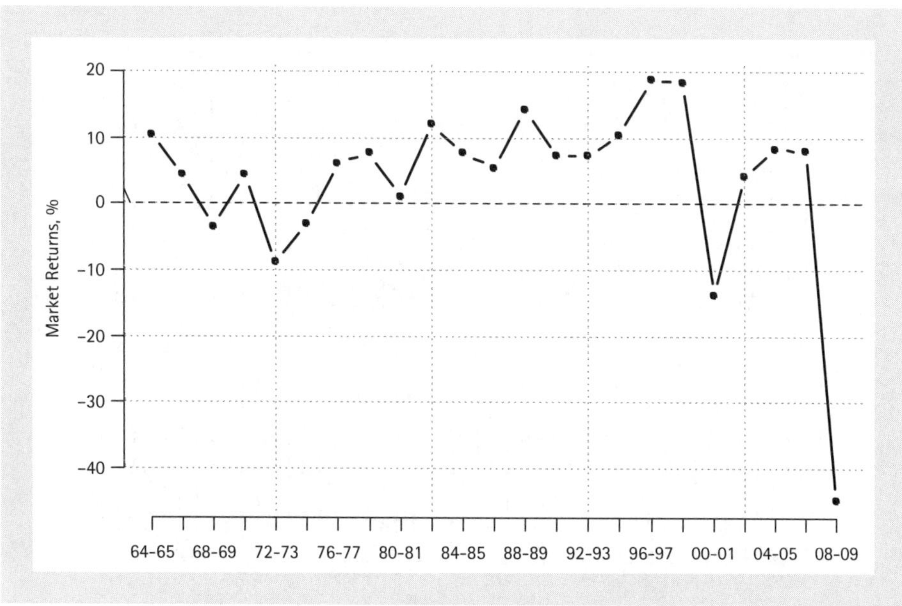

FIGURE 11.D3 Annualized mean excess market returns.

total capitalization virtually vanish for the four years following the market crash of 1987. We note that the 1% largest sized firms (mega-caps) had market capitalizations whose minimum value grew from about \$3B in 1965–1966 to a minimum value of about \$60B in 2006–2007, while the 1% smallest sized firms (nano-caps) had market capitalizations whose maximum value grew from only about \$1.3M in 1964–1965 to only about \$9M in 2006–2007.

The mean two-year market returns in excess of the risk-free rate in Figure 11.D3 show local minima at market events superimposed on a positive linear trend from 1968–1969 to 1998–1999, followed by an extreme minimum when the dot-com bubble burst and the even more extreme minimum (−45%) in 2008–2009.

APPENDIX E

NON-NORMALITY OF THE LIQUID STOCKS

The presence of stock return outliers that result in differences between OLS and robust betas is indicative of non-normal returns. To determine the extent of non-normality among the liquid stocks used in our study we first computed Jarque–Bera (JB) test statistics for each two-year interval in each size group.[19] The resulting cross-sections of the test statistics are displayed in Figure 11.E1 where the horizontal solid lines near the bottom of each panel are located at the

[19] The JB non-normality test statistic is given by $JB = \left(\frac{n}{6}\right) SK^2 + \left(\frac{n}{24}\right)(K-3)^2 \sim \chi_2^2$ where $SK = \hat{\sigma}^{-3}\frac{1}{n}\sum_1^n (r_t - \bar{r}_t)^3$, $K = \hat{\sigma}^{-4}\frac{1}{n}\sum_1^n (r_t - \bar{r}_t)^4$ and $\hat{\sigma}^2 = \frac{1}{n}\sum_1^n (r_t - \bar{r}_t)^2$.

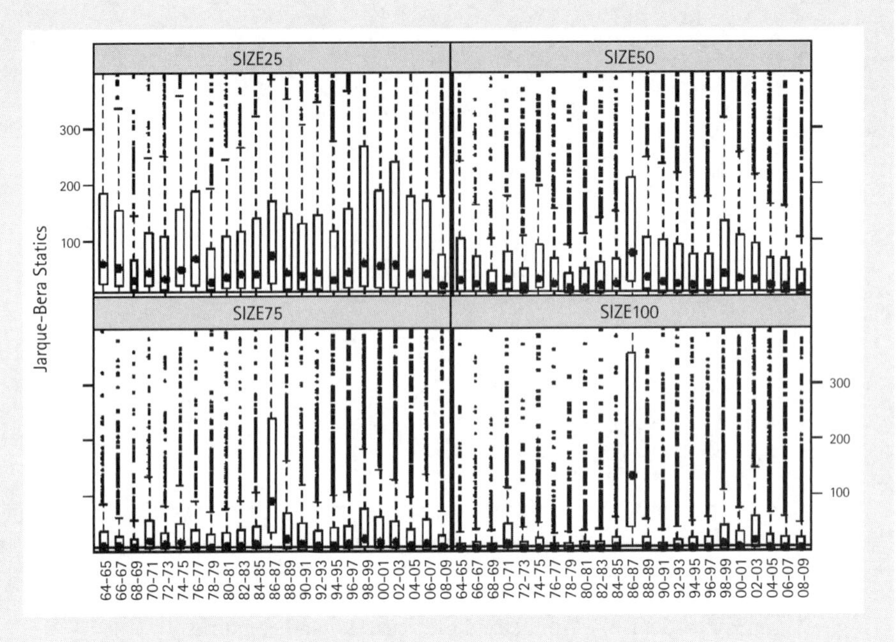

FIGURE 11.E1 Jarque–Bera tests of normality of excess stock returns.

upper 1% point (value equal 9.2) of the approximating chi-square distribution with two degrees of freedom for the JB statistic.

Figure 11.E1 reveals that the proportion of stocks with non-normal returns decreases with increasing firm size, which is hardly surprising. Furthermore one sees that the cross-sections of the JB statistics during 1986–1987 are outliers for the three largest size groups, and it turns out that this is due to the single weekly return outlier due to Black Monday.

To facilitate comparisons of non-normality across time and size groups, Figure 11.E2 displays the JB statistics as in Figure 11.E1 except with the Black Monday outlier removed and with the vertical range of the SIZE75 and SIZE100 groups reduced to 150 for better visualization of the bulk of the cross-section distribution (and the SIZE25 and SIZE50 ranges left as in Figure 11.E1). For the SIZE25 group the normality hypothesis is rejected for over 75% of the stocks in all time periods except 2008–2009 where the percentage of rejection is close to 75%. Even for the SIZE50 group normality is rejected for at least 75% or nearly 75% of the firms across all time periods.

Clearly the largest size group SIZE100 exhibits the least non-normality over time, with normality rejected for less than half the firms in all time periods except 1970–1971, 1998–1999 and 2002–2003. However it may be surprising to some readers to see that ignoring these three anomalous time periods, normality is rejected for over 25% of the SIZE100 firms during all other time periods and normality is rejected for close to 50% of these firms in many of the other time periods. In other words, substantial non-normality is more present in the returns of large size firms than one might have imagined.

Also, there are some interesting temporal patterns of the cross-section distributions of the JB statistics. For example non-normality increases across all size groups during the dot-com

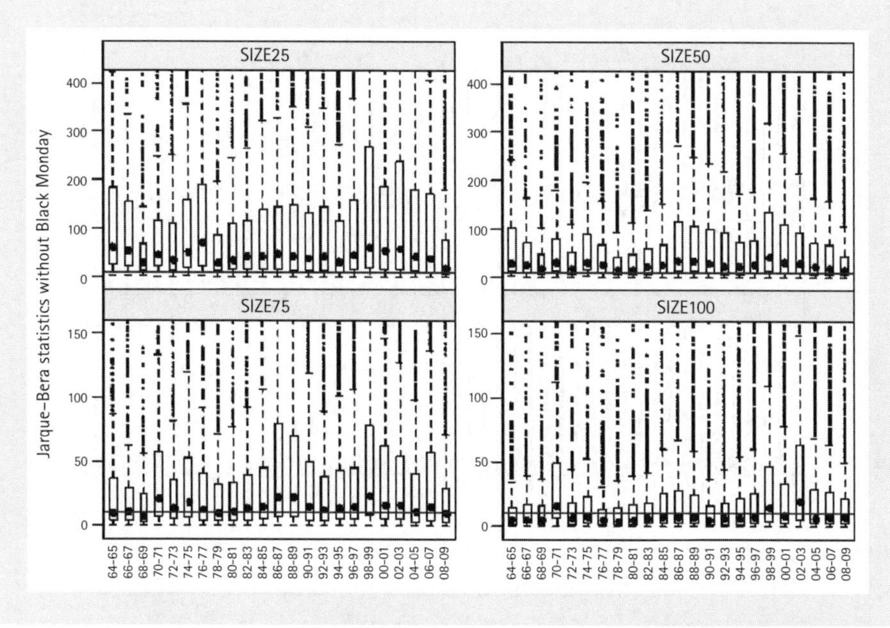

FIGURE 11.E2 Jarque–Bera tests without 1987 Black Monday outlier.

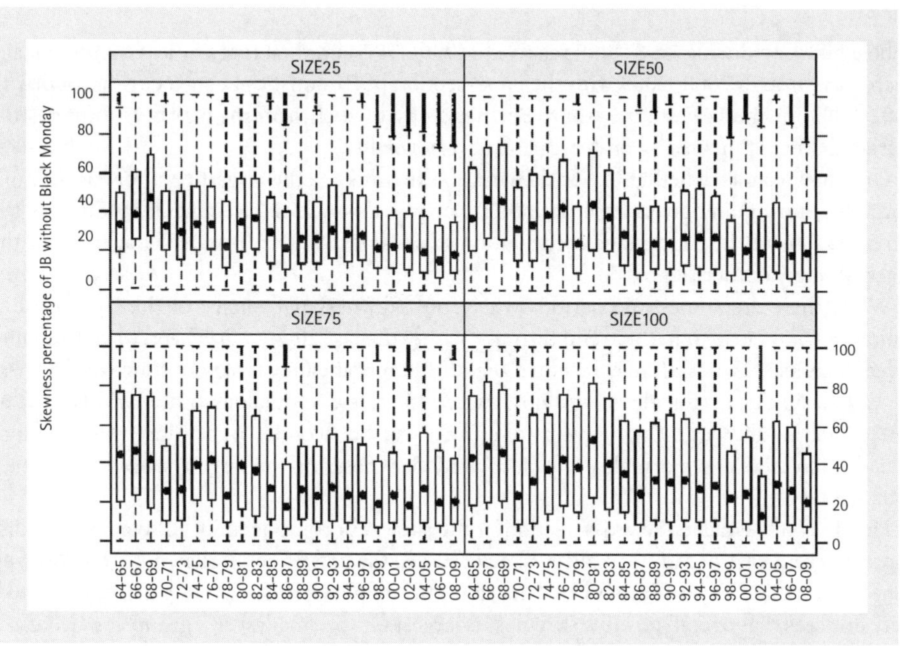

FIGURE 11.E3 Skewness percentages of JB statistic without 1987 Black Monday outlier.

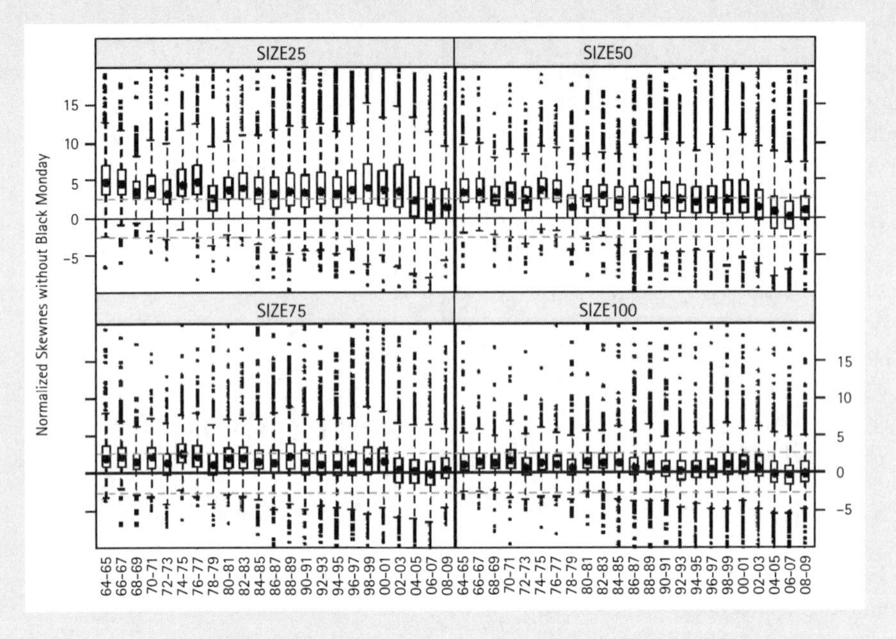

FIGURE 11.E4 Normalized skewness without 1987 Black Monday outlier.

bubble build-up during 1998–1999 relative to 1996–1997, and then more or less monotonically decreases through 2008–2009 with the cross-section of JB statistics being a curious outlier in 2002–2003 for the largest size group. Further study of such patterns may reveal interesting market drivers of increasing or decreasing non-normality.

One may wonder whether either skewness or kurtosis are the largest components of non-normality during any given time period. To answer this question, Figure 11.E3 displays the cross-sections of the percentage contribution of skewness to the JB statistic, again with the Black Monday outlier removed.

While there are some time periods where the skewness percentage of the JB statistic is around 50% or close to it, the trend during roughly the last 20 years has been toward smaller percentages of skewness. It may be noted that the temporal patterns of percentage of skewness are rather similar across all size groups, except for a few anomalous time periods such as 2002–2003 for the largest size group (one can't help but wonder what cause the combination of increased non-normality but decreased skewness for the largest size group during 2002–2003).

Finally, to investigate the cross-section of the skewness component itself, Figure 11.E4 displays the cross-sections of normalized skewness, i.e., the coefficient of skewness standardized to be approximately a standard normal distribution when the returns are normally distributed. Here one sees that overall positive skewness is largest for the smallest size group and decreases to very moderate levels for the largest size group. The temporal patterns are again rather similar across all size groups and one notices a decrease in skewness across all size groups during 2004–2009 relative to earlier time periods.

References

Bailer, H.M. (2005). Robust estimation of factor models in finance. PhD Dissertation. University of Washington, Seattle.

Barnes, M.L. and Hughes, A.W. (2002). A quantile regression analysis of the cross-section of stock market returns. *No. 02-2, Working Papers from Federal Reserve Bank of Boston.*

Blume, M.E. (1975). Betas and their regression tendencies. *Journal of Finance*, ***30*** (3), 785–795.

Bowie, D.C. and Bradfield, D.J. (1998). Non-normality and robust estimation of beta coefficients. *Journal of Business Finance and Accounting*, ***25*** (3&4), 439–454.

Bradfield, D. (2003). Investment basics XLVI. On estimating the beta coefficient. *Investment Analysts Journal*, ***57***, 47–53.

Bradley, B.O. and Taqqu, M. (2003). Financial risk and heavy tails. In. S.T. Racheve (ed.) *Handbook of Heavy-Tailed Distributions in Finance*. Elsevier, Amsterdam.

Chan, L.K. and Lakonishok, J. (1992). Robust measurement of beta risk. *Journal of Financial and Quantitative Analysis*, ***27*** (2), 265–282.

Cloete, G.S., de Jongh, P.J., and de Wet, T. (2002). Combining Vasicek and robust estimators for forecasting systematic risk. *Investment Analysts Journal*, ***55***, 37–44.

Connolly, R.A. (1989). An examination of the robustness of the weekend effect. *Journal of Financial and Quantitative Analysis*, ***24*** (2), 133–169.

Connor, C., Goldberg, L., and Korajczyk, R. (2010). *Portfolio Risk Analysis*. Princeton University Press, Princeton.

Cornell, B. and Dietrich, J.K. (1978). Mean-absolute-deviation versus least-squares regression estimation of beta coefficients. *Journal of Financial and Quantitative Analysis*, ***13***, 123–131.

Fama, E.F. and French, K.R. (1992). The cross-section of expected stock returns. *Journal of Finance*, ***47***, 427–466.

Genton, M.G., and Ronchetti, E. (2008). Robust prediction of beta. In E.J. Kontoghiorghes, B. Rustem, and P. Winker (eds), *Computational Methods in Financial Engineering*, Essays in Honour of Manfred Gilli, Springer, 147–161.

Hampel, F.R., Ronchetti, E.M., Rousseeuw, P.J., and Stahel, W.A. (1986). *Robust Statistics: The Approach Based on Influence Functions*. New York: John Wiley & Sons, Inc.

Huber, P.J. (1964). Robust estimation of a location parameter. *The Annals of Mathematical Statistics*, ***35***, 73–101.

Huber, P.J. (1973). Robust regression: asymptotics, conjectures and Monte Carlo. *The Annals of Statistics*, ***1***, 799–821.

Huber, P.J. (1981). *Robust Statistics*. New York: John Wiley & Sons, Inc.

Knez, P.J. and Ready, M.J. (1997). On the robustness of size and book-to-market in cross-sectional regressions. *Journal of Finance*, ***4*** (52), 1355–1382.

Koenker, R. and Bassett, G. (1978). Regression quantiles. *Econometrica*, ***46***, 33–50.

Lintner, J. (1965). The valuation of risk assets and the selection of risk investments in stock portfolios and capital budgets. *Review of Economics and Statistics*, ***47***, 13–37.

Maronna, R.A., Martin, R.D., and Yohai, V.J. (2006). *Robust Statistics: Theory and Methods*. New York: John Wiley & Sons, Ltd.

Martin, R.D. and Simin, T.T. (2003). Outlier-resistant estimates of beta. *Financial Analysts Journal*, ***59***, 56–69.

Martin, R.D., Yohai, V.J., and Zamar, R.H. (1989). Min-max bias robust regression. *The Annals of Statistics*, ***17***, 1608–1630.

Mills, T.C. and Coutts, J.A. (1996). Misspecification testing and robust estimation of the market model: estimating betas for the FT-SE industry baskets. *The European Journal of Finance*, **2** (4), 319–331.

Rachev, S.T., Fabozzi, F.J., and Menn, C. (2005). *Fat-Tailed and Skewed Asset Return Distributions: Implications for Risk Management, Portfolio Selection and Option Pricing*. John Wiley & Sons, New York.

Rousseeuw, P.J. (1984). Least median of squares regression. *Journal of the American Statistical Association*, **79**, 871–880.

Rousseeuw, P.J. and Leroy, A.M. (1987). *Robust Regression and Outlier Detection*. John Wiley & Sons, New York.

Rousseeuw, P.J. and Yohai, V.J. (1984). Robust regression by means of S-estimators, robust and nonlinear time Series. *Lectures Notes in Statistics* (ed. J. Franke, W. Härdle, and R.D. Martin) **26**, 256–272.

Sharpe, W.F. (1964). Capital asset prices: A theory of market equilibrium under conditions of risk. *Journal of Finance*, **19**, 425–442.

Sharpe, W.F. (1971). Mean-absolute-deviation characteristic lines for securities and portfolios. *Management Science*, **18** (2), B1–B13.

Svarc, M., Yohai, V.J., and Zamar, R.H. (2002). Optimal bias-robust M-estimates of regression. In *Statistical Data Analysis Based on the L1 Norm and Related Methods* (ed. Y. Dodge), pp. 191–200. Birkhäuser, Basle.

Vasicek, O.A. (1973). A note on using cross-sectional information in Bayesian estimation of security betas. *The Journal of Finance*, **28** (5), 1233–1239.

CHAPTER 12

THE INFORMATIONAL CONTENT OF FINANCIAL OPTIONS FOR QUANTITATIVE ASSET MANAGEMENT: A REVIEW*

DANIEL GIAMOURIDIS
AND GEORGE SKIADOPOULOS

12.1 Introduction

The view that informed investors might choose to trade derivatives has been shared by both academics and practitioners from as early as the introduction of options trading in the early 1970s. Black (1975) claims that "... Since an investor can get more action for a given investment in options than he can by investing directly in the underlying stock, he may choose to deal in options when he feels he has an especially important piece of information ...". In the same spirit, Manaster and Rendleman (1982) argue that investors may regard options as a superior investment vehicle to the underlying stocks for the purposes of revealing information regarding equilibrium stock values. They base their argument on a number of practical issues including the lower trading costs in the option market relative to the stock market, the ease of short-selling a stock through a long put option position and a short call option position as opposed to borrowing the stock in the cash market, and the direct access to implementing leverage in the option market as opposed to maintaining margin accounts with tight requirements in the cash market. Furthermore, a theoretical rationale for why option prices may contain useful information is presented by Back (1993) who develops a model for continuous insider trading that also includes call options. Back (1993) concludes that trades in the option

* We would like to thank Dimitris Flamouris, Eirini Konstantinidi, and Alexandros Kostakis for useful comments. Because of space limitations some contributions have not been given the attention they deserve. Any remaining errors are our responsibility alone.

and the underlying asset convey different types of information and thus the existence of the option implies that a richer class of signals can be received by the market.

Arguments such as those presented above have stimulated a substantial amount of empirical and – to a lesser extent – theoretical research. A large body of this literature includes papers that use the information from option markets to forecast the future volatility of the underlying asset. This is done by means of the implied volatility, i.e. the volatility of the underlying asset that equates the market option price to the corresponding Black and Scholes (1973) one (see Poon and Granger 2003, for a review). The main motivation of studies in this line of research is that option contracts are forward-looking contracts since they have payoff functions that depend on the future value of the underlying index. Hence, market option prices are expected to incorporate the views of market participants about potential future outcomes of the underlying asset price. In this respect, market option prices may be more informative than historical data since future patterns may differ from past ones. A generalization of this idea suggests that the whole distribution of the underlying asset price can be extracted from the market option prices (see Breeden and Litzenberger 1978); the horizon of the distribution corresponds to the options expiry date. This distribution is termed an implied distribution (also called a risk-neutral distribution). In principle, the (risk-adjusted) implied distribution can be used to forecast the distribution of the underlying asset price (see for example Bliss and Panigirtzoglou 2004; Anagnou-Basioudis, Bedendo, Hodges, and Tompkins 2005).

In this chapter, we review the literature that deals with the informational content of market option prices. Our focus is on studies that are primarily concerned with the use of option implied information in the context of quantitative asset management. We touch upon a number of aspects that arise in the daily efforts of professional portfolio managers including stock selection, portfolio construction, risk measurement, and management. The implications for the investment process are also discussed. Due to space limitations, the review is to some extent biased towards the more recent literature. The chapter is structured as follows. Section 12.2 discusses stock selection ideas that are based on the prices of equity options. Section 12.3 explains the way that option implied distributions can be used for asset allocation purposes and reviews the associated literature. Section 12.4 reviews the literature that has examined how market option prices can be used in portfolio risk management. Section 12.5 outlines the use of options for market/style timing. Section 12.6 discusses articles that focus on the information content of option trading activity rather than market option prices, and Section 12.7 concludes.

12.2 Stock Selection Based on Option Prices

This section reviews articles that have investigated the use of option-related information as a stock selection factor. We identify five different themes. First, investment strategies that are based on the discrepancy between observed stock price and option implicit stock prices are discussed. Then, we review papers that investigate whether the information contained in the differences between out-of-the money (OTM hereafter) and at-the-money (ATM hereafter) implied volatilities can be used to form profitable strategies. The third theme builds upon deviations of the implied volatilities of same-strike and maturity put and call options. The last two subsections present stock selection ideas based on idiosyncratic implied volatility and option prices prior to corporate events, respectively.

12.2.1 Observed Stock Prices vs. Option-Implicit Stock Prices

To the best of our knowledge, Manaster and Rendleman (1982) are the first authors who have studied empirically the conjecture that option prices may contain useful information for the future values of the underlying asset. Based on the Black and Scholes (1973) model they computed the price of the stock that equates the theoretical value of the option with its market price, i.e. the implied stock price. They argued that the Black and Scholes (1973) approach suggests that the implied price should be the value of the underlying stock for which a continuously revised option-bond portfolio would be a perfect substitute for the stock. Therefore, in the case where implied stock prices differ significantly from observed stock prices, traders will arbitrage it away, and as a result implied and observed stock prices will converge. The authors argue that the investment vehicle that provides the greatest liquidity, the lowest trading costs, and the least restrictions will play the predominant role in the market's determination of the equilibrium stock price and discuss why the option markets are superior to the stock markets in these respects. The empirical analysis is undertaken in the context of an investment strategy that ranks stocks according to the magnitude of the discrepancy between the traded and the implicit stock price and forms portfolios which are held for one day. The results indicate that a portfolio of stocks in the top quintile of percentage discrepancies, i.e. the implicit price is higher than the actual price, outperforms a portfolio of stocks in the bottom quintile of discrepancies by an economical and statistically significant 0.065% return (Table V, p. 1054).[1]

12.2.2 Slope of the Implied Volatility Curve

Rather than looking at implied equity prices Xing, Zhang, and Zhao (XZZ 2010) focus on the predictability of the slope of the implied volatility smirk.[2] In particular, standing

[1] Peterson and Tucker (1988) extend this idea to the currency markets and find that the proportional deviation between implied and simultaneously observed spot exchange rates is a significant determinant of subsequent returns on foreign currency holdings. Furthermore, they show that an *ex ante* trading rule based on implied rates is sufficient to generate significant economic profits.

[2] At any given point in time and any given expiry option contract, the implied volatility smirk is defined to be the negative relationship between the implied volatility and the strike price. This negative

on time t and for any given option's expiry date, they define the slope of the implied volatility smirk as:

$$skew_{i,t} = vol_{i,t}^{OTMP} - vol_{i,t}^{ATMC} \tag{12.1}$$

where $skew_{i,t}$ is a measure that proxies the slope of the implied volatility smirk of the ith underlying stock, $vol_{i,t}^{OTMP}$ and $vol_{i,t}^{ATMC}$ are the implied volatilities of an OTM put and ATM call options, respectively, all measured at time t. The authors conjecture that investors tend to choose out-of-the-money puts to hedge their stock positions against possible future negative jumps. Therefore, OTM puts become more expensive prior to large negative jumps. As a result, firms with steeper volatility smirks should earn lower subsequent returns compared to firms with flatter volatility smirks. To empirically investigate this hypothesis, they construct a long-short trading strategy based on the *skew* measure (12.1). In particular, each week they sort all firms traded in NYSE/AMEX/NASDAQ into decile portfolios based on the last week (Tuesday close to Tuesday close) average of *skew*. Portfolio 1 includes firms with the lowest *skews*, and portfolio 10 includes firms with the highest *skews*. Then, they skip one day and compute the next week (Wednesday close to Wednesday close) return of decile portfolios. Using value weighting, the portfolio with the lowest skews has a weekly return in excess of the risk free rate of 0.24% (13.18% annualized), and the portfolio with the highest skews has a weekly return in excess of the risk free rate of 0.08% (3.99% annualized). The long-short portfolio return is 0.16% per week (9.19% annualized) with a t-statistic of 2.19. The respective alpha values computed through the Fama and French (1996) three-factor model (FF3 hereafter) adjusting for market, size, and value risks are 0.10%, −0.11%, and 0.21% per week (10.90% annualized) the latter with the t-statistic of 2.93. Robustness checks indicate that after controlling for the predictive ability of known variables such as the difference between the historical and implied volatility, size, book-to-market ratio, past six-month equity returns, the stocks' historical volatility, stock turnover, and the put-call call ratio, the predictive power of the skew is still economically large and statistically significant.

A subsequent study by Rehman and Vilkov (2008) uses the Bakshi, Kapadia, and Madan (2003) model-free measure to explore the stock-specific information content of the option price cross-sections. This measure captures the skewness of a stock's risk-neutral return distribution. Low (high) skewness values, i.e. large negative (positive) skewness values, are associated with expensive OTM put (call) options and should therefore predict negative (positive) future returns for the underlying stock. The authors argue that this sentiment measure should contain less noise than the one used in XZZ since it is based on the entire option price cross-section (as opposed to only two moneyness ranges, i.e. one OTM put option and one ATM call option). To confirm that their proposed measure captures the forward looking stock-specific sentiment in an

relationship has been documented empirically in both equity and index option markets (see e.g., Skiadopoulos 2001).

economically significant way, they analyze the returns of a monthly rebalanced portfolio that consists of a long position in stocks with relatively high skewness and a short position in stocks with relatively low skewness. They find that the magnitude of the out-performance, on average, is 0.45% per month on a risk-adjusted basis or about 5.53% per year. Risk-adjustment is made with a four-factor model (FF4 hereafter) which includes market, size, value, and momentum risks (see Carhart 1997). In addition, the authors explore the longer term predictive power of skewness through similar portfolios that are held for up to six months. They find that skewness predicts the cross-section of stock returns up to five months from the date of portfolio formation. However, the alpha decreases monotonically over time. Similar results for the persistence of the skew's predictive ability are presented also in XZZ. When contrasting the results of the two papers, it is not easy to conclude which one of the sentiment factors is superior to the other. On the one hand, portfolio strategies based on the measure presented in XZZ use a factor that is easy to construct and generates an annualized abnormal return of 6.52% (risk-adjusted through FF4) for a four-week holding period. On the other, the stock selection factor used by Rehman and Vilkov (2008) uses the entire cross-section of options and hence is more complicated in terms of calculations but less prone to estimation error. The associated portfolio strategy generates an abnormal annualized return equal to 5.53% annualized (risk-adjusted through FF4) for a four-week holding period.

12.2.3 Deviations of Implied Volatilities

Cremers and Weinbaum (2010) hypothesize that deviations from put-call parity in options on individual stocks may reflect the trading activity of informed investors who trade first in the option markets and subsequently in the stock markets. To test their hypothesis empirically, they use a volatility spread variable VS that measures deviations from put-call parity by means of the weighted difference in implied volatilities between call and put options (with the same strike price and maturity), i.e.:

$$VS_{i,t} = \sum_{j=1}^{N_{i,t}} w_{j,t}^{i} \left(IV_{j,t}^{i,calls} - IV_{j,t}^{i,puts} \right) \tag{12.2}$$

where j refers to the jth pair of put and call options and thus indexes both strike prices and maturities, $w_{j,t}^{i}$ are weights computed as the average open interest in the call and put, $N_{i,t}$ denotes the number of pairs of options on stock i on day t, and $IV_{j,t}^{i}$ denotes the Black and Scholes (1973) implied volatility (adjusted for dividends and the possibility of early exercise since they use an American options data set). Intuitively, when the markets anticipate a rise in the price of the underlying stock, they should charge a higher premium for call options whereas a higher insurance premium should be charged for investors wishing to buy protection via put options when prices are expected to drop. Hence, a positive difference in implied volatilities between call and put options (i.e. positive *VS*) should predict positive future returns and vice versa. The authors find that the next-day, -week, and four-week abnormal returns (risk-adjusted by the FF4 model) on the long/short hedge portfolio, i.e. a portfolio that buys stocks with expensive call options and sells stocks with expensive put options, are 0.38% (with a t-statistic of 27.2), 0.50% (with a t-statistic of 8.01), and 0.73% (with a t-statistic of 4.82), respectively. Another interesting result from the empirical analysis is the finding on the relationship between future stock prices and the levels and changes in volatility spreads. The authors find that the next-week and four-week abnormal returns (risk-adjusted by the FF4 model augmented with the systematic co-skewness factor of Harvey and Sidiqque, 2000) on the long/short hedge portfolio, i.e. a portfolio that buys stocks with expensive call options and sell stocks with expensive put options, are 0.21% (with a t-statistic of 3.33) and 0.51% (with a t-statistic of 3.35) respectively. Another interesting result from the empirical analysis is the finding on the relationship between future stock prices and the levels and changes in volatility spreads. The authors find that the long/short portfolio that buys stocks with high and increasing volatility spreads, and sells stocks with low and decreasing volatility spreads, earns an abnormal return (risk-adjusted by the FF4 model augmented with the systematic co-skewness factor of Harvey and Sidiqque, 2000) of 0.50% per week (with a t-statistic of 3.76) including the first overnight period. Similar results are obtained for the four-week rebalancing case, i.e. the abnormal return is 0.99% (t-statistic of 2.37). However, the authors carry out an analysis and conclude that the predictability of the volatility diminishes in the latter years of their sample yet does not disappear particularly for nest-day returns.

Bali and Hovakimian (2009) test whether there is a negative cross-sectional relation between firm-level returns and the volatility risk premium. Their hypothesis is motivated by the empirical evidence of a negative volatility risk premium (see, e.g., Bakshi and Kapadia 2003a; Bakshi and Kapadia 2003b; Bali and Engle 2007). They find that stock selection based on the magnitude of the difference between the realized and implied volatility of a stock can generate significant portfolio returns; the realized volatility is measured over a month and the implied volatility is the average volatility implied by call and put option prices of the same strike and maturity observed at the end of the same month. In particular, a trading strategy that buys stocks in the lowest realized-implied volatility discrepancy quintile and shorts stocks in the highest realized-implied volatility discrepancy quintile produces average returns of 0.60% to 0.73% per month (risk-adjusted through FF3). These results are consistent with the conjecture that the realized-implied volatility spread is a proxy for volatility risk. They also develop a stock selection strategy that is based on the difference between call and put option implied volatilities just as in Cremers and Weinbaum (2010). In accordance with them, they argue that equity prices move away from their fundamental values in the case where call option prices exceed the levels implied by put-call parity due to irrational behavior and limits to arbitrage. Their stock selection strategy entails buying stocks in the highest call-put implied volatility spread quintile, and selling stocks in the lowest call-put implied volatility spread quintile. The strategy generates average returns in the range of 1.05% to 1.49% per month that are highly significant.

Doran and Krieger (2009) study the information content of different parts of the implied volatility skew. They define five measures each one capturing a different portion of the implied volatility skew. One, AMB, calculates the difference between the mean implied volatilities of the option pair whose strike prices are above the current underlying price and the option pair whose strike prices are below the current underlying price. This measure is claimed to capture the information contained in the tails of the volatility skew. Two others, COMA and POMA, capture the difference between the OTM and ATM volatilities of calls and puts, respectively. They are motivated as measures capturing the right and middle side of the volatility skew for call, and the left and middle side of the volatility skew, for put options. The last two measures are simplified measures of Cremers and Weinbaum (2010) and XZZ. The first captures the information contained in the middle of the volatility skew, and the second uses information across the left of the put and middle of the call volatility skew. To construct the measures, the authors use only options that expire in the second month following the trading day the measures are calculated. Firms are sorted into quintiles by the calculated measures, and returns are calculated for each quintile over the following month. The empirical analysis concludes that information about the future return is contained at various parts of the volatility skew, most notably in two places. First, future underlying returns are positively linked to the higher differences in the volatilities between ATM calls and puts. Second, higher returns are positively related to more negative skews as measured on the left-hand side of the volatility skew, between OTM and ATM puts. However, much of the analysis in this paper offers counter-intuitive results. One example is the finding that negative skews are associated with higher returns. Another counter-intuitive result presented in the analysis is that high AMB stocks underperform low AMB stocks.

12.2.4 Idiosyncratic Implied Volatility

Another idea of stock-selection based on option implied information is developed by Diavatopoulos, Doran, and Petersen (DDP 2009). DDP define the idiosyncratic portion of implied volatility and explore the returns of portfolios of stocks formulated on the basis of stocks' idiosyncratic implied volatility. The idiosyncratic portion of implied volatility is extracted from the following relationship:

$$\sigma^2_{IV,j,t} = \beta^2_j \sigma^2_{IV\_M,t} + \sigma^2_{IV\_idio,j,t} \tag{12.3}$$

where $\sigma^2_{IV\_M,t}$ is the implied market variance measured by the VIX index on day t, $\sigma^2_{IV,j,t}$ is the implied total variance for firm j at time t, and β^2_j is the squared market beta from the estimation of a single factor model (see Sections 12.4.1 and 12.4.2 for a description of market beta and VIX, respectively). The authors form quintile portfolios based on $\sigma^2_{IV\_idio,j,t}$ and study their monthly returns. In principle, stocks associated with higher (idiosyncratic) risk should deliver higher returns. They find that a portfolio of stocks with high idiosyncratic implied volatility generate a statistically significant abnormal return of 1.51% per month (adjusted by the FF4 model). Furthermore, the hedge portfolio that is the portfolio that also shorts stocks in the low implied volatility quintile, i.e. stocks with low idiosyncratic risk, yields a statistically significant abnormal return of 1.40% per month. The authors also compare their results with the results obtained from a similar exercise where the sorting variable is the realized idiosyncratic volatility. They conclude that when implied and realized idiosyncratic volatility are directly compared with each other, implied idiosyncratic volatility is positively linked to future returns but realized idiosyncratic risk is not. The main result in DDP, i.e. the documentation of a positive relationship between idiosyncratic implied volatility and future returns, seems to be more intuitive than the results presented in the literature that examine the predictability of idiosyncratic volatility (see, e.g. Ang, Hodrick, Xing, and Zhang 2006); the latter concludes that stocks with low idiosyncratic volatility outperform stocks with high idiosyncratic volatility.

12.2.5 Implied Volatilities Around Corporate Events

On the side of the literature aiming to identify candidate stocks for equity long/short portfolio strategies, there are some articles exploring the information content of option prices prior to specific corporate events. The basic idea is that the option market may contain information about the outcome and effects of a corporate event and therefore the direction of a firm's stock price.

A relatively unexplored work by Bar-Yosef and Sarig (1992) demonstrates how option prices can be used to determine dividend surprises that are often exploited by event-driven portfolio managers. The authors define a dividend surprise by subtracting dividend expectations imputed from pre-announcement option prices from dividend expectations imputed from post-announcement option prices, that is:

$$\Delta IDIV = PC(DIV)^A - PC(DIV)^B \tag{12.4}$$

where $PC(DIV)^A$ and $PC(DIV)^B$ denote the put-call parity implied dividend after and prior to the dividend announcement, respectively. In the case where $\Delta IDIV$ is positive this would indicate that market participants expect an increase in disseminated future dividends, and hence an increase in the future stock price. Although not explicitly tested, a portfolio strategy that would exploit these findings should involve buying stocks with positive dividend surprises and sell stocks with negative dividend surprises.

Recent work by Diavatopoulos, Doran, Fodor, and Peterson (DDFP 2008) focuses on another corporate event that is the earnings announcement. In particular, they posit that changes in stock return skewness and kurtosis implied by option prices before the earnings announcement should be related to future stock and option returns. This is important for a portfolio manager who is interested in predicting the direction and size of the surprise so as to exploit part of the empirically documented pre-announcement drift phenomenon (see Bernard and Thomas 1989), i.e. the increase in stock price prior to the earnings announcement date. DDFP measure implied skewness and implied kurtosis by means of the approach developed by Bakshi, Kapadia, and Madan (2003). Then, they calculate changes in implied skewness and kurtosis over periods leading to the earnings announcement, that is changes between the values observed 30 days prior to the earnings announcement date and 20, 10, and 5 days prior to the earnings announcement date. Their analysis concludes that implied skewness and kurtosis changes over the 30-day period prior to the earnings announcement date are strongly related to future stock and option returns up to the earnings announcement date. In particular, the top performing quintile basket of stocks in the periods $[-4, 1]$, $[-9, 1]$, and $[-19, 1]$ (notation is read as the period starting four days prior the announcement day and ending one day after the announcement day, and so on) is the one associated with the greater increases in implied skewness (and greater increases in implied kurtosis). These results suggest that portfolio managers wishing to speculate on the earnings announcement return or even take advantage of the pre-announcement period return may use implied skewness (or kurtosis) in their stock selection process. Earlier work linking option prices with earnings announcement includes Pattel and Wolfson (1981) and Ho (1993). The former study finds that the average standard deviations of stock returns implied by pre-announcement option prices exhibit a time-series profile which anticipates the stock price behavior. The latter study finds that the security prices of firms with a traded option anticipate annual accounting earnings changes prior to the announcement day.

12.3 Forming Optimal Portfolios by Using Information from Options

This section reviews papers that suggest ways of using information from option markets for the purposes of constructing optimal portfolios. The first subsection outlines the setting, and the second introduces the motivation for the development of this literature and the relevant papers.

12.3.1 The Setting

Let a myopic investor stand at time t with initial wealth W_t and investment horizon over the period$[t, t+1]$. The investor wishes to optimally allocate her wealth between n assets with return vector $R = (r_1, r_2, \ldots, r_n)'$ and joint cumulative distribution function (CDF) $F(r_1, r_2, \ldots, r_n)$. Her end-of-period wealth is given by

$$W_{t+1} = W_t \times (1 + r_p) \tag{12.5}$$

where r_p denotes the portfolio return, with $r_p = a'r$ and $a = (a_1, a_2, \ldots, a_n)'$ being the portfolio weights assigned to the corresponding n assets. The investor's preferences are described by a utility function $U(W_{t+1})$, where $U'(\cdot) > 0$ and $U''(\cdot) < 0$. The optimal portfolio choice a^* is defined to be the solution to the following problem:

$$\max_{\{\alpha\}} E_t[U(W_{t+1})] = \max_{\alpha_t} \int \int \ldots \int^U (W_{t+1}) dF_t(r_1, r_2, \ldots r_n)$$
$$s.t. \sum_{i=1}^{n} a_i = 1. \tag{12.6}$$

Obtaining the optimal portfolio weights by solving Equation (12.6) is also termed direct maximization (see, e.g., Adler and Kritzman 2007; and Sharpe 2007) and requires estimation of the CDF.

Alternatively, the optimal portfolio weights can be obtained by indirect maximization of expected utility: first, the utility function is approximated by a Taylor series expansion truncated to a desired order. Then, the expected value of the expansion is maximized with respect to the portfolio weights. To fix ideas, let $\overline{W}_{t+1}$ be the mean value of the future wealth. Then, at any point in time t, the expected utility approximated by a Taylor series expansion of infinite order k around $\overline{W}_{t+1}$ is given by

$$E_t[U(W_{t+1})] = E_t\left[\sum_{k=0}^{\infty} \frac{U^{(k)}(\overline{W}_{t+1})(W_{t+1} - \overline{W}_{t+1})^k}{k!}\right]. \tag{12.7}$$

Under rather mild conditions (see Garlappi and Skoulakis 2008 and the references therein), Equation (12.7) can be rewritten as

$$E_t[U(W_{t+1})] = \sum_{k=0}^{\infty} \frac{U^{(k)}(\overline{W}_{t+1})}{k!} E_t[(W_{t+1} - \overline{W}_{t+1})^k]. \tag{12.8}$$

Then, for a given choice of k, the optimal portfolio can be formed by maximizing Equation (12.8) with respect to the portfolio weights. For instance, the standard mean-variance Markowitz optimal portfolio corresponds to the case where $k = 2$. Higher order moments may also be considered (e.g., skewness and kurtosis for $k = 3, 4$, respectively; see e.g. Jondeau and Rockinger, 2006, for a nice exposition of the impact of incorporating higher order moments in an asset allocation setting). Equation (12.8) shows that in the case of indirect maximization the estimation of the moments of the portfolio returns PDF is required.

12.3.2 The Forward-Looking Approach

There is a vast literature that deals with the estimation of the PDF/moments of portfolio returns in either the direct or indirect maximization case (see DeMiguel, Garlappi, and Uppal 2009). All of the proposed estimators require historical data (backward–looking approach). Inevitably, the estimated parameters are very sensitive to estimation errors (see, e.g., Chopra and Ziemba 1993). This may lead to significant miscalculation of the optimal portfolio strategy. As a response, there is a developing literature that suggests

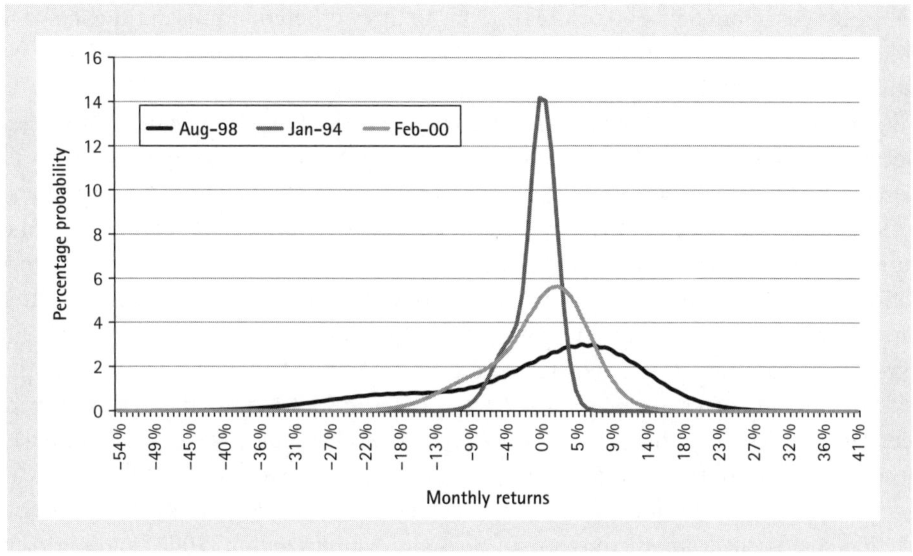

FIGURE 12.1 Risk-neutral option-implied distributions.

using implied PDFs/implied moments extracted from market option prices instead of relying only on historical data; Kostakis, Panigirtzoglou, and Skiadopoulos (KPS 2009) term this a *forward-looking approach* to asset allocation.

To fix ideas, let $c_t(K, T)$ be the price of a European call option at time t written on an asset with price S_t that expires at time T $(t \leq T)$ with strike price K and payoff function $c_T(K, T) = \max[S_T - K, 0]$. Assuming deterministic interest rates, the call price is given by (see Björk, 2004 for a detailed discussion)

$$c_t(K, T) = e^{-r(T-t)} E_t^Q[\max(S_T - K, 0)] = e^{-r(T-t)} \int_0^{\infty} \max(S_T - K, 0) f_t(S_T) dS_T \quad (12.9)$$

where the expectation of the options payoff is formed at time t under the so-called risk-neutral probability measure Q; and $f_t(S_T)$ denotes the T-expiry implied risk-neutral PDF of the asset price standing at time t. Differentiating the call option price twice with respect to the strike price yields (see Breeden and Litzenberger 1978):

$$f_t(S_T) = e^{r(T-t)} \frac{\partial^2 c_t(K, T)}{\partial K^2} \Big|_{S_T = K} . \quad (12.10)$$

The extraction of an implied PDF can be done at any point in time t via the model-free formula shown in Equation (12.10).[3] Figure 12.1 shows one-month horizon implied

[3] However, even though Equation (12.6) is model-free, its implementation is not. This is because it requires the existence of market call option prices across a continuum of strike prices; this is not the case in practice. Therefore, various implementation techniques have been proposed in the literature; these effectively suggest alternative schemes to interpolate across available market option prices and extrapolate beyond them (see Jackwerth 2004, for an excellent review).

PDFs extracted from S&P 500 futures options in three different points in time: January 1994, August 1998, and February 2000 (see Panigirtzoglou and Skiadopoulos 2004, for a study of the dynamics of implied PDFs over time).

So far in the literature, four papers have taken a forward-looking approach to asset allocation. The first by KPS (2009) develops an approach that uses implied PDFs to form optimal portfolios via direct and indirect maximization of expected utility. Doing so, KPS take into account the empirically encountered deviations of the portfolio returns distribution from normality. Their forward-looking approach requires transformation of the risk-neutral PDF to its physical (risk-adjusted) analogue since the latter is required in Equation (12.6). Moreover, such a transformation is necessary to obtain non-trivial allocations.[4] The transformation of the implied PDF is feasible since the risk-neutral and corresponding risk-adjusted PDFs are related via the pricing kernel (see, e.g., Ait-Sahalia and Lo 2000, for a detailed explanation); the latter is uniquely specified once a utility function for the representative investor is assumed in a complete market setting and the risk-aversion coefficient is estimated. KPS extract the risk aversion coefficient using the method of Bliss and Panigirtzoglou (2004) and perform the change of probability measure. They test the out-of-sample empirical performance of their method compared to the standard backward-looking approach. To this end, they consider an asset universe that consists of a risky (S&P 500) and risk-free asset. Various performance measures and utility functions (including behavioral finance ones) are employed. KPS find that the forward-looking approach dominates the backward-looking one under all measures. For instance, their approach yields a typical increase in the Sharpe ratio of the order of 0.2 per annum. Furthermore, in the case where transaction costs are included, the investor is still better off by 1–3% per annum.

In a subsequent paper, DeMiguel, Plyakha, Uppal, and Vilkov (DPUV 2011) focus on a mean-variance setting and calculate minimum-variance optimal portfolios by using implied volatilities and option implied correlations as inputs.[5] They consider a portfolio consisting of a large number of U.S. stocks to assess whether information from option markets can improve the out-of-sample performance of the formed optimal portfolios. To this end, they use a number of performance measures and benchmark portfolios based on historical data. They find that the use of implied volatilities or implied correlations *per se* does not improve portfolio performance. Interestingly though, the introduction of the volatility risk premium and option-implied skewness in the portfolio formation yields optimal portfolios that earn greater Sharpe ratios than the portfolios based on historical information. Their motivation for using these option-elements is that stocks with low volatility (implied skewness) risk premium outperform those with high volatility (implied skewness) risk premium as has been discussed in Section 12.2.3.

[4] These trivial solutions will occur in a Markowitz mean-variance paradigm. This is because under the risk-neutral probability measure, the expected return equals the risk-free rate. Hence, the risk-premium is zero and consequently a risk-averse investor will place all her money in the risk-free asset.

[5] An option implied correlation is defined to be the value of the correlation coefficient that equates the variance of the returns of a portfolio with the option implied variance of the portfolio.

However, there are two important differences between DPUV and KPS: First, DPUV constrain their analysis in a mean-variance setting and examine only myopic portfolios, whereas KPS take into account the whole PDF to calculate the optimal myopic portfolios and present also an extension to an intertemporal asset allocation problem. Second, DPUV need to assume a certain parametric dependence between the optimal portfolio weights and option-implied factors; this may prove a restrictive assumption.

Ait-Sahalia and Brandt (ASB 2008) also develop a forward-looking approach to portfolio formation. Their approach is developed in an intertemporal asset allocation setting for a non-myopic investor where multiple risky assets exist (risk-free asset, stock, and bond), i.e.,

$$\max_{\{\alpha_s | t \leq s \leq T\}} E_s[U(W_T)] \tag{12.11}$$

subject to a process that governs the dynamics of wealth over time (Merton 1971). Their algorithm relies on the martingale representation theory that converts a dynamic asset allocation problem to a static one (see Campbell and Viceira 2003). This approach requires the multivariate implied and historical PDF as inputs (i.e. the pricing kernel) and delivers the optimal consumption path over time; the performance of their approach has not been examined from a portfolio manager's perspective, though, since no formulas are derived for the optimal portfolio weights.[6]

Finally, Jabbour, Peňa, Vera, and Zuluaga (JPVZ 2008) calculate optimal portfolio weights using implied PDFs. However, their definition of optimality differs from the previous three papers in that the optimal portfolio is defined to be the one that minimizes the portfolio's Conditional Value-at-Risk (CVaR, also known as expected shortfall, see Rockafellar and Uryasev, 2000) over all possible implied PDFs, so that the existing market option prices an be replicated. Intuitively, their idea is the following: CVaR is defined as the average portfolio loss calculated over the portfolio losses that have exceeded Value-at-Risk (VaR), i.e.,

$$CVaR(F_R, a) = -E[r_p \,|r_p \leq -VaR] = -\frac{\int_{-\infty}^{-VaR} z f_{r_p}(z) dz}{F_{r_p}(-VaR)} \tag{12.12}$$

where $F(\cdot)$ is the real-world CDF of portfolio returns, and the one-day VaR_t is estimated at day $(t-1)$ at coverage probability $\alpha\%$, where $\alpha\%$ is the percentile defined as

$$\Pr[r_{p,t} \leq -VaR_t(a)] = a. \tag{12.13}$$

JPVZ perform a two-dimensional search (in weights and PDFs) so that the optimal portfolio weights correspond to the minimum CVaR calculated under the *implied* PDF; the latter is not extracted independently as in the other two papers but instead is used as

[6] The authors estimate the multivariate implied PDF by extracting the marginal implied PDFs and linking them through an assumed copula function. An alternative way to estimate the multivariate implied PDF would be to use data on basket options; unfortunately, these options are not traded heavily as yet.

a constraint in the above nonlinear problem. The JPVZ approach is an interesting one given that CVaR is a coherent measure of risk (see Artzner, Delbaen, Eber, and Heath 1999) and its concept may not sound abstract to a practitioner as the expected utility paradigm might do. The authors run some preliminary empirical tests in a two-asset universe to evaluate the performance of their algorithm in terms of the sensitivity of the estimated parameters to changes in the data and delivered Sharpe ratios as compared to that derived by a naïve $1/N$ diversification strategy where a fraction $1/N$ of the total wealth is allocated to each one of the N assets.

12.4 Estimating Risk by Using Information from Options

This section reviews papers that use option information for the purposes of estimating the beta coefficient and Value-at-Risk (VaR). The accurate estimation of both these concepts is of paramount importance to practitioners.

12.4.1 Beta Coefficient

The beta coefficient β_i of the ith asset is defined as the covariance of the returns r_i of the ith asset with the returns r_m of the market portfolio divided by the variance of the returns of the market portfolio, i.e.,

$$\beta_i = \frac{Cov(r_i, r_m)}{Var(r_m)}. \tag{12.14}$$

Equation (12.14) can be re-written as

$$\beta_i = \rho_{iM} \left(\frac{Var(r_i)}{Var(r_m)} \right)^{1/2} \tag{12.15}$$

where ρ_{iM} denotes the correlation between the returns of the ith asset and these of the market portfolio.

The accurate estimation of beta is of great importance to the industry since it can be used to (i) measure the systematic risk of an asset, (ii) calculate the cost of capital via the CAPM model and subsequently evaluate equities, and (iii) measure the abnormal performance (i.e. alpha) of a portfolio manager. To this end, a large literature has been developed to estimate beta accurately (see Chang, Christoffersen, Jacobs and Vainberg, (CCJV) 2009, for a list of references). Given that the proposed estimators rely on past data, the issue whether the estimated beta is mis-estimated arises again just as in the case of optimal portfolio choice. As a response to this, a beta forward-looking literature that employs information from market option prices has emerged. French, Groth, and Kolari (1983) first proposed a hybrid beta estimator that uses historical returns to estimate the correlation term in Equation (12.15) and the implied volatilities of options written on the ith asset (equity option) and the index (index option) that proxies the market portfolio. Buss and Vilkov (2009) also proposed a beta estimator that uses information from historical and options data (historical correlations and implied volatilities of index and equity options) based on a multi-factor return model where structure is posed on the dynamics of pairwise correlations between stocks. CCJV improve on the hybrid beta estimator by developing a beta estimator that relies solely on market option data (option-implied beta).[7] They derive an expression that relates the beta to the implied volatilities of the index and equity options and the implied from options (risk-neutral) skewness coefficients $Skew_i$ and $Skew_m$ of the asset and index returns, respectively. In particular, they show that

$$\beta_i = \left(\frac{Skew_i}{Skew_m}\right)^{1/3} \left(\frac{Var(r_i)}{Var(r_m)}\right)^{1/2}. \tag{12.16}$$

CCJV propose calculating the risk-neutral moments that appear in Equation (12.16) by means of the risk-neutral moment expressions developed by Bakshi, Kapadia, and Madan (2003).[8] These expressions are model-free, however their implementation requires the existence of European plain vanilla options trading across a continuum of strikes which is not the case in practice. Therefore, interpolation and extrapolation schemes should be used. This is a similar hurdle to the case where the model-free result of Breeden and Litzenberger (1978, equation (12.10)) needs to be implemented. In fact, Equation (12.16) can alternatively be implemented by using the risk-neutral moments obtained from extracted risk-neutral distributions.

It should be noted that the derivation of Equation (12.16) is based on two rather debatable assumptions: the first is that a single-factor model holds, i.e.,

$$r_i = a_i + \beta_i r_m + \varepsilon_i \tag{12.17}$$

where ε_ι is an idiosyncratic shock assumed to have mean zero and be independent of the market return. The second is that the skewness of ε_ι is zero. In addition, its implementation requires that options are traded on the asset whose beta one is looking for. Despite these constraints, the CCJV option implied beta can in principle respect the data generating process of the ith asset returns because of its inherent forward looking property and its properties should be explored further.[9]

[7] Siegel (1995) also suggested the creation of a type of derivative (called an exchange option) that would allow the computation of betas based solely on options data. However, this type of option is not yet traded and hence his method cannot be implemented.

[8] There is a caveat at this point. Equation (12.16) is written in terms of the moments (variance and skewness) of the real-world PDF. Replacing the real-world moments with the risk-neutral ones presents a conceptual problem (see CCJV for a discussion). This problem also arises in the French, Groth, and Kolari (1983) and Vilkov and Buss (2009) approaches.

[9] CCJV consider a number of stocks and find that in many cases their option implied beta forecasts the 180 day *ex post* realized beta more accurately than a historical (rolling-window) beta does. However, Buss and Vilkov (2009) find that the CCJV beta estimator performs worse than a historical estimator in the case where a 90-day horizon is considered. In addition, they find that hybrid beta estimators outperform historical and the CCJV estimators.

Husmann and Stephan (2007) also estimate beta by using information only from market option prices. First, they derive a beta estimator assuming that the index and equity returns are bivariately normally distributed. Then, the inputs of their estimator are back out from calibrating a CAPM option pricing model to market option prices. Finally, Fouque and Kollman (2009) have derived an expression to estimate beta by using information from option implied volatilities where a continuous time setting with stochastic volatility is assumed. Their beta formula is based on a linear interpolation of the implied volatility skew, which may be thought to be a restrictive assumption though.

12.4.2 Value-at-Risk (VaR)

Information from market option prices can also be used to calculate risk measures such as the VaR and CVaR that are used both for risk management, as well as for asset allocation purposes (e.g., in a mean-CVaR setting instead for the standard mean-variance one, see, e.g., Giamouridis and Vrontos 2007).

Any parametric VaR model requires as an input the variance of the portfolio returns (see Christoffersen 2003, for an introduction to VaR models, and Angelidis and Skiadopoulos 2008, and Giamouridis and Ntoula 2009, for empirical applications). To this end, an implied volatility index can be used. An implied volatility index represents the implied volatility of a synthetic option written on a stock index that has a fixed time to maturity. It is constructed by using the market prices of plain vanilla call and put options traded across a number of strike prices and expiry dates that surround the targeted time to maturity.[10] Nowadays, there is a number of implied volatility indices traded in various exchanges (e.g., VIX, VXO, VXN, VXD, VDAX, VCAC, etc., see Dotsis, Psychoyios, and Skiadopoulos 2007, and Konstantinidi, Skiadopoulos, and Tzagkaraki 2008, for a description of the indices and their properties).[11] Giot (2005a) uses the VXO and VXN indices to calculate the VaR for the S&P 100 and NASDAQ 100 portfolios. He finds that the corresponding VaR models pass various backtesting tests even though they perform similarly to the standard J.P. Morgan RiskMetrics VaR model (see Alexander 2001, for a review of the model).

Interestingly, Ait-Sahalia and Lo (2000) first suggested calculating VaR from implied rather than real-world distributions since the option implied VaR (termed Economic VaR, E-VaR) may be a more accurate estimate than the historical VaR (they call it statistical VaR, SVaR). Next, Panigirtzoglou and Skiadopoulos (2004) developed a model for the dynamics of implied PDFs and found that it can be used to calculate accurately the E-VaR. Following this line of research, Alentorn and Markose (2008) calculated the E-VaR for the FTSE-100 and found that outperformed S-VaR calculated

[10] A commonly used algorithm is the one used for the construction of VIX, see the VIX white paper (at http://www.cboe.com/micro/VIX/vixwhite.pdf). Skiadopoulos (2004) also provides an algorithm for the construction of an implied volatility index in emerging markets.

[11] The primary reason for the introduction of implied volatility indices is to underly implied volatility derivatives (see, e.g., Psychoyios and Skiadopoulos 2006, for a review of the literature and an examination of the hedging effectiveness of volatility derivatives by means of a simulation application).

by means of historical simulation. Essentially, the authors conclude that the advantage of E-VaR is that it "responds quickly to market events and in some cases even anticipates them."

12.5 Market and Style Timing

Option markets may contain information that is useful for timing asset allocation or style rotation decisions. A number of papers have explored whether implied volatility indices can serve as leading indicators of the stock market, i.e. to forecast the future stock returns. Their motivation to do so stems from the well-documented negative correlation between changes of the implied volatility index and changes in the underlying asset price (leverage effect). Therefore, an increasing volatility index is associated to a falling stock market and hence it can be regarded as a barometer of the investor's fear (see Whaley 2000). Based on this stylized fact, Copeland and Copeland (1999) apply two trading strategies where an increase in the VXO index over its three-month moving average triggers (i) buying value stocks and selling growth stocks (BARRA's indices) and (ii) buying large-cap stocks and selling small-cap stocks (S&P futures and Value Line futures). The strategies yield positive returns. However, their results are not reported on a risk-adjusted basis and hence no safe conclusions can be drawn about the profitability of these strategies. Giot (2005b) attempts to identify whether regimes of high (low) values for VXO correspond to positive (negative) future S&P 100 stock returns for holding periods up to 60 days. His rationale is based again on the leverage effect, i.e., a high (low) level of the index would indicate an oversold stock market. His findings confirm that this is the case. The previous two studies investigate the properties of implied volatility indices as a marketing tool at a stock index level. Benerjee, Doran, and Peterson (2007) run predictive regressions and find that VIX forecasts future stock returns of NYSE stock portfolios formed on size, book-to-market and beta, as well; the evidence is stronger for longer holding period returns (60 days rather than 30 days). Future research should apply a trading strategy to assess the economic significance of their results.[12]

12.6 The Use of Information in Option Trading Activity

The literature we have thus far discussed focuses on studies that explore the potential uses of option prices for stock selection, portfolio construction, risk measurement/

[12] Diavatopoulos, Doran, and Peterson (2009) find that the idiosyncratic implied volatility of stock options predicts the one-month ahead future underlying stock returns by means of predictive regressions. Again, no trading strategy has been applied.

management, and market/style timing. There is also an extensive literature concerned with the information conveyed by the options trading activity, primarily options trading volume, regarding future stock returns. This section reviews some representative studies of this strand.

Easley, O'Hara, and Srinivas (EOHS 1998) is perhaps the most well-known study that investigates the linkages between the underlying equity and option markets by emphasizing the crucial role of option transaction volume as a statistic for technical analysis. The authors develop a market microstructure model that offers an explanation about why the volume of particular types of option trades might be indicative of information-based trading and therefore constitute a useful source of information for other investors. Next, EOHS analyze transaction data to classify whether an option trade is a buyer- or a seller-initiated trade based on which price point of the bid-ask spread a trade occurs. For example, trades occurring in the upper half of the bid-ask spread are classified as buyer-initiated trades. "Positive news" trades are call option buys or put option sales. "Negative news" trades are put option buys or call options sales. The authors find that it is this "positive news" or "negative news" option volumes that have predictive power for future stock price movements. In fact, the predictability pattern found in the paper is asymmetric and supportive of the hypothesis that options markets are more attractive venues for traders acting on "bad" news.[13] Pan and Poteshman (2006) provide additional empirical evidence for the predictability of option volume for future stock prices. Their study uses option trades that are initiated by buyers to open new positions as in EOHS. The core variable for the empirical analysis is the put-call ratio defined to be the number of put option contracts purchased to open new positions divided by the total number of option contracts – put and call options – purchased to open new positions. As this ratio approaches one, a bearish signal is conveyed: "fresh" put options are bought presumably on the basis of negative information. On the other hand, a bullish signal is revealed in the case where the ratio approaches zero: "fresh" call options are bought on the basis of positive information. The authors find that during their sample period, the stocks in the lowest quintile put-call ratios outperform those in the highest quintile put-call ratios by over 0.40% per day and 1% per week on a risk-adjusted basis. When the stock returns are tracked for several weeks, the level of predictability gradually dies out, indicating that the information contained in the option volume eventually gets incorporated into the underlying stock prices.

A recent study by Roll, Schwartz, and Subrahmanyam (2009) combines options and stock trading volume in a measure termed the options-to-stocks trading volume ratio (O/S hereafter). For options and the underlying stock of a given firm, O/S is defined to be the ratio between the total volume of trading in the options of the firm listed in the market and the corresponding volume of trading in the stock market; the ratio is calculated over a given calendar period, usually a day. The authors study the way that O/S varies across time and companies. To trigger a trading strategy one should

[13] A basic argument for this hypothesis is that it is easier to trade negative views by means of long put or short call option positions as opposed to selling short stocks that should be borrowed.

not look at variation of this variable *per se* but in conjunction with another variable of interest. For instance, the authors find that O/S increases sharply prior to the earnings announcement date and high O/S and high Cumulative Abnormal Returns (CARs) before earnings announcements imply smaller CARs following the announcements. The rationale is that informed traders prefer trading in the options than the stock market. Therefore, the increase of O/S indicates that the number of informed traders who ride on the increasing CARs increases up to the announcement date. After the announcement date the whole information has been incorporated in the stock price resulting in a decrease in CARs.

A number of authors have also looked at the informational role of option volume around corporate events. Amin and Lee (1997) for example find that abnormal option volume is observed in the three to four days before the quarterly earnings announcement and that the buy/sell activities of option trades foreshadow subsequent earnings news. In particular, active-side option trades are found to be associated with positive returns, suggesting that initiators of option trades bring private information to market in line with EOHS. Donders, Kouwenberg, and Vorst (2000) conclude that trading volume in options reacts faster and stronger to earnings announcements than stock volume; this suggests that investors anticipate price reactions in the underlying stock and try to take advantage through leverage. Cao, Chen, and Griffin (2005) study option volumes prior to takeovers; options written on stocks of the target firm are considered. They conclude that short-term OTM call options which could be the most profitable trade should a takeover announcement arises (since they will become in-the-money due to the increase in the stock price of the acquired firm), experience the largest increase in volume and buyer-initiated volume. Similar findings are presented by Jayaraman, Frye, and Sabherwal (2001) who study both the volume of option contracts traded and the open interest prior to the announcement of a merger or an acquisition. Arnold, Erwin, Nail, and Nixon (2006) find that the options market is the preferred venue – relative to the cash equity market – for traders attempting to profit on anticipated tender offer announcements.

12.7 Conclusion

The view that informed investors might choose to trade derivatives has been entertained by both academics and practitioners from as early as the introduction of options trading in the early 1970s. This chapter has reviewed recent as well as representative prior papers that discuss uses of the option markets implicit information for quantitative equity portfolio management. The reviewed articles cover a wide range of aspects of the quantitative investment process including stock selection, portfolio construction, risk measurement, and market/style timing. Attention has been drawn to papers that deal with the information content of option prices. In addition, we have discussed articles that use the information content of the options trading volume as an equity quant factor.

An overview of the results of these papers suggests that stock markets may not be efficient in the case where stock trading strategies are formed based on information encountered in option markets. This implies that option prices seem to contain information that hasn't been discounted in the underlying equity prices since quantitative equity portfolio managers may have not sufficiently utilized it in their investment process. The merits of using option implied information for equity portfolio management may go beyond the first order effect, i.e., the portfolio's strategy profitability, discussed in the majority of the papers. In particular, we believe that an important aspect of stock selection based on option implicit information is that it generates trading ideas in the large-cap space where portfolio managers struggle to find original ideas.

We would like to thank Dimitris Flamouris, Eirini Konstantinidi, and Alexandros Kostakis for useful comments. Because of space limitations some contributions have not been given the attention they deserve. Any remaining errors are our responsibility alone.

References

Adler, T. and Kritzman, M. (2007). Mean-variance versus full-scale optimization. *Journal of Asset Management*, 7, 302–311.

Ait-Sahalia, Y. and Lo, A.W. (2000). Nonparametric risk management and implied risk aversion. *Journal of Econometrics*, **94**, 9–51.

Ait-Sahalia, Y. and Brandt, M.W. (2008). Consumption and portfolio choice with option-implied state prices. NBER: Working paper.

Alexander, C. (2001). *Market Models: A Guide to Financial Data Analysis*. John Wiley, New York.

Alentorn, A. and Markose, S. (2008). Generalized extreme value distribution and extreme economic value at risk (EE-VaR). In *Computational methods in Financial Engineering*. Essays in Honor of Manfred Gilli (ed. J. Kontoghiorghes, B. Rustem, and P. Winker). (Springer, Berlin).

Amin, K.I. and Lee, C.M.C. (1997). Option trading, price discovery and earnings news dissemination. *Contemporary Accounting Research*, **14**, 153–192.

Anagnou-Basioudis, I., Bedendo, M., Hodges, S.D., and Tompkins, R. (2005). Forecasting accuracy of implied and GARCH-based probability density functions. *Review of Futures Markets*, **14**: 41–66.

Ang, A., Hodrick, R., Xing Y. and Zhang, X. (2006). The cross-section of volatility and expected returns. *Journal of Finance*, **61**, 259–299.

Angelidis, T. and Skiadopoulos, G. (2008). Measuring the market risk of freight rates: A value-at-risk approach. *International Journal of Theoretical and Applied Finance*, **11**, 447–469.

Arnold, T., Erwin, G., Nail, L., and Nixon, T. (2006). Do option markets substitute for stock markets? Evidence from trading on anticipated tender offer announcements. *International Review of Financial Analysis*, **15**, 247–255.

Artzner, P., Delbaen, F., Eber, J.M., and Heath, D. (1999). Coherent measures of risk. *Mathematical Finance*, **9**, 203–228.

Back, K. (1993). Asymmetric information and options. *Review of Financial Studies*, **6**, 435–472.

Bakshi, G. and Kapadia, N. (2003a). Delta-hedged gains and the negative volatility risk premium. *Review of Financial Studies*, **16**, 527–566.

Bakshi, G. and Kapadia, N. (2003b). Volatility risk premium embedded in individual equity options. *Journal of Derivatives*, **11**, 45–54.

Bakshi, G., Kapadia, N. and Madan, D. (2003). Stock return characteristics, skew laws, and differential pricing of individual equity options. *Review of Financial Studies*, **10**, 101–143.

Bali, T.G. and Engle, R.F. (2007). Investigating ICAPM with dynamic conditional correlations. Baruch College and New York University: Working paper.

Bali, T. and Hovakimian, A. (2009). Volatility spreads and expected stock returns. *Management Science*, **55**, 1997–1812.

Banerjee, P.S., Doran, J.S. and Peterson, D.R. (2007). Implied volatility and future portfolio returns. *Journal of Banking and Finance*, **31**, 3183–3199.

Bar-Yosef, S. and Sarig, O.H. (1992). Dividend surprises inferred from option and stock prices. *Journal of Finance*, **47**, 1623–1640.

Bernard V. and Thomas J. (1989). Post-earnings-announcement drift: Delayed price response or risk premium? *Journal of Accounting Research*, **27**, 1–36.

Björk, T. (2004). *Arbitrage Theory in Continuous Time* (second edition). *Oxford University Press*, Oxford.

Black, F. (1975). Fact and fantasy in the use of options. *Financial Analysts Journal*, **31**, 36–41; 61–72.

Black, F. and Scholes M. (1973). The pricing of options and corporate liabilities. *Journal of Political Economy*, **81**, 637–654.

Bliss, R.R. and Panigirtzoglou, N. (2004). Option-implied risk aversion estimates. *Journal of Finance*, **59**, 407–446.

Breeden, D.T. and Litzenberger, R.H. (1978). Prices of state-contingent claims implicit in option prices. *Journal of Business*, **51**, 621–651.

Buss, A. and Vilkov, G. (2009). Option-implied correlation and factor betas revisited. Goether University: Working paper.

Cao, C., Chen, Z. and Griffin, J.M. (2005). Informational content of option volume prior to takeovers. *Journal of Business*, **78**, 1073–1109.

Campbell, J.Y. and Viceira, L.M. (2003). *Strategic Asset Allocation: Portfolio Choice for Long-Term Investors*. Oxford University Press, Oxford.

Carhart, M.M. (1997). On persistence in mutual fund performance. *Journal of Finance*, **52**, 57–82.

Chan, K.Y., Chung, P., and Fong, W. (2002). The informational role of stock and option volume. *Review of Financial Studies*, **15**, 1049–1075.

Chang, B.-Y., Christoffersen, P., Jacobs, K., and Vainberg, G. (2009). Option-implied measures of equity risk. McGill University: Working paper.

Chopra, V.K. and Ziemba, W.T. (1993). The effect of errors in means, variances and covariances on optimal portfolio choice. *Journal of Portfolio Management*, **19**, 6–11.

Christoffersen, P. (2003). *Elements of Financial Risk Management*. Academic Press, New York.

Copeland, M.M. and Copeland, T.E. (1999). 'Market timing: style and size rotation using the VIX'. *Financial Analysts Journal*, 55: 73–81.

Cremers, M. and D. Weinbaum (2010), Deviations from put-call parity and stock return predictability. *Journal of Financial and Quantitative Analysis*, **45**, 335–367.

DeMiguel, V., Garlappi, L., and Uppal, R. (2009). How inefficient are simple asset allocation strategies? *Review of Financial Studies*, **22**, 1915–1953.

DeMiguel, V., Plyakha, Y., Uppal, R., and Vilkov, G. (2011). Improving portfolio selection using option-implied volatility and skewness. Goethe University: Working paper.

Diavatopoulos, D., Doran, J. S., Fodor, A. and Peterson, D. R. (2008). The information content of Implied skewness and kurtosis changes prior to earnings announcements for stock and option returns. Working paper: available at SSRN: http://ssrn.com/abstract=1309613

Diavatopoulos, D., Doran, J.S., and Peterson, D.R. (2009). The information content in implied idiosyncratic volatility and the cross-section of stock returns: evidence from the option markets. *Journal of Futures Markets*, **28**, 1013–1039.

Donders, M.W., Kouwenberg, R., and Vorst, T.C.F. (2000). Options and earnings announcements: An empirical study of volatility, trading volume, open interest and liquidity. *European Financial Management*, **6**, 149–171.

Doran, J.S. and Krieger, K. (2009). Implications for asset returns in the implied volatility skew. *Financial Analysts Journal*: forthcoming.

Dotsis, G., Psychoyios, D., and Skiadopoulos, G. (2007). An empirical comparison of continuous-time models of implied volatility indices. *Journal of Banking and Finance*, **31**, 3584–3603.

Easley, D., O'Hara, M., and Srinivas, P. (1998). Option volume and stock prices: Evidence on where informed traders trade. *Journal of Finance*, **53**, 431–465.

Fama, E. and French, K. (1996). Multifactor explanation of asset pricing anomalies. *Journal of Finance*, **51**, 55–84.

Fouque, J.-P. and Kollman, E. (2009). Calibration of stock betas from skews of implied volatilities. University of California, Santa Barbara: Working paper.

French, D., Groth, J., and Kolari, J. (1983). Current investor expectations and better betas. *Journal of Portfolio Management*, **10**, 12–17.

Garlappi, L. and Skoulakis, G. (2008). Taylor series approximations to expected utility and optimal portfolio choice. University of Texas at Austin: Working paper.

Giamouridis, D. and Ntoula, I. (2009). A comparison of alternative approaches for determining the downside risk of hedge fund strategies. *Journal of Futures Markets*, **29**, 244–269.

Giamouridis, D. and Vrontos, I.D. (2007). Hedge fund portfolio construction: A comparison of static and dynamic approaches. *Journal of Banking and Finance*, **31**, 199–217.

Giot, P. (2005a). Implied volatility indexes and daily Value-at-Risk models. *Journal of Derivatives*, **12**, 54–64.

Giot, P. (2005b). Relationships between implied volatility indexes and stock index returns. *Journal of Portfolio Management*, **31**, 92–100.

Harvey, C., and Siddique, A. (2000). Conditional skewness in asset pricing tests. *Journal of Finance*, **55**, 1263–1295.

Ho, L.-C.J. (1993). Option trading and the relation between price and earnings: a cross-sectional analysis. *Accounting Review*, **68**, 368–384.

Husmann, S. and Stephan, A. (2007). On estimating an asset's implicit beta. *Journal of Futures Markets*, **27**, 961–979.

Jabbour, C., Peña, J.F., Vera, J.C., and Zuluaga, L.F. (2008). An estimation-free, robust CVaR portfolio allocation model. *Journal of Risk*, **11**, 57–78.

Jackwerth, J. (2004). Option-implied risk-neutral distributions and risk aversion. *Research Foundation of AIMR, CFA Institute.*

Jayaraman, N., Frye, M., and Sabherwal, S. (2001). Informed trading around merger announcements: An empirical test using transaction volume and open interest in options market. *Financial Review*, **36**, 45–74.

Jondeau, E. and Rockinger, M. (2006). Optimal portfolio allocation under higher moments. *European Financial Management*, **12**, 29–55.

Konstantinidi, E., Skiadopoulos, G., and Tzagkaraki, E. (2008). Can the evolution of implied volatility be forecasted? Evidence from European and US implied volatility indices. *Journal of Banking and Finance*, **32**, 2401–2411.

Kostakis, A., Panigirtzoglou, N., and Skiadopoulos, G. (2011). Market Timing with option-implied distributions: A forward-looking approach. *Management Science*, forthcoming.

Manaster, S. and Rendleman, R.J. (1982). Option prices as predictors of equilibrium stock prices. *Journal of Finance*, **37**, 1043–1057.

Merton, R.C. (1971). Optimal consumption and portfolio rules in a continuous-time model. *Journal of Economic Theory*, **3**, 373–413.

Pan, J. and Poteshman, A. (2006). The information in option volume for future stock prices. *Review of Financial Studies*, **19**, 871–908.

Panigirtzoglou, N. and Skiadopoulos, G. (2004). A new approach to modeling the dynamics of implied distributions: Theory and evidence from the S&P 500 options. *Journal of Banking and Finance*, **28**, 1499–1520.

Patell, J.M. and Wolfson, M.A. (1981). The ex ante and ex post price effects of quarterly earnings announcements reflected in option and stock prices. *Journal of Accounting Research*, **19**, 434–458.

Peterson, D. and Tucker, A. (1988). Implied spot rates as predictors of currency returns: A note. *Journal of Finance*, **43**, 247–258.

Poon, S.-H. and Granger, C.W.J. (2003). Forecasting volatility in financial markets: A review. *Journal of Economic Literature*, **26**, 478–539.

Psychoyios, D. and Skiadopoulos, G. (2006). Volatility options: Hedging effectiveness, pricing, and model error. *Journal of Futures Markets*, **26**, 1–31.

Rehman, Z. and Vilkov, G. (2008). Option-based sentiment for portfolio decisions. Goethe University, Frankfurt: Working paper.

Rockafellar, R.T. and Uryasev, S. (2000). Optimization of conditional value-at-risk. *Journal of Risk*, **2**, 21–41.

Sharpe, W.F. (2007). Expected utility asset allocation. *Financial Analysts Journal*, **63**, 18–30.

Siegel, A. (1995). Measuring systematic risk using implicit beta. *Management Science*, **41**, 124–128.

Skiadopoulos, G. (2001). Volatility smile consistent option models: A survey. *International Journal of Theoretical and Applied Finance*, **4**, 403–437.

Skiadopoulos, G. (2004). The Greek implied volatility index: Construction and properties. *Applied Financial Economics*, **14**, 1187–1196.

Whaley, R.E. (2000). The investor fear gauge. *Journal of Portfolio Management*, **26**, 12–17.

Xing, Y., Zhang, X., and Zhao, R. (2010). What does individual option volatility smirk tell us about future equity returns? *Journal of Financial and Quantitative Analysis*, **45**, 641–662.

CHAPTER 13

PARAMETER UNCERTAINTY IN ASSET ALLOCATION*

CAMPBELL R. HARVEY, JOHN C. LIECHTY, AND MERRILL W. LIECHTY

13.1 The Setting

In the traditional mean-variance asset allocation problem, the investor is presumed to have complete knowledge of the inputs, *i.e.*, exact knowledge of expected returns, variances, and covariances. Most often this assumption is considered innocuous, ignored, or perhaps not fully understood by asset managers. There have been many advances in dealing with parameter uncertainty.[1] In an important recent article, Markowitz and Usmen (2003) report the results of an experiment which compares the performance of two competing methods for determining optimal portfolio weights, where each method explicitly accommodates the uncertainty in the parameter estimates. We revisit this comparison.

In the first approach, portfolio weights are found by integrating out these uncertainties using Bayesian methods. In the second, a competing set of weights is obtained using the Resampled Efficient Frontiers^{TM} method found in Michaud (1998).[2] Markowitz and Usmen (2003) conduct an experiment using synthetic data and find that the resampled weights perform better than the weights implied by a Bayesian method.

* We appreciate the detailed comments of the referees.

[1] Estimation error has been examined by Klein and Bawa (1976), Bawa *et al.* (1979), Jobson and Korkie (1980 and 1981), Chen and Brown (1983), Jorion (1985 and 1986), Frost and Savarino (1986), Michaud (1989), and Britten-Jones (1999).

[2] Several authors have considered resampling, including Bey *et al.* (1990), diBartolomeo (1991 and 1993), Jorion (1992), Broadie (1993), Michaud (2001), Herold and Maurer (2002), Scherer (2002, 2006) Christie (2005), Harvey *et al.* (2006), and Mostovoy and Satchell (2006).

We revisit the same investment experiment, with two main differences from the way the experiment was conducted by Markowitz and Usmen (2003). First, while they use uniform prior distributions for the mean and covariance, we use a hierarchical Bayesian model with diffuse, conjugate prior distributions that mimic uniform prior distributions. This facilitates the second and more important difference, *i.e.*, the use of a Markov Chain Monte Carlo (MCMC) algorithm, as opposed to an Importance Sampling algorithm. While both approaches are used in the literature, the MCMC algorithm is almost always preferred in part because of well documented problems that can arise with regards to the variance of Importance Sampling approximations, see Robert and Casella (1998) and Bernardo and Smith (1994). In addition, Markowitz and Usmen (2003) probably used too few samples to approximate these high dimensional integrals.

Under the MCMC inference method, we find that the results from the investment experiment sharply differ from the original experiment. In our rematch, there are many cases where weights from the Bayesian method perform better than weights from the resampling method, using the same performance criteria as the initial experiment. In this rematch, we found that the Bayesian method does better at low levels of risk aversion and the resampling method does better at high levels of risk aversion. We provide the economic intuition for the role of risk aversion.

We also consider a second asset allocation setting, a one-step ahead version of the investment problem, which is more relevant from the investor's perspective. In this competition, additional returns are generated and one-step ahead portfolio returns are calculated for all of the different historical data sets. We find that the Bayes approach dominates the resampled efficient frontier approach when the data are drawn from a distribution that is consistent with the data in each history, *i.e.*, drawn from the predictive distribution conditional on each history. Our results lead us to conjecture that the resampled frontier approach has practical merit when the future returns are not consistent with the historical returns (*e.g.*, when the underlying statistical model has been misspecified or the data is drawn from a distribution other than the predictive distribution) or when the investor has a very long investment horizon, as implied by the criteria used in the initial experiment, and is not very risk averse. Later we explore why risk aversion impacts the success of these approaches for both competitions.

The chapter is organized as follows. In Section 13.2, we review the simulation competition and the set of utility functions that are considered. We briefly review the equivalent Resampled Efficient Frontier^{TM} approach that we use in Section 13.3, and we discuss our modification of the specification of the Bayesian investor in Section 13.4. In Section 13.5, we explore the one-step ahead investment problem and conclude with a discussion of the results and potential reasons for the differences between the original experiment and the new experiment. We also discuss settings where the resampled frontier approach may offer a more robust solution to the portfolio allocation problem. Some concluding remarks are offered in Section 13.7.

13.2 The Investment Experiment

We conduct a simulated asset allocation with two investors and a referee, following Markowitz and Usmen (2003). The referee generates 10 "true" parameter sets for a multivariate normal density. Each "true" parameter set summarizes the behavior for a group of eight asset returns in the sense that for each "truth" the monthly percent returns for these eight assets are assumed to be *i.i.d.* multivariate normal with means, variances, and covariance given by the corresponding "true" set of parameters. As in the original experiment, we mimic the asset allocation task discussed by Michaud (1998), where the assets that are being considered are a collection of six equity indices (Canada, France, Germany, Japan, United Kingdom, and United States) and two bond indices (United States Treasury bond and a Eurodollar bond).

The referee starts with an original set of parameters, which are the Maximum Likelihood Estimates (MLEs) of the mean and covariance for these eight assets based on their monthly percent returns over the 216 months from January 1978 to December 1995; see Chapter 2 of Michaud (1998) for the exact values. The referee then generates 10 sets of perturbed parameters, or "truths," by generating 216 draws from a multivariate normal density using the original parameters and a new random seed; the perturbed or "true" parameters are the MLEs from each corresponding sets of draws. Using each of the 10 truths, the referee then generates 100 histories (each with 216 simulated observations), which form the basis of the experiments, see Figure 13.1 for a summary. To be more explicit, let μ_{OP} and Σ_{OP} be the mean 8-vector and 8×8 covariance matrix, respectively, representing the original parameters. The referee creates the ith set of "true" parameters (μ_{Ti}, Σ_{Ti}), by generating 8-vectors

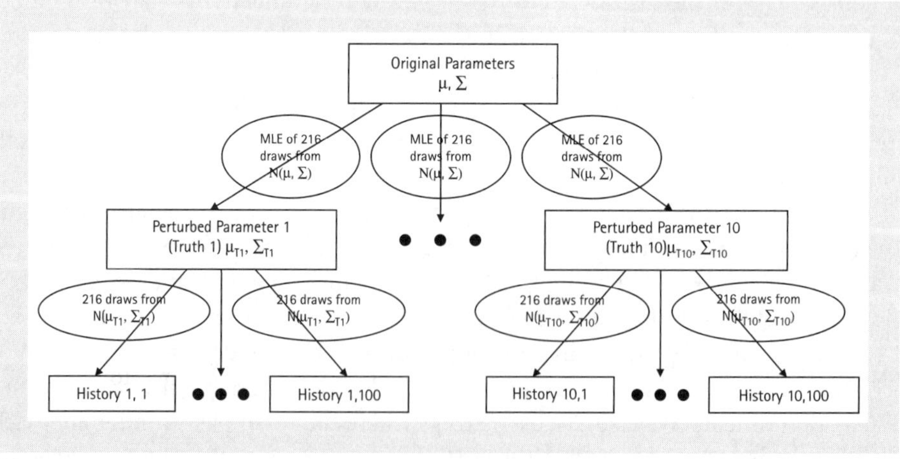

FIGURE 13.1 Graphical representation of the histories and truths used both in this chapter and in Markowitz and Usmen (2003).

$$r_{in} \sim N\left(\mu_{OP}, \Sigma_{OP}\right), \text{ for } n = 1, .., 216 \tag{13.1}$$

and letting

$$\mu_{Ti} = \frac{1}{216}\sum_{n=1}^{216} r_{in} \text{ and } \Sigma_{Ti} = \frac{1}{216}\sum_{n=1}^{216}\left(r_{in} - \mu_{Ti}\right)\left(r_{in} - \mu_{Ti}\right)'. \tag{13.2}$$

For each (μ_{Ti}, Σ_{Ti}), the referee generates 100 histories, where the kth history for the ith set of "true" parameters is as follows:

$$H_{ik} = \left\{r_{ikn} : r_{ikn} \sim N\left(\mu_{Ti}, \Sigma_{Ti}\right), n = 1, .., 216\right\}. \tag{13.3}$$

The asset allocation experiment is played as follows. The referee gives each investor a simulated history and the investors tell the referee the portfolio weights that they believe will maximize the expected utility under three different utility functions; the utility functions are given by:

$$u_{\lambda}\left(\omega, r_{n+1}\right) = \omega' r_{n+1} - \lambda\left(\omega'\left(r_{n+1} - E\left[r_{n+1}|H\right]\right)\right)^2, \ \lambda = \{0.5, 1.0, 2.0\}, \tag{13.4}$$

where $E\left[r_{n+1}|H\right]$ is the predictive mean given history H, ω are the portfolio weights, r_{n+1} are the predictive returns (*e.g.*, the distribution of returns for the next month, month 217, conditional on the observed returns, months 1–216), and λ reflects risk aversion and takes three different values. In addition to returning the optimal portfolio weights, the investors also tell the referee their own estimate of the expected utility using their optimal weights. The referee compares each investors' weights by calculating the investors' expected utility using the true parameter values in place of the predictive mean and covariance. For each of the 100 histories, the investor with the weights that result in a higher expected utility, using the true parameter values, is determined to have won.

As shown in Markowitz and Usmen (2003) and Harvey *et al.* (2006), the expected utility of (13.4), given a specific history H, is a function of predictive moments (mean and covariance). The predictive mean is equal to the posterior mean, which will be very close to the MLE estimate of μ (the historical average returns). The predictive covariance matrix, however, is composed of *two* different summaries of uncertainty: (1) the posterior mean of Σ, which will be very close to the MLE estimate of Σ (the historical covariance matrix of the returns) and (2) the posterior mean of the *covariance* of μ, which reflects our uncertainty with respect to the mean returns μ given the data that has been observed. So Σ captures both the covariance of the return as well as summarizing the inherent uncertainty in estimating the average return or the uncertainty with respect to μ. (See Appendix 13.A.1 for more details.)

The Bayes investor finds the weights, ω_B, which maximize the expected utility with respect to the predictive moments for each history, while the Michaud investor finds the weights, ω_M, using the resampling scheme. The referee compares both sets of weights assuming the true parameters used to generate the history, μ_T, Σ_T, are the predictive mean and covariance, or

$$Eu_{1\lambda}\left(\omega|H\right) = \omega'\mu_T - \lambda\omega'\Sigma_T\omega. \tag{13.5}$$

Before describing the details of how the Michaud and Bayes investors obtain their portfolio weights, it is worth observing that the referee and two investors are not using consistent frameworks. The Bayes investor uses a utility function based on predictive returns and the Michaud investor uses a utility function based on parameter estimates. The referee evaluates performance based on the "true" parameters, which ignores the contribution to Σ that comes from the inherent uncertainty regarding the "true" average return. If this extra variance is missing, the estimate for the portfolio variance will be lower than it should be, which will lead to suboptimal portfolio allocation.

13.3 The Resampling Investor

As in the original experiment, we consider the basic version of the resampled frontier approach. Markowitz and Usmen (2003) form the resampled frontier by calculating the resampled weights for an appropriate grid of portfolio standard deviations. In our experiment, we implement the alternative, but equivalent approach, of constructing a resampled frontier by calculating portfolio weights for a range of linear utility functions, see Michaud (1998: 66) for a discussion. The advantage of using this version of the resampling approach is that the resampled frontier only needs to be calculated for values of λ that are of interest to the referee and there is no need to calculate the frontier for a grid of portfolio standard deviations.

For each history H_{ik}, the Michaud investor uses the corresponding standard parameter estimates μ_{ik} and Σ_{ik} and generates 500 additional histories, which we will denote as resampled histories H^R_{ikm}, by drawing 216 *i.i.d.* multivariate normal draws using μ_{ik} and Σ_{ik}. For each resampled history, a discrete approximation of the efficient frontier is calculated, or a set of 101 weights describing the efficient frontier based on the standard estimates from each resampled history are calculated. Next, the set of weights which gives the highest utility value is selected for each resampled history.

The Michaud weights are equal to the average of the best weights for each resampled history.[3] Stated more explicitly, in the original experiment, the Michaud investor calculates an efficient frontier for each resampled history,[4] H^R_{ikm}, and for a discrete grid of 101 equally spaced portfolio standard deviations $(\sigma_{ikm,\min}, \sigma_{ikm,1}, \ldots, \sigma_{ikm,99}, \sigma_{ikm,\max})$, they calculate a set of weights $W_{ikm} = (\omega_{ikm,\min}, \omega_{ikm,1}, \ldots, \omega_{ikm,99}, \omega_{ikm,\max})$ that maximize the portfolio expected return for the corresponding standard deviation; these weights form a discrete estimate of the efficient frontier for the corresponding resampled history, H^R_{ikm}; one draw from the resampled frontier. In the original experiment, for each value of λ, the Michaud investor selects the weights as follows,

[3] This approach is guaranteed to produce weights that result in an expected utility that is less than the maximum expected utility because the resampled weights will be different from the Bayes weights (see Harvey *et al.* (2006) for a discussion).

[4] Each resampled efficient frontier is based on μ^R_{ikm} and Σ^R_{ikm}, which are the standard estimates based on H^R_{ikm}.

$$\omega_{\lambda ikm} = \arg\max\left\{\omega'\mu^R_{ikm} - \lambda\omega'\Sigma^R_{ikm}\omega : \omega \in W_{ikm}\right\}. \tag{13.6}$$

Then the "resampled" weights, $\overline{\omega}_{\lambda ik}$, reported by the Michaud investor for the kth history associated with the ith "truth," are the average optimal weights over the corresponding resampled histories, or

$$\overline{\omega}_{\lambda ik} = \frac{1}{500}\sum_m \omega_{\lambda ikm}. \tag{13.7}$$

Alternatively, the maximized weights for each μ^R_{ikm} and Σ^R_{ik} and for each λ can be obtained directly by solving the standard quadratic programming problem of

$$\omega_{\lambda ikm} = \arg\max\left\{\omega'\mu^R_{ik} - \lambda\omega'\Sigma^R_{ik}\omega : 0 \leq \omega, \sum_p \omega_p = 1\right\}. \tag{13.8}$$

Finding the optimal weights for each λ in this fashion has two advantages: first it requires fewer optimizations (3 compared to 101) and it obtains a set of weights for each resampled history which is at least as good as the weights using the original experiment.

13.4 The Bayes Investor

In our new setting, the Bayes investor will use a different approach for calculating the expected utility. In both the original and current experiment, the Bayes investor assumes that asset returns are *i.i.d.* and follow a normal distribution with mean μ and covariance matrix Σ; see Appendix 13.A.2 for an exact specification of the model.

We modify the Bayes investor in two ways: we alter the prior distribution and we use the MCMC algorithm. In the original experiment, the Bayes investor assumes a uniform prior distribution on μ and Σ, where the distributions are truncated to include all "reasonable" parameter values. This allows equal probability, *a priori*, over the range of possible parameters, reflecting a diffuse prior distribution. In our current experiment, we assume diffuse conjugate prior distributions for μ and Σ or

$$\mu \sim N\left(\overline{\mu}, \tau^2 I\right), \tag{13.9}$$

and

$$\Sigma^{-1} \sim Wishart\,(\nu, SS), \tag{13.10}$$

where $\overline{\mu} = 0$, $\tau^2 = 100$, $SS = I$, $\nu = 5$, and I is an identity matrix. The intuition is as follows. The prior distribution for a model parameter, such as μ, is considered to be conjugate, if the resulting distribution, conditional on the data and the remaining parameters, is the same type of distribution as the prior distribution (*e.g.*, if the prior for μ is a Normal distribution, then the distribution for μ, conditional on Σ and the data, is also a Normal distribution). By picking appropriate values for τ^2, ν, and SS, these distributions can be such that they are diffuse, and have no impact on the final parameter estimates. Both the uniform prior and the diffuse conjugate prior are equivalent with regards to the information they bring to the analysis. However, the conjugate prior makes it easier to do the MCMC calculations. While the calculations could still be done with a uniform prior, they would be more cumbersome. Hence the reason for choosing the conjugate prior is purely computational. See Bernardo and Smith (1994) for a more complete discussion of prior distributions. See Appendix 13.*A*.2 for a discussion of how both model specifications are similarly diffuse.

The most important difference between the original experiment and our experiment is the use of the Markov Chain Monte Carlo (MCMC) algorithm to estimate the expected utility; see Gilks *et al.* (1998) for a discussion of the MCMC algorithm. In the original experiment, the Bayes investor used an Importance Sampling scheme, based on 500 draws from a proposal distribution to approximate the expected value of (13.4) (see Appendix 13.*A*.1 for more details); while the Importance Sampler has attractive computational properties, it can result in integral estimates with unbounded or extremely large variances, which is problematic because the weights for points with high posterior probability can be large, leading to infrequent selection from the proposal distribution; see Bernardo and Smith (1994) and Robert and Casella (1998).

To contrast the two inference approaches, the MCMC algorithm generates samples from the predictive density and uses these draws to approximate the expected utility integral, where the Importance Sampling scheme generates draws from an alternative density and reweights these draws in order to approximate the integral with respect to the predictive density. In other words this MCMC algorithm samples directly from the predictive density, whereas the Importance Sampler obtains samples from the predictive density in a round-about way. An important difference between our implementation of the MCMC algorithm and Markowitz and Usmen's (2003) implementation of the Importance Sampler has to do with the number of samples that were used. In the original experiment, they used only 500 samples, whereas we use 25,000 draws from the predictive density. The relatively small number of draws, with respect to the dimension of the space being integrated over (44 dimensions), is one potential reason for the differences in the two experiments.[5]

[5] In order to explore the robustness of the results from the original experiment, we opted to use the MCMC algorithm and have the Bayes investor generate samples from the posterior distribution and in turn generate samples from the predictive distribution for each draw from the posterior distribution. (Even though we are using conjugate priors, the joint, posterior density of μ and Σ is non-standard and cannot be integrated out analytically; hence the need to take a sampling based approach (MCMC) to integrate out the parameters with respect to the predictive density.) The approximation of the expected utility for the Bayes investor is calculated by taking the average utility based on the draws from the predictive density. For each history, the Bayes investor finds and reports the weights that maximize this average utility; see Appendix 13.*A*.3 for the exact formulas.

13.5 Results of the New Setting

The results using the MCMC algorithm for inference and using the original performance criteria (i.e., evaluating each weight using the proposed "true" parameter values as the predictive mean and covariance as detailed in (13.5)) are markedly different from the results reported from the original experiment. In the original experiment, the Michaud investor won for every "truth" and for every value of λ in that the portfolio weights reported by the Michaud investor gave a larger average utility over the 100 histories as evaluated by the referee. In the new experiment, the Bayes investor wins for 7 out of the 10 histories when $\lambda = 0.5$, and the Michaud investor wins for 8 out of 10 histories and for 6 out of 10 histories when $\lambda = 1$ and 2, respectively; see Table 13.1 for a summary of the results.[6]

The main difference between the original experiment and the current experiment comes from the choice of inference used by the Bayes investor (*i.e.*, the difference between using the Importance Sampling and the MCMC algorithms to approximate the expected utility). As a result, investors should use caution when determining which approach to use for selecting an optimal portfolio in practice.

In the original experiment, the referee chooses a criterion that handicaps the Bayes investor and that reflects an investment strategy that is much different from the investment strategies pursued in practice. Specifically, the investors select an optimal set of weights based on a history and then the referee uses a criterion that is not consistent with that history (he/she evaluates the weights using the "true" mean and covariance, which are different from the predictive mean and covariance associated with the history). This would be reasonable, if the investor does not expect future returns to match historical returns. Since this is not the case in the original experiment, the Bayes investor is handicapped as he/she is operating under the assumption that the future returns distribution will match the past returns distribution, and it is interesting that even with this handicap the Bayes investor performs at a comparable level to the Michaud investor.

From an investment perspective, the referee's criterion implicitly assumes that each investor is going to take their derived weights and hold a portfolio based on these weights until all uncertainty from the parameter estimates is gone. Stated differently, the referee is determining the performance of a set of portfolio weights by assuming that each investor will hold their respective portfolio forever (or at a minimum for the rest of the investor's life). It is inconceivable that a real world investor will never adjust their portfolio.

13.5.1 One Period Ahead Asset Allocation

In order to explore the performance of these two approaches in a setting that is more relevant to an investor with a shorter investment horizon and where the Bayes investor

[6] Table 13.1 follows the same format as Table 13.3 in Markowitz and Usmen (2003).

Table 13.1 Investor's choice of portfolio.

Panel A: EU averaged over 100 histories, for each of 10 truths

λ:	0.5	0.5	0.5	0.5	1	1	1	1	2	2	2	2
Investor:	Bayes	Bayes	Michaud	Michaud	Bayes	Bayes	Michaud	Michaud	Bayes	Bayes	Michaud	Michaud
Eval. by:	Investor	Referee	Investor	Referee	Investor	Referee	Investor	Referee	Investor	Referee	Investor	Referee
Truth 1:	0.02036	0.01916	0.02019	0.01902	0.01800	0.01684	0.01840	0.01714	0.01403	0.01293	0.01508	0.01366
Truth 2:	0.01214	0.01046	0.01186	0.01032	0.01006	0.00854	0.01024	0.00866	0.00700	0.00585	0.00755	0.00599
Truth 3:	0.00739	0.00487	0.00710	0.00486	0.00617	0.00418	0.00635	0.00421	0.00464	0.00333	0.00515	0.00326
Truth 4:	0.01623	0.01362	0.01599	0.01360	0.01457	0.01251	0.01480	0.01246	0.01194	0.01036	0.01279	0.01072
Truth 5:	0.01167	0.01035	0.01143	0.01014	0.00926	0.00790	0.00966	0.00827	0.00598	0.00483	0.00694	0.00551
Truth 6:	0.00830	0.00632	0.00804	0.00622	0.00663	0.00494	0.00683	0.00500	0.00431	0.00315	0.00486	0.00312
Truth 7:	0.00763	0.00481	0.00736	0.00491	0.00597	0.00374	0.00613	0.00372	0.00400	0.00252	0.00438	0.00222
Truth 8:	0.00966	0.00692	0.00935	0.00693	0.00812	0.00593	0.00827	0.00594	0.00578	0.00419	0.00638	0.00427
Truth 9:	0.01021	0.00699	0.00993	0.00699	0.00841	0.00578	0.00865	0.00580	0.00613	0.00430	0.00665	0.00407
Truth 10:	0.00751	0.00512	0.00724	0.00504	0.00606	0.00402	0.00646	0.00450	0.00413	0.00271	0.00513	0.00349
Mean	0.01111	0.00886	0.01085	0.00880	0.00932	0.00744	0.00958	0.00757	0.00679	0.00542	0.00749	0.00563
Std. Dev.	0.00425	0.00464	0.00429	0.00459	0.00401	0.00425	0.00405	0.00428	0.00344	0.00349	0.00358	0.00370
No. times better		7		3		2		8		4		6

Notes: Panel A shows averages of estimated and expected utility achieved by the two investors. Specifically, for risk aversion $\lambda = 0.5, 1.0$, and 2.0, as indicated by the row labeled "Lambda", and for each investor, and as indicated by the row labeled "Investor".

Table 13.1 Continued

Panel B: Number of "wins" out of 100 histories, for each of 10 truths

λ: Investor: Eval. by:	0.5 Bayes Referee	0.5 Michaud Referee	1 Bayes Referee	1 Michaud Referee	2 Bayes Referee	2 Michaud Referee
Truth 1:	73	27	20	80	6	94
Truth 2:	70	30	41	59	24	76
Truth 3:	54	46	43	57	46	54
Truth 4:	61	39	61	39	26	74
Truth 5:	75	25	14	86	8	92
Truth 6:	66	34	43	57	42	58
Truth 7:	40	60	51	49	79	21
Truth 8:	52	48	53	47	32	68
Truth 9:	53	47	40	60	71	29
Truth 10:	63	37	15	85	9	91
Avg. No. wins	60.7	39.3	38.1	61.9	34.3	65.7
No. times better	9	1	3	7	2	8

Notes: Panel B reports the number of "wins" out of 100 histories, for each of the 10 truths.

Table 13.1 Continued

Panel C: Standard deviation of EU over 100 histories, for each of 10 truths

λ:	0.5	0.5	0.5	0.5	1	1	1	1	2	2	2	2
Investor:	Bayes	Bayes	Michaud	Michaud	Bayes	Bayes	Michaud	Michaud	Bayes	Bayes	Michaud	Michaud
Eval. by:	Investor	Referee	Investor	Referee	Investor	Referee	Investor	Referee	Investor	Referee	Investor	Referee
Truth 1:	0.00418	0.00124	0.00419	0.00119	0.00399	0.00108	0.00405	0.00108	0.00362	0.00081	0.00373	0.00083
Truth 2:	0.00338	0.00126	0.00339	0.00108	0.00315	0.00108	0.00320	0.00102	0.00247	0.00059	0.00267	0.00074
Truth 3:	0.00281	0.00081	0.00283	0.00077	0.00246	0.00057	0.00257	0.00080	0.00193	0.00042	0.00212	0.00076
Truth 4:	0.00322	0.00106	0.00323	0.00089	0.00280	0.00080	0.00293	0.00074	0.00258	0.00064	0.00256	0.00076
Truth 5:	0.00439	0.00182	0.00438	0.00171	0.00391	0.00126	0.00401	0.00131	0.00307	0.00074	0.00333	0.00088
Truth 6:	0.00332	0.00097	0.00332	0.00081	0.00302	0.00075	0.00310	0.00070	0.00240	0.00039	0.00254	0.00053
Truth 7:	0.00319	0.00082	0.00320	0.00066	0.00286	0.00056	0.00295	0.00057	0.00219	0.00038	0.00235	0.00061
Truth 8:	0.00308	0.00051	0.00306	0.00045	0.00287	0.00049	0.00290	0.00059	0.00251	0.00029	0.00259	0.00071
Truth 9:	0.00375	0.00087	0.00379	0.00074	0.00340	0.00057	0.00351	0.00068	0.00274	0.00039	0.00293	0.00069
Truth 10:	0.00262	0.00138	0.00259	0.00124	0.00241	0.00092	0.00246	0.00120	0.00183	0.00063	0.00222	0.00090
Avg. Std. Dev.		0.00107		0.00095		0.00081		0.00087		0.00053		0.00074
No. times better		0		10		6		4		10		0

Notes: Panel C reports the standard deviation of the expected utility over 100 histories, for each of the 10 truths.

is not handicapped, we conducted a new experiment. In this out-of-sample asset allocation, the referee assumes that the investor will only hold the portfolio for one period and where the referee draws returns that are consistent with the history that has been presented to the investor (i.e., the return is drawn from the predictive density, given the history).

To be more precise, for each history H_{ik}, both investors calculate weights as described in Sections 13.3 and 13.4. The referee draws 100 asset returns for the next period ($n = 217$) from the predictive distribution

$$r_{ik217} \sim N\left(\mu_{|H_{ik}}, \Sigma_{|H_{ik}}\right),$$

and using the Michaud investors weights, $\omega_{MH_{ik}}$, and Bayes investors weights, $\omega_{BH_{ik}}$, the referee calculates the portfolio return for each draw

$$R_{Mik} = \omega'_{MH_{ik}} r_{ik217} \quad \text{and} \quad R_{Bik} = \omega'_{BH_{ik}} r_{ik217}. \tag{13.11}$$

The referee calculates the investors utility for each "truth" (for each i), by calculating the mean and variance of the one-step ahead portfolio returns and putting that into the quadratic utility function, or given a λ and estimates of the portfolio mean and variance calculated in the usual way

Table 13.2 EU calculated using one-step ahead draws from predictive distributions.

λ:	0.5	0.5	1	1	2	2
Investor:	Bayes	Michaud	Bayes	Michaud	Bayes	Michaud
Eval. by:	Referee	Referee	Referee	Referee	Referee	Referee
Truth 1:	0.01929	0.01926	0.01612	0.01597	0.01150	0.01054
Truth 2:	0.00968	0.00959	0.00742	0.00703	0.00439	0.00348
Truth 3:	0.00595	0.00578	0.00457	0.00425	0.00255	0.00168
Truth 4:	0.01491	0.01472	0.01278	0.01248	0.00962	0.00869
Truth 5:	0.01078	0.01067	0.00778	0.00764	0.00394	0.00326
Truth 6:	0.00667	0.00660	0.00472	0.00455	0.00212	0.00153
Truth 7:	0.00628	0.00615	0.00430	0.00416	0.00176	0.00129
Truth 8:	0.00826	0.00790	0.00639	0.00610	0.00372	0.00290
Truth 9:	0.00852	0.00821	0.00632	0.00608	0.00351	0.00284
Truth 10:	0.00639	0.00610	0.00445	0.00408	0.00201	0.00050
Grand mean	0.00967	0.00950	0.00749	0.00723	0.00451	0.00367
Std.Dev.	0.00434	0.00438	0.00395	0.00397	0.00333	0.00330
No. times better	10	0	10	0	10	0

Notes: This table shows averages of expected utility calculated from one-step ahead draws from predictive distributions for each investor. Specifically, for risk aversion $\lambda = 0.5, 1.0$, and 2.0, as indicated by the row labeled "Lambda", and for each investor, and as indicated by the row labeled "Investor".

$$\mu_{port_i} = \frac{1}{10,000}\sum_{kn} R_{ikn} \text{ and } \Sigma_{port_i} = \frac{1}{10,000}\sum_{kn}\left(R_{ikn} - \mu_{port_i}\right)^2. \tag{13.12}$$

Each investor's utility is given by

$$E[u_\lambda] = \mu_{port} - \lambda\Sigma_{port}. \tag{13.13}$$

In the one-step ahead asset allocation experiment, using the draws from the "predictive" density, the Bayes investor wins for all of the "truths"; the Bayes investor has a higher expected utility for 10 out of 10 "truths" for all of the utility functions, see Table 13.2 for a summary.

The results of the experiment show that the Bayesian approach will outperform and potentially dominate the resampling approach, depending on the perspective that the investor wants to adopt. If the investor assumes that the distribution of future returns will match the distribution of past returns and the investor has a short investment time horizon, then they should avoid the resampling approach; alternatively, if there is some ambiguity about the distribution of past returns and the investor has a very long time horizon, the resampling approach has some advantages.

13.5.2 Interpreting the Relative Performances: Bayes vs. Resampling

In replaying the original experiment, it appears that there may be a pattern in the performance of the two approaches. The difference in the average expected utility between the two approaches across all of the histories is influenced by the investor's risk aversion (or λ). In the original experiment, as the investor's risk aversion increases (λ gets bigger), the resampling approach performs better on average, see Figure 13.2.

In contrast, although the Bayes approach dominates in the new experiment, the level of dominance increases as the investor becomes more risk averse.

The influence of risk aversion on the difference in performances is much larger for the new experiment than for the original experiment and it is in the opposite direction. The economic reason for these differences can be understood by investigating how the average portfolio mean and the average portfolio variance (the two components of the quadratic utility function) change as a function of λ. As the investor becomes more risk averse, the average portfolio mean and variance, for both approaches across both experiments, decreases as we would expect. However, the decrease in the average variance and the average mean for the Bayes approach is larger (particularly the decrease in the average variance) when compared with the resampling approach, see Table 13.3. This gives us the key insight that while the resampling approach tends to result in a larger average portfolio mean, this comes at the expense of a larger average portfolio variance, and this difference in the average variance increases dramatically as an investor's risk aversion increases.

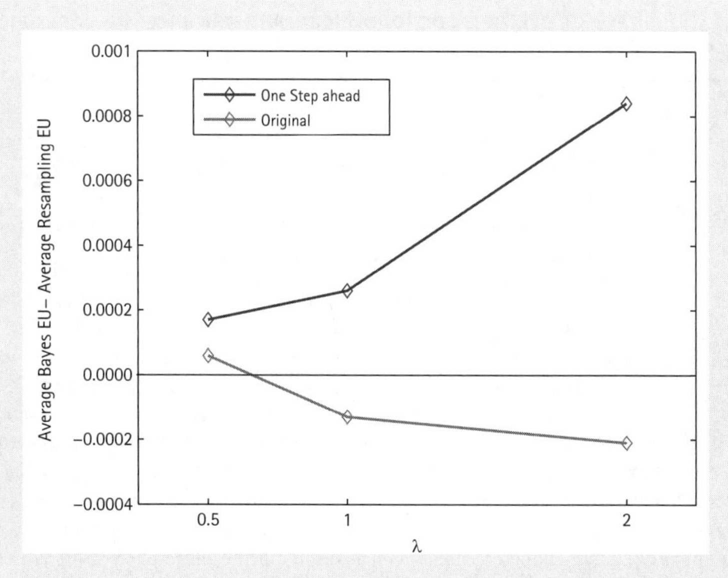

FIGURE 13.2 Difference in the average expected utility (Bayes – Resampling) as a function of risk aversion (or λ). Results are for the original experiment and for the new experiment (or one-step ahead experiment).

The two can be framed in terms of the investment time-frame: a long-term investor in the original experiment and a short-term investor in the new or one-step ahead experiment. While investors in both experiments use the same amount of information (216 data points) to find their weights, the referee uses very different criteria for each experiment. In the original experiment the referee evaluates weights using the "true" parameters, which implies that the investor is holding the portfolio for a very long time. By using the "true" parameters, the referee is ignoring the extra variance that comes from the uncertainly about the estimates of the average return. As a result the average portfolio variance for the original or long-term experiment are smaller than the average portfolio variance from the second or one-step ahead experiment, again see Table 13.3. The most striking difference between the two experiments is in terms of the average portfolio variance. For both the Bayes and resampling approach, the average portfolio variance is roughly twice as large for the new experiment when compared with the original experiment. In the original experiment, the smaller variances from the Bayes strategy does not compensate for the relative change in mean, which results in the resampling strategy performing slightly better as λ increases. However, for the new experiment the average portfolio variances are roughly doubled while the average portfolio means are only marginally better (on the order of 1.2 times larger). As a result the naturally smaller portfolio variance of the Bayes strategy becomes increasingly important and leads to the dominant performance of the Bayes approach.

Table 13.3 Summary of average portfolio mean and variance, by experiment and approach.

		$\lambda = 0.5$	$\lambda = 1$	$\lambda = 2$
Original experiment	Bayes: Average portfolio mean	0.0102	0.0094	0.0081
	Resampling Ave. portfolio mean	0.0100	0.0098	0.0091
	Bayes: Average portfolio variance	0.0026	0.0020	0.0013
	Resampling Ave. portfolio variance	0.0025	0.0022	0.0017
One-step ahead experiment	Bayes: Average portfolio mean	0.0124	0.0113	0.0095
	Resampling Ave. portfolio mean	0.0120	0.0117	0.0109
	Bayes: Average portfolio variance	0.0054	0.0038	0.0025
	Resampling Ave. portfolio variance	0.0049	0.0045	0.0036

Notes: The striking difference between the two experiments is the difference in the average portfolio variance. For both Bayes and resampling approach, the average portfolio variance is roughly twice as large for the new experiment (one-step ahead) when compared with the original experiment, again see Table 13.1. In the original experiment, the smaller variances from the Bayes strategy does not compensate for the relative change in mean, which results in the resampling strategy performing better. However, for the new experiment, the average portfolio variances are roughly doubled while the average portfolio means are only marginally better (on the order of 1.2 times larger). As a result the naturally smaller portfolio variance of the Bayes strategy becomes increasingly important. We feel that the new experiment is the proper way to asses the performance of both of these methods as both strategies are calibrated conditional on the historical data and they have to account for both uncertainly due to unexplained randomness and uncertainty due to our inability to predict the mean.

All investors will have to deal with making asset allocation decisions in the face of both the unexplained uncertainty and uncertainty about the mean. In addition, the dramatic difference in the average portfolio variance obtained by using the Bayes approach demonstrates the value of the Bayes approach as the uncertainty facing the investor increases and/or as the investor becomes more averse to risk.

13.6 A Deeper Look

We further explore the differences between Bayes and resampling at a very simple level. While we agree that there are some overlapping elements to our Bayesian approach and the resampling approach, there are some substantial differences that merit closer attention. The main difference is that the resampling approach breaks from the traditional optimization framework of maximizing an expected utility and instead takes the expectation of weights that maximize a utility; stated simply the resampling approach maximizes and then averages instead of maximizing an average (or an expected return).

This is a fundamental departure from the seminal framework proposed originally by Markowitz (1959).

We wish to focus our discussion on the differences in optimization approaches and within that framework discuss the role of various investment scenarios (referees) that could be used to assess the performance of an asset allocation strategy.

There are three components to both of the approaches being considered: (1) generation of random parameters, (2) the optimization framework used to determine an optimal set of investment weights, and (3) the investment scenario used to determine how well the resulting weights perform. The first issue is important, but not of real interest as the Monte Carlo approach used in the resampling methodology can be viewed as an approximation to the MCMC sampler used to generate posterior draws of the mean and covariance matrix.

13.6.1 The Resampled Optimization Approach

The second point is of substantial interest as this point represents a major break from the traditional (or more accurately characterized, the dominant) approach to optimal decision making. Part of the challenge with past discussions of the resampled optimization approach, is that these discussions have been restricted to finding weights for long-only portfolios (i.e., the weights are constrained to be positive). If we lift this restriction, then we can derive analytic results which help clarify the differences between the resampled optimization approach and the traditional optimization approach. To illustrate, in a way that is directly comparable with the resampling approach, we will show differences using the assumption that investors' utilities are a function of parameter values.

Traditionally, an investor will choose weights, ω, that maximize their expected utility $u(\omega, \mu, \Sigma)$, or assuming quadratic utility they would solve the following problem:

$$\omega_T = argmaxE\left[u\left(\omega, \mu, \Sigma\right)|H_O\right] = argmax\left(\omega' E\left[\mu|H_O\right] - \lambda\omega' E\left[\Sigma|H_O\right]\omega\right)$$

where the subscript T denotes the traditional approach and R denotes the resampled approach, H_O represents the observed history, $E\left[\mu|H_O\right]$ are the expected returns, $E\left[\Sigma|H_O\right]$ is the variance-covariance matrix, and λ is the risk aversion of the investor; using simple calculus we can obtain the standard set of optimal weights

$$\omega_T = \frac{E\left[\Sigma|H_O\right]^{-1} E\left[\mu|H_O\right]}{2\lambda}.$$

An investor, who is following the resampling approach, inverts the traditional order and they use the following weights

$$\omega_R = \frac{1}{N}\sum_{i=1}^{N} \omega_i^*\left(\mu_i, \Sigma_i\right) \tag{13.14}$$

where

$$\omega_i^* = argmax\left(\omega'\mu_i - \lambda\omega'\Sigma_i\omega\right) = \frac{\Sigma_i^{-1}\mu_i}{2\lambda},$$

$$\mu_i, \Sigma_i \sim f\left(\mu, \Sigma|H_O\right),$$

where $f(\mu, \Sigma|H_O)$ represents the parameter uncertainty given the history H_O. A direct comparison of the weights that result from the two approaches is instructive:

$$\omega_T = \frac{1}{2\lambda}\left(\frac{1}{N}\sum_{i=1}^{N}\Sigma_i\right)^{-1}\left(\frac{1}{N}\sum_{i=1}^{N}\mu_i\right) = \frac{1}{2\lambda}\overline{\Sigma}^{-1}\overline{\mu} \tag{13.15}$$

and

$$\omega_R = \frac{1}{N}\sum_{i=1}^{N}\frac{\Sigma_i^{-1}\mu_i}{2\lambda} = \frac{1}{2\lambda}\overline{\Sigma^{-1}\mu}, \tag{13.16}$$

where $\overline{\Sigma}^{-1}\overline{\mu}$ is product of the averages, and $\overline{\Sigma^{-1}\mu}$ is the average of the products.

To help understand the differences consider the single-asset case where an investor can either invest in a single risky asset or in the risk free asset. In this case, the resampled investor weight will always be larger, in absolute value, than the traditional investor, or $Pr(|\omega_R| > |\omega_T|) = 1$; this is a simple consequence of Jensen's inequality. The intuition for this can be seen from the fact that μ and Σ are essentially uncorrelated and that small values of Σ, when inverted, will have an increasingly larger impact than large values of Σ. This can be seen by recalling that as $\Sigma \to 0$, $(1/\Sigma) \longrightarrow \infty$. Hence, averaging over $(1/\Sigma)$ will result in a larger value than taking one over the average of Σ.[7]

13.6.2 Selecting the Referee

Since we have derived the weights, we can explicitly calculate the expected utility for both investors and compare their performance, if we can determine an appropriate investment scenario or stated differently if we can agree on an acceptable referee. The key to understanding the referee's perspective is to recall that the investor creates their weights, ω_T and ω_R, from moments based on the observed history H_O (e.g., $\mu = E[\mu|H_O]$) and the referee can use a different history, H_{REF}, to evaluate the performance of the weights. For example, if we continue with our single-asset example, the expected utility becomes:

[7] Jensen's inequality simply says that for a convex function, the function of the average will be less than the average of the function.

$$EU_T = E\left[u\left(\omega_T, \mu, \Sigma\right)|H_{REF}\right] = \frac{1}{2\lambda}\left(\overline{\Sigma}^{-1}\overline{\mu}E\left[\mu|H_{REF}\right] - \frac{\left(\overline{\Sigma}^{-1}\overline{\mu}\right)^2 E\left[\Sigma|H_{REF}\right]}{2}\right) \tag{13.17}$$

and

$$EU_R = E\left[u\left(\omega_R, \mu, \Sigma\right)|H_{REF}\right] = \frac{1}{2\lambda}\left(\overline{\Sigma^{-1}\mu}E\left[\mu|H_{REF}\right] - \frac{\left(\overline{\Sigma^{-1}\mu}\right)^2 E\left[\Sigma|H_{REF}\right]}{2}\right). \tag{13.18}$$

Using simple algebra, we can explicitly determine when the traditional approach will have a higher expected utility; $EU_T > EU_R$ when

$$E\left[\Sigma|H_{REF}\right]^{-1} E\left[\mu|H_{REF}\right] < \frac{1}{2}\left(\overline{\Sigma}^{-1}\overline{\mu} + \overline{\Sigma^{-1}\mu}\right) = \overline{\Sigma}^{-1}\overline{\mu} + \Delta, \tag{13.19}$$

where $\Delta = 1/2\left(\overline{\Sigma^{-1}\mu} - \overline{\Sigma}^{-1}\overline{\mu}\right)$, $\overline{\mu} = E\left[\mu|H_O\right]$, $\overline{\Sigma} = E\left[\Sigma|H_O\right]$, and as noted above, $Pr\left(\Delta > 0\right) = 1$.

There are three referees that we would like to consider, the Predictive (or One Step Ahead) Referee, the Truth Referee, and the Random Referee. The Predictive Referee uses the observed history, $H_{REF} = H_O$, or the predictive distribution based on the observed history (which is the only history available to the investor), hence

$$E\left[\mu|H_{REF}\right] = E\left[\mu|H_O\right] = \overline{\mu}$$

and

$$E\left[\Sigma|H_{REF}\right] = E\left[\Sigma|H_O\right] = \overline{\Sigma}.$$

Based on (13.19), the traditional approach will always win, with probability 1. We are willing to concede that the Predictive Referee is backwards looking, in that he/she uses just the observed history to assess performance, but we are not willing to concede that this is a circular argument. It simply points out that the traditional approach always beats the resampled approach, when the objective function being maximized is used to assess performance.

The Truth Referee uses the parameters, μ_{True}, Σ_{True}, that were used to generate the history, which is equivalent to using an infinite history, or

$$H_{REF} = H_\infty = \left\{r_\tau, \tau = 1, \ldots, \infty : r_\tau \sim f(r|\mu_{True}, \Sigma_{True})\right\}.$$

Hence, the resulting moments are the true parameters, or $E[\mu|H_\infty] = \mu_{True}$ and $E[\Sigma|H_\infty] = \Sigma_{True}$. While the Truth Referee is often assumed to be the best referee, he/she has the fatal flaw that the investor must hold the portfolio forever; only at that point will there be no variability in the parameter estimates and only then will the investor's utility agree with the utility used by the Truth Referee. We do not find this infinite time horizon scenario to be a creditable scenario, even if others feel this is viable.

The Random Referee acknowledges the shortcoming of the Predictive and Truth Referee and assumes that the investor will hold the portfolio for a finite amount of time, e.g., the amount of time equal to the original history. Over this future time a new history based on the true parameters μ_{True}, Σ_{True}, will be generated, or

$$H_{REF} = H_{Rand} = \{r_\tau, \tau = 1, ..., \tau_{Rand} : r_\tau \sim f(r|\mu_{True}, \Sigma_{True})\}$$

and

$$H_{Rand} \neq H_O.$$

For the Random Referee, the resulting moments, $\mu_{Rand} = E[\mu|H_{Rand}] \cong \overline{\mu}_{Rand}$ and $\Sigma_{Rand} = E[\Sigma|H_{Rand}] \cong \overline{\Sigma}_{Rand}$, will be used to assess the weights. It is worth noting that in the limit, as the size of the new history goes to infinity ($\tau_{Rand} \to \infty$) the Random Referee becomes the Truth Referee.

The resulting empirical moments, $\overline{\mu}_{Rand}$, $\overline{\Sigma}_{Rand}$, can be viewed as random variables drawn from the same distribution as the original empirical moments, $\overline{\mu}$, $\overline{\Sigma}$, or

$$(\overline{\mu}_{Rand}, \overline{\Sigma}_{Rand}), (\overline{\mu}, \overline{\Sigma}) \sim f(\mu, \Sigma|\mu_T, \Sigma_T).$$

This means that the Traditional approach will do better than the Resampled approach more than 50% of the time. To see this recall that $EU_T > EU_R$ when

$$E[\Sigma|H_{REF}]^{-1}E[\mu|H_{REF}] = \overline{\Sigma}^{-1}_{Rand}\overline{\mu}_{Rand} < \overline{\Sigma}^{-1}\overline{\mu} + \Delta$$

and realize that both $\overline{\Sigma}^{-1}_{Rand}\overline{\mu}_{Rand}$ and $\overline{\Sigma}^{-1}\overline{\mu}$ have the same distribution. A simple symmetry argument requires that if $\Delta > 0$, then

$$Pr(\overline{\Sigma}^{-1}_{Rand}\overline{\mu}_{Rand} - \overline{\Sigma}^{-1}\overline{\mu} < \Delta) > 0.5$$

or

$$Pr(EU_T > EU_R) > 0.5.$$

Finally, because $Pr(\Delta > 0) = 1$, due to Jensen's inequality, the Random Referee will, more times than not, declare the traditional optimization approach to be better than the resampling optimization approach, which is not surprising given the overwhelming acceptance of the traditional decision science definition that an optimal decision is one that maximizes expected utility.

13.6.3 Minor Points

There are a few other minor points of criticism that might be relevant to the study we have undertaken with this rematch.

We readily acknowledge that we use a variation of the resampled approach emphasized by Markowitz and Usmen (MU) (2003), but in doing so we followed recommendations explicitly given by the proponents of the resampled approach. For example, we used the λ-associated resampling algorithm instead of the rank-ordered algorithm. When the λ-associated method is put forth in Michaud (1998) they say, "As a practical matter, the choice between the two approaches may simply be a matter of convenience." (Michaud 1998: 67).

Another important issue to consider is that of sample size. We (as well as Markowitz and Usmen, 2003) follow the recommendations given by Michaud (1998) for the resampled method which says that 500 Monte Carlo samples should be used to find the resampled efficiency portfolio. We think that this value is much too small, but the reader should recall that this is the particular recommendation that was given previously by Michaud for this specific set of data. For a proper Bayesian analysis, 500 samples are much too restrictive. Therefore, we use the recommended number of samples from each discipline, 500 for the resampled method and (something much bigger) 25,000 for the Bayesian method. We would like to note that it is not our recommendation to integrate over 44 dimensions with a sample size of 500. Finally, we would like to remind the reader that our primary purpose was not to determine whether the guidelines put forward for the resampled approach were optimal.

13.7 Conclusion

Our chapter re-examines the asset allocation simulation that pits a Bayesian investor against an investor that uses the resampling approach advocated by Michaud (1998). In the original experiment, Markowitz and Usmen (2003) find that the resampling investor always wins. We level the playing field by allowing the Bayes investor to use a more standard technique to approximate the moments of the predictive distribution. With this minor change, it ends up essentially even.

We also offer an investment setting that more closely approximates the practical situation that investors face – a one-step ahead portfolio allocation. Here our results depend on the distributional assumptions. If the future distribution is just like the past, the Bayes investor always outperforms. However, if there is a change in the distribution (*i.e.*, the predictive distribution is different from the historical distribution), the resampling investor shows advantages.

The dominant performance of the Bayes investor, for the one-step ahead experiment, comes about because the investor faces more uncertainty (they have uncertainty about both the variability of the returns and about their ability to predict the mean) and because the Bayes approach results in a smaller average portfolio variance as the investor's risk aversion increases.

The Bayesian and resampling literature consider a broader interpretation of risk by focusing on parameter uncertainty. The Bayesian handles parameter uncertainty by averaging over parameter values in a way that is consistent with the data, the assumed distribution, and the prior beliefs, whereas the resampler resorts to a Monte Carlo simulation to deal with the uncertainty.

There is another type of risk sometimes referred to as ambiguity. One can think of this as uncertainty about the distribution or uncertainty about the basic model. That is, while we might have a prior for a particular distribution, there are many possible distributions. Our results show that the resampling approach shows some robustness to distributional uncertainty. Our future research will focus on a Bayesian implementation to handle this type of certainty.

APPENDIX

Details for Bayesian analysis

13.A.1 Posterior Moments

Conditional on diffuse priors and the data gives a posterior density, $f(\mu, \Sigma|H)$, for each history. The predictive distribution, for the next observation in a history, is obtained by integrating out the model parameters with respect to the posterior density,

$$f(r_{n+1}|H) = \int_{\mu,\Sigma} f(r_{n+1}|\mu, \Sigma) f(\mu, \Sigma|H)\, d\mu d\Sigma. \tag{13.A1}$$

As shown in Markowitz and Usmen (2003) and Harvey *et al.* (2006), the expected value of the utility given in (13.4) and a specific history H becomes,

$$E\left[u_\lambda(\omega, r_{n+1})\,|H\right] = \omega'\hat{\mu} - \lambda\omega'\hat{\Sigma}\omega - \lambda\omega' Cov\left(\mu - \hat{\mu}\right)\omega, \tag{13.A2}$$

where $\hat{\mu}$ is the predictive mean, which is equal to the posterior mean,

$$\hat{\mu} = E\left[r_{n+1}|H\right] = E\left[\mu|H\right], \tag{13.A3}$$

and where the predictive covariance matrix can be rewritten as the sum of the posterior mean of Σ and the posterior mean of the covariance of $\mu - \hat{\mu}$, or

$$\hat{\Sigma} = E\left[\Sigma|H\right] \text{ and } Cov\left(\mu - \hat{\mu}\right) = E\left[\left(\mu - \hat{\mu}\right)\left(\mu - \hat{\mu}\right)'|H\right]. \tag{13.A4}$$

Parameter uncertainty is taken into account by including this extra term $Cov\left(\mu - \hat{\mu}\right)$ in the predictive covariance.

13.A.2 Model Specification

The Bayes investor assumes that all returns follow a normal probability model, or

$$f(r|\mu, \Sigma) = |\Sigma|^{-1}\left(\frac{1}{2\pi}\right)^{\frac{p}{2}} \exp\left[-\frac{1}{2}(r-\mu)'\Sigma^{-1}(r-\mu)\right], \tag{13.A5}$$

where p is the number of assets, and assumes a set of diffuse conjugate priors for μ and Σ, or

$$\mu \sim N\left(\overline{\mu}, \tau^2 I\right), \tag{13.A6}$$

and

$$\Sigma^{-1} \sim Wishart\,(\nu, SS). \tag{13.A7}$$

By choosing diffuse hyper-parameters, the conjugate prior specification can be made to mimic the uniform prior specification used in the original experiment. (For example by letting $\overline{\mu} = 0$ and letting τ^2 be large, the prior for μ becomes essentially constant over the range of "reasonable" parameter values. The same can be obtained for Σ^{-1}, by letting $\nu = p + \delta$, letting $SS = \delta I$, and letting δ be small.) To illustrate how both modeling approaches can result in equally "objective" diffuse priors over the range of "reasonable" parameters values, consider a prior on μ. When there is only one asset, μ is a scalar. If we assume that the range of "reasonable" values for μ is between -100 and 100, then the uniform prior is given by

$$f_{UniformPrior}(\mu) = \frac{1}{200} I\left\{-100 < \mu < 100\right\}, \tag{13.A8}$$

where $I\{\}$ is the indicator function, see Figure 13.A1 for a graphical representation. If we assume a conjugate prior for μ, which is the Normal distribution, and set the hyper-parameters (or parameters of this prior distribution) to be equal to 0 for the mean and τ^2 for the variance, or

$$f_{ConjugatePrior}(\mu) = \frac{1}{\sqrt{2\pi}\tau} exp\left\{-\frac{\mu^2}{2\tau^2}\right\}, \tag{13.A9}$$

then the difference between these two prior specifications, for the "reasonable" values for μ disappears as τ^2 increases, see Figure 13.A1 for an illustration. Similar prior specifications can be chosen for the covariance matrix Σ.

13.A.3 Approximating Expected Utility

In order to approximate the expected utility, with respect to the predictive distribution, the Bayes investor generates samples from the posterior distribution

$$\mu^m, \Sigma^m \sim f\left(\mu, \Sigma | H, \overline{\mu}, \tau^2, n, SS\right), \tag{13.A10}$$

and in turn generates samples from the predictive distribution for each draw from the posterior distribution,

$$r_{n+1}^{m,\varrho} \sim f\left(r | \mu^m, \Sigma^m\right). \tag{13.A11}$$

In the implementation for the new experiment, the Bayes investor ran the MCMC algorithm for a burn-in of 10,000 iterations (to allow the MCMC algorithm converge in distribution) and then generated 25,000 draws from the posterior and predictive densities (*i.e.*, one sample from the predictive density for each posterior draw). The approximation of the expected utility for the Bayes investor is calculated as follows,

$$E\left[u_\lambda\left(\omega, r_{n+1}\right)|H\right] \cong \frac{1}{25,000}\sum_{m,\varrho} \omega' r_{n+1}^{m,\varrho} - \lambda\left(\omega'\left(r_{n+1}^{m,\varrho} - \hat{\mu}\right)\right)^2, \tag{13.A12}$$

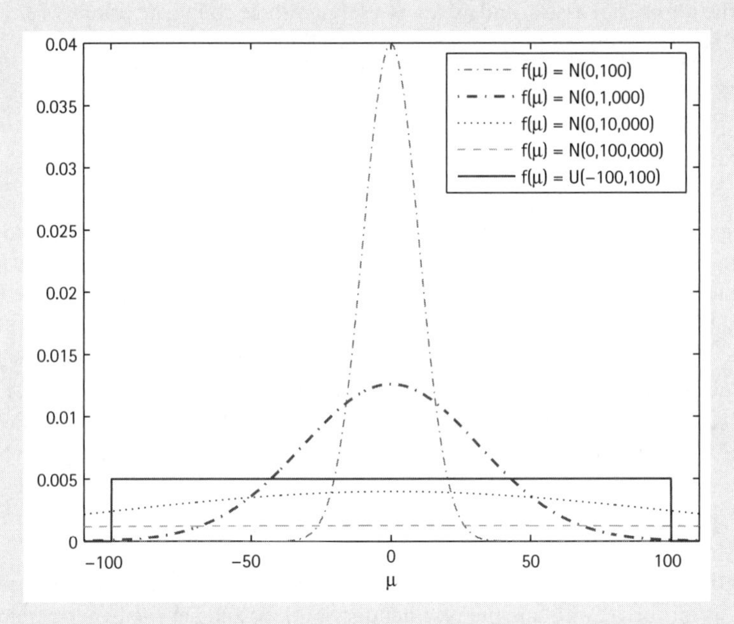

FIGURE 13.A1 Several normal densities, and one uniform density that could be used as priors for μ. A normal density can be a non-informative prior by setting the standard deviation to be large. Markowitz and Usmen (2003) use a uniform density as their non-informative prior.

where

$$\hat{\mu} \cong \frac{1}{25,000} \sum_{m,\varrho} r_{n+1}^{m,\varrho}. \tag{13.A13}$$

For each history, the Bayes investor finds and reports the weights that maximize (13.*A*12).

Glossary

Conjugate prior – a prior distribution for a parameter, where the resulting full-conditional distribution (the distribution conditional on the remaining parameters and the data) is from the same family of distributions as the prior distribution. For example, for the models considered in this chapter, if we assume μ follows a Normal distribution, before observing any data, then the distribution of μ conditional on Σ and the data is a Normal distribution.

Diffuse Bayesian analysis – summary of parameter distributions, assuming a Bayesian model, where the prior distributions are chosen to be vague or non-informative.

Diffuse prior – a prior distribution that is vague or non-informative, where the information provided by the data dominates the information provided in the prior.

Hierarchical Bayesian model – a statistical model that is specified in a hierarchical fashion; typically the distribution of the observed data is given conditional on a set of parameters (random variables) and the (prior) distribution of these parameters is given conditional on another set (or hierarchy) of parameters.

Importance Sampling – A Monte Carlo technique for sampling, where samples are drawn from a proposed distribution and then are re-weighted according to a target distribution in order to obtain a sample from the target distribution.

Inverse Wishart distribution – a family of distributions for covariance matrices. To contrast with the Normal distribution, if excess returns r are Normally distributed, this describes the distribution of returns; in contrast an inverse Wishart distribution describes the distribution of Covariance matrices.

Markov Chain Monte Carlo (MCMC) – Monte Carlo integration using Markov Chains. Samples from a distribution of interest (for example a posterior distribution) are obtained by repeatedly sampling from the distribution of each parameter, conditional on the most recently sampled values of the remaining parameters and the data. This forms a Markov Chain that results in samples from the distribution of interest.

Predictive distribution (density) – the distribution of the data in the future, conditional on all of the observed data and the prior distributions. For example, the distribution of tomorrow's excess returns, conditional on a set of historical excess returns and prior beliefs.

Prior distribution – a distribution placed on a parameter before any data is observed. This can represent an expert's prior opinion or be vague and non-informative.

Posterior distribution – the distribution of the model parameters, conditional on all of the observed data and the prior distributions. For example, the distribution of the average excess returns μ and the covariance matrix Σ conditional on a set of historical excess returns and prior beliefs.

References

Bawa, V.S., Brown, S.J., and Klein, R.W. (1979). *Estimation Risk and Optimal Portfolio Choice.* North-Holland, New York.

Bernardo, J.M. and Smith A.F.M. (1994). *Bayesian Theory*. John Wiley, New York.

Bey, R., Burgess R., and Cook, P. (1990). Measurement of estimation risk in Markowitz portfolios. University of Tulsa, unpublished paper, October 1990.

Britten-Jones, M. (1999). The sampling error in estimates of mean-variance efficient portfolio weights. *Journal of Finance*, **LIV**, 655–671.

Broadie, M. (1993). Computing efficient frontiers using estimated parameters, *Annals of Operations Research: Financial Engineering*, **45**, 21–58.

Chen, S.-N. and Brown, S.J. (1983). Estimation risk and simple rules for optimal portfolio selection, *The Journal of Finance*, **38**, 1087–1093.

Christie, S. (2005). Strategic and tactical asset allocation in the presence of sampling error. Unpublished paper (Macquarie University).

diBartolomeo, D. (1991). Estimation error in asset allocation, Unpublished paper, May 30, 1991.

diBartolomeo, D. (1993). Portfolio optimization: The robust solution. Prudential Securities Quantitative Conference, December 21.

Frost, P.A. and Savarino J.E. (1986). An empirical Bayes approach to efficient portfolio selection. *The Journal of Financial and Quantitative Analysis*, **21**, 293–305.

Gilks, W.R., Richardson, S., and Spiegelhalter, D.J. (1998). *Markov Chain Monte Carlo In Practice.* Chapman and Hall, New York.

Harvey, C.R., Liechty, J.C., and Liechty, M. W. (2008a). Bayes vs. resampling: A rematch. *Journal of Investment Management*, **6**, 29–45.

Harvey, C.R., Liechty, J.C., and Liechty, M.W. (2008b). Letter to the Editor. *Journal of Investment Management*, **6**, 114.

Harvey, C.R., Liechty, J.C., Liechty, M.W., and Müller, P. (2010). Portfolio selection with higher moments. *Quantitative Finance*, **10**, 469–485.

Herold, U. and Maurer, R. (2002). Portfolio choice and estimation risk: A comparison of Bayesian approaches to resampled efficiency. Working paper (Johann Wolfgang Goethe University).

Jobson, J.D. and Korkie, B. (1980). Estimation for Markowitz efficient portfolios. *Journal of the American Statistical Association*, **75**, 544–554.

Jobson, J.D. and Korkie, B. (1981). 'Putting Markowitz theory to work'. *Journal of Portfolio Management*, 7, 70–74.

Jorion, P. (1985). International portfolio diversification with estimation risk. *Journal of Business*, **58**, 259–278.

Jorion, P. (1986). Bayes–Stein estimation for portfolio analysis. *Journal of Financial and Quantitative Analysis*, **21**, 279–292.

Jorion, P. (1992). Portfolio optimization is practice. *Financial Analysts Journal*, **48**, 68–74.

Klein, R.W. and Bawa, V.S. (1976). The effect of estimation risk on optimal portfolio choice. *Journal of Financial Economics*, **3**, 215–232.

Markowitz, H.M. and Usmen, N. (2003). Resampled frontiers versus diffuse Bayes: An experiment. *Journal of Investment Management*, **1**, 9–25.

Michaud, R.O. (1989). The Markowitz optimization enigma: Is "optimized" optimal? *Financial Analysts Journal*, **45**, 31–42.

Michaud, R.O. (1998). *Efficient Asset Management.* Harvard Business School Press, Boston.

Michaud, R.O. (2001). *Efficient Asset Management: A Practical Guide to Stock Portfolio Optimization and Asset Allocation.* Oxford University Press, New York.

Michaud, R.O. and Michaud, R. (2008). Letter to the Editor. *Journal of Investment Management*, 6, 113–114.

Mostovoy, D., and Satchell, S.E. (2006). Robust inference in quantitative finance - especially robust optimization. Alpha Strategies Investment Seminar Presentation, Duke University.

Robert, C.P. and Casella, G. (1998). *Monte Carlo Statistical Methods.* Springer Verlag, New York.

Scherer, B. (2002). Portfolio resampling: Review and critique. *Financial Analysts Journal*, **58**, 98–109.

Scherer, B. (2006). A note on the out of sample performance of resampled efficiency. *Journal of Asset Management*, 7, 170–178(9).

PART V

RISK MANAGEMENT

CHAPTER 14

EQUITY FACTOR MODELS: ESTIMATION AND EXTENSIONS

DAN DIBARTOLOMEO

14.1 INTRODUCTION

Factor models are a convenient and popular way to represent the common properties of equity securities and their returns. Such models can be used to describe the observed past and forecast the future magnitudes and variability of stock returns, either at the individual security or portfolio level. There are four commonly used estimation methods for equity factor models, each of which has its own strengths, weaknesses, and issues of parameterization. There are also many useful extensions of basic equity factor modeling, including customizing such models to improve their intuitiveness to investors, making the models more adaptive to changes in financial market conditions, and extending the equity factor approach to other matters of investor interest such as the credit risk associated with corporate bonds.

The most popular representation of a factor model is Equation (14.1).

$$R_{it} = \Sigma_{j=1 \text{ to } n} B_{ijt} F_{jt} + e_t \qquad (14.1)$$

where

R_{it} = the return on security i during period t;
B_{ijt} = the exposure of security i to factor j during period t;
F_{jt} = the return to factor j during period t;
e_t = the residual return of security i during period t.

The first possible use of such a model is to forecast future returns for a particular security. In a *return model*, we hope to identify factors where the mean of the distribution of each of the factor return time series (the F_{jt} values) is statistically significantly different from zero. After identifying factors where the expected value of the future factor returns is meaningfully positive or negative on average, we can select securities to hold that have appropriately signed exposures to those factors (the B_{ijt} values) to produce positive return expectations. It should be noted that the exposure values add linearly across securities within a portfolio so Equation (14.1) applies equally well to stock portfolios and to individual stocks.

The second possible use of such a model is to forecast the dispersion or risk for an individual security or a portfolio. To the extent that either the factor returns or the factor exposures vary through time, we would expect resultant time-series variation in the returns to the security or portfolio. In a risk model, we want to select the set of factors that explains as much of the variation of the security as possible without concern for the requirement that the central tendency of the distribution of the factor returns be significantly non-zero. For example, we might know of a factor X that has very positive returns ($+F_{xt}$) in some periods and large magnitude negative ($-F_{xt}$) returns in other periods, but has a mean close to zero. Such a factor would be an attractive candidate for inclusion in a *risk model*, but probably not in a *return model*.

A third possible use of a model based on Equation (14.1) is a *timing model*. Consider a factor K where the mean of its time series is close to zero. Even with a mean close to zero, we can still add to our investment returns by successfully predicting in which future periods factor K's return (F_{kt}) will be positive and in which future periods it will be negative. We can then choose securities for investment that have the appropriate sign on the factor exposure (B_{ijt}) at the appropriate times to produce positive returns. While it would appear at first glance that the same factors that would be appropriate for *risk models* would be appropriate for *timing models*, this is not quite true. In *risk models*, we would typically assume that the factor return time series (F_{jt} values) are a random variable. In *timing models* we would have to assume that the same factor return time series are somewhat predictable, and hence not entirely random.

In asset pricing theory *return models* based on Equation (14.1) are used to describe whether a particular return generating process is in equilibrium or to reveal an anomaly. The theoretical justification for this framework comes from the arbitrage pricing theory put forth by Ross (1976) and in related papers such as Chen, Roll and Ross (1986) and Burmeister and Wall (1986). If a model represents equilibrium, the distribution of the residual returns (e_t) will have a mean that is not statistically significantly different from zero. Such models imply that financial markets are efficient and that there are close ties between risks undertaken and the returns achieved. If the distribution of the residual returns has a non-zero central tendency, the factor or combination of factors in use is said to represent an anomaly.

14.2 Factor Representation of Equity Portfolio Risk

There is an overriding rationale for representing the covariance of security returns with a factor model rather than by simple statistical estimation of historically observed covariance. By expressing the covariance structure in the form of a factor model, we filter out historic occurrences that are not likely to be repeated in the future. For example, we might have two firms that are completely unrelated except by the fact that both their respective CEOs are killed in the same plane crash. If the two firms both experience negative returns by virtue of this tragedy, the sample covariance values will make the firms appear positively related. By expressing the covariance across firms through an appropriate factor structure, we are able to mitigate the inaccuracy that would otherwise arise. We should always recall that for any factor representation of covariance, we can calculate the numerically equivalent full covariance matrix across the set of assets, as described in diBartolomeo (1998).

One thing in common across all models is the similar formula by which the expected return variance of a portfolio is calculated. There are three standard methods used to estimate the parameters of such a model. A useful overview of equity factor models of risk and the strengths and weaknesses of the various estimation processes can be found in Scowcroft and Sefton (2006).

$$V_p = E\left[\Sigma_{i=1 \text{ to } n}\Sigma_{j=1 \text{ to } n}B_{it}B_{jt}\sigma_i\sigma_j p_{ij} + \Sigma_{k=1 \text{ to } m}{\varepsilon_k}^2\right] \tag{14.2}$$

where

V_p = expected return variance of the portfolio;
m = the number of securities in the portfolio;
n = number of factors in the model;
B_{it} = the exposure of the portfolio to factor i at time t;
P_{ij} = the correlation of returns between factor i and factor j;
σ_i = the standard deviation of returns to factor i;
ε_k = standard deviation of asset specific returns to security k;
E = the expectations operator.

Among practitioners, the most popular type of model is an *endogenous* specification in Equation (14.2). These models are also known as "fundamental models" because the factors used in such models are typically observable fundamental characteristics of stocks such as market capitalization, dividend yield, and P/E ratio. In such a model, we can observe the exposure values (the *B*'s) in an unambiguous fashion. For example, we can readily observe that a high P/E stock is a high P/E stock and a low P/E stock is a low P/E stock. We can equally observe that a large market capitalization company is large and a small capitalization company is small. While we may choose to put both

P/E and market capitalization on a common scale (such as cross-sectional Z-scores) as a matter of convenience, the key issue is that we are not making any estimates of the B values. They can be observed exactly.

In an endogenous model, we do need to statistically estimate the factor return volatility (the σ_j) values and the correlations (P_{ij}) among the factor returns. The estimation process is usually done as a cross-sectional regression analysis, the result of which is a set of returns to the chosen factors during a particular time period. By repeating this process over a series of time periods, we obtain our needed parameters. As such, any errors in our factor risk estimates will arise in these factor return covariance terms.

Alternatively, we could use an *exogenous* specification of the model as in

$$V_p = E\left[\Sigma_{i=1 \text{ to } n}\Sigma_{j=1 \text{ to } n}B_iB_j\sigma_i\sigma_jp_{ij} + \Sigma_{k=1 \text{ to } m}\varepsilon_k{}^2\right]. \tag{14.3}$$

In such a model, we relate stock returns to observable driving factors. These could be macroeconomic factors such as interest rates or oil prices, or they could be market variables such as the spread in monthly returns between two stock indices (e.g., the spread between the Russell 1000 and Russell 2000 as a measure of the relative performance in the U.S. of large capitalization and small capitalization portfolios). With an exogenous specification, we can directly observe the factor returns for each time period from which we can immediately calculate the factor covariance terms. In this case we need to do statistical estimation of how these driving factors impact the return behavior of individual stocks. This is normally accomplished by doing a separate time series regression analysis of the returns of a particular stock (dependent variable) against the returns of the chosen factors (independent variables). In this method errors arising from statistical estimation will occur in the exposure coefficients (the B values). These exposure values (the B's) are considered fixed and do not vary across time. Market participants often perceive this as a very reasonable assumption. For example, one would not expect that the degree of sensitivity of an oil company's return to changes in oil prices would vary dramatically over time.

It is important to note that the original intent of endogenous models was to relate firms to endogenous factors, and the endogenous factors to the true, pervasive effects that were generally macroeconomic in nature. This two-level process was advocated because it was believed that an assumption that exposure coefficients were fixed over time was not sufficiently responsive to potential changes in the nature of firms. For example, the extent to which a particular firm was sensitive to changes in interest rates might change dramatically if a firm issued a large amount of floating-rate bond debt to finance acquiring another firm. Rosenberg and Guy (1976) argued that beta coefficients for stocks could be better estimated from investment fundamentals, but did not argue that relative returns to fundamental characteristics were the true risks that mattered to investors. Even with this fundamental view of the firm, the important factor remains changes in interest rates, and not the time series variation in the relative return behavior of low debt and high debt firms.

The third method of estimation is the use of a *blind* factor model, also called an *implicit or statistical* factor model as in

$$V_p = E\left[\Sigma_{j=1 \text{ to } n} B_j^2 \sigma_j^2 + \Sigma_{k=1 \text{ to } m} \varepsilon_k^2\right]. \tag{14.4}$$

In this model we make no preconceived choice of factors. We simply carry out a statistical analysis that will estimate both the exposure coefficients (the B values) and the factor return covariance terms. There are a number of different statistical techniques for carrying out such a process, the best known of which is principal components analysis. In order to make a functional model without imposing any external views as to the nature of the factors, we are required to make the assumption that all the correlations among the different factors are orthogonal by construction. This assumption simplifies the expression for the covariance among factors.

There is much debate among theoreticians and financial market participants as to which of these processes is most effective in *ex ante* forecasting of portfolio return variation. Even if we believe that no one type of model is inherently superior to another, we may choose a particular specification for reasons other than simply the predictive power of the model. Investment personnel may find the factors chosen for a particular model to be more intuitive than others. Market conditions differ from country to country and often dictate differing degrees of diversification within portfolios. The availability, quality, and accounting standards for company fundamental data vary greatly from country to country. Finally, investors may have high or low turnover portfolio strategies. The right choice of model specification will maximize the advantages and minimize the disadvantages, conditional on the market and strategy being pursued by the investor.

One consideration is the asset specific risks (the ε terms) that are typical in a market. In large, transparent markets like the U.S., the degree of stock specific return (and risk) is much greater. This usually means that the explanatory power of market movements for individual stock returns (r-squared) is less. In short, we actually can explain less of what is going on, so we need to be more cautious in our assumptions about how well our model works.

Another way to say this is that the cross-sectional dispersion of returns is greater within each time period. This also means that there is more potential for active managers to produce superior returns by picking individual stocks, rather than market timing. This leads active managers to take far more concentrated "bets" in a market like the U.S. as compared to other countries where asset specific risk is lower. In a market where asset specific risks are low, the returns of all stocks tend to be bunched relatively closely together. There is therefore little to be gained by taking big bets on individual stocks, so more diversified portfolios are sensible.

This gives us a reason to prefer one type of model specification to another. If we are running a highly concentrated portfolio, an endogenous specification is often considered preferable. The exposures of even a single stock are known exactly. As all the potential for errors resides in the factor covariance matrix, the risk estimates of a diversified portfolio or a concentrated portfolio are apt to have about the same level of correctness.

On the other hand, an exogenous specification puts the potential for errors in the exposure coefficients of the individual stocks. If our interest is running a concentrated portfolio with only a few names, the potential for errors in the exposure coefficients is substantial. However, since our exposure coefficients are normally best linear unbiased estimators, the errors in the exposure coefficients will diversify away as the portfolio is diversified. This means we may prefer an exogenous specification for broadly diversified portfolios.

While global accounting standards are starting to be applied to a small set of large companies around the world, the accuracy of accounting data is so suspect in many countries that local investors refuse to believe the numbers. This lack of willingness to believe company specific information drives the differences in r-squared across markets. This issue is more fully explored by Morck, Yeung, and Yu (2000) and Jin and Myers (2004).

When we are operating in a global portfolio context, another property of fundamental data often makes an endogenous model less attractive. There are wide differences in accounting standards across countries. For example, pension liabilities are handled very differently in Germany and Japan, making comparison of price/book ratio values for stocks in these two countries problematic. One way around this is to normalize the price/book ratio within country. Unfortunately, "in country" normalization leads to other problems. If we normalize something like market capitalization within country, we get the puzzling result that the largest stocks in Poland would be considered to have extremely large capitalization in a factor representation, while in a global context these stocks would be considered quite small.

Proponents of implicit factor models argue that all of these specification issues can be simply avoided by using a blind factor specification. In effect, we are going to let the data tell us what factors we need to use. While this is a very appealing idea, there are a number of possible pitfalls that must be carefully weighed. First, in order to estimate an implicit factor model we must make the assumption that the driving factors just happen to be uncorrelated with one another. If you asked a group of professional investors what they think are important drivers of stock behavior you would likely get answers like P/E ratios, dividend yields, growth rates, beta, and sector membership, among others. None of these happen to be uncorrelated with the others.

The second problem with blind factor models is that they do not give us any intuition as to what the actual underlying drivers of the market may be. Few active managers are prepared to take large bets on something like "factor 6" without knowing what factor 6 is in the real world. While it is possible to map implicit factor exposure coefficients onto real-world factors using a statistical estimation akin to returns-based style analysis, the reasonableness of mapping orthogonal factor loadings onto non-orthogonal real-world factors is often quite limited.

The most serious problem with blind factor models is that it greatly amplifies sample period dependence. We usually estimate risk models over some past sample period. If we use a specified factor model, whether endogenous or exogenous, we can estimate the model over many past periods of time in order to come up with our best estimates of future factor volatilities and correlations. In an implicit factor model, there is little likelihood that factor 6 estimated over the past five years, and factor 6 estimated during the five years from 1990 to 1995, would represent the same real-world economic driver. As such, all of our information about future factor covariance values is solely dependent on the sample period.

Consider a sample period of time when growth stocks and value stocks had little difference in their relative returns. An implicit factor model would say that growth/value simply didn't matter and it would not be represented in the model. In a specified factor model, we could consider the factor that the growth/value relationship (however you choose to define it) did matter a lot throughout many prior sample periods. We could therefore make an informed judgment as to how much volatility to expect in growth/value factor in the future, rather than simply assume it drops out because it wasn't important in the most recent sample. The other dimension of sample dependency is addressed by Miller (2006), where it is argued that blind factor models often lack the statistical power to identify factors that impact only a subset of the population of firms.

Random matrix theory has also been used to demonstrate that blind factor models often incorrectly identify factors where there is no true underlying structure of the observed returns. Bouchard *et al.* (2000) simulate time series of returns which are known to be uncorrelated random variables and then try to estimate a blind factor in the data. Since the return time series are uncorrelated by construction, no common factors should be found. However, they find that blind models often mistake random coincidences (noise) in the returns to be real correlations that should be represented as factors. They provide an approximation formula that can be used to discriminate between blind factors that are likely to arise from real economic drivers and those that may arise from over-fitting.

Some researchers such as Scowcroft and Sefton (2006) and Menchero and Mitra (2008) have suggested that a generally satisfactory factor specification is a *hybrid* of the specified and implicit factor methods. For example, one could use an exogenously specified model to capture all the aspects of investment risk that we believe are persistent across time and across markets. We can then take the small amount of risk not explained by specified factors and use implicit factors to estimate the risk of emerging new factors (e.g. Internet stocks) or other transient effects in the markets.

14.3 Regime Switching and Conditional Models

Time horizon is also an important factor. Imagine a situation where the CEO of an important company were killed in a plane crash. While this tragedy might have only a small impact on share volatility in the long run, the effect could be very substantial in the short-run. Although it has always been the tradition of the investment industry to talk about return volatility in annual units, there has always been ambiguity as to whether we are really forecasting annual risk (the risk expected over the upcoming year), or the *annualized value* of risk over some shorter time horizon. Given the extreme volatility that has been present in equity markets from time to time, making the differences between short-term and long-term risk levels more explicit will be an important advantage to investors in trying to adapt their portfolios to rapid changes in market conditions. For example, rather than focusing on the traditional risk forecast horizon of a year, we might prefer a much shorter horizon, such as the *annualized value of the risk over the next two weeks*. The transition between annual and annualized values of risk requires attention to the autocorrelation properties of the security returns as described in Shah (2008).

One approach to addressing shifts in factor volatility and correlation conditions has been traditional "regime-switching" models. In this approach, we simply estimate the entire model two or more times based on observations of different ranges of historical data. A particular estimation of the model might be based on data drawn from typical conditions, while another estimation might be based on data only drawn from periods of economic recession or other unusually stressful or volatile conditions. We then use the estimated model that appears to have been generated from historical data most similar to current conditions. A good discussion of regime-switching models is provided by Kritzman, Lowry, and Van Royen (2001).

While regime-switching models are widely used in asset allocation decisions, their use in equity factor applications is limited by the fact that the period of existence of particular firms can be quite short, so no data may be available for the desired periods. For example, many firms created during the so-called "tech bubble" at the turn of the millennium have never existed in a period of high price inflation.

A different approach is embodied in the concept of conditional models that are based on a vector of state variables. This approach allows any chosen model to adapt rapidly to changes in market conditions, but to retain the existing factor definitions and factor exposures. In effect, we ask ourselves how are market conditions today different from what they were on average during the period of history used to estimate the usual model. To judge the degree of difference, an information set of state variables is defined that describes contemporaneous aspects of the financial conditions but that are not normally used in the risk model. Such variables might include the implied volatility of options on stock indexes (e.g., VIX) and bond futures, yield spreads between different credit qualities of bonds, and the cross-sectional dispersion of stock returns among different sectors and countries.

In mathematical terms, we can think of this process as built around a vector we'll call theta. For each important element of the risk model (e.g., the volatility of a factor), there will be a corresponding element in the vector theta. Each element of the vector has a default value of one. We multiply each element of the model by its corresponding element in theta in order to reflect changes in state variables. For example, if a firm's manufacturing plant were to be destroyed in a flood, it would take many observations of returns to make a new estimate of how the covariance of this firm with returns of other firms had changed due to the changed circumstances. However, if the firm in question had traded options we might immediately observe a change in the stock volatility implied by the prices of the traded options. The relative change in the implied volatility as compared to past values of implied volatility would be reflected in the theta vector and could help to immediately adjust our risk expectations for this firm, as described in diBartolomeo and Warrick (2005).

Using news itself to condition factor risk estimates has also been explored recently. In diBartolomeo, Mitra, and Mitra (2009), the content of textual news flows through a news service (e.g., Dow Jones, Bloomberg, Reuters) is analyzed for length, frequency, and sentiment. They conclude that conditioning on news content adds meaningfully to the responsiveness of risk estimates, even beyond the use of implied volatility for securities with liquidly traded options.

14.4 Alignment of Return and Risk Models

There are a number of reasons why investment managers might wish to view the returns and risks of a particular financial market through a factor model that is particular to their needs. One concern that quantitative asset managers often have is a potential for misalignment that may occur if the risk model and the return model are based on different factors. They fear that in this case, the risk model might detract from the ability of the manager's return forecast to add value in portfolio construction.

A recent paper addressing this issue is Stefek and Lee (2008) in which benchmark relative expected return (alpha) is decomposed into factor and residual components using a procedure similar to that proposed by Bulsing, Sefton, and Scowcroft (2004). Stefek and Lee argue that if the risk model is complete in the sense that residual returns are uncorrelated, any residual alpha arising from a common factor has to be an estimation error. Ceria, Stubbs, Renshaw, and Schmieta (2006) come at the problem from the opposite direction, assuming that residual alpha is not an estimation error in the forecast returns but rather arises from an omitted factor in the risk model. In both papers, a penalty is introduced into the optimization objective to compensate for the assumed bias. It should be noted that to the extent that the manager's return forecasts are based on security specific (i.e., fundamental) analysis rather than common factors, these methods may detract from returns by compensating for a non-existent bias.

A similar problem exists in that fundamentally oriented equity portfolio managers often find the factors in commercially available models to be unintuitive. They want to customize their view of risk to they way they view the world, structuring the decomposition of risk and return into factors that seem understandable and relevant to them. A related issue arises because risk managers often wish to express risk limits on portfolios and trading desks in terms of broad conceptual categories that may not align with specific factors in available models. For example, one might say "Not more than 40% of the tracking variance of a portfolio can come from oil price related effects." If the risk model in use is endogenous, there is generally no easy way to describe this within the model. A similar argument is put forward in the context of performance attribution. Mirabelli (2010) argues that attribution of past portfolio returns should be a "decision-based" approach in which the factors of the model are designed to reflect the actual strategic process of the portfolio manager.

If we assume that the risk model is complete in that residuals are uncorrelated and no relevant factors have been omitted, then revising a factor model to make it more intuitive is quite tractable. We can simply map any user selected factors onto the complete set of factors and then reverse the relationships to add to intuition. A few important properties of a risk model follow from the assumption of completeness:

1. The values of asset specific risks in the given model are uniquely correct. If the factor model accounts for all covariance among securities, the idiosyncratic risks will be the same for any factor covariance matrix that also accounts for all covariance among securities. We can therefore leave the asset specific risks alone when we add new factors.
2. Returns to any new common factor can be expressed as an exact linear combination of the original factors
3. The risk of any portfolio will remain the same even if we express the risk using different factors

Let us consider a simple example. We'll assume an original model with three factors (F_1, F_2, and F_3) to which a user would like to revise with new two factors (U_1 and U_2). Our usual expression for the return on a stock (Equation 14.1) would be:

$$R_{it} = B_{i1}F_{1t} + B_{i2}F_{2t} + B_{i3}F_{3t} + e_{it} \tag{14.5}$$

Now we can introduce the user-defined factors. From property 2 we have that

$$U_{jt} = C_{j1}F_{1t} + C_{j2}F_{2t} + C_{j3}F_{3t} \tag{14.6}$$

where

U_{jt} = return to user factor j during period t;
C_{jn} = exposure of user factor j to original factor n.

Note that there is no residual in this expression since we know that returns to the user factors must be an exact combination of the returns to the factors of any complete model. Since there is no assertion of causality in Equation (14.6), it is equally legitimate to reverse the sides and express the return to the original factors as linear combinations of the returns to the user factors. However, since we have no expectation that the user factors represent a complete model a residual comes back into the expression when we estimate the relationship by a regression.

$$F_{jt} = D_{j1}U_{1t} + D_{j2}U_{2t} + f_{jt} \tag{14.7}$$

where

D_{jn} = the exposure of factor F_j to user-defined factor U_n;
f_{jt} = return to factor F_j that is residual to the set of user factors.

We can now proceed with our normal factor covariance model estimation on the augmented five factor model. Our five factors are now the return time series to our two user-defined factors (U_1, U_2) and three additional factors (f_1, f_2, and f_3) that replace the original F time series. The additional factors f_1, f_2, and f_3 are the portion of the F time series that could not be explained by the user-defined factors. We can now estimate the covariance matrix of the five factors in the usual fashion.

If a user kept adding new user-defined factors that were not linear combinations of other user factors, the f_{jt} values would continue to get smaller and smaller, until the unexplained portion of the original factors became statistically insignificant. In effect, the user will have entirely replaced the original model. The key caveat is that the number and properties of the return time series to the user defined factors be such that Equation (14.7) can be reliably estimated for each of the original factors by regression. The user-defined factors must be limited in number, not too correlated for the available amount of historical data, and be compliant with typical statistical estimation concerns about outliers.

The benefit of this process is that we need not do any statistical estimation in order to get factor exposures (B values) for individual securities to our new factor structure in which we have replaced the set of F factors with the set of $U + f$ factors. The factor exposures of individual securities to factor f_i will be the same as for the corresponding F_i. To obtain factor exposures to the new user-defined factors, we substitute our expressions for each F term in Equation (14.5) with the corresponding right-side of Equation (14.7). By collecting like terms we obtain B values for individual securities with respect to the user-defined factors U.

14.5 Equity Factor Exposure of a Corporate Bond

In many ways it is intuitive to think of a corporate bond as being a combination of a riskless bond and the equity of the issuing firm. Low credit quality bonds (i.e., high yield, "junk") are often treated by investors as a sort of middle ground between owning a bond and owning the stock of the issuing firm. Other securities such as convertible bonds and preferred stocks obviously also share some of the properties of both equity and debt. As such, it is often useful to know the equity factor exposure of a corporate bond.

Since Merton (1974) the "contingent claims" framework for bond default has provided a conceptual linkage between corporate bonds and the equity of the issuer. The classic Merton process is based on the idea that stockholders of a limited liability company hold two options. The first option is a call option on the assets of the firm, with a strike price of the value of the firm's debt and an expiration date of the maturity of the debt. The shareholders can choose to own the assets of the firm outright by paying off the debt.

The second option is a put option on the firm's assets, with a strike price of the value of the firm's debt and an expiration date of the maturity of the debt. If the value of the assets of the firm falls below the value of the debt, the stockholders can simply walk away and give the lenders (bondholders) the assets of the firm in lieu of payment. The bondholders are short this put option.

In the original Merton formulation, the options are assumed to be European options expiring at the maturity date of the bond. Subsequent papers by Black and Cox (1976) and Leland and Toft (1996) extend the practicality of the method to allow for bond default before maturity, multiple bond issues from the same issuer, the potential for technical defaults (e.g., violating a covenant with respect to a balance sheet ratio), and the frictional costs of bankruptcy proceedings. To the extent that a company can issue new bonds, these options may be treated as a perpetual American option. A computational framework for evaluating perpetual American options is provided in Yaksick (1998).

The general context for combining equity factor models and contingent claims models of bond default is provided in diBartolomeo (2010). Depending on the willingness to endure technical complexity, a variety of pricing models can be used to value the options, allowing for inclusion of stochastic processes for volatility and interest rates. If we make the simplifying assumptions that interest rates are fixed for the option term (consistent with Black–Scholes) and we also assume that the equity dividend payments of the firm are inconsequentially small, the approximate equity factor exposures of a corporate bond are given by

$$\%R_{\text{bt}} \sim (-(T-B)/B)^*(\Delta_{\text{p}}/\Delta_{\text{c}})^*[\Sigma_{j=1 \text{ to } n} B_j F_{jt}] + e_t] \tag{14.8}$$

where

R_{bt} = the return on bond b during period t;
T = the value of the bond if it were riskless;
B = the market value of the bond;
Δ_p = the delta of the shareholder put option;
Δ_c = the delta of the shareholder call option.

Essentially, the equity factor exposure of the bond is given as the factor and residual exposures of the equity itself (the last of the three portions) times two scaling coefficients. The first scaling coefficient represents the approximate return on the bond per unit change in the value of the options. The second scalar is just the ratio of the delta values for the shareholder put and call options. To the extent that the value of the bond, the value of the riskless bond, and the delta of the call are strictly non-negative, and the delta of the put is strictly non-positive, we obtain the intuitive result that the bond's exposure to equity factors is always non-negative.

14.6 Conclusions

Equity factor models have become ubiquitous within the institutional asset management community. They are routinely used to estimate the potential benchmark relative returns of equity securities and portfolios. Such models are even more pervasive in the estimation of equity portfolio risk. Equity factor models offer numerous advantages over simple historical observation in providing understandable linkages between security characteristics and subsequent returns, and filtering out much of the random noise affecting returns. Most importantly such models help clarify the distinction between return generating processes that impact a particular security, and processes which are in common across many firms.

Despite the popularity of such models, there is no broad consensus as to the best estimation methods for such models. In recent years, techniques have become available to make such models respond more rapidly to changes in financial market conditions. In addition, methods have been available to transform the strategic perspective of a given model to a different perspective so as to be more intuitive or in greater alignment with the strategy underlying portfolio decisions.

References

Black, F. and Cox, J.C. (1976). Valuing corporate securities: Some effects of bond indenture provisions. *Journal of Finance*, **31**, 351–367.

Bouchard, J.-P., Cizeau, P., Laloux L., and Potters, M. (2000). Random matrix theory and financial correlations. *International Journal of Theoretical and Applied Finance*, **3**, 391–397.

Bulsing, M., Scowcroft, A., and Sefton, J. (2004). Understanding forecasting: A unified framework for combining both analyst and strategy forecasts. *UBS Global Quantitative Research*.

Burmeister, E. and Wall, K. (1986). The arbitrage pricing theory and macroeconomic factor measures. *Financial Review*, **21**, 1–20.

Ceria, S., Renshaw, A.A. Stubbs, R.A., and Schmieta, S. (2006). Axioma alpha factor method: Improving risk estimation by reducing risk model portfolio selection bias. *Axioma, Inc. Research Report* (March).

Chen, N.-F., Roll R., and Ross, S. (1986). Economic forces and the stock market. *Journal of Business*, **59**, 383–403.

diBartolomeo, D. (1998). Optimization with composite assets using implied covariance matrices. Northfield Working Paper, http://www.northinfo.com/documents/58.pdf.

diBartolomeo, D. and Warrick, S. (2005). Making covariance based portfolio risk models sensitive to the rate at which markets reflect new information. In *Linear Factor Models* (eds. J. Knight and S. Satchell). Elsevier Finance, Amsterdam.

diBartolomeo, D., Mitra, G., and Mitra, L. (2009). Equity portfolio risk estimation using market information and sentiment. *Quantitative Finance*, **9**, 887–895.

diBartolomeo, D. (2010). Equity risk, credit risk, default correlation and corporate sustainability. *Journal of Investing*, **19**, 128–133.

Jin, L. and Myers, S. (2004). R-squared around the world: New theory and new tests. Harvard/MIT Working paper.

Kritzman, M., Lowry, K., and Van Royen, A.-S. (2001). Risk, regimes, and overconfidence. *The Journal of Derivatives*, **8**, 32–43.

Lee, J.-H. and Stefek, D. (2008). Do risk factors eat alphas? *The Journal of Portfolio Management*, **34**, 12–24.

Leland, H. and Toft, K.B. (1996). Optimal capital structure, endogenous bankruptcy, and the term structure of credit spreads. *Journal of Finance*, **51**, 987–1019.

Menchero, J. and Mitra, I. (2008). The structure of hybrid factor models. *Journal of Investment Management*, **6**, 1–14.

Merton, R.C. (1974). On the pricing of corporate debt: The risk structure of interest rates, *Journal of Finance*, **29**, 449–470.

Miller, G. (2006). Needles, haystacks and hidden factors. *Journal of Portfolio Management*, **9**, 9–22.

Mirabelli, A. (2010). The decomposition versus the decision – evaluation of active risk-adjusted returns. Opturo working paper.

Morck, R., Yeung B., and Yu, W. (2000). The information content of stock markets: Why do emerging markets have synchronous stock price movements? *Journal of Financial Economics*, **58**, 215–260.

Rosenberg, B. and Guy, J. (1976). Prediction of beta from investment fundamentals. *Financial Analyst Journal*, **32**, 60–72.

Ross, S. (1976). The arbitrage theory of capital asset pricing. *Journal of Economic Theory*, **13**, 341–360.

Scowcroft, A. and Sefton, J. (2006). Understanding factor models. *UBS Global Quantitative Research*.

Shah, A. (2008). Short term risk from long term models. Northfield News (October) (http://www.northinfo.com/documents/312.pdf).

Yaksick, R. (1998). Expected optimal exercise time of a perpetual American option: A closed form solution, *Journal of Financial Engineering*, **4**, 55–73.

CHAPTER 15

FIXED INCOME INVESTMENT RISK

KENNETH WINSTON

The terms "fixed income" (U.S. usage) or "fixed interest" (U.K. usage) are used to describe an asset class containing, but not limited to, debt instruments. In many cases these terms are fantastically misleading, since many fixed income instruments are neither fixed nor income-generating.

These instruments are characterized by contractual exchanges of money ("cash flows") between two or more parties where the flows are contingent on well-defined future events. At a minimum these events include a party's ability to pay. The cash flows may also be dependent on levels of market variables such as interest rates, foreign exchange rates, or a measure of inflation such as the Consumer Price Index. Cash flows can be linked to virtually anything measurable – for example, some catastrophe bonds are tied to weather events.

We define risk as lack of information about the future. This lack of information may take the form Frank Knight (1921) specified as risk – that is, a situation where we know all possible outcomes and their associated probabilities, such as a roulette wheel. Our definition of risk also includes what Knight referred to as uncertainty – a situation where we don't know the probabilities associated with all the outcomes, or where we don't even know all the possible outcomes. Perhaps the most common mistake in mathematical finance is to think that markets display Knightian risk, when in fact they display Knightian uncertainty.

Even apparently well-defined outcomes can contain uncertainty. For example, a zero coupon bond is scheduled to pay a fixed amount, say $100, at some point in the future. If we are sure that the bond will pay the $100 on time and in full, we would appear to have a situation where the outcome is not only well-defined but in fact certain. But prevailing interest rates and the value of money can change over the life of the bond, so the outcome – receiving $100 – can have a different meaning than expected when the bond was issued.

If we're not sure of repayment, then we may receive some amount (the recovery amount) at some point in the future. In extreme situations, the rule of law can be suspended or abrogated entirely. A government can decree debt forgiveness, a practice that dates back thousands of years. It can provide extra support for troubled assets or it can confiscate healthy assets. It can alter the rules for mortgage payments, thereby affecting mortgage prepayment speeds and default levels. A party to a complex security where many parties have competing interests can sue, leading to delays in court and an unexpected decision imposed by a judge. A bondholder may end up with unexpected collateral, like a fleet of rusting oceangoing freighters seized from a shipping company that defaulted on its bonds. The set of outcomes can become far wider than we might have anticipated, leading us further into Knightian uncertainty and away from Knightian risk.

The use of the word "fixed" in "fixed income" indicates a desire for certainty. Some aspects of the fixed income market lend themselves to comparatively narrow outcomes. For example, interest rates in stable economies are virtually never negative and virtually never above 20% per year. Rates outside this range can occur, but they indicate an unstable economy. On the other hand, rates of return on equity have no comparable predetermined range even in a stable economy.

The vast size and complexity of the fixed income market leads to changing relationships between its parts. In this chapter, we will survey the component parts of the global fixed income market and will focus on risks arising from interest rates and credit spreads.

15.1 The Fixed Income Universe

As with most financial markets, the fixed income market consists of primary instruments (often called "cash" instruments) and derivatives. According to the International Monetary Foundation's Global Financial Stability Report (IMF 2010), at the end of 2009 the global debt market totaled U.S. $92 trillion, of which $55.7 trillion was privately issued and $36.4 trillion was publicly issued. The geographic breakdown is shown in Table 15.1. World public debt was 77% of the capitalization of the entire world equity market, while world private debt was 18% larger than the world equity market.

While overall debt monotonically increased in the 2000s, the ratio of public debt to total debt remained range-bound as shown in Figure 15.1.

In fixed income markets (including foreign exchange), over-the-counter ("OTC") derivatives dwarf exchange-traded derivatives in notional size. OTC derivatives are contracts between two parties where there is counterparty credit risk – it is not certain that both parties will honor their contractual obligations. Exchange-traded derivatives have minimal counterparty risk, since exchanges use capital cushions and collateral (margin) collection to avoid defaults.

Table 15.1 World markets, 2009.

Area	GDP	Stock Market Capitalization	Public Debt	Private Debt	Total Debt
WORLD	57,843.4	47,188.9	36,403.4	55,679.0	92,082.4
European Union	15,373.1	10,013.4	10,076.4	23,479.6	33,556.0
France	2,656.4	1,894.8	1,749.2	3,410.3	5,159.5
Germany	3,338.7	1,292.4	1,850.0	3,893.1	5,743.1
Italy	2,118.3	655.8	2,217.5	2,888.0	5,105.5
Spain	1,467.9	1,434.5	745.7	3,030.4	3,776.1
United Kingdom	2,178.9	2,796.4	1,238.5	3,473.8	4,712.3
All Others	3,612.9	1,939.5	2,275.5	6,784.0	9,059.5
North America	15,455.1	16,754.1	10,484.0	23,036.1	33,520.1
Canada	1,336.1	1,676.8	1,005.8	862.3	1,868.1
United States	14,119.1	15,077.3	9,478.2	22,173.8	31,652.0
Japan	5,068.9	3,395.6	9,657.4	2,263.5	11,920.9
Developed Asia	1,603.8	4,308.5	723.6	1,063.3	1,786.9
Emerging Markets	17,962.0	9,909.8	4,895.6	2,723.3	7,618.9
Asia	7,876.0	5,434.6	2,448.9	1,498.6	3,947.5
W. Hemisphere	3,964.8	2,194.8	1,492.4	838.4	2,330.8
Middle East	1,974.3	753.5	151.9	113.6	265.5
Africa	883.4	559.3	98.2	79.9	178.1
Europe	3,263.5	967.6	704.2	192.8	897.0

Notes: (IMF 2010, Table 15.3, "Selected Indicators on the Size of Capital Markets, 2009.") About 5% of the world economy is not reflected in the regions shown. Numbers in $U.S. billions.

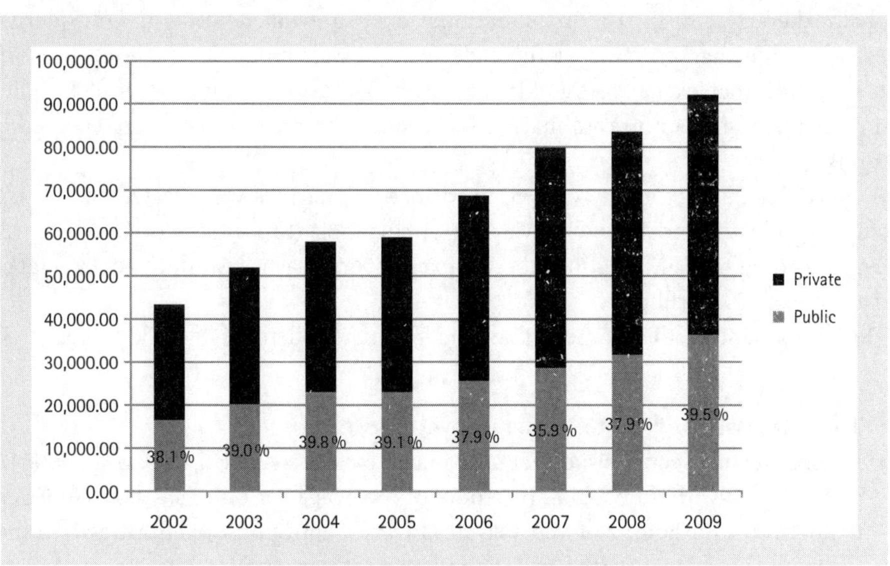

FIGURE 15.1 Public and private debt.

Source: Global Financial Stability Reviews, IMF.

Table 15.2 Global over-the-counter derivatives markets, 2009.

Item	Notional	Gross Market Value
Total	614,674	21,583
Foreign Exchange	49,196	2,069
Interest Rate	449,793	14,018
Equity-linked	6,591	710
Commodity	2,944	545
Credit Default Swaps	32,693	1,801
Single name	21,917	1,243
Multi-name	10,776	559
Unallocated	73,456	2,440

Notes: (IMF 2010, Table 4, "Global Over-the-Counter Derivatives Markets: Notional Amounts and Gross Market Values of Outstanding Contracts.") Numbers in $U.S. billions.

Derivatives' notionals – particularly interest rate derivatives' notionals – are many times as large as global fixed income markets. A typical plain vanilla interest rate swap involves one party paying at a floating rate (often LIBOR, the London InterBank Offered Rate) while the other party pays at a fixed rate. The notional may be $1 billion, but if LIBOR is at 3% and the fixed leg is paying 2.8%, then only 0.2% of $1 billion ($2 million) is exchanged annually.

Table 15.2 shows the International Monetary Foundation's data on the notionals as well as the market values of over-the-counter derivatives at the end of 2009. Globally there was $615 trillion of notional exposure taken through OTC derivatives, while the market value of these derivatives was about $22 trillion. The IMF also indicated that exchange-traded derivatives had a gross notional of $73 trillion and (by construction) no gross market value since the market values are covered by margins.

A more detailed taxonomy of U.S. fixed income markets was created by the U.S. Securities Industry and Financial Markets Association (SIFMA) as of December 31, 2009. According to SIFMA (2010), the US fixed income cash (non-derivatives) market had a value of $34.8 trillion.

The components of the U.S. cash fixed income market defined by SIFMA are:

- **Treasury**: issued by the U.S. federal government.
- **Federal agency securities**: direct debt issued by agencies such as GNMA, FNMA, and FHLMC without backing by a pool of mortgages or other assets. Before September 2008, the latter two were private Government-Sponsored Entities, but since then they have been placed in U.S. government conservatorship. Many consider this an effective guarantee by the U.S. Treasury.

- **Agency Residential Mortgage-Backed Securities (RMBS):**
  - **Pools**: Securities backed by mortgage pools assembled by, and guaranteed by, the above-named agencies (and hence effectively by the U.S. Federal Government since September 2008).
  - **Structures**: CMOs (Collateralized Mortgage Obligations) and other structures referencing agency RMBS. Structures redirect cash flows, so for example IOs are claims on interest payments only, and POs are claims on principal payments only.
- **Municipal bonds**: Issued by sub-federal level governments (such as states, cities, and port authorities) to finance projects such as schools and infrastructure. Most municipal bonds are free of U.S. federal tax. The most notable group of taxable municipal bonds are BABs ("Build America Bonds"), whose interest payments, while taxable, are subsidized by the U.S. Federal Government.
- **Corporate debt**: issued by private corporations.
- **Money markets**: short-term instruments including commercial paper, bankers acceptances, and large time deposits in banks.
- **Non-agency mortgage-related**:
  - **RMBS**: Securities backed by mortgage pools assembled by private institutions. Usually the collateral is of lower quality than agency mortgages. There are also structures referencing non-agency collateral (CMOs, IOs, POs, CDOs).
  - **CMBS (Commercial Mortgage-Backed Securities)**: referencing commercial (as opposed to single-family residential) mortgage pools; issued privately and usually not containing a borrower prepayment option.
- **Asset-backed securities**: securities whose cash flows are gathered from a large pool of underlying debts such as auto loans, credit card receivables, home equity loans, manufacturing, student loans, and collateralized debt obligations (CDOs).

Figure 15.2 shows SIFMA's breakdown of the U.S. fixed income market.[1]

Relationships between these sectors is a central fact of the fixed income market. Borrowing by the government can crowd out corporate and asset-backed borrowing. Defaults by corporate borrowers can cause a flight to safety, inflating the value of safety assets such as highly rated government bonds and lowering rates. In the U.S., lower rates can cause mortgage borrowers to prepay, flooding the holders of mortgage-backed securities with cash. The cash will mostly be put back into longer-term fixed income instruments – especially Treasurys – driving the prices of those securities up, lowering rates, and increasing still further the incentive to prepay. Local versions

[1] SIFMA's $34.8 trillion is higher than the $31.7 trillion reported by the IMF for the U.S. Debt levels changed rapidly in 2008–2009, possibly accounting for discrepancies between SIFMA and the IMF. For example, neither SIFMA nor the IMF seems to be exactly synchronized with the debt reported by the United States Treasury (U.S. Treasury 2010). The Statement of Public Debt as of the end of 2009 showed $7.8 trillion in debt held by the public (probably the figure that SIFMA and IMF intended), and $12.3 trillion total debt including intragovernmental holdings such as the Social Security Trust Fund. By September 2010 these figures were $9 and $13.6 trillion, respectively.

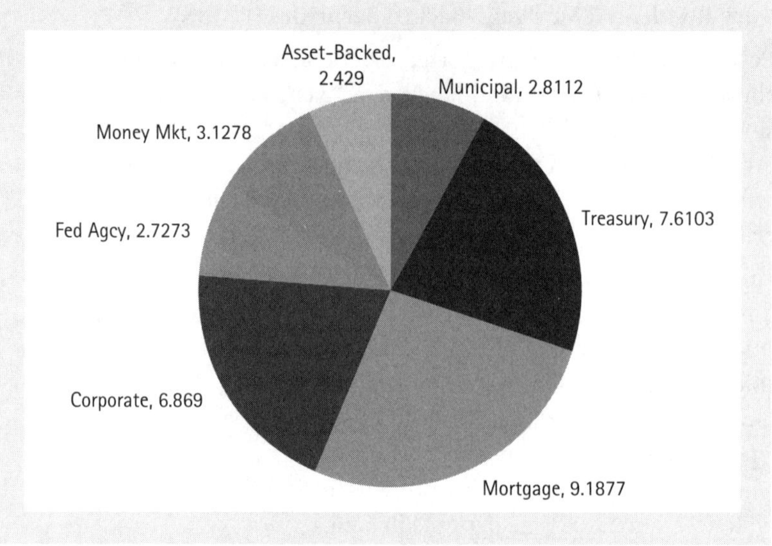

FIGURE 15.2 U.S. fixed income, 31 December 2009, $ trillions.

of sector interplay take place in every country, although various sectors can be different in size and legal status. (For example, there are no other mortgage sectors as huge as the U.S.'s, and in most countries there is no material mortgage bond market.) Cross-border relationships compound the number of interactions that need to be understood.

15.2 Interest Rate Risk

A fixed income instrument consists of a series of future cash flows $f_1, \ldots, f_n$ that may occur at future times $t_1, \ldots, t_n$. Sources of risk are:

- the sizes of the flows (f_i may be variable, due to known or unknown dependencies on parameters whose values are not known at the current time);
- the timing of the flows (t_i may be variable);
- whether or not the flows will actually occur as agreed (credit risk; the payer may default);
- in what form the flows will occur (optionality – one party may have the choice of changing the nature and timing of the flows).

In this section, we'll assume that none of these sources of risk are present. We will assume that we know with certainty each f_i and t_i at time zero.

Consider for example a simple bullet bond: a lender gives a borrower an amount, often calibrated to 100 units of currency (say \$100). The borrower agrees to pay interest periodically during the life of the bond at a fixed rate. Let's assume a 10 year maturity, with 20 payments of \$2.50 each six months. The 20th payment of \$2.50 coincides with the repayment of \$100 principal.

Based on the assumptions we made above, we know that the borrower will definitely make every scheduled payment on time and in full. In that case, this would seem to be a riskless situation – per Frank Knight's prescription, we know all the outcomes to the penny, and we know with certainty (absent default) that they will happen.

But this is not in fact a riskless situation. We don't know what the future holds in terms of other choices, which in effect determine the value of the money we will receive. While we know that we will receive \$2.50 (say) 18 months from now, we don't know whether or not we could have done better. Suppose that six months after the bond we've just described was issued, just after it pays its first \$2.50 interest payment, a new default-free bond worth \$100 is issued maturing exactly at the same time as the first bond (now 9.5 years in the future) and paying fixed interest payments every six months just like the first bond. However, the new bond's rate is 6% a year, or \$3 every six months.

The old bond isn't as appealing as the new bond. In fact if we could go long the new bond and short the old bond, our net investment would be zero but we'd make with certainty \$0.50 every six months for the next 9.5 years. Even if it is not possible to short the old bond, it will certainly be less attractive than the new bond and will command a lower price. Thus the value of the old bond has to be less than \$100.

This situation illustrates one of the most basic risks in fixed income – if we do have a truly fixed income instrument, then if the prevailing level of interest rates changes, the value of our instrument changes. In our example, a rough estimate of the new value can be obtained from elementary bond mathematics.[2] When future cash flows $f_1, \ldots, f_n$ will definitely occur at future times $t_1, \ldots, t_n$, we can discount the cash flows to the present at a yield y in order to determine the current price P of the bond:

$$P = \sum_{i=1}^{n} \frac{f_i}{(1+y)^{t_i}}. \tag{15.1}$$

In our example, $n = 19$ as there are 19 half-year periods left in the life of the bond. $f_1 = f_2 = \ldots = f_{18} = 2.5$, and $f_{19} = 102.5$ as the final payment includes both interest and principal. In this case the prevailing level of interest rates tells us that the yield y must be .03 per half-year.[3] This creates a geometric series that we use to solve for P:

$$P = 2.5\frac{1 - 1.03^{-19}}{.03} + \frac{100}{(1.03)^{19}} = 92.84. \tag{15.2}$$

[2] There are many expositions of basic fixed income mathematics. Two excellent sources are Wise and Bhansali (2010) and Fabozzi (2006).

[3] Of course 3% per half-year isn't exactly the same as 6% per year, but there are many subtleties as to how discount factors are applied. By using 3% per half-year we have chosen the proper discounting method in this case.

The price of the bond has fallen to 92.84 because rates have gone up, meaning it is no longer competitive. Similarly if rates fall to 4%, the price of the bond will go up (to $107.84) because it is more attractive than bonds issued at the going rate.

If a simple bullet bond is a par bond (its price is 100), then its coupon rate (6% a year in our example) equals its yield y. If the price is not 100, then – using the observed market price P as in input rather than an output – we can solve for the yield y that causes the two sides of Equation (15.1) to be equal.

15.3 Yield Curves

We referred above to "the prevailing level of interest rates," but in fact there are many prevailing interest rates. In many countries, the rates at which the government borrows money establish a set of benchmarks from which other borrowings are measured. In the United States, the Treasury borrows money at many different maturities, from a day to 30 years. These rates are summarized in the U.S. Treasury yield curve, which is a graph of current U.S. Treasury interest rates (on the vertical axis) versus the times to maturity (on the horizontal axis). No issuer has instruments maturing every single day from the present to 30 years in the future, so as we will see below yield curves are interpolated between actual observations and sometimes extrapolated beyond the existing observations. Figure 15.3 shows a U.S. Treasury curve. The dark ("par") line indicates the yields of active Treasury bills, notes and bonds from 1 month to 30 years (360 months).

To obtain (say) the 10-year point on the par curve, we observe the current price of a U.S. Treasury 10-year bond together with the bond's fixed coupon rate. These parameters are input to Equation (15.1) in order to obtain the bond's yield y, which is the value

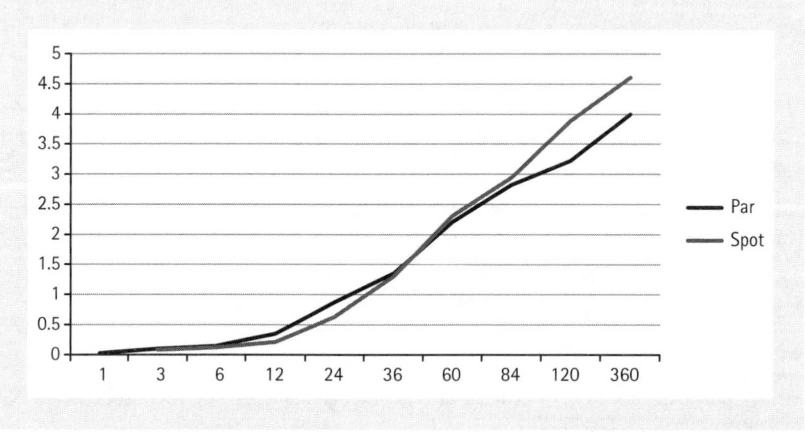

FIGURE 15.3 U.S. Treasury actives (par) and spot curves, November 2009.

Source: Bloomberg, U.S. Treasury actives

placed on the curve. Originally bonds close in price to 100 were used – hence the name "par curve."

The par curve is widely used but it contains a flaw. It's apparent from Figure 15.3 that yields differ at different maturities. Yields far into the future are above 4%, while yields close to the present are below 1%. So cash flows that will be received soon should be discounted at a lower rate than cash flows to be received later. However Equation (15.1) contemplates only one discount rate for all cash flows, averaging a number of different discount rates across the life of the bond.

We can cleanse the curve of temporal mixing by creating or observing a *spot* or *zero* curve. A zero (or zero-coupon bond) is a bond that has only one cash flow: a return of principal at maturity. This simple structure avoids complications arising from different discounting of interim cash flows. A zero curve can be obtained from direct observation of zero-coupon bonds, or from disassembling cash flows of bullet bonds using a process called "bootstrapping." The U.S. Treasury spot (zero) curve is shown in the lighter line in Figure 15.3.

We can use the spot curve to discount each cash flow of a bond with the appropriate rate. Equation (15.1) becomes

$$P = \sum_{i=1}^{n} \frac{f_1}{(1+z_{t_i})^{t_i}}. \tag{15.3}$$

The single yield (discount factor) y has been replaced by multiple spot rates z_{t_i} taken from the spot curve and matched to the time of the cash flow. An instrument priced with Equation (15.3) is said to "price off the spot curve." The spot curve is often upward-sloping, while Equation (15.1) assumed a flat curve.

Spot curves contain implicit predictions of what spot rates will be in the future. These predictions are called *forward curves.* To derive a forward curve, consider the value $V(s,f)$ of a bond that will originate s ("start") years in the future and pay \$1 when it matures f ("finish") years from now, where $s \leq f$. The behavior of such a bond can be replicated in two parts:

- Buy a zero originating today paying \$1 at maturity f years from now. We denote that zero's value as $V(0,f)$.
- Sell short a quantity q of a zero originating today and paying \$1 at maturity s years from now, where $q = V(0,f)/V(0,s)$.

The quantity q is chosen so that the two-bond portfolio has zero value today; s years from now the short bond position will be worth q and the long bond will be worth $V(s,f)$ since it will mature in $f - s$ more years and pay \$1. Thus in the absence of arbitrage we must have $V(s,f) = V(0,f)/V(0,s)$.

Translating this into annualized yields and using straightforward notation we have

$$(1+y(s,f))^{s-f} = \frac{(1+y(0,f))^{-f}}{(1+y(0,s))^{-s}} \tag{15.4}$$

The yields on the right-hand side are obtained from the current spot curve. This defines the forward yield $y(s,f)$ of the zero originating s years from now and paying \$1 f years from now.

15.4 Curve Interpolation

To compute spot and forward curves, we must have yields available to serve as discount rates at each cash flow. Typically, however, even the largest issuers will have a comparatively small finite number of bonds – perhaps 30 – available from which to observe prices and yields. To address this problem, a number of interpolation methods have been suggested to fill in yield curves between observed maturities.

An interpolation function $yi(y_1, \ldots, y_k, t_1, \ldots, t_k, t)$ produces yields for any maturity t (where $t_k \geq t \geq 0$) from a finite number of observed yields $y_1, \ldots, y_k$ at maturities $t_1 < \ldots < t_k$. Hagan and West (2006) note several desired properties for interpolation methods, including:

- the input points should equal the output points – i.e., $yi(y_1, \ldots, y_k, t_1, \ldots, t_k, t) = y_j$ if $t = t_j$;
- the interpolation function yi is continuous in t; and
- assuming the inputs allow it, forward curves based on the function yi do not contain negative yields.

Interpolation methods range from simple linear connection to spline functions.

Another approach to producing continuous yield curves is to note that although there may be (say) $k = 30$ observed points at which market prices can be obtained, there are rarely 30 degrees of freedom in the shape of the yield curve. By suspending Hagan and West's first interpolation condition – an exact match of the interpolated curve at the input points – we can usually find a curve that very closely matches the input points but that depends on far fewer than 30 parameters. One class of curve fitting models was originated by Nelson and Siegel (1987):

$$yi(f) = \beta_0 + \beta_1 \frac{\tau}{f}\left(1 - \exp\left(-\frac{f}{\tau}\right)\right) + \beta_2 \frac{\tau}{f}\left(1 - \exp\left(-\frac{f}{\tau}\right)\left(1 + \frac{f}{\tau}\right)\right). \quad (15.5)$$

While later examples of this class use more parameters, the Nelson–Siegel version uses the four parameters β_0, β_1, β_2, and τ, which can be fitted to observed inputs $y_1, \ldots, y_k, t_1, \ldots, t_k$ to provide in most cases a good fit.[4] These parameters have straightforward intuitive explanations:

[4] For a discussion of how to estimate the parameters of interpolation methods, see Diebold and Li (2006).

- As $f \to \infty$, all terms except for β_0 approach zero, so β_0 is the yield level at the long end of the curve.
- As $f \to 0$, yi approaches $\beta_0 + \beta_1$, so β_1 is the opposite of the slope between the yield at the short end of the curve and the yield at the long end of the curve.
- β_2 determines yield levels in the middle ("belly") of the curve.
- τ controls how fast the levels transition from short end to belly to long end.

Litterman and Scheinkman (1991) also noted dimension reduction in yield curves. If we form a $k \times k$ covariance matrix based on k observed yields (where as above k might be 30 or more), a principal components analysis usually shows that well over 90% of the variability is accounted for by the first three principal components. These often correspond to – or can be easily rotated into – three intuitive factors:

- **Level**: the average yield across all maturities. This is sometimes proxied by a middle point such as the 10-year yield.
- **Slope (or steepness)**: the difference between short maturity yields and long maturity yields.
- **Twist (or curvature)**: the level of a butterfly long-short-long position at short, medium, and long maturities, respectively.[5]

This is similar to the intuition behind the Nelson–Siegel approach – most of the behavior of a yield curve is determined by some combination of short, medium, and long-term maturities.

15.5 The Instantaneous Forward Rate and One-Factor Models

Observations about dimension reduction and interpolation indicate that there isn't a large gap between (1) observable market prices of a discrete number of bonds, and (2) a properly fitted smooth continuous function describing a yield curve. Thus we will assume that there is a smooth curve yi that closely matches observed inputs $y_1, \ldots, y_k, t_1, \ldots, t_k$.

From such a function yi, we can define an instantaneous forward rate $fi(s) = yi(s,f)$ as the limiting value of the quantity defined on the left-hand side of (15.4) as s and f get closer and closer together. The instantaneous forward rate fi embodies all the information about the spot curve and forward curves. For example, it is not hard to see that under reasonable conditions, we can retrieve any forward rate $yi(s,f)$ from the instantaneous forward rate:

[5] Litterman and Scheinkman used slightly different specifications of their three factors, but they generally span the same vector space and have the same intuitive meanings as the factors listed here.

$$yi(s,f) = \int_{t=s}^{t=f} fi(t)dt. \tag{15.6}$$

The instantaneous forward rate automatically enforces the no-arbitrage conditions used to derive Equation (15.4) – the value of the forward $V(s,f)$ must equal the ratio $V(0,f)/V(0,s)$. Thus the instantaneous forward rate – also called the short rate – is often a convenient way to describe the yield curve.

A large class of models is based on specifying the stochastic evolution of the short rate. These models are usually used to generate multiple paths over which today's yield curve could evolve. Instruments priced off this yield curve can then be evaluated using Expression (15.3) or some variant in which additional uncertainties are present. This class of models allows Monte Carlo simulations of complex instruments to be run in order to characterize the distribution of responses to changes in the yield curve. Of course like any models these depend on sometimes oversimplified assumptions, most often a dependence on a Brownian motion to generate processes that are empirically non-normal.

One-factor models of the short rate have the form

$$dr = \mu(r,t)dt + \sigma(r,t)d\beta. \tag{15.7}$$

Here r is the short rate and β is a Brownian motion (a draw from a normal distribution with mean 0 and variance t over a time period of length t). μ and σ are deterministic functions. More complex models involving two or more sources of randomness can be used. LIBOR market models use observed market prices of LIBOR-based interest rate derivatives to infer the possible evolution of yield curves (Rebonato 2002).

Many short rate models derive from the original one due to Vasicek (1977). Vasicek noted that interest rates have no long-term drift and must revert to some long-term mean. He therefore used a mean-reverting Ohrnstein–Uhlenbeck process (Ohrnstein and Uhlenbeck 1930):

$$dr = a(b - r)dt + \sigma d\beta. \tag{15.8}$$

This model captures the intuition that there is a long-term average short rate (b), and the more the current rate strays from the long-term average, the stronger will be the tendency to mean-revert. The parameter a controls the speed at which mean reversion occurs. Volatility σ is a constant. Rendleman and Bartter (1980) used a different approach and took what most now believe was a step backward by using a process similar to the lognormal process that Bachelier proposed in 1900 for equity prices:

$$dr = \mu r dt + \sigma r d\beta. \tag{15.9}$$

However this process can drift to large negative or large positive short rates. This is inconsistent with empirical observation and economic sense.

Cox, Ingersoll, and Ross (1985) combined the mean reversion of an Ohrnstein–Uhlenbeck process with an adjustment for the fact that the volatility of changes in rates is larger as rates get larger. This model can be obtained by assuming that the short rate $r = s^2$, enforcing positive short rates. s in turn is assumed to follow the Vasicek process (15.8) with long-term mean $b = 0$. Applying Itô's lemma to $r = s^2$ and $ds = -asdt + \sigma d\beta$ gives a process of the form[6]

$$dr = c(d - r)dt + \sigma\sqrt{r}d\beta. \tag{15.10}$$

The square-root adjustment in the volatility term appears to be supported by empirical patterns.

The Ho and Lee (1986) model allows fitting to the current curve:

$$dr = \alpha(t)dt + \sigma d\beta \tag{15.11}$$

where $\alpha(t)$ is constructed so that r will match the current nonstochastic short rate curve at the current time and then drift from there. The Hull and White (1990) model

$$dr = (\alpha(t) - ar)dt + \sigma d\beta \tag{15.12}$$

combines the intuition of Ho and Lee (fitting to the current curve) and of Vasicek (Ohrnstein–Uhlenbeck mean reversion).

Black, Derman and Toy (1990) combine a lognormal process with curve fitting and an Itô volatility adjustment. They further incorporate data from the interest rate derivatives market to fit rate volatilities as well as short rate levels:

$$dr = \left(\alpha(t) + \frac{\sigma^2}{2}\right) rdt + \sigma rd\beta. \tag{15.13}$$

Black and Karasinski (1991) force non-negative rates by substituting the logarithm of short rates for short rates themselves in Vasicek's model (15.8). They further fit both current rates and volatilities into the parameters a, b and σ (which are functions, not constants):

$$dln(r) = (b - a\,ln(r))dt + \sigma d\beta. \tag{15.14}$$

Models currently in use allow varying degrees of calibration to market observables and generally avoid or discourage negative rates and long-term drift to unrealistically high rates. An economy with interest rates tending toward infinity is unsustainable, as is an economy with zero or negative interest rates. While negative or very large positive interest rates can exist for short periods under unusual conditions, they can't be sustained.

[6] Cox, Ingersoll, and Ross ("CIR") developed their model based on a rather complex general equilibrium model which is a complete intertemporal description of a continuous time competitive economy. The simple connection between Cox–Ingersoll–Ross and Vasicek was pointed out by Attilio Meucci.

15.6 Empirical Interest Rate Distributions

Data from the U.S. Federal Reserve shows that the lowest constant maturity U.S. Treasury 10-year rate observed between the beginning of 1962 and the end of 2009 was 2.08% on December 18, 2008; the highest was 15.84% on September 30, 1981.

Central bank policy, momentum in the economy, and other factors cause interest rates to have persistence. For example, Figure 15.4 shows that from the late 1970s to the mid-1980s, rates were significantly higher than at other times during the sample. Toward the end of the sample, extreme accommodative measures from the U.S.'s central bank (the Federal Reserve) – along with risk averse flight to quality – brought rates to unusually low levels.

Taking first differences of rates removes much of the persistence in levels, as we see in Figure 15.5.

While Figure 15.5 is symmetric about zero, it also reveals volatility regimes in rates. The beginning of the sample period – from 1962 to 1966 – shows unusually low rate volatility, while the early 1980s show high volatility. The same factors that cause persistent levels also cause large moves and signal more or less uncertainty about the economy, and therefore about the volatilities of rates. For example, the biggest single-day drop was a 75bps change from 10.15% to 9.40% on October 20, 1987 – a flight-to-quality reaction to the largest-ever stock market drop the previous day (Carlson 2006). On a relative basis, the biggest single day move was a drop from 3.02% to 2.51% from March 17 to March 18,

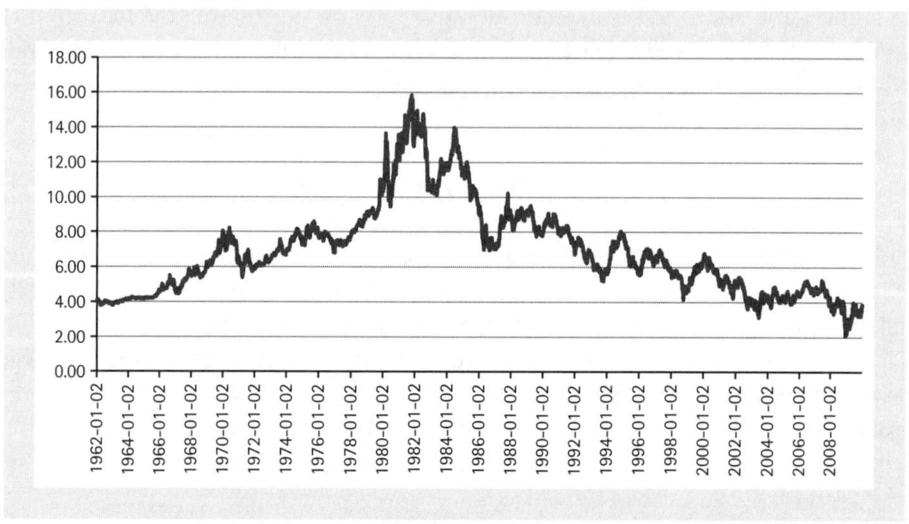

FIGURE 15.4 Constant maturity U.S. Treasury 10-year rates, 1962–2009.

Source: Federal Reserve (FRED database), series DGS10 constant maturity 10-year Treasury rates.

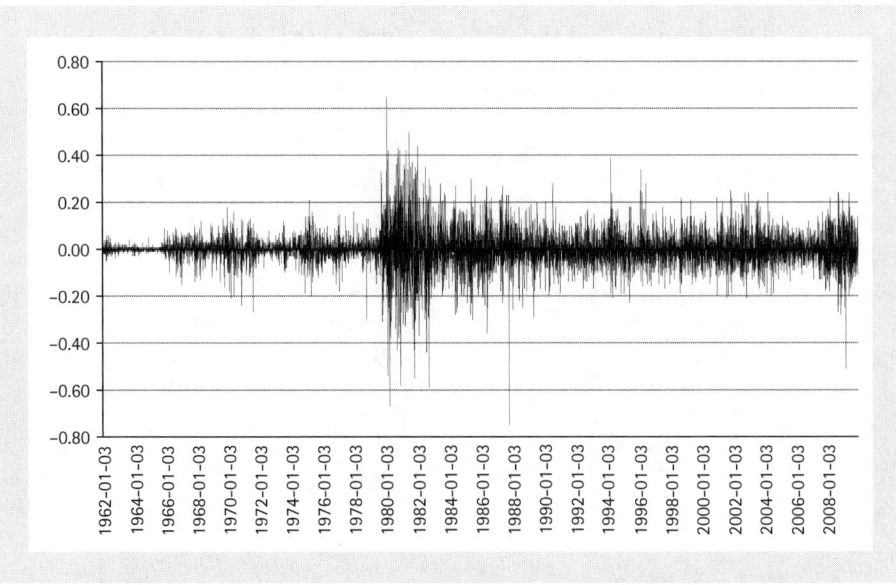

FIGURE 15.5 First differences of constant maturity U.S. Treasury 10-year rates.

2009. This reflected an announcement by the Federal Reserve of massive quantitative easing, including the purchase of up to \$300 billion of long-term Treasurys. Both of these moves marked significant changes in subsequent rate volatility levels. While some of the apparent higher volatility in the 1980s is level dependent, volatility regimes are present even when levels are removed – extreme moves in 2008 and 2009 were larger on a relative basis than extreme moves in the 1980s.

In practice a simple normalization of rate moves works well to account for volatility regime changes. Define the trailing 21-business-day (approximately a business month) standard deviation as

$$\sigma_t = \sqrt{\frac{1}{21}\sum_{s=t-20}^{t}(dr_s)^2}. \tag{15.15}$$

Here dr_s is the arithmetic change in rates (i.e. what is shown in Figure 15.5) at day s. The normalized time series dr_t/σ_{t-2} has smoother characteristics than the first difference series dr_t. Table 15.3 shows that normalization significantly lowers the kurtosis, indicating that volatility clusters explain some of the behavior. A further simple adjustment for first-order autocorrelation makes the series of changes in 10-year interest rates close to a slightly fat-tailed distribution – for example, a Student's t distribution with six degrees of freedom.

As we noted above, among others Litterman and Scheinkman (1991) pointed out that the shape of the yield curve is also variable, with the slope between short term rates and mid-to-long term rates being roughly the second most important factor after the overall level of rates. The slope – which we will represent by the difference between constant

Table 15.3 Comparison of U.S. Treasury 10-year rate first differences 1962–2009 – Original and normalized.

Statistic	dr_t	dr_t/σ_{t-2}
Count	11982	11961
Min	-.75%	-9.34
Max	+.65%	+7.43
Mean	0	.0243
Standard deviation (daily)	.0683%	1.134
Serial correlation	.0786	.1339
Skewness	-.2847	.0842
Excess Kurtosis	9.5843	3.637
Jarque-Bera	45942	6618
Chi-squared	0	0

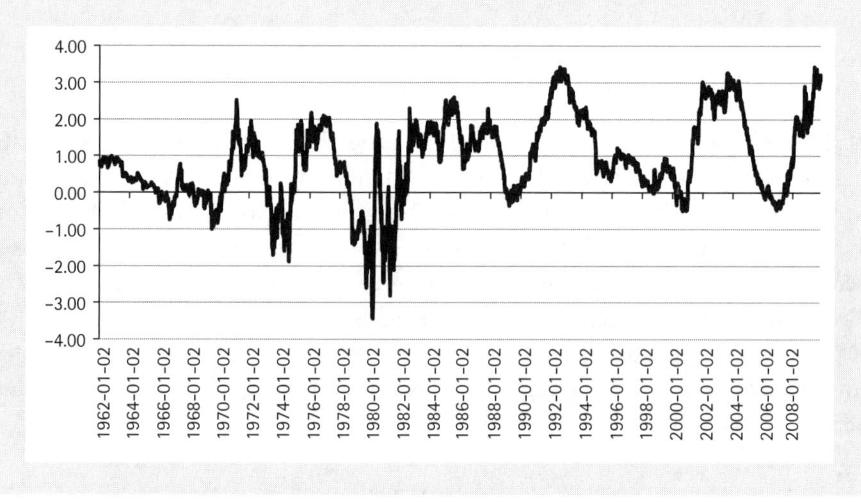

FIGURE 15.6 10 year minus 1 year U.S. Treasury slope, 1962–2009.

Source: Federal Reserve (FRED database), series DGS10 and DGS1.

maturity 10 year U.S. Treasury rates and constant maturity one-year rates[7] – was positive 79% of the time from the beginning of 1962 to the end of 2009. The most steeply inverted curve (where 10-year rates were lower than one year rates) had a 3.44% drop (March 26, 1980), while the steepest upward slope was a symmetric 3.43% on June 10, 2009.

Daily 1–10 year slopes are shown in Figure 15.6.

One-year rates are considerably more fat-tailed than 10-year rates. The kurtosis of daily changes in one-year rates over the 1962–2009 period was 22.5. Even after adjusting

[7] It is customary to use the 2 year – 10 year slope, but 2-year constant maturity data is only available starting in 1976.

for volatility regimes by dividing by trailing, non-overlapping 21-day volatility, the kurtosis of the normalized series remained high at 12.9 over this period. One reason for this persistent fat-tailed behavior is the more direct influence of central bank policy on one-year rates. In the belly and the long end of the curve, smoothing takes place as market participants price in expected policy shocks over time. With recent quantitative easing measures targeting longer-term rates, some of the insulation from shocks at longer-term rates may become frayed.

Another variable factor is the correlation between changes in the 10-year rate and changes in the ten-minus-one year slope. As we noted above, these roughly correspond to the first two principal components of the covariance matrix between different observed yields on the yield curve. The correlation between principal components is zero by construction. However Figure 15.7 shows that the trailing 252 business day (approximately one year) correlations between the 10-year rate and the ten-minus-one-year slope vary considerably.

During very low-rate environments such as the year 2009, virtually all variation in the slope is due to the 10-year rate, so the correlation between 10-year rates and ten-minus-one-year slopes is close to one. In these periods the principal components do not correspond well to the simple specification of levels and slopes. We can test whether there is meaningful persistence in the correlations between levels and slopes by an extension of the normalization process we used above.

For each trailing 21-day period ending at period t, form the covariance matrix

$$C_t = \begin{pmatrix} \sigma_t^2 & c_{1,10} \\ c_{1,10} & \theta_t^2 \end{pmatrix}. \tag{15.16}$$

Here σ_t^2 is the square of Expression (15.15); θ_t^2 is the analogous variance of one-year rate changes; and $c_{1,10}$ is the covariance of one-year rates with 10-year rates over the 21 days

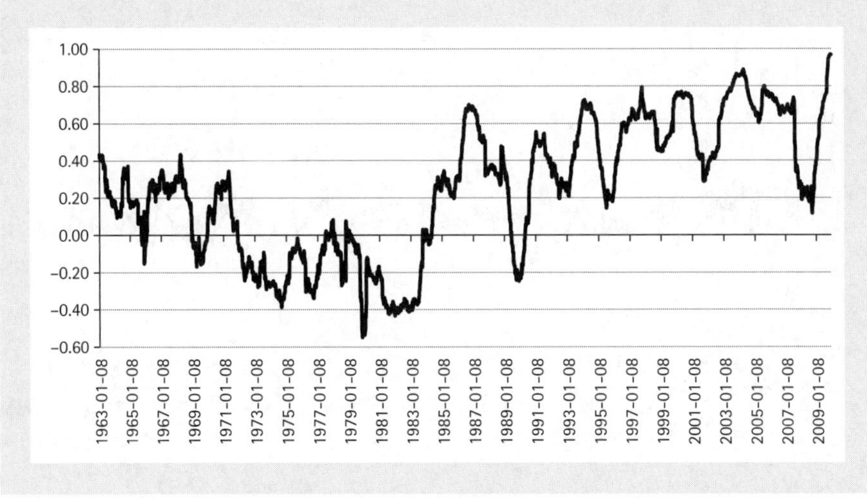

FIGURE 15.7 Rate/slope correlations, 1963–2009.

ending at day t. We do not use ten-minus-one-year slope changes here because they are a linear transformation of the directly observed rates so there is no new information in using them. We Cholesky factor C_t:

$$C_t = \begin{pmatrix} \sigma_t & 0 \\ c_{1,10}/\sigma_t & \sqrt{\theta_t^2 - \frac{c_{1,10}^2}{\sigma_t^2}} \end{pmatrix} \begin{pmatrix} \sigma_t & c_{1,10}/\sigma_t \\ 0 & \sqrt{\theta_t^2 - \frac{c_{1,10}^2}{\sigma_t^2}} \end{pmatrix} = R_t R_t'. \tag{15.17}$$

Let v_t be the 2-vector of observations of the change in the 10-year rate from day $t-1$ to day t, together with the change in the one-year rate over the same period. Then we can normalize v_t by multiplying by the inverse of the non-overlapping Cholesky factor:

$$w_t = R_{t-2}^{-1} v_t. \tag{15.18}$$

The normalization is the same as the one we carried out above in the first component – the 10-year rate is divided by its lagged 21-day standard deviation. The second component is a linear combination of 10-year rate and the one-year rate which almost always has a positive weight on the 10-year rate change and a negative weight on the one-year rate change. The correlations between the two components of w_t over time are shown in Figure 15.8.

These correlations have a far smaller range and are far more stable than the pre-normalization correlations in Figure 15.7, showing that there is persistence in the covariance matrix between one-year rates and 10-year rates. Thus while it might be too literal to expect that rate levels and slopes are always good proxies for the first and second principal components of the covariance matrix of a yield curve, it does appear that a slowly changing linear combination of one-year and 10-year rates can usually capture

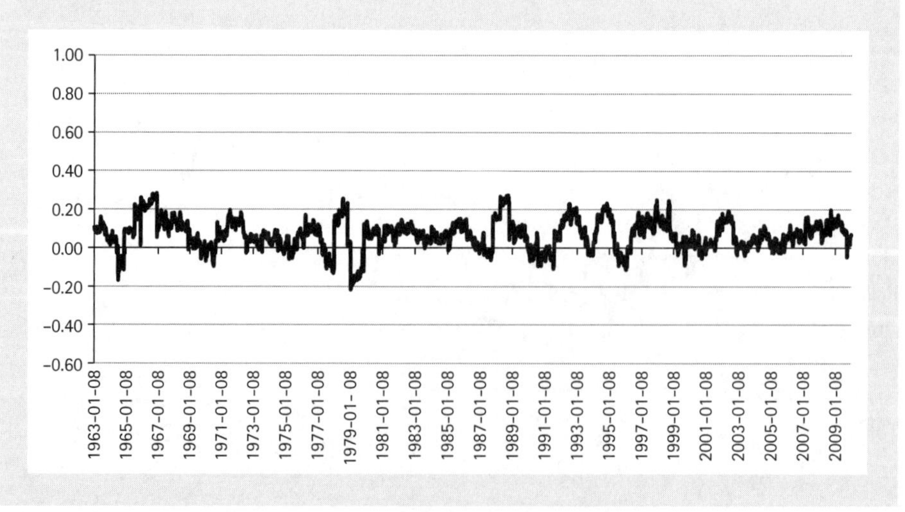

FIGURE 15.8 Normalized series correlations, 1963–2009.

a second and largely independent dimension of yield curve variability from 10-year rates alone.

15.7 Portfolio Duration and Convexity

A very simple measure of a fixed income instrument's risk is its time to maturity. A bondholder who is scheduled to be fully repaid within a week has – all other things being equal – less risk than a bondholder who is not scheduled to be fully repaid for 30 years.

In 1938 Frederick Macaulay pointed out that there was a better way to measure time-based exposure. A zero-coupon bond – one paying a single lump sum at its maturity date – differs from a coupon-paying bond maturing on the same date. The coupon-paying bond has already delivered some of the money it has promised by the time it gets to maturity, so it has whittled down the exposure. Macaulay's concept of duration captured this idea by measuring the average time at which cash flows would be received by the bond. A zero has duration equal to time to maturity, but a coupon-paying bond has a duration that is less than the time to maturity.

Using the standard fixed income pricing identity in Expression (15.1) above, we can define the Macaulay duration D by weighting each cash flow by the time it arrives, and normalizing by the price P:

$$D = \sum_{i=1}^{n} \frac{t_i f_i}{(1+y)^{t_i}} / P. \tag{15.19}$$

An expression like the right-hand side of (15.19) can also be obtained by taking the derivative of (15.1) with respect to yield:

$$\frac{dP}{dy} = -\frac{1}{1+y} \sum_{t=1}^{n} \frac{t_i f_i}{(1+y)^{t_i}} = -\frac{1}{1+y} DP. \tag{15.20}$$

Equation (15.20) provides a second intuition about duration: it relates price changes to yield changes. We can rearrange (15.20) into a finite difference approximation (ignoring higher order terms) and obtain

$$\frac{dP}{P} \approx -D_m dy \tag{15.21}$$

where D_m is modified duration, or Macaulay duration divided by $1+y$. Thus a bond with 4 years' modified duration will go down in price approximately 40 bps (i.e. its current price will be multiplied by .996) when its yield goes up by 10 bps.

In addition to ignoring higher order terms, (15.21) oversimplifies in other ways. The bond's own yield y is not directly observable. The only market observable in expressions (15.1) and (15.19)–(15.21) is the bond's price P. These expressions merely repackage the price and the cash flow structure of the bond into yield and duration. However, many market participants use duration to relate the price movement of a bond to movements in the general level of interest rates. Thus the last sentence of the previous paragraph might morph into a statement like: "...a bond with 4 years' modified duration will go down in price approximately 40 bps...when the U.S. Treasury 10-year rate goes up by 10 bps." This assumes that the movements of the bond's own yield y and U.S. Treasury 10-year rates are highly correlated.

Clearly not all bond yields move in lockstep with the U.S. Treasury 10-year rate. The variability of Rate/Slope correlations shown in Figure 15.7 would not exist if the one-year and the 10-year rates moved in lockstep. The variability in Figure 15.7 arises mainly from one factor – time to maturity – since the issuer is in both cases the U.S. Treasury. Many other factors such as the credit of the issuer, optionality in the bond, variable cash flows, foreign exchange rates, and liquidity can assert themselves in lowering the reliability of the relationship between a benchmark rate like the U.S. Treasury 10-year and the yield of a particular bond.

Using Expression (15.3), we can compute the price $P(dz)$ of the instrument under the assumption that the entire curve is translated upward by a small amount dz. This computation may be difficult, as the cash flows f_i may not be constant and may depend in complex ways on the perturbed curve. We can obtain an effective duration D_e from a general price function $P(\,)$ that takes these features into account:

$$D_e = -\frac{P(dz) - P(-dz)}{2P\,dz}. \tag{15.22}$$

To get more detailed information on responses to changes in different parts of the curve from which the instrument is priced, we can perturb only one of the discount rates z_{t_i} in a process analogous to (15.22). The duration obtained in this way is a *partial duration* D_{t_i}. A vector of partial durations sampled at several tenors along the curve can provide more information than a single number.

However we are still faced with a fundamental problem: durations – no matter how they are defined and now matter how many parts of the yield curve we sample – do not easily mix. For example, Japanese Government Bonds ("JGBs") are considered default-free as are U.S. Treasurys. However Figure 15.9 shows that changes in JGB 10-year rates do not have consistent correlation with changes in U.S. Treasury rates.[8]

A portfolio containing just three instruments – a U.S. Treasury one-year bond; a U.S. Treasury 10-year bond; and a Japanese Government 10-year bond – can react

[8] Correlations were formed on a trailing 12 month basis to avoid asynchronous trading issues present in daily data. JGB rates were obtained from the Japanese Ministry of Finance (http://www.mof.go.jp/english/bonds/interest_rate/data.htm). JGB nine-year rates were used until 10-year rates became available in July 1986. The correlations are based on arithmetic changes in rates month-over-month.

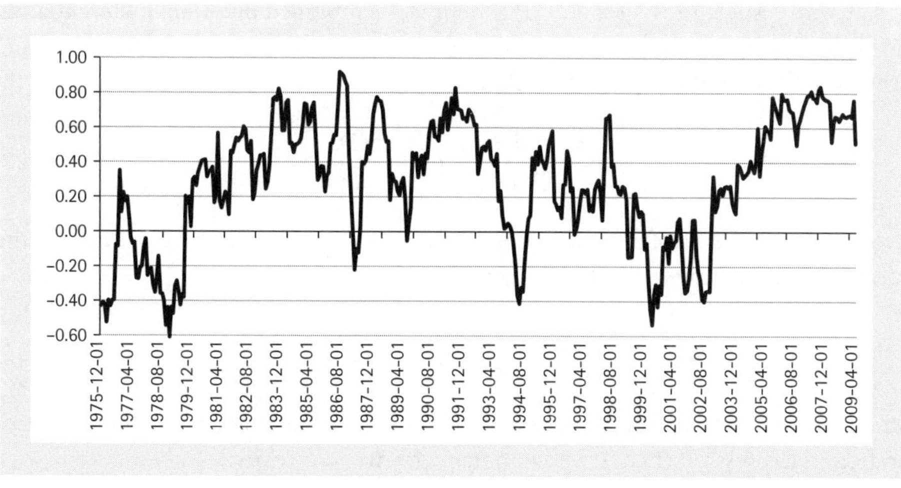

FIGURE 15.9 U.S. Treasury/Japanese Government bond correlations, 1976–2009.

very differently at different times to a change in the general level of U.S. interest rates. Proper management of interest rate risk requires at the very least an understanding of several key rate durations and an understanding of the relationships between durations arising from different segments of the fixed income market. Since these relationships are not static, the actions taken to manage interest rate risk may vary sharply in different periods. For example Figure 15.9 shows that in the late 1970s, JGBs were negatively correlated with U.S. Treasurys. In that period JGB duration would cancel some U.S. Treasury duration. On the other hand, JGBs were highly correlated with U.S. Treasurys in the late 2000s, so their durations in that period were additive. While much of the variation in JGB/U.S. Treasury yields is due to the dollar/yen exchange rate, there are many other factors influencing the relationship.

Fixed income market participants often form a single aggregate portfolio duration by taking the duration of each instrument in a portfolio and multiplying it by the percentage weight that instrument occupies in the portfolio; these products are then summed. However, as we have seen, aggregate portfolio duration attempts to encapsulate in a single number what is in fact a multi-dimensional set of influences. Relationships between influences are time-varying and no static mapping can be made between these different dimensions. More sophisticated fixed income market participants look beyond simple aggregate portfolio duration and take into account expected relationships between the different segments of the portfolio in order to estimate interest rate risk.

Expression (15.21) can be a good local approximation, but when moves in yields are large the higher-order terms can become significant. In particular the second-order term can produce noticeable deviations from Expression (15.21) for any bond more complicated than a zero-coupon bond. Expression (15.20) indicates that the first derivative of price with respect to yield is $-D_m P$, where D_m is modified duration. Differentiating this expression again gives an expression for *convexity*, which is related to the second derivative of price with respect to yield:

$$C = \frac{1}{P}\frac{d^2P}{dy^2} = D_m^2 - \frac{dD_m}{dy}. \tag{15.23}$$

If we expand the terms of dP in a Taylor series up to second order, we can improve the approximation in Expression (15.21) to obtain:

$$\frac{dP}{P} \approx y_0 - D_m dy + \frac{1}{2}C(dy)^2. \tag{15.24}$$

In the same way we used a perturbation of a complex pricing function to obtain effective duration in Expression (15.22), we can obtain effective convexity:

$$\begin{aligned} C_e = \frac{1}{P}\frac{d^2P}{dy^2} &\approx \frac{1}{P}\left(\frac{P(2dw) - P - P + P(-2dw)}{4(dw)^2}\right) \\ &= \frac{1}{P}\left(\frac{P(dz) + P(-dz) - 2P}{(dz)^2}\right). \end{aligned} \tag{15.25}$$

The approximation is obtained by perturbing Expression (15.22) up and down by a small quantity dw. We set $dz = 2dw$ to make the expression simpler, obtaining the quantity on the right of Expression (15.25).

The fact that prices can depend on multiple factors can cause even more problems for convexity than it does for duration. A multiple-factor price function might be written $P(dy_1, dy_2, \ldots, dy_k)$ where the dy_i's are changes in the various factors that affect the bond. Approximation (15.24) then generalizes to a vector/matrix expression:

$$\frac{dP}{P} \approx y_0 - \overrightarrow{D_m}'\overrightarrow{dy} + \frac{1}{2}\overrightarrow{dy}'H\overrightarrow{dy} \tag{15.26}$$

where H is a Hessian matrix of cross-convexities. As the number of factors expands, this matrix rapidly becomes difficult for a human to grasp, but given the changing nature of relationships between factors it is usually not possible to use simple historical projection to estimate these easily. In many cases cross-convexities are ignored in the hope that they are not significant. This hope is not always realized.

The problems we noted with combining individual security durations to form a portfolio level duration become even more pronounced if we attempt to extend the Taylor series approximation to price change to the second order. The number of parameters to be estimated is quadratic in the number of influences on yields, rapidly leading to an intractable problem. Models that attempt to extract orthogonal factors, reducing the number of required parameters down to linear, are usually necessary in order to be able to make testable predictions of future behaviors of portfolios.

15.8 Credit Risk

We have seen that interest rate risk is multi-dimensional and depends at the very least on tenor and the economy and currency from which default-free bonds are issued. If we remove the assumption that the bonds are default-free, further dimensions of risk become apparent.

Bond issuers need to demonstrate to lenders that they have a reasonable chance of repaying the money loaned to them, or they simply won't be able to borrow. Thus insisting on a good fiscal position is the first line of defense against default for any bond lender. However, if fiscal positions deteriorate, governments possess a unique set of powers that corporations can't use: governments can increase taxes; can expropriate or sell property; and (if the government controls the currency in which the bond was issued) can simply create money to pay back bondholders in debased currency.

Even with these powers, governments can and do default. A somewhat whimsical saying – "Corporations default because they have to; governments default because they want to" – refers to the special powers of government. But as the saying implies, at some point a government may decide that the pain to its citizens from exercising its special powers outweighs the pain it will endure from defaulting on its bonds. The consequences of defaulting likely include being frozen out of debt markets or having to pay higher yields in the future. Government defaults therefore include an extra element of Knightian uncertainty over corporate defaults. While we might plausibly think that a large sample of corporate issuer behavior will, under appropriate conditions, allow us to infer a reasonably complete set of outcomes and probabilities, we have little hope that the highly idiosyncratic behavior of politicians will be similarly amenable to analysis. It does not suffice to calculate balance sheets and national income to calculate probabilities: one must discern the will of the government as well.

While government defaults involve both fiscal and political calculations, corporate defaults are more purely fiscal. If, as we observed in the previous paragraph, observations of large numbers of corporate bond issuers all operating under a rule of law that they can't change constitute an example of Knightian risk, then we have would have known outcomes and known probabilities. But it is immediately apparent that this is not true – the rule of law does in fact change over time even in stable countries. The economic environment changes too: for example since its inception the United States has changed from an emerging market with an agrarian economy, to an industrial economy, to a developed market with a service economy.

While many things change over time, there are factors that remain the same. And entity that spends a very large percentage of its income on debt service is probably in trouble. This was as true in ancient Egypt as it is in the modern world. Similarly the ratio of debt outstanding to the total value of an enterprise is clearly universally important.

Ratings agencies like Moody's and Standard and Poors have been classifying corporate credit quality using long-lasting criteria for decades. While these agencies have been

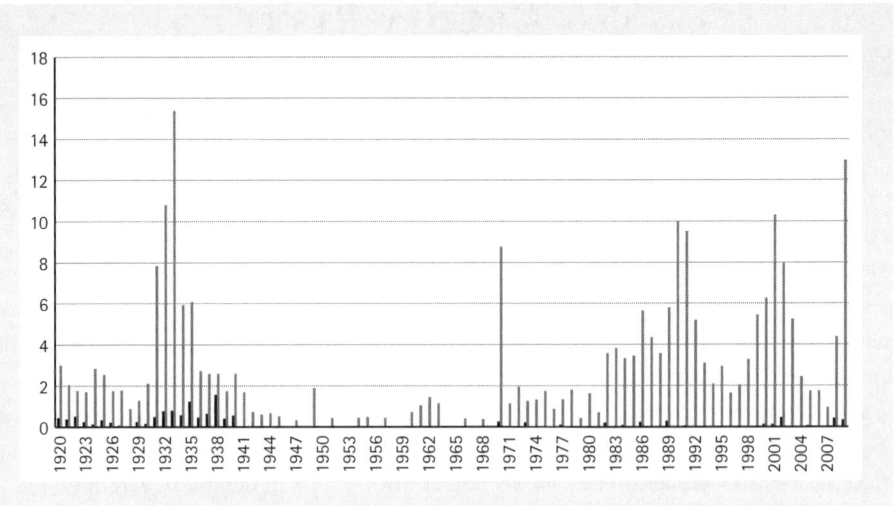

FIGURE 15.10 Moody's default rates, 1920–2009.

Source: (Moodys 2010, Exhibit 31)

taken to task for the reliability of their ratings of non-corporate debt such as asset-backed and structured securities, the basic corporate credit rating function has been reasonably stable for almost a century.

Corporate bonds have long been divided into investment grade bonds – those that, in the opinion of the rating agency, have a very low chance of defaulting – and speculative grade bonds that have a higher chance of default.[9] What constitutes a "low chance of defaulting" and a "higher chance of default" varies with the economic climate: agencies do not directly estimate probabilities when they assign ratings to corporate bonds. Instead they observe characteristics such as debt service to income, debt to enterprise value, and capital structure (that is, how many other obligations have higher or lower priority than the one being rated).

Figure 15.10 shows that default frequencies vary with the general economic climate: the larger bars are the percentages of speculative grade bonds defaulting each year, while the barely visible smaller bars that sometimes are to the left of the larger bars are the percentages of investment grade bonds defaulting each year.

Over the 90 years 1920–2009, the average default rate of investment grade bonds was 0.15% per year, while the average default rate of speculative grade bonds was 2.774% per year. For investment grade bonds the worst default rate in that period was 1.579% in 1938. Thus investment grade defaults, even in the Great Depression, were relatively rare. Figure 15.10 shows that investment grade median and mode default rates are zero.

[9] Until the 1980s, speculative grade bonds were not widely issued. Instead, an investment grade bond migrated to speculative grade status as the firm's fiscal situation deteriorated – it was a "fallen angel." Starting in the 1980s, speculative grade bonds became more widely available as direct issuance rather than as migrated investment grade bonds.

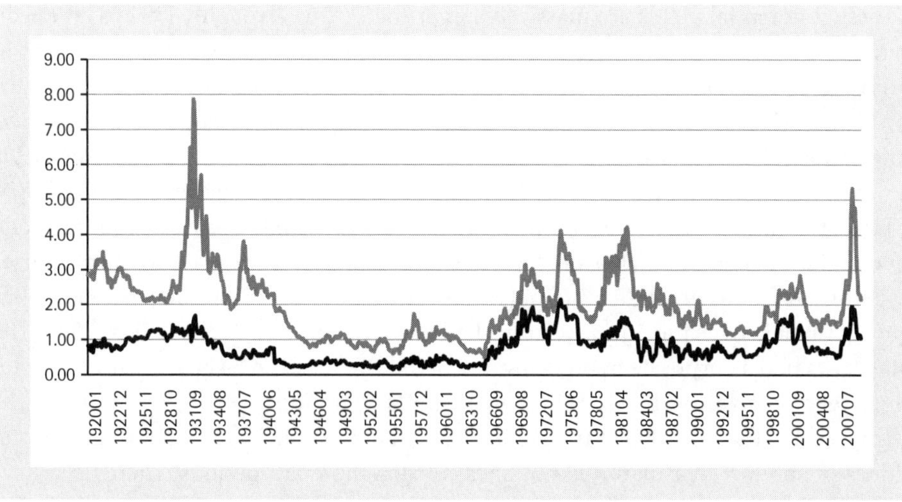

FIGURE 15.11 Differences between IG corporate bond yields and comparable U.S. Treasurys, 1920–2009.

Source: U.S. Federal Reserve. Series AAA (Moody's seasoned AAA corporate bonds) and BAA (Moody's seasoned Baa corporate bonds).

Notes: The top line is the difference between BAA bond yields and the Treasury rate; the bottom line is the difference between AAA bond yields and the Treasury rate. The Treasury rate is the average rate of all Treasury issues over 10 years. (United States Federal Reserve, 1943 and 1996), supplemented with downloads in 2010 of Moody's series and data collected by Michael Bazdarich. In addition to data, I am indebted to Dr. Bazdarich for many useful comments.

Bonds with credit risk should pay higher interest rates than identical bonds without credit risk; lenders need to be compensated for the possibility of default. For example, U.S. corporate bonds pay more than U.S. Treasurys with similar characteristics. When corporate bonds did default in the period 1982–2009, recovery rates averaged approximately 43% for investment grade bonds and 37% for speculative grade bonds. A rough calculation of the average loss rate for investment grade bonds is therefore 0.15% times 43%, or 6.45 bps a year. Due to the nature of averaging, our rough calculation is not quite right, but for the period 1982–2009 (Moody 2010), Exhibit 23 calculates loss rates directly and obtains a number very close to this: 6bps as the average loss rate in the year after bonds are rated investment grade.[10]

Thus long-term investors in U.S. investment grade bonds would have been compensated for their losses due to default if they had received an extra 6 or so basis points a year over U.S. Treasurys. In fact they generally received more than that. Figure 15.11 shows the extra yield (over comparable Treasurys) received by investment-grade corporate bonds: the lower line shows highest-rated investment-grade bonds (Aaa), and the higher line shows the extra yield received for lowest-rated (Baa).

[10] Recovery rates show the amount obtained by the lender in the event of default. A recovery rate of 43% means the lender is paid 43 cents per dollar originally loaned. (Moody's (2010), Exhibit 22 for senior unsecured bonds, averaged over years 1–5.)

These differential yields are massively larger than 6 bps – roughly 139 bps a year on average.[11] However, yields alone do not tell us how much compensation an investor in corporate bonds would have received, among other reasons because index reconstitution masks price moves. If a bond drops in rating, it will almost always go down in price. However, it will also then be excluded from the set of bonds used to compute the yields shown in Figure 15.11, unrealistically failing to penalize an investor for the price drop.

To see how much an investor would have been compensated for investing in corporate bonds versus comparable Treasurys, we need a total return index. Total return indices for corporate bonds are difficult to obtain for the full period shown in Figure 15.11, but data is available over the 20 years from the beginning of 1990 to the end of 2009. The data shows that a corporate bond investor would have received 54 bps a year more total return than an investor in U.S. Treasurys of similar duration.[12]

This result – that the total returns of investment grade bonds are higher than the total returns of similar Treasurys – is not always true. There are periods where Treasurys outperform investment grade bonds on a total return basis, especially during flight-to-safety conditions such as the fourth quarter of 2008. However, it appears that during most long periods, the total returns on corporate bonds are higher than the total returns on Treasurys.

The total return characteristics of speculative grade bonds versus U.S. Treasurys and speculative grade defaults are also time-period dependent. In the modern era where speculative grade bonds were issued directly rather than coming about as a result of a drop in the rating of an investment-grade bond, the loss rate was 304 bps/year (Moody's 2010, Exhibit 23). On a total rate of return basis, high yield bonds returned 139 bps/year more than comparable Treasurys over the last 15 years.[13] Unlike bonds in investment grade indices, bonds in high yield indices do not usually migrate out of the index before the index is penalized for the initial price drop due to default or impending default. Thus the performing bonds in the high-yield index not only made up for the 304 bps/year, but also provided 139 bps of further outperformance.

Most financial markets display risk aversion and require compensation for bearing risk above the simple expectation of loss. So we should not be surprised if there is extra compensation for bearing the risk of default. One way to think about the compensation for bearing default risk was suggested by Merton (1974). This "structural model" of default is one of the pillars of modern finance (as is its author, a Nobel Laureate) and has spawned thousands of subsequent investigations.

[11] 139 bps is the average of the two series shown in Figure 15.11 (79 bps and 198 bps for Aaa and Baa, respectively). The option-adjusted spread from the Barcap U.S. Aggregate Corporate series of investment-grade bonds from 1990–2009 was a similar 130 bps (Bloomberg series LUACOAS).

[12] The difference between the annual rate of return of the Barcap US IG Corporate Index (LUACTRUU) and the annual rate of return of the Barcap U.S. Treasury Index (LUATTRUU) was 59 bps/year. The corporate index had a slightly longer duration, so this figure was scaled down.

[13] Bloomberg series CSIYUS for the 15 years 1995–2009. It is coincidental that the 139 bps figure for high yield bonds outperforming U.S. Treasurys over this period is the same as the one cited in the previous footnote.

Merton's structural model notes that in a corporation, bondholders' claims on assets are superior to equity holders' claims. The value of a corporate enterprise can be written $V = D + E$, where V is the overall enterprise value, D is the principal amount of debt the company owes, and E is the remaining equity. To illustrate Merton's point, assume that there is only one kind of debt which matures at one time T in the future. If at time T the value V of the enterprise is greater than the principal amount D of the debt, then debt holders will be repaid and equity holders will have assets worth $V - D = E$. If, however, the value V is less than D, then the equity holders will receive nothing and the debt holders will seize the entire value V of the corporation.

The payoff pattern to the equity holders at time T is $\max(0, V - D)$. This is the payoff pattern of a call option on an underlying asset V with strike price D. The basic option conversion equation

$$V - Call = e^{-rT}D - Put \tag{15.27}$$

can therefore be used to value the risk of credit default. The left-hand side of the equation removes the equity holders' value from the overall value V of the enterprise. That leaves the debt holders' value on the right-hand side. The expression $e^{-rT}D$ is the value of a default-free zero-coupon bond such as a U.S. Treasury bond. Thus the right-hand side of Expression (15.27) shows that bondholders will need additional compensation over U.S. Treasury bonds, and that additional compensation will equal the value of a put option struck at the principal value D of the debt and maturing at time T. Often the volatility of the firm's equity is used as an input to an option pricing formula to obtain the value of the put.

Does the value of the put obtained from the structural model explain the extra compensation received by investment grade bond investors in many time periods? Numerous empirical tests have been conducted leading to a clear conclusion: the structural model explains only a small portion of the extra compensation for investment grade bonds. None of the many refinements and follow-ups to the Merton structural model has definitively answered the "credit spread premium puzzle" – why is the compensation for taking investment grade credit risk as large as it is?

Krainer (2004) reviews some of the explanations for the credit spread – tax treatment, bond market illiquidity, and generally changing levels of systemic risk aversion that can't be diversified away. Current explanations either fail to explain empirical behavior fully, or require fitting so that they don't produce any testable hypothesis or prediction.

In Figure 15.11 we obtained a spread between the yields of corporate bonds and U.S. Treasury bonds simply by subtracting. An extension of Expression (15.3) is often used to extract a spread that takes into account the term structure of interest rates

$$P = \sum_{i=1}^{n} \frac{f_i}{(1 + z_{t_i} + s)^{t_i}}. \tag{15.28}$$

Just as yield y is defined by Expression (15.1), so spread s is defined by Expression (15.28). Inputs to Expression (15.28) are the market observable price P of a bond, the cash flow structure of the bond, and the discount rates z_{t_i} obtained from prices of default-free bonds used to make up the spot curve. The output of Expression (15.28) is the number s that makes it an equality. The spread s may embody small influences – such as the difference between on-the-run (recently issued) U.S. Treasurys and off-the-run (seasoned) U.S. Treasurys. Or it may embody very large differences – the bond being priced could be a defaulted Polish corporate issue while the basic curve could be the U.S. Treasury curve.

Expression (15.28) contemplates a single spread s at all times; a further refinement could be to allow s to be time-varying and to form a spread curve. If the spread s introduced in Expression (15.28) is uncorrelated with the discount curve z_{t_i} and/or is small compared to the curve discount factors, then Expression (15.28) is a useful way to organize knowledge about default-free interest rates and the additional factors that go into defining the spread. On the other hand, if s is very large in size and/or volatility, then Expression (15.28) may not be a useful way of organizing knowledge about the bond being priced. For example, the price of a defaulted Polish bond will have almost no relationship to movements in the U.S. Treasury curve: it is far more likely that price movements of such a bond will respond mainly to idiosyncratic developments in the particular defaulted company's fortunes. Terms like z_{t_i} are likely in this case to be irrelevant in Expression (15.28), as all the price movement will be captured in movements of s.

While structural credit models attempt to use the capital structure of the firm to explain credit default risk, reduced form models first introduced by Jarrow and Turnbull (1992) use market observable data rather than corporate-finance-observable data. Thus with a reduced form model, market observables such as index volatilities and economic data may be used to calibrate processes that estimate the value of the spread s obtained from Expression (15.28).

Volatility is a common theme in both reduced form models and structural models of credit risk. The value of the option on the right-hand side of Expression (15.27) depends on the volatility of the enterprise value, while reduced form models almost always use equity volatility as an explanatory factor for credit spreads. The correlation between the CBOE VIX index of implied volatilities from U.S. S&P 500 index options was 62% with Aaa spreads (the bottom line in Figure 15.11) and 69% with Baa spreads from 1986–2009,[14] confirming that over long periods of time a large portion of credit spread movement is due to changes in market volatility. The connection is most pronounced during market shocks when both volatilities and credit spreads suddenly expand; during other times the connection can be more tenuous.

The correlations between default-free rate movements and corporate credit spread movements between 1920 and 2009 are shown in Figure 15.12. While most decades have a correlation near −60%, the 1930s and the 2000s show that unusual economic stress, together with fiscal and monetary response, can cause a regime shift. There was no

[14] (http://www.cboe.com/micro/vix/historical.aspx). Based on an older methodology (VXO) with monthly data from June 1986 to Decemeber 1989, and current methodology monthly from January 1990 to December 2009.

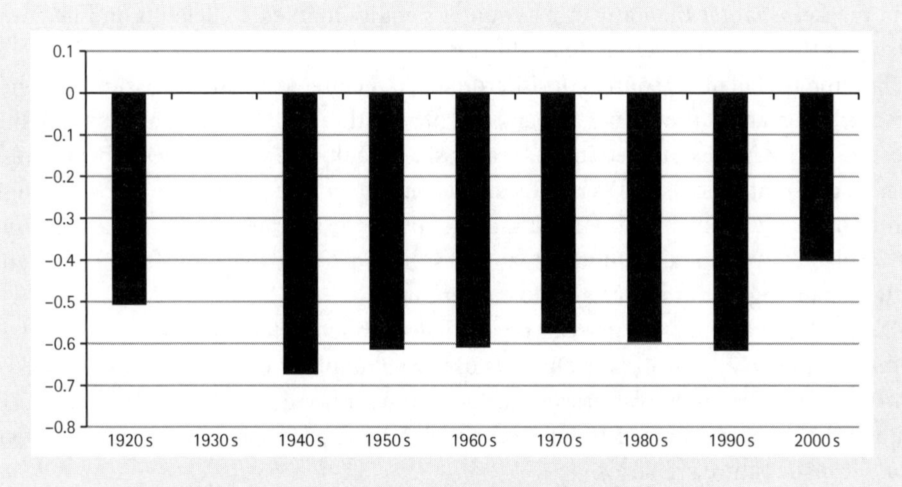

FIGURE 15.12 Rate/spread change correlations by decade.

correlation at all between rates and spreads in the 1930s, and the correlation between rates and spreads in the two years 2007–2008 was a statistically insignificant −11%.

Credit risk, like other aspects of the fixed income market, responds to multiple influences in ways that change in different economic regimes. The most obvious explanation of credit spreads is that they compensate for the possibility of loss given default. However, even after adding compensation not only for the average default loss, but also for aversion to taking the risk of default loss, credit-risky bond holders in the U.S. have often received more than has been required by these factors.

Part of this may be due to survivor bias: the fact that the U.S. would not have a major break in its legal or economic system over this period was not known at the beginning of the period. Holders of Chinese or Russian bonds issued in the early 1900s were certainly not overcompensated for holding credit-risky bonds compared to (say) U.S. Treasurys. Credit spreads' relationships with key influences such as default-free interest rates and equity market volatility therefore change as economic regimes change, especially as the possibility of changes to, or complete rupture in, the economic and legal system seem more likely.

15.9 Conclusions

The global fixed income market is large and diverse. Public and private debt is twice as large as the global equity market, and is 60% larger than world GDP. The components of the global fixed income market are so large that movements in these components have major impacts on economic conditions everywhere. For example, the U.S. mortgage debt market is larger than any other country's equity market, so defaults and hedging related to this market reverberate worldwide.

If we remove all other sources of risk from fixed income instruments, assuming complete certainty about the timing and amount of all future cash flows, we are left with the most basic risk in this market: interest rate risk. Default-free yield curves show interest rates at different tenors, and generally show some structure arising from no-arbitrage conditions. However, since the fixed income market is a dealer market dependent on the availability of capital to function, at times there can be departures from consistent patterns ranging from minor to complete rupture.

Future paths of interest rates can be simulated under a class of models that started with Vasicek (1977). More recent models use large numbers of observations of market data such as prices and volatilities in the government bond and/or LIBOR markets to calibrate their parameters. The future paths can be used to price instruments under many realistic future scenarios.

While there may be a large number of observations making up a default-free yield curve, generally there is a smaller number – usually between three and six – of key parameters or principal components that capture most of the information in the yield curve. Two key components – level and slope – show changing volatility and correlation parameters over long periods. However, adjusting these components by normalizing for recent past volatility and correlation behavior produces more well-behaved series, showing that recent relationships have persistence.

A common technique in fixed income analysis to use duration, a measure of a bond's response to changes in yields, to produce a description of an entire portfolio's response to change in yields. Since different bonds' yields respond to different influences, combining durations can be problematic. Fixed income risk is multi-dimensional and cannot be reduced to a single number.

If bonds have uncertainty about whether the borrower will be able to pay all the scheduled cash flows on time and in full, credit risk arises. In the U.S., average losses due to credit defaults are often lower than the compensation that credit-risky bond holders receive in the form of extra yield over similar default-free bonds. Part of this increased yield is payment for taking on risk; part is a result of the factors that make total returns of indices disproportionate to yield differences; but there remains a credit spread premium puzzle where the size and variability of credit spreads is often larger than theoretical models can explain. Managing credit risk, like managing interest rate risk, requires an understanding of changing relationships as economic regimes shift.

References

Black, F., Derman, E., and Toy, W. (1990). A one-factor model of interest rates and its application to treasury bond options. *Financial Analysts Journal*, **46**, 24–32.

Black, F. and Karasinski, P. (1991). Bond and option pricing when short rates are lognormal. *Financial Analysts Journal*, **47**, 52–59.

Carlson, M. (2006). A brief history of the 1987 stock market crash. Federal Reserve Board Finance and Economics Discussion Series, http://www.federalreserve.gov/Pubs/feds/2007/200713/200713pap.pdf

Cox, J., Ingersoll, J., and Ross, S. (1985). A theory of the term structure of interest rates. *Econometrica* **53**, 385–407.

Diebold, F.X. and Li, C. (2006). Forecasting the term structure of government bond yields. *Journal of Econometrics*, **130**, 337–364.

Fabozzi, F. (2006) *Fixed Income Mathematics*, McGraw-Hill, New York.

Hagan, P. and West, G. (2006). Interpolation methods for curve construction. *Applied Mathematical Finance* 13(2), 89–129.

Ho, T. and Lee, S.B. (1986). Term structure movements and pricing interest rate contingent claims. *Journal of Finance*, **41**, 1011–1029.

Hull, J. and White, A. (1990). Pricing interest-rate derivative securities. *The Review of Financial Studies*, **3**, 573–592.

International Monetary Fund, Global Financial Stability Report (October 2010). (http://www.imf.org/external/pubs/ft/gfsr/2010/02/pdf/text.pdf Statistical appendix http://www.imf.org/external/pubs/ft/gfsr/2010/02/pdf/statappx.pdf).

Jarrow, R. and Turnbull, S. (1992). Credit risk: Drawing the analogy. *Risk Magazine* **5**(9), 63–70.

Knight, F. (1921). *Risk, Uncertainty and Profit*. Houghton Mifflin, New York.

Krainer, J. (2004). "What determines the credit spread?" http://www.frbsf.org/publications/economics/letter/2004/el2004-36.pdf

Litterman, R. and Scheinkman, J. (1991). Common factors affecting bond returns. *Journal of Fixed Income*, **1**, 54–61.

Merton, R.C. (1974). On the pricing of corporate debt: The risk structure of interest rates. *Journal of Finance*, **29**, 449–70.

Moody's Investor Service (2010). *Corporate Default and Recovery Rates, 1920–2009*.

Nelson, C. and Siegel, A. (1987). Parsimonious modeling of yield curves. *Journal of Business* **60**(4), 473–479.

Rebonato, R. (2002). *Modern Pricing of Interest-Rate Derivatives: The LIBOR Market Model and Beyond*. Princeton University Press, Princeton.

Rendleman, R. and Bartter, B. (1980). The pricing of options on debt securities. *Journal of Financial and Quantitative Analysis*, **15**, 11–24.

SIFMA (Securities Industry and Financial Markets Association), www.sifma.org/ uploadedFiles/Research/Statistics/SIFMA_USBondMarketOutstanding.xls accessed October 2010.

Uhlenbeck, G. and Ornstein, L. (1930). On the theory of Brownian motion. *Physical Review* **36**, 823–41.

United States Federal Reserve (1943, 1966). *Banking and Monetary Statistics* (http://fraser.stlouisfed.org/publications/bms_supp/issue/1562/download/6044/Section_12.pdf).

United States Treasury (2010). Statement of Public Debt, http://www.treasurydirect.gov/govt/reports/pd/mspd/mspd.htm accessed October, 2010.

Vasicek, O. (1977). An equilibrium characterisation of the term structure. *Journal of Financial Economics* **5**, 177–188.

Wise, M. and Bhansali, V. (2010). *Fixed Income Finance*. McGraw-Hill, New York.

CHAPTER 16

RISK MANAGEMENT FOR LONG-SHORT PORTFOLIOS*

THOMAS HEWETT AND KENNETH WINSTON

In this chapter we examine the differences between distributions associated with long-short investing and those associated with long-only investing. We take the difference of two geometric Brownian motions – which is not itself a geometric Brownian motion – to represent long-short outcomes. We don't suggest that this is the most realistic model of fund returns, but we are able to obtain a surprising amount of insight while providing a base for further analysis.

Previous hedge fund literature (Getmansky, Lo, and Makarov 2004; Kat and Lu 2005) concentrates on the statistical properties of hedge fund return series, such as the consequences of investing in illiquid securities and infrequent data sampling. Other work uses style analysis and factor models for hedge fund returns (Brown and Goetzmann 2003; Fung and Hsieh 1999, 2001, 2002, 2003; Dor and Jagannathan 2002; Kat and Palaro 2005; Agarwal and Naik 2004; Bondarenko 2004) to examine the nature of the option-like returns resulting from certain hedge fund investment strategies.

Others have employed continuous stochastic processes to analyze options contingent on hedge fund returns – for example to price fee structures (Goetzmann, Ingersoll, and Ross 2001) or options on hedge funds (Atlan, German, and York 2006). Our approach is similar to that of Kritzman and Rich (1998, 2002) in that we reverse this process and use insights from the pricing of options (Kirk 1995; Carmona and Durrleman 2003; Lee 2004) to draw conclusions about hedge fund risks.

A linear combination of lognormal distributions is not itself lognormal. This is common knowledge, but is often ignored in finance. When a covariance matrix C, whose (i, j) entry is the covariance σ_{ij} between the log-returns of the ith security and the

* We gratefully acknowledge comments by Andrey Ukhov, Petter Kolm, and Lisa Goldberg. All errors remain the responsibility of the authors.

log-returns of the jth security, is formed, many analysts assume that a portfolio with weight vector w is lognormally distributed with variance $w^T Cw$.

In the context of long-only portfolios (positive linear combinations), if security returns are similar in magnitude or the portfolio is rebalanced, then log-returns are not too different from simple returns, and this assumption may not be too far off. However, this approximation breaks down for long-short portfolios, where portfolio value may go negative. Thus when shorts are permitted one cannot compute distributional risk metrics such as value-at-risk by simply choosing a multiple of the standard deviation according to the inverse of the standard cumulative normal distribution function. That will never get us to negative values since the worst case for a lognormal distribution is zero.

In practice it is unlikely that a portfolio would be allowed to go bankrupt unless there was a gap move that could not be managed. Instead, the portfolio would be modified with stop losses, lowered leverage, lowered volatility, or other risk management techniques. Our intention in this chapter is to present a tractable model for when unmanaged long-short portfolios go bankrupt or otherwise achieve an unacceptable result. From this model we can investigate the effectiveness of different risk management techniques. We will derive approximations for the distribution of terminal value and the stopping time to a drawdown barrier as well as the probability of achieving a given terminal value conditional on avoiding a specified drawdown level.

As an application of these methods, we consider a simple form of risk management – keeping leverage constant – and show how that affects the distribution of outcomes. In a future publication we intend to examine alternative risk management techniques and their impacts on the return process.

16.1 The Standard Multivariate Lognormal Model

We first make the mathematically tractable assumption that there is a long portfolio,L, and a short portfolio, S, that follow correlated geometric Brownian motion (hereafter "GBM") according to

$$\frac{dL}{L} = \alpha_L dt + \sigma_L dZ_L \quad \frac{dS}{S} = \alpha_S dt + \sigma_S dZ_S \quad dZ_L dZ_S = \rho dt. \tag{16.1}$$

We will assume throughout that both the long and short portfolios are themselves long-only portfolios – they consist of non-negative holdings of assets that have a minimum value of zero. The actual portfolio we hold at time t is $L(t) - S(t)$. We assume an initial normalizing budget constraint $L(0) - S(0) = 1$ and denote leverage by $\lambda(t) = \frac{L(t)+S(t)}{L(t)-S(t)}$. Thus initial leverage is the sum of the longs and the shorts.

The vector $(L(t), S(t))$ follows a multivariate lognormal distribution. If we wish to mimic the familiar long-only portfolio risk/return calculation based on a weighted sum of simple constituent returns, we may proceed as follows. The expected values of annual simple returns are (see Law and Kelton 2000 or Aitchison and Brown 1957):

$$E(L(1)/L(0)) - 1 = \bar{\alpha}_L = \exp(\alpha_L) - 1$$
$$E(S(1)/S(0)) - 1 = \bar{\alpha}_S = \exp(\alpha_S) - 1.$$

The variances of, and correlation between, $L(1)$ and $S(1)$ are given in terms of the GBM parameters of (16.1) by:

$$\bar{\sigma}_L^2 = Var(L(1)) = \exp(2\alpha_L)\left(\exp\left(\sigma_L^2\right) - 1\right)$$
$$\bar{\sigma}_S^2 = Val(S(1)) = \exp(2\alpha_S)\left(\exp\left(\sigma_S^2\right) - 1\right)$$
$$\bar{\rho} = Cor(L(1), S(1)) = \frac{\exp(\rho\sigma_L\sigma_S) - 1}{\sqrt{\left(\exp\left(\sigma_L^2\right) - 1\right)\left(\exp\left(\sigma_S^2\right) - 1\right)}}.$$

The portfolio expected return and variance may be derived from the initial weight vector $(L(0), -S(0))$ and the moments above as

$$\bar{\alpha}_P = L(0)\bar{\alpha}_L - S(0)\bar{\alpha}_S$$
$$\bar{\sigma}_P^2 = L(0)^2\bar{\sigma}_L^2 + S(0)^2\bar{\sigma}_S^2 - 2\bar{\rho}\bar{\sigma}_L\bar{\sigma}_S L(0)S(0).$$

We can define these quantities formally, but the assumption that $L(1) - S(1)$ follows a lognormal distribution with these moments is incorrect. Nevertheless, as we noted above many analysts implicitly do this.

If we ignore this problem and persist in attempting to recover the parameters of a supposed (but nonexistent) underlying GBM

$$\frac{d(L - S)}{L - S} = \alpha_P dt + \sigma_P dZ_P$$

we may invert the parameter transformations above to obtain

$$\alpha_P = \ln(1 + \bar{\alpha}_P)$$
$$\sigma_P^2 = \ln\left(1 + \frac{\bar{\sigma}_P^2}{(1 + \bar{\alpha}_P)^2}\right).$$

This is similar to, although not exactly the same as, the Fenton–Wilkinson approximation (Fenton 1960), which originated in signal processing. Signal processing analysts have noted that the Fenton–Wilkinson approximation breaks down when parameters are not close to zero.

Consider the parameters in Table 16.1. They describe a skilled long-short manager – one with 300 bp skill in picking good long investments and 200 bp skill in picking bad

Table 16.1 Sample parameter set.

Parameter	Description	Value
α_L	Long side drift	3%
σ_L	Long side volatility	20%
α_S	Short side drift	−2%
σ_S	Short side volatility	15%
ρ	Long/short correlation	0.80
L(0)	Initial long	3.5
S(0)	Initial short	2.5
	Derived parameters	
$\bar{\alpha}_L$	Transformed long drift	3.05%
$\bar{\sigma}_L$	Transformed long volatility	20.82%
$\bar{\alpha}_S$	Transformed short drift	−1.98%
$\bar{\sigma}_S$	Transformed short volatility	14.79%
$\bar{\rho}$	Transformed correlation	0.80
$\bar{\alpha}_P$	Portfolio expected simple return	15.61%
$\bar{\sigma}_P$	Portfolio simple return volatility	48.80%
α_P	Assumed lognormal portfolio drift	14.50%
σ_P	Assumed lognormal portfolio volatility	40.49%

short investments. The long and short sides are 80% correlated, and initial leverage is 6 – a very risky portfolio. All time-dependent parameters are annualized.

We generated 100,000 values of $L(1) - S(1)$ using a Monte Carlo simulation where

$$L(T) = L(0)\exp\left(\left(\alpha_L - \sigma_L^2/2\right)T + \sqrt{T}\sigma_L\left(Z_1\sqrt{(1+\rho)/2} + Z_2\sqrt{(1-\rho)/2}\right)\right)$$

and

$$S(T) = S(0)\exp\left(\left(\alpha_S - \sigma_S^2/2\right)T + \sqrt{T}\sigma_S\left(Z_1\sqrt{(1+\rho)/2} - Z_2\sqrt{(1-\rho)/2}\right)\right)$$

where Z_1 and Z_2 are independent draws from an N(0,1) distribution and $T = 1$. Figure 16.1 shows the difference between the simulated portfolio density and the assumed lognormal fit. Clearly they are significantly different.

Deviations from normal become even more pronounced as time T increases, correlation decreases, leverage increases, and volatility increases. Thus we need a better model of long-short portfolio behavior.[1]

[1] For low correlation and approximately equal long and short volatility, the difference of two lognormal random variables more closely resembles a normal distribution than a lognormal. Hence the Gaussian spread option pricing model proposed by Shimko. See Carmona and Durrleman (2003) for details.

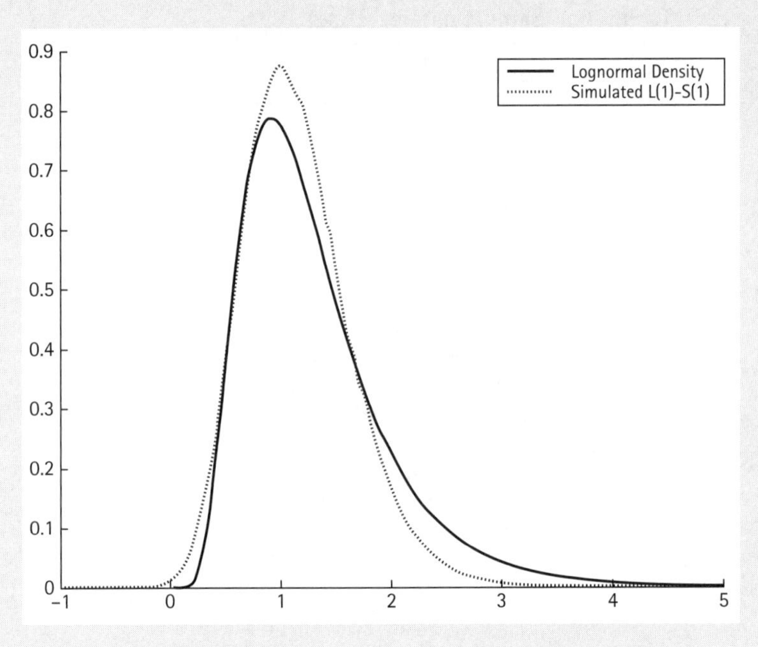

FIGURE 16.1 Lognormal vs. difference of lognormal.

16.2 Ratio Analysis

In this section, we consider the ratio $\frac{L(T)}{S(T)}$. Bankruptcy (or worse) may be characterized by the condition[2] $\frac{L(T)}{S(T)} \leq 1$. This line of reasoning is fruitful because a ratio of lognormal random variables is itself lognormal. First we derive the process followed by $f = \frac{L}{S}$. By Itô's lemma

$$df = \nabla f \bullet d(L,S)' + \frac{1}{2} d(L,S) H(f) d(L,S)'$$

$$S^2 df = (S, -L) \bullet d(L,S)' + \frac{1}{2} d(L,S) \begin{pmatrix} 0 & -1 \\ -1 & \frac{2L}{S} \end{pmatrix} d(L,S)'$$

where $H(f)$ denotes the Hessian matrix of second-order derivatives of f. Substituting for dL and dS and simplifying gives

$$\frac{df}{f} = \left(\alpha_L - \alpha_S + {\sigma_S}^2 - \rho\sigma_L\sigma_S\right) dt + \sigma_L dZ_L - \sigma_S dZ_S$$

[2] From a practical perspective, this is a somewhat unsatisfactory characterization of bankruptcy as one may have $L(T) \to 0$ and $S(T) \to 0$ while $\frac{L(T)}{S(T)} \gg 1$. This will be addressed in the next section.

or

$$\frac{df}{f} = Adt + \Sigma dZ$$

where

$$\begin{aligned} A &= \alpha_L - \alpha_S + \sigma_S^2 - \rho\sigma_L\sigma_S \\ \Sigma^2 &= \sigma_L^2 + \sigma_S^2 - 2\rho\sigma_L\sigma_S \\ \Sigma dZ &= \sigma_L dZ_L - \sigma_S dZ_S \end{aligned} \tag{16.2}$$

so

$$f = f(0)\exp\left((A - \Sigma^2/2)T + \Sigma Z\sqrt{T}\right)$$

where $Z \sim N(0,1)$.

16.2.1 Terminal Distribution

Thus the long-short ratio is itself lognormal, and it follows that its distribution is given exactly by

$$P(L(T)/S(T) \leq r) = P\left(Z \leq \frac{\ln\left(\frac{r}{f(0)}\right) - (A - \Sigma^2/2)T}{\Sigma\sqrt{T}}\right) = N(D_1) \tag{16.3}$$

where N(·) is the standard cumulative normal distribution function and

$$D_1 = \frac{\ln\left(\frac{rS(0)}{L(0)}\right) - (A - \Sigma^2/2)T}{\Sigma\sqrt{T}}.$$

Figure 16.2 illustrates the response of (16.3) to a range of volatilities – with the remaining parameters as specified in Table 16.1. It is evident from Figure 16.2 that for large values of the volatility parameters the effect on the failure probability of increasing long vol, σ_L, and short vol, σ_S, is quite different. For high enough values of σ_L, increasing σ_S reduces the failure probability. This is due to the asymmetry of the Itô adjustment in the drift equation of (16.2), which contains an additional term increasing in σ_S.

16.2.2 Stopping Time

The probability of failure as expressed in (16.3) does not reflect economic reality since it is a terminal value that does not take into account the absorbing barrier of bankruptcy or termination by a client. The probability measured in (16.3) fails to account for paths that dip temporarily below the threshold level but recover by the end of the time horizon. To address this, we calculate the stopping time for drawdown to the threshold, r, namely:

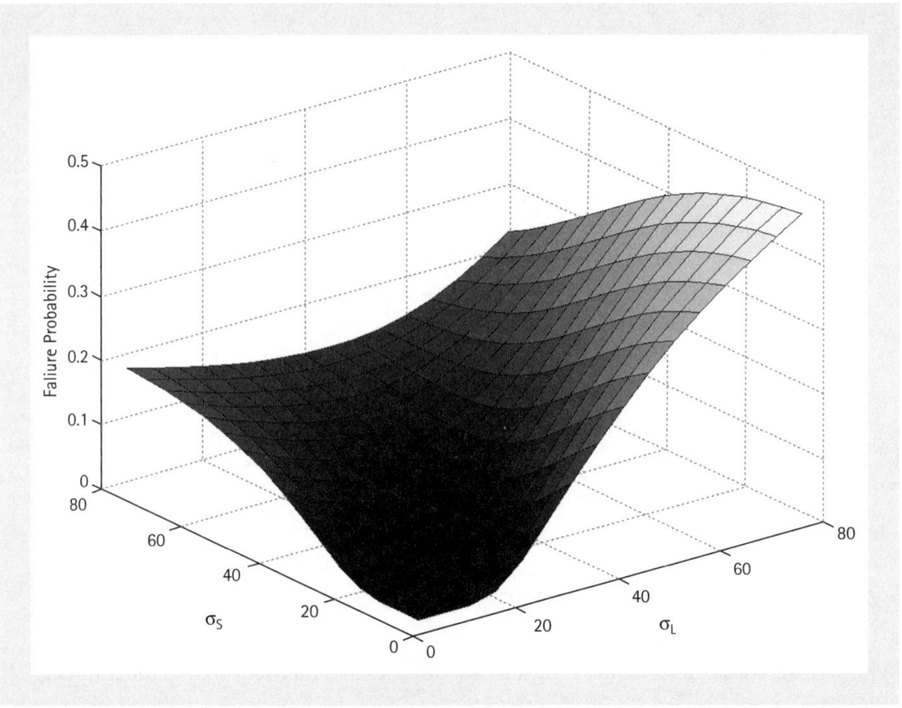

FIGURE 16.2 Equation (16.3): $P(L(T)/S(T) < r)$, $r = 1$, $T = 1$, $\lambda = 6$, GBM per Table 16.1.

$$\tau_r = inf\{t : t > 0, L(t)/S(t) \leq r\}.$$

This is a well-known problem – variously called the first passage, absorbing barrier, or stopping time problem. The standard tool for this problem – found, for example, in Musiela and Rutkowski (1998) – computes the cumulative distribution function of the minimum value achieved by an arithmetic Brownian motion over an interval.

M&R Corollary 3.3 Let $g = at + sW$ be an arithmetic Brownian motion driven by a Wiener process, W, and let $m_T^g = \underset{u \in [0,T]}{inf} (g(u))$. Then for every y < 0,

$$P\left(m_T^g \geq y\right) = N\left(\frac{-y + aT}{s\sqrt{T}}\right) - \exp(2ay/s^2)N\left(\frac{y + aT}{s\sqrt{T}}\right).$$

We apply this result to the arithmetic Brownian motion $g(t) = \ln(f(t)) - \ln(f(0))$. By Itô's lemma $dg = (A - \Sigma^2/2)dt + \Sigma dZ$. Assuming $L(0)/S(0) \geq r$, we have

$$\begin{aligned}
&\tau_r \geq T \\
&\Leftrightarrow \forall u < T : \tfrac{L(u)}{S(u)} \geq r \\
&\Leftrightarrow \forall u < T : g(u) \geq -\ln(f(0)/r) \\
&\Leftrightarrow \forall u < T : m_T^g \geq -\ln(f(0)/r).
\end{aligned}$$

It follows from the result above that

$$P\left(\inf_{t\in[0,T]}\left(\frac{L(t)}{S(t)}\right)\leq r\right)=P\left(\tau_r\leq T\right)=1-P\left(m_T^g\geq-\ln\left(\mathrm{f(0)}/_\mathrm{r}\right)\right)$$
$$=N(D_1)+\left(\frac{L(0)}{rS(0)}\right)^{1-\frac{2A}{\Sigma^2}}N(D_2) \tag{16.4}$$

where

$$D_1=\frac{\ln\left(\frac{rS(0)}{L(0)}\right)-(A-\Sigma^2/2)T}{\Sigma\sqrt{T}}$$

as above and

$$D_2=D_1+2\frac{\left(A-\Sigma^2/2\right)\sqrt{T}}{\Sigma}.$$

Thus the probability of hitting the absorbing barrier is the failure probability (16.3) – that is, $N(D_1)$ – plus another positive term representing the probability of dipping below the barrier level prior to T.

Figure 16.3 shows the volatility dependence of this incremental probability, namely the difference between (16.4) and (16.3). The remaining parameters are the same as those in Table 16.1. The surface is complex, but generally shows increasing incremental probability in short volatility. In long volatility, incremental probability increases to a point, and then tails off at very high levels. As we've indicated above, this asymmetry between long volatility and short volatility arises from expression (16.2).

16.3 Difference Analysis

We now extend the previous section's results to the arithmetic value of the long-short portfolio at time T, $L(T)-S(T)$. Bankruptcy may be characterized equivalently in ratio terms or in difference terms as

$$\frac{L(T)}{S(T)}\leq 1 \text{ or } L(T)-S(T)\leq 0.$$

If the only condition we care about is complete bankruptcy, there is no point in looking at the difference, since the ratio analysis suffices. However, as noted in the footnote above, one may have $L(T)\to 0$ and $S(T)\to 0$ while $\frac{L(T)}{S(T)}\gg 1$. For example we could start with say \$100 million of capital and lose both on the long and on the short side in such a way that we never actually went bankrupt, but ended up with two cents worth of longs and one cent worth of short. This would have a perfectly acceptable long-short ratio but would presumably be a matter of concern for an investor with an interest in

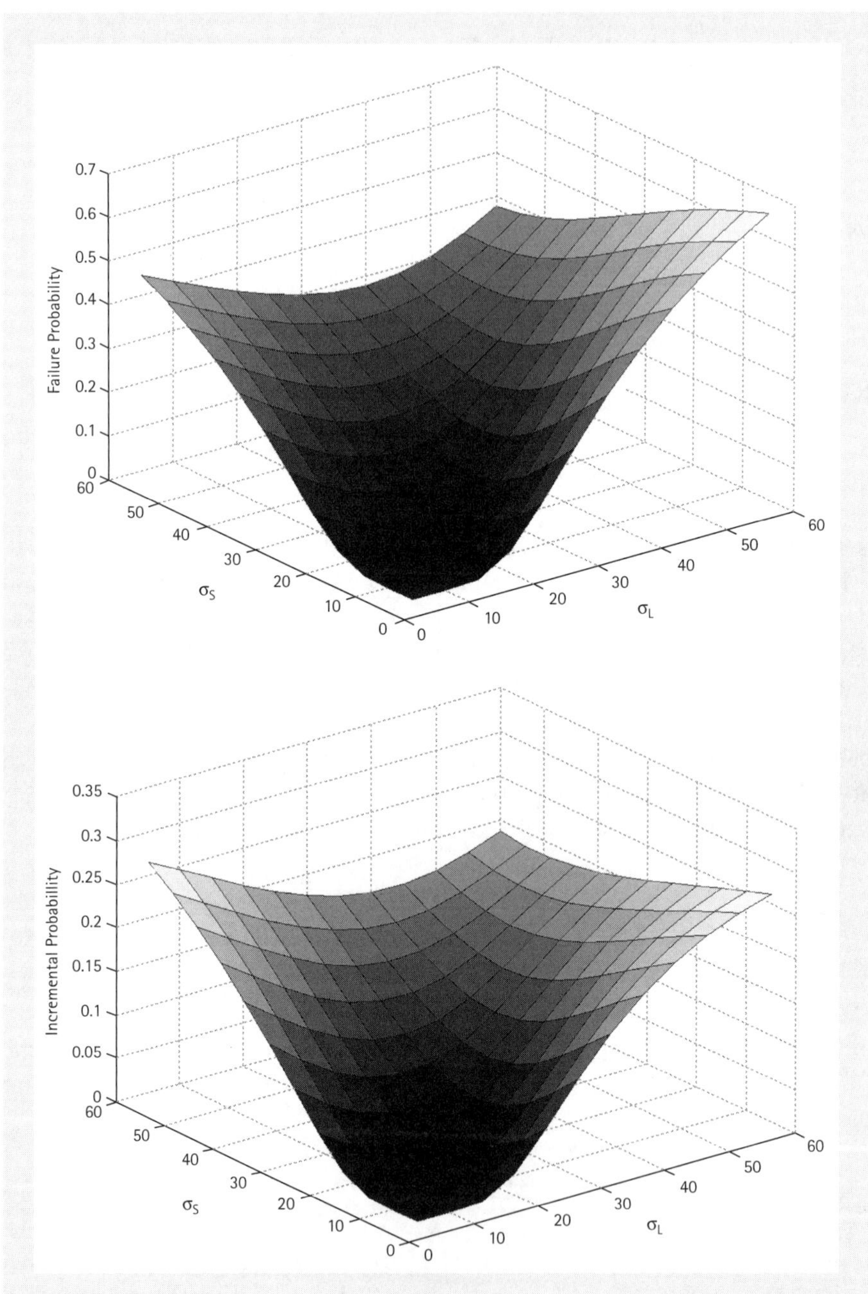

FIGURE 16.3 (a) Equation (16.4), $r = 1$, $T = 1$, $\lambda = 6$, GBM per Table 16.1; (b) Equations (16.3) and (16.4), $r = 1$, $T = 1$, $\lambda = 6$, GBM per Table 16.1.

$L(t) - S(t)$. Therefore, to better reflect economic reality, we should study the condition $L(T) - S(T) \leq k$.

16.3.1 The Kirk Approximation

As we have noted previously, the difference between two lognormals in not a tractable distribution. In particular, there is no closed form analytic expression for $P(L(t) - S(t) < k)$. This problem manifests itself when one attempts to price spread options in the Black–Scholes framework - a problem for which there is no known closed form solution.[3] We may, however take advantage of an approximation due to Kirk (1995) and first applied in the pricing of commodity spread options. This approach is based on the simple observation that the conditions $L(T) - S(T) \leq k$ and $L(T)/(S(T) + k) \leq 1$ are equivalent. The approximation comes in assuming that $S(t) + k$ follows a GBM.[4] In particular:

$$\begin{aligned} \frac{d(S+k)}{S+k} &= \left(\frac{S}{S+k}\right)\frac{dS}{S} = \frac{S}{S+k}\left(\alpha_S dt + \sigma_S dZ_S\right) \\ &\approx \frac{S(0)}{S(0)+k}\left(\alpha_S dt + \sigma_S dZ_S\right). \end{aligned} \tag{16.5}$$

As we will use the adjustment factor in this approximation frequently, we define the scale factor

$$SF = \frac{S(0)}{S(0)+k}.$$

This approximation works remarkably well, as we will show with Monte Carlo analysis. The appendix discusses the efficacy of this approximation.

16.3.2 Terminal Distribution

Applying the approximation (16.5) to the terminal distribution formula (16.3) we get

$$P(L(T) - S(T) \leq k) = P(L/(S+k) \leq 1) \approx N(\hat{D}_1) \tag{16.6}$$

[3] See (Haug 1998).

[4] This is not appropriate when k is negative. In this case a slightly different transformation is required as described in the appendix.

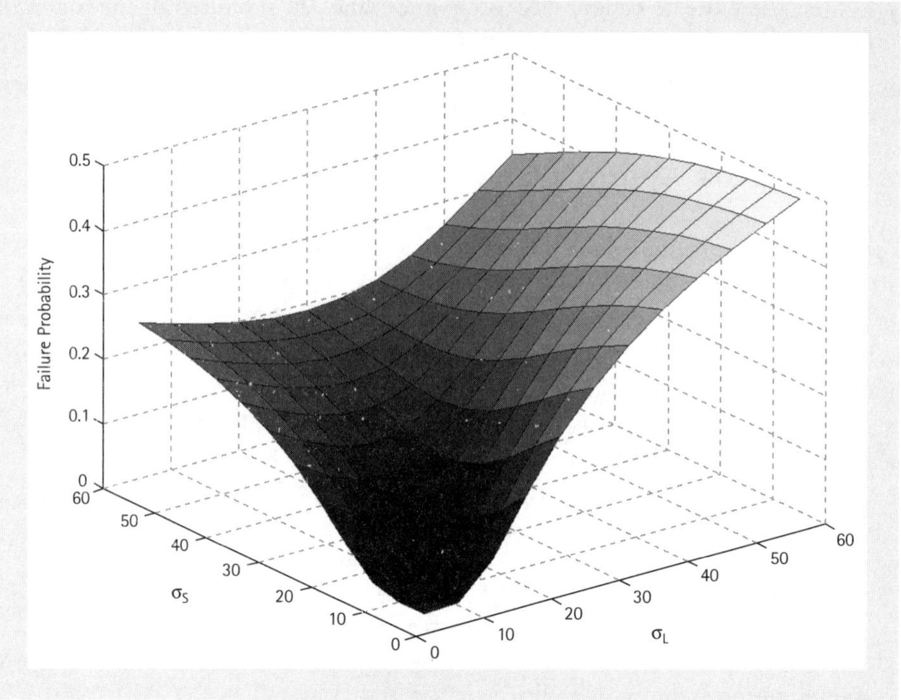

FIGURE 16.4 Equation (16.6) $P(L(T) - S(T) < k)$, $k = 0.5$, $T = 1$, $\lambda = 6$, GBM per Table 16.1.

where

$$\hat{A} = \alpha_L - SF\alpha_S + SF^2{\sigma_S}^2 - \rho\sigma_L\sigma_S SF$$

$$\hat{\Sigma}^2 = {\sigma_L}^2 + SF^2{\sigma_S}^2 - 2\sigma_L\sigma_S\rho SF$$

$$\hat{D}_1 = \frac{\ln\left(\frac{S(0)+k}{L(0)}\right) - (\hat{A} - \hat{\Sigma}^2/2)T}{\hat{\Sigma}\sqrt{T}}.$$

Note that (16.6) with $k = 0$ is the same as (16.3) with $r = 1$; that is, in the case of complete bankruptcy there is no approximation and the ratio and difference conditions coincide. The interesting differences come when k becomes larger than zero.[5] It is likely that a portfolio experiencing a 50% drawdown in a year would go out of business, so Figure 16.4 shows the probability surface with parameters similar to those in Figure 16.2, but with $k = .5$ instead of $k = 0$ $(r = 1)$.

[5] Differentiating (16.6) with respect to k, we obtain an approximate density function for $L(T) - S(T)$: $\varphi(k) \approx \frac{SF^2\sigma_S^2\left(\hat{\Sigma}+\hat{D}_1\sqrt{T}\right)-SF\left(\hat{\Sigma}\alpha_S T+\rho\sigma_L\sigma_S\hat{D}_1\sqrt{T}\right)+\hat{\Sigma}}{(S(0)+k)\hat{\Sigma}^2\sqrt{2\pi T}}\exp\left(-\hat{D}_1^2/2\right).$

16.3.3 Stopping Time to Drawdown Level, k

Mimicking our development in Section 16.2, we derive the stopping time to a minimum level k. We denote

$$\tau_k = inf\{t : t > 0, L(t) \leq S(t) + k\}$$

and obtain

$$\begin{aligned} P\left(\inf_{t\in[0,T]} (L(t) - S(t)) \leq k\right) &= P(\tau_k \leq T) \\ &\approx N(\hat{D}_1) + \left(\frac{L(0)}{S(0)+k}\right)^{1-\frac{2\hat{A}}{\hat{\Sigma}^2}} N(\hat{D}_2) \end{aligned} \tag{16.7}$$

where

$$\hat{D}_1 = \frac{\ln\left(\frac{S(0)+k}{L(0)}\right) - (\hat{A} - \hat{\Sigma}^2/2)T}{\hat{\Sigma}\sqrt{T}} \quad \text{and} \quad \hat{D}_2 = \hat{D}_1 + 2\frac{(\hat{A} - \hat{\Sigma}^2/2)\sqrt{T}}{\hat{\Sigma}}.$$

We note that (16.7) allows one to compute the risk metric described by Kritzman and Rich (2002) as the "Continuous Value at Risk", namely the quantile of the maximum loss distribution over the interval $[0, T]$. While VaR represents a loss at a fixed horizon, in our notation we may write for a quantile level q:

$$ContVaR_T^q = Max_k\{L(0) - S(0) - k | P(\tau_k < T) \leq 1 - q.\}.$$

This quantity may be derived by solving (16.7) for the k that causes the expression to equal $1 - q$. Unfortunately there is no analytic solution as k appears in the formula for $\hat{D}_1$. However, we may solve for k numerically.

As we saw with the ratio analysis, the difference between (16.7) and (16.6) is a positive quantity. Figure 16.5 graphs the added probability of failure due to this term; that is, due to the presence of an absorbing barrier. Comparing Figure 16.5 to Figure 16.3, one notes higher incremental probabilities.

Figures 16.2–16.5 have been based on the parameters of Table 16.1 with leverage of 6, but Figure 16.6 shows that the added probability of failure can be significant with lower leverage of 2, especially at higher volatilities.

As we expect, negative correlation is harmful in long-short portfolios as shown in Figure 16.7.

16.3.4 Monte Carlo Simulations

While the long-short ratio formulas (16.3) and (16.4) are exact, the difference formulas (16.5)–(16.7) are approximations. To assess the performance of the approximations above we performed a number of Monte Carlo simulations. First we examined

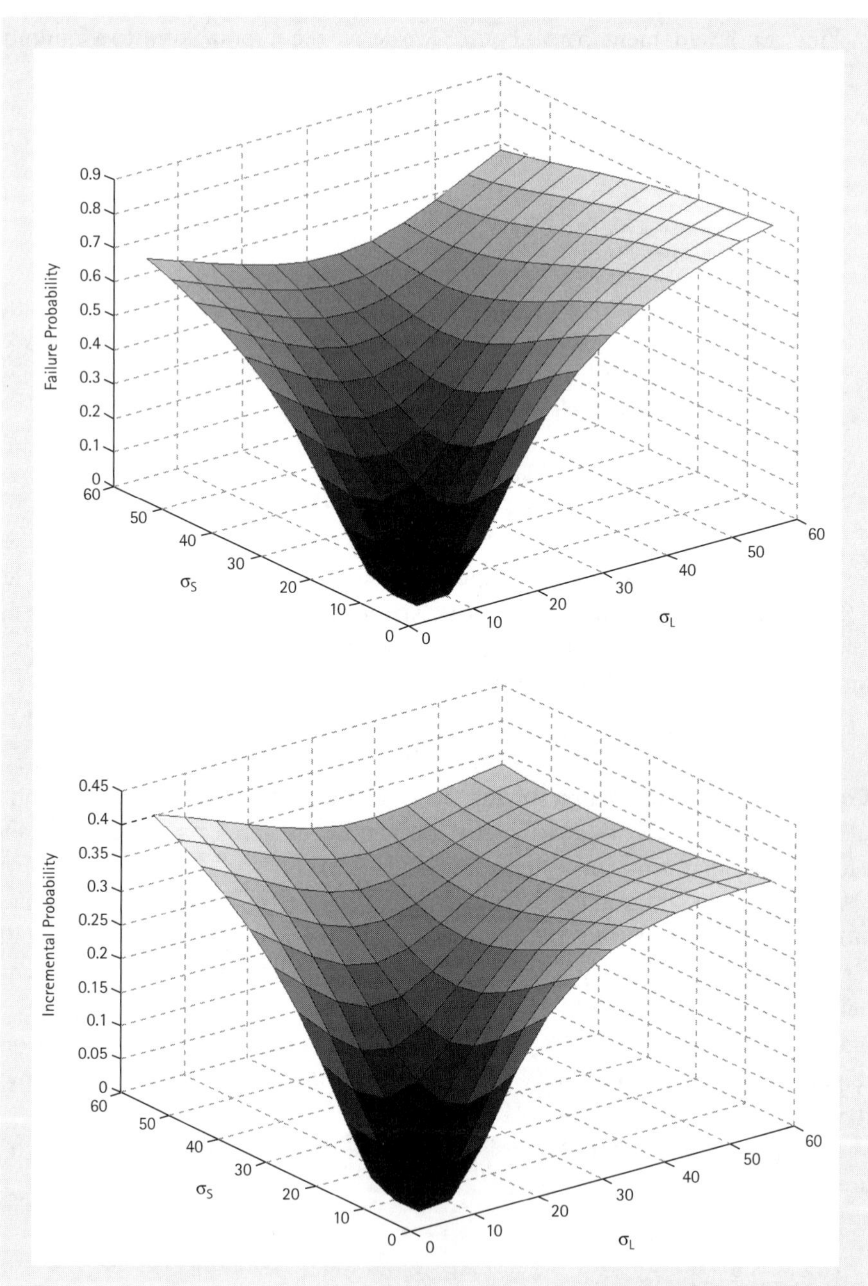

FIGURE 16.5 (a) Equation (16.7), $k = 0.5,\ T = 1,\ \lambda = 6,\ \rho = 0.8$, GBM per Table 16.1; (b) Equations (16.6) and (16.7) $k = 0.5,\ T = 1,\ \lambda = 6,\ \rho = 0.8$, GBM per Table 16.1.

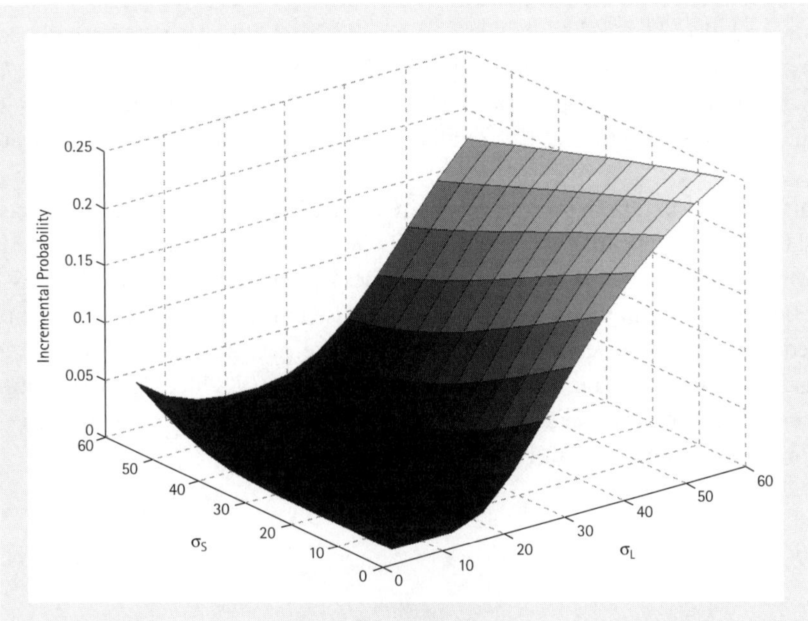

FIGURE 16.6 Equations (16.6) and (16.7), $k = 0.5$, $T = 1$, $\lambda = 2$, $\rho = 0.8$, GBM per Table 16.1.

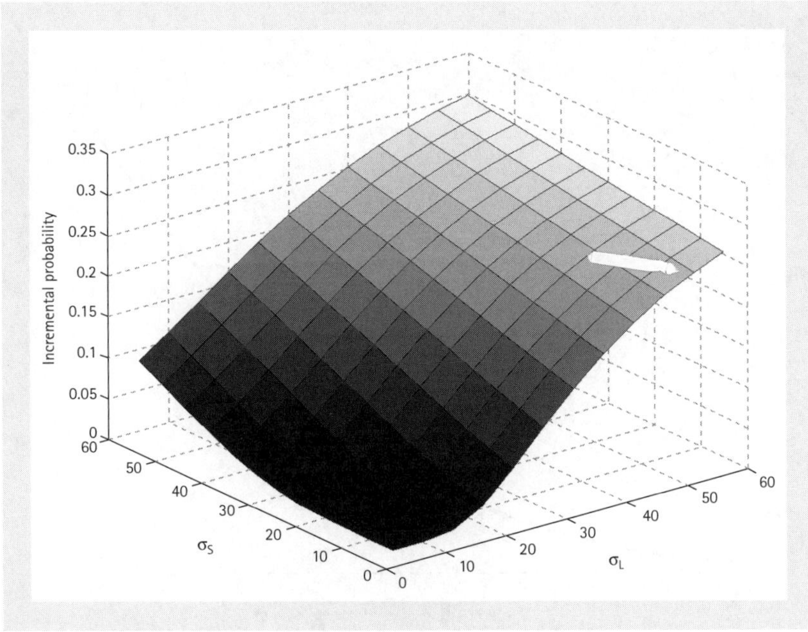

FIGURE 16.7 Equations (16.6) and (16.7), $k = 0.5$, $T = 1$, $\lambda = 2$, $\rho = -0.5$, GBM per Table 16.1.

Equation (16.6). 10,000 random draws were taken from a bivariate lognormal distribution and $P(L(T) - S(T) < k)$ was estimated from the simulated results as well as from (16.6) for a variety of combinations of the parameters $\alpha_L, \sigma_L, \alpha_S, \sigma_S, \rho, T$ as well as the initial leverage parameter $\lambda(0) = L(0) + S(0)$. We found no significant differences between (16.6) and the simulated results. Typical results are illustrated in Figures 16.8–16.10.

We also use simulation to test the approximation in (16.7). The time horizon was subdivided into time steps of 0.001 years and the Brownian motions were evolved. Stopping times were recorded when these discretized series breached the barrier $L(T) - S(T) < k$. 10,000 paths were simulated and the resulting distributions of the stopping times are recorded below for a variety of combinations of the parameters $\alpha_L, \sigma_L, \alpha_S, \sigma_S, \rho, T, k$ as well as the initial leverage parameter $\lambda(0) = L(0) + S(0)$. Once again, we found no significant differences between the simulated results and the approximation in (16.7). Typical results are illustrated in Figures 16.11–16.13.

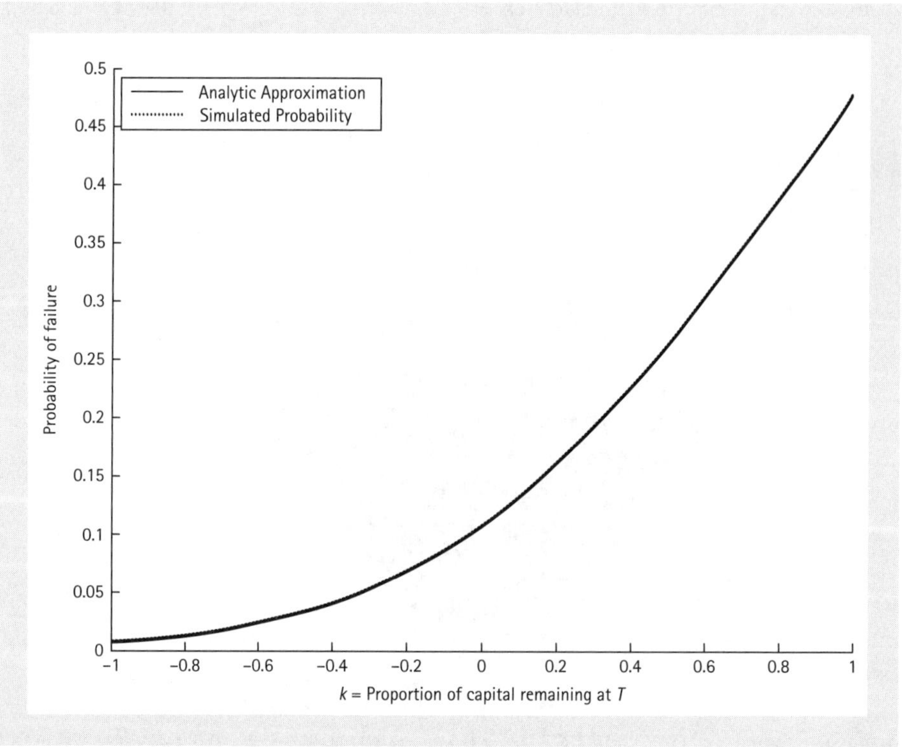

FIGURE 16.8 Equation (16.6): Horizon value CDF, $\alpha_L = 4\%$, $\sigma_L = 20\%$, $\alpha_S = 2\%$, $\sigma_S = 15\%$, $\rho = 30\%$, $L(0) = 4.5$, $S(0) = 3.5$, $T = 1$.

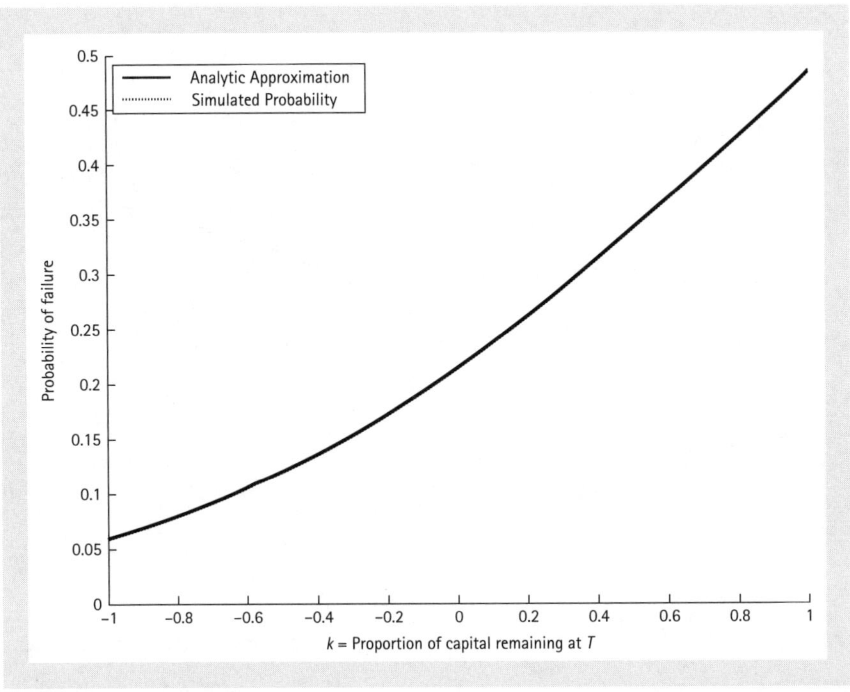

FIGURE 16.9 Equation (16.6): Horizon value CDF, $\alpha_L = 4\%$, $\sigma_L = 20\%$, $\alpha_S = 2\%$, $\sigma_S = 15\%$, $\rho = 80\%$, $L(0) = 4.5$, $S(0) = 3.5$, $T = 1$.

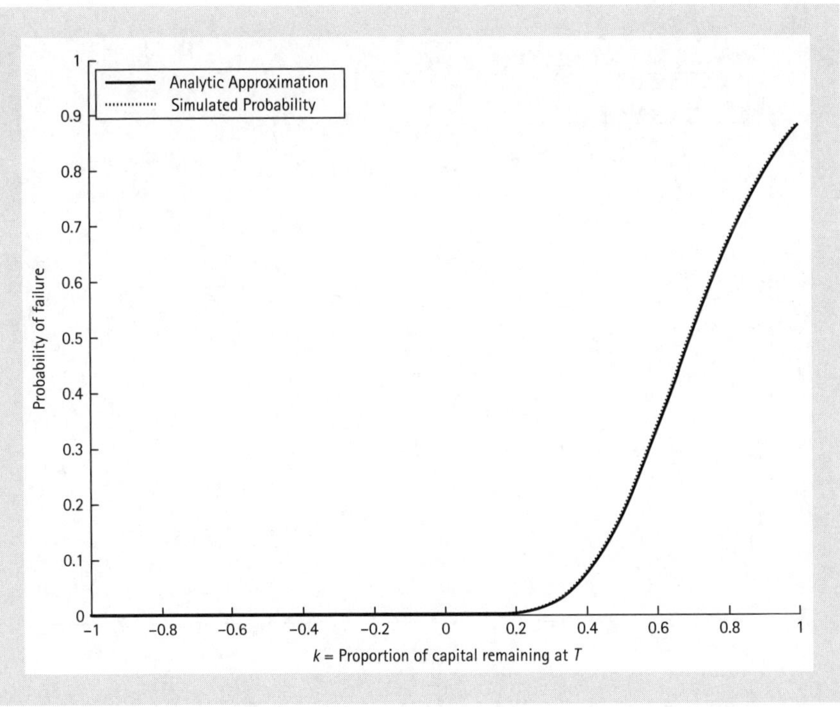

FIGURE 16.10 Equation (16.6): Horizon value CDF, $\alpha_L = -20\%$, $\sigma_L = 20\%, \alpha_S = 2\%$, $\sigma_S = 15\%$, $\rho = 30\%$, $L(0) = 1.5$, $S(0) = 0.5$, $T = 1$.

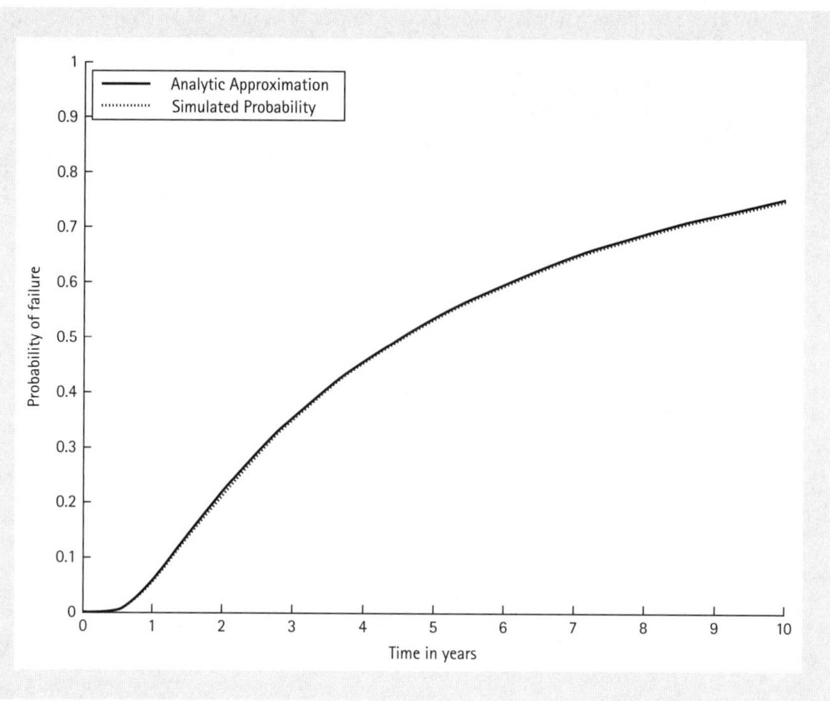

FIGURE 16.11 Equation (16.7): Stopping time CDF, $\alpha_L = -2\%$, $\sigma_L = 20\%, \alpha_S = 2\%$, $\sigma_S = 15\%$, $\rho = 30\%$, $L(0) = 1.5$, $S(0) = 0.5$, $K = 0.5$.

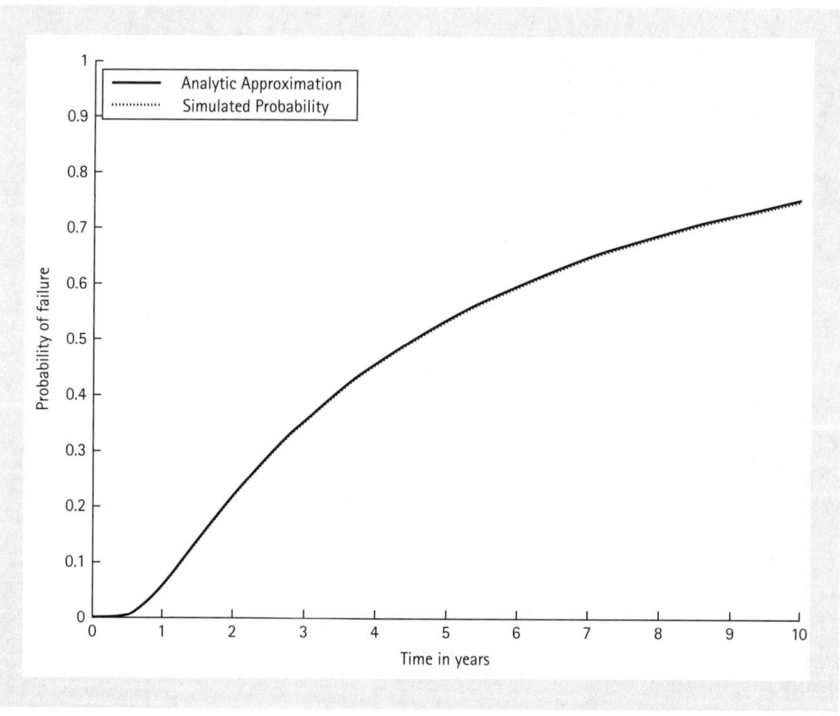

FIGURE 16.12 Equation (16.7): Stopping time CDF, $\alpha_L = 4\%$, $\sigma_L = 20\%$, $\alpha_S = 2\%$, $\sigma_S = 15\%$, $\rho = 80\%$, $L(0) = 2.5$, $S(0) = 1.5$, $K = 0.8$.

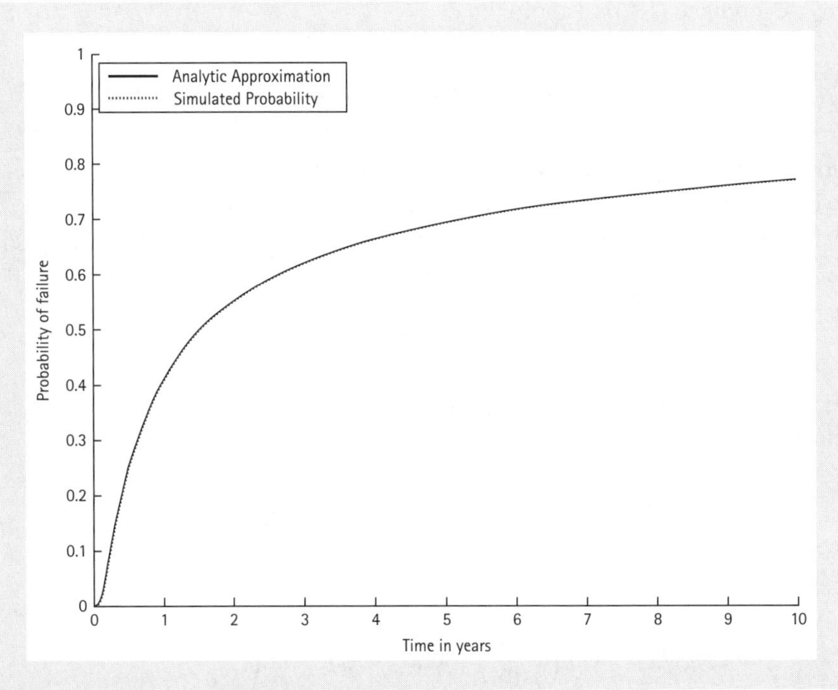

FIGURE 16.13 Equation (16.7): Stopping time CDF, $\alpha_L = 4\%$, $\sigma_L = 20\%$, $\alpha_S = 2\%$, $\sigma_S = 15\%$, $\rho = 0\%$, $L(0) = 4.5$, $S(0) = 3.5$, $K = 0.2$.

16.4 Terminal Distribution Conditional on Surviving an Absorbing Barrier

Our four key formulas so far have progressed as follows. First we computed:

(16.3) Terminal probability of failure defined by a ratio: $L(T)/S(T) < r$.

We then noted that the terminal probability is overly optimistic since any path that fails at any time between $t = 0$ and $t = T$ would stop, so we derived:

(16.4) Probability of ratio failure at any time: $L(t)/S(t) < r$ for some $0 < t < T$.

While the ratio analysis is convenient analytically, the difference analysis is more economically meaningful, hence we approximated:

(16.6) Terminal probability of failure defined by a difference: $L(T) - S(T) < k$.

Finally, we modified (16.6) to approximate

(16.7) Probability of difference failure at any time: $L(t) - S(t) < k$ for some $0 < t < T$.

While the results thus far are informative regarding portfolio downside risk, we also wish to assess the probability of achieving a desired wealth level. Thus we now characterize the terminal distribution of portfolio value given that we avoid failure along the barrier at k. That is, we compute the joint probability

$$P(K, k) = P(L(T) - S(T) \leq K, \forall t \in [0, T] : L(t) - S(t) > k)$$

where we assume that $k < L(0) - S(0)$ and $k < K$.

Define

$$f(t) = \frac{L(t)}{S(t) + k} \quad \text{and} \quad F(t) = \frac{L(t)}{S(t) + K}.$$

and define

$$g(t) = -\ln\left(\frac{f(t)}{f(0)}\right) \quad \text{and} \quad G(t) = \ln\left(\frac{F(t)}{F(0)}\right).$$

These are approximated by standard arithmetic Brownian motions according to

$$dG \approx (\hat{A}(K) - \hat{\Sigma}(K)^2/2)dt + \hat{\Sigma}(K)dZ_G$$

$$dg \approx (-\hat{A}(k) + \hat{\Sigma}(k)^2/2)dt + \hat{\Sigma}(k)dZ_g$$

using the obvious extensions of the "hat" notation introduced after formula (16.6). Here

$$\hat{\Sigma}(K)dZ_G = \sigma_L dZ_L - \frac{\sigma_S S(0)}{S(0) + K} dZ_S$$

and

$$\hat{\Sigma}(k)dZ_g = -\sigma_L dZ_L + \frac{\sigma_S S(0)}{S(0) + k} dZ_S.$$

The joint probability we seek can be expressed in this notation as

$$P(K, k) \approx P(G(T) \leq -\ln(F(0)), \underset{t \in [0,T]}{Max}\, g(t) \leq \ln(f(0))).$$

To calculate this we invoke results by Lee (2004) derived for the purpose of pricing barrier options contingent on multiple assets. Lee shows that if $(X_1(t), X_2(t))$ is a bivariate linear Brownian motion with drift (μ_1, μ_2) and covariance structure $\begin{pmatrix} \sigma_1^2 & \psi\sigma_1\sigma_2 \\ \psi\sigma_1\sigma_2 & \sigma_2^2 \end{pmatrix}$ and $M_2(s, t) = \underset{\tau \in [s,t]}{Max}\, X_2(\tau)$, then

$$P(X_1(T) \le x, M_2(s,t) \le m) = \Phi_3\left(\frac{x-\mu_1 T}{\sigma_1\sqrt{T}}, \frac{m-\mu_2 t}{\sigma_2\sqrt{t}}, \frac{m-\mu_2 s}{\sigma_2\sqrt{s}}, \psi\sqrt{\frac{t}{T}}, \psi\sqrt{\frac{s}{T}}, \sqrt{\frac{s}{t}}\right)$$

$$-\exp\left(\frac{2\mu_2 m}{\sigma_2^2}\right)\Phi_3\left(\frac{x-\mu_1 T}{\sigma_1\sqrt{T}} - \frac{2\psi m}{\sigma_2\sqrt{T}}, \frac{-m-\mu_2 t}{\sigma_2\sqrt{t}}, \frac{m+\mu_2 s}{\sigma_2\sqrt{s}}, \psi\sqrt{\frac{t}{T}}, -\psi\sqrt{\frac{s}{T}}, -\sqrt{\frac{s}{t}}\right)$$

where $\Phi_3(a, b, c, \rho_{12}, \rho_{13}, \rho_{23}) = P(Z_1 \le a, Z_2 \le b, Z_3 \le c)$ is the trivariate cumulative distribution function for a standard normal vector, (Z_1, Z_2, Z_3), with correlation matrix $\begin{pmatrix} 1 & \rho_{12} & \rho_{13} \\ \rho_{12} & 1 & \rho_{23} \\ \rho_{13} & \rho_{23} & 1 \end{pmatrix}$.[6]

To obtain from our problem the parameters required to apply Lee's result, we compute the correlation between G and g:

$$\hat{R} := Cor(dZ_G, dZ_g)$$

$$= \frac{-1}{\hat{\Sigma}(K)\hat{\Sigma}(k)}\left[\sigma_L^2 - \rho\sigma_L\sigma_S S(0)\left(\frac{1}{S(0)+K} + \frac{1}{S(0)+k}\right) + \frac{\sigma_S^2 S(0)^2}{(S(0)+K)\,(S(0)+k)}\right].$$

In our application:

$$X_1 = G,\ X_2 = g,\ x = -\ln(F(0)),\ m = \ln(f(0)),\ s = 0,\ t = T,$$

$$\mu_1 = \hat{A}(K) - \hat{\Sigma}(K)^2/2,\ \mu_2 = -\hat{A}(k) + \hat{\Sigma}(k)^2/2,\ \sigma_1 = \hat{\Sigma}(K),\ \sigma_2 = \hat{\Sigma}(k),\ \psi = \hat{R}.$$

Substituting these values into Lee's result, we obtain

$$P(X_1(T) \le x, M_2(0,T) \le m) = \Phi_3\left(\frac{x-\mu_1 T}{\sigma_1\sqrt{T}}, \frac{m-\mu_2 T}{\sigma_2\sqrt{T}}, \mathrm{sgn}(m).\infty, \psi, 0, 0\right)$$

$$-\exp\left(\frac{2\mu_2 m}{\sigma_2^2}\right)\Phi_3\left(\frac{x-\mu_1 T}{\sigma_1\sqrt{T}} - \frac{2\psi m}{\sigma_2\sqrt{T}}, \frac{-m-\mu_2 T}{\sigma_2\sqrt{T}}, \mathrm{sgn}(m).\infty, \psi, 0, 0\right).$$

Because $s = 0$ and $\mathrm{sgn}(m) = 1$, the trivariate normal cdf reduces to a bivariate normal cdf, so we obtain

$$P(K,k) \approx \Phi_2\left(\frac{x-\mu_1 T}{\sigma_1\sqrt{T}}, \frac{m-\mu_2 T}{\sigma_2\sqrt{T}}, \psi\right) - \exp\left(\frac{2\mu_2 m}{\sigma_2^2}\right)$$

$$\Phi_2\left(\frac{x-\mu_1 T}{\sigma_1\sqrt{T}} - \frac{2\psi m}{\sigma_2\sqrt{T}}, \frac{-m-\mu_2 T}{\sigma_2\sqrt{T}}, \psi\right)$$

[6] Standard statistical packages frequently do not provide two- and three-dimensional normal cdf functions. West (2005) provides algorithms for the two-dimensional case and references for three-dimensional algorithms. Our application in fact reduces to the two-dimensional case, which is covered by West's Figure 16.7.

which in our original notation becomes

$$P(K,k) \approx \Phi_2(\hat{D}_1(K), -\hat{D}_1(k), \hat{R}) - \left(\frac{L(0)}{S(0)+k}\right)^{1-\frac{2\hat{A}(k)}{\hat{\Sigma}(k)^2}}$$

$$\Phi_2\left(\hat{D}_1(K) - \frac{2\hat{R}\ln\left(\frac{L(0)}{S(0)+k}\right)}{\hat{\Sigma}(k)\sqrt{T}}, \hat{D}_2(k), \hat{R}\right). \qquad (16.8)$$

Note that as $K \to \infty$, $\hat{D}_1(K) \to \infty$, so the bivariate normal cdf in (16.8) reduces to a univariate function and (16.8) reduces to one minus (16.7). This confirms that the sum of the stopping probability and all non-stopping probabilities is one.

16.4.1 Monte Carlo Simulations – Terminal Distribution with Absorbing Barrier

As in the case of approximations (16.6) and (16.7), the Monte Carlo tests for (16.8) demonstrate that the approximation is remarkably good – see Figures 16.14–16.16.

We ran the Monte Carlo simulation varying the number of paths as well as the number of time steps on each path and it is clear that for time steps in the range of 100–10,000 per year, the discretization error caused by misclassifying paths that hit the absorbing barrier between mesh points is greater in magnitude than the approximation error in (16.8). The figures presented use 10,000 paths and 10,000 steps per path. In Figures 16.14–16.16, we plot the probability of "failure" represented by $P(K,k)$ comparing the estimate (16.8) with the Monte Carlo solution. As a check, the graphs also include $P(\tau_k < T) + P(K,k)$ (that is, formula 16.7 plus formula 16.8) which should converge to 1 as $K \to \infty$.

The probability of "success," i.e., of avoiding k on $[0,T]$ and exceeding K at T is given by $S(k,K,T) = 1 - P(\tau_k < T) - P(K,k)$. An example of this surface is given in Figure 16.17.

16.5 Constant Leverage

Our analysis so far has concerned an unmanaged portfolio. At $t = 0$ we create a portfolio with specified long and short sides, but for later t the portfolio drifts according to the dictates of the Brownian processes without any interference from the portfolio manager. This is a stylized base case applicable over short time horizons. Over longer horizons it is not representative of the way portfolios are managed in practice. In a subsequent paper we intend to investigate the impact on stopping times and success probabilities of a

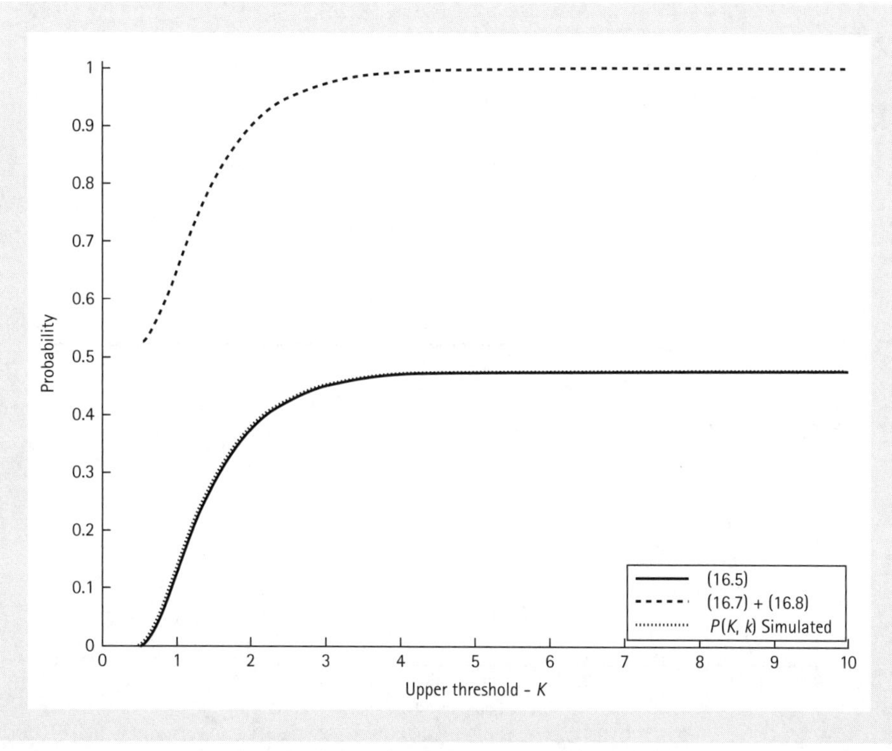

FIGURE 16.14 Equation (16.8): Failure probability, $\alpha_L = 0\%$, $\sigma_L = 20\%$, $\alpha_S = 0\%$, $\sigma_S = 15\%$, $\rho = 50\%$, $L(0) = 2$, $S(0) = 1$, $T = 5$, $k = 0.5$.

variety of risk management techniques. Here we will look at a simple case – maintaining constant leverage – because it offers closed form solutions.

We assume that a manager continuously rebalances the portfolio allocation to L and S such that at all times, $\frac{L+S}{L-S} = \lambda$ for a constant λ. Then $L = \frac{\lambda+1}{2}(L - S)$ and $S = \frac{\lambda-1}{2}(L - S)$. In other words, a constant proportion $\frac{\lambda+1}{2}$ of portfolio equity is invested in L and a constant proportion $\frac{\lambda-1}{2}$ is shorted in S. The SDE for the portfolio value P is given by

$$\frac{d(P)}{P} = \frac{\lambda+1}{2}\left(\frac{dL}{L}\right) - \frac{\lambda-1}{2}\left(\frac{dS}{S}\right)$$

(see Fernholz and Shay 1982, eqn. 15), so

$$\frac{d(P)}{P} = \alpha_\lambda dt + \sigma_\lambda dZ$$

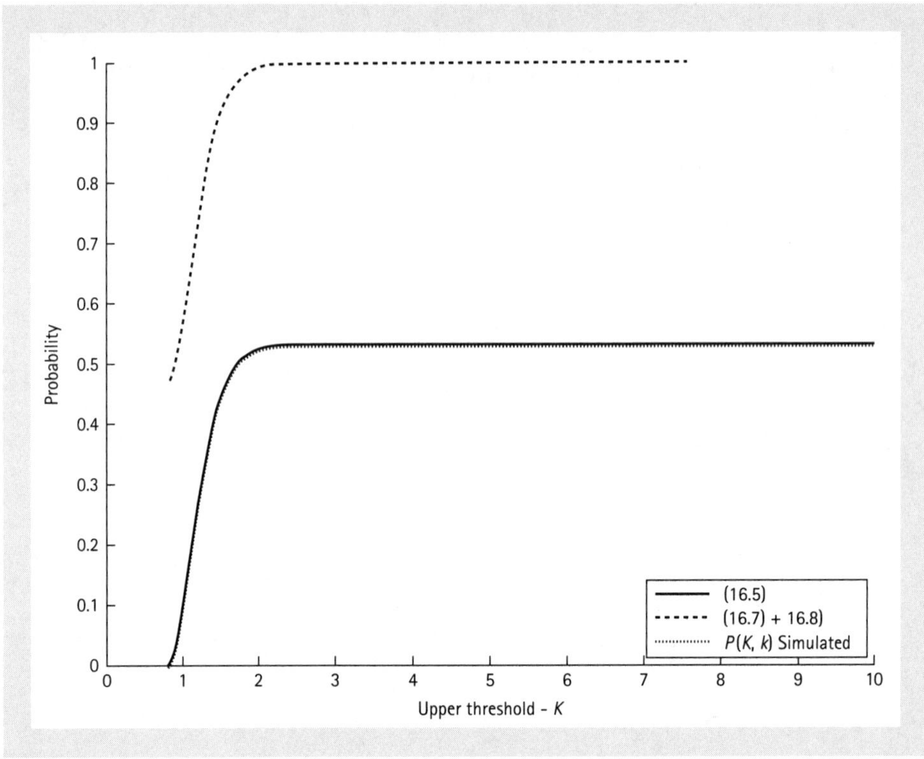

FIGURE 16.15 Equation (16.8): Failure probability $\alpha_L = 4\%$, $\sigma_L = 20\%$, $\alpha_S = 2\%$, $\sigma_S = 15\%$, $\rho = 0\%$, $L(0) = 1.5$, $S(0) = 0.5$, $T = 1$, $k = 0.8$.

where Z is a standard Wiener process and

$$\sigma_\lambda dZ \equiv \sigma_L \frac{\lambda+1}{2} dZ_L - \sigma_S \frac{\lambda-1}{2} dZ_S$$

$$\alpha_\lambda = \alpha_L \frac{\lambda+1}{2} - \alpha_S \frac{\lambda-1}{2}$$

$$\sigma_\lambda^2 = \frac{1}{4}\left((\lambda+1)^2\sigma_L^2 - 2(\lambda^2-1)\rho\sigma_L\sigma_S + (\lambda-1)^2\sigma_S^2\right).$$

Thus we see that in the constant leverage case the portfolio process is a GBM. Therefore we may apply the earlier result on Brownian stopping from Musiela and Rutkowski (1998, Appendix B3) to derive the cumulative distribution for the stopping time

$$\tau_k = inf\{t : t > 0, L(t) - S(t) \leq k\}$$

namely

$$P(\tau_k \leq T) = N(\breve{D}_1) + k^{\frac{2\alpha_\lambda}{\sigma_\lambda^2}-1} N(\breve{D}_2) \tag{16.9}$$

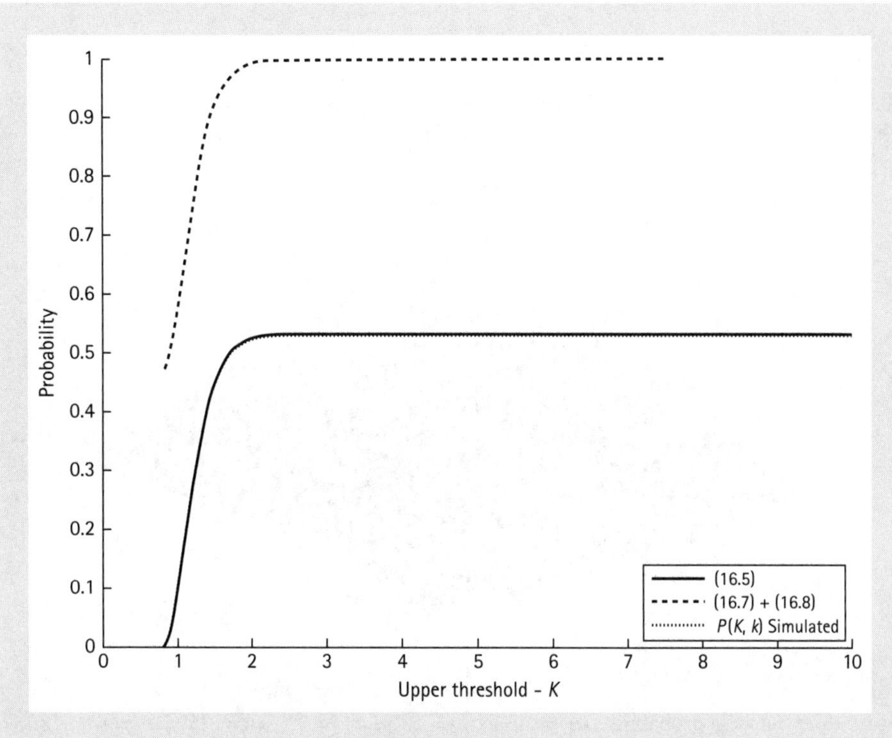

FIGURE 16.16 Equation (16.8) Failure probability, $\alpha_L = 0\%$, $\sigma_L = 20\%$, $\alpha_S = 0\%$, $\sigma_S = 15\%$, $\rho = -20\%$, $L(0) = 3$, $S(0) = 2$, $T = 5$, $k = 0.2$.

where

$$\breve{D}_1 = \frac{\ln(k) - \left(\alpha_\lambda - \sigma_\lambda^2/2\right) T}{\sigma_\lambda \sqrt{T}}, \; \breve{D}_2 = \frac{\ln(k) + \left(\alpha_\lambda - \sigma_\lambda^2/2\right) T}{\sigma_\lambda \sqrt{T}}. \tag{16.10}$$

To compute the cumulative probability distribution conditional on avoiding the absorbing barrier (failure) at k:

$$P(K,k) = \Pr(L(T) - S(T) \leq K | \forall 0 \leq t \leq T, L(t) - S(t) > k)$$

(Musiela and Rutkowski 1998, Appendix B3) gives

$$P(K,k) = N(d_1) - k^{\frac{2\alpha_\lambda}{\sigma_\lambda^2} - 1} N(d_2) \tag{16.11}$$

where

$$d_1 = \frac{-\ln(K) + \left(\alpha_\lambda - \sigma_\lambda^2/2\right) T}{\sigma_\lambda \sqrt{T}}, \; d_2 = \frac{\ln(k^2/K) + \left(\alpha_\lambda - \sigma_\lambda^2/2\right) T}{\sigma_\lambda \sqrt{T}}. \tag{16.12}$$

Since the constant leverage portfolio is a GBM, this is an effective risk management technique for avoiding total bankruptcy as the portfolio value is in fact lognormally

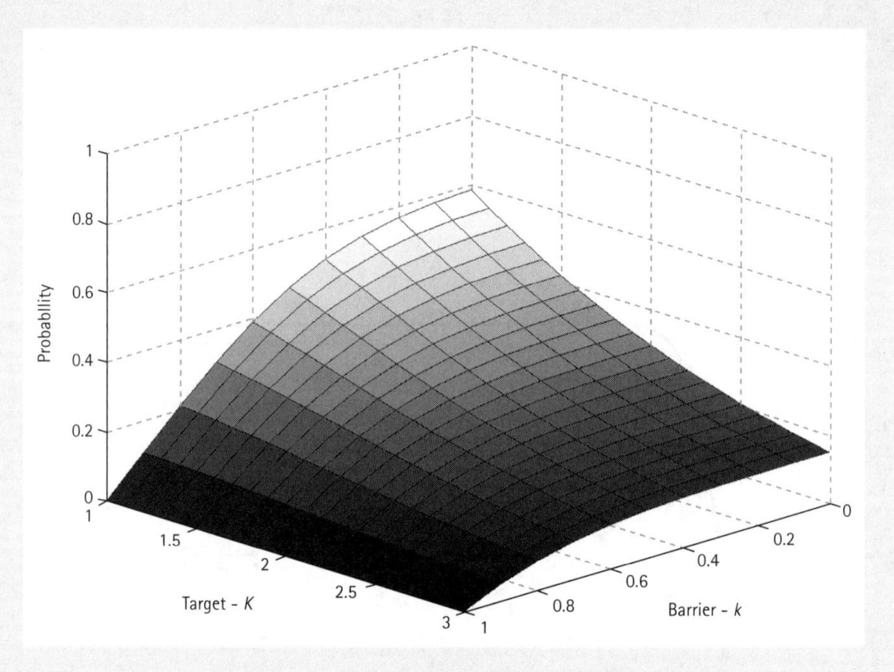

FIGURE 16.17 Success probability, $\alpha_L = 4\%$, $\sigma_L = 20\%$, $\alpha_S = 2\%$, $\sigma_S = 15\%$, $\rho = 0\%$, $L(0) = 1.5$, $S(0) = 0.5$, $T = 10$.

distributed. This is apparent in (16.9), where setting $k = 0$ gives negative infinite arguments to the cumulative normals and thus gives zero probability of hitting the absorbing barrier.

Since the unmanaged portfolio represented by (16.7) can have positive probability of attaining $k = 0$ or less, one might expect that the constant leverage portfolio would have less chance of very poor results, more chance of middling results, and less chance of very good results. However, the relationship between the constant leverage portfolio and the unmanaged portfolio is complex. Consider the surface in Figure 16.18, representing the incremental success probability associated to managing with constant leverage.

The green area in the front right of the surface is the impossible region where $K < k$. For values of $k > 0.6$, constant leverage has less chance of producing low values of K but a larger chance of producing high values. For $k < 0.6$, there is a spike in the front left area of the surface that indicates a higher chance of low values of K for constant leverage, followed by a drop in the middle area, followed by greater chances of constant leverage producing large values of K.

All other things being equal, it is desirable for a risk management technique to sell winners and buy losers. If there is a crowded trade – many funds or banks have similar long-short positions – then if they all have risk management techniques telling them to buy winners and sell losers, a destructive cycle will emerge in which the reaction to

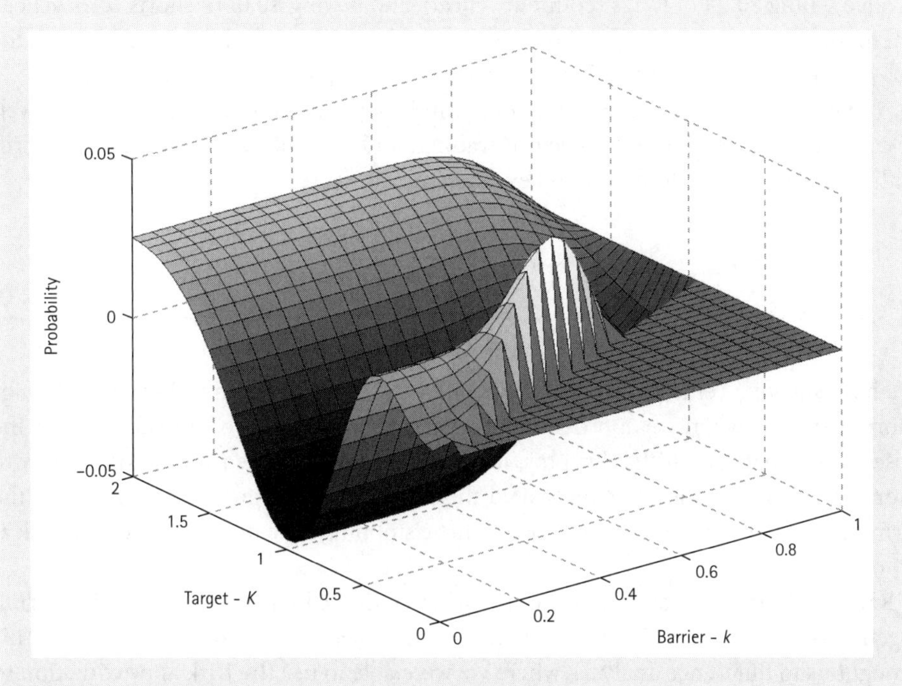

FIGURE 16.18 Incremental success probability, $k = 1$, $T = 1$, $\lambda = 6$, $\rho = 0.8$, GBM per Table 16.1.

market movements makes them worse. Even if this systemic problem does not occur, at the very least executing trades against the market will be expensive at the individual fund level.

Given that there is a budget constraint, there is no risk management technique that is always countercyclical. Consider a fund worth \$1 with \$2 of longs and \$1 of shorts, for a leverage of $\lambda = 3$. Suppose asset values are generally rising, so the longs go up \$0.1 and the shorts go up \$0.04. In this case the fund rises in value from \$1 to \$1.06. To maintain constant leverage in this case we would sell \$0.02 of shorts (a desirable countercyclical trade) and buy \$0.02 of longs (an undesirable procyclical trade). However a series of such moderate moves is less likely to cause a destructive spiral than an abrupt stop loss.

The best way to avoid the systemic and individual fund consequences of crowded trades is simply to avoid crowded trades in the first place. Hedge funds should take care that they are not doing the same strategy everyone else is doing; banks should too. Another approach would be to have a cash buffer that is used to avoid or lower trading into a crowded procyclical trade. Suppose in our example of the previous paragraph we had \$1 of cash in addition to our \$2 long and \$1 short, and we intend to keep the risky/cash balance at 50% each while maintaining a leverage of 3 in the risky portion. Given the move described in the previous paragraph (and assuming a zero return on cash), we would want to end up with $L = 2.06$, $S = 1.03$, and cash $C = 1.03$. This would involve selling \$0.04 of longs (countercyclical), and buying \$0.01 of shorts (procyclical, but moderately). Depending on how much we value countercyclicality, we could let the risky/cash percentage vary within bounds to avoid even more procyclical trading.

As a public policy measure, regulators or industry groups may require certain levels of cash buffer to moderate procyclical trading, and may allow leverage limits to drift within certain bounds to further relieve systemic pressure.

16.6 Conclusions

We have shown a remarkably high probability of failure from un-risk-managed long-short portfolios when we approximate the arithmetic difference. We started with the observation that for full bankruptcy, it suffices to look at when the ratio of longs to shorts drops below one. This motivated the development of an exact solution for the terminal distribution and for the more realistic stopping time problem when we look at ratios.

Ratio analysis does not handle the case when both the long and the short side shrink together – they might maintain a high ratio while the difference dwindles to zero. This brought us to difference analysis, where we were able to use the Kirk approximation to transform the difference analysis to the previous case so the results from ratio analysis could be used. We noted that the approximation agrees remarkably well with Monte Carlo simulations for most reasonable parameter sets. Finally, we looked at a joint distribution that took into effect avoiding failure, while allowing for success in the form of exceeding a specified terminal wealth.

In practice, long-short portfolios would not be allowed to drift unchecked towards absorbing barriers as we have assumed. Long before bankruptcy could result, one would hope that a responsible portfolio manager or a vigilant risk manager would take action. A variety of forms of action are possible – for example deleveraging or rebalancing the holdings of the long and short portfolios so as to manipulate their drift, volatility, and correlation. Since we have specified continuous processes, this kind of risk management would generally be effective. Our formula (16.8) provides a way of assessing the impact of such a rebalance on the risk and return profile of the portfolio.

Finally we analyzed a specific risk management regime – keeping leverage constant. Constant leverage is equivalent to constant proportions in the long and the short sides – that is, a rebalanced portfolio. This portfolio has a different success surface than the unmanaged portfolio and never goes bankrupt. However, in Figure 16.18 we see a complex relationship between the constant-leverage portfolio and the unmanaged portfolio. Determining which is preferable would depend on exact parameter values and a specification of an objective function.

In subsequent investigations, we intend to examine the sensitivity of our results to the introduction of a variety of risk management paradigms as well as more general price processes. Jump diffusion processes, in addition to capturing in a more realistic way the kurtotic nature of real-world distributions, allow for the possibility of gapping past an absorbing barrier and hence complicate the life of the risk manager who presumably requires continuous processes to be effective. Finally we are curious as to whether these results can be used to arrive at strategies that dynamically manage the covariance of the long and short portfolios to enhance alpha capture and/or risk efficiency.

APPENDIX

Effectiveness of the Kirk Approximation

Why is it that the approximate equations (16.5)–(16.7) and (16.8) prove so accurate under Monte Carlo testing? Recall that the inexact step in the analysis is approximation (16.5) which assumes that $S(t) + k$ follows a GBM. To derive some intuition as to why this assumption does not degrade the accuracy of (16.5) ff. we look at sample paths of $S(t)$ simulated according to (16.5), both exactly and with the Kirk approximation with the same driving Wiener process. A typical path pair is given in Figure 16.A1.

We note that, even for a relatively large k value of .5, the paths differ only very slightly and the difference is not noticeably systematically biased positive or negative. As a result, when we

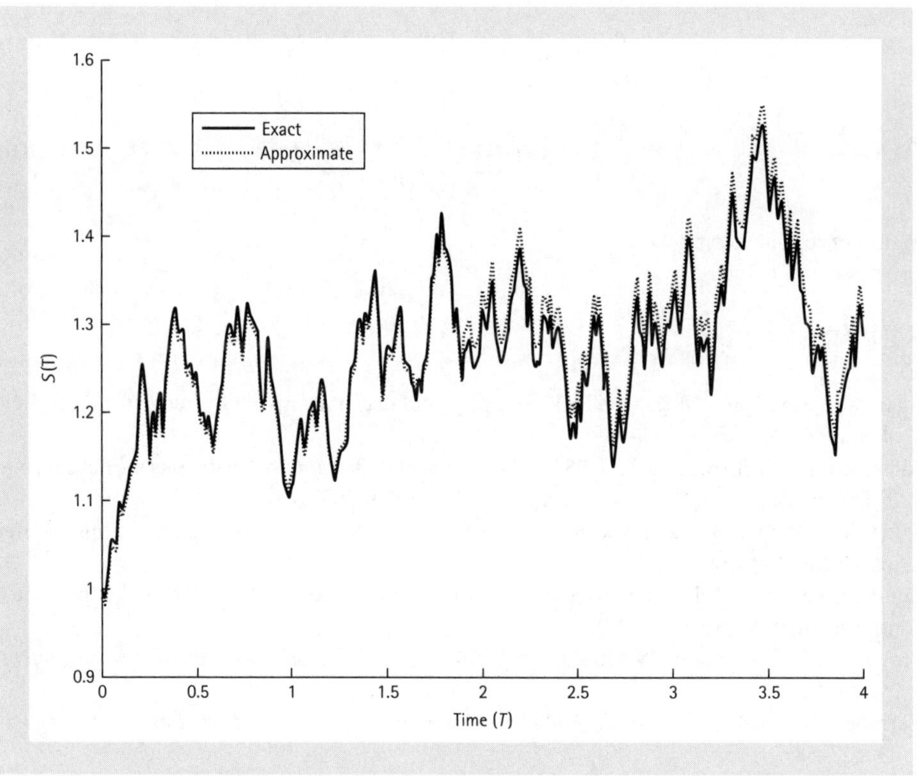

FIGURE 16.A.1 Exact and approximate paths of $S(T)$, $\alpha_S = 2\%$, $\sigma_S = 20\%$, $K = 5$.

measure probabilities of the form (16.6), (16.7) and (16.8), over all possible paths, the "error" coming from the difference in the path trajectories tends to cancel out in the averaging process over multiple paths, resulting in accurate estimates for the various probabilities.

When k is negative, the Kirk approximation on the short process may not work. Drawdowns to negative asset levels are nonsensical, so why do we mention this? In the event that a portfolio comprises a significant cash position, C, it may be preferable to absorb cash into the constant k than into the long or short portfolios. The right-hand side of the inequality $L(t) - S(t) < k - C$ can be negative. We note the condition $L(t) - S(t) < k$ can also be rewritten $(L(t) - k)/S(t) < 1$, where the numerator is positive. We then use the Kirk approximation on the process for L-k, obtaining

$$\begin{aligned}\frac{d(L-k)}{L-k} &= \left(\frac{L}{L-k}\right)\frac{dL}{L} = \frac{L}{L-k}(\alpha_L dt + \sigma_L dZ_L) \\ &\approx \frac{L(0)}{L(0)-k}(\alpha_L dt + \sigma_L dZ_L).\end{aligned} \tag{16.5}$$

The adjustment factor analogous to SF is

$$LF = \frac{L(0)}{L(0)-k}.$$

Rather than the "hat" substitutions, we would use "tilde" substitutions

$$\begin{aligned}\tilde{A} &= LF\alpha_L - \alpha_S + {\sigma_S}^2 - \rho\sigma_L\sigma_S LF \\ \tilde{\Sigma}^2 &= LF^2{\sigma_L}^2 + {\sigma_S}^2 - 2\sigma_L\sigma_S\rho LF \\ \tilde{D}_1 &= \frac{\ln\left(\frac{S(0)}{L(0)-k}\right) - (\tilde{A} - \tilde{\Sigma}^2/2)T}{\tilde{\Sigma}\sqrt{T}}\end{aligned}$$

in the appropriate formulas.

References

Agarwal, V. and Naik, N. (2004). Risks and portfolio decisions involving hedge funds. *Review of Financial Studies*, **17**, 63–98.

Aitchison, J. and Brown, J.A.C. (1957). *The Lognormal Distribution, with Special Reference to its Use in Economics*. Cambridge University Press, Cambridge.

Atlan, M., German, H., and Yor, M. (2006). Options on hedge funds under the high-water mark rule. Preprint.

Bondarenko, O. (2004). Market price of variance risk and performance of hedge funds. http://ssrn.com/abstract=542182

Brown, S. and Goetzmann, W. (2003). Hedge funds with style. *Journal of Portfolio Management*, **29**, 101–112.

Carmona, R. and Durrleman, V. (2003). Pricing and hedging spread options. *SIAM Review*, **45**, 627–685.

Dor, A. and Jagannathan, R. (2002). Understanding mutual fund and hedge fund styles using return based style analysis. NBER Working Paper No. W9111.

Fenton, L. F. (1960). The sum of log-normal probability distributions in scatter transmission systems. *IRE Transactions in Communications*, **8**, 57–67.

Fernholz, R. and Shay, B. (1982). Stochastic portfolio theory and stock market equilibrium. *Journal of Finance*, **XXXVII** (2), 615–622.

Fung, W. and Hsieh, D. (1999). A primer on hedge funds. *Journal of Empirical Finance*, **6**, 309–331.

Fung, W. and Hsieh, D. (2001). The risk in hedge fund strategies: Theory and evidence from trend followers. *Review of Financial Studies* **14**, 313–341.

Fung, W. and Hsieh, D. (2002). The risk in fixed-income hedge fund styles. *Journal of Fixed Income* **12**, 6–27.

Fung, W. and Hsieh, D. (2003). The risk in hedge fund strategies: Alternative alphas and alternative betas. *Managing the Risks of Alternative Investment Strategies* (ed. L. Jaeger). Euromoney, Brussels.

Getmansky, M., Lo, A.W., and Makarov, I. (2004). An econometric model of serial correlation and illiquidity in hedge fund returns. *Journal of Financial Economics*, **74**, 529–609.

Goetzmann, W., Ingersoll J., and Ross, S. (2001). High-water marks and hedge fund management contracts. Yale ICF Working Paper No. 00–34.

Haug, E.G. (1998). *The Complete Guide to Option Pricing Formulas*. McGraw Hill, New York.

Kat, H. and Lu., S. (2005). Some statistical properties of hedge fund returns. In *Handbook of Hedge Funds* (eds. Jochen Kleeberg). Uhlenbruch Verlag, Berlin.

Kat, H. and Palaro, H. (2005). Who needs hedge funds? A copula-based approach to hedge fund return replication. Alternative Investment Research Centre Working Paper No. 27.

Kirk, E. (1995). Correlation in energy markets. *Managing Energy Price Risk*. Risk Publications/Enron, London: pp. 71–78.

Kritzman, M. and Rich, D. (1998). Risk containment for investors with multivariate utility functions. *The Journal of Derivatives*, **5**, 28–44.

Kritzman, M. and Rich, D. (2002). The mismeasurement of risk. *Financial Analysts Journal*, **58**, 91–99.

Law, A. and Kelton, W. (2000). *Simulation Modeling and Analysis* (third edition). McGraw Hill, New York.

Lee, H. (2004). A joint distribution of two-dimensional Brownian motion with an application to an outside barrier option. *Journal of the Korean Statistical Society*, **33**, 245–254.

Musiela, M. and Rutkowski, M. (1998). *Martingale Methods in Financial Modeling*. Springer Verlag, Berlin.

West, G. (2005). Better approximations to cumulative normal functions. *Wilmott Magazine*, May 2005: 70–76.

PART VI

MARKET STRUCTURE AND TRADING

CHAPTER 17

ALGORITHMIC TRADING, OPTIMAL EXECUTION, AND DYNAMIC PORTFOLIOS

PETTER N. KOLM AND LEE MACLIN

17.1 Introduction

Almost 50 years ago, the ascent of portfolio theory brought with it a new language for considering the trade-off between risk and reward. A similar change is taking place today. As portfolio managers, traders, and market makers struggle to make sense of a Niagara of innovations, a new language is evolving for describing execution quality, performance analytics, and efficient portfolio management strategies, as well as many other aspects of algorithmic trading.

Vast changes in trading technology and the growth of alternative execution venues such as dark pools and crossing networks have fueled the search for better algorithmic trading tools. Both traditional broker dealers and software vendors are rushing to fill this gap, but are finding that the new tools are not always easy to integrate into existing frameworks. The impediments are often conceptual as well as infrastructure related.

While the term algorithmic trading is still often used to describe a wide range of automated trading strategies – some are based on mathematical principles and others are simple mechanical rules – increasingly, practitioners are turning to the mathematics of algorithmic trading for measurable improvement in performance. The growing field of algorithmic trading typically includes market impact modeling, execution risk analytics, optimal execution, cost-aware portfolio construction, and dynamic portfolio management. Other terms that are often associated with algorithmic trading are statistical arbitrage, smart order routing, program trading, and high frequency trading.

In this chapter, we first discuss the main ideas of algorithmic trading, order book mechanics and market impact, and then present a simple decision framework for choosing execution strategies. Next, we turn to portfolio optimization with market impact costs, combining execution and portfolio risk, and dynamic portfolio analysis. We introduce a multi-period portfolio optimization model that incorporates permanent and temporary market impact costs, and alpha decay. We close the chapter with a discussion of the high frequency infrastructure arms race, crossing networks and anti-gaming, and their impact on the markets.

17.2 Market Impact and the Order Book

The bid side of the *limit book* consists of resting bids to buy a certain number of shares of stock at a certain price. The offer side consists of resting offers to sell a certain number of shares of stock at a certain price. These *limit orders* rest in the book and provide liquidity as they wait to be matched with non-resting orders, which represent a demand for liquidity. The three most common types of non-resting orders are market orders, marketable limit orders (if they fill completely), and fill-or-kill orders.

A *market order* is a demand for an immediate execution of a certain number of shares at the best possible price. To achieve the best possible price, a market order sweeps through one side of the limit order book – starting with the best price – matching against resting orders until the full quantity of the market order is filled or the book is completely depleted.

Unlike a market order, a *marketable limit order* can be executed only at a specified price or better. For example, a marketable limit order to buy 100 shares at \$90.01 can match with a resting limit order to sell 200 shares at \$90.00. The trade print – the price at which the trade would take place – would be \$90.00.

A *fill-or-kill order* is a limit order that must be filled immediately in its entirety, or it is canceled. In other words, a fill-or-kill order does not guarantee a fill price. Rather, it guarantees a fill at the specified price or better, or not at all.

The following stylized examples illustrate how market orders to sell interact with resting limit orders to buy. In addition, these examples show how market impact costs arise at the market microstructure level.

Figure 17.1 shows the idealized market impact of a 200-share market order to sell. The x- and y-axes display the time and price, respectively.

The bid side of the limit order book contains bids to buy a certain number of shares of stock at a certain price. Resting limit orders – orders that sit in the order book – are said to *provide liquidity* by mitigating the market impact of orders that must be filled immediately. The state of the book establishes a *pre-trade equilibrium* (1), which

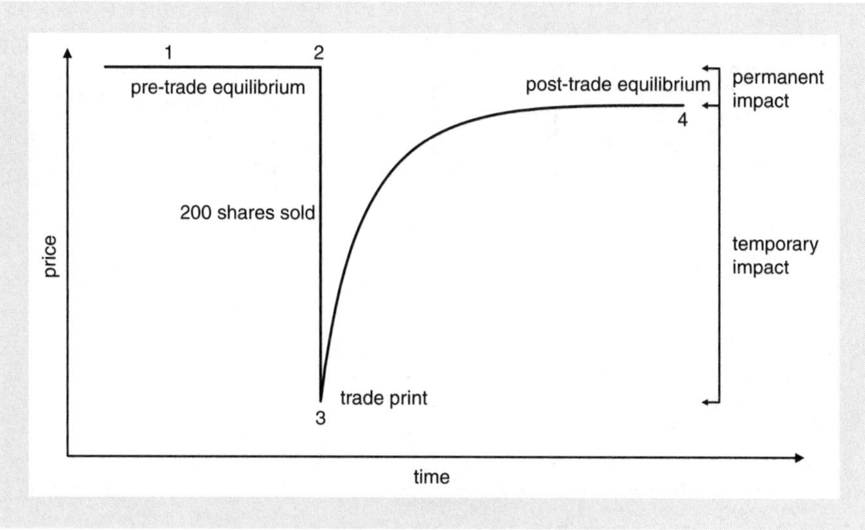

FIGURE 17.1 Idealized market impact model showing sell of 200 shares.

is disturbed by a market order to sell 200 shares (2). Market orders must be filled immediately, and therefore represent a demand for liquidity.

As the sell order depletes the bid book by matching with limit orders to buy, it obtains an increasingly less favorable (lower) trade price, resulting in the trade print (3). Assuming no other trading activity, over time liquidity providers replenish the bid book to (4), which is the *post-trade equilibrium.*

The difference between (4) and (1) is an information-based effect called *permanent market impact.* It is the market's response to information that a market participant has decided not to own 200 shares of this stock. This effect is typically modeled as immediate and linear in total number of shares executed. Huberman and Stanzl (2004) show that, if the effect were not linear and immediate, buying and selling at two different rates produces an arbitrage opportunity.

The difference between (3) and (4) is called *temporary market impact.* The trader who initiated the trade is willing to obtain a less favorable fill price (3) to get his trade done immediately. This *cost of immediacy* is typically modeled as linear or square root. Under the assumption of square root impact, with all other factors held constant, a trade of 200 shares executed over the same period of time as a trade of 100 shares would have square root of two times more temporary impact per share.

Figure 17.2 shows what would happen if the same trader were willing to wait some time between trades. The trade print from the previous figure is shown as a reference point (p). As in Figure 17.1, a pre-trade equilibrium (1) is disturbed by a 100 share market order to sell (2). As the market order depletes the bid book by matching with limit orders to buy, it obtains a fill price (3). Over time (t), liquidity providers refill the bid book with limit orders to buy. But the new post-trade equilibrium (4) is lower than the pre-trade equilibrium because it incorporates the information of the executed market order.

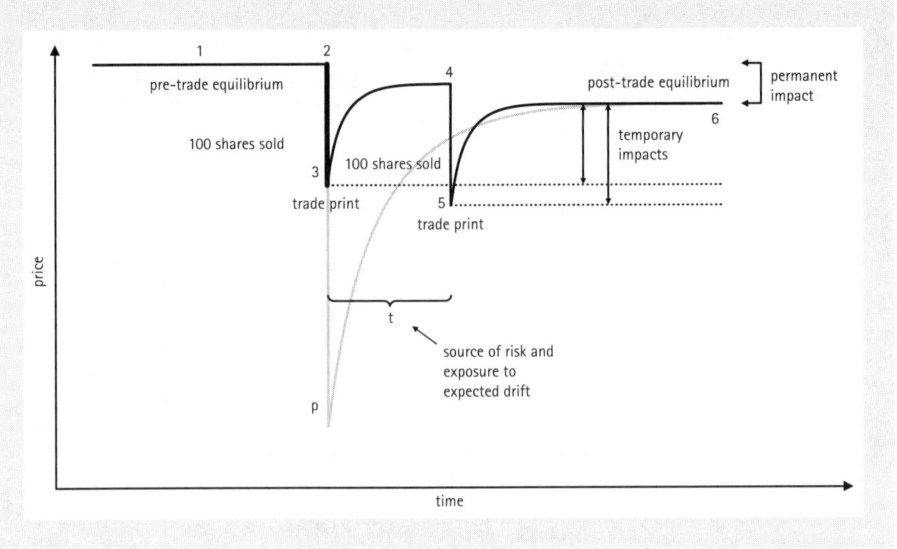

FIGURE 17.2 Idealized market impact model showing two sells of 100 shares each.

Our trader then places another market sell order for 100 shares (4) and obtains a trade print (5). Over time the temporary impact – (5) minus (6) – decays and results in a new post-trade equilibrium (6). As the permanent impact is assumed to be linear and immediate, the post-trade equilibrium is shown to be the same for one order of 200 shares as it is for two orders of 100 shares each.

17.3 Optimal Execution

While our trader waits between trades (t), he incurs price risk – the risk that his execution will be less favorable due to the random movement of prices. In this context, a *shortfall*, below referred to as C, is the difference between the effective execution price and the arrival price – the prevailing price at the start of the execution period. If we use the variance of shortfall, $Var(C)$, as a proxy for risk, a trader's aversion to risk establishes a trade-off between expected shortfall and the variance of shortfall. In the first scenario, he pays a higher cost – the difference between (p) and (6) – to eliminate risk. In the second scenario, he pays a lower cost – the average of the differences between (3) and (6), and (5) and (6) – but takes on a greater dispersion of shortfalls associated with the waiting time between trades (t). This is the trade-off considered in the seminal paper of Almgren and Chriss (2000).

The general form of the optimal execution problem is finding the best trade-off between the effects of risk, market impact, and alpha by minimizing risk-adjusted costs relative to a pre-specified benchmark over the trading period T. The first formulations of this problem go back to the seminal papers by Bertsimas and Lo (1998) and Almgren and Chriss (2000). In the latter, it is assumed that stock price follows the arithmetic random walk

$$S_k = S_{k-1} + \sigma\tau^{1/2}\xi_k$$

for $k = 1, \ldots, N$, where σ is the volatility of the asset, $\tau = T/N$, and ξ_k are independent random variables with zero mean and unit variance. When there is trading, the stock price is affected by linear permanent and temporary impacts. The permanent impact is linear in the number of shares traded, n_k, between $t_{k-1} = (k-1)\tau$ and $t_k = k\tau$:

$$S_k = S_{k-1} + \sigma\tau^{1/2}\xi_k - \gamma n_k.$$

The temporary impact is linear in the average rate of trading, n_k/τ, and only affects the effective price, $\tilde{S}_k$, in the current period

$$\tilde{S}_k = S_{k-1} - \eta \cdot \frac{n_k}{\tau}.$$

The parameters γ and η are referred to as the permanent and temporary market impact cost coefficients, respectively.

If we assume that the agent has quadratic utility, his optimal execution problem takes the form.[1]

$$\min_{x_1,\ldots,x_{T-1}} [E(C) + \lambda Var(C)]$$

where C is the cost of deviating from the arrival price benchmark and $\lambda > 0$ is his risk aversion. The solution is given by the trade schedule x_t $(n_k = x_{k-1} - x_k)$ that represents the number of shares that remains to be traded between t_{k-1} and t_k.

For instance, let us consider selling X shares. That is, we want $x_0 = X$ and $x_T = 0$. Then the solution is given by

$$x_t = X\frac{\sinh(\kappa(T-t))}{\sinh(\kappa T)}$$

where $\kappa = \sqrt{\frac{\lambda\sigma^2}{\eta}}$.

Note that the solution is effectively the decaying exponential $X\exp(-\kappa t)$ adjusted such that $x_T = 0$. The solution does not depend on permanent market impact because it is linear in trade size, not the rate of trading. The urgency of trading is embodied in κ. This parameter determines the speed of liquidation independent of the order size X. For a higher risk aversion parameter or volatility – for example, representing increased perceived risk – the speed of trading increases as well. All other factors held constant, a higher expected temporary market impact encourages slower trading, while a higher expected risk or risk aversion encourages faster trading.

[1] Bertsimas and Lo (1998) proposed an algorithm for the optimal execution problem that finds the minimum expected cost of trading over a fixed period of time for a risk neutral trader, $\lambda = 0$, facing an environment where price movements are serially uncorrelated.

Similar to classical portfolio theory, as λ varies the resulting set of points $(Var(C;\lambda), E(C;\lambda))$ traces out the *efficient frontier of optimal trading strategies*. The two extreme cases $\lambda = 0$ and $\lambda \to \infty$ correspond to the minimum impact strategy – trading at a constant rate throughout the execution period – and the minimum variance strategy – a single execution of the entire target quantity at the start of the execution period.

Another factor that influences the decision to trade more quickly or more slowly is the expectation of price change.[2] For the purpose of execution, a *positive alpha* is an expectation of profits per share per unit time for unexecuted shares. A faster execution captures more of the profits associated with this expectation of price change. A *negative alpha* is the expectation of losses per share per unit time for unexecuted shares. A slower execution incurs less of the losses associated with this expectation of price change. For example, a trader has positive alpha if he expects prices to move lower while he is executing his sell orders. He may choose to front-weight his trade schedule – execute more rapidly at the beginning of the execution period – to obtain better execution prices. Similarly, a seller who believes that prices are moving higher may back-weight his trade schedule or delay the execution.

The model outlined above is a common starting point for an optimal execution strategy referred to as Arrival Price. The following section provides a general decision framework for choosing between this and four other common algorithmic trading strategies.

17.4 Algorithmic Trading Strategies

The five most popular algorithmic trading strategies – *Arrival Price*, *Market-On-Close*, *Participation*, *Time-Weighted Average Price* (*TWAP*), and *Volume-Weighted Average Price* (*VWAP*) – cumulatively comprise a large fraction of all trading volume. Though, at first, these strategies may appear to be entirely unrelated, they do, in fact, reflect traders' divergent beliefs about the best way to measure and minimize risk-adjusted costs of execution.

Typically, risk-adjusted costs are computed as follows. At the end of an execution period, the average price per share of executed shares is compared to a benchmark price. The difference between the execution price and the benchmark price is called a shortfall, which is frequently modeled as having three factors.

The first factor is the random movement of prices. All else held constant, a risk averse trader would prefer unexecuted shares to be exposed to less return volatility.

The second factor is the temporary market impact of a trader's own execution, which is sometimes referred to as the liquidity premium. As traders buy (sell), they temporarily

[2] Under certain simplifying assumptions, it is straightforward to extend the model presented here to incorporate this effect. For example, see the original paper by Almgren and Chriss (2000).

deplete available liquidity and thereby drive up (down) the price of the shares they execute. This results in a less favorable execution.

The third factor is any expectation of price change due to exogenous factors. For example, during an execution period, a trader may expect prices to move higher due to the activity of other traders.

The first factor represents risk, while the second and third factors are costs. Given a utility function and a risk aversion parameter, a trader can translate the risk of a proposed execution strategy into a certainty equivalent cost. This is the dollar amount that a trader would agree to pay to eliminate execution risk.

The three costs – the certainty equivalent cost of risk, any expectation of a trader's own market impact, and any expectation of price change driven by exogenous factors – are then summed to obtain a risk-adjusted cost for the proposed execution strategy. The best execution strategy is the one with the lowest risk-adjusted costs.

Market participants who want to minimize risk-adjusted costs – whether explicitly, as above, or using a less rigorous (rule-of-thumb) approach – are confronted with a series of decisions, which are then used to determine the execution strategy that best fits their preferences. The process can be described as having four steps: (1) choosing the lowest risk strategy; (2) choosing the lowest cost strategy; (3) modeling the expectation of price change; and (4) finding the trade-off between risk and costs that is most compatible with one's appetite for risk. These steps are discussed in greater detail below.

17.4.1 Choosing Lowest Risk Strategy

The first decision a trader must make is related to his view of risk. Given a benchmark price and an execution risk model, traders must decide on the type of execution that is expected to expose their positions to the smallest risk. The concept of a benchmark price is discussed in the following paragraphs.

As explained above, a benchmark price is the price to which execution prices are compared. Sometimes, a benchmark is selected for traders. For instance, a fund-of-funds client of a hedge fund might choose a benchmark to gauge the hedge fund's execution quality. At other times, the benchmark is self-imposed. This is the case when portfolio managers within a fund choose a benchmark for measuring the performance of their traders.

There are three popular benchmarks. The arrival price is the prevailing price when a parent order first arrives at a trading desk. The VWAP price is the dollar value – price multiplied by size – of all trades in the market during a certain period divided by the total number of shares traded in that period. The closing price is simply the price of the last trade – or series of trades – of the day.

The most compelling reason for choosing a benchmark is its use in performance evaluation. For example, if a trader's performance is evaluated by comparing his execution prices to the VWAP price, minimizing risk-adjusted shortfall relative to other benchmarks will unnecessarily increase the dispersion of shortfalls relative to the VWAP benchmark.

There are situations in which the additional risk may be an acceptable trade-off for a reduction in costs. However, if the trade-off becomes routine, it is likely that the evaluator has chosen the wrong benchmark. For example, suppose that a strategy with a strong expectation of positive price change on unexecuted shares is benchmarked to VWAP. An opportunity to capture some of the profits associated with an expectation of price change may compel a trader to execute buys faster than would be optimal if the only concern were risk. In this case, arrival price may serve as a more appropriate benchmark.

For each benchmark, there is a theoretical execution that carries the lowest associated risk. For an arrival price benchmark, as discussed in the previous section, it is the immediate transaction of the entire target quantity as soon as the parent order arrives at the trading desk.

For a VWAP benchmark, the lowest risk execution is obtained by trading one's own shares in the same fractional volume pattern as the market. For instance, if the market is expected to trade 10% of total daily volume between 11 a.m. and 11:30 a.m., traders seeking to minimize deviation from the VWAP benchmark should trade 10% of their day's target quantity over the same period of time. For any given day, the fractional volume prediction is noisy. This makes it impossible to eliminate all risk relative to the VWAP benchmark while still executing the full target quantity.

If traders were willing to give up the certainty of executing their full target quantity – if they were willing to trade an uncertain, smaller, or larger number of shares – they could completely eliminate the risk of deviating from a VWAP benchmark. This is one of the objectives of a participation strategy. For example, traders using this strategy may decide that they will trade one share for every 100 shares traded in the market. If 100,000 shares are then observed to have traded in the market, the traders in this example will execute their own 1,000 shares.

Finally, in the case of a closing price benchmark, the lowest risk is associated with a single execution of the full target quantity in the last few seconds of the day.

17.4.2 Choosing Lowest Cost Strategy

To determine the lowest cost strategy, traders must first decide which model of market impact is most compatible with their views. The most popular model of market impact is the *rate of trading model* of the type described in Almgren, Thum *et al.* (2005) discussed in the next section.

In a rate of trading model, temporary market impact is a function of one's own rate of trading expressed as a fraction of the absolute trading activity of the market. However, there is some disagreement as to whether the absolute trading activity of the market should be a static, historical value – such as the average daily volume over the last 10 days – or the absolute trading volume expected to actually occur in the time period of a trader's own execution. In other words, a trader who believes the latter may use a different expectation of the market's trading activity from 12 p.m. to 1 p.m. than from 1 p.m. to 2 p.m., whereas a trader who believes the former would use the same value for both periods.

One popular interpretation of the model is that the markets are relatively efficient with respect to the relationship between trading volume and volatility, which are typical inputs of the model. This view implies that if trading activity increases (decreases), it is the result of an increase (decrease) of available information, which carries with it an increase (decrease) of volatility. Therefore, any reduction in impact that results from more trading volume would be offset by an increase in impact due to increased volatility. In this view, executing more shares at a time of day that historically sees more volume does not necessarily result in a reduced impact, which implies that the lowest impact cost is achieved by the lowest absolute, not relative rate of trading. The lowest absolute rate of trading can be realized by distributing one's orders evenly over time. This is called a *time-weighted average price* (TWAP) execution.

The other interpretation of the rate of trading model is that the markets are not efficient with respect to the relationship of volatility and volume, in which case an expectation of increased volume without a commensurate increase in volatility is an opportunity to lower one's relative rate of trading, and hence lower one's overall expected temporary impact. In this view, VWAP execution is expected to result in the lowest temporary market impact costs. In a VWAP execution, a trader places his orders in the same fractional volume pattern as the market.

17.4.3 Choosing Model of Price Change

Passive or indexed traders are motivated by a need to reduce risk, free up capital for redemptions, or increase holdings to accommodate new capital. In this case, the relevant trade-off is a compromise between risk and costs and no alpha model is necessary.

For directional traders – traders who have a view regarding future prices – expectation of price change is the primary motivation for trading. In most models of expectations – often called *alpha* models – the signal is either constant or decaying. In other words, the peak of the expectation occurs at the beginning of the trading period, with the largest price changes expected to occur around the time a signal to trade is first received.

When deliberately trading against the consensus – buying (selling) when the majority of investors are selling (buying) – a trader is said to have negative alpha. For such traders, waiting to execute will result in more favorable prices. Value investors and mean reversion traders are good examples of this group.

When executing with the consensus, a trader is said to have positive alpha. For such traders, waiting to execute will result in less favorable prices. Trend followers and event traders fall into this second category.

Just as with risk and impact models, alpha models are an important consideration in choosing an execution benchmark. A mismatch between alpha models and a choice of benchmark may result in sub-optimal performance.

For instance, consider a directional trader with positive alpha who wants to buy some number of shares of stock XYZ. Suppose he is benchmarked to VWAP. As he begins to execute, his prediction is gradually realized as the price of stock XYZ moves up for all market participants. If he is executing his shares in the same fractional volume pattern as the market, he will closely track the price obtained by others. This price will reflect his failure to profit from the price move he correctly predicted, a move which was not – by definition – anticipated by other market participants. The arrival price benchmark – rather than the VWAP benchmark – more appropriately reflects this trader's sense of urgency.

In general, negative alpha – the expectation of more favorable fill prices on deferred executions – is best used with a deferred benchmark, such as market-on-close. A positive alpha – the expectation of less favorable fills for deferred executions – is more compatible with the arrival price benchmark. Finally, if a trader has no view about directional price change, he should choose the VWAP benchmark.

17.4.4 Choosing an Algorithmic Execution Strategy

The final step in the process of choosing an algorithmic execution strategy is finding the appropriate compromise between impact, risk, and alpha loss. This trade-off is relatively straightforward under the assumptions of the model by Almgren and Chriss discussed in the previous section. In their model, alpha is assumed to be positive and constant throughout the execution period. The benchmark price is the arrival price, and market impact is linear in the rate of trading. As we saw earlier, the trade-off between risks and costs can be described in the following three dimensions. A higher (lower) alpha or higher (lower) risk aversion both compel faster (slower) trading, while a higher (lower) expectation of market impact compels slower (faster) trading.

As previously explained, the trade-off becomes less obvious – and in some cases even contradictory – when a mismatched set of benchmarks and objectives are used.

Tables 17.1 and 17.2 are decision tables that can be used to choose a benchmark price and the appropriate execution strategy. The top of each table shows decisions. A column in the top half is a set of decisions. The bottom half of each table shows actions that are appropriate for a given set of decisions. For example, in Table 17.1, column 1 represents the following decision set:

- There is no expectation of price change (alpha).
- Maintaining a trade schedule that mimics the market volume pattern is believed to result in the lowest market impact costs.
- The execution period has a set start time.
- The execution period has a set end time.

Table 17.1 Decision table to choose the appropriate benchmark and execution strategy.

Decisions	No alpha	y	y	y			
	Positive alpha				y	y	
	Negative alpha						y
	Min impact = volume weighted trading	y	y				
	Min impact = time weighted trading			y	y	y	
	Set end time	y		y	y	y	y
	Set end quantity	y		y	y	y	y
Benchmark	Choose VWAP benchmark	1	1				
	Choose Arrival Price benchmark				1	1	
	Choose closing price benchmark						1
	Choose TWAP benchmark			1			
Execution Strategy	Choose VWAP execution strategy	2					
	Choose back-weighted execution						2
	Choose TWAP strategy			2			
	Choose Participation strategy		2				
	Choose Arrival Price strategy				2	2	

Looking at column 1 in the bottom of the same table, it can be seen that the following actions are the result from the above decisions:

- *Choose VWAP benchmark.*
- *Choose the VWAP execution strategy.*

Tables 17.1 and 17.2 do not include all possible combinations for the reason that some of them are either counterproductive or very unlikely to arise. For example, it would be counterproductive for a market participant with a strong positive alpha to choose a closing price benchmark. As previously explained in this section, such a choice would hide the true risk-adjusted costs of this execution.

When a benchmark is not imposed by managers or investors, a market participant can use Table 17.1 to choose the appropriate combination of benchmark and execution strategy. Having chosen an executions strategy and benchmark, a market participant would then use Table 17.2 to further adjust the trade-off between risk and costs.

Table 17.2 Decision table to choose appropriate refinements once the benchmark and strategy have been set.

	Strategy:	AP			Part			MOC			VWAP			TWAP		
Benchmark	Arrival Price	y	y	y												
	VWAP				y	y	y				y	y	y	y	y	y
	Closing Price							y	y	y						
Alpha Structure	Positive alpha	y	y	y								y				
	No alpha	y		y	y	y	y									
	Negative alpha							y	y	y						
Objectives	Reduce risk	y			y			y			y			y		
	Reduce alpha loss		y			y			y			y			y	
	Reduce impact			y			y			y			y			y
Action	Move start time closer to end time							1	1							
	Move start time further from end time						1			1						
	Move end time closer to start time											1			1	
	Move end time further from start time												1			1
	Front-weight execution	1	1									2			2	
	Flatten execution			1						2						
	Back-weight execution							2	2							
	Place fewer market orders			2			2			3	1		2	1		2
	Place fewer limit orders	2						3								
	Increase participation rate				1											
	Decrease participation rate						3									

17.5 Market Impact Models

An impact model is used to predict changes in price due to trading activity. This expectation of price change may be used to inform execution and portfolio construction decisions. Several well known models have been proposed. For example, see Hasbrouck (1991), Fabrizio, Farmer *et al.* (2003), and Almgren, Thum *et al.* (2005).

The main feature of the model in Almgren, Thum *et al.* (2005) is that it explicitly and separately estimates the permanent and temporary market impact costs. The authors use a proprietary data set obtained from Citigroup's equity trading desk in which a trade's direction – buyer or seller initiated – is known. Note that for most public data sets, trade direction is not available and has to be estimated by a classification algorithm. Classification errors in algorithms such as Lee and Ready (1991), and Ellis, Michaely *et al.* (2000) introduce a bias that typically produces an overestimate of the true trading cost.

In Almgren, Thum *et al.*, trades serve as a proxy for trading imbalance. The authors assume that, some time after the complete execution of a parent order, only permanent impact remains. This allows them, for each order of n_t shares, to separate the resulting impact into its permanent (I_t^{perm}) and temporary $\left(I_t^{temp}\right)$ components

$$I^{perm}(n_t) = \gamma \cdot \sigma_t \cdot \left|\frac{n_t}{V_t}\right|^{\alpha} + \varepsilon_t^{perm}$$
$$I^{temp}(n_t) = \eta \cdot \sigma_t \cdot \text{sign}(n_t) \cdot \left|\frac{n_t}{V_t \cdot T}\right|^{\beta} + \varepsilon_t^{temp}$$

where V_t is the average daily volume, σ_t is the one-day standard deviation, T is the fraction of the day over which the trade is executed, and ε_t^{perm} and ε_t^{temp} are unexplained residual terms.

Using a large set of trades, the model parameters $\alpha, \gamma, \beta, \eta$ can be estimated, giving the following qualitative results. First, permanent impact cost is linear ($\hat{\alpha} \cong 1$) in trade size. Second, temporary impact cost is roughly proportional to the square root – Almgren *et al.* find $\hat{\beta} \cong 3/5$ – of the fraction of volume represented by one's own trading during the period of execution. Hence, for a given rate of trading, a less volatile stock with large average daily volume has the lowest temporary impact costs.

17.6 Portfolio Optimization with Market Impact Costs

The objective of the portfolio allocation process is to find an optimal trade-off between return and risk. Traditionally, this was done independently of trading cost considerations, as the control and management of trading costs were handled separately by the trading desk. This suboptimal approach would often lead to target portfolio holdings that would incur large trading costs, in some cases having a severe impact on realized risk-adjusted returns. By directly incorporating transaction costs into the portfolio allocation process, resulting portfolios are more cost effective and show improvement in terms of realized risk-adjusted returns.

To illustrate how market impact cost can be incorporated into a single-period portfolio position, we consider a simple extension of standard mean-variance optimization. Suppose that the current portfolio holdings in dollars are w_0 and we want to determine the new holdings w, given a vector of expected returns μ, a covariance matrix of returns Σ, and a risk aversion coefficient λ.[3] The mean-variance problem with market impact costs then takes the form

$$\begin{aligned}
&\max_{w} w'\mu - \lambda w'\Sigma w - TC(x) \\
&\text{s.t.} \quad w'e + TC(x) \leq w_0' e \\
&w \in C, \quad e = (1, 1, \ldots, 1)'
\end{aligned}$$

where $x = w - w_0$ are the trades, and C is a linear convex constraint set The objective function combines the standard mean-variance utility with a market impact cost function. The modified budget constraint states that the market impact costs have to be financed from existing holdings.

For instance, using the market impact model of the previous section the transaction cost function would take the form

$$TC(x) = \sum_i TC_i(x_i) = \sum_i |x_i| \cdot \left[\frac{1}{2} I^{perm}\left(\frac{x_i}{S_i}\right) + I^{temp}\left(\frac{x_i}{S_i}\right) \right]$$

where S_i is the current price of stock i We observe that the individual terms of the transaction cost function are of the form $TC_i(x_i) = a_i \cdot |x_i|^{8/5} + b_i \cdot |x_i|^2$.

Although this is a specific example, it is in general true that transaction cost functions involve nonlinear (and non-quadratic) functions. While the portfolio allocation problem without transaction costs is a quadratic program (QP), with transaction costs it is a nonlinear program (NP) and thus more time-consuming to solve, especially for a large number of assets.

There are two main approaches to handle this. One can proceed as in, for example, Ceria, Takriti *et al.* (2008) and use a specialized solver to directly solve these types of problems, or one can solve a QP relaxation of the problem. Kolm (2010) show that there is no loss in accuracy by solving a problem where the market impact function has been approximated by a simple linear/quadratic function. Their key argument is that market impact data is *very* noisy and estimated market impact models therefore have large estimation errors. They show that the error that results from approximating the nonlinear market impact function with a linear/quadratic function is smaller than

[3] While the estimation of these quantities is very important in practice, a discussion of these issues is beyond the scope of this chapter. See Fabozzi, Kolm, Pachamanova, and Focardi (2007), for an overview of the most common approaches used in practice to estimate the inputs to portfolio optimization problems.

the estimation error. A benefit of the approximation is that it can be solved very quickly with standard QP or SOCP solvers.

17.7 Combining Execution and Portfolio Risk

Optimal execution algorithms have less value to a portfolio manager if analyzed separately from the corresponding returns earned by his trading strategy. In fact, high transaction costs are not bad *per se* – they could simply prove to be necessary for generating superior returns. At present, the typical sell side perspective of algorithmic trading does not take expectation of profits or the client's portfolio objectives into account. Needless to say, this is an important component of execution and, if not correctly accounted for, will lead to suboptimal execution and portfolio performance.

The decisions of the trader and the portfolio manager are based on different objectives. The trader decides on the timing of the execution, breaking large parent orders into a series of child orders that, when executed over time, represent the correct trade-off between opportunity cost, market impact, and risk. The trader sees only the trading assets, whereas the portfolio manager sees the entire portfolio, which includes both the traded and non-traded positions.

In general, the optimal execution framework of Almgren and Chriss (2000), described in an earlier section of this chapter, is not appropriate for the portfolio manager. The portfolio manager's task is to construct a portfolio by optimizing the trade-off between opportunity cost, market impact, and risk for the full set of trading and non-trading assets.

Engle and Ferstenberg (2007) proposed a framework that unites these objectives by combining optimal execution and classical mean-variance optimization models. In their model, trading takes place at discrete time intervals as the portfolio manager rebalances his portfolio holdings w_t at times $t = 0, 1, \ldots, T$, subject to changing expected returns, μ_t, and risk (as measured by the covariance matrix of returns), Ω_t, until he reaches the portfolio that reflects his final view $w_T = \frac{1}{2\lambda}\Omega_T^{-1}\mu_T$. The joint dynamic optimization problem has the form

$$\max_{\{w_t\}} \left\{ \sum_{t=1}^{T} \left(w_T'\mu_T - \lambda w_T'\Omega_T w_T\right) - \sum_{t=1}^{T} \left\{\Delta w_t'\tau_t + (w_T - w_{t-1})'\mu_t \right.\right.$$
$$\left.\left. +\lambda (w_T - w_{t-1})'\Omega_t (w_T - w_{t-1})\right\} + 2\lambda \sum_{t=1}^{T} (w_T - w_{t-1})'\Omega_t w_T \right\}$$

where $\tau_t = \tau_t(\Delta w_t)$ is the temporary market impact function (for simplicity of exposition we ignore permanent impacts). This is a dynamic programming problem that has to be solved by numerical techniques.

Each one of the three terms in the objective function above has an intuitive interpretation. The first term represents the standard mean-variance optimization problem. The second term corresponds to the optimal execution problem. The third term is the covariance between the remaining shares to be traded and the final position. In the single-asset case, the third term is positive (negative) for buying (selling) orders, which implies that risk is reduced (increased). If this term is ignored – which happens when portfolio allocation and optimal execution are performed separately – the measurement of total risk is incorrect.

17.8 Dynamic Portfolio Analysis

The antithesis of the small delta continuous trading approach is embodied in the idea of *lazy portfolios*, in which portfolios are rebalanced infrequently to reduce market impact costs. The first argument against lazy portfolios is that as time passes, the weights drift further and further away from optimal target holdings, in both alpha and risk dimensions. Second, use of an optimizer after long holding periods tends to produce large deviations from current holdings. When executed – often relatively quickly – these deviations result in significant market impact costs.

Engle and Ferstenberg (2007) show that to correctly measure risk we must take both existing positions and unexecuted shares into account. This idea unites execution risk with portfolio risk. Portfolio construction and optimal execution are similarly united by incorporating market impact costs directly into the portfolio construction process.

Ideally, the portfolio manager would like to solve a problem similar in nature to the Merton (1969) multi-period consumption-investment problem, that in addition takes market impact costs and changing probability distributions for a large universe of securities into account.[4] This *dynamic portfolio* or *small delta continuous trading* problem represents the next step in the evolution of institutional money management.

However, in practice multi-period models are seldom used. There are several reasons for that. First, it is often very difficult to accurately estimate return/risk for multiple periods, let alone for a single period. Second, multi-period models tend to be computationally burdensome, especially if the universe of assets considered is large. Third, the most common existing multi-period models do not handle real world constraints. In practice, the majority of managed portfolios are subject to all kinds of constraints (e.g. industry, sector, turnover, and tracking error constraints). For these reasons, it is most common to use single-period models to rebalance the portfolio from one period to another.

[4] As has been pointed out by Sneddon (2005), the dynamic portfolio problem differs in several important ways from the classical multi-period consumption-investment problem. First, the return probability distributions change throughout time. Second, the objective functions for active portfolio management do not depend on predicted alpha/risk, but rather on realized return/risk. Third, the dynamics of the model may be far more complex, including market impact costs and changing alpha.

The classical papers of Merton (1969, 1990) and Campbell and Viceira (2002) illustrate that single-period portfolio choice policies are in general not optimal in multi-period settings as they do not capture intertemporal effects and hedging demands. Return predictability and market impact naturally give rise to inter-temporal hedging demands for assets, and investors need to look beyond just the next period when optimally allocating across assets. For instance, market impact costs from trades in the current period have an effect on prices in subsequent periods.

In this section we discuss a multi-period framework that allows us to jointly model return predictability (alpha) and its decay, and permanent and temporary impact costs. The models of Grinold (2006), Engle and Ferstenberg (2007), and Garleanu and Pedersen (2009) are special cases of this model. A detailed description of this model, that also incorporates standard portfolio constraints, is presented by Kolm (2010). Kolm and Maclin (2010) report computational experiments and simulations using this model.

We consider a discrete time economy with N risky securities. Suppose that price changes $r_{t+1} \equiv p_{t+1} - p_t$ are given by

$$r_{t+1} = \mu_t + \alpha_t + \varepsilon^r_{t+1}$$

where μ_t are the fair security returns (the return that correctly compensates for the risk of holding each security), α_t are predictable excess returns, and ε^r_{t+1} is an unpredictable residual term with $E_t\left(\varepsilon^r_{t+1}\right) = 0$ and $Var_t\left(\varepsilon^r_{t+1}\right) = \Sigma$. The investor forecasts "alphas" using a factor model with K mean reverting factors ($K \ll N$)

$$\alpha_t = Bf_t + \varepsilon^\alpha_t$$

$$\Delta f_{t+1} = -Df_t + \varepsilon^f_{t+1}.$$

In the first equation, $f_t \in \mathbb{R}^K$ represents the factors, $B \in \mathbb{R}^{N\times K}$ the factor loadings, and ε^f_t the idiosyncratic components. This specification generalizes a standard static factor model, making it time-dependent. The second equation specifies the temporal behavior of the factors. Here $D \in \mathbb{R}^{K\times K}$ is a positive definite matrix of mean-reversion coefficients. Intuitively, the greater the elements of this matrix the faster the factors' mean revert to zero. Furthermore, we assume $E_t\left(\varepsilon^\alpha_{t+1}\right) = E_t\left(\varepsilon^f_{t+1}\right) = 0$, $Var_t\left(\varepsilon^f_{t+1}\right) = \Sigma^f$, $Var_t\left(\varepsilon^\alpha_{t+1}\right) = \Sigma^\alpha$, and that the error terms $\varepsilon^r_t, \varepsilon^\alpha_t, \varepsilon^f_t$ are mutually independent. This is similar to the setup in Garleanu and Pedersen (2009). We will now expand this model by incorporating temporary and permanent market impact costs.

We denote the investor's holdings at time t by w_t. Any trading in our economy is subject to both temporary and permanent impacts. Following Almgren and Chriss (2000) – which was discussed in an earlier section – we model the costs associated with trading an amount of $\Delta w_t = w_t - w_{t-1}$ shares as a cost against the investor's alpha, that is

$$\begin{aligned}\alpha_t &= Bf_t + \varepsilon^\alpha_t + \underbrace{\Pi\Delta w_t}_{\text{permanent}} + \underbrace{H\Delta w_t}_{\text{temporary}} - H\Delta w_{t-1} \\ &= Bf_t + \varepsilon^\alpha_t + \Pi w_t + H(\Delta w_t - \Delta w_{t-1})\end{aligned}$$

where $\Pi, H \in \mathbb{R}^{N \times N}$. Note that the term $H(\Delta w_t - \Delta w_{t-1})$ reverses the effect of a trade from one period to the next, making the impact of $H\Delta w_t$ effective for one period only (single period impact). Therefore, we refer to $H\Delta w_t$ as the temporary component and $\Pi \Delta w_t$ as the permanent component.

In most practical applications temporary impacts do not decay instantaneously over a single period but rather last for several. If we would like our temporary impact component to decay over multiple periods, we can achieve this by modeling the alpha process as

$$\alpha_t = Bf_t + \varepsilon_t^{\alpha} + (\Pi + H)\Delta w_t - h_t$$

where the new state variable h_t is defined by

$$h_t = Gh_{t-1} + (I - G)H\Delta w_{t-1} + \varepsilon_t^h.$$

Here the matrix $G \in R^{N \times N}$ (with $\|G\| < 1$) determines how fast the temporary impact decays. We assume $E_t\left(\varepsilon_t^h\right) = 0$, and $Var_t\left(\varepsilon_t^h\right) = \Sigma^h$.

The investor solves the following multi-period version of the mean-variance problem

$$\max_{\Delta x_1, \Delta x_2, \ldots} E\left[\left\{\sum_{t=1}^{T-1} (1-\rho)^t (x_t'\alpha_t - \frac{\lambda}{2} x_t' \Sigma x_t - \frac{1}{2} \Delta x_t' \Lambda \Delta x_t)\right\} + (1-\rho)^T (x_T'\alpha_T - \frac{\lambda}{2} x_T' \Sigma x_T)\right]$$

where $\rho \in (0,1)$ is a discount factor, λ is a risk aversion coefficient, Σ is the covariance matrix of returns, Λ is a diagonal matrix of positive entries representing a quadratic transaction cost, and w_0 are the initial portfolio holdings.

This objective function together with the dynamics turns out to be a stochastic linear-quadratic (LQ) regulator problem. In this model, the trade size Δw_t is the control variable and the optimal policy is linear in the "augmented state" variable, s_t,

$$\Delta w_t = L_t s_t$$

where the control matrices L_t are determined from the dynamics and problem parameters. The calculation of the control matrices is straightforward and only involves a few matrix operations. For some more details, we refer the reader to the appendix.

A full mathematical analysis of this model is beyond the scope of this chapter. Instead, we discuss the intuition behind the main results here.

The main results can be grouped into alpha and transaction-cost related effects, respectively. Let us first consider the effect of the alpha dynamics. As one would expect, the model prefers securities with high alphas, and securities that decay slowly relative to other securities. Of course, these are the assets with higher loadings to the more persistent factors. If either alpha decreases or its decay increases, the resulting holdings decrease, and vice versa. We refer to the optimal portfolios determined without trading costs (for each t) as the *target portfolios*.

First, we discuss effects related to transaction costs. In the sole presence of one-period temporary market impact cost, the optimal trade is proportional to the difference between the current and target portfolio holdings. When temporary market impact costs last for more than one period – and/or in the presence of permanent market impact costs – the optimal trade is proportional to the difference between current portfolio holdings and a dynamically modified optimal target portfolio (from here on referred to as the *dynamic target portfolio*). This dynamic target portfolio is different from the optimal target portfolio above, as it incorporates the transient and persistent frictional effects from trading into security prices.

Dynamic portfolio analysis changes the perception of traditional portfolio management – from a static to a dynamic view. Portfolios are moving targets that we are attempting to optimally track to balance the trade-off between risk-adjusted returns and trading costs while accounting for the persistent effects of both. We do this by choosing the optimal rate of trading. Kolm and Maclin (2010) illustrate that the dynamic portfolio framework presented here is computationally within full reach using a standard PC, even for quite large portfolios. In addition, they address the important practical challenge of accurately estimating the model parameters.

17.9 The High-Frequency Arms Race[5]

These sophisticated high-frequency trading firms, representing about 2% of the approximately 20,000 trading firms in the U.S., are believed to the responsible for almost three-quarters of all U.S. equity trading volume. These businesses include hundreds of the most secretive prop shops, proprietary trading desks at the major investment banks, and about 100 or so of the most sophisticated hedge funds, see Iati (2009). The TABB Group estimates that total annual profits of these high-frequency trading firms were about $21 billion in 2009, see Tabb and Iati (2009).

An often-quoted – but unattributed – fact is that a one millisecond reduction in latency is worth about $100 million per year for some exchanges and high-frequency trading firms. Needless to say, this is a substantial amount of money. Should companies be willing to pay this amount of money?

The main argument is that by being faster they can react to changes in the market before everyone else, thereby gaining an advantage. Their competitive advantage arises from being able to process and disseminate information sooner and faster than other market participants. This so-called "millisecond game" involves using anything from

[5] The area of algorithmic and high-frequency trading has been rapidly developing over the last few years, and is continuing to do so. The facts and comments reported in this section are based on the information available as of the time of writing. As this landscape is continuing to change and evolve, so may the facts.

faster computers located closer to the exchanges,[6] to the use of highly specialized software, in which, for example, the message packet sizes have been optimized.

17.9.1 Latency

Certainly, one part of being faster means reducing *latency*. While latency is a very important component of high-frequency trading, there is no common and agreed-upon definition. One definition considers the so-called end-to-end latency, which is sometimes referred to as total latency and consists of two components: (1) exchange latency, and (2) member latency. The former is the latency associated with the price discovery and dissemination from the exchange, while the latter refers to the time it takes to get the information to the firm and process it. These two components can in turn be further broken down into the following steps.

1. price dissemination and distribution at the exchange;
2. transmission of price information from the exchange to the firm;
3. preparation of the order at the firm;
4. distribution of the order to the exchange;
5. placement of the order in the order book;
6. order acknowledgment from the exchange;
7. final report on order execution from the exchange.

A survey conducted by Greene and Robin (2008) concluded that the timings for each one of the steps above varies quite a bit from exchange to exchange, and from firm to firm. The results from the survey are as follows: (1) 500 microseconds – 5 milliseconds,[7] (2) 4–5 milliseconds, (3) + (4) around 100 milliseconds,[8] (5) 5–25 milliseconds,[9] and (6) 500 microseconds – 2 milliseconds.[10] The study did not address (7).

Remote location data transfers are an important part of latency. These transfers are typically between the firm and the exchange, but may involve other parties as well (or multiple exchanges). With the current technology available these transfers can be done

[6] This practice is referred to as *colocation*. As of August 2009, at NASDAQ about 100+ firms colocated their servers at a rate of about $7,000 per rack and month.

[7] NASDAQ (1 millisecond), BATS Trading (400–500 microseconds), LSE (2 milliseconds), NYSE (2–5 milliseconds), Deutsche Börse (2 milliseconds).

[8] According to the study, some firms reported that they can handle prices within 2–3 milliseconds.

[9] Average/median execution times: LSE (8–14 milliseconds), NYSE (10–25 milliseconds), NASDAQ (15 milliseconds), BATS Trading (5 milliseconds). However, the study reports that outliers can be up to 250–500 milliseconds for execution.

[10] This is a confirmation that the order has been *received* at the exchange, and not necessarily that it has been placed on the book: BATS Trading (500 microseconds), LSE (1 millisecond), NASDAQ (1 millisecond), NYSE (2 milliseconds).

in about 7 milliseconds between New York and Chicago, and in about 35 milliseconds between the West and East coasts.[11]

Many high-frequency traders are concerned with latency. An example is high-frequency liquidity providers that profit from the spread (about a cent for the most liquid stocks) and the rebate (also referred to as the "maker taker" fee). Market participants that place resting limit orders – orders that are added to the limit book – are offered a rebate from the exchange if their quotes result in trades. This is part of their compensation for providing liquidity. Today, most markets offer rebates as a form of volume discount to attract high-frequency traders. For example, in July 2009 Direct Edge paid a rebate of 0.25 cents per share to subscribing firms that provide liquidity and charged liquidity takers a fee of 0.28 cents.

Every time the exchange publishes an update to the limit book, the fastest firms are able to respond by updating their quotes accordingly. By being first at the new price, their limit orders receive time priority over subsequent orders at the same price, and hence are more likely to match incoming marketable orders. A successful execution provides them with a small gain that includes the spread and the rebate (if any).

The problem of latency affects not only the opportunity to capture profit, but also the trade-off between risk and market impact. Suppose that a trader executes orders according to a trade schedule that is expected to result in 80% limit fills and 20% market fills. This trader would not want the ratio of limit to market orders to drop significantly lower than 4-to-1. But this is exactly what might happen as a result of a high latency. As time passes, quotes move around. The higher the latency, the greater the potential dispersion of real prices around the observed stale quote. To take an extreme example, if the bid at the open is \$91.01, a limit order to buy at \$91.01 placed at 3:59 p.m. – nearly 6½ hours later – is almost as likely to be at the new bid as it is to be at the new offer. When a limit order to buy falls at the offer, it is a marketable limit order, and will match against the offers to sell at that price. Hence, an execution meant to provide liquidity, thereby capturing the spread and earning a rebate, will achieve neither of those objectives. This is yet another reason that high-frequency traders who expect large limit fill rates should be mindful of the latency of their trading infrastructures.

17.9.2 Algorithmic Trading and Liquidity

The most critical component of an exchange is to be able to provide market participants with liquidity. For the purposes of this discussion, we can loosely define liquidity as: (1) the ability to *trade quickly* without significant price changes, and (2) the ability to *trade large volumes* without significant price changes.

[11] These are one-way transfers as reported by Barr (2008). At the speed of light it would take about 11 milliseconds at the shortest distance from the East Coast to the West Coast (this is 2,092 miles or 3,347 kilometers, and is from (approximately) Jacksonville, FL to San Diego, CA. The speed of light is 299.792458 kilometers/millisecond.

There is an ongoing debate both in the technical as well as popular press whether high-frequency traders enhance market efficiency and provide increased liquidity.

Decreasing latency changes the competitive factors in the demand and supply of liquidity and how quotes are updated to reflect public information. High-frequency traders consume liquidity when it is cheap and supply liquidity when it is expensive, thereby smoothing out liquidity over time. As high-frequency traders compete by trying to provide the best quotes, they move the market towards its efficient price.

Hendershott, Jones *et al.* (2008) show that increased algorithmic trading leads to narrower quoted and effective spreads for large-cap stocks. The narrower spreads result from a decrease in the amount of price discovery associated with trades (i.e. a decrease in adverse selection).

Interestingly, Hendershott, Jones *et al.* (2008) suggest that the revenues of liquidity suppliers also increase with high-frequency trading. This is consistent with the idea that algorithmic liquidity suppliers have a form of market power as they introduce their new algorithms and are able to capture some of the surplus for themselves.

High-frequency traders are often blamed for the recent increase in market volatility. A recent study by Riordan and Hendershott (2009) in the 30 DAX stocks on the Deutsche Börse seems to indicate the opposite. In particular, they find no evidence that algorithmic traders demanding liquidity during times of low liquidity increased volatility. In addition, they also show that when algorithmic traders do not supply liquidity, there is no impact on volatility.

Obviously, there are physical limitations as to how much latency can be decreased. Standard arguments of economic theory suggest that over time through competition the profit margins of algorithmic trading will decrease. Most market participants will, at some point have about the same technological infrastructure, but not necessarily the same algorithms. As in many other areas, it will come down to who has the best – the smartest – algorithms. Some believe that the true edge in algorithmic trading is already coming from the use of superior algorithms – not necessarily the fastest algorithms, but those able to make the better decisions.

As trading platforms and tools proliferate, traders have more options for getting their orders to market, as well as growing concerns that as the number of contact points increases, so does information leakage. The problem of information hiding is more acute for the most advanced trading strategies.

For example, consider the multi-period optimization frameworks by Engle and Ferstenberg (2007) and Kolm (2010). The executing entity, which is often a broker dealer, must have full knowledge of all portfolio positions, even static positions for which it is not executing orders. Few, if any hedge funds are willing to share full portfolio information with their broker's algorithmic trading desk.

One solution is the idea of *third party hosting*, where the analytics server sits not at the broker dealer's location but at a third party site. The server is controlled entirely by the client. The broker dealer has limited access to the machine after market hours. In this way, the broker dealer can check total volume transacted and update strategy parameters, while the client has no fear of exposing an entire portfolio to the analysis.

17.9.3 Crossing Networks and Anti-Gaming

Falling trade sizes and increased transparency have made it difficult for large traders to hide information from smaller, more agile market participants. *Crossing networks* and *invisible orders* are a direct response to the argument that easily accessible and transparent electronic markets are bad for large traders.

A crossing network is essentially a hidden limit book where market participants can place large orders that – unlike orders placed in the open markets – are not immediately visible to other traders. Unlike an open exchange, crossing networks do not publish a price, instead they rely on the prices published by a designated open exchange.

Suppose two counter-parties – one a buyer and the other a seller – place large, offsetting orders in a crossing network. If these orders have no limit price – no minimum or maximum price at which they will execute – they will cross right away at the mid-quote price of a reference exchange. This mid-quote cross is frictionless in that neither side incurs market impact. However, after a cross occurs, both sides typically pay the crossing network fee. The fee can be substantial, but, for large traders, who would otherwise incur substantial market impact, is completely justified.

When orders placed in a crossing network fail to immediately find a counter-party, they may be added to one side of the network's limit book. For example, if an order to buy 5,000 shares joins another order to buy 10,000 shares but the offer book is empty, the two orders sit in the bid book until a sell order is received. The same might happen if orders have limit prices that prevent them from crossing.

The advent of limit orders in crossing networks makes these networks much more like open exchanges. Similarly, the introduction of dark orders – orders that are not displayed in the order book – makes exchanges look more like crossing networks. The difference between the two is that open exchanges are limited in what they can do to protect their orders from gaming.

In the context of crossing networks, *gaming* is the act of trading in a way to profit from information about order flow. The type of gaming that is familiar to most market participants is front running – buying (selling) a smaller number of shares before another trader's larger buy (sell) order is executed, then selling (buying) to cover the position, hence profiting from the market impact of the larger order.

Another type of gaming is called *gaming the quote*. In this strategy, the gamer uses small orders to manipulate the public exchange mid-quote that is used by a crossing network to obtain a price at which its internal orders are crossed. For example, if the best bid and offer are \$91.01 and \$91.03, respectively, placing a small bid at \$91.02 changes calculations of the mid-quote. If a large order placed in the network finds a counter-party for a mid-quote cross, the cross will take place at the new, manipulated mid-quote.

There are a number of strategies for limiting gaming in crossing networks. A minimum size requirement is an example of a simple but effective anti-gaming strategy. Allowing only large orders limits the amount of gaming that can profitably take place. Along with a size requirement, some networks have a minimum time requirement.

Specifying a minimum time that orders must spend in a crossing network before they can be removed (cancelled) protects the network's clients from active traders.

Yet another anti-gaming measure prevents orders of vastly different sizes from seeing each other in the network. Under this scheme, an order to buy 10,000 shares may be allowed to cross with part of an order to sell 20,000 shares, but an order to buy 100 shares would not.

The three anti-gaming measures described thus far are effective against front running, but not against gaming the quote. A strategy that is specifically designed to address the latter problem is the *volatility filter*. In this strategy, the network allows no crosses to take place when the quotes in a reference exchange are too volatile. It is assumed that it would be too expensive for gamers to manipulate the quote in an open exchange for long periods of time. Hence, if periods of small but rapid quote changes are filtered out, so is most of this type of gaming.

The emergence of nearly 40 crossing venues has created a new type of liquidity fragmentation. For example, if a 10,000 share order to buy is sitting in the bid book of network A, it will not match with a 10,000 share order to sell in network B. *Crossing aggregators* are broker dealers who strategically distribute large client orders across multiple crossing venues in an attempt to address the problem of liquidity fragmentation. By having orders in many or all of the different crossing venues at once, aggregators have more information about potential imbalances than would an individual trader. For example, when one client's order to buy fails to cross in a particular network, aggregators know that the likely imbalance in that network is on the buy side, and is probably larger than their own order. This piece of information may cause them to direct more sell orders to that network than they otherwise would.

As is the case with crossing venues, gaming is a big concern for crossing aggregators. When aggregators expose their clients' orders to a badly protected crossing network, they are in fact exposing all of their clients' orders on the same side to gaming. Hence, anti-gaming initiatives are a top priority for aggregators today.

17.10 Summary

In this chapter, we provided an overview of the main ideas of algorithmic trading, order book mechanics, and market impact, as well as a simple decision framework for choosing execution strategies. Next, we turned to portfolio optimization with market impact costs, first reviewing a stylized single-period model and then introducing a new multi-period portfolio optimization model that incorporates permanent and temporary market impact costs, and alpha decay. We closed the chapter with a discussion of the high-frequency infrastructure arms race, crossing networks, and anti-gaming, and their impact on the markets.

It is nontrivial for portfolio managers and other market participants to adapt to the new environment of algorithmic trading. There are still many challenges ahead in this field – both of a conceptual as well as of an infrastructure related nature – that make this area of finance attractive both from a business and from an academic perspective.

APPENDIX

In this appendix we provide a sketch of the analytical details underlying the multi-period framework with return predictability (alpha) and its decay, and permanent and temporary impact costs. The problem can be formulated as a linear-quadratic-Gaussian (LQG) control problem, where the state equations are linear and the cost function is quadratic. Its solution follows closely that of the standard theory (see, for example, Åström (2006). We summarize the results here. Further details are presented by Kolm (2010).

(a) State dynamics: First, we observe that the dynamics of the state variables of the problem (f_t, w_t, and h_t) are linear. It is convenient to define the "augmented state" variable $s_t = (f_t, w_t, h_t)'$, Now, observe that its dynamics are given by

$$\begin{aligned} s_t &= \begin{pmatrix} I-D & 0 & 0 \\ 0 & I & 0 \\ 0 & 0 & G \end{pmatrix} s_{t-1} + \begin{pmatrix} 0 \\ I \\ (I-G)H \end{pmatrix} \Delta w_t + \begin{pmatrix} \varepsilon_t^f \\ 0 \\ \varepsilon_t^h \end{pmatrix} \\ &= \hat{A} s_{t-1} + \hat{B} \Delta w_t + \varepsilon_t \end{aligned}$$

where

$$Var_{t-1}(\varepsilon_t) = \begin{pmatrix} \Sigma_f & 0 & 0 \\ 0 & 0 & 0 \\ 0 & 0 & \Sigma_h \end{pmatrix}.$$

(b) Objective function: The objective function was defined in the main text. Each summand is quadratic and can be rewritten as follows

$$\begin{aligned} x_t'\alpha_t - \frac{\lambda}{2} x_t' \Sigma x_t - \frac{1}{2} \Delta x_t' \Lambda \Delta x_t &= x_t' \left(Bf_t + \varepsilon_t^\alpha + (\Pi + H)\Delta x_t - h_t \right) \\ &\quad - \frac{\lambda}{2} x_t' \Sigma x_t - \frac{1}{2} \Delta x_t' \Lambda \Delta x_t \\ &= \begin{pmatrix} s_t \\ \Delta x_t \end{pmatrix}' \begin{pmatrix} R & S \\ S' & Q \end{pmatrix} \begin{pmatrix} s_t \\ \Delta x_t \end{pmatrix} + O(\varepsilon_t^\alpha) \\ &\equiv c(s_t, \Delta x_t) + O(\varepsilon_t^\alpha) \end{aligned}$$

where

$$R = \begin{pmatrix} 0 & \frac{1}{2}B' & 0 \\ \frac{1}{2}B & -\frac{\lambda}{2}\Sigma & -\frac{1}{2}I \\ 0 & -\frac{1}{2}I & 0 \end{pmatrix}, \quad S = \begin{pmatrix} 0 \\ \frac{1}{2}(\Pi + H) \\ 0 \end{pmatrix} \text{ and } Q = -\frac{1}{2}\Lambda.$$

The objective function can therefore be written as

$$\max_{\Delta x_1, \Delta x_2, \ldots, \Delta x_{T-1}} E\left[\sum_{t=1}^{T-1} (1-\rho)^t c(s_t, \Delta x_t) + (1-\rho)^T C(s_T)\right]$$

where $c(s, \Delta x)$ is defined above, $C(s) = s'Rs$, and $R = R' \geq 0, S \geq 0, Q = Q' > 0$.

(c) The control: Together, the linear dynamics in (a) and the quadratic objective function in (b) define an LQG problem. Applying standard results from the theory of LGQ problems (see, for example, Åström (2006), the optimal control is the linear control given by

$$\Delta x_t = L_t s_t,$$

Here $L_t = -(Q + (1-\rho)\hat{B}' K_{t+1} \hat{B})^{-1}(S + (1-\rho)\hat{B}' K_{t+1} \hat{A}), t < T$, where K_t satisfies the Riccati equation

$$K_t = R + (1-\rho)\hat{A}' K_{t+1} \hat{A} - (S' + (1-\rho)\hat{A}' K_{t+1} \hat{B})$$
$$(Q + (1-\rho)\hat{B}' K_{t+1} \hat{B})^{-1}(S + (1-\rho)\hat{B}' K_{t+1} \hat{A})$$

References

Almgren, R. and Chriss, N. (2000). Optimal Execution of Portfolio Transactions. *Journal of Risk*, **3**(2): 5–39.

Almgren, R., Thum, C. Hauptmann, E., and Li, H. (2005a). Direct Estimation of Equity Market Impact. *Risk*, **18**: 57–62.

Almgren, R., Thum, C. Hauptmann, E., and Li, H. (2005b). Equity Market Impact. *Risk*, **18**(7): 57–62.

Åström, K.J. (2006). *Introduction to Stochastic Control Theory*, Dover Publications, London.

Barr, J. (2008). Low latency: What's it all about? 451 Market Insight Service.

Bertsimas, D. and Lo, A.W. (1998). Optimal Control of Execution Costs. *Journal of Financial Markets*, **1**(1): 1–50.

Campbell, J.Y. and Viceira, L.M. (2002). *Strategic Asset Allocation: Portfolio Choice for Long-Term Investors*. Oxford University Press, New York.

Ceria, S., Takriti, S., Tierens, I., and Sofianos, G. (2008). Incorporating the Goldman Sachs shortfall model into portfolio optimization. Axioma's Breakfast Research Seminar Series, New York.

Ellis, K., Michaely, R., and O'Hara, M. (2000). The accuracy of trade classification rules: Evidence from NASDAQ. *The Journal of Financial and Quantitative Analysis*, **35**(4): 529–551.

Engle, R.F. and Ferstenberg, R. (2007). Execution risk. *Journal of Portfolio Management*, **33**(2): 34–44.

Fabozzi, F.J., Kolm, P.N. Pachamanova, D., and Focardi, S. M. (2007). *Robust Portfolio Optimization and Management*. John Wiley, New York.

Fabrizio, L., Farmer, J.D. and Rosario, N.M. (2003). Master curve for price-impact function. *Nature*, **421**, 129.

Garleanu, N.B. and Pedersen, L.H. (2009). Dynamic trading with predictable returns and transaction costs. SSRN eLibrary.

Greene, J. and Robin, P. (2008). The competitive landscape for global exchanges: What exchanges must do to meet user expectations. Cisco exchanges survey.

Grinold, R. (2006). A dynamic model of portfolio management. *Journal of Investment Management*, **2**, 5–22.

Hasbrouck, J. (1991). Measuring the information content of stock trades. *The Journal of Finance*, **46**(1), 179–207.

Hendershott, T.J., Jones, C.M. and Menkveld, A.J. (2008). Does algorithmic trading improve liquidity? SSRN eLibrary.

Huberman, G. and Stanzl, W. (2004). Price manipulation and quasi-arbitrage. *Econometrica* **72**(4), 1247–1275.

Iati, R. (2009). *The Real Story of Trading Software Espionage*. Advanced Trading, New York.

Kolm, P.N. (2010a). Multi-period portfolio optimization with market impact, alpha decay, and constraints. Mathematics in Finance Working Paper Series, New York University, Courant Institute of Mathematical Sciences.

Kolm, P.N. (2010b). Portfolio optimization with market impact costs. Mathematics in Finance Working Paper Series. Courant Institute of Mathematical Sciences, New York University.

Kolm, P.N. and Maclin, L. (2010). A practical multi-period portfolio optimization model with market impact costs. Mathematics in Finance Working Paper Series, Courant Institute of Mathematical Sciences, New York University.

Lee, C.M.C. and Ready, M.J. (1991). Inferring trade direction from intraday data. *The Journal of Finance*, **46**(2), 733–746.

Merton, R.C. (1969). Lifetime portfolio selection under uncertainty: The continuous-time case. *The Review of Economics and Statistics*, **51**(3), 247–257.

Merton, R.C. (1990). *Continuous-Time Finance*. Blackwell Publishers, London.

Riordan, R. and Hendershott, T. (2009). Algorithmic trading and information. Working Paper.

Sneddon, L. (2005). *The Dynamics of Active Portfolios*. Westpeak Global Advisors, Boulder, CO.

Tabb, L. and Iati, R. (2009). *Equity Trading in Transition: New Business Models for a Brave New World*. Tabb Group Westborough, MA.

CHAPTER 18

TRANSACTION COSTS AND EQUITY PORTFOLIO CAPACITY ANALYSIS*

YOSSI BRANDES, IAN DOMOWITZ, AND VITALY SERBIN

18.1 Introduction

In 1991, research by Perold and Salomon focused the attention of academics and practitioners on the effect of the size of assets under management (AUM) on fund performance. The bulk of the ensuing literature documents an inverse relationship between a fund's size and its net return. The dominant explanation blames diminishing returns on rising turnover costs as fund size increases.

Turnover is required to exploit informational advantages, but performance deteriorates as fund managers turn over larger volumes of stock, incurring higher explicit and implicit transaction costs.[1] This observation leads to the *capacity problem*, or more

* We are grateful to Milan Borkovec and Lorelei Skillman for helpful comments, and to Michael Chigirinskiy for expert research assistance. Any opinions expressed herein reflect the judgment of the individual authors at this date and are subject to change, and they do not necessarily represent the opinions or views of Investment Technology Group, Inc. The information contained herein has been taken from trade and statistical services and other sources we deem reliable, but we do not represent that such information is accurate or complete, and it should not be relied upon as such. The analyses discussed herein are derived from aggregated ITG client data and are not meant to guarantee future performance or results. This report is for informational purposes and is neither an offer to sell nor a solicitation of an offer to buy any security or other financial instrument. This report does not provide any form of advice (investment, tax, or legal).

[1] See Wermers (2000) on informational advantages and Perold and Salomon (1991) and Vangelisti (2005) on performance.

generally, to *capacity analysis*, which has been defined in different ways over time. It may be understood simply to describe the dependence between equity portfolio performance and size of fund. Alternatively, capacity analysis may be the study of ways to increase a fund's assets under management for a given target level of return. The term has even been applied specifically to the identification of an optimal level of turnover for every level of assets under management. By any of these definitions, capacity analysis remains an important topic, used by plan sponsors in manager search, by chief investment officers to determine growth options, and by portfolio managers to calibrate turnover levels.

We build on the work of Kahn and Shaffer (2005) and Bull, Serbin, and Zhu (2009), who are concerned with ways in which the range of a fund size might be extended while remaining efficient. We introduce the use of expected transaction costs, on a stock-specific basis, at the portfolio construction stage. In previous work, transaction costs are applied after portfolio optimization is completed, to simply compute net returns. Controlling for transaction costs while rebalancing the portfolio allows the maintenance of a significantly larger fund size, relative to previous practice, and permits a higher level of turnover than would be possible otherwise.

We begin with an overview of the current state of equity portfolio capacity analysis in Section 18.2. As thinking advances from simply adding assets to a fixed portfolio strategy to consideration of stock-specific implementation costs, an explicit link is established among trading costs, portfolio optimization, and turnover. Consideration of implementation costs as an integral part of portfolio construction leads to the formulation of a Markowitz-style optimization problem in Section 18.3.

The results of modeling net return at different levels of AUM are described in Section 18.4. Explicit controls for stock-specific expected transaction costs minimize adverse effects of fund size on net return, and increase the potential informational advantages accruing to higher turnover. The benefits of including expected costs in portfolio optimization increase with fund size itself.

Taxes and trading strategy are taken up in Section 18.5. The role of taxes in portfolio construction is old ground, of course. We use this particular extension largely to reconcile differences in calculated turnover levels from our analysis with that observed in the mutual fund industry.[2] The role of trading strategy is more interesting. Accounting for expected implementation costs leads to turnover levels which strike a balance between the timely exploitation of new information and the avoidance of excessive costs. Trading strategy directly affects those costs, and therefore has a potentially important effect on capacity analysis. Although our basic results remain qualitatively the same for a wide class of expected cost estimates, quantitative conclusions can differ sharply with changes in trading strategy. We illustrate this point through a comparison of aggressive and passive trading behavior. Trading strategy becomes increasingly important as fund size grows.

[2] See, for example, Jeffrey, and Arnott (1993).

18.2 Past is Prologue: Capacity Analysis Today

18.2.1 The Current State of Play

We have all seen announcements concerning the closure of funds to new investment, on the grounds that the limitation of further AUM growth preserves current fund performance. As academic authors and practitioners more fully documented the relationship between AUM growth and decline in realized return, attention shifted to explanations of underlying causes. The winner of the intellectual debate was the effect of implementation cost, and its close cousin, turnover, on fund performance. In hindsight, this was an obvious conclusion. After all, investment performance reflects two factors: the underlying investment strategy of the portfolio manager and the execution costs incurred in realizing those objectives.

The stock-specific nature of implementation costs led to a definition of fund capacity in terms of the capacity of an individual investment strategy. For fixed portfolio strategies, this point is illustrated in Figure 18.1, which is based on four trade lists representing distinct size-segments of the U.S. equity universe: equally weighted and market-cap weighted large-cap stocks (SP500) as well as equally weighted and market-cap weighted small-cap stocks (R2000). Trading an equally weighted R2000 list costs noticeably more

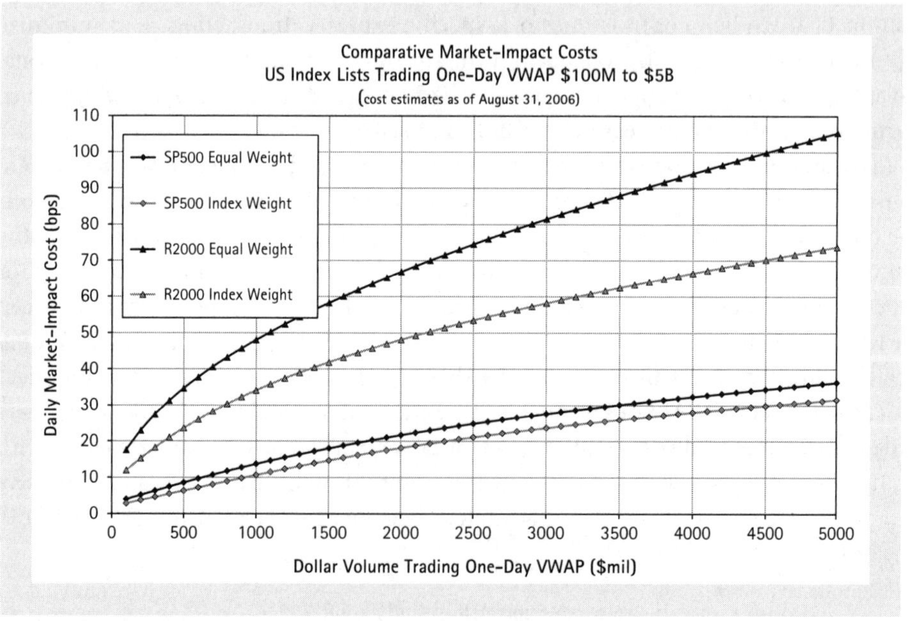

FIGURE 18.1 Daily market-impact costs for U.S. indices trade lists up to $5 billion.

than an index-weighted list, as more dollar volume is pushed into the less liquid names. Asset classification is routinely influenced by this sort of evidence.[3]

Liquidity, measured in terms of implementation costs, can be affected by changing the breadth of the portfolio or by changing the investable universe. In turn, liquidity effects differ depending on the investment strategy, implying that capacity is a strategy-specific phenomenon.

Consideration of strategy has a logical extension to the method of implementation itself, namely trading. Given the evolution of transaction cost analysis (TCA), the incorporation of trading strategies into stock-specific trading cost estimates was slow. As a result, any focus on implementation cost in portfolio construction was on assumed fixed costs and turnover.[4] Even as such assumptions were replaced by better information over time, market-impact costs were taken into account only in the "scoring" process to determine net returns, diminishing the importance of the trading strategy proper. In other words, transaction costs were simply subtracted from expected portfolio returns after portfolio strategy in terms of names and quantities was determined. The emphasis remained on turnover, which was treated as the only real choice variable, conditional on an investment strategy and estimates of underlying implementation costs. Intuitively, this made sense, if only because turnover acted as a multiplier of costs and as an implicit penalty function in analytical frameworks.

One can get a long way with turnover. In Bull, Serbin, and Zhu (2009), a long-short manager, using the S&P 500 as the investable universe, is modeled as an imperfect alpha forecaster, who rebalances monthly. In their framework, it is possible to derive optimal turnover levels for VWAP trading strategies, illustrated in Figure 18.2.

Due to transaction costs, the paper return dominates the returns of the portfolios at all AUM and turnover levels except zero. When turnover is very low, all four AUM levels exhibit almost a linear increase in net return. As turnover climbs past 20%, net returns for the larger AUM portfolios peak and drop quickly. For the $10 billion portfolio, net return is maximized at 3.40% with 40% turnover, while the $20 billion portfolio is maximized at 2.50% net return with 34% turnover. The $2 billion portfolio achieves a net return closer to 6%, and lower AUM levels approach the paper return, which includes neither commission costs nor market-impact costs.

This type of result motivates the idea of an efficient frontier for turnover, illustrated in Figure 18.3. If turnover is held constant, the manager moves from point A straight down to point B. In order to achieve the highest return in this scenario, the manager decreases turnover to move to point C. Point B represents not just an inefficient portfolio but an inefficient *strategy* that is paying too much in market-impact costs from excessive turnover relative to skill level in forecasting alpha.

[3] For example, the ordering of the international markets from least to most expensive in the fixed-dollar trade terms coincides with available floats. McDonald and Richardson (2006) suggest that index providers' decision to classify South Korea as an "emerging" market is largely for the convenience of institutional investors. With South Korea in their universe, emerging market funds can grow much larger without facing prohibitive turnover and maintenance costs, since South Korean stocks are much more liquid relative to stocks from other emerging markets.

[4] See Bogle (1994), for an early example.

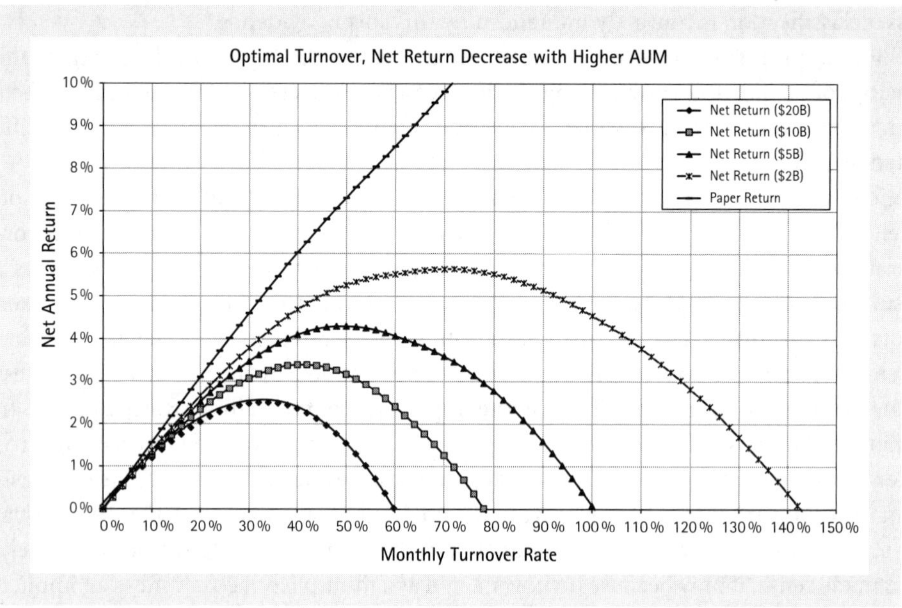

FIGURE 18.2 Optimal turnover rates for different levels of assets under management.

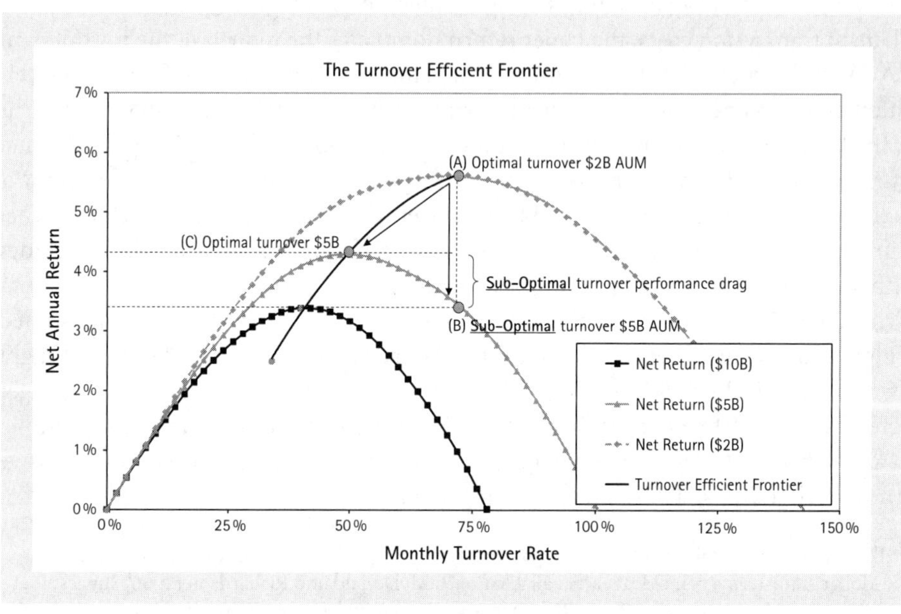

FIGURE 18.3 Turnover optimality.

Isolation of causal factors in the form of transaction costs makes possible the idea that fund capacity analysis could be done *ex ante*. In short, expected implementation cost joins expected return in portfolio planning and execution.

The focus shifts as a consequence. The capacity problem can be recast as a simple variant of the classical Markowitz optimization problem. The Fundamental Law of Active Management is also revisited by Coppejans and Madhavan (2007) and Bull, Serbin, and Zhu (2009), from which some theoretical insights may be interpreted in capacity terms. For example, if the information coefficient is reinterpreted as the correlation between predicted and realized *net* alphas, then increasing AUM is accompanied by decreasing forecasting ability, and by a reduced correlation between risk-adjusted alphas and active portfolio weights.

At this point in the evolution of capacity analysis, turnover is a simple multiplier of the fixed costs of transacting. Bringing the turnover decision into the capacity problem requires some explicit link among trading costs, portfolio optimization, and turnover itself. We now turn briefly to the evidence that suggests such a link exists.

18.2.2 Portfolio Optimization and the Cost of Trading

The introduction of implementation costs into portfolio formation began with properly accounting for net, as opposed to "paper" returns after the composition of the portfolio was determined. In the simplest case, transaction cost analysis in portfolio construction is limited to the idea that costs simply eliminate part of the notional or "paper" return to an investment strategy, and therefore, costs should be controlled at the level of the trading desk only. Research on how to generalize and solve the portfolio construction problem in the presence of transaction costs dates all the way back to 1970, however.[5] The focus in most of the published papers has been on technical formulations and the mechanics of problem solving.

The economic implications of incorporating implementation costs directly into portfolio optimization are explored theoretically by Engle and Ferstenberg (2007) and on an empirical level by Borkovec, Domowitz, Kiernan, and Serbin (2010). One of the optimization problems investigated in the latter work revolves around a two-year monthly rebalancing of a market and dollar neutral equity portfolio through August 2008, with the stock universe defined as the Russell 2000 Value Index. Stock specific transaction costs are included in the formulation of the problem, forcing the various optimization stages to recognize implementation cost at each step. Details with respect to the precise problem, its solution, and results can be found in the reference. For our purposes here, Figures 18.4 and 18.5 yield links between the use of transaction costs as an explicit part of portfolio strategy construction and turnover. In the charts, we refer to the solution of the problem, including transaction costs *ex ante*, as being *cost aware*, while the *non-cost-aware* portfolio is optimized setting costs to zero and then subtracting expected costs from returns. The dotted lines delineate 95% statistical confidence bands.

[5] See, for instance, Pogue (1970).

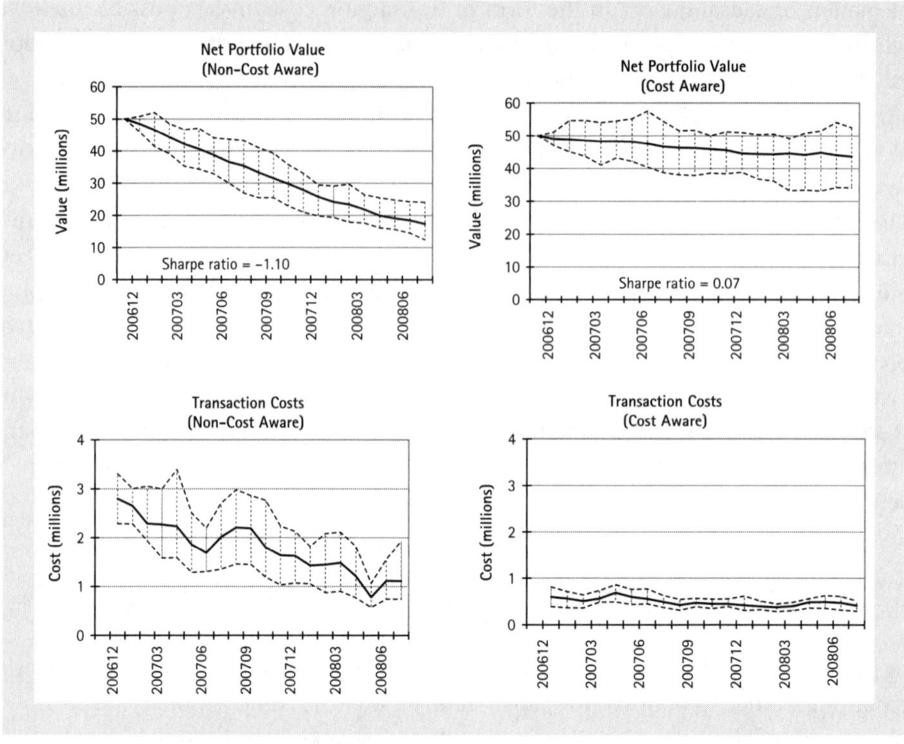

FIGURE 18.4 Net performance based on monthly rebalancing.

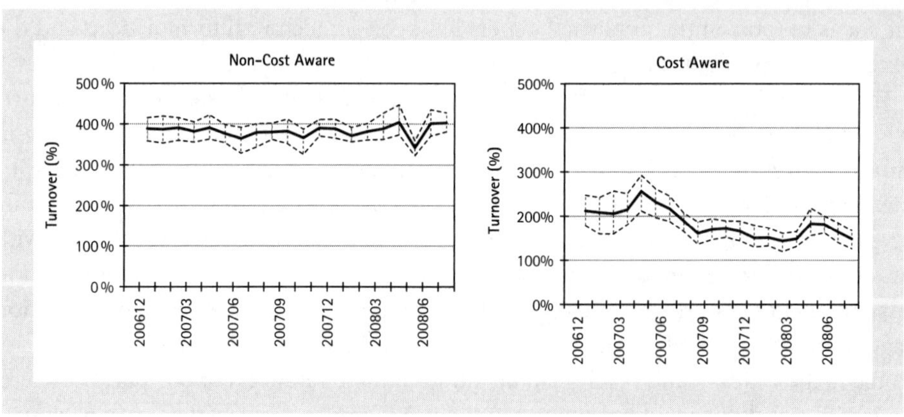

FIGURE 18.5 Turnover comparisons based on monthly rebalancing.

In Figure 18.4, the non-cost-aware rebalancing strategy loses on average more than 50% of its initial portfolio value by the end of the out-of-sample period, which translates into a negative Sharpe ratio of about −1.10. In contrast, the cost-aware portfolio performs much better, yielding a modest but positive Sharpe ratio of 0.07. The average dollar costs of implementing the cost-aware rebalancing strategy are two to four times lower than the costs of implementing the non-cost-aware strategy.

The costs of implementing the cost-aware rebalancing strategy remain lower despite the fact that its portfolio size starts to exceed the size of the non-cost-aware portfolio by as much as 50% in the last several months of the period considered. This is an important point in the context of capacity analysis. Another change shows up in turnover, depicted in Figure 18.5.

Turnover is calculated in percentage terms in this particular example, as dollars traded relative to the monthly portfolio basis. In a long-only portfolio, this statistic would have a maximum value of 200%. That value is doubled for the long-short portfolio with a 2:1 leverage ratio, i.e. the case in which the portfolio is 100% long and 100% short in dollar terms.[6] The total portfolio turnover goes down from almost 400% for the non-cost-aware to 250% and even 150% in the later months for the cost-aware rebalancing strategy. In other words, the cost-aware portfolio consistently exhibits significantly lower turnover and the monthly differences in this example can be as large as 270%.

We learn two lessons from this example, both applicable to capacity analysis. First, consideration of implementation costs as an integral part of portfolio construction matters, at least in the case of that amenable to a Markowitz-style methodology. In the context of capacity, similar integration offers the possibility of increasing fund size for any given level of required return. Second, the same method jointly determines expected cost, net returns, and turnover, and does so in such a way as to further reduce the cost to the portfolio. The implication here is what we have been looking for: turnover should not be considered a simple cost multiplier effect in a capacity analysis setting. We now turn to an investigation of both these points, beginning with the formulation of an appropriate optimization framework.

18.3 The Optimization Problem

We consider a fund manager, who rebalances a portfolio every month subject to a typical set of constraints, augmented by penalties for turnover and trading transaction costs. Portfolio net returns are used as the yardstick by which we compare alternative combinations of turnover levels and fund sizes.

[6] In fact, the long-short portfolio turnover can occasionally exceed 400% when, for example, the short side outperforms the long side in the month following the optimization date, thus reducing the net portfolio basis.

Table 18.1 Parameter values used in the optimization problem.

Portfolio wealth, W	\$100mln, \$250mln, \$500mln, \$1bln, \$2bln, \$5bln
Max. allocation weight, ϖ	5%
Monthly turnover bounds, t	10%, 20%, 30%, 50%, 70%, 100%, 130%
Annualized risk constraint σ	35%
Trading cost aversion coefficient τ	0, 5, 10, 15, 20, 30, 50

Every month, starting from December 2003 and ending in December 2008, we form a random portfolio of 100 stocks out of the eligible stock universe. The universe consists of all U.S. stocks with a market capitalization exceeding \$78 million, the approximate cutoff for the Russell 2000 index as of the time of writing this chapter. We also require a trading price above \$1 and no more than 10 missing returns in the last 60 months as of each portfolio formation date. This is admittedly an arbitrary choice, but any similar cutoff does not change the qualitative nature of the results. We add an additional restriction, that the half-spread for each stock does not exceed the 95th percentile of all half-spreads for the Russell 3000 universe for each month in the out-of-sample period. This requirement excludes extremely illiquid stocks, which are very expensive to trade. We consider six portfolio wealth levels ranging from \$100 million to \$5 billion, documented in Table 18.1.

After the random portfolio is formed at the beginning of each month, we run the following optimization problem:

$$\begin{aligned} &\max_{\omega} \widehat{\mu}' \omega - \tau \frac{TC(W)}{W} \\ &\omega' \Sigma \omega \leq \sigma^2 \\ &\sum_{i=1,n} \omega_i = 1, \; 0 \leq \omega \leq \varpi \\ &\sum_{i=1,n} \left| \omega_i - \omega_{i,0} \right| \leq t \end{aligned} \tag{18.1}$$

where $\omega_{i,0}$ is the initial allocation of the asset i, $i = 1, \ldots, 100$, ω^I is the vector of benchmark weights, and the remaining notation is contained in Table 18.1.[7]

The vector $\hat{\mu}$ in (18.1) represents the portfolio manager's estimate of expected returns. We simulate this alpha-forecasting process by drawing $\hat{\mu}$ from a statistical distribution given by:

$$\hat{\mu}_{i,t} = IC \cdot \mu_{i,t}^{observed} + \left[\Sigma_{\mu}{}^{1/2} \right]_i \cdot \sqrt{1 - IC^2} \cdot \varepsilon_i, \quad i = 1, \ldots, n, \tag{18.2}$$

[7] We also considered a tracking-error constrained problem in which the first constraint in (18.1) is replaced by $(\omega - \omega^I)' \Sigma (\omega - \omega^I) \leq \vartheta^2$. These results are quite similar and are not reported here.

where $\mu_{i,t} = R_{i,t} - r_f$, $R_{i,t}$ is the realized return for security i in month t, r_f is the risk-free rate, Σ_μ is the diagonal of the return covariance matrix, IC is the information coefficient (i.e. the proxy for the money manager's forecasting ability), and $\varepsilon \sim N(0,1)$. We report results for $IC = 5\%$, roughly corresponding to an average forecasting ability.

Expected costs, TC, are derived from ITG's Agency Cost Estimator (ACE^{TM}). Generation of these costs relies on a transparent methodology, and permits stock-specific estimates, which can be matched against expected returns.[8] We assume a 10% volume participation rate strategy throughout. Using a different price impact model leads to similar qualitative conclusions, if the alternative model embodies a concave relationship between unit costs and volume. On the other hand, trading strategy affects implementation costs. Our results will suggest that taking expected costs into account matters a great deal, and trading strategy has a quantifiable effect on the investment strategy overall. We will, therefore, return to the role of trading strategy in Section 18.5.

The covariance estimates are provided by the monthly U.S. model from the suite of ITG risk models. The model is estimated using time-series on a per-stock basis. The factor covariance matrix is scaled using an option-implied adjustment coefficient to provide forward-looking risk forecasts. The covariance matrix Σ of stock returns is computed as:

$$\Sigma = V^T F V + D \tag{18.3}$$

where F is the factor covariance matrix, V is the matrix of factor loadings, and D is the diagonal matrix of asset-specific variances.

Solving the optimization problem, we obtain an optimal portfolio which we hold for one month, record its return, and then perform optimization again. At the end of December 2008, we have a time series of 60 monthly portfolio returns. We repeat this exercise 25 times: we draw 25 random portfolios and average the out-of-sample statistics across time (except for the first month when we start from cash) and portfolios. We repeat this exercise for different combinations of parameter values presented in Table 18.1.

18.4 Trading Costs, Turnover, and Capacity

We model the interaction between turnover levels and net return at different levels of fund size. Since we introduce the transaction cost penalty τ in the objective function, this relationship is described in terms of realized (as opposed to target) turnover.[9]

[8] A complete description of the model, and results comparing expected to actual costs, are contained in ITG Inc. (2007). A more concise overview is contained in Bull, Serbin, and Zhu (2009).

[9] Choosing high values for transaction cost penalty makes the turnover constraint non-binding. In that case, the composition of the optimal portfolio is determined mainly by the value of the transaction cost penalty, resulting in a virtually flat relationship between net returns and the turnover constraint.

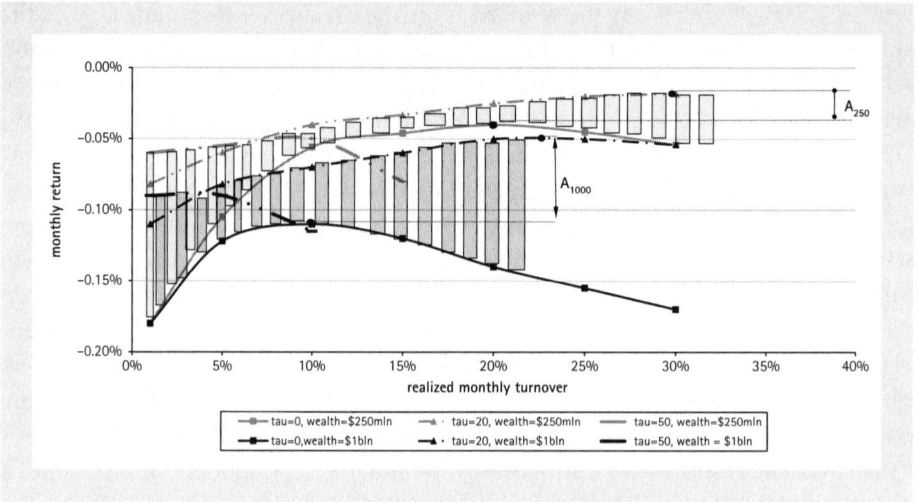

FIGURE 18.6 Return vs. realized turnover for different portfolio wealth.

Figure 18.6 illustrates the central results of this exercise. Realized turnover is plotted along the horizontal axis and the associated out-of-sample net return appears along the vertical axis. We show this relationship for two levels of fund wealth ($250mln and $1Bn) and for three values of the transaction cost penalty coefficient ($\tau = 0$, 20, and 50). The solid lines represent results corresponding to $\tau = 0$, which in turn means that transaction cost estimates are applied to yield net returns only post-optimization, accounting for implementation cost but playing no direct role in portfolio construction. Dashed curves track results when such costs are introduced directly into the optimization problem, i.e. corresponding to $\tau > 0$.

Increasing portfolio size leads to lower out-of-sample net returns. This result is not new, but the context is now important. Previous results implicitly contain the assumption that transaction costs enter only through the calculation of net return, post-optimization. Once that assumption is relaxed, the game changes markedly.

In particular, by picking an appropriate value for the cost aversion coefficient, τ, it is possible to minimize adverse affects of the fund size on net return. Applying transaction cost estimates post-optimization is inferior to including these costs when setting up the rebalancing problem. The net returns for a $1Bn fund with $\tau = 20$ are almost as high as the net returns for a $250mln fund which ignores transaction costs ($\tau = 0$).

To see this more clearly we mark the distance A, which is the difference between the highest net return with $\tau = 0$ and the highest net return with $\tau > 0$. This distance is the largest for the biggest portfolio ($A_{1000} \sim 0.09\%$ or almost 1.1% annualized) and the smallest for the smallest portfolio ($A_{250} \sim 0.025\%$, over 0.3% annualized). More generally, the area between the solid and dotted lines roughly represents the gain obtained by allowing τ to deviate from 0 (shown by the difference lines for $250mln and $1Bn wealth levels).

Comparing the size of the shaded areas, we conclude that the benefits of controlling for transaction cost increase with the fund size. Stock-specific transaction costs (and not turnover *per se*) effectively determine the capacity at which the fund remains profitable. The relative sizes of the shaded areas also depend on the turnover range: for low turnover levels (up to 25%) the benefits of setting $\tau > 0$ are slightly larger for a smaller fund, while the situation reverses when turnover levels exceed 25–30%.[10]

Transaction cost controls allow higher turnover levels, which translates into higher returns. For example, while optimal turnover levels for $\tau = 0$ are 18%, 14%, and 10% (for the \$250mln, \$500mln, and \$1Bn portfolios, respectively), these levels become 36%, 32%, and 25%, respectively, once τ is set to 20. Net return now peaks at a higher turnover level, which is consistent with the academic literature. That work identifies two major factors behind maintaining optimal turnover levels: the speed of release and homogeneity of information concerning the firm, and transaction costs.[11] The positive relationship between the turnover level and net return can be related to information, as more trading is required to efficiently process new information. In practice this could be true only if the benefits of increased trading are not overwhelmed by accompanying transaction costs.

A higher net return is achieved not purely by increasing turnover, but by doing so in a cost-effective way. This is illustrated in Figure 18.7, which shows the median trading volume associated with portfolio rebalancing (expressed as a percentage of average daily dollar volume, ADDV) versus realized turnover. The slope of the line decreases dramatically when the coefficient of cost aversion is increased. While the slope is close to 1 for $\tau = 0$, it is virtually zero when $\tau = 30$, measuring the slope over the turnover range between 0 and 30% per month. Achieving this type of result might include, for example, selection of more liquid stocks with similar alpha characteristics and spreading the portfolio across more names. This helps to achieve the benefits of running a high-turnover strategy while avoiding to a large extent transaction costs associated with it. Our findings echo the theoretical predictions of Coppejans and Madhavan (2007), who note that controlling for transaction cost helps to maintain portfolio breadth and turnover, both of which have a positive impact on alpha.

Higher turnover levels are not always possible, however. Some of the curves in Figures 18.6 and 18.7 are shorter then the others. The shortest ones correspond to the highest values of τ. For instance, with $\tau = 20$, a \$250mln portfolio can increase its turnover to 75%, while a \$1Bn portfolio with $\tau = 20$ can grow turnover only to 55%. In other words, setting τ too high limits the turnover range as a large coefficient of cost aversion completely dominates turnover constraints. With high values of τ (e.g. $\tau = 50$), realized turnover can grow to only around 20% per month for a \$250mln portfolio and to only 10% per month for a \$1Bn portfolio.

[10] The actual turnover constraints used to plot Figure 18.6 are different from the realized turnover values shown on the chart. The 1-to-1 correspondence between realized and actual turnover holds only for the $\tau = 0$ line. While the same number of turnover constraints was used for $\tau > 0$, the resulting lines span a shorter range of realized turnover than the $\tau = 0$ line.

[11] See, for example, Karpoff (1986) and Domowitz, Glen, and Madhavan (2001).

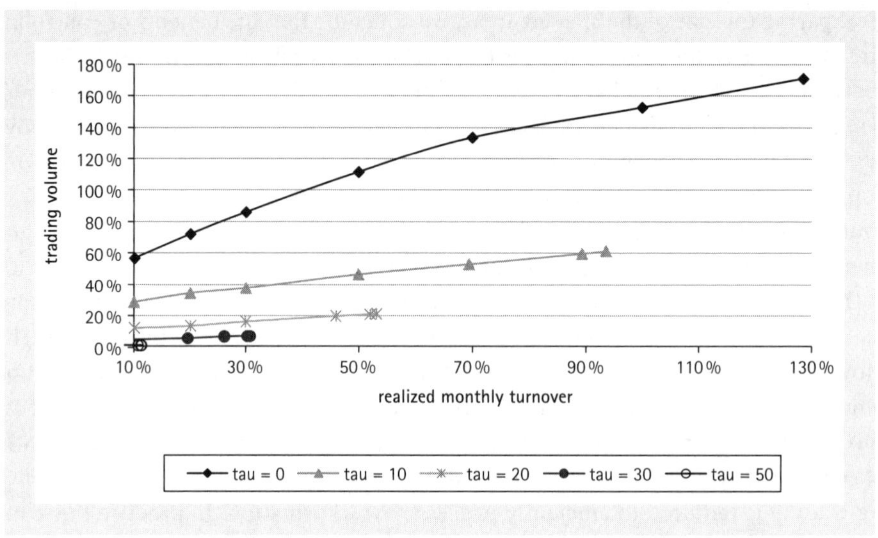

FIGURE 18.7 Median trading volume, % of ADDV vs. realized turnover, $1Bn portfolio.

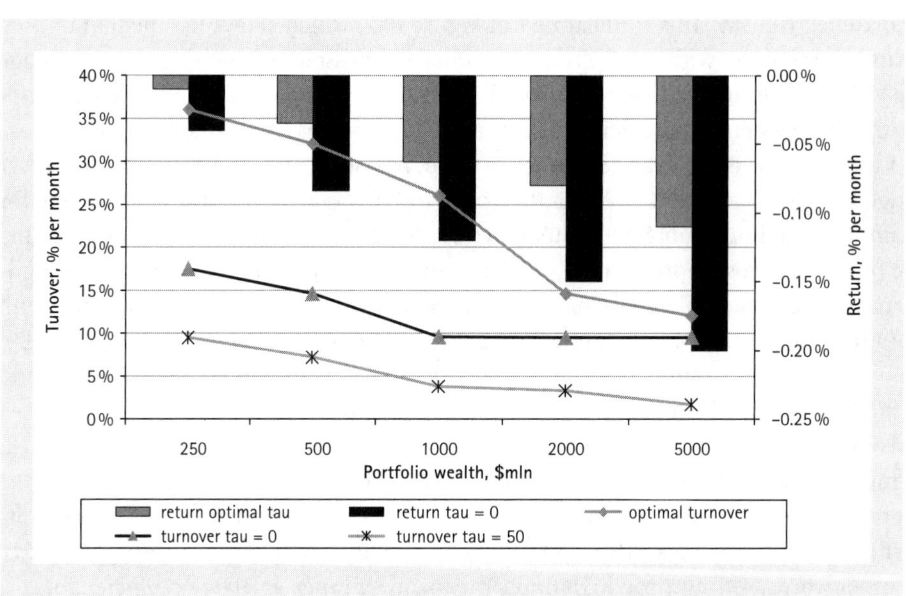

FIGURE 18.8 Optimal turnover for a given τ and portfolio wealth.

It is instructive to look at how turnover varies with the wealth level. For the purpose of this discussion, optimal turnover is defined as the level corresponding to the highest out-of-sample net return. Figure 18.8 depicts this definition of optimal turnover as a function of fund size. Three turnover levels are shown, corresponding to the use of the optimal coefficient of cost aversion, the absence of cost control (coefficient of cost aversion τ is set to zero), and a curve for which $\tau = 50$. We also show the corresponding net returns. Two observations are immediately visible from the chart.

First, the optimal turnover level goes down as the fund size increases. This is intuitive and reflects other results available in the literature. In the broader framework considered here, such a result must be interpreted only in the context of a fixed level of implementation cost penalty, however. The implications of varying that penalty bring us to the second point.

Higher turnover levels are achieved by picking the right transaction cost penalty at each particular level of the fund wealth. For example, suppose that the fund manager does not include transaction costs into the rebalancing problem for a \$500mln fund. In order to increase the fund size to \$2Bn and still maximize net return, the manager should decrease turnover from 15% per month to 10% while giving up some net return (from −0.08% to −0.15% per month). However, if growing the fund were accompanied by introducing effective cost controls (setting $\tau = 20$), the fund manager could keep turnover at 15% per month, which preserves net return. Careful modeling of transaction costs during portfolio rebalancing allows reaping the informational benefits of maintaining the same turnover level with more wealth, extending the effective range of the fund's capacity.

Figure 18.9 provides another illustration that the effect of turnover on the fund's net returns and capacity follows from the more fundamental link originating in transaction cost control. There, we show all turnover levels for a \$500mln fund.

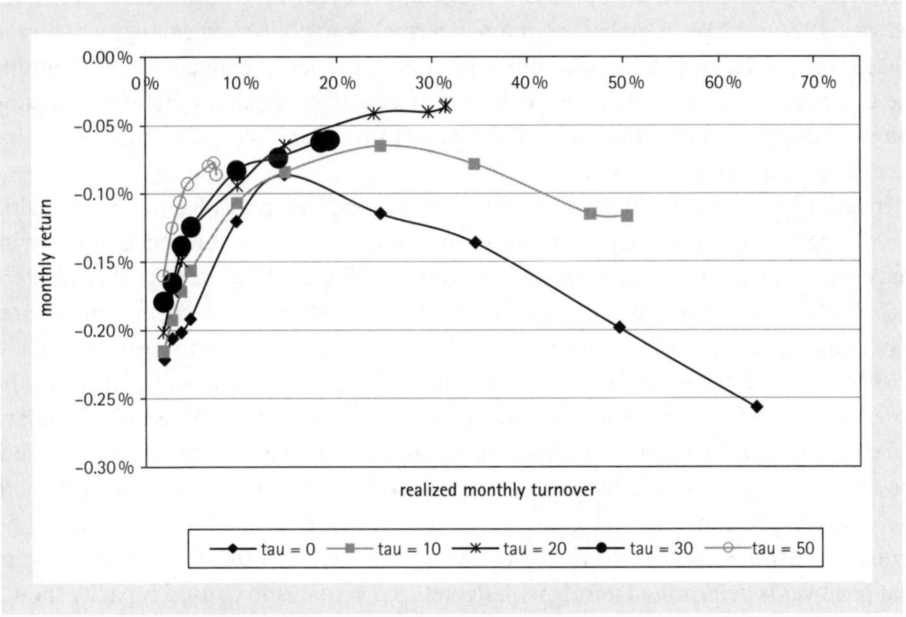

FIGURE 18.9 Pre-tax net return vs. realized turnover.

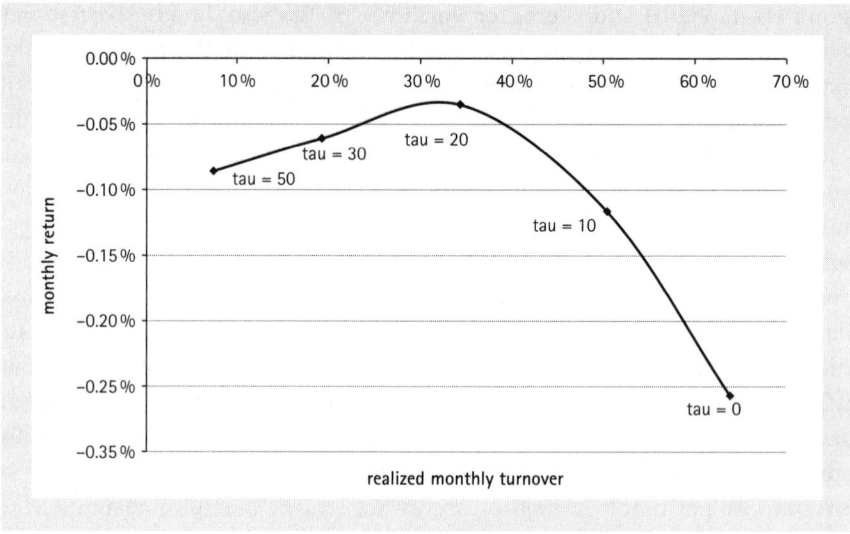

FIGURE 18.10 Monthly return vs. realized turnover.

Maximization of net return solely through turnover is not generally possible. Without adjusting the coefficient of cost aversion, there is no guarantee that any chosen level of turnover would result in the highest net return. Fixing the cost aversion coefficient and then shifting the turnover level up or down also would not work, because the optimal cost aversion coefficient is different for each turnover level. For example, when the turnover level is 0–10% the optimal τ is 50, but it becomes 30 for a turnover range between 10% and 20%. A global optimum in terms of portfolio performance is achieved by setting $\tau = 20$, with the maximum supported turnover of about 30–32%. Running the combination of 30–32% turnover and $\tau = 20$ strikes a balance between utilizing informational advantages that come with a higher turnover level while guarding against excessive implementation costs.

In order to achieve the highest possible return for a given portfolio and fund wealth, the manager may ignore turnover constraints, and improve performance, if costs are managed through the coefficient of cost aversion. Figure 18.10 depicts this idea for a \$500mln fund. Traversing through the values of cost aversion coefficient ensures traversing through all relevant turnover levels. Only return corresponding to the highest possible realized turnover level for each value of τ (where we would end up in the absence of turnover constraint) is shown. The values of τ are marked on the chart. Varying only the cost penalty coefficient we are able to arrive at the same sweet spot for a \$500mln fund (which is $\tau = 20$, and turnover $\sim$ 32%) as we did by varying *both* the cost penalty and turnover constraint. Since turnover levels for the optimization problem illustrated on Figure 18.10 were never set explicitly, this illustrates the point that turnover is determined jointly with net returns. Expansion of fund capacity should advance through the direct control of stock-specific transaction costs.

18.5 Taxes, Trading Strategy, and Turnover

18.5.1 A Role for Taxes

Optimal turnover levels reported in the previous section are higher than the typical turnover levels observed in the mutual fund industry. Average fund sizes in the large-cap blend, mid-cap blend, and small-cap blend categories are \$2.3Bn, \$850mln, and \$600mln, respectively, and the average turnover levels are 80%, 90%, and 95% per year, respectively.[12] Simulation runs for a \$500mln fund reported in the previous section indicate an optimal turnover level of 30–32% per month. There are features of our "experimental design" which may account for this, of course, including but not limited to over-optimism with respect to innovations in the alpha generating process on a month-by-month basis.

We offer another reconciliation of the difference in turnover levels by considering taxes. This point has been made by Jeffrey and Arnott (1993), who demonstrate that realized capital gains taxes play a substantial role in the calculation of net returns.[13]

Assuming a combined federal, state, and local tax rate of 35% and a 6% annual asset growth, those authors estimate that an investor would lose 2.1% per year to taxes if the fund's turnover is kept at 100%. Going back to the basic problem setup described in Section 18.3, we change the way we compute realized out-of-sample net returns by approximating taxes to be paid on realized capital gains. We do not consider taxes at the optimization stage; we simply subtract taxes when calculating out-of-sample return. We will return briefly to this point below.

We assume capital gain taxes to be a simple function of turnover. We calculate turnover as it is defined by the SEC, i.e. the lesser of purchases or sales for one year divided by the average of portfolio wealth during this year.[14] Denote total portfolio purchases in dollars in year y as:

[12] The source is Morningstar, using information taken from their web site, www.morningstar.com

[13] They find, for example, that increasing turnover from 25% to 50% requires an additional 63 basis points in return to offset the increase in taxes, and an additional 45 basis points in return to offset the increase in taxes when moving from 50% to 100% turnover.

[14] Since the goal of this section is to compare simulated turnover levels with the levels observed in the mutual fund industry, we now adhere to a slightly simplified version of the SEC definition on the Form N-3 which is required to be filed by investment management companies under the Securities Act of 1933 and the Investment Company Act of 1940. It is different from the values shown in the earlier sections where we calculated turnover per the last constraint in (18.1).

$$b^y = \sum_{i=1,..,n} \sum_{m=1,..,12} b^y_{i,m} \tag{18.4a}$$

and total portfolio sales in dollars as:

$$s^y = \sum_{i=1,..,n} \sum_{m=1,..,12} s^y_{i,m} \tag{18.4b}$$

where $b^y_{i,m}$ and $s^y_{i,m}$ are the dollar amounts of asset i bought and sold, respectively, within month m of year y.

We then aggregate monthly portfolio returns r_t in order to arrive at the fund wealth at the end of year y (or at the beginning of year $y+1$):

$$C^{y+1} = C^y \prod_{t=1}^{12} (1 + r_t) \tag{18.5}$$

where C_y and C_{y+1} are the portfolio wealth at the beginning of year y and $y+1$, respectively.

Taking (18.4)–(18.5) into consideration, we calculate turnover in year y as:

$$to^y = \min\left(\frac{b^y}{(C^y + C^{y+1})/2}, \frac{s^y}{(C^y + C^{y+1})/2}\right). \tag{18.6}$$

While capital gains taxes depend on the holding period, we assume that the taxable part of realized capital gain for year y is proportional to the annual turnover in that year. This assumption is consistent with the one used in Jeffrey and Arnott (1993) in which the authors assume a "hockey stick" relationship between turnover and holding period. At the same time, the taxable part of the capital gain cannot be more than 100% of the total. We approximate taxes G^y for year y as:

$$\begin{aligned} G^y &= g^y(C^{y+1} - C^y), && \text{if}(C^{y+1} - C^y) > 0 \\ G^y &= 0, && \text{if}(C^{y+1} - C^y) \leq 0 \end{aligned} \tag{18.7}$$

where $g^y = to^y$, if $to^y < 1$ and $g^y = 1$, if $to^y \geq 1$.

Using a tax rate of 15% ($t_{rate} = 0.15$), we calculate the realized annual net return as:

$$R^y = \frac{C^{y+1} - C^y - t_{rate}G^y}{C^y}. \tag{18.8}$$

At the end of December 2008, we have a time series of five annual portfolio returns. Repeating this exercise 25 times, we have 25 random portfolios whose out-of-sample statistics we average across time (except for the first month when we start from cash) and across portfolios. We repeat this exercise for different combinations of parameter values presented in Table 18.1.

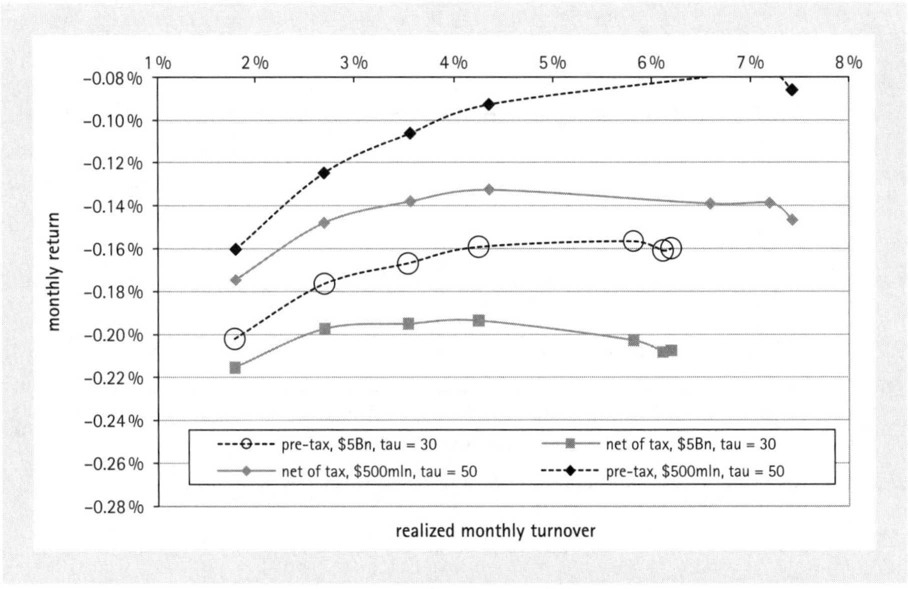

FIGURE 18.11 Net return vs. realized turnover.

We present only a simple illustration of how taxes affect the results. In Figure 18.11 we show pre- and post-tax returns for two combinations of fund size and cost aversion coefficient: $500mln/$\tau = 50$ and $5Bn/$\tau = 30$.[15]

Applying taxes reduces net return by design, of course. It also reduces the optimal level of turnover: from 5.8% per month to 4.25% per month for a $5Bn fund and from 7.2% to 4% for a $500mln fund. Both values of after-tax turnover are now in line with the turnover prevailing in the industry.

Taking taxes into account does not always lead to reduced optimal turnover. The maximum fraction of capital gains which could be taxed is 100%. If optimal turnover ignoring taxes is above 100%, introducing taxes does not make a difference. This happens for some combinations of smaller fund sizes (< $1Bn) and smaller values of cost aversion coefficient ($\tau < 30$).[16]

The tax results here are preliminary, suggesting that for a representative fund size and reasonable value of cost aversion, taxes can reconcile theoretical turnover with the data. Properly including taxes in fund strategy requires the incorporation of position-specific tax considerations at the portfolio optimization stage, in the same way as we have treated transaction costs. A full development of this line of thought is beyond the scope of this chapter, however, and must await further research.

[15] The evidence for other fund sizes and other parameter values is qualitatively similar and not reported here.

[16] Jeffrey and Arnott (1993) also make this point. They note that the marginal impact of taxes diminishes as turnover increases, disappearing at 100% turnover, and advise that taking taxes into account is most critical for low turnover ranges.

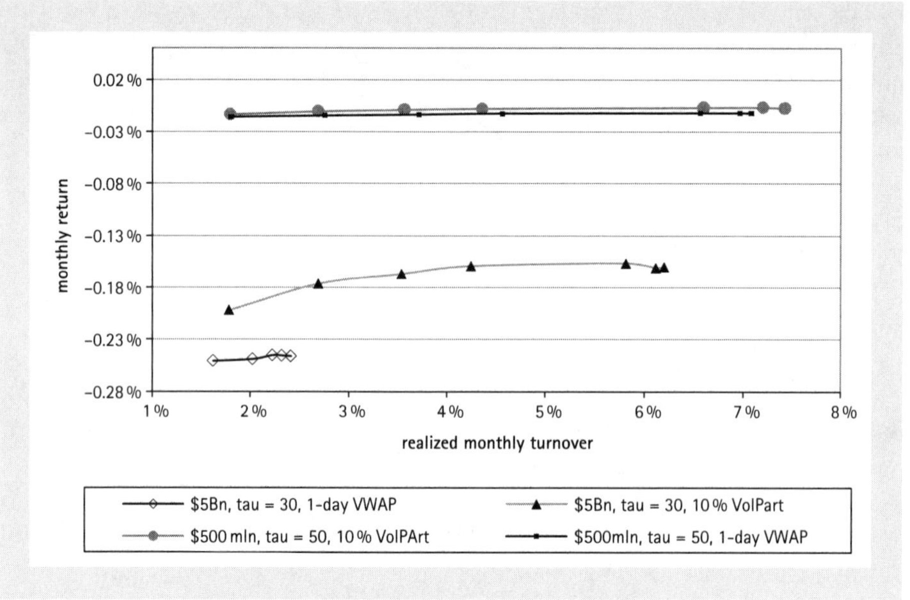

FIGURE 18.12 Net return vs. realized turnover.

18.5.2 Trading Strategy and Turnover

Accounting for expected implementation cost leads to turnover levels which strike a balance between the timely exploitation of new information and the avoidance of excessive costs. It follows that accounting for transaction cost is an integral part of the portfolio formation process, and that trading strategy has an important place within investment strategy. In Section 18.4, we noted that the use of alternative price impact models leads to similar qualitative conclusions with respect to capacity and turnover, if the alternative model embodies a concave relationship between unit costs and volume. Nevertheless, trading strategy affects implementation costs. Quantitative differences in capacity, for alternative assumptions concerning trading strategy, can be substantial.

In order to illustrate this point, we now employ a more aggressive trading strategy than used in Section 18.4, enforcing a single-day trading horizon with respect to the implementation of an investment decision. In Figure 18.12 we demonstrate the effect of running a one-day value-weighted average price strategy (commonly known as one-day VWAP). We present the resulting relationship between net return and realized turnover for two combinations of fund size and cost aversion coefficients: a $5Bn fund with $\tau = 30$, and a $500mln fund with $\tau = 50$.

For a $5Bn fund, using the more aggressive trading strategy results in lower net returns, but also dramatically shifts the range of optimal turnover values towards zero. In fact, the magnitude of the shift exceeds the one resulting from considering taxes. We mark the optimal turnover levels for a 10% volume participation strategy with a grey line, and those for a one-day VWAP strategy with a black line. The dotted line corresponds to the $\tau = 30$ curve for the \$5Bn fund in Figure 18.11. The optimal turnover level for a \$5BN fund and $\tau = 30$ is 5.8% monthly. Taking taxes into consideration shifts this value to 4.25% per month, while running the one-day VWAP strategy shifts it even further, to 2.4% per month.

For a \$500mln fund, however, the difference between running one-day VWAP and 10% volume participation strategies is negligible. Trading volumes for a smaller fund are low enough that the main component of cost is the bid-ask spread and, therefore, any trading strategy would produce a similar result.

In summary, the tactics of trading matter in the context of the overall investment strategy. The degree of importance of this observation depends itself on fund size, becoming increasingly relevant as AUM increases.

18.6 Concluding Remarks

Capacity research has come a long way since its formal inception, most notably moving from reactive to proactive analysis. There are two new lessons to be learned from the current work.

The previous focus on turnover as a choice variable, and on its role as a proxy for implementation cost, is misplaced. Considering stock-specific transaction costs at the portfolio construction stage enables higher turnover levels, which themselves are determined through the interaction of alpha predictions and expected cost estimates. Managing the fund at a higher turnover level allows for faster processing of new information which, in conjunction with effective cost control, leads to superior net return.

The second point is closely related to the first: excluding trading strategy from portfolio construction negatively impacts returns and reduces the capacity of the fund. Lack of consideration of trading and its costs also distorts capacity analysis, and biases capacity choice downwards in general.

The use of an explicit optimization framework to reach such conclusions is both a strength and a limitation. The ability to explicate the problem formally in such a way as to isolate the contributions of individual components is part of the strength, as well as the ability to replicate and extend results. Such models are also used widely in certain segments of the asset management community, and are extensible to investment problems involving dynamic substitution of similar assets. The limitation is also fairly clear, namely that a variety of stock-picking exercises are precluded from explicit analysis.

Nevertheless, we believe that the basic lessons derived within such a framework are intuitive and more generally valid. Establishing this point is an interesting direction for future work, widening the practical value of the exercise.

References

Bogle J. (1994). *Bogle on Mutual Funds: New Perspectives for the Intelligent Investor.* Irwin Professional Publishing, Burr Ridge, IL.

Borkovec, M., Domowitz, I., Kiernan, B., and Serbin, V. (2010). Portfolio optimization and the cost of trading *Journal of Investing*, **19**(2), 63–76.

Bull, P., Serbin, V., and Zhu, H. (2009). The capacity of liquidity-demanding equity strategies. *Journal of Portfolio Management*, **36**(1), 78–89.

Coppejans, M. and Madhavan, A. (2007). The value of transaction cost forecasts: Another source of alpha. *Journal of Investment Management*, **5**(1), 65–78.

Domowitz, I., Glen, J., and Madhavan, A. (2001). Liquidity, volatility and equity costs across countries and over time. *International Finance*, **4**(2), 221–255.

Engle, R. and Ferstenberg, R. (2007). Execution risk: It's the same as investment risk, *Journal of Portfolio Management*, **33**(2), 46–59.

Grinold, R. and Kahn, R. (2000). The efficiency gains of long–short investing. *Financial Analysts Journal*, **56**(6), 40–53.

ITG Inc. (2007) ITG ACE – Agency Cost Estimator, available at http://www.itg.com/news_events/papers/ACE_White_Paper_200705.pdf

Jeffrey, R. and Arnott, R. (1993). Is your alpha big enough to cover its taxes: The active management dichotomy, *Journal of Portfolio Management*, **19**(3), 15–25.

Kahn, R. and Shaffer, J. (2005). The surprisingly small impact of asset growth on expected alpha. *Journal of Portfolio Management*, **32**(1), 49–60.

Karpoff, J. (1986). A theory of trading volume. *The Journal of Finance*, **41**(5), 1069–1087.

Korajczyk R. and Sadka R. (2004). Are momentum profits robust to trading costs? *The Journal of Finance*, **59**(3), 1039–1082.

McDonald, I. and Richardson, K. (2006). For South Korea, "emerging" label can be a burden. *Wall Street Journal*, July 12.

Perold, A. and Salomon, R. (1991). The right amount of assets under management. *Financial Analysts Journal*, **47**(3), 31–39.

Pogue, G. (1970). An extension of the Markowitz portfolio selection model to include variable transactions' costs, short sales, leverage policies and taxes. *Journal of Finance*, **25**(5), 1005–027

SEC (2007). Registration statement of separate accounts organized as management investment companies, available at http://www.sec.gov/about/forms/formn-3.pdf

Vangelisti, M. (2006). The capacity of an equity strategy. *Journal of Portfolio Management*, **32**(2), 44–50.

Wermers, R. (2000). Mutual fund performance: An empirical decomposition into stock-picking talent, style, transactions costs, and expenses. *Journal of Finance*, **55**(4), 1655–1695.

PART VII

INVESTMENT SOLUTIONS

CHAPTER 19

PENSION FUNDS AND CORPORATE ENTERPRISE RISK MANAGEMENT

MICHAEL PESKIN

19.1 Introduction

Corporations raise equity capital, borrow money from the markets, and then invest the proceeds in their operations to generate a profit. We can gain insight by considering a corporation as a hedge fund[1] that has both long and short positions. The corporation's borrowing can be considered a short position in the bond market, while its operations can be considered a long position. To maximize profit per unit of risk, the corporation needs to manage its profits (growth in shareholder wealth) and the "basis risk"[2] between its operations and its debt. The success of the corporation will be determined in part by its success in managing the debt-to-equity ratio, that is, the ratio of its obligations to creditors and its shareholder wealth. The defined benefit pension plan can play a significant role in effective debt-to-equity management. The unfunded pension liability is a debt of the corporation. However, unlike most debt – where the nominal amount owed remains fixed – the pension debt can change radically with asset and liability performance. Companies that sponsor defined benefit pension plans tend to regard their plans as net risk contributors. If the risk is properly hedged and managed the pension plan can become a valuable risk management tool.

This chapter explains how the liquid pool of pension assets can be strategically and tactically invested to manage the combined pension and corporate risks to the joint benefit of the plan sponsors (shareholders) and plan participants. Risks that are innate

[1] Hedge funds use a wide range of investment techniques involving utilizing both long and short positions and hedge risks (hence the name).

[2] "Basis risk" refers to the mismatch risk between assets and liabilities. Such basis risk creates the potential for an adverse move in net value upon the repricing of assets and liabilities when economic or market conditions change.

to the corporation cannot easily be reduced as changes in the business model would usually be required. However, the risks taken in the liquid pool of pension assets can be changed quickly, dramatically, and as often as required. These assets provide an avenue for the corporation to manage both its pension and corporate risk to improve corporate performance significantly.

To manage pension assets effectively within a corporate enterprise framework, it is necessary to understand the relationship between the pension plan and the corporation in an increasingly sophisticated world. The most active and sophisticated market participants set the stock price of corporations. These investors tend to focus on the real economics of corporations and take advantage when antiquated accounting conventions (such as current pension accounting) misrepresent value.

In order to increase shareholder wealth, corporations need to increase the return they offer to investors per unit of risk that they add. Corporations that take risks that do not deliver a compensating return to their shareholders can increase their value merely by hedging these risks.[3] Any risk taken must compensate for the increased possibility of bankruptcy and/or the loss of tax shield that adds friction cost. Corporations generate revenue by taking many risks, some of which are necessary to the business model but that subtract value as they are not properly compensated. The efficient hedging of such risks adds value to shareholders and plan participants.

However, hedging at the corporate level may be inhibited by asymmetric payoffs, tax rules, and accounting that may mark only one side of the hedge to market. A pension plan does not subject the corporation to these asymmetries and therefore provides an excellent vehicle for hedging. In addition, such enterprise risk management is beneficial to the plan participants in most circumstances and thus is economically sound from a pension fiduciary perspective.

Effective financial management thus requires an integration of pensions into corporate finance. This integration is easy and practical to implement and can add considerable value to shareholders and plan participants.

We present a brief summary of eleven contributors to a comprehensive approach. The remainder of the chapter goes into more depth for each of these contributors.

1 **Enterprise and Pension Management**

The primary goal of corporate management is to maximize share price. Managing the debt-to-equity ratio is a critical component. Debt includes the outstanding bonds, short term debt, and creditors – as well as the after-tax unfunded portion of the pension plan.

If debt-to-equity ratios are excessive, access to capital markets and opportunistic investing can be restricted, valuable tax shields can be lost, and bankruptcy can result. These threats create friction costs, such as loss of continuity and efficiency, legal fees, and transaction delays. Yet running with too low a debt-to-equity ratio may imply inefficient investment in the future of the company and too low a return

[3] To the extent that the price of hedging is determined by liquid capital market instruments.

on capital. Enterprise management through the pension plan is likely to increase market valuation.

Pension promises are a form of corporate debt collateralized by pension assets. The net pension debt is the after-tax unfunded liability, and will be viewed as an integral part of the firm-wide debt-to-equity ratio and risk characteristics.

2 **Comparison of Termination, Funding, and Accounting Liabilities**

There are three liability measures in common usage:

A. Funding liabilities – used to determine pension contribution requirements.
B. Accounting liabilities – used for income statement and balance sheet reporting.
C. Termination liabilities – used to calculate the amount of money necessary to fully defease (permanently eliminate the pension plan liabilities from the corporate balance sheet, with no further obligation from the corporation).

All three measures calculate a liability by discounting future benefit payments. They differ in the nature of the pension obligations discounted and the discount rates used.

3 **Contributions and Funding Considerations**

Many companies need to concern themselves with liquidity. An appropriate liquidity measure is the ratio of near-term cash demands (including pension contribution requirements) to the corporate "Free Cash Flow" (FCF)[4] plus liquid assets. The near-term required contributions are determined in accordance with the Pension Protection Act of 2006 (the "PPA"). Thus, liquidity and debt-to-equity management may require differing investment strategies.

Strong companies should have well funded pension plans. Corporations with low borrowing costs should consider buying back their pension debt (prefunding), even if they have to borrow. Unfunded pension liabilities (adjusted for tax) are a debt of the corporation. Funding, or making a contribution to the pension plan, should be considered the equivalent of a debt buyback. For example, when GM contributed $18.5 billion to its pension plan in 2003, it received a tax deduction on that contribution. It expunged gross pension debt of $18.5 billion but also reduced its future tax deductions. The net debt expunged was exactly the same as if GM had bought back its other debt with the net amount ($18.5 billion minus the tax deduction).[5] Funding rules require a minimum level of pension debt buyback each year. It is accretive to value for corporations with low borrowing costs to fund more rapidly.

4 **Corporate Income and Balance Sheet Accounting**

Many investors focus on reported rather than economic earnings and corporations tend to follow suit. Pension accounting currently allows the expected rate of return on investments to be recognized as an income item in reported earnings

[4] Free Cash Flow (FCF) is the cash available for distribution among all securities holders of an organization.

[5] See Peskin (2010).

(this anomaly in the accounting rules is expected to be removed in 2012 or soon thereafter). The most active and sophisticated investors are aware of the issues with reported earnings and see through to the real economic earnings of the corporation. Corporations need to manage to the economics, not the reported accounting measures, to add value to shareholders.

5 **Corporate Risk Factors**
The corporation has many risks innate to its business model. Some of these risks are managed at the corporate level. However, accounting and tax considerations can inhibit effective risk management. The pension plan can be an effective tool for managing and diversifying many of the risks as it is not subject to the same tax and accounting rules as the corporation.

6 **Corporate Finance Theory**
Corporate finance theory maintains that a corporation is a vehicle that passes performance through to the individual shareholders. This implies that value cannot be added to shareholders by including equities in the company's pension portfolio, as they can easily alter their own equity exposure. Second-order effects, such as Black and Tepper Tax Arbitrage (explained in detail below), do add value. As will be discussed later, significant additional value can be created by managing corporate risks through the pension plan.

7 **Impact of Pension Benefit Guarantee Corporation ("PBGC")**
The PBGC guarantees a certain level of benefits to participants if the pension plan is underfunded in the event of corporate bankruptcy. The PBGC provides a further level of security to plan participants. This should be considered when making investment and funding decisions.

8 **Pension Plan Investments and Asymmetric Payoffs**
Pension plans themselves do not bear risk. Instead, the individual investors in the corporation, creditors, and plan participants are the primary bearers of pension plan risk. Their risk/return tradeoffs can be asymmetric. For example, the inability of shareholders to extract surplus from the plan at full value disproportionally reduces its value to shareholders. The participants experience asymmetry in the cost of a loss of funded status due to the existence of the PBGC.

9 **Impact of Capital Market Pricing.**
The capital market pricing of corporations makes pension surplus and other traditional asset/liability efficient frontiers produce erroneous answers that overweight risk premiums and underweight risk. A focus on overall debt-to-equity is a huge improvement. Furthermore, everything that enters into the debt-to-equity ratio (both pension and corporate assets and liabilities) is impacted by capital market pricing. Asset allocation must be flexible and vary with debt-to-equity ratios as well as the price of hedging risk.

10 **Debt-to-Equity Management Through the Pension Plan**
The optimal investment strategy for the pension plan should be to minimize the potential loss of benefits to participants (the fiduciary obligation of the plan) and

to maximize the value of the company. This dual objective may occasionally present conflicts. The route to achieving these goals as well as resolving conflicts is to manage the overall debt-to-equity ratio of the company (inclusive of after-tax pension unfunded liabilities). The pension plan provides an excellent vehicle for this kind of management.

11 **Macroeconomic Impacts on Investment Strategy**
The current economy is unusual and marked by a high level of uncertainty. This chapter differentiates between uncertainty and risk in the way that Frank Knight described in the 1920s. Uncertainty can arise as a result of a few decisions made by central banks and key politicians, and has a profound effect. Risk, on the other hand, arises as a natural consequence of a multitude of people making decisions about their futures and a reasonable probability distribution can be found to describe the possible outcomes. Uncertainty, however, does not allow for the determination of a probability distribution of outcomes with any confidence.

The required asset allocation for adding value differs between macroeconomic environments. In particular, periods of uncertainty require hedging and a more tactical and dynamic approach to investing.

Each of these eleven components plays an important role in assessing how defined benefit pension plans can be used to manage a corporation's debt-to-equity ratio. We now discuss each of these components in greater depth.

19.2 Enterprise and Pension Management

The goals of corporate pension management are: (1) to manage the plan in the interest of participants (the primary fiduciary obligation); and (2) to maximize the value of the corporation. The pension plan consists of a liability (deferred compensation in the form of retirement income to employees[6]) and related assets. The objective of this chapter is to demonstrate that there is significant untapped added value, to both shareholders and participants, available through appropriate financial management. The added value emanates largely from a reduction in the correlation between the pension plan and the corporation's equity.

Historically, pension assets were managed independently of both the corporation and the pension liabilities. More recently, some pension plans have been managed against a pension liability benchmark. This is called asset liability management (ALM) or more popularly, liability driven investing (LDI). The next step in this evolution is investing pension assets to manage the overall debt-to-equity ratio of the corporation. The

[6] Whether or not the provision of lifetime pension income is the optimal corporate strategy for providing compensation is beyond the scope of this chapter.

questions that arise with respect to pension debt are: What is the actual pension debt? How should this debt be priced? How can pension investment management reduce the economic cost of the debt? What is the potential increase in stock price if the pension plan is managed appropriately?

To answer these questions it is necessary to start with a focus on pension debt.

19.2.1 Establishing the Appropriate Pension Debt

There are differences between pension debt and the other debts of a corporation. For example, it is more difficult to establish the price of pension debt than it is to establish the price of a corporate bond. A company can usually enter the market and buy back its bonds at a price set by the open market. However, a corporation cannot buy back its pension obligation in the same manner.

To eliminate or defease its pension liability, a corporation must terminate the plan. This requires the purchase of annuities issued through an insurance company to cover the benefits accrued to date. A corporation has a right to terminate its plan and is only responsible for the cash flows associated with the termination liabilities. Of these cash flows, only the unfunded portion is debt.[7] Sometimes a pension plan provides for an increase in benefits upon termination. Such increases are equivalent to a "poison pill" and can make it more expensive to terminate the plan. These increases in liabilities are usually best ignored for the purpose of establishing the appropriate debt as the plan can be operated without triggering such increases.

19.2.2 Pricing the Pension Debt

Unfunded liabilities are included in debt-to-equity and other leverage calculations by ratings agencies, credit, and equity markets. Often the debt used in these calculations is the accounting liability, which includes projections in future pay and uses an artificial discount rate.[8]

Since unfunded pension liabilities are unsecured debts of the corporation and are similar to an unsecured bond, they should be priced at the corporation's unsecured borrowing cost.[9] This implies that the unfunded liability cash flows should be valued differently in corporations with differing credit strengths. For example, an identical unfunded liability cash flow projection for an A rated corporation can have markedly

[7] Many financial experts regard the entire liability as a debt and treat pension assets as a corporate asset. This is an augmented balance sheet approach. The IASB and the FASB have a common convention; they treat the liabilities minus the assets as a debt. This chapter adopts that convention to avoid unnecessary conflict with the accounting.

[8] For a seminal paper introducing a market-based valuation of pension liabilities, see Exley, Mehta, and Smith (1997).

[9] Peskin (1989).

Table 19.1 Present value of duration 14 liability – Impact of discount rate.

Credit rating:	AA	A	B
Discount rate:	4.50%	6.00%	8.00%
Present value of liability	$100.00	$82.50	$65.71

Table 19.2 Leveraging effect of the asset liability relationship on the pension.

$million	Starting	Liability valuation increases 20%	Asset valuation decreases 20%	Combined effect
Pension assets	800	800	640	640
Pension liabilities	1,000	1,200	1,000	1,200
Pension underfunding (Debt)	200	400	360	560

The combined impact of the increase in pension liability valuation and decrease in pension asset valuation increases the pension underfunding from $200 million to $560 million.

different costs to shareholders than the same liability of a B rated corporation. Similarly, the value to pension plan participants also differs. Ignoring the PBGC guarantee for a moment, participants will only receive the promised benefits if the corporation does not default. Table 19.1 shows the present value of a liability with a 14 year duration at different discount rates.[10]

19.2.3 Risk Associated with the Pension Debt

Unlike a corporate bond, pension debt is leveraged. A $1 billion pension plan with $800 million in assets has an unfunded liability of $200 million. This underfunding (debt) is calculated by subtracting the assets from the liabilities which effectively levers the debt. This is illustrated in Table 19.2:

There are three factors impacting the pension plan's contribution to the debt-to-equity ratio of the corporation:

(i) the size of the pension plan relative to the size of the corporation;
(ii) the basis risk (asset/liability mismatch) associated with the pension asset allocation;
(iii) the correlation between the basis risk and the enterprise value;

[10] For a thorough discussion of the economic-based pricing of liabilities that takes into account real and inflation components, see Waring and Siegel (2007).

The economic debt of the pension plan is the unfunded accrued liability cash flows discounted at the unsecured borrowing cost of the corporation. There is, however, another important addition/subtraction to the economic value due to the basis risk and its correlation with the corporation. The security of participants and the stock price can both usually be increased by reducing the overall debt-to-equity risk. Such a decrease in risk is accomplished by reducing the correlation between the basis risk and the corporation. This is expanded on in Section 19.10 (Debt-to-Equity Management Through the Pension Plan) below.

19.3 Comparison of Termination, Funding, and Accounting Liabilities

A pension plan sponsor uses three different definitions of liabilities associated with the plan: termination, accounting, and funding (required under the PPA) liabilities. The most effective means of managing the corporation's overall debt-to-equity is via the unfunded termination liabilities. Most companies, however, focus on managing accounting and/or funding liabilities. It is thus necessary to discuss and compare all three. Table 19.3 compares the three liabilities.

Table 19.3 Liability measurement – Key differentiating features.

	Liability type		
	Accounting	Funding	Economic/ Termination
Application	Financial Reporting	Determination of contributions	Market valuation
Discount rate	High Quality Credit	High quality credit using blending/interpolation method proscribed under Pension Protection Act	Swap
Is discount rate hedgeable?	No	No	Yes
Salary projected to retirement date to determine liabilities?	Yes, at assumed wage inflation	No	No

Notice that while all three definitions of liability use service to the current date, funding and termination (defeasance) liabilities are calculated using current pay (Accrued Benefit Obligation or "ABO"). However, accounting liabilities measure pension benefit obligations based on projected future pay (Projected Benefit Obligation or "PBO").

As discussed above, termination liabilities are key to managing the debt-to-equity ratio. Accounting liabilities are used to determine balance sheet and income statement reporting. PPA liabilities are used to determine contribution requirements.

19.3.1 Funding Rules (PPA)

The projected benefit cash flows used in funding (PPA) calculations are accrued to date without future pay increases or benefit accruals. They differ from termination cash flows only in the vesting assumptions: all participants vest on termination.

The funding liability, used to determine the minimum required contribution, is calculated by discounting projected benefits at a hypothetical long duration "A" rated corporate bond curve that projects credit spreads far into the future.[11] Due to its hypothetical and uninvestible nature, this curve cannot be used to hedge actual liabilities over an extended period. However, the high credit component in the curve provides a buffer for corporations in difficult economic scenarios when credit spreads widen, reducing contribution requirements counter-cyclically at a time when the corporation may be struggling. For example, in October 2007 the PPA curve spread was 128 basis points. Following the credit collapse the spread widened to 424 basis points, substantially reducing funding liabilities.[12]

Credit spreads are linked to equity market pricing and volatility. Generally, a rise in credit spreads is likely to be accompanied by a fall in equity prices including the sponsoring corporation's own equity. Thus the debt-to-equity ratio of the corporation is likely to rise. Hedging credit is counter-productive to managing the debt-to-equity ratio of the corporation. Credit is an opportunistic rather than a hedging asset class. The only time it makes sense to hedge the credit component in the PPA curve is when credit spreads have ballooned in a credit crisis, as was the case in late 2008. The potential subsequent contraction in credit spreads could cause PPA liabilities to rise more than assets. This would result in additional contribution requirements by the corporation. In general, credit should be considered an opportunistic asset which rarely mitigates debt-to-equity risk.

[11] The resulting curve is known as the "PPA Curve." Applicable law permits use of "A" to "AAA" credit, which effectively results in companies using "A."

[12] PPA curve spread information may be obtained via comparison of historic rate data available for applicable U.S. Treasury rates on www.federalreserve.gov and PPA rates on www.irs.gov

Table 19.4 Example: Active employee total compensation and accounting.

Effects Direct Compensation	Deferred Compensation Accounting	Deferred Compensation Termination	Total Economic Compensation
$100,000	$40,000	$20,000	$120,000
One year later, changes in the economy result in a necessary increase in economic compensation to $130,000. At the same time, the value of the deferred compensation increased by $25,000 leaving a balance of $105,000 to be paid in direct compensation.			
$105,000	$40,000	$25,000	$130,000

Total compensation increased by 8%. However, only a 5% increase was necessary in direct compensation as the deferred compensation had financed the remaining 3%. The accounting reflects future direct compensation and does not recognize the change in direct compensation. The accounting does not recognize that future direct compensation is based on the value of the pension plan.

19.3.2 Accounting

Accounting liabilities are calculated using a credit spread that assumes a rate of default equivalent to an AA rated bond portfolio.[13] Accounting liabilities therefore also have an artificial exposure to long duration credit and are thus subject to the same hedging limitations as the funding liabilities discussed above. In addition, the accounting liabilities are based on PBO projected pay.

Although total compensation is set by market forces, companies have control over direct pay and can therefore manage increases in deferred compensation by reducing direct compensation. Table 19.4 illustrates this:

19.3.3 Termination

Termination liabilities for traditional defined benefit pension plans are sensitive to interest rates and the sponsoring corporation's credit. Termination liabilities are calculated using the fully collateralized AAA rate. U.S. Treasury and other long duration low credit risk instruments play a significant role in managing pension debt.

[13] See Financial Accounting Statement (FAS) 87, Paragraph 44A, regarding guidance on assumed discount rate, stating the objective as measurement of "the single amount that, if invested at the measurement date in a portfolio of high-quality debt instruments, would provide the necessary future cash flows to pay the accumulated benefits when due." "High-quality" is generally viewed as satisfied by a AA rating. See also Emerging Issues Task Force Topic D-36, "Selection of Discount Rates Used for Measuring Defined Benefit Pension Obligations and Obligations of Postretirement Benefit Plans Other Than Pensions."

Defined benefit pension liabilities are the present value of the pension promises, or deferred compensation, made to participants. These future obligations have traditionally taken the form of a life annuity based on pay at or near a participant's retirement. The present value of a stream of contingent cash flows can be obtained by either (1) discounting those cash flows at the appropriate risk adjusted discount rate, where rates may be adjusted upward for contingencies such as the possibility of default; or (2) creating a "reference portfolio" consisting of market instruments with identical cash flows and contingencies.[14]

19.3.4 Comparison

While the projected cash flows for funding and termination liabilities are similar, the discount rate differs substantially. Compared to the AAA rate used for termination liabilities, the funding liabilities are calculated using a credit spread that assumes a rate of default equivalent to an A rated bond portfolio. For the accounting liability, that assumption is equivalent to an AA rated bond portfolio. This higher discount rate tends to make this liability lower than the termination liability, thus offsetting to varying extents the effects of future pay increases.[15]

As discussed, the economic liabilities are determined by calculating the funded (collateralized) liabilities at collateralized borrowing costs and the unfunded liabilities at the sponsor's unsecured cost of borrowing. The three liabilities discussed above do not

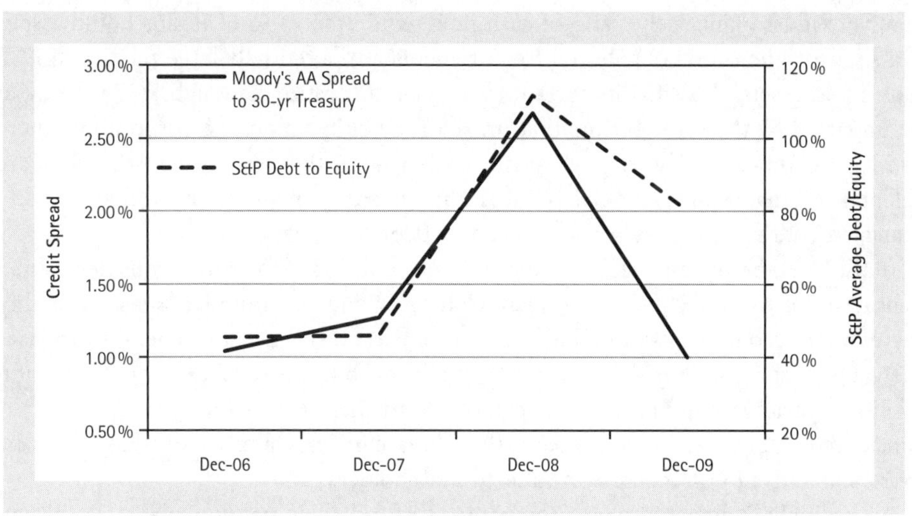

FIGURE 19.1 Credit spreads and debt-to-equity year-end values.

[14] See Peskin and Moore (2002).

[15] For an in-depth discussion regarding use of ABO in the economic view of liabilities, see Bader (2003) and Kopcke (2006).

necessarily reflect economic liabilities, although termination liabilities are the closest to presenting an accurate picture. While accounting and funding liabilities are important for determining near-term cash flow requirements and near-term income and balance sheet numbers, termination liabilities are more accurate (as well as more hedgeable and more consistent) for economic measurements. Thus, there is little reason, except in unusual circumstances, to hedge either the funding or accounting liabilities. It is more important to hedge the termination liabilities. Figure 19.1 shows the strong link between credit spreads and debt-to-equity, illustrating that it is wasteful to hedge against credit spreads falling.

Even termination, the simplest of these three liabilities, is difficult to hedge. For instance, currently there is no hedge against improving longevity. In addition, pension plan design often exacerbates this problem, also ensuring that there is no matching instrument in the capital market. For example, a cash balance plan that provides a crediting rate that is greater than the return on cash is not hedgeable.

19.4 Contributions and Funding Considerations

Companies must ensure that they can meet nearer term cash flow needs in all scenarios (particularly those where borrowing is expensive or unavailable). As a company's cash requirements may vary by scenario and the FCF may also be highly variable, the company must manage the ratio of cash flow requirements to FCF plus liquid assets. If a sponsor's pension contribution requirements are potentially large relative to FCF plus liquid assets, then it is important to manage this ratio. Although FCF is likely to be impacted by the same factors that impact the equity value of a corporation, there can be differences in the shorter term. Furthermore, the pension contributions are calculated using funding (PPA) liabilities rather than economic liabilities. Thus liquidity management may differ from management of debt-to-equity.

In this current low interest rate environment, sponsors increasingly consider issuing debt in order to fund the pension plan. Collateralizing an unfunded pension liability increases the economic value of the pension promise; however, it also generally increases the value to shareholders due to the potential tax arbitrage, reduction, or elimination of PBGC variable rate premiums and increase in the tenure of the overall debt.[16] If considered and implemented properly, the increase in associated funding costs may be more than offset by an increase in value to shareholders.[17]

Accordingly, it benefits many companies to fund their pension plans faster than regulations require. The three major potential advantages are:

[16] The borrowing is an increase in debt but is offset by the reduction in the unfunded pension liability, and therefore does not affect the overall debt of the corporation.

[17] For an analysis of relevant factors, see Peskin (2010).

19.4.1 Tax Arbitrage

Pension debt is equivalent to corporate debt with the advantage that earnings in the pension trust are tax free. Thus, if a company borrows money at the corporate level and funds the pension plan with the proceeds, the net cost of debt to the corporation will be reduced if the after-tax cost of debt is lower than the liability matching Treasury bond return. For example, if a company has a cost of borrowing of 5% and a 30% tax rate, it can borrow at an after-tax rate of 3.5%. If the long bond rate is 4%, then the cost of borrowing at the corporate level will be lower than the cost of debt of the pension plan, so it would benefit the corporation to fund the plan.[18]

19.4.2 PBGC Premiums

The PBGC currently charges a variable rate premium of $9 per $1000 of underfunding.[19] Financially strong companies, with low borrowing costs, do not benefit from the PBGC variable rate premium, since the PBGC insurance is unlikely to ever be tapped. The premium can be eliminated by fully funding the pension plan.

19.4.3 Extending the Tenure of the Debt

Current funding rules amortize the unfunded portion of pension liabilities over a seven-year period. A financially strong company can borrow for a much longer period, fund the plan with the proceeds, and thus extend its overall debt tenure to reduce near-term liquidity considerations.

The same principles can be applied to financially weak companies, although with different outcomes. If the benefits are largely guaranteed by the PBGC, then funding the plan more rapidly than the required minimums would not benefit participants or shareholders. The price of the pension promise would increase quite significantly because of the collateralization.

19.5 Corporate Income and Balance Sheet Accounting

A company's income and balance sheet are important to its valuation. A common way to value corporations is to apply a multiple to the earnings of the company using

[18] For a detailed example, see ibid.

[19] Section 4006.3(b)(1) of *The Employee Retirement Income Security Act of 1974* ("ERISA").

an expected price/earnings ("PE") ratio. This multiple will take both the growth and riskiness of earnings into account. Generally, the riskier the earnings are, the lower the multiple. The pension plan provides an excellent vehicle for managing earnings volatility, which tends to increase the multiple and thus the stock price.

However, there is considerable debate about which earnings should enter into the valuation and thereby contribute to stock price. In particular, current pension cost accounting is largely ignored by sophisticated investors because current accounting permits the *expected* rate of return on investments to be recognized as an income item for the pension sponsor. Pensions appear to have a lower cost when invested in risky assets like equities, with higher expected rates of return as compared to bonds. This effect led to high equity exposure in many U.S. and U.K. pension plans. Sophisticated investors recognize that the increased accounting earnings produced by higher risk assets result in greater risk and thus reduce the multiple. Proposed International Accounting Standards Board (IASB) rules remove this poor accounting[20] with the Financial Accounting Standards Board (FASB) expected to follow suit soon thereafter.

In addition, balance sheet accounting does not differentiate between collateralized and unfunded pension obligations. Both are valued using a hypothetical AA corporate curve, which will undervalue the collateralized portion of the liabilities and can either undervalue or overvalue the unfunded portion of the liabilities, depending on the financial strength of the sponsor. Thus, the pension obligation reported on the balance sheet does not accurately reflect the economics.

As mentioned above, the reported liability has a further flaw in that it takes into account future pay increases (using PBO vs. ABO). Such future pay increases are properly viewed as a part of future compensation and are not a current economic liability of shareholders. For instance, the company can reduce the direct pay of participants to compensate for any change in the value of the pension plan or terminate the employee and/or the plan.[21]

There is some debate about the possible effects accounting changes will have on equity prices.[22] Many believe that this debate ended in the 2000–2002 recession, when the largest traders, such as hedge funds, saw through these accounting issues and adjusted prices accordingly. Additionally, changes in FASB requirements for pension balance sheet accounting helped transition the market toward mark-to-market rather than expected return reporting.[23] Analysts, particularly sell-side analysts, have had to reconcile balance sheet (based on mark-to-market) with the pension earnings (based on expected returns) and have increasingly shifted to adjust the earnings. A recent example

[20] Proposed amendments to IAS 19 are expected to be finalized in 2011 and implementation likely not before 2012. See IASB Press Release, "IASB proposes improvements to defined benefit pensions accounting," April 29, 2010.

[21] For a seminal paper arguing this contingency component to the benefit promise, see Bodie (1990).

[22] For background regarding pension accounting and the impact of anticipated reforms on equity valuations, see Zion and Carcache (2005).

[23] FAS 158 requires balance sheets to include a mark-to-market reporting of plan funded status. FAS 87 permitted footnote presentation of plan funded status.

is Honeywell, which switched toward mark-to-market accounting[24] and experienced an immediate bump in Honeywell's stock price despite the accounting losses introduced (other reasons could have accounted for this but were not apparent).

19.6 Corporate Risk Factors

The corporation has many risks innate to its business model. A common risk is beta or market risk. The beta of a company varies dramatically over time and between companies and industries as shown in Figure 19.2.

A corporation can invest its pension assets to mitigate these risks and increase its return per unit of risk. Investing within an enterprise risk framework can have a significant impact on the corporation's stock price when pension assets are large. As a rule of thumb, assets in excess of 10% of the market capitalization of the corporation are large enough to have significant impact. In addition, these investments are beneficial to both the shareholders and participants.

Traditionally, defined benefit pension plans promise life annuities far out into the future. This promise is the equivalent of a long bond issuance. This bond contributes significant interest rate risk to the corporation. To manage this risk, some investment in long duration bonds is necessary. As the corporation will have other interest rate risks (e.g., stemming from operations and other debt), it may not be valuable to fully hedge the interest rate risk in the pension plan. It is valuable for strong companies to hedge or diversify some of their beta and other factor risks emerging from operations.[25]

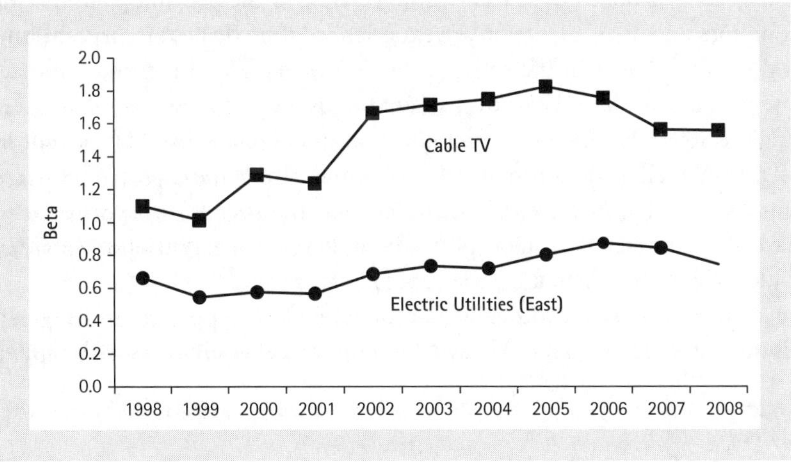

FIGURE 19.2 Historical beta – Selected industries.

[24] See Honeywell press release, "Honeywell Announces Change in Pension Accounting and Plans for 2011 Pension Funding," November 16, 2010.

[25] See Peskin and Hueffmeier (2008).

Interestingly, it does not pay shareholders to hedge a weak or near bankrupt company as the stock price will be driven by the option value. Participants, however, could still benefit from hedging.

Corporations have some risks that cannot be diversified. Beta, or market risk, is the key non-diversifiable risk component. Companies also have diversifiable risks that can be diversified by investors and are specific to the company or to its industry. The non-diversifiable risk (beta) should be reduced to a minimum, as a general rule, as such risks have no benefit to shareholders. The market risk premium can be obtained easily and cheaply directly by the shareholders.[26] The beta at the company level adds to the potential for the loss of the tax-shield or bankruptcy, which have real costs to shareholders and employees. It also pays corporations to hedge or diversify many of their idiosyncratic risks even though these can be diversified by investors. The reason, once more, is that they add to the potential loss due to the loss of the tax shield and bankruptcy (Merton and Perold 1993).[27]

19.7 Corporate Finance Theory

Corporate finance theory is a branch of financial economics that views the corporation as a pass-through entity. The corporation is owned by shareholders and, to some extent, lenders, who share in the gains and losses. Modigliani and Miller, Proposition I, is one of the cornerstones of this theory, stating that under certain pure conditions (i.e., no taxes or transaction costs) it is irrelevant whether the corporation raises capital through debt or equity.[28]

Classical theory extends this "pass through" view to the pension plan, holding that plan economics and asset allocation are experienced directly by the corporation shareholders through changes in the share price.[29] For example, if a corporation seeks to reallocate plan assets out of U.S. government bonds and into other equity issuers (e.g., by buying the S&P 500), the first-order effect on shareholders would be a shift in their personal portfolio allocation from bonds to equities. While the expected return of their portfolios is increased, so is the risk. A shareholder wanting more exposure to equities could have made the change in allocation in his or her personal portfolio. Merely shifting shareholders along the efficient frontier does not add value.[30]

However, there is a second-order effect called the Black Tepper tax arbitrage. It states that, if individuals are taxed more heavily on bonds than equities (as with capital gains

[26] For a comparison of the pension and sponsoring corporation as a source of equity return, see Gold and Hudson (2003).

[27] See Merton and Perold (1993).

[28] See Modigliani and Miller (1958).

[29] The concept of integrating the pension into a corporate "augmented balance sheet" was introduced by Treynor (1972).

[30] The level of systematic equity risk present in pensions has been shown to be fairly accurately reflected in capital market pricing. See Jin, Jin, Merton, and Bodie (2006).

treatment), then shareholders are better off with bonds in the pension plan and stocks in their individual portfolios.[31]

Developments in corporate finance theory have indicated that value is created for the shareholders by shorting beta in the pension plan.[32] The value of a company to shareholders depends on its additive return vs. its additive risk to the shareholders' portfolio. Anything that provides returns or diversifies risk beyond what the shareholders can do themselves is beneficial. This has been used as an argument to support investment in alternative asset classes as they may increase the potential for diversification.

A reduction in beta risk adds value if the reduction in expected earnings is less than a shareholder would need to give up if they reduced beta (equity exposure) directly in their own portfolio. This holds true for most companies because the increase in potential for both the loss of a tax shield and bankruptcy reduces asset value (friction cost).

An additional gain can be achieved by shareholders if companies can efficiently hedge some of their specific risks (such as a multi-national corporation hedging currency risks). This is valuable because shareholders can diversify the idiosyncratic risks themselves but they cannot eliminate the friction costs in the firm arising from volatility. Many companies do hedge direct operational risks but do not hedge additional economic or statistical risks due to the accounting, cash flow, and tax treatment of the hedges.[33]

19.8 Impact of the Pension Benefit Guarantee Corporation (PBGC)

The Pension Benefit Guarantee Corporation was established under ERISA in response to the default of Studebaker that left many retirees and active participants without pensions. The PBGC provides benefits in the event a corporation defaults at a time when the pension plan is underfunded. Like all taxpayer guarantees, the establishment of the PBGC has several unintended consequences, some of which can impact investment strategy.

As previously discussed, funded liabilities are priced close to U.S. treasury rates and unfunded liabilities are priced at the unsecured borrowing cost of the corporate sponsor. Financially weaker companies could be demotivated to fund their plans and reduce risk. In some cases, the safety net of the PBGC could incentivize such companies to give greater pension benefits in lieu of cash compensation at a time when they need to attract or retain employees, but do not have the ability to offer competitive

[31] See Black (1981).

[32] Gold (2007).

[33] Note that Modigliani–Miller corporate finance theory (Propositions I and II) does not apply here because the conditions of their propositions do not hold.

salaries. These unintended consequences of the PBGC impact all plan sponsors who may have to bear increased premiums as well as taxpayers who may have to bail out the PBGC.[34]

In addition to the costs of funding the plan, financially weak companies with underfunded pension plans are not motivated to derisk their plans. Very weak companies will tend to trade like an option. Shareholders stand to gain much more from the upside of a risky investment than they stand to lose from the downside, as the share price cannot go below zero. This is a clear situation where the interest of shareholders and plan participants are not aligned. If participants are not protected by the PBGC, they would gain by derisking the plan.

19.9 Pension Plan Investments and Asymmetric Payoffs

When assessing returns vs. risk it is important to consider any asymmetries that may apply. Returns in the pension plan may translate into returns to shareholders or participants in a very nonlinear way. For example, as discussed above companies that are near bankruptcy trade like options. The price of an option rises with volatility because the potential upside benefits the shareholders but the potential downside is limited, as the stock price cannot go below zero. The rest of the losses are borne by creditors, bondholders, and taxpayers through the PBGC. Hence, it may be beneficial to shareholders to take risk in the pension plan. Asymmetries change with funded status and the strength of the company. While option pricing is the theoretically right tool to use, Table 19.5 illustrates the concept.

We've previously noted that financially weak companies are motivated to underfund their plans as the PBGC assumes most of the risk. Taking investment risk may have a positive impact on stock price for such weak companies.

Asymmetry in the opposite direction may arise when a company has a well-funded pension plan and the excise tax makes surplus difficult for shareholders to recover. In such cases additional surplus may have little value, whereas the emergence of a deficit would need to be funded by shareholders.[35] The return realized by shareholders would be considerably lower than the return realized by the plan. On the other hand, if a company can pass costs on to a third party, it may make sense to take risk if the reduction in expected cost helps to win a contract and the third party is responsible for making up investment losses. This is often the situation in government contracting.

[34] The PBGC premium structure and incentives has been argued to be a significant driver to the recent PBGC crisis. See Bodie (2006).

[35] For an in-depth discussion of this asymmetry, see Peskin (1997).

Table 19.5 Corporate asymmetry example.

		Outcomes: Assets Not Matched to Liabilities			Outcomes: Assets Matched to Liabilities	
	Current	Assets Up 20%	Assets Down 20%	Current	Assets Up 20%	Assets Down 20%
Corporate Assets	$1,000	$1,200	$800	$1,000	$1,200	$800
Corporate Liabilities (Debt)	$1,000	$1,000	$1,000	$1,000	$1,200	$800
Equity	$0	$200	$0	$0	$0	$0
Probability of Outcome		50%	50%		50%	50%
Expected Value of Outcome		$100	$0		$0	$0
Stock Price*	$50 =	50%* $100	+ 50% * $0	$0 =	50% * $0	+ 50%* $0

*In reality, stock price would be a bit higher to reflect the value of volatility to options.

19.10 Impact of Capital Market Pricing

Investment in risky assets is only justified if it increases the risk/return tradeoff to shareholders of the company by more than is available to the shareholders investing for themselves. It is insufficient to focus on returns, volatility of returns, and correlations. Using a surplus (or any other pension asset vs. pension liability) efficient frontier gives erroneous answers. Such an approach tends to overweight the value of risk premia and underweight the associated risks. To illustrate this point, let's consider U.S. Treasuries versus equities. Treasury bonds outperform equities in periods of recession when people are poorer, many are unemployed, corporate borrowing costs (spreads to treasuries) are high, spending and corporate profits are down, and cash is king. Equities outperform bonds in bull markets when people are richer, corporations have high profits and easy access to credit.

U.S. Treasuries are "riskless" in the sense that the coupon and principal will be paid as promised. The U.S. can always print money and therefore will not default.[36] The price of treasuries is set by the marketplace.[37] The market also prices contingent cash flows that change over time based on the state of the world. The *equity risk premium* is the excess expected return that equities have over treasuries. While equities usually outperform treasury bonds, they tend to do so when capital is readily available and thus less valuable. On the other hand, when treasury bonds outperform equities, often in a recession, the loss of capital due to falling equity prices can be particularly painful. The equity risk premium is compensation for this phenomenon. Some of the premium also stems from a natural human aversion to risk.

Asset allocation must account for the price of risk set by the marketplace or highly inefficient results (reduction in stock price) can ensue. The price of risk should be monitored as does the price of insuring risk (hedging). The asset allocation in the pension plan is an excellent tool to execute such risk management.[38]

19.11 Debt-to-Equity Management Through the Pension Plan

The optimal investment strategy for a pension plan should be to minimize the potential loss of benefits to participants (the fiduciary obligation of the plan) and to maximize the

[36] The U.S. may well reduce the real payoff to lenders by depreciating the currency (i.e., inflation) but will not default in a strict sense.

[37] This can break down in unusual times when central bank intervention can control interest rates to an abnormal extent as is the case at the time of writing (fall of 2010).

[38] For a further discussion of capital market pricing implications on pension asset allocation, see Peskin and Hueffmeier (2006).

value of the stock of the corporation. This dual objective may occasionally conflict. The route to achieving these goals, as well as to resolving conflicts, is to manage the overall debt-to-equity ratio of the company.

Participants will only lose accrued pension benefits promised to date on the joint occurrence of bankruptcy of the corporation and an underfunded pension plan. Managing the debt-to-equity ratio to mitigate the potential for bankruptcy will help avoid any such loss. Furthermore, such management should improve the pension plan's performance when the corporation's operation is performing poorly, thereby reducing the potential for the joint occurrence of bankruptcy and an underfunded plan.[39]

For example, consider a company that generates its revenue in the U.S. but has costs tied to raw material prices driven by emerging market demand. U.S. growth is beneficial to such a company (sales will increase) and emerging market growth would be detrimental (increased costs). Therefore, the corporation is effectively long the U.S. equity market and short emerging equity markets. Strategic investing in the pension plan to mitigate this exposure (i.e. buying emerging market equities and selling U.S. equities) can reduce the corporation's overall risk without compromising expected earnings. The pension plan provides an excellent vehicle for such economic hedging.

Competitive forces are likely to pressure corporations to adopt many of the successful practices of hedge funds. Among these practices, shorting can be a valuable tool in hedging risk. A corporation is naturally "long" certain risks that are innate to its business model. Many of these risks are statistical in nature and cannot be hedged at the corporate level due to accounting and tax treatment. They can, however, be hedged in the pension plan.

Corporate debt – with the exception of pension underfunding – tends to be fairly stable. Equity capitalization can move with several factors, some of which are market driven (beta and industry beta) and some of which are idiosyncratic (specific to the firm).

Unlike other debts of the corporation, unfunded pension liabilities are leveraged. Interest rate and equity values (risky assets) can significantly affect the unfunded liabilities. If the pension plan is large relative to the corporation, the pension liability will be a significant risk requiring hedging. The plan can and should also be used to hedge other corporate risks.

Corporate equity value can be enhanced by increasing the return per unit of risk to shareholders. A reduction in risk can lead to a higher equity valuation by diminishing the costs that come with an increasing debt-to-equity ratio (bankruptcy friction costs, loss of the tax shield, and opportunity cost).[40] Expected returns might be further increased if the plan has more efficient access to investments or investor skills that allow shareholders to expand their efficient frontiers (complete markets), which would be experienced by them as alpha (excess returns not explained by risk). Alpha generating investments that also hedge corporate risks are of particular value.

[39] Peskin and Hueffmeier (2008).

[40] See Merton (2006).

Table 19.6 Debt-to-equity ratio: Impact of hedging strategies.

	Liability Valuation Increases 20%, Asset Valuation Decreases 20%, Corporate Equity Decreases 20%			
	Starting	No Hedge	Pension Assets Matched to Liabilities	Pension Assets Matched to Liabilities, Pension Debt Matched to Corporation
Corporate Equity	1,000	800	800	800
Pension Assets	800	640	960	1,008
Pension Liabilities	1,000	1,200	1,200	1,200
Pension Underfunding	200	560	240	192
Debt-to-Equity Ratio	**20%**	**70%**	**30%**	**24%**
Corporate Equity	1,000	1,200	1,200	1,200
Pension Assets	800	640	960	912
Pension Liabilities	1,000	1,200	1,200	1,200
Pension Underfunding	200	560	240	288
Debt-to-Equity Ratio	**20%**	**47%**	**20%**	**24%**

Stability in the debt-to-equity ratio should translate into a higher multiple, and thus a higher stock price.

Many corporations hedge some of their risks at the corporate level. However, they are limited by tax and accounting rules that fail to recognize the parallel between both sides of the hedge. This limitation is not present in the pension plan, where accounting and tax recognition is not immediate. Risks which may be hedged in the plan could include currency, operations, and financing costs.[41]

The overall impact on a corporation's debt-to-equity, if both pension liabilities and corporate risk are hedged, is illustrated (in steps) in Table 19.6.

Reducing the risk of the corporation has a further advantageous effect. The borrowing cost and the borrowing capacity of a firm is impacted by the riskiness of the firm. If risk is reduced then borrowing cost will decrease and borrowing capacity will increase.[42] The increase in borrowing capacity allows the firm to take further advantage of the tax deduction on debt. Thus, stock price will be further advantaged.

19.12 Macro-Economic Impacts on Investment Strategies

At the time of writing, the world economy is in the process of establishing a new equilibrium following a credit meltdown and in the early stages of a process of a

[41] See Berner, Boudreau and Peskin (2006).

[42] Ibid.

massive deleveraging. Deleveraging results in lower real GDP growth, perhaps even negative growth. Low growth is likely to be accompanied by unemployment and falling real income. It is also likely to give rise to significant government and central bank intervention in an attempt to mitigate (reduce, export, or otherwise transfer) economic hardship. With all of their unknowns and connectedness, global macroeconomic drivers are playing an increasingly important role in pension performance.

To better understand the impacts of the macroeconomy on pension investing, it is helpful to first define risk vs. uncertainty.[43] Risk arises as a natural consequence of a multitude of people making personal financial, purchasing, saving, investing, and business decisions. While the future is unknown, a reasonable probability distribution of possible outcomes can be determined from past experience. Uncertainty, on the other hand, arises when decisions made by a few central bankers and key politicians have a profound effect on capital market prices.[44] With uncertainty, there is insufficient data to determine a probability distribution of outcomes.

The major forces for deflation are well established. The two largest are: the large supply of significantly lower paid skilled and unskilled labor in the emerging economies and the bursting of the credit bubble. The bursting of the credit bubble results in a fall in spending. Consumers are unable to continue to spend both their incomes and future incomes (borrowing against their homes, credit cards, etc.). Instead, they will have to constrain spending to their current income after saving for retirement. Furthermore, the rise in unemployment, due to extensive layoffs as companies anticipate the decline in sales, adds to deflationary pressures.

Some elements of the macroeconomy are known with great confidence. For example, the massive debt in the U.S., Europe, and Japan must be paid down, defaulted on, or inflated away. The aging and longer living populations of Japan, China, and most of Europe will lead to fewer people supporting more dependents.

To mitigate deflation, central banks around the world have printed money, spent and borrowed to increase money supply. However, central banks only have the power to increase the monetary base and have little control over the aggregate GDP, which is the aggregate money supply (monetary base times the multiplier). This is shown in Figure 19.3.

Any action to increase the multiplier is not precise and could result in debt growing faster than GDP, or could succeed and result in GDP growing faster than debt. If the multiplier grows, central banks must reduce liquidity or high inflation will ensue. A deeper deflationary recession could result if the reduction in liquidity occurs too quickly.

High unemployment and/or inflation in food prices causes unrest and gives rise to tensions both geopolitically (between countries) and politically (within countries). This is likely to cause a growth in tension with further pressures for government intervention.

[43] The distinction between risk and uncertainty was first developed by Frank Knight (1921).

[44] Ibid.

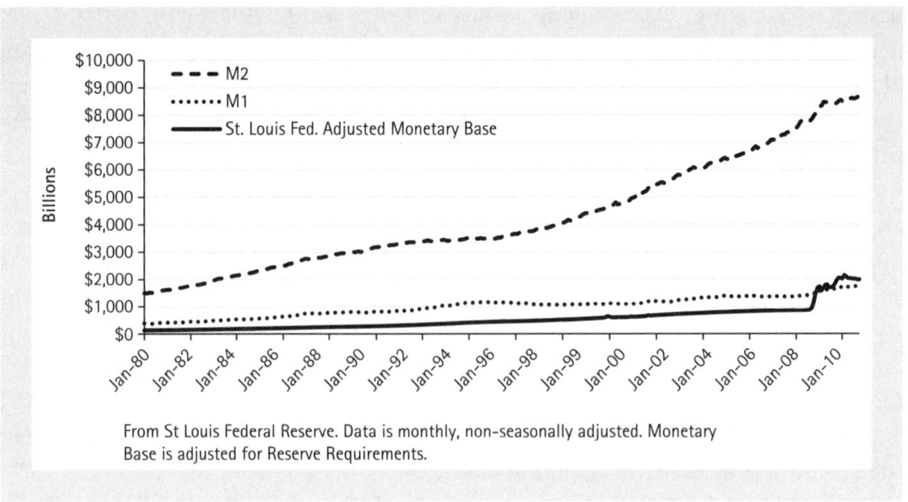

FIGURE 19.3 Money supply measures.

The current uncertainty creates an environment with four possible scenarios: stagflation, heating, recession, or innovation. The occurrence of one does not necessarily preclude moving to another. Figure 19.4 shows the quadrants and the associated scenarios.

Each of these emerging quadrants will have a dramatically different impact on a corporation's debt-to-equity ratio. Strategic asset allocation – setting fixed targets to equity exposures and fixed income – is inappropriate during such a stressed economic environment. Some degree of tactical/dynamic investment is necessary to manage debt-to-equity ratios.

For example, a high-beta corporation with a large pension plan should hedge against recession as this environment can cause debt-to-equity ratios to balloon. However, in the emergence of an inflationary environment, the same corporation should reduce its deflation hedge to take advantage of the emerging inflationary environment to reduce its debt. Emerging inflation is likely to persist as central banks will react slowly for fear of causing a recession. But at some point, central banks will have to react to inflation, whereupon the corporation should begin to reinstate its deflationary hedge.

Corporations with large pension plans and high beta are likely to find that the recessionary scenario has the largest impact on the debt-to-equity ratio. Debt will rise as interest rates fall at the same time that the corporation's value and income declines.

To avoid a precipitous impact on the debt-to-equity ratio, corporations should hedge against both debt and equity declines through investments in long treasuries and short equity beta. The cost of hedging may be significant as interest rates are at low levels and options are expensive but are a necessary insurance. Furthermore, the hedge can result in significant losses with emerging inflation or rising sovereign risk. Inflation will

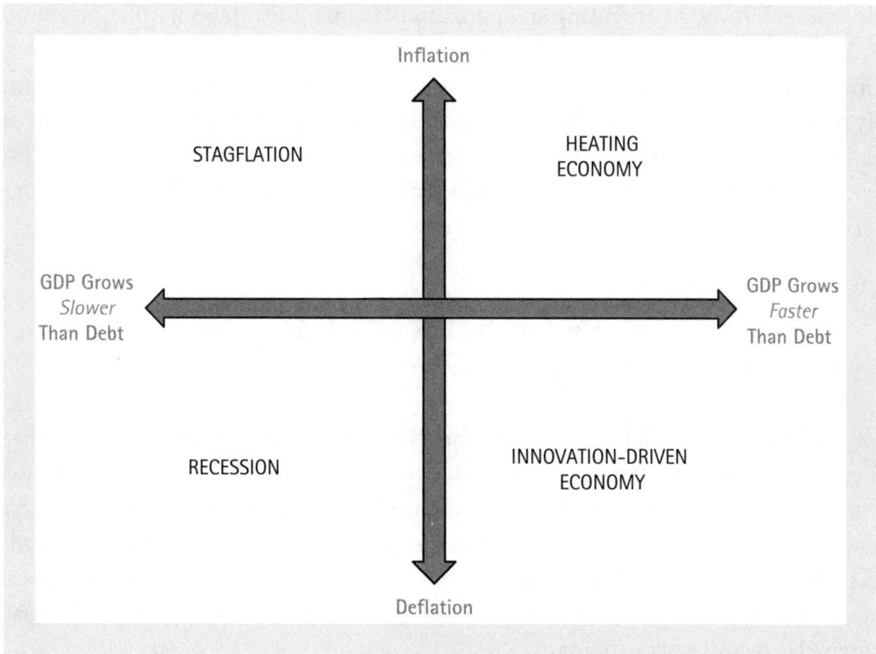

FIGURE 19.4 Footnote overview of economic framework – Description of four quadrants.

Recession
This is the most feared quadrant where stimulus fails to counter the impact of deleveraging and the economy stagnates, resulting in poor equity returns and volatility, deflation, low interest rates, and chronic unemployment.

Stagflation
Stagflation occurs when stimulus fails to promote growth and the byproduct is inflation and a falling dollar. In this quadrant, the macroeconomy would experience a trajectory of higher inflation, higher interest rates, and poor real equity returns coupled with high volatility.

Heating Economy
Heating is experienced when stimulus succeeds and produces growth in GDP. The dollar declines experienced are more than offset by the growing economy. This quadrant would experience a significant decline in unemployment resulting in strong equity returns as consumer spending rebounds and moderate inflation as the Federal Reserve withdraws liquidity slowly to avoid recession.

Innovation-Driven Economy
A significant innovation, such as a new energy source, is necessary for this quadrant to emerge. The macroeconomy in this quadrant would experience excellent equity returns and low inflation. The emergence of this quadrant is highly unlikely in the near term.

likely emerge slowly,[45] presenting an opportunity to take advantage of inflation's natural erosion of the debt markets, including pension liabilities, by reducing the hedge.

Uncertain macro-environments offer many opportunities. Any government action is likely to have some predictable consequences. These can be tapped with appropriate tactical investments. A purely strategic investment approach, with fixed exposures to asset classes, will not succeed in either hedging or exploiting the predictable consequences of government action.

19.13 Summary

Managing the pension plan in an enterprise framework is advantageous to both shareholders and pension participants. In particular, stock price and the financial security of participants can be enhanced by managing the corporation's debt-to-equity ratio through the pension plan. This will increase stock price by reducing the likelihood of bankruptcy or loss of tax shield and their associated friction costs. It also reduces the joint probability of corporate bankruptcy and pension underfunding, which increases the financial security of participants.

- The economic debt of the pension plan is the unfunded accrued liability cash flows discounted at the unsecured borrowing cost of the corporation. There is, however, another important addition/subtraction to the economic value due to the basis risk between the assets and liabilities and its correlation with the corporation. The lower the correlation with the corporation the less return the basis risk needs to generate to be valuable. Negatively correlated basis risk can have negative returns and still be valuable.
- Liquidity management is important to many companies and is achieved by managing the ratio of cash demands (including pension contributions) to free cash flow plus liquid assets. The resulting investment strategy may differ somewhat from the management of debt-to-equity.
- Corporations with low costs of borrowing should fund their plans faster than regulations require even if it requires borrowing to do so.
- Pension accounting does not sufficiently reflect the economics to be an effective management tool for either participant financial security or for increasing the value of the corporation.
- The asymmetric payoff to shareholders and participants should be recognized and managed to enable valuable arbitrages.
- Capital market pricing sets the price of "hedging" as well as the risk premiums. The price is an important factor in determining the risk/return tradeoff of investment/hedging strategies.

[45] At the time of this writing, inflation appears to be rising.

- The pension plan provides an excellent vehicle to manage the overall corporate debt-to-equity ratio as it provides a liquid pool of assets with symmetric tax and accounting treatment allowing for hedging of corporate economic risks.
- The reduction in overall corporate risk should allow for lower borrowing costs and increased borrowing capacity.
- The pension plan allows for a rapid response to emerging macroeconomic scenarios and anticipated effects of government intervention, allowing for opportunistic returns and avoidance of emerging pitfalls.

References

Bader, L. (2003). Treatment of pension plans in a corporate valuation. *Financial Analysts Journal*, May/June, 19–24.

Berner, R., Boudreau, B., and Peskin, M. (2006). "De-risking" corporate pension plans: Options for CFOs. *Journal of Applied Corporate Finance*, **18**, 25–35.

Black, F. (1980). The tax consequences of long-run pension policy. *Financial Analysts Journal*, July–August, 21–30.

Bodie, Z. (1990). The ABO, the PBO, and pension investment policy. *Financial Analysts Journal*, September–October, 27–38.

Bodie, Z. (2006). On asset-liability matching and federal deposit and pension insurance. Federal Reserve Bank of St. Louis Review, July/August 2006, **88**(4), 323–29.

Exley, C., Mehta, S., and Smith, A. (1997). The financial theory of defined benefit pension schemes. *British Actuarial Journal*, **3**, 835–966.

Gold, J. (2007). The intersection of pensions and enterprise risk management (http://www.pensionfinance.org/papers/TheIntersectionofPensionsandEnterpriseRiskManagement.pdf).

Jin, L., Merton, R., and Bodie, Z. (2006). Do a firm's equity returns reflect the risk of its pension plan? *Journal of Financial Economics*, **81**, 1–26.

Knight, F.H. (1921). *Risk, Uncertainty and Profit*. Harper, New York.

Kopcke, R.W. (2006). Managing the risk in pension plans and recent pension reforms. Federal Reserve Bank of Boston, MA: Hart, Schaffner & Marx; Houghton Mifflin Co. Discussion Paper, November 2006 (06–7).

Merton, R.C. (2006). Allocating shareholder capital to pension plans. *Journal of Applied Corporate Finance*, Winter.

Merton, R.C. and Perold, A.F. (1993). Theory of risk capital in financial firms. *Journal of Applied Corporate Finance*, Fall, 16–32.

Modigliani, F. and Miller, M. (1958). The cost of capital, corporation finance, and the theory of investment. *American Economic Review*, **48**(3), 261–297.

Peskin, M.W. (1989). Corporate finance approach to pensions and other employee retirement benefits. *Morgan Stanley Pension Issues & Insights*, October, pp. 1–4.

Peskin, M.W. (1997). Asset allocation and funding policy for corporate-sponsored defined-benefit pension plans. *Journal of Portfolio Management*, Winter, 66–73.

Peskin, M.W. and Moore, J. (2002). *Discount Benchmarks for Defined Benefit Pension Plans*. Morgan Stanley, New York.

Peskin, M.W. and Hueffmeier, C. (2006). The emerging pension paradigm – Part I. *Investment Management Journal*, November.

Peskin, M.W. and Hueffmeier, C. (2008). Asset-liability management within a corporate finance framework. *Investment Management Journal*, August.

Peskin, M.W. (2010). Issue debt to fund DB plan: The GM 2003 decision. *Society of Actuaries Presentation*, March.

Tepper, I. (1981). Taxation and Corporate Pension Policy. *Journal of Finance*, **36**, 1–13.

Treynor, J.L. (1972). [using pseudonym, Walter Bagehot], Risk and reward in corporate pension funds. *Financial Analysts Journal*, January–February, 80–84.

Waring, B.M. and Siegel, L.B. (2007). Don't kill the golden goose! Saving pension plans. *Financial Analysts Journal*, **63**, 31–45.

Zion, D. and Carcache, B. (2005). The magic of pension accounting, Part III. Credit Suisse First Boston Equity Research, February.

CHAPTER 20

PRICING EMBEDDED OPTIONS IN VALUE-BASED ASSET LIABILITY MANAGEMENT*

ROY P. M. M. HOEVENAARS

20.1 Introduction

Asset liability management (ALM) studies play a key role in important financial policy decisions of pension schemes, insurance companies, endowments, and other institutional investors. Traditionally, academic and practical research on ALM focuses on the simulation of stochastic and deterministic scenarios of the future balance sheet (see Boender 1997; Ziemba and Mulvey 1998 and Boender, Dert, Heemskerk; Hoek 2007). As the fair valuation of pension liabilities has become regulatory practice in many countries over recent years, market-consistent valuation of pension liabilities has attracted attention in the literature (see Kortleve, Nijman, and Ponds 2006; Nijman and Koijen 2006; Bodie 2006; De Jong 2008, 2009; Pelsser and Vlaar 2009). Next to that, the increased risk awareness due to the recent financial crisis and the advent of mark-to-marked accounting are two of many reasons that traditional defined benefit plans worldwide are redesigning their pension deals (see Ambachtsheer 2007). Pension redesign will inevitably lead to risk transfers between stakeholders.

These transfers can be detected with the help of a relatively new approach – so-called "Value-based ALM" – which essentially is based on applying option-pricing

* The views expressed in this chapter are those of the author and do not necessarily reflect those of the employer and colleagues. I gratefully acknowledge Theo Kocken, Roderick Molenaar, and Eduard Ponds for fruitful discussions and comments on earlier versions of this chapter.

techniques in an ALM context. Roots date back to the 1970s (Sharpe 1976) and applications of contingent claim analyis to real-life problems in the fields of pensions and insurance as in Blake (1998); Steenkamp (1998); and Chapman, Gordon, and Speed (2001). Recently, vigourous applications in the field of pension redesign of collective pension schemes include Ponds (2003); Kocken (2006); Kortleve and Ponds (2006); Hoevenaars and Ponds (2008); and Hoevenaars, Kocken, and Ponds (2009). Any collective pension arrangement between an employer and its employees can be stated in terms of contingent claims which can be valued within a contingent claim analysis framework. The value of all claims equals the value of assets covered by the contract. Policy changes lead to changes in the value of the claims. Value-based ALM identifies such embedded options on the balance sheet of a complex long-term commitment as if it were a negotiable financial contract. Changes in the fair values of the embedded options reveal risk transfers between the stakeholders. It provides an objective way to identify and quantify the shifts in risk positioning, and the potential amount of compensation one group of stakeholders should pay when they bear less risk in a redesigned pension plan such as the transition to collective DC. That said, insights into the risk exposure of the different groups of stakeholders contributes to the transparency of complex pension deals. It helps the discussion for a fair and transparent pension fund redesign.

How does value-based ALM relate to classical ALM as prescribed by financial theory and practice? Classic ALM analysis focuses on the financial position and balance sheet and is based on the probability distributions of key pension fund variables over a certain horizon. Econometric models are used to create projections of economic scenarios regarding the development of equity markets, interest rates, and inflation in the future (see Hoevenaars, Molenaar, Schotman, and Steenkamp 2008; Van Rooij, Siegmann, and Vlaar 2004; and Amenc, Martellini, and Ziemann 2009). This results in a series of probability distributions for the most important variables of a pension fund such as the funding ratio and the extent to which indexation is awarded. The information from the probability distributions is used to weigh risks on one hand (e.g., probability of a funding shortfall) versus the expected return on the other (e.g., the expected percentage of indexation awarded to the participants and the expected average paid contribution). By adjusting control variables such as the allocation to investment classes, a derivatives overlay, and the contribution rate, it is possible to look for the most acceptable solution. Given that a pension plan has different stakeholders (employers, employees, retirees, and future participants) with different and sometimes conflicting interests, there is no uniform set of objectives leading to an optimal result. Instead, this situation calls for a highly complex analysis of multiple criteria where diverse interests need to be reconciled.

With value-based ALM, the financial policy is not only evaluated in terms of the uncertain future financial position and balance sheet, but also in terms of the exposure of the beneficiaries to the total risk embedded in the pension deal. By determining all contributions, payments, and investment returns in each of the future scenarios and calculating their present value with the stochastic discount rate belonging to each of these scenarios, it is possible to determine the present economic value of these cash flows. Economic value can be understood as the present financial value of uncertain future cash flows. For example, this relates to the value of future indexation flows and contributions. The absolute and relative changes of the economic values of the future commitments in the pension deal from a change in the policy parameters reveals the changes in risk positions of the different groups of stakeholders. In short, classical ALM optimizes the policy, while value-based ALM can be used to ensure that this takes place on fair economic terms between stakeholders.

This chapter is organized as follows. The next section identifies contingent claims and embedded options on the balance sheet of a collective defined benefit pension scheme. Section 20.3 describes an econometric model for the risk and return dynamics. We use the model for classical ALM and the consistent pricing of embedded options. Sections 20.4.1 illustrates the application of embedded options to pension fund redesign. We use the embedded indexation and employer guarantee options to calculate the employer share in risk. In turn, this forms the basis for the monetary compensation required when the employer withdraws as a risk taker. Such a shift from a typical defined benefit plan to a collective defined contribution plan should cost the employer, in this illustration, a lump sum payment of 12% of the accrued pension obligations and an increase in the contribution rate of 4% of pay. Section 20.4.2 illustrates the application of embedded options to asset management. A change in the investment strategy from a calendar rebalancing to a fixed strategic asset allocation towards a more dynamic asset allocation which is driven by a risk constraint of the funding ratio increases the participant share in total risk. The employer share in risk decreases substantially in the example under consideration. Section 20.5 concludes.

20.2 Contingent Claims as Embedded Options

Framing DB pension plans as aggregates of embedded options builds on the work of Sharpe (1976), Ponds (2003), Kocken (2006), and Hoevenaars (2008), among others. Below we identify embedded options on the balance sheet of a funded collective pension scheme. To that purpose we rewrite the balance sheet such that it reveals the implicit payoffs and claims to the stakeholders.

We define the excess on the balance sheet (E_t) as the market value of the assets (A_t) minus the market value of the liabilities (L_t): $E_t = A_t - L_t$. During a year the asset side changes due to pension payments (P_t), inflow from contributions (C_t), and investment returns (R_t). Changes on the liability side result from new accrued pension claims (N_t), pension payments, and indexation (I_t). In other words,

$$A_t = A_{t-1}(1 + R_t) + C_t - P_t \tag{20.1}$$

$$L_t = L_{t-1} + N_t + I_t - P_t. \tag{20.2}$$

In an arbitrage-free world the present value of future investment returns equals one ($\mathsf{E}_t\,(M_{t+1}(1 + R_{t+1}))$). Following the asset pricing literature (e.g. Cochrane 2001) the present value of the excess at $t + \tau$ can be written as

$$V_t\,(E_{t+\tau}) = \mathsf{E}_t\left(M^*_{t+\tau}E_{t+\tau}\right) \tag{20.3}$$

$$= A_t - L_t - V_t\left(\Delta I_{t,t+\tau}\right) - V_t\left(\Delta N_{t,t+\tau} - \Delta C_{t,t+\tau}\right) \tag{20.4}$$

where $M^*_{t+\tau} = M_{t+1} \cdots M_{t+\tau}$ is the corresponding stochastic discount factor for payoffs in period $t + \tau$. In general, high values of the stochastic discount rates are assigned to bad scenarios, and low values are assigned to good scenarios. As a consequence payoffs during bad times are more valuable than payoffs during good times. This reflects the prevailing risk aversion in the market which implies that payoffs during bad times are more valuable than payoffs during good times. The option pricing framework described in this chapter accommodates complex real-world path-dependent policy decisions and investment strategies. $V_t\left(\Delta I_{t,t+\tau}\right)$, $V_t\left(\Delta N_{t,t+\tau}\right)$, and $V_t\left(\Delta C_{t,t+\tau}\right)$ represent the present value of the indexation, new accrued pension claims, pension payments, and contributions during the time period $(t, t + \tau)$. Accordingly, the change in the balance sheet between t and $t + \tau$ is

$$V_t\left(\Delta I_{t,t+\tau}\right) + V_t\left(\Delta E_{t,t+\tau}\right) + V_t\left(\Delta N_{t,t+\tau} - \Delta C_{t,t+\tau}\right) = 0. \tag{20.5}$$

Equation (20.5) identifies three types of options in these plans: indexation, shortfall-related, and contribution-related. Each type is further described in the definitions that follow.

Indexation option Indexation is either a hard guarantee or conditional on the plans funded status. In the latter case, annual updates are determined by a graduated indexation. If the nominal funding ratio is equal to or lower than the lower limit of the graduated scale, no indexation is awarded. If the nominal funding ratio is equal to or higher than the upper limit of the graduated scale, full indexation is awarded, and possibly supplemented with previous unawarded indexations. With funding ratios between the lower and upper limit, indexation reductions are imposed proportionate to the funding ratio. Conditional indexation can be interpreted as a string of put options for the fund written by the participants and maturing at several months in the future. Whenever the financial position deteriorates such that full indexation is not longer sustainable, the put option becomes in-the-money and the fund can exercise the option. This leads to conditional indexation. Equivalently, the put-call parity implies that the conditional indexation option can also be interpreted as a call option for the participants written by the fund. From this perspective the conditional indexation policy implies that participants implicitly have the right to claim indexation according to the indexation policy. The economic value of this conditional indexation method is called the indexation option. The embedded indexation option discloses the future indexation potential and is path-dependent on the market variables. It depends on the indexation policy.

Shortfall option (employer guarantee) Employers usually have a hard or moral obligation to act as guarantor in situations involving a nominal funding shortfall. This guarantee has financial value. The employer has effectively written a series of complex put options, the exercise price being a nominal funding ratio of 100%. Valuing these options requires determining the annual probability of a nominal funding shortfall and the size of each shortfall that occurs over the entire settlement period of the existing rights. These future funding shortfall estimates can then be valued in present-value units of money. The employer may or may not have a right to withdraw excess surplus. Even without this right, restitution can still be obtained indirectly through contribution reductions (e.g., exercising the contribution reduction option).

Contribution option The contribution rate in DB schemes should, in principle, be equal to the costs of the new accrual of pension rights, taking into account the expected return on investments. We will call this contribution rate the plans uniform contribution. The basis of this is the uniform contribution rate, which can also be used as a risk management instrument. Although it is not fixed, it includes a variable component (positive or negative) that depends on the funded status of the fund. The resulting contribution option value is the net outcome of the economic values of contingent contribution increases and reductions. The contribution rate option is particularly valuable if there is a conditional contribution rate policy or at times of contribution holidays like the ones we have seen in the past for some pension funds. Note that the contribution option in Equation (20.5) also includes changes in the actuarial characteristics of the pension scheme participants.

Other embedded options naturally result from the (changes in the) pension deal. One option that is always present as soon as the (corporate) sponsor is not default-free is the pension put. Kocken (2006) extensively describes this pension put in a value-based ALM application to pension fund redesign.[1] It entails the credit exposure of the participants if the fund defaults on its commitments. The higher the default risk of the parent, the lower the value of the employer guarantee to the beneficiaries and consequently the higher the pension put. The pension put is in fact an option on two joint events: a shortfall in the pension funding ratio and a default of the parent company at the same time. Another option embedded in Equation (20.5) is a surplus related option. Most pension funds do not explicitly assign the right to withdrawn excess surpluses from the fund. That said, a high value surplus option is more attractive for the entrance of new participants in the future. Hoevenaars (2008) studies the change in this option value to identify the attractiveness of the pension fund for future stakeholders and entrance of future generations. Hoevenaars and Ponds (2008) and Hoevenaars, Molenaar, and

[1] See Steenkamp (1998) for an analysis of the pension put from the perspective of the parent company.

Ponds (2010) demonstrate value-based generational accounting when there are many age cohorts in a collective pension scheme. Another embedded option reveals itself in the recent credit crisis. As the funding ratio of many pension funds dropped below 100%, the regulator required a recovery plan for the near future. Cutting pension rights to increase the current funding ratio was sometimes evaluated as a possible solution when there was a severe drawdown. Such a conditional cut was not even considered among the policy instruments a few years ago. In the current economic challenging times, it becomes an extremely expensive embedded option for the current beneficiaries who are close to retirement and who have built up many pension rights over the years.

The key question is: how are the various options allocated amongst stakeholders? The content of the pension contract is very important to this question since it sets out consequences of any change in the financial position of the fund for fixing premiums, indexation policy, and so on. For every existing pension fund with a pension contract that specifically states what party will bear what part of the risk going either up or down, this contract can be translated in concrete, embedded options. A pension contract is not always conclusive and all options are not always neatly allocated between employer and employee. The surplus option in particular, the biggest part of the upside (the call), usually receives little attention in terms of ownership rights. For a pension design to be fair per stakeholder, the options it writes to the pension fund (e.g, indexation by the beneficiaries) should equal the option this stakeholder receives. In this respect, it would be fair in the simple case of a pension fund with only an indexation option (beneficiaries) and employer guarantee (parent).[2] As a result, the analysis in this chapter will not include the surplus option as undefined ownership and the analysis shall focus on the risk element assumed by employers and employees. Equation (20.5) also demonstrates the zero-sum character in value terms. This means that policy changes lead to value transfers between the three components in Equation (20.5), but do not create additional value.

20.3 Pricing Embedded Options in ALM

The return dynamics is based on a vector autoregressive (VAR) model and builds on Hoevenaars (2008). An attractive property of a VAR model is that it enables us to distinguish long-term and short-term risk properties of asset classes (see Campbell, Chan, and Viceira 2003). Along the lines of Cochrane and Piazzesi (2005) we extend the VAR system with the pricing kernel to derive an affine term structure of interest rates. In

[2] That the surplus option is divided over these two stakeholder groups in the same ratio as the ratio indexation option/employer guarantee. See Kocken (2006) for practical examples of this principle.

this way we construct a consistent economic environment applicable to strategic asset allocation and fair value ALM.[3]

The ALM framework is based on a simulation study which projects the development of the pension fund in many future scenarios. The policy horizon for the classic ALM analysis is 20 years.[4] As this chapter focuses on fair value in ALM, we have suppressed the degree of complexity of the investment universe. The investment universe consists only of a MSCI world stock index and zero-coupon nominal bonds with a constant maturity of 10 years. Furthermore, we assume that wage inflation equals price inflation, so that real wage growth is zero.[5]

The relevant economic factors z_t in the model include the one-month interest rate, the 10-year zero coupon rate, price inflation, stock returns in excess of the one-month interest rate, and the corresponding dividend yield. Returns on a rolling 10-year constant maturity bond portfolio are constructed from the nominal term structure.

Formally, the VAR is written as:

$$z_{t+1} = c + Bz_t + \Sigma\zeta_{t+1}$$

where $\zeta_{t+1} \sim N(0, I)$.

To derive an affine term structure of interest rates, we use the no-arbitrage assumptions, and we specify the pricing kernel as

$$-\log M_{t+1} = \delta_0 + \delta_1 z_t + \frac{1}{2}\lambda_t'\lambda_t + \lambda_t'\zeta_{t+1}$$

where λ_t are time-varying prices of risk which are affine in the state variables. M_{t+1} is the stochastic discount factor which can be used for the valuation of embedded options in the pension deal. The short rate $(\delta_0 + \delta_1 z_t)$ is assumed to be the observable one-month interest rate $\left(y_t^{(1)}\right)$ which is also included in the VAR such that $y_t^{(1)} = \delta_0 + \delta_1 z_t$. To achieve consistency between the VAR and the short rate dynamics we let $\delta_0 = 0$ and $\delta_1' = (1, 0, 0, 0, 0)$.

The affine class of term structure models states that (nominal) yields on an n-period zero coupon bond are linear in the state variables.

$$y_t^{(n)} = -\frac{A_n}{n} - \frac{B_n'}{n} z_t. \tag{20.6}$$

[3] Obviously, the concept of embedded options in the pension deal is not exclusively related to the VAR model for the return dynamics. Other econometric model specifications can be used to create arbitrage-free scenarios.

[4] An infinite horizon for the pension contract and pension fund would be hard to justify. We choose to evaluate the fund position at a finite horizon. On the one hand, we aim for insights about the implications of a pension policy at various horizons. On the other hand, it makes no sense to simulate too far into the future, because we have only a limited amount of historical data to estimate the return dynamics. A 20 year horizon reveals implications for short, medium, and long horizons.

[5] The assumption of a real wage growth of zero avoids the problem of valuation in an incomplete market. As there are no wage-indexed assets, risk relating to real wage growth is not priced into the market. De Jong (2008) discusses several methods to value wage-indexed cashflows in an incomplete market.

The scalar A_n and $(n \times 1)$ vector B_n are defined under the no-arbitrage condition and can be solved recursively when $A_0 = B_0 = 0$, such that

$$A_n = -\delta_0 + A_{n-1} + B'_{n-1}(c - \Sigma\lambda_0) + \tfrac{1}{2}B'_{n-1}\Sigma\Sigma' B_{n-1}$$

$$B_n = -\delta_1 + (B - \Sigma\lambda_1)' B_{n-1}.$$

Equation (20.6) describes the whole term structure of nominal interest rates. The constant part of the risk premia λ_0 influences A_n, and the time-varying component Λ_1 influences B_n. As a consequence, λ_0 only affects the average level of the term structure of interest rates and the term spread. Λ_1 introduces time-variation in the term structure and term spreads. This modeling framework ensures that the term structure model in (20.6) and the VAR have identical implications for the one-month interest rate and the 10-year zero coupon rate. The return dynamics of the VAR are reflected in and consistent with the modeled term structure of interest rates.

For our empirical analysis we use monthly European data. All data start in 1973:01 and end in 2006:12. German zero coupon yields are from the Deutsche Bundesbank, and the price inflation (non-seasonally adjusted) is from Datastream. MSCI world stock returns (in euros and dollar hedged) and the corresponding dividend yield are from Factset. Summary statistics are provided in panel (a) of Table 20.1. The equity risk premium of 4.26% implies a Sharpe ratio of 0.29.

Parameter estimates of the VAR are also summarized in Table 20.1. Stock returns are explained by the dividend yield, the 10-year yield, lagged stock returns, and inflation. The dividend yield captures mean reversion in stock returns: dividend yields rise if stock prices decline. A higher dividend yield predicts an increase of stock returns next period. The higher R^2 of inflation (0.17) reveals that this series is better explained than stock returns ($R^2 = 0.06$). Besides its own lag, inflation is explained by one-month interest rates and the dividend yield. Furthermore inflation is an important driver for the other variables in our system. An increase in inflation predicts an increase in interest rates and dividend yield. On the contrary, inflation is negatively related to next period stock returns.

Stochastic scenarios are constructed by forward iterating the VAR. As the historical inflation (3.03%) is well above the current long-term inflation target of the European Central Bank (2%), we transform the constant term of the VAR (c) for the scenario generation ($c = (I - B)\mu'$). In the same way we transform λ_0 and calibrate the level of term structure of nominal interest rates A_n such that the expected value of the future spot interest rate k periods from now equals the current implied forward rate. The average of the future interest rate scenarios is thus in line with current market expectations. The average equity risk premium and dividend yield in the scenarios is pinned down at the historical averages. The classical results include a set of probability distributions for all relevant ALM output variables in each future year. Asset returns are used to determine the returns on the asset mix. Interest rates are used to compute the present value of liabilities, and inflation scenarios are employed to index the liabilities.

Table 20.1 Summary statistics and VAR estimation results.

(a) Summary statistics	(y^1)	(π)	(y^{120})	(x_s)	(dy)	
μ	5.36	2.86	6.64	4.53	3.58	
σ	2.60	1.14	1.66	14.44	1.35	
(b) VAR estimates (B)	(y^1_t)	(π_t)	$\left(y^{120}_t\right)$	$(x_{s,t})$	(dy_t)	(R^2/p)
y^1_{t+1}	0.95	0.02	0.04	−0.00	−0.01	0.96
	(60.14)	(2.46)	(1.57)	(−0.88)	(−1.02)	(0.00)
π_{t+1}	0.46	0.09	−0.01	0.01	0.09	0.17
	(4.00)	(1.70)	(−0.00)	(1.41)	(1.68)	(0.00)
y^{120}_{t+1}	0.01	0.01	0.97	0.00	−0.00	0.98
	(1.64)	(1.90)	(71.73)	(0.70)	(−0.12)	(0.00)
$x_{s,t+1}$	−0.82	−1.28	−6.16	0.10	2.71	0.06
	(−0.53)	(−1.91)	(−2.20)	(2.07)	(3.53)	(0.00)
dy_{t+1}	−0.00	0.01	0.05	−0.00	0.98	0.99
	(−0.10)	(2.12)	(1.75)	(−1.33)	(125.08)	(0.00)
(c) VAR estimates $(\Sigma'\Sigma)$	(y^1)	(π)	(y^{120})	(x_s)	(dy)	
y^1	0.04					
π	−0.04	0.30				
y^{120}	0.19	0.12	0.02			
x_s	−0.05	0.02	−0.12	4.10		
dy	0.07	−0.01	0.14	−0.91	0.04	

Notes: Panel (a) provides summary statistics of the data. Annualized means and standard deviations are provided for the entire sample (1973:01–2006:12). Variables are one-month euribor (y^1), 10-year zero coupon yield (y^{120}), price inflation (π), MSCI world stock returns in excess of one-month euribor (x_s) and dividend yield (dy). Panel (b) contains parameter estimates (B) of the VAR with t-values between parentheses. Panel (c) contains cross-correlations of the innovations with monthly standard deviations on the diagonal $(\Sigma'\Sigma)$.

M_{t+1} can be used as the stochastic discount factor for valuation of embedded options in the pension deal.[6]

20.4 Fair Value in ALM

We illustrate value-based ALM in the context of pension redesign (based on Hoevenaars, Kocken, and Ponds 2009) and asset management (based on Hoevenaars 2008).

[6] Alternatively option values can be computed in a risk-neutral economy by changing the numeraire. In the empirical part we find that in our model setup with time-varying risk opportunities less scenarios are required for a high degree of accuracy in the risk neutral Q-world, than in the P-world. In order to relax the computational burden we numerically compute the option values in the Q-world.

20.4.1 Pension Plan Redesign and Fair Risk Transfers

The advent of mark-to-market accounting and increased risk awareness are two of many reasons that corporations are retreating as risk takers in their traditional defined benefit (DB) plans and shifting pension-related risk to the beneficiaries. In the United Kingdom, this has usually meant switching to individual schemes for new entrants. In the Netherlands, a collective element has been maintained through inter-generational risk pooling arrangements among plan participants, leading to the creation of collective defined contribution (CDC) plans. The employer is still contributing into the same pension scheme but with a fixed contribution rate and no employer's guarantee. The beneficiaries bear all the risks and for the rest, the scheme is not changed and often not closed to new entrants. That said these shifts are often negotiated without a clear quantitative assessment of the risk transfers between the various stakeholders.

When valuing risk transfers in these cases, a split must occur between accrued rights already paid for by the employer and beneficiaries and new rights to be accrued in future. The reason for this split is that a policy shift affects both the already accrued pension rights of existing participants and the pension rights to be accrued in future potentially in a different way. In this section and the next we follow Hoevenaars, Kocken, and Ponds (2009) and show the effect of policy changes on the embedded options by splitting the existing and future rights. They demonstrate that a shift from a typical defined benefit plan to a collective defined contribution plan should cost the employer a lump sum payment of 12% of the accrued pension obligations and an increase in the contribution rate of 4% of pay.

The valuation calculations assume a typical pension fund with the following characteristics. The investment policy consists of 50% risk-bearing assets (e.g., equities, property, and others) and 50% nominal government bonds. The lower limit of the graduated indexation scale is 100% nominal funding ratio and the upper limit of the graduated indexation scale is 135%. The contribution rate is set at 17% on the basis of a prudently estimated real investment return.

The employer guarantee is equal to the sum of the underlying put options with various terms, taking into account the entire settlement period of the pension rights. In the case of a pension fund with a current nominal funding ratio of 130%, the employer guarantee is worth approximately 12% of nominal obligations. The skew in Figure 20.1 shows that the value of the employer guarantee is inversely related to the size of the current funding ratio and that the value rises faster if this funding ratio falls. Many other factors also go into determining the value of the guarantee, such as the selected asset mix and various policies (e.g., the indexation formula) agreed upon between stakeholders in the pension fund; see Hoevenaars and Ponds (2008) for an analysis under various asset mixes, indexation, and contribution policies. A particularly interesting factor to consider is how results change according to the investment policy of the pension fund. Figure 20.2 shows how the skew evolves in the surface of the employer guarantee option prices for various asset mixes and various levels of the current funding ratio. In general,

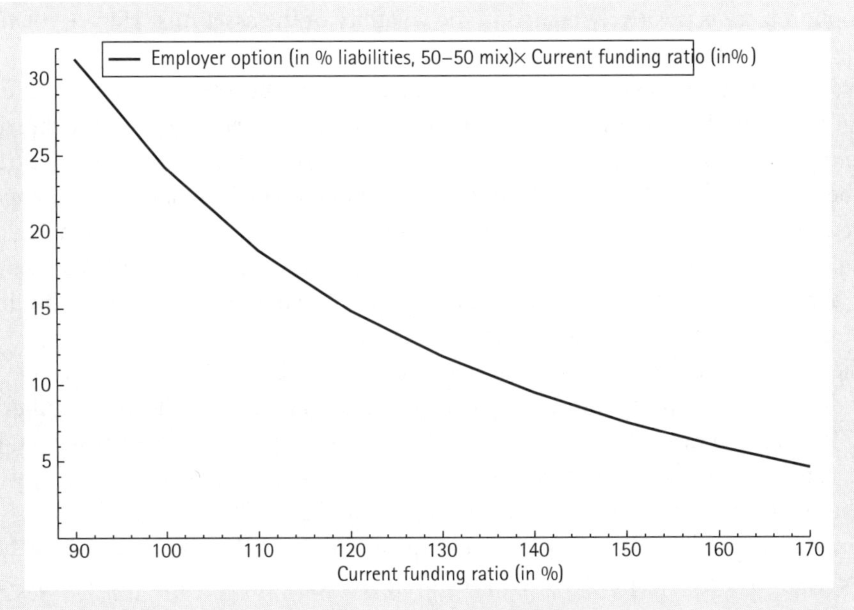

FIGURE 20.1 Employer guarantee option for a 50-50 equity-bond mix. Employer guarantee option price embedded in the current pension deal as a percentage of the pension liabilities and as a function of the current funding ratio for a 50–50 equity-bond mix.

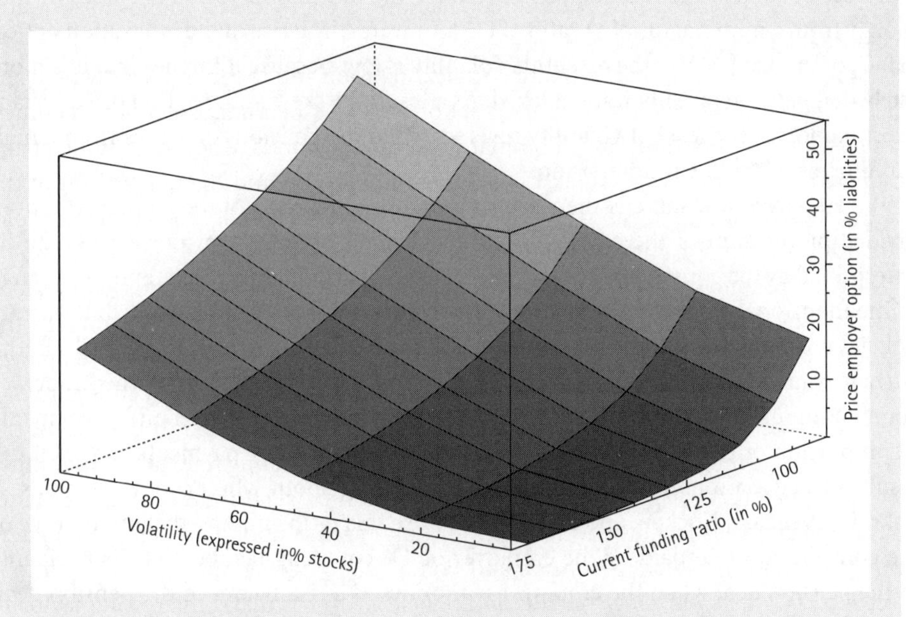

FIGURE 20.2 Employer guarantee option suface. Surface of employer guarantee option price embedded in the current pension deal as a percentage of the pension liabilities and as a function of the current funding ratio and the volatility of the asset mix.

the option price is positively related to the volatility of the asset mix. Higher volatility in the asset mix leads to a higher option price.

In theory, if the employer contributes the calculated risk buyoff amount into the fund, it can then use this amount to buy derivatives from another party so that the risks formerly carried by the employer are now transferred to other parties. In practice, risks will be transferred only in part to third parties through financial markets. This happens somewhat because the products are not easily obtainable in this exact form in the market and also because plan participants may be willing to bear part of the risk themselves. This applies mostly to funds with relatively young members and a reasonably high amount of – fixed or variable – contribution income.

The employer share in the total pension risks in the current pension deal may be very different from the employer-employee ratio for paying the uniform contribution rate. The pension deal identifying what stakeholders are responsible for when, and to what extent, with respect to absorbing shortfalls or surpluses is important. A value can be assigned to these arrangements using the option method previously discussed, leading to values of the employer and participant options in the risk-bearing structure. These options are a composite of the previously described shortfall, contribution, and indexation options.

The employer option comprises: the value of its commitment to make up a nominal shortfall, the net value of the right to receive a contribution reduction, and the obligation to pay a contribution increase in line with the pension deal. The participant option has indexation and contribution elements. Figure 20.3 shows how the indexation option increases in value if the funding ratio declines. The indexation option becomes in-the-money from a nominal funding ratio of 135% onwards. The rise of the indexation option value goes much faster if the asset mix volatility is low, because it implies that it is more likely that pensions are not fully indexed. As a result the skew in the option price surface as a function of the level of volatility reverses when the pension fund goes from a high funding ratio to a low funding ratio.

The employer risk share is then determined using the ratio of the employer option, divided by the sum of the employer and participant options. Obviously, this ratio is determined by the constituents of the employer and participant options, and can change tremendously when a conditional cut of pension rights or flexible contribution rate policies are embedded in the pension deal. This ratio reveals who bears the risks in the current pension deal. It permits a quantitative framework to determine the monetary compensations for a pension redesign to be divided between employer and participants in proportion of the risk incurred. Nowadays, such monetary payments are often the results of negotiations without a clear understanding about who bears what kinds of risks. Hoevenaars, Kocken, and Ponds (2009) use this ratio and find that an increase of the contribution rate paid by the employer of 4% compensates the other participants in the pension deal when the employer withdraws as a risk bearer in the pension deal. In the calculations, the indexation and shortfall options of the existing rights were used to determine the share of risk. Other embedded options like the contribution option could be easily included in the analysis. Other valuation factors include the choice of

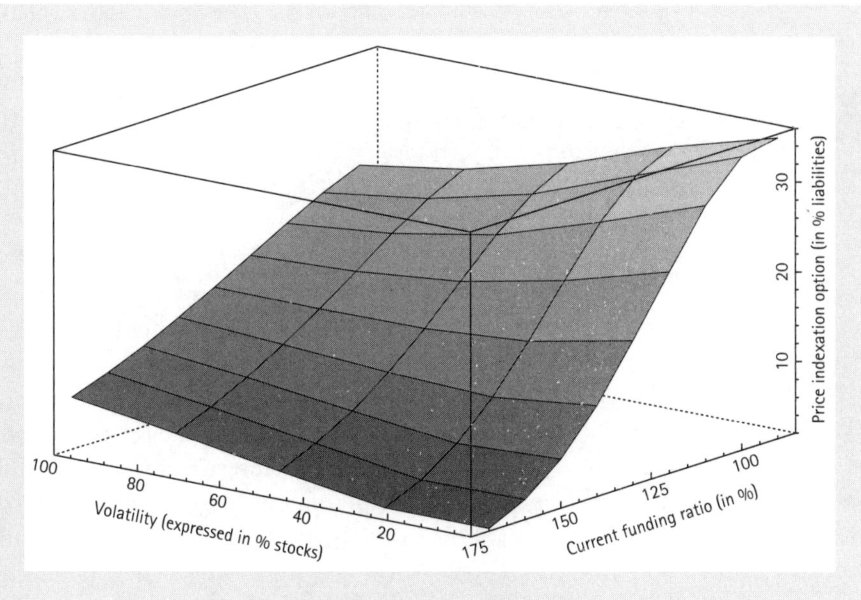

FIGURE 20.3 Indexation option surface. Surface of indexation option price embedded in the indexation policy of the current pension deal as a percentage of the pension liabilities and as a function of the current funding ratio and the volatility of the asset mix.

investment mix, the size of the funding ratio at the time of employer withdrawal, and actuarial factors such as the future development of participants.

An interesting phenomenon reveals itself in Figure 20.4 with respect to the influence of asset allocation on the employer share of total risk. The employer share of the total risk undertaken in the pension fund initially decreases with an increasing funding ratio, but it increases for higher volatile asset mixes. In other words, when the asset mix of the pension fund has a low volatility, the employer share exhibits a skew-like pattern versus the current funding ratio. When the asset mix is more volatile, the employer share exhibits a smile-like pattern versus the current funding ratio. Why does this local minimum in the smile happen, for example in the case of a 50–50 equity-bond mix? The explanation lies in the structure of options. The indexation option is a digital option because plan members receive either full indexation, partial indexation, or no indexation. This implies there is a maximum on the options value. The maximum of the indexation option is the difference between liabilities discounted at real rates (which corresponds to the upper limit of the graduated indexation scale of 135%) minus liabilities discounted at nominal rates. When funding ratios are very high, the indexation option is worth little compared to the employer guarantee. At lower funding ratios, the indexation option gains faster in value than the employer guarantee, but at some point gets closer to its maximum value. That said, the employer guarantee continues to increase in value when funding ratios drop further, prompting the employer share in total risk to increase again.

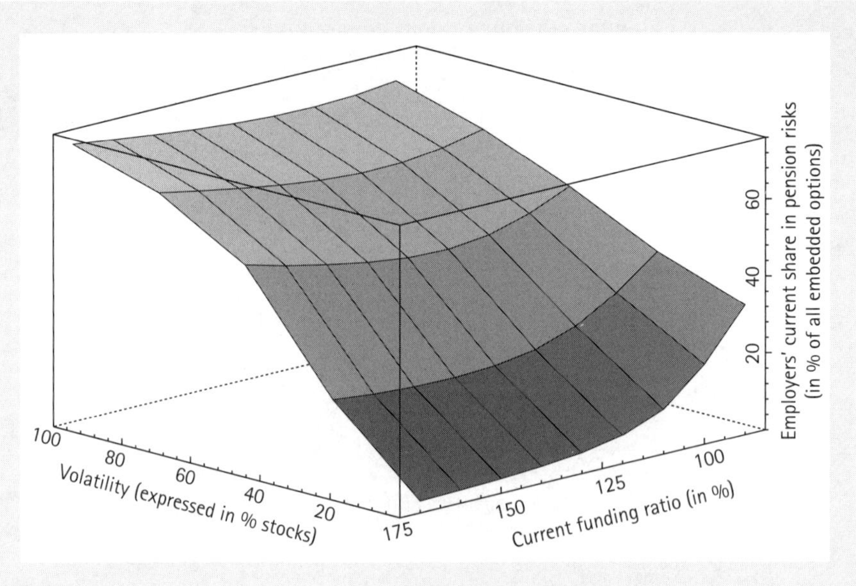

FIGURE 20.4 Employer share in total risk. Employer share in pension risks embedded in the current pension deal expressed as the value of the employer option values as a percentage of the employer and participant option values embedded in the current pension deal.

20.4.2 Asset Management and Embedded Options

Long-term investment strategies are being re-evaluated since the recent deterioration of the financial position of many institutional investors from falling stock returns and declining interest rates. Traditionally, most pension funds adapt a so-called calendar rebalancing to a fixed strategic asset allocation. Tactical asset allocation and market timing often accounts for only a small part of the risk budget. This section explores the tradeoffs when a pension fund chooses a dynamic asset allocation which is driven by the financial position in terms of the funding ratio. Obviously, the menu of dynamic strategies is large. In order to demonstrate the insights from the embedded options we compare a simple dynamic strategy to a traditional calendar rebalancing.

Our stylized ALM framework is representative of a stand-alone funded collective defined benefit-like pension plan. It is an average-wage plan with the goal to fully index liabilities with price inflation. Workers acquire for each year of service 2% of their pensionable wage as new accrued pension rights. The financial position of the fund is represented by the funding ratio which is defined as the ratio of the market value of the assets to the present value of the pension liabilities. The discount rates for the latter are nominal interest rates, because pension payments are guaranteed without inflation compensation. It is evident that the attractiveness of policy variants depends on the initial funding ratio. Many pension funds around the world have a deficit in real terms, but a surplus in nominal terms. For the empirical part we therefore set the initial

Table 20.2 Calendar rebalancing and dynamic mix.

Solvency position	*(i)*	*(ii)*
$Fnom_{t+1}$	1.13	1.11
$Fnom_{t+10}$	1.31	1.05
$P(Fnom_{t+1} < 100)$	0.07	0.00
$P(Fnom_{t+10} < 100)$	0.02	0.15
$Pw(Fnom_{t+10} < 100)$	0.30	0.21
Indexation quality		
IR_{t+1}	0.34	0.29
IR_{t+10}	0.54	0.14
$P(IR_{t+1} < 80)$	0.96	1.00
$P(IR_{t+10} < 80)$	0.97	0.99
$P(FI_{t+10})$	0.41	0.03

Notes: Summary statistics of the financial situation based on the ALM model with an initial funding ratio of 115% under two different investment frameworks: (*i*) calendar rebalancing, (*ii*) dynamic mix. The selected output variables for the solvency position include the median of the nominal funding ratio (*Fnom*), probability of under funding in the next year ($P(Fnom < 100)$), and probability of under funding within the next ten years ($Pw(Fnom < 100)$). The indexation quality is summarized by the median indexation result (*IR*), the probability of an indexation result less than 80% ($P(IR < 80)$), and the probability on full indexation in a year (*P(FI)*).

nominal funding ratio at 115%. Such a starting position clearly reveals the tradeoffs between the probability of a nominal deficit and the real inflation ambition later on in this chapter. The indexation and contribution policy are as described in the previous section.

We specify the reference strategy as a constant 50–50 equity-bond mix. The duration of the bond allocation is around eight years, and the duration of the liabilities is around 16 years. The expected return on this investment mix is 6.4% per year with 10% volatility.[7] Calendar rebalancing strategies exploit (short-term) mean reversion. Assets which have risen relative to other assets are sold at the end of the year, and vice versa. Calendar rebalancing strategies buy assets as markets have relatively fallen, and sell assets as markets have risen.

The ALM output variables in Table 20.2 suggest that an increase of the nominal funding ratio is anticipated, but that there are also substantial downside risks. The probability of insolvency in the next year exceeds 2.5% which is a commonly used risk tolerance set by regulators. There is a 30% probability that the fund will be underfunded within the next 10 years. According to the scenarios there is a chance that the funding ratio drops below 90% in the next year. Furthermore, the ALM study indicates that under the return assumptions used there is only a 41% chance that pension payments can be fully indexed by price inflation ($P(FI_{t+10})$), and pension payments can on average be adjusted for half

[7] In the scenarios for the next 10 years the average stock and bond return are 7.4% and 3.7%, respectively.

of the price inflation in the long run (IR_{t+10}). Clearly, the 50% equity allocation is not sufficient under the return expectations used to pursue the long run goal of the pension fund.

An alternative investment strategy is a dynamic mix. Now, the fund adapts the same constant 50–50 equity-bond constant mix as in the reference strategy, but now changes the asset allocation whenever the probability of underfunding within one year exceeds 2.5%. This strategy reacts to downside risks, and adjusts them if they are unacceptable in the eyes of the board or a regulatory framework. The dynamic mix switches between a risky and a hedge portfolio based on an *ex ante* risk measure. The return on the asset mix is

$$R_t = \left(1 - \alpha_t^{(h)}\right) R_t^r + \alpha_t^{(h)} R_t^h \tag{20.7}$$

where R_t^r and R_t^h are returns on the risky and the hedge portfolio, respectively. The hedge portfolio closely tracks the growth of the nominal liabilities. The hedge portfolio entails purchasing a bond that replicates the liabilities. As we construct a hypothetical bond with the same duration as the nominal liabilities (around 16 years) there may be some mismatch risk due to convexity effects. In accordance with the reference strategy the risky portfolio is a 50–50 equity-bond mix. The allocation to the hedge portfolio $\left(\alpha_t^{(h)}\right)$ is optimized numerically such that the probability of underfunding equals the risk constraint. In contrast to the reference strategy equities are sold and the duration is extended whenever equity markets or interest rates fall and the probability of underfunding exceeds 2.5%. As risky assets are sold when the funding ratio approaches 100%, there is high chance that the pension fund evolves in a "solvency trap." In that case there will be a lower return potential and the duration extension will lead to losses if interest rates rise, but the financial position is protected for severe drawdowns.

Relative to calendar rebalancing the dynamic mix leads to an improvement of the risk profile in the short run, but a worsening in the long run (see Table 20.2). In the short run the probability of underfunding in the next year (close to 0%) improves, and according to the scenarios it is very unlikely that the funding ratio drops below 97%. The higher probability on long run insolvency is not directly comparable to the case of calendar rebalancing, because drawdowns are much less severe. The value of the shortfall options (in Figure 20.5) explicitly accounts for this, because they express the probability in terms of economic value. The solvency trap makes the situation look worse from a return perspective. The reduction of the return potential inevitably leads to a decrease of the funding ratio towards 105% over 10 years. Furthermore, this investment strategy has a worse indexation quality (the expected indexation result is 14%).

This naturally then begs the question: Which stakeholders bear the risks in the pension deal when the investment strategy changes from a calendar rebalancing to a dynamic mix? A comparison of the embedded options values reveals that risks are transferred from the employer towards the participants. The value of the indexation option increases. When the funding ratio is below 135% the indexation option is in-the-money and indexation payments are partly cut. The solvency trap implies that

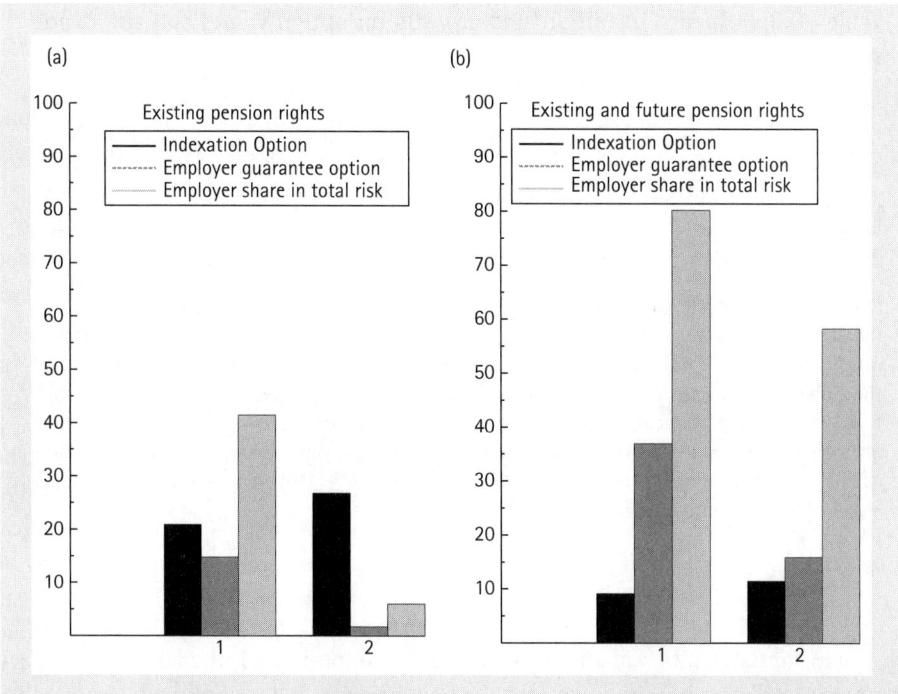

FIGURE 20.5 Option values and risk exposure under different investment strategies. Embedded option values and employer share in risk under two different investment frameworks: (*i*) calendar rebalancing, (*ii*) dynamic mix. Part (a) includes the existing pension rights only; part (b) considers a pension fund in continuity during the next 20 years.

this seems to happen more often than with the calendar rebalancing. Downside risks for the employer are reduced to a large extent, and severe drawdowns (below a 95% funding ratio) are very unlikely. As a result the employer guarantee option loses in value. Figure 20.5(a) shows that the employer share in the risk of the existing pension rights decreases from 41% to 6%. Table 20.3 demonstrates that this risk transfer seems fairly robust to the initial funding ratio. Both the employer guarantee and indexation option lose in value when the initial funding ratio increases. The table reveals that the impact on the option values of a shift in investment strategies gets smaller when the initial funding ratio increases, because the delta and gamma of the underlying options reduces. A switch from a calendar rebalancing to a dynamic mix at higher funding ratios leads to an increase of the value of the indexation option and a reduction of the value of the employer guarantee, but if the current funding ratio is higher this occurs at a lower rate. As a result the employer share in risk is roughly the same regardless of the initial funding ratio. That said, the participant bears the remainder and largest part of the risk in the existing rights.

Of course the analysis above heavily relies on the employer not defaulting on his obligations to pay up for any shortfall in the nominal funding of the fund. If default

Table 20.3 Influence of initial funding ratio on option values and risk exposure.

	115%	135%	155%
△ Index option (ii)-(i)	+6	+3	+1
△ Empl option (ii)-(i)	−13	−8	−5
Employer share (i)	41	41	43
Employer share (ii)	6	6	6

Notes: Changes in the embedded options from different investment frameworks: (*i*) calendar rebalancing, (*ii*) dynamic mix. The results are based on the ALM model with an initial funding ratio of 115%. The first and second lines represent the change of the indexation option and the employer guarantee option for the existing rights (in %-points) when the fund would shift from a calendar rebalancing to a dynamic asset allocation, respectively. The third and fourth lines give the employer share in total risk (in % of current rights) in the pension deal for a calendar rebalancing and dynamic asset allocation, respectively. The columns demonstrate the effect of the initial funding ratio.

risk is substantial (quite realistic in today's real economic life), the above mentioned pension put will become significant for the beneficiaries. In that case a dynamic policy may be beneficial to the beneficiaries, reducing their pension put whilst increasing the indexation option. The net value of these two effects decides the usefulness of such a policy from the beneficiaries' perspective. This analysis is outside the scope of this overview.

Another interesting insight reveals itself in Figure 20.5(b) where we consider the situation of a pension fund in continuity, so accruing pension rights in the future and accumulating inflows from contribution payments. In this case the option values only reflect the payoffs in the next 20 years. The overall picture does not change. Again the employer bears a smaller part of the risk in the pension deal (from 80% to 58%). Why is the employer share so much higher when we include future rights and focus on the next 20 years? The explanation lies in horizon effects in the payoff structure of the underlying options.[8] More than 60% of the payoffs of the indexation option for the existing pension rights are beyond 20 years from now. New rights hardly affect its value, because their share in the indexation payoff relative to the existing rights is small. As such, the value of the indexation option in part (b) is about 30% of the value in part (a). The employer guarantee option, on the other hand, increases, because the assets under management increase from contribution inflows and the accrual of new pension rights. A 1% point underfunding when assets under management have increased, for example, leads to a higher value of the employer option when it is expressed relative to the current existing rights. Overall, this leads to a reduction of the employer share in risk.

[8] Obviously, actuarial factors also have an effect, because they determine the future composition of the participants in the fund.

20.5 Conclusion

The classical ALM approach plays a central role in financial policy decisions of many institutional investors and consultancy firms. Probability distributions of ALM indicators like the funding ratio and inflation compensation lack the insights with respect to the exposure of the different groups of stakeholders to risks in the pension deal. That is where value-based ALM adds an extra dimension. Valuation of the embedded options reveals each stakeholder's share in total pension risk, and as such it identifies who bears the risks implied by a proposed policy change.

In current times were pension redesign and traditional investment strategies are being re-evaluated, value-based ALM can greatly strengthen future negotiations about changes in financial policy. Insights into risk transfers from pension redesign help the contruction of a "fair" and transparent pension deal. Nevertheless, policy changes which are a zero-sum game in option terms do not automatically lead to a "fair" pension system, because insights into the historical costs and rewards (e.g., contribution holidays) are not incorporated in the analysis. This chapter has demonstrated that the value of contractual claims of the various stakeholders in the pension deal can be objectively determined. Its applications encompass situations where pension rights are cut when the funding ratio drops below a threshold; the investment strategy is changed towards inflation insurance in the long-term; intergenerational risk sharing changes due to a shift from traditional defined benefit to collective defined contribution; or the investment framework is changed.

In all these cases, option pricing techniques can be used to quantify the risk transfers between different groups of stakeholders. The analysis above can be extended easily to a large group of cohorts of beneficiaries instead of only employer versus one group of beneficiaries (see Hoevenaars and Ponds 2008). The price of the embedded risks can be high relative to the built-up pension rights, and the distribution of the embedded option values among the different stakeholders critically depends on the pension deal, market variables, investment policies, and the current financial situation of the fund. Clearly, the employer and beneficiary shares in risk depend on the embedded options in the pension deal. Current discussions about conditional cuts in pension rights and flexible contribution rates can easily be incorporated into the value-based ALM framework outlined above. In this way value-based ALM identifies who bears what kinds of risks in an objective way.

References

Ambachtsheer, K.A. (2007). *Pension Revolution, A Solution to the Pensions Crisis,* John Wiley & Sons, New York.

Amenc, N., Martellini, L., and Ziemann, V. (2009). Inflation-hedging properties of real assets and implications for asset-liability management decisions. *Journal of Portfolio Management,* 35, 94–110.

Blake, D. (1998). Pension schemes as options on pension fund assets: Implications for pension fund management. *Insurance: Mathematics and Economics*, **23**, 263–286.

Bodie, Z. (2006). Fair value accounting and pension benefit guarantees. In *Fair Value and Pension Fund Management* (ed. N. Kortleve, T.E. Nijman, and E. Ponds). Elsevier Publishers, Amsterdam.

Boender, C.G.E. (1997). A hybrid simulation/optimization scenario model for asset-liability management. *European Journal of Operations Research*, **99**, 126–135.

Boender, C., Dert, C., Heemskerk, F. and Hoek, H. (2007). Scenario approach of ALM. In *Handbook of Asset Liability Management* (ed. S.A. Zenios and T.Z. Ziemba). North Holland, Amsterdam.

Campbell, J.Y., Chan, Y.L., and Viceira, L.M. (2003). A multivariate model for strategic asset allocation. *Journal of Financial Economics*, **67**, 41–80.

Chapman, R.J., Gordon, T.J., and Speed, C.A. (2001). Pensions, funding and risk. *British Actuarial Journal*, **74**, 605–663.

Cochrane, J.H. (2001). *Asset Pricing*. Princeton University Press, Princeton.

Cochrane, J. and Piazzesi, M. (2005). Bond risk premia. *American Economic Review*, **95**, 138–160.

De Jong, F. (2007). Pension fund investments and the valuation of liabilities under conditional indexation. *Insurance: Mathematics and Economics*, **42**, 1–13.

De Jong, F. (2008). Valuation of pension liabilities in incomplete markets. *Journal of Pension Economics and Finance*, **7**, 277–294.

Hoevenaars, R.P.M.M. (2008). *Strategic Asset Allocation and Asset Liability Management*. Datawyse, Maastricht, The Netherlands.

Hoevenaars, R.P.M.M., Kocken, T.P., and Ponds, E.H.M. (2009). Pricing risk in corporate pension plans: Understanding the real pension deal. *International Journal of Pension Management*, **2**, 56–63.

Hoevenaars, R.P.M.M., Molenaar, R.D.J., and Ponds, E.H.M. (2010). Public investment funds and value-based generational accounting. In *Central Bank Reserves and Sovereign Wealth Management* (ed. A. Berkelaar, J. Coche, and K. Nyholm). Palgrave Macmillan, London.

Hoevenaars, R.P.M.M., Molenaar, R.D.J. Schotman, P.C. and Steenkamp, T.B.M. (2008). Strategic asset allocation with liabilities: Beyond stocks and bonds. *Journal of Economic Dynamics and Control*, **32**, 2939–2970.

Hoevenaars, R.P.M.M. and Ponds, E.H.M. (2008). Valuation of intergenerational transfers in funded collective pension schemes. *Insurance: Mathematics and Economics*, **42**, 578–593.

Kocken, T.P. (2006). *Curious Contracts: Pension Fund Redesign for the Future*. Den Bosch, Tutein Nolthenius.

Koijen, R.S.J. and Nijman, T.E. (2006). Valuation and risk management of inflation-sensitive pension rights. In *Fair Value and Pension Fund Management* (ed. N. Kortleve, T.E. Nijman, and E. Ponds). Elsevier Publishers, Amsterdam.

Kortleve, N., Nijman, T.E., and Ponds, E. (2006). *Fair Value and Pension Fund Management*. Elsevier, Amsterdam.

Kortleve, N. and Ponds, E. (2006). Pension deals and value-based ALM. In *Fair Value and Pension Fund Management* (eds. N. Kortleve, T.E. Nijman, and E. Ponds). Elsevier Publishers, Amsterdam.

Pelsser, A.A.J. and Vlaar, P. (2009). Market consistent valuation of pension liabilities. Netspar Panel Paper.

Ponds, E.H.M. (2003). Pension funds and value-based generational accounting. *Journal of Pension Economics and Finance*, **2**, 295–325.

Rooij, M. Van, Siegmann, A., and Vlaar, P. (2004). PALMNET: A pension asset and liability model for the Netherlands. DNB research memorandum WO no 760.

Sharpe, W.F. (1976). Corporate pension funding policy. *Journal of Financial Economics*, 3, 183–193.

Steenkamp, T.B.M. (1998). *Het Pensioenfonds in een Corporate Finance Perspectief (The Pension Fund From a Corporate Finance Perspective)*. Ph.D. Thesis, Vrije University Amsterdam.

Ziemba, T.Z. and Mulvey, J.M. (1998). *Worldwide Asset and Liability Modelling*. Cambridge University Press, Cambridge.

CHAPTER 21

ASSET LIABILITY MANAGEMENT FOR SOVEREIGN WEALTH FUNDS

FRANCIS BREEDON AND ROBERT KOSOWSKI

21.1 Introduction

Sovereign wealth funds (SWFs) are an increasingly important investor group in global capital markets. It is estimated that in 2009 SWFs held around U.S.$ 3 trillion of assets and are expected to more than triple in size over the next decade (Chhaochharia and Laeven 2009). Despite the importance of this investor group relatively few normative or positive studies have been carried out on the asset allocation of SWFs.

The objective of this chapter is to discuss optimal asset allocation for sovereign wealth funds. Our discussion aims at a summary of the relevant theoretical literature that may guide SWF optimal asset allocation decisions. Our focus on the *financial asset liability management objective* of SWFs differs from the objective of many recent papers on SWFs which examine the political and strategic objectives of SWFs. Nevertheless, we are careful to highlight real-world institutional and political constraints and also provide empirical evidence on actual SWF asset allocations. This section provides a definition of SWFs and describes the differences between the sub-groups of *commodity* and *excess reserve* funds. Section 21.2 discusses optimal asset and currency allocation for commodity funds in a simplified framework that ignores liabilities. Section 21.3 discusses optimal asset and currency allocation for commodity funds in an asset-liability matching framework. Section 21.4 discusses optimal asset allocation for excess reserve funds. Section 21.5 concludes.

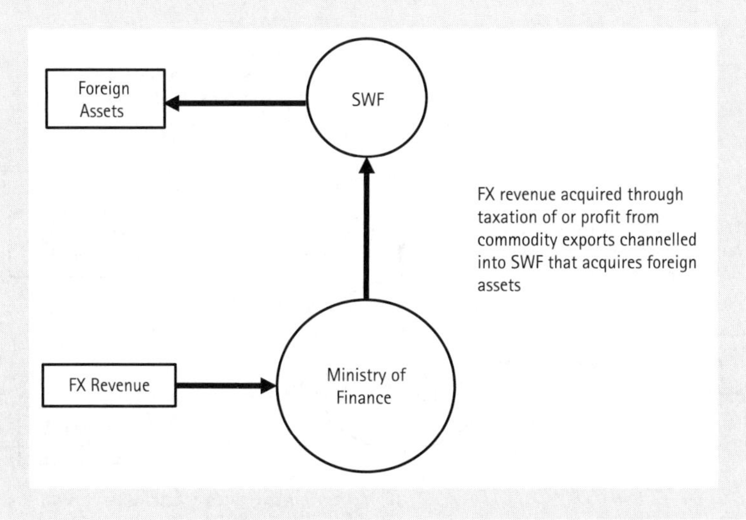

FIGURE 21.1 Stylized commodity fund.

21.1.1 Some Definitions

Despite being widely discussed, there is no accepted definition of what a sovereign wealth fund actually is. In this chapter we use the definition put forward by the U.S. Treasury (2007) that states that an SWF is "a government investment vehicle which is funded by foreign exchange assets, and which manages those assets separately from the official reserves of the monetary authorities (the central bank and reserve-related functions of the finance ministry). SWF managers typically have a higher risk tolerance and higher expected return than traditional official reserve managers."

Following U.S. Treasury definitions once again, this chapter will focus on the two broad categories of SWFs

- *Commodity funds (CF)* – Commodity funds are financed through foreign currency earnings on commodity exports (either owned or taxed by the government). They can serve many different purposes, including stabilization of government revenues and the balance of payments, but our focus is on their intergenerational saving role. Figure 21.1 present a simplified diagram of their operation.
- *Excess reserve funds (ERF)* – Funds in this group are financed through transfers of assets from foreign exchange reserves. This transfer generally occurs following a period of persistently large current account surplus and/or capital account deficit which results in significant reserve accumulation.[1] This reserve accumulation allows the country concerned to transfer "excess" foreign exchange reserves to

[1] Whilst commodity exports clearly contribute to the current account surplus, commodity funds rarely engage in prolonged intervention relying instead on direct FX revenue.

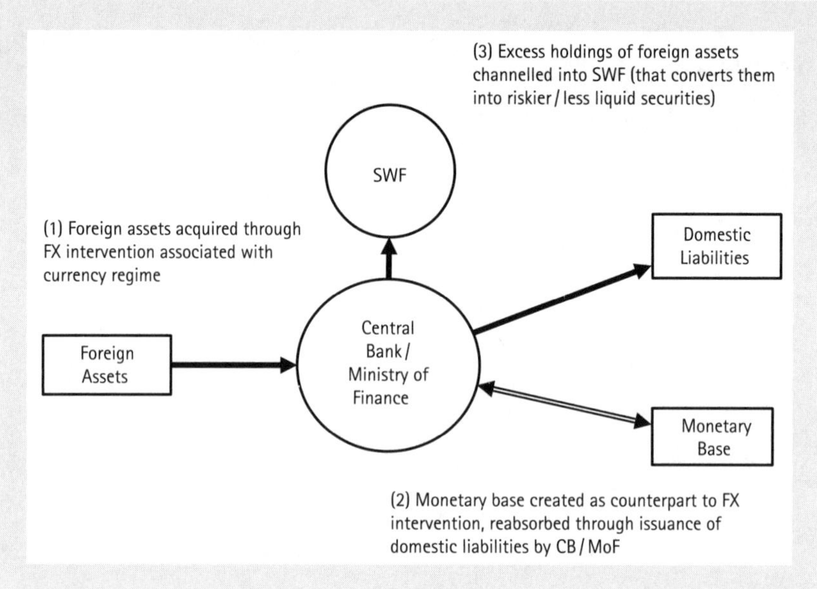

FIGURE 21.2 Stylized excess reserve fund.

stand-alone funds. Since reserve accumulation must generally be sterilized (i.e. the domestic currency created to purchase foreign assets is re-absorbed through local currency debt issuance[2]), excess reserve funds can be thought of as being financed through borrowed funds.[3] See Figure 21.2.

To illustrate these two categories Table 21.1 shows recent data for the largest examples of both types of fund. The table illustrates that commodity funds are dominated by oil exporters whilst excess reserve funds tend to be located in East Asia.

21.2 Strategic Asset Allocation for Commodity Funds

21.2.1 The Economics of Commodity Funds

The main purpose of a commodity based sovereign wealth fund is to create a permanent income stream out of a temporary one and so allow consumption smoothing over

[2] Sterlization need not involve bond issuance. In the case of China, for example, the majority of the local currency creation associated with foreign currency purchases has been absorbed by increased bank reserve requirements.

[3] Several studies have examined the role of the government in managing assets and commodity related revenue (see Amuzegar 2005; Kalyuzhnova and Kaser 2006; Mehrara and Oskoui 2007; Petersen and Budina 2003; and Habibi 1998).

Table 21.1 The growth of SWFs (assets under management $bn).

	1999	2000	2001	2002	2003	2004	2005	2006	2007	2008
Total assets (1)+(2)	86	123	150	484	797	1,023	1,364	1,793	2,547	2,915
Of which: total external assets	86	123	150	484	765	972	1,302	1,738	2,375	2,712
Total: Commodity funds (1)	28	48	74	408	600	795	1,088	1,475	1,960	2,321
Algeria	n.a.	4	6	6	8	14	29	46	49	64
Chile	28						1	9	14	20
Kazahstan				2	4	5	8	14	20	28
Kuwait	n.a.	n.a.	n.a.	94	115	140	160	200	250	265
Norway		43	69	85	148	192	238	306	384	326
Russia	n.a.					19	44	82	181	209
Saudi Arabia	n.a.	n.a.	n.a.	21	37	60	126	197	271	433
Venezuela	n.a.						8	19	33	33
Oman		n.a.	n.a.	n.a	n.a	1	3	5	8	8
Qatar		n.a.	n.a.	.1	.2	10	20	35	56	60
UAE		n.a.	n.a.	200	286	354	452	571	708	875
Total: Excess reserve funds (2)	59	75	76	75	197	229	276	318	587	594
China	0	0	0	0	0	0	0	0	200	200
Hong Kong	59	75	76	75	74	78	77	88	98	98
Malaysia	0	0	0	0	0	13	15	18	26	26
Korea	0	0	0	0	0	0	20	20	20	25
Singapore	n.a.	n.a.	n.a.	n.a.	123	137	163	182	223	245

Source: Alberola and Serena (2008) and authors' calculations and classifications.

time (in fact, across generations). The stabilization of fiscal revenues can be considered a sub-objective of this broader aim. In principle, this objective could be most effectively obtained through a long-term total return swap (TRS) with a counter-party. The resource rich country would buy an over-the counter (OTC) swap in which it receives a fixed and permanent cash flow each period and the counter-party would receive the variable and temporary revenues from the exploitation of the natural resource. Of course in practice such a swap is not realistic due to the size of the contract, the long-term uncertainty, as well as control issues, but it is instructive to consider it to illustrate the economic objective. In the absence of such a long-term contract the government has to optimally manage its exhaustible resources as well as its SWF. In resource economics with a closed economy, **Hartwick's rule** defines the amount of investment into assets such as infrastructure, knowledge, stocks, etc., that is needed to exactly offset declining stocks of non-renewable resources and so smooth consumption (Hartwick 1977). This investment is undertaken so that the standard of living is maintained into the indefinite future. Hartwick's rule – often abbreviated as "invest resource rents" – requires that a nation invest all rent earned from exhaustible resources currently extracted, where "rent" is defined along paths that maximize returns to owners of the resource stock.[4] Okumura and Cai (2007) present an open-economy model with explicit microeconomic foundations and derive the Hartwick rule with the additional implication that resource rents should be invested in overseas assets.

As well as consumption smoothing the accumulation of foreign assets by commodity funds has the additional benefit that it helps mitigate the "Dutch disease" whereby real exchange rate appreciation caused by the exploitation of the resource crowds out other non-resource based tradable production.[5] By stabilizing the real exchange rate (through FX outflows that at least partially offset the FX inflows associated with the resources) a commodity fund can also help stabilize the production side of the economy.

It is helpful to outline the broad framework within which the financial objectives of a commodity fund can be examined. The optimal asset allocation for a commodity fund can be derived within the country's external balance of payments framework. To illustrate the basic idea, Table 21.2 presents a simplified balance sheet of a natural resource-rich country.

The asset side of the balance sheet is transformed over time from the present value of the resource still underground into the market value of international financial assets and other investments. Although the expenditure by the SWF could take the form of pension payments, health care costs, etc., ultimately such expenditure must result in an excess of domestic absorption over domestic non-oil production (i.e., net imports) and so the ultimate liability of the fund is a stream of future imports funded by returns from assets (these returns begin as revenue from resource extraction but eventually become income

[4] Dixit *et al.* (1980) extends Hartwick's rule by suggesting that keeping the present discounted value of total net investment constant over time is necessary and sufficient for constant utility.

[5] The Dutch disease refers to the proposition that an increase in revenues from natural resources will deindustrialize a nation's economy by raising the real exchange rate, which makes the manufacturing sector less competitive.

Table 21.2 Simplified balance sheet.

Assets	Liabilities
Present value of natural resources underground ⇓	Present value of country's future liabilities (excess of national non-oil spending over national non-oil production)
Present value of financial assets and other investments (i.e. the commodity fund)	

from financial assets). In essence, the SWF can be viewed as a centralized institutional investor that aims to convert the temporary income from commodity extraction into a permanent one for the country's citizens and so despite being run and ultimately dispersed by the government can be viewed as independent of other elements of fiscal policy.

It is clear from the above example that risks faced by commodity funds stem from both the stochastic movement in asset and liability values. The fund's objective is to (1) *maximize the return* on assets while (2) *matching liabilities* to reduce the risk of an asset-liability mismatch *over time*.[6]

Although the asset-liability management framework is clearly the correct one to apply, most studies on SWF optimal asset allocation have purely focused on hedging risks that occur on the asset side of the balance sheet. More specifically these studies examine how the commodity price risk associated with as yet unextracted resources can be hedged (unconditionally) through optimal diversification across non-commodity financial assets. We will first discuss the simplified case of optimal asset allocation without liabilities before turning to the more comprehensive asset-liability management.

21.2.2 Commodity Price Risk and Strategic Asset Allocation Framework for Commodity Funds

The asset allocation framework typically consists of an objective function that implies a preference for the highest return for a given level of risk. For simplicity many studies assume simple mean-variance preferences. The asset universe of a commodity fund differs from other investment managers in that commodity price risk enters the portfolio variance through its covariance with other assets since the country is exposed to commodity price uncertainty due to the as yet unexploited resources.

[6] This discussion shows that all SWFs have at least implicit liabilities. Some SWFs related to sovereign pension funds (SPFs) have explicit liabilities in the form of future pension liabilities.

Here, we discuss risk minimization before turning to maximization strategies. Commodity producing countries' current income and un-extracted commodity assets are sensitive to commodity price risk and so SWFs may have an incentive to hedge this risk. Hausmann and Rigobon (2003) attempt to quantify this risk and estimate that a one standard deviation shock to the oil price can represent an income shock worth 6% of GDP for a country in which oil represents around 20% of the economy. Since claims on as yet un-extracted commodity wealth are not tradable, other ways to hedge commodity price risk have to be considered. The degree of hedging required is, however, not straightforward to calculate. It depends both on how permanent commodity price movements tend to be, and how large the countries exposure to the un-extracted resource actually is.[7] This latter consideration not only requires some estimate of how much of the resource remains, it is also important to consider how much of the fund's returns will be used to purchase the commodity once the country's own stock is depleted. So far, three methods of hedging commodity price risk have been used or proposed in a framework without liabilities: (i) hedging in derivatives markets, (ii) bilateral hedging arrangements, and (iii) indirect hedging through other financial instruments.

Hedging directly in financial markets One of the most recent examples of hedging in derivatives markets is provided by Mexico which starting in July 2008 bought 330m barrels worth of oil put options for 2009, securing a minimum price of $70 for the country's crude oil exports.[8] An earlier example of such hedging is the State of Texas which in 1991 started a hedging program for the tax revenue it receives from oil production. While this may seem the most obvious route through which hedge commodity price risk, it is clear that in many cases the hedging demand of a large commodity producer will dwarf the available liquidity in derivatives markets. Indeed, some dealers suspect that Mexico's hedging programe may have exacerbated the decline in oil prices during some periods since the option writers such as Wall Street banks, need to sell futures – pushing down prices – to hedge themselves against their option exposures (*Financial Times*, 13 November 2008). Devlin and Titman (2004) propose that to deal with this problem, an international agency such as the World Bank should help create securities that are linked to oil prices and are attractive to major investment funds – acting in a similar (but not identical) way to Fannie Mae and Freddie Mac in the mortgage market.

Bilateral hedging deals Since non-commodity SWFs tend to be commodity importers and so may usefully hedge future commodity imports (see below), there may be capacity for the two types of funds to enter into bilateral swap agreements based on commodity prices. Indeed, in February 2009 China and Russia were reported to have struck a

[7] Barnett and Vivanco (2003) present some evidence of mean reversion which also seems to be present in futures prices.

[8] Augustin Carstens, Mexico's finance minister, said the cost of the initiative was about $1.5bn. In November 2008, with international oil prices at about $55 a barrel, the present value of the hedging initiative was about $9.5bn. (*Financial Times*, November 13, 2008, article "Mexico hedges to protect oil revenues.")

long-term oil deal, in which China lends $25 billion to two Russian energy companies in exchange for an expanded supply of Russian oil.[9] According to the *Wall Street Journal*, the supply deal – which represents about 300,000 barrels a day, or nearly 10% of China's current volume of oil imports – is to last 20 for years.

Indirect hedging through other financial instruments An alternative to the hedging schemes described above is to incorporate commodity price risk into the optimal asset allocation by treating the commodity as one of the assets. Gintschel and Scherer (2008) demonstrate how oil price risk can be partially hedged by changing country or sector weightings in the fund's benchmark portfolio. In their empirical results they find that a fund of equal size to remaining reserves can reduce oil price risk by up to 50% (10% if short sales are not allowed) through this means. Scherer (2009a) extends this framework by introducing background risk for an SWF in the form of oil reserve uncertainty. Scherer (2009b) ends the one-period analysis of Gintschel and Scherer (2009) and applies the Campbell and Viceira (2002) strategic asset allocation framework without liabilities to the portfolio choice problem of a SWF.[10]

21.2.3 Liquidity Premia

The above discussion has been largely focused on (commodity price) risk minimization. Of course, in practice the objective is to maximize risk-adjusted returns which implies that certain risk exposures need to be chosen to generate return. What makes SWFs different from other investors and what risk exposures are more suitable for SWFs? One of the key determinants of risk-preferences is the investment horizon. SWFs have very long investment horizons and can therefore be argued to be able to bear certain types of risk. In that repect, some argue that they are similar to university endowments and so should hold similar assets[11] (e.g. Pascuzzo 2008). The long investment horizon implies that the liquidity needs of SWFs are not as acute as those of other investors, thus permitting SWFs to invest in illiquid assets that may earn a liquidity premium.

21.2.4 Political and Strategic Considerations

21.2.4.1 *Activist Investors*

The balance of payments framework outlined above focuses on a purely financial objective function for the SWF. However, non-financial objectives such as political and other

[9] China, Russia strike $25 billion, oil pact. *Wall Street Journal*, Feburary 18, 2009, http://online.wsj.com/article/SB123488153527399773.html

[10] For background on strategic asset allocation, see Chapter 13 in this volume.

[11] The spending cuts forced upon Harvard and Stanford university as a result of the 2007–2009 financial crisis and the poor performance of illiquid assets in their portfolios reveals that university endowments may not be as long-term invests as previously argued, though.

strategic considerations may also affect the investment behaviour of SWFs (Summers, 2007; Gieve, 2008). As Chhaochharia and Laeven (2009) point out, one concern relates to the issue of whether SWFs target militarily and technologically strategic industries. Many recent papers examine the political and strategic objectives of SWFs while we focus on the asset liability management objective.

21.2.4.2 *Market Failure and Securing Food or Land Resources*

As explained above the ultimate objective of a SWF is to smooth consumption and achieve intergenerational transfers. The accumulation of financial assets presupposes functioning markets for consumption goods such as food products. Another consideration that may guide the investment behaviour of sovereign wealth funds and that highlights the role of liabilities, is food security. Future food imports are a key component of the balance of payments identity. If markets fail, due to other governments' intervention in the form of export restrictions, then there may be a role for SWFs' accumulation of land in other countries.[12] In a April 2009 International Food Policy Research Institute report, von Braun and Suseela Meizen-Dick note recent farmland purchases in developing countries (such as the Philippines, Sudan, Ukraine, Kenya, Tanzania, and Pakistan) by China, South Korea, India, Saudi Arabia, Libya, Bahrain, UAE, and Kuwait.

21.2.5 Optimal Currency Allocation for Commodity Funds in the Presence of Liabilities

The above asset allocation discussion does not pay special attention to the issue of currency allocation. However, currency allocation is important for diversification from the asset allocation perspective and also has an effect on asset liability management.

The simplified balance sheet in Table 21.1 can help us examine what role currency allocation should play in a commodity fund's asset liability management decisions. Table 21.1 frames the objective of the commodity fund as choosing assets such that the present value of the assets matches the liabilities. A rigorous analysis of the commodity fund's optimal asset allocation policy must take into account the role of liabilities and therefore requires an analysis of the country's balance of payments. In order to express the objective in terms of the returns on the assets and the returns on liabilities, we may assume that currently the fund's assets are sufficient to match the liabilities (the funding ratio is one). Therefore, the objective becomes selecting a portfolio of assets whose returns are positive on average and highly correlated with the returns on liabilities.

What is the interpretation of the asset and liabilities returns in the context of the balance of payments? The macroeconomic literature provides us with a framework for analysis. The net foreign asset (NFA) position of a country is the value of the assets that

[12] Many countries imposed food export bans in 2008. (Fresh export bans deepen food crisis. *Financial Times*, April 16, 2008.)

the country owns abroad, minus the value of the assets owned by foreigners. The traditional balance of payment identity ignores valuation effects and views changes in net foreign assets as being fully captured by the current account. The recent macroeconomic literature – see Clarida (2006) for a survey – studies the implications of a new balance of payment identity, which considers the role of asset price changes and valuation effects. This research stresses that NFAs equal the current account plus valuation effects due to changes in asset prices of assets held abroad.

Current external imbalances can be compensated either by future trade surpluses (the trade channel) or by future favorable returns on the net foreign asset position (the valuation channel) of the home country. The accumulation identity for net foreign assets – see Gourinchas and Rey (2007), for example – between periods t and $t-1$ captures the impact of the trade and the valuation channel on a country's net foreign asset holdings:

$$NFA_{t+1} = R_{t+1} \times NFA_t + NX_{t+1} \tag{21.1}$$

where NX_{t+1} represents net exports, defined as the difference between exports X_{t+1} and imports M_{t+1} of goods and services, NFA_t measures net foreign assets, defined as the difference between gross external assets and gross external liabilities, measured in the domestic currency, and R_{t+1} denotes the return on the net foreign asset portfolio, a combination of the (gross) return on assets and the (gross) return on liabilities. Equation (21.1) is sometimes referred to as the accumulation identity and implies that the net foreign asset position is determined by net exports and the return on the net foreign asset portfolio in the previous period.[13] The importance of valuation effects has increased over the last few years. According to Gourinchas and Rey (2007), the gross stocks of cross-border assets and liabilities have increased dramatically from roughly 50% of world GDP in the early 1990s to more than 120% a decade later. Therefore, gains and losses on those assets have significant effects on the balance of payments.

Equation (21.1) highlights the importance of asset management and illustrates the conversion of natural resources into permanent foreign income and the role of the commodity fund's currency allocation. In the early years of the fund's existence NX_{t+1} is positive as resource exports X_{t+1} are likely to exceed imports M_{t+1}. As natural resources are exhausted over time NX_{t+1} can be expected to fall and become negative (as the country begins to consume the income from assets). To ensure that the current external balance is positive at any given point it is crucial that NFA_{t+1} (consisting to a large extent of fund assets) fulfill certain conditions. First, for a given level of risk, the mean return on the NFA, R_{t+1}, should be as high as possible. In particular the mean return should match the increase in net imports. Second, the risk measures should reflect the fund's objectives such as minimizing the unconditional volatility (or standard deviation) of R_{t+1} as well as a maximizing the (negative) correlation between R_{t+1} and NX_{t+1}. The reason for the correlation objective is that the external balance can be expected to be

[13] Note that the accumulation identity ignores other elements that affect the balance of payments such as unilateral transfers, capital account transactions, and errors and omissions.

adversely affected in a scenario where the value of net foreign assets drops while net exports suddenly fall at the same time. Of course, a country's commodity fund is not the only entity that can accumulate net foreign assets. However, given the size of many SWFs it is realistic to assume that in many commodity-rich countries, the commodity fund accounts for the majority of net foreign assets.[14]

The framework outlined above will help us to review the literature on optimal asset allocation. This literature can be viewed as determining optimal portfolio weights and currency allocations given a set of returns on assets R^n_{t+1} without considering the return on liabilities R^l_{t+1}. The asset management (AM) and portfolio choice literature's conclusions regarding optimal currency allocations are model specific and are derived for representative investors based on a specific set of assumptions about variables such as (i) investors' risk preferences, (ii) exchange rate movements, (iii) asset returns, and (iv) market integration (see for example, Solnik 1974; Sercu 1980; Stulz 1981; Adler and Dumas 1983; and Black 1989, 1990). There is empirical evidence that several of the underlying theoretical assumptions are not fulfilled in practice – PPP, for example. Market capitalization weighting schemes are only (theoretically) optimal under very restrictive assumptions. It is important to note that despite the questionable theoretical assumptions of these models they provide the theoretical foundation of different forms of market capitalization weighting schemes that are followed by some large institutional investors including SWFs.[15] The benchmark for the Norwegian Petroleum Fund (Global Pension Fund or GPF), for example, is based on a regional allocation and then market-capitalization or value weighted benchmarks for both fixed income and equities securities within each region. The Kuwait Investment Authority also uses market-capitalization weighted equity indices as benchmarks for its equity portfolios.

Recent empirical evidence on optimal currency hedging (Resnick 1988; Bekaert and Hodrick 1992; Glen and Jorion 1993; Campbell, Serfaty-de Medeiros, and Viceira 2008) is mixed but suggests that market capitalization weighting may not be optimal in terms of risk minimization, even if complete currency hedging is allowed for. Added to this, other research shows that market-capitalization weighted equity and fixed income indices tend to underperform benchmarks based on alternative schemes (Arnott, Hsu, and More 2005; Arnott, Hsu, Li, and Shepherd 2008). One explanation for this is that market capitalization tends to underweight value stocks. Overall, it appears that standard market capitalization weighting schemes – though widely used – are not appropriate for commodity funds, not least because hedging currency risk back into domestic currency is precluded by the fund's underlying objective of offsetting capital inflows associated with the resource.

[14] Alberola and Serena (2008) examine the subcomponents of sovereign external assets further by distinguishing between public and private capital flows in the following balance of payments identity: Current Account Balance + Capital Inflows – Private Capital Outflows = Change in Sovereign Wealth Fund Assets + Change in Reserves = Change in Sovereign External Assets.

[15] Ugano (2000) reviews the operational modalities and experience of different oil funds. Chhaochharia and Laeven (2008) examine investment strategies and performance of sovereign wealth funds.

21.2.6 Currency Allocation – ALM Perspective and Breedon and Kosowski (2009)

The asset liability management (ALM) literature addresses the shortcomings of traditional portfolio choice models that ignore liabilities. The ALM literature explicitly takes into account the role of liabilities and the resulting additional hedging demands. Given that commodity funds exist to provide resources to match future liabilities (in the form of future imports), it is crucial to examine how conclusions regarding optimal portfolio choice and currency hedging change as assets and liabilities are explicitly modeled. The conclusions from this literature are similar to the AM literature in that optimal portfolio weights and hedging policies crucially depend on (i) investor's (inter-termporal) risk preferences with respect to assets and liabilities, (ii) the correlation between returns on assets and liabilities, (iii) the impact of exchange rate risk on assets and liabilities, and (iv) the time-variation in assets and liabilities. Optimal portfolio allocations eventually depend on a scheme's specific asset and liabilities; see, for example, Sharpe and Tint (1990); Rudolf and Ziemba (2004); Van Binsbergen and Brandt (2006); Nijman and Swinkels (2007); and Detemple and Rindisbacher (2008).

The asset liability management (ALM) literature examines both assets and financial liabilities and models the return on assets R^n_{t+1} and the return on liabilities R^l_{t+1} discussed in the context of Equation (21.1). However, this literature does not model net exports NX_{t+1} as part of the liabilities. Our framework in Equation (21.1) above clearly shows that the objective function of the commodity fund should include NX_{t+1}. Breedon and Kosowski (2009) were the first to examine the role of optimal currency allocations in the context of the commodity fund's asset liability matching problem represented by the country's net foreign assets NFA_t and net exports NX_{t+1} over time.

21.2.7 Optimal Currency Allocation in the Asset-Liability Management Context

The asset-liability management problem faced by a commodity fund is a complex dynamic optimization problem. For simplicity, however, we will abstract from the dynamic nature of the problem and assume that either the relative import weights are going to remain constant over time or continue their recently observed trend. This will allow us to make assumptions about future liabilities.

Sharpe and Tint (1990) and Nijman and Swinkels (2007) use surplus optimization as a method to reflect the presence of liabilities and its effect on optimal portfolio choice. Breedon and Kosowski (2009) build on this framework to examine the optimal currency allocation of the Norwegian GPF. The authors discuss the conditions under which Norway's net import mix can be expected to affect the optimal asset and currency allocation. They then derive the optimal currency allocations and examine the risk-return properties of using currency allocations that match liabilities instead of using market-capitalization based currency allocations. In order to assess the historical performance of the net import portfolio, Breedon and Kosowski (2009) construct 20 years of bond and equity returns for the relevant countries that trade with Norway. A comparison of the existing Norwegian benchmark portfolio and the net important portfolio shows that the net import portfolio generates economically significantly higher returns and Sharpe ratio and appears to match the fund's liabilities well.

Figure 21.3 shows estimates of Norway's net import shares since 1960 (five-year moving averages in order to iron out short-term erratic movements). Encouragingly, these shares are generally quite stable given that they represent the balance of two large numbers. The importance of net imports from the Eurozone and – to a lesser extent – Sweden is clear throughout the sample. Net imports from the U.S. and U.K. are more variable in importance whilst China, which was barely represented prior to 1990, has risen dramatically in importance over the last 20 years to over 10% of net imports.

Using historic net imports as a guide, Breedon and Kosowski (2009) construct a net import weighted portfolio to assess its properties relative to the current allocation used by the fund. Figure 21.4 shows the cumulative returns on the net import weighted portfolio and the current benchmark.

In addition to evidence on the superior performance of the net import weighted asset portfolio, Breedon and Kosowski (2009) also show that the net import weighted portfolio has better liability matching properties. The authors calculate the correlation between

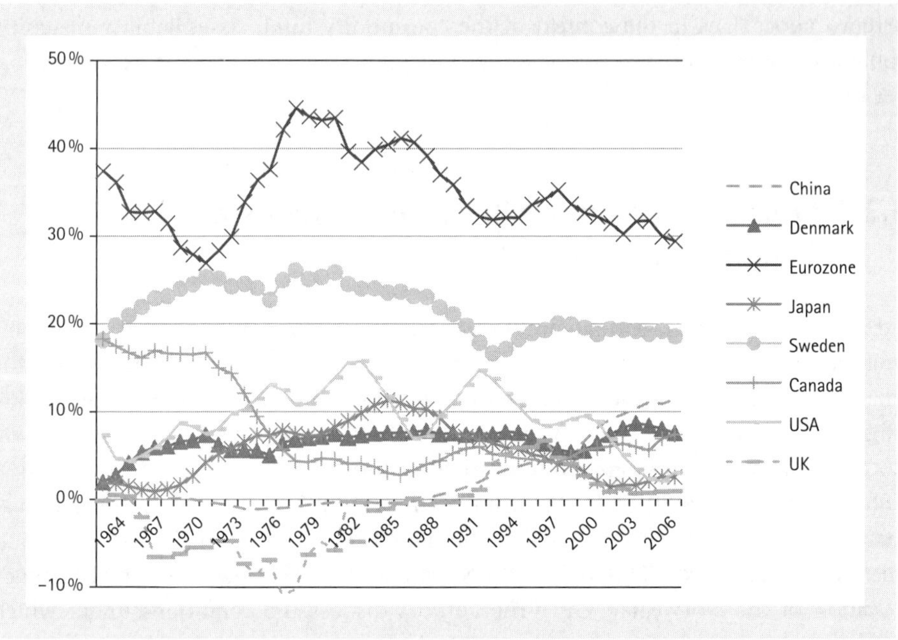

FIGURE 21.3 Net non-oil import shares (selected countries).

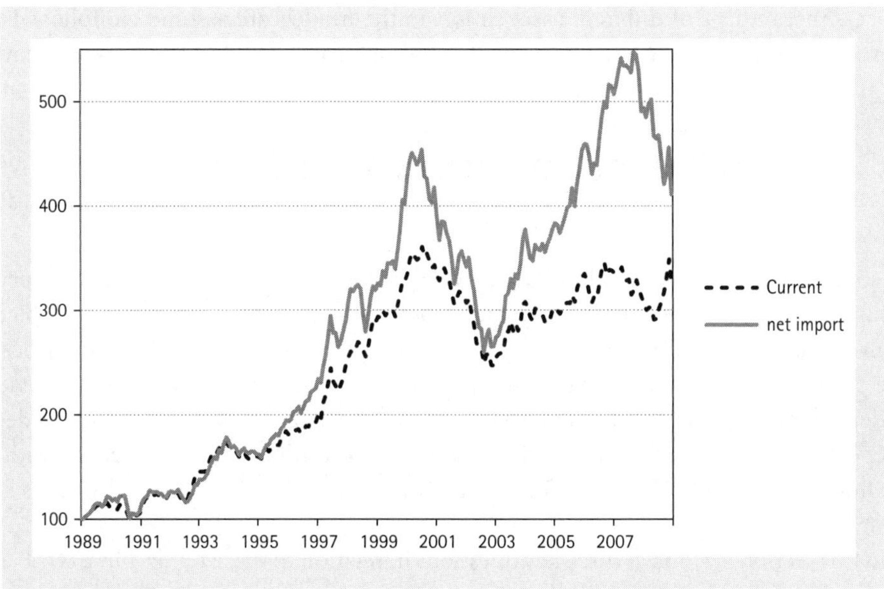

FIGURE 21.4 Cumulative returns on current GPF and alternative (net import weighted) portfolio from 1989 to 2009 (in NOK terms); see Chart 5 in Breedon and Kosowski (2009).

assets and liabilities which is the key metric in the ALM approach. Four alternative measures of liabilities over three time horizons are used and show that net import portfolios consistently outperform the current benchmark in terms of correlation with liabilities (with the exception of two short-term indicators). Overall, the correlation results seem to indicate the net import portfolio has some power to hedge against real exchange rate risk compared with the current currency allocation adopted by the GPF.

21.2.8 Dynamic Asset Liability Management Without Parameter Uncertainty

For simplicity we have assumed above that the commodity fund solves a static investment problem. In a more general multi-period asset-liability problem the agent maximizes inter-temporal expected utility defined over a surplus. This leads to potential hedging demands; see for example, Rudolf and Ziemba (2004) for an extension of the Sharpe and Tint (1990) framework to a dynamic setting; other examples include Boulier *et al.* (1995); Sundaresan and Zapatero (1997); Carirns (2000); Van Binsbergen and Brandt (2006); and Detemple and Rindisbacher (2008). In practice, however, the difficulty of precisely forecasting surplus returns given a set of state variables in the presence of parameter uncertainty may mean that hedging demands are small and the optimal multi-period solution under uncertainty may be close to the static solution (Barberis 2000). Second, normative conclusions from dynamic models are based on the stochastic process that returns of different asset classes in the models are assumed to follow. For these reasons it seems reasonable to adopt a static approach to ALM as described above.

21.3 Excess Reserve Funds

In comparison with commodity-based SWFs, those that arise due to excess reserve accumulation are more controversial and more complex to analyse. The key problem from the asset allocation perspective is that the purpose of these funds is unclear. Are they – as some would argue – simply the by-product of a strategy of currency undervaluation (i.e. excess foreign assets acquired through persistent, and one-sided, intervention) or do they serve a similar purpose to commodity funds in dealing with a medium-term "windfall" of excess domestic saving/capital inflows or are they for self-insurance purposes?

In this section we look at three key questions in relation to these funds. First, what are they and how are they financed? Second, why do some countries split the management of their foreign assets between a standard central bank reserves management function and a sovereign wealth fund? Third, what factors lie behind the accumulation of foreign assets that these funds manage? Having looked at these questions we then draw some tentative conclusions as to what asset allocation is most appropriate for such funds.

21.3.1 What is an Excess Reserve Fund?

As discussed above, these funds have generally arisen in East Asian economies in which persistent current account surpluses are not matched by private sector capital outflows. Figure 21.5 compares the balance of payments of the major commodity fund countries with those of the major excess reserve countries. The current account of these two groups is similar in the sense that they both generate large surpluses (though the commodity group tends to run a larger surplus). The key difference is in the capital and financial account where the commodity fund currencies have net capital outflows that nearly mirror the current account surplus whilst for excess reserve fund countries, capital outflows fall well short of the current account surplus and balance is maintained through significant reserve accumulation. It is this reserve accumulation that finances the excess reserve funds.

In the case of commodity funds, the financing of the fund is through government revenues generated by commodity exports and so there is a simple correspondence between the current account surplus, government revenues, and the financing of the fund. In the case of excess reserve funds, this is not the case as the current account surplus is generated by the private sector. This means that the reserve accumulation that finances the fund must itself be financed through borrowing from the private

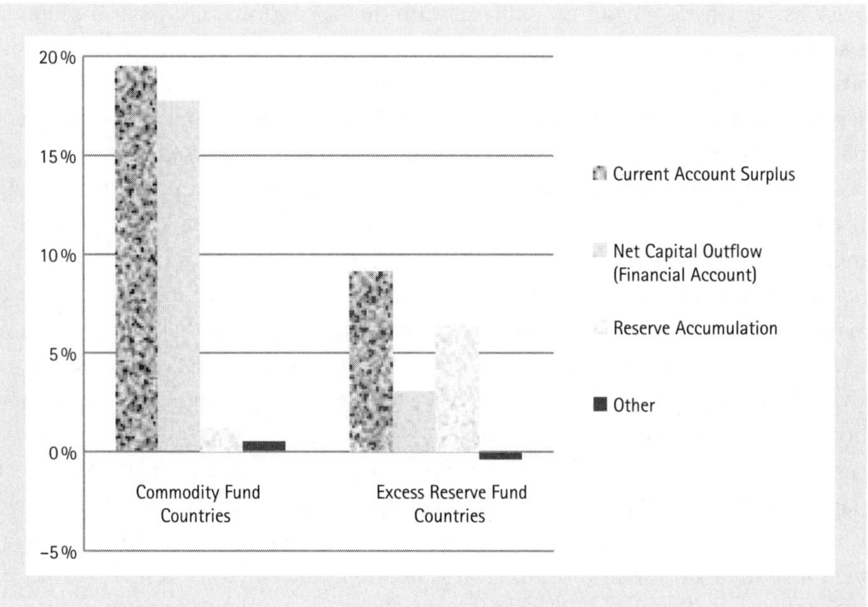

FIGURE 21.5 Balance of payments for sovereign wealth fund countries (1997–2007 average, % of GNI).

Notes: Commodity fund group = Norway, Saudi Arabia, Kuwait. Excess Reserve Group = Singapore, China, South Korea. Source: IFS

sector (or possibly other means as in the case of China). This process, called sterilization, usually requires the central bank to create local currency debt (or run down its stock of local currency assets) in order to fund its reserve accumulation. Without such sterilization the reserve accumulation would, by default, be funded by base money creation.

21.3.2 Why do SWFs that Manage Excess Reserves Arise?

Since excess reserve funds are financed by reserve accumulation by the central bank, it is natural to ask why these purchases are not maintained as reserves held by the central bank as would conventionally be the case. All central banks have established reserve management functions and in fact many countries with extremely high levels of foreign exchange reserves do not have excess reserve funds.

Aizenman and Glick (2008) set out a simple model to explain why excess reserve funds arise. Their starting point is to note that foreign exchange asset holdings have a dual purpose in most countries. Reserves both reduce the risk of sudden stops (crises in which access to foreign currency is cut off) and can be a source of government revenue. They assume that the central bank is preoccupied by reducing the risk of sudden stops given their responsibility for financial stability. This preoccupation makes them prefer low risk assets whose payout are more certain during periods of crisis – a preference that seems to accord with standard central bank practice of holding relatively short duration government securities. At low levels of reserves, this practice also fits with the preferences of agents in the economy since the cost of sudden stops far outweighs the income from a small reserves holdings. However, as reserves grow the income forgone by not investing in higher yielding but risky assets becomes more important and rather than trying to change the investment behavior of the central bank, the government establishes a SWF with a sole aim of maximizing risk-adjusted returns (i.e. with no direct concern of the financial stability motive for holding foreign currency). In this framework, the allocation between the FX reserves manager and the SWF is a function of (a) the size of reserves, (b) the cost of sudden stops, (c) the impact of reserve holdings on the risk of sudden stops, and (d) the extra return available from risky investments. Although Aizenman and Glick (2008) do not explicitly model why a separation between the reserves manager and SWF is desirable (rather than, say, a mandate for reserves management that reflects both financial stability and return maximization objectives), they note that central bank governors are far more likely to be sacked for failing to prevent a sudden stop than for failing to generate high returns of reserves. They also note that the expertise of central banks is generally in financial stability rather than asset management. However, neither explanation seems entirely consistent with the common practice of allowing central banks to run sovereign wealth funds as a distinct function from reserves management.

21.3.3 Why do Excess Reserves Arise?

Whilst the balance between financial stability and revenue may help explain why SWFs arise in the presence of excess reserves, they do not explain why these reserves arise in the first place. Unfortunately, there is no widely accepted explanation for rapid reserve accumulation by these countries. Probably the most commonly cited explanation for excess reserve holding is as a by-product of what has been termed a "mercantilist" foreign exchange policy (Aizenman and Lee 2007). Mercantilism in this context means aiming to maintain an undervalued exchange rate in order to encourage growth and investment in export industries. Such a policy can be maintained either through capital controls and/or persistent one-sided currency intervention (i.e. persistent sales of local currency and purchases of foreign currency).

A possible alternative explanation is that these funds act as a conduit for excess domestic savings to be channelled into foreign investments. Certainly, all of the excess reserve countries have savings rates far above those of comparable countries at the same stage of development and given that financial development in these economies is still not complete, it is plausible to suggest that there are neither sufficient domestic investment opportunities nor reliable private sector mechanisms for channelling these

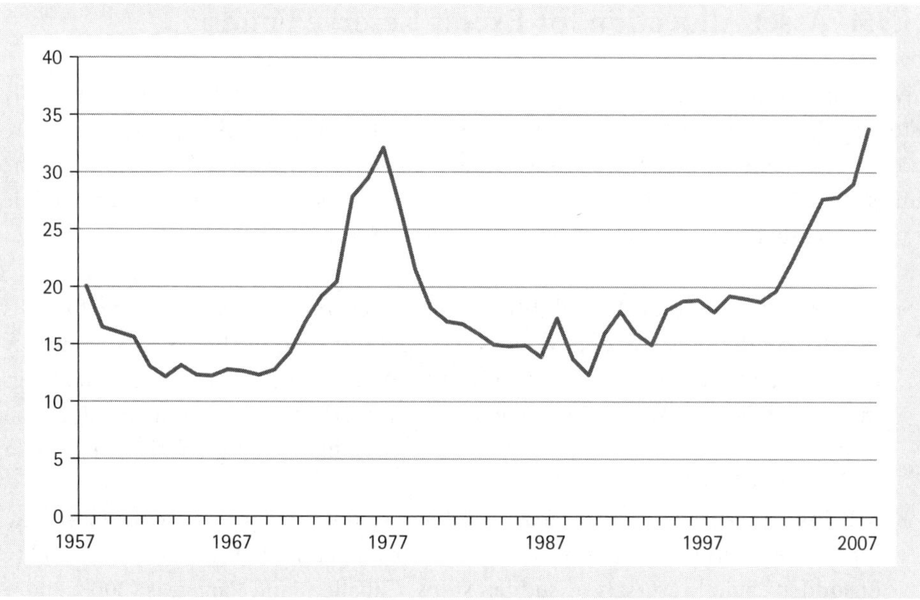

FIGURE 21.6 Ratio of reserves to M2 for developing economies (%).

Note: Sum of all developing IMF member country non-gold reserves divided by M2. Source: IFS

saving overseas (though it is hard to square this explanation with the presence of capital controls in many of these countries).

Thus whilst all studies on the opportunity cost of reserves find that the returns achieved on foreign currency holdings are far outweighed by the cost of borrowing and diverting resources away from domestic investment (see for example Rodrik 2006), this is not so clearly the case in the excess reserve fund countries which tend to have low domestic interest rates. Prasad and Wei (2005), for example, argue that the return on foreign investments may outweigh domestic borrowing costs in the case of China.

Another alternative is that this very high level of reserves holding is needed for self-insurance purposes in a world of large cross-border capital flows. Thus reserves channelled into these funds could still be thought as having some financial stability purpose. Figure 21.6 provides some intriguing evidence for the self-insurance explanation for rapid reserve accumulation. It shows the average reserves to M2 ratio for developing and emerging economies over the 50 years from 1957 to 2007; it is often argued that this ratio is the most appropriate measure of reserves adequacy (Obstfeld, Shambaugh and Taylor 2009). Since it is normally suggested that this ratio should be around 20% for developing economies, it is clear that there have been two periods of "excess" reserve holding over this period. The first occurred in the middle to late 1970s in the run up to the debt crisis of the early 1980s. The second occurred in the 2000s before the credit crunch. The run up in reserves prior to these two crises either shows remarkable prescience on behalf of developing country central banks or that financial market bubbles are periods of excess capital flows and so encourage reserve accumulation.

21.3.4 Asset Allocation for Excess Reserve Funds

Given our discussion above, it is apparent that excess reserve funds do not fit as easily into an ALM framework as commodity funds since the liabilities of such funds are not clear (though the managers of such funds may have a clearer understanding of the fund's objectives than outside observers). Given this problem, we present three possible frameworks that could by applied to excess reserve funds.

- **ALM relative to domestic liabilities** Since the purpose of excess reserve funds is unclear (in the sense of identifying when, and on what, the funds will eventually be spent) and since these funds usually involve the creation of a domestic liabilities in the form of sterilization instruments it would seem the simplest asset allocation framework would involve maximizing return and minimizing volatility relative to these domestic liabilities.
- **Self-insurance** If the excess reserve fund has a similar purpose to official reserves, then the allocation of the fund should be considered in relation to the possibility of sudden capital reversals or sudden stops. Caballero and Panageas (2003, 2004) discuss the problem that central banks in emerging market economies can face as a result of sudden reversal of capital inflows. They note that hoarding international reserves can be used to smooth the impact of such reversals, but that these reserves are rarely sufficient and always expensive to hold. They argue that adding richer hedging instruments to the portfolios held by central banks can significantly improve the efficiency of the anti-sudden stop mechanism. Caballero and Panageas (2003) provide an example based on a simple quantitative hedging model, where optimally used options and futures on the S&P100's implied volatility index (VIX) increases the expected reserves available during sudden stops by as much as 40%.
- **Commodity fund style of asset-liability management** It is likely that, in practice, excess reserve funds will in fact eventually be used to finance future net import purchases when excess savings cease or a long-term (rather than sudden a short-term) capital reversal occurs. If this is the case, then it seems reasonable for them to consider a net import weighting scheme similar to the one discussed above in the case of commodity funds.

21.4 Empirical Evidence on SWFs Actual Asset Allocation and Portfolio Holdings

Following our normative discussion of the commodity fund's asset allocation we now turn to a positive analysis and review empirical work on SWF's actual asset allocation.

One of the most comprehensive recent studies on the determinants of actual investment allocations by sovereign wealth funds has been carried out by Chhaochharia and Laeven (2009) who collect data on about 30,000 equity investments by sovereign wealth funds during the period 1997–2007. The authors use both country-level and firm-level analysis to identify the key determinants of SWFs investment decisions.[16] The focus is in particular on geographical proximity and cultural factors that may influence decisions. The authors' main findings are that (i) SWFs tend to invest in countries that share similar cultural traits, suggesting that SWFs bias their investments to the familiar. Chhaochharia and Laeven (2009) hypothesize that this preference for investing in the familiar may indicate the exploitation of informational advantages, or simply a tendency to feel affinity with the familiar. Second, this cultural bias is found to (i) be more pronounced for SWFs than for other global and institutional investors and (ii) tends to disappear with repeated investments in the same country, suggesting that informational asymmetries disappear over time as investors become more acquainted with local culture. The authors also report that SWFs display significant industry biases, in particular that they hold a disproportionately large fraction of their stocks in oil companies. The authors interpret this evidence as being consistent with the SWFs targeting technologically strategic industries. SWFs also tend to invest more in large-cap stocks, consistent with prior evidence on investments by institutional investors (Kang and Stulz, 1997; Coval and Moskowitz, 1999).

Several other studies focus on the performance of SWF investments as opposed to the determinants of these investment decisions. Bartolotti *et al.* (2008) examine data on about 1,200 SWF investments and report that these investments tend to exhibit positive abnormal returns upon announcement but significantly negative long-term abnormal returns. Several other papers document similar results. Kotter and Lel (2008) analyze data on 163 SWF investments and find that these investments exhibit positive abnormal returns. They also show that the degree of transparency of the fund is negatively associated with the size of these abnormal returns. Dewenter *et al.* (2009) and Fernandes (2009) also find that the firm value increases when SWFs acquire equity stakes. Bernstein *et al.* (2009), instead, focus on private equity investments of SWFs, and find that they tend to invest when equity prices are relatively high. Balding (2008) examines the portfolios of the Singaporean and Norwegian SWF in detail and other SWFs using aggregate data.

Bernstein, Lerner and Schoar (2009) examine the private equity investment strategy across sovereign wealth funds and how they depend on the funds' organizational structure. They find evidence of trend chasing behavior by SWFs which tend to invest at home when domestic prices are high and abroad when foreign prices are high. Funds see the P/E ratio of their domestic investment drop in the year after the investment while the P/E ratio of their foreign investments tends to rise after the same period. The authors

[16] It is important to note that they do not solely focus on commodity funds or excess reserve funds but also include pension funds (from countries such as Ireland and New Zealand).

examine the role of corporate governance structure and geographical origin of funds on the investment outcome.

21.5 Conclusions

Sovereign wealth funds represent a large and growing investor group that face unique challenges in asset management. In this chapter we set out to describe an optimal asset allocation for sovereign wealth funds in a simple asset liability management (ALM) framework. In the case of commodity funds (wealth funds that are funded by revenues from resource extraction) the framework is simple to analyse and implement. Using the case of the Norwegian Petroleum Fund, we demonstrate that our proposed allocation framework produces superior risk and return outcomes relative to the current allocation. Additionally, on the asset side, a commodity price hedging scheme to guarantee the value of the as yet un-extracted resource would also be worthwhile for these funds (though challenging to implement in practice, given the scale of hedging required). In the case of excess reserve funds (funded by foreign currency acquired through intervention), ALM is more problematic since the future liabilities of these funds are often not clearly defined.

References

Adler, M. and Dumas, B. (1983). International portfolio selection and corporation finance: A synthesis. Journal of Finance, **46**, 925–984.

Aizenman, J. and Glick, R. (2007). International reserves: Precautionary versus mercantilist views theory and evidence, *Open Economies Review* **18**(2), 191–214.

Aizenman, J. and Glick, R. (2008). Sovereign wealth funds: Stylized facts about their determinants and governance. NBER Working Papers 14562.

Alberola, E. and Serena, J.M. (2008). Sovereign external assets and the resilience of global imbalances. Documentos de Trabajo No. 0834, Bance De España.

Amuzegar, J. (2005). Iran's oil stablization fund: A misnomer. *Middle East Economic Survey*, 48.

Arnott, R.D., Hsu, J.C., and Moore, P., 2005. Fundamental indexation. *Financial Analyst Journal*, **61**. Available at SSRN: http://ssrn.com/abstract=604842.

Arnott, R.D., Hsu, J.C., Li, F., and Shepherd, S.D. (2008). Applying valuation-indifferent indexing to fixed income. Available at SSRN: http://ssrn.com/abstract=1263246

Caballero, R.J. and Panageas, S. (2003). Hedging sudden stops and precautionary recessions: A quantitative framework. NBER Working Paper 9778.

Caballero, R.J. and Panageas, S. (2004). Contingent reserves management: An applied framework. Federal Reserve Bank of Boston, No. 05-2.

Campbell, J. and Viceira, L. (2002). *Strategic Asset Allocation*. Oxford University Press, Oxford.

Cheung, H., (2007). China's foreign exchange reserve allocation. State Street Global Advisors, General Investing Essay and Presentation.

Chhaochharia, V. and Laeven, L.A. (2009). Sovereign wealth funds: Their investment strategies and Performance. Available at SSRN: http://ssrn.com/abstract=1262383

Davis, V., Ossowski, R., Daniel, J., and Barnett, S. (2003). Stabilization and savings funds for nonrenewable resources: Experience and fiscal policy implications. In *Fiscal Policy Formulation and Implementation in Oil-Producing Countries* (ed. J. Davis, R. Ossowski, and A. Fedelino). International Monetary Fund, Washington, DC.

Devlin, J. and Titman, S. (2004). Managing oil price risk in developing countries. *World Bank Research Observer*, **19**.

Dixit, A., Hammond, H., and Hoel, M. (1980). On Hartwick's rule and regular maxi-min paths of capital accumulation and resource depletion. *Review of Economic Studies*, **47**(2), 551–556.

Gintschel, A. and Scherer, B. (2008). Optimal asset allocation for sovereign wealth funds. *Journal of Asset Management*, **9**, 215–238.

Gourinchas, P.-O., and Rey, H. (2007). From world banker to world venture capitalist: U.S. external adjustment and the exorbitant privilege. In *G7 Current Account Imbalances: Sustainability and Adjustment* (ed. R.H. Clarida). University of Chicago Press (for NBER), Chicago.

Habibi, N. (1998). Fiscal response to fluctuating oil revenues in oil exporting countries of the middle east. Economic Research Forum Working Paper.

Hartwick, J.M. (1977). Intergenerational equity and the investing of rents from exhaustible resources. *American Economic Review*, **67**(5), 972–974.

Hausmann, R. and Rigobon, R. (2003). An alternative explanation of the resource curse. In *Fiscal Policy Formulation and Implementation in Oil-Producing Countries* (ed. J. Davis, R. Ossowski, and A. Fedelino). International Monetary Fund, Washington, D.C.

Kalyuzhnova, Y. and Michael K., (2006). Prudential management of hydrocarbon revenues in resource rich transition economies. *Post Communist Economies*, **18**, 167–187.

Leibowitz, M.L., Kogelman, S., and Bader, L.N., (1993). Asset performance and surplus control: A dual-shortfall approach. *Journal of Portfolio Management*, Winter, 28–37.

Mehrara, M. and Kamran N.O. (2007). The sources of macroeconomic fluctuations in oil exporting countries: A comparative study. *Economic Modelling*, **24**, 365–379.

Mody, A. and A.P.M. (2005). Growing up with capital flows, *Journal of International Economics*, **65**(1), 249–266.

Obstfeld, M., Shambaugh, J.C., and Taylor, A.M. (2010). Financial stability, the trilemma, and international reserves. *American Economic Journal: Macro Economics*, **2**, 57–94.

Okumura, R. and Cai, D. (2007). Sustainable constant consumption in a semi-open economy with exhaustible resources. *Japanese Economic Review*, **58**, 226–237. Available at SSRN: http://ssrn.com/abstract=986783 or doi:10.1111/j.1468-5876.2007.00348

Pascuzzo, P. (2008). Best practice asset allocation and risk management for sovereign wealth funds. Mercer Report.

Petersen, C. and Budina, N. (2003). Governance framework of oil funds: The case of Azerbaijan and Kazakhstan. Prepared for the Workshop on Petroleum Revenue Management.

Prasad, A., Rajan, R., and Subramanian, A. (2007). Foreign capital and economic growth. Brookings Papers on Economic Activity, Economic Studies Program, The Brookings Institution, vol. 38, pages 153–230.

Prasad, E.S. and Wei, S.-J. (2005). The Chinese approach to capital inflows: Patterns and possible explanations. IMF Working Paper, 05/79.

Rodrik, D. (2006). The social cost of foreign exchange reserves. *International Economic Journal*, Korean International Economic Association, **20**(3), 253–266.

Rudolf, M. and Ziemba, W.T. (2004). Intertemporal surplus management. *Journal of Economic Dynamics and Control*, **28**, 975–990.

Scherer, B. (2009a). Portfolio choice for oil-based sovereign wealth funds. EDHEC Business School Working Paper.

Scherer, B. (2009b). a note on portfolio choice for sovereign wealth funds. EDHEC Business School Working Paper.

Sharpe, W.F. and Tint, L.G. (1990). Liabilities: A new approach. *Journal of Portfolio Management*, Winter, 5–10.

Solnik, B. (1974a). The international pricing of risk: an empirical investigation of the world capital market structure. *Journal of Finance*, **29**, 365–378.

Solnik, B. (1974b). An equilibrium model of the international capital market. *Journal of Economic Theory*, **8**, 500–524.

Solow, R.M. (1974). Intergenerational equity and exhaustible resources. *Review of Economic Studies*, Vol. 41, Symposium on Economics of Exhaustable Resources, pp. 29–45. Oxford University press.

Stulz, R. (1981). A model of international asset pricing. *Journal of Financial Economics*, **9**, 383–406.

US Treasury. (2007). Appendix 3: Semi-annual report on international economic and exchange rate policies. http://www.treas.gov/offices/international-affairs/economic-exchange-rates/

Van Binsbergen, J.H. and Brandt, M.W. (2006). Optimal asset allocation in asset and liability management. Working Paper. Fuqua School of Management, Duke University.

INDEX